Peter FitzSimons is a journalist with the *Sydney Morning Herald* and *Sun-Herald*, and a busy events and motivational speaker. He is the author of twenty-eight books, including *Tobruk, Kokoda, Batavia, Eureka, Ned Kelly, Gallipoli, Victory at Villers-Bretonneux* and biographies of Douglas Mawson, Nancy Wake, Kim Beazley, Nick Farr-Jones, Les Darcy, Steve Waugh and John Eales, and is one of Australia's biggest selling non-fiction authors of the last fifteen years. He lives with his wife, Lisa Wilkinson, and their three children in Sydney.

Also by Peter FitzSimons

Nancy Wake: a Biography of Our Greatest War Heroine
Kim Beazley
Nick Farr-Jones
Nene: the Queen of the Magazine Wars
The Rugby War
A Simpler Time
John Eales: the Biography
Steve Waugh
The Ballad of Les Darcy
Little Theories of Life
Tobruk
And Now for Some Light Relief
Kokoda
Charles Kingsford Smith and Those Magnificent Men
Mawson
Batavia
Eureka
Ned Kelly
Gallipoli
Victory at Villers-Bretonneux

PETER FITZSIMONS

FROMELLES & POZIÈRES

IN THE TRENCHES OF HELL

WILLIAM HEINEMANN: AUSTRALIA

A William Heinemann book
Published by Penguin Random House Australia Pty Ltd
Level 3, 100 Pacific Highway, North Sydney NSW 2060
www.penguin.com.au

First published by William Heinemann in 2015
This paperback edition published in 2016

Addresses for the Penguin Random House group of companies can be found at global.
penguinrandomhouse.com/offices.

National Library of Australia
Cataloguing-in-Publication entry

FitzSimons, Peter, author
Fromelles and Pozières: in the trenches of hell/Peter FitzSimons

ISBN 978 0 14378 330 5 (paperback)

Fromelles, Battle of, Fromelles, France, 1916
World War, 1914–1918 – Campaigns – France – Fromelles
World War, 1914–1918 – Campaigns – France – Pozières
World War, 1914–1918 – Campaigns – France
World War, 1914–1918 – Participation, Australian

940.4144

Front cover: Members of the 24th Battalion in a trench. (AWM EO3138).
Back cover: Field of poppies, photo by John Benestone.
Cover design by Adam Yazxhi/MAXCO
Internal design and typesetting by Xou Creative, Australia
Printed in Australia by Griffin Press, an accredited ISO AS/NZS 14001:2004 Environmental Management System printer

Penguin Random House Australia uses papers that are natural, renewable and recyclable products and made from wood grown in sustainable forests. The logging and manufacturing processes are expected to conform to the environmental regulations of the country of origin.

To the Bishop boys, Bert, Ray and Billy, and all those who so bravely served with them. We dips our lids.

In Hell's Trenches . . .
23/7/16

My darlings, the gods only know if I am writing for the last
time. We have now been two days in the front trenches.
It is not really a trench, but a little ditch, shattered with
shells – not the slightest cover and no protection. We
have lost fifty men in two days, and life is unendurable.
*From a German soldier's letter found blowing around the Pozières
battlefield after the second day of battle (Charles Bean, Official
History of Australia in the War of 1914–1918, Vol. III)*

CONTENTS

Part Three: End Game

LIST OF MAPS

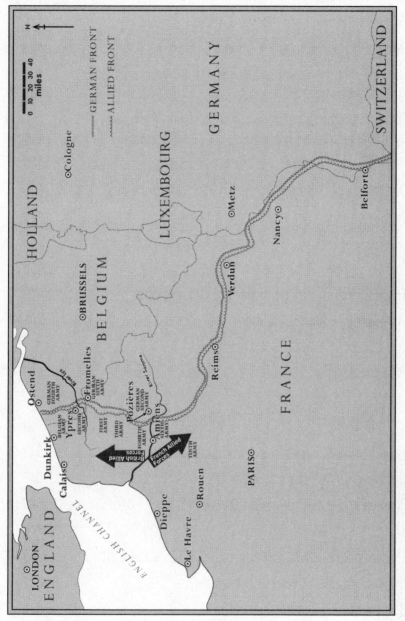

Western Front at the end of 1914

BACKGROUND AND ACKNOWLEDGEMENTS

Fromelles? Pozières? Something to do with the Western Front in the First World War, weren't they?

I mean, as a little boy, my Second World War veteran father taught me the most famed First World War poem – *In Flanders fields, the poppies blow,/ Between the crosses, row on row,/ That mark our place; and in the sky/ The larks, still bravely singing, fly/ Scarce heard amid the guns below* – and I gathered Fromelles was in French Flanders, yes?

And, yes, later on at high school, there might have been passing reference to both battles in Rex Ward's Modern History class, but after that faded, there was little left in my memory, let alone my heart, other than a vague presentiment that they had been important conflicts. While Gallipoli came up again and again – in conversation, on the TV, in the papers, in books – Fromelles and Pozières were no more than names that occasionally I would see referred to in passing, in the same breath as Bullecourt, Passchendaele, Polygon Wood, Villers-Bretonneux and the like . . . you know, key battles in the fight for the whole Western Front?

No?

Well, me neither. As a younger man, I could never quite get my head around what the whole thing had been about, beyond the fact that our own 'weird mob' were with the Allies on one side, and the Germans were on the other side. And I gathered the slaughter had been unimaginable.

Interest slowly grew, however.

For the 80th anniversary of Armistice in 1998, I interviewed for *The Sydney Morning Herald* Paul Fischer, a 101-year-old former French soldier on the Western Front who'd become a Professor at the Sorbonne, before moving to Australia with his wife in the early 1960s to be close to their only daughter. He lived just 50 metres down the hill from my home on Sydney's Lower North Shore, and his story quite stunned me.

'I remember many things,' he told me. 'The bombardments, the screaming, the death, *c'était terrible, mais vraiment terrible! Le capitaine* would lift his arm to signal to make ourselves ready to attack, and when he dropped it, we had to scramble up and out and follow our bayonets towards *les Allemandes*.'

Back then, he said, he looked on every sunrise as if it would be his last, and for the vast majority of his comrades, it was. And yet here he was, *eight decades* later, still going strong – ish – apart from the nightmares still powerful enough to wake him in the night, with only his wife of 63 years, Lynette, able to hold him, to calm him, to assure him, *cherie*, that it was over, that he was not back there once more.

This, clearly, was a man who had known things, seen things, experienced things, of which I had not the slightest conception.

A couple of years later, while writing the biography of Wallaby captain John Eales, I was entranced by the words with which Wallaby coach Rod Macqueen had inspired his charges before the 1999 World Cup Final. In the dressing room with just two minutes to go before going out onto the field at Cardiff, Macqueen cited the team's visit to Villers-Bretonneux the previous year, before quoting the special order of one-time Victorian clergyman Lieutenant F. P. Bethune to his men before the battle: 'This position will be held, and the section will remain here until relieved . . . The enemy cannot be allowed to interfere with the programme. If the section cannot remain here alive, it will remain here dead, but in any case it will remain here. Should any man, through shell shock or other cause attempt to surrender, he will remain here dead. Should all guns be blown out, the section will use Mills grenades, and other novelties. Finally, the position, as stated, will be held.'[1]

For the second time, I felt a flicker of interest in the Western Front, and yet still that interest was nothing as to how absorbed I subsequently became in doing a biography on Nancy Wake, and books on Kokoda,

Tobruk and Gallipoli. It was the book on the Anzacs at the Dardanelles, of course, that got me interested in Fromelles and Pozières. For while researching the reminiscences of many Gallipoli veterans who'd gone on to those battles, a constant theme was that the Dardanelles was 'a picnic' compared with those first two battles the Australians had engaged in in France.

I knew how bad Gallipoli was, so what must the Western Front truly have been like for them to say that? And so it began. From first reading up on those battles, I was stunned at just what occurred, and went from there with the same aim as always: to bring the whole thing back to life. The late, great American novelist E. L. Doctorow once noted, 'The historian will tell you what happened. The novelist will tell you what it felt like.'[2]

It is for you to judge my success or otherwise, but I strain to do both. As noted in my previous work, I want to make my account read like a novel filled with accurate, raw detail and quotations, perching on 2000 or so firm footnotes to show that it is nevertheless real. For the sake of the storytelling, I have occasionally created a direct quote from reported speech in a newspaper, diary or letter, just as I have changed pronouns and tenses to put that reported speech in the present tense – and occasionally assumed generic emotions where it is obvious, even though that emotion is not necessarily recorded in the diary entries, letter, etc. I have also occasionally restored swearing words that were blanked out in the original newspaper account due to the sensitivities of the time. Always, my goal has been to determine what were the most likely words used, based on the documentary evidence presented, and what the *feel* of the situation was. Once again in this book, as noted in the endnotes, I have taken documented detail from one time frame and placed it in a slightly later time – as the situation was almost exactly the same.

For the same reason of remaining faithful to the language of the day, I have stayed with the imperial system of measurement and used the contemporary spelling.

I have, of course, prized primary documents above all else, but many books have been great sources both for overall understanding and for pointing to where the treasure troves of those primary documents lay. A list of all books used is in the Bibliography, but beyond the combined works of 'The Master' – Charles E. W. Bean – I am indebted to the work of English academic Peter Barton for his book *The Lost Legions of Fromelles*, which is a **masterpiece**, particularly on the German side of the equation. It is, quite simply, without peer, and I highly commend his book to those who wish to know more. For emotion and feel, I loved the memoir of the 55th Battalion's Bert Bishop, *The Hell, the Humour and the Heartbreak*, and have drawn heavily from it. I thank the Bishop family for providing wider raw material. I also loved Eddie Rule's book, *Jacka's Mob*, and have used details from it to bring the Pozières story, particularly, to life. For the purely personal German side of the account, Jack Sheldon's anthology, *The German Army on the Somme*, was invaluable, as were the reminiscences of General Richard Ludwig Wellmann in *Mit der 18. Reserve-Division in Frankreich*.

My friend Dr Peter Pedersen has written three books that have covered the battles of Fromelles and Pozières, complete with great maps and diagrams. Whenever I was lost in a maze of muddy trenches – which was frequently – they were a great resource, both for information and for getting my bearings. Ditto my friends Les Carlyon and his book *The Great War*; Ross McMullin with his biography of *Pompey Elliott*, together with his wonderful account of the lives of Geoff McCrae, Tom Elliott and George Challis, *Farewell Dear People*; and particularly Ross Coulthart and his book *Charles Bean*. Lambis Englezos could not have been kinder sharing his detailed knowledge of Fromelles, as was Ward Selby, and their vetting of the manuscript for errors was invaluable. I thank all of them for their generosity of spirit in sharing their knowledge with me, and steering me back on course when I was drifting – along with Australia's most esteemed historian Professor David Day for his general counsel, and friendship.

I owe deep gratitude to Edward Bean LeCouteur and Anne Marie Carroll, the grandchildren of Charles Bean and owners of the copyright in his diaries and papers, for their kind permission to quote from the great man.

I also gratefully acknowledge all the friendly and helpful staff members at the State Library of New South Wales in Sydney (including Jan-Amanda Harkin, who showed initiative tracing a missing volume of a magazine), and Katrina Nicolson at the Shrine of Remembrance in Melbourne. In Germany, special thanks to Dr Dieter Storz and Carmen Böhm at *Bayerisches Armeemuseum* (Bavarian Army Museum) in Ingolstadt; Johannes Moosdiele-Hitzler at *Bayerisches Hauptstaatsarchiv, Abteilung IV, Kriegsarchiv* (Bavarian Main State Archive, Department IV, War Archive) in Munich; Melanie Wehr at the *Bundesarchiv, Abteilung Militärarchiv* (National Archive, Department Military Archive) in Freiburg; Christoph Albers at the *Zeitungsabteilung* of *Staatsbibliothek zu Berlin* (Newspaper Department of the Berlin State Library); Dr Verena Türk at *Landesarchiv Baden-Württemberg* (State Archive Baden-Württemburg) in Stuttgart; Steffi Wolf at *Deutsche Nationalbibliothek* (German National Library) in Leipzig; Dr Carolin Weichselgartner at *Archiv der Deutschen Kapuzinerprovinz* (Archive of the German Capuchin Province) in Altötting; Edith Kaes from the *Kreisgemeinschaft Rastenburg* (Society of Rastenburg); and freelance researcher Dr Oliver Hemmerle, who lives in Germany and France. In the United Kingdom, I thank Diana Manipud at King's College London Archives; Andrew Gough at the British Library; Tricia Buckingham at the Bodleian Libraries; and, back home, all the research staff at the mighty Australian War Memorial research centre . . . to name but a few!

As ever, I have put this book together with the help of a marvellous team of researchers, the majority of whom have worked with me, and substantially with each other, for many years. So complex has been the material, so difficult to synthesise into a coherent, accurate account, I have never had to rely on this team more, to dig for the gold nuggets and bring them to the surface for examination. The major digger for the Diggers, trawling through diaries and letters, was Dr Noel Boreham – I respectfully think of him as 'Noel the Diary Mole' – who spent enormous slabs of time finding so many of the original accounts and quotes you will find herein.

Sonja Goernitz, meanwhile, is a dual German–Australian citizen with whom I have worked for one good decade now, starting with my book *Tobruk* in 2005. For this book too, not only her research and referencing skills and her familiarity with German history, culture and language were invaluable, but also her record-keeping drive.

The first person I sat down to talk to about Australia's involvement in these battles was Dr Peter Williams, a Canberra military historian who had hugely helped me with *Gallipoli* and whose special field is precisely this. With him using salt and pepper shakers as battle sites, and a knife as the Somme River, I achieved the first glimmer of strategic understanding of the whole affair. He has worked with me on the manuscript since and, though we differ on a few points – the worth of General Haig for starters, but *don't* get me started – his depth and width of knowledge, and further familiarity with the literature on the subject and the highways and byways of the archival records have been invaluable.

Only late in the piece did it come up that one of his own books was about mistakes appearing in the stats used in Kokoda accounts, including (*sniff*) mine. This time, I was glad he was on my side, and he was particularly strong in sorting out just what the correct figures and facts were, from the many conflicting accounts. (I was also grateful to tour the actual battlefield sites in January 2015, in the company of English historian and First World War specialist Dr Andrew Thomson.)

Libby Effeney is a PhD student from Deakin University. In my last book, I lauded her for her intellect, work ethic, creative nous and drive to get to the bottom of things. Ditto. Of all my favourite notations to researchers, foremost was 'LME PR', as in 'Libby Marea Effeney, please resolve' – using the intellect and patience I don't possess to wade into this tangle of differing accounts with footnotes from everywhere and come up with a sole, solid quote sourced to an original document we ideally have a screenshot of. Bingo. Done. Move on.

Double ditto for Henry Barrkman, who again, in my book on Gallipoli, I described as 'an angel of accuracy, a demon for detail, whose impact on this manuscript was immense'. His strength in this book, as ever, lay in challenging the accepted version of events until such times as original documentation proved it, up to and including cross-checking the Official War Diaries. Beyond that, in the endless maze of primary documentation, most of it complicated and much of it contradictory, he proved expert at picking the eyes out of it – including analysing, excerpting and referencing material from the National Archives at Kew, and elsewhere – to sort out what *actually* happened, and in what chronological order. A bravura performance.

As ever, I also relied on other specialists in their fields, including my wonderfully assiduous long-time researcher at the Australian War Memorial, Glenda Lynch, together with her fellow researcher, Jane Robertson; Dr Michael Cooper, for medical history; Gregory Blake, for his assistance in all matters to do with firearms and artillery; Bryce Abraham, who was particularly expert on the story of Albert Jacka; Colonel Steve Larkins and Tony Agars for their help with the Russell Bosisto story; and Mat McLachlan for vetting the whole manuscript, as did Michael Ball. My thanks also to the descendants of the Australian soldiers Archie Barwick, Russell Bosisto, Harry Paulin, Percy Cherry and August Band. Gentlemen, they did you proud, and treasure your memories still.

As to illustrations and maps, I am once more indebted to Jane Macaulay, whose great work you will see throughout. My colleague at *The Sydney Morning Herald* Harriet Veitch was as sharp as ever in preliminary copy-editing, spotting inconsistencies and errors while also untangling hopelessly twisted sentences and eliminating many grammatical errors. I have always treasured the story of Raymond Chandler writing to his publisher in 1947, re the proofreader, that 'when I split an infinitive, God damn it, I split it so it will stay split . . .' but in my own case I need help to spot the split infinitive in the first place.

My thanks also, as ever, to my highly skilled editors, Kevin O'Brien and Brandon VanOver, who treated my work with something more than just due diligence: namely, passion and great skill. I am grateful, as ever, to my long-time publishers Ali Urquhart and Nikki Christer, who were encouraging throughout, particularly Ali, whose instinct proved as sure as ever.

And finally, of course, my gratitude and love to my wife, Lisa, for her belief, support, encouragement and understanding of just how much, when I am truly launched, my books possess me, and in some ways *our* lives.

All up, I hope this moves you as it does me.

Peter FitzSimons
Neutral Bay, Sydney
September 2015

PROLOGUE

I adore war. It's like a big picnic without the
objectlessness of a picnic. It's all the best fun. I have
never felt so well or so happy, or enjoyed anything so
much. It just suits my . . . barbaric disposition. The
fighting-excitement vitalizes everything, every sight
and word and action. One loves one's fellow-man
much more when one is bent on killing him.[1]
Captain the Honourable Julian Henry Francis Grenfell,
1st Royal Dragoons, 3 November 1914, in a letter
home. He had less than six months to live.

Arthur Balfour: Consider the casualties. There must have
been nearly 10,000 men lost in these engagements.
Lord Kitchener: Eight thousand seven hundred at Neuve
Chapelle, but it isn't the men I mind. I can replace the
men at once, but I can't replace the shells so easily.[2]
This conversation recorded in the diary of Frances Stevenson, 4 April 1915

It was a bit over a century ago.

At the highest spot on Pozières Ridge, overlooking the Valley of the
Somme in northern France, there was a windmill. Rusty and rustic,
yes, but it worked well, turning softly with the breeze and grinding the
wheat for flour, just as it was meant to do, and just as it had done at this
spot for three centuries since 1610.[3]

The forebear of the farmer upon whose land it now stood had placed
it precisely there as it was the highest, windiest spot on his farm, indeed
the highest spot in a 12-mile radius, and he was content with it. It

1

was all part of the natural order of things. The birds flew, the dogs barked, the cows gave their milk, Madame Farmer gave birth to their children and that windmill clicked over as regularly as the passage of the seasons, the passing of the years.

What were the chances that its sails would soon be turned not by the breeze but by the winds of war?[4] What was the likelihood they would suddenly spin, pushed by the concussive force of shells falling nearby, shells that would soon blow the whole windmill apart? And what probability that thousands of other farmers who hailed and sailed from the other side of the planet – strangers with guns, coming from strange places with stranger still names such as Gunning, Gundagai, Gunbar and Goondiwindi – would fight for their lives, *sacrifice* their lives, to secure the site on which the rubble of the windmill stood, against the claims of more thousands of men coming from a neighbouring country, equally desperate to deny them?

Infinitesimally small.

But it all happened, and herein lies a tale . . .

In the northern summer of 1914, the Great War hit Europe and her attendant empires like a vicious thunderstorm on a shining day. The sky darkened, the tension crackled, the thunder boomed and, yes, the winds blew. And then the storm hit with a force unparalleled in human history. Within the space of one week from 28 July 1914, Germany and Austria-Hungary were at war with Serbia, Russia, Great Britain, France and Belgium, and suddenly ten million soldiers were on the move. Cities fell to the beat of foreign boots, buildings and bridges were destroyed, and, even in the first few weeks, tens of thousands of citizens and soldiers were slaughtered.

Perhaps the most extraordinary thing was the number of people who – instead of being devastated by this turn of events – were completely thrilled by it. There is no better example of this strange phenomenon than a poorly educated, out-of-work, 25-year-old Austrian artist, barely surviving in Munich, living off his mediocre talent. For, right on the cusp of the Great War breaking out, this artist was said to be standing in Munich's main square, the Odeonsplatz, to hear the pro-war speakers up to and including Kaiser Wilhelm II, and was overjoyed as never before in his life. 'The sword must now decide,' the Kaiser had told his people,[5] and now he, Adolf Hitler, was going to be one of the millions with the honour of lifting that sword for Germany.

After the Germans flooded into Belgium and France, and the million soldiers in the five French armies and the 100,000 soldiers of the British Expeditionary Force under Field Marshal Sir John French surged forward to meet them, 80,000 soldiers on the Allied side were killed in the *first month*. On just one day, 22 August 1914, over 25,000 French soldiers were slaughtered in battle.

By early September, seven German armies, totalling one and a half million men, had fought all the way to the River Marne, a tributary of the Seine, east of Paris. The residents of the French capital were so convinced that the city was about to fall – the Germans were just 30 miles away – that no fewer than a million Parisians fled, including the French Government, which announced that its new seat of power was in Bordeaux.

Just when it looked as though France was to face cataclysmic defeat, the French reserve turned up at the front – 6000 of them, in Parisian taxicabs, ever after to be known as *les taxis de la Marne* – and were able to hold the Germans off. Some figures stood especially tall. There was the Commander-in-Chief of the entire French Armed Forces on the Western Front, the jowly, red-faced and white-haired General Joseph 'Papa' Joffre, who exuded such confidence that, no matter how dire the circumstances, he still insisted on six-course banquet lunches at his General Headquarters (GHQ) in Vitry-le-François, followed by an hour's nap, and *then* he would deal with the war. But he makes an impression all right. 'There never was anyone less like the ordinary conception of a great soldier, than Joffre,' wrote Colonel John Charteris, Chief Intelligence Officer under British General Sir Douglas Haig, in a letter home. 'He is a very big person, very placid in appearance, almost benevolent, slow in his movements and in his speech, and has remarkable eyes – very steady and still. He keeps his eyes fixed on you all the time you are with him, not glaring, or unfriendly, but just as if he were determined that no change of expression should pass unnoticed.'[6]

Joffre's leading officer in the line was General Ferdinand Foch, the Commander of the Ninth Army, who evinced equal *savoir faire,* even in the worst of battles. 'My centre is giving way, my right falling back; the situation is excellent,' he reported to Joffre during the First Battle of the Marne. *'J'attaque.'*[7]

There were heavy casualties, but Foch was sanguine on the subject, famously noting, 'It takes 15,000 casualties to train a major general.'[8] More than mere machine guns, what counted for him was *le caractère*: men with the courage to attack, come what may.

In such views, he was joined by a couple of significant British officers of the British Expeditionary Force. Commander of the 5th Infantry Brigade Brigadier-General Richard Haking – a Boer War veteran and former Professor specialising in tactics and strategy at the British Army Staff College, who in both capacities had become ever closer to General Haig – had even written a textbook on it. *Company Training* was a work that many of the younger British officers had studied closely. 'There is one rule which can never be departed from and which will alone lead to success,' Haking had asserted in the book, and now asserted to all and sundry on the front in person, 'and that is always to push forward, always to attack . . .

'The importance of the attack, as compared with any other form of military operation, is so vast that it practically swamps the remainder . . .

'The only weapon which can possibly lead us to success is the spirit of offensive from the highest to the lowest.'[9]

He was strongly supported in this by his friend, ally and superior officer General Haig, who also passionately believed in the virtues of offensive actions over defensive. 'The idea that a war can be won by standing on the defensive and waiting for the enemy to attack is a dangerous fallacy,' Haig would say, 'which owes its inception to the desire to evade the price of victory.'[10]

If that price was tens of thousands of your own soldiers dead, so be it. That was as regrettable as it was unavoidable, if you actually were prepared to do what it took to win. Both Haig and Haking were, and it was part of the bond between them.

Taking the opposite approach to all of them, however, was another French officer, the dashing bachelor Brigadier-General Henri-Philippe Pétain, who, like Foch, had lectured at the French Army College, *L'École de Guerre*, for years. As one who understood better than most the power of machine guns and artillery, Pétain preached the virtues of a well-prepared defence, that the best way to kill the enemy was to pick your battleground, lace it with machine guns and heavy artillery, and lure your enemy onto it. When you had to attack, it should only be done after the artillery had carried out the essential work of softening up the defenders.

One of Pétain's officers, Lieutenant Charles de Gaulle, agreed, noting how the old-world tactics of his confrères stood no chance in this new world of military machinery now killing its enemies on an industrial scale. 'With affected calm,' de Gaulle would write of his experiences at this time, 'the [French] officers let themselves be killed standing upright, some obstinate platoons stuck their bayonets in their rifles, bugles sounded the charge, isolated heroes made fantastic leaps, but all to no purpose. In an instant it had become clear that not all the courage in the world could withstand this fire.'[11] Of the quality of Pétain's leadership, de Gaulle had no doubt, later writing that he 'showed me the meaning of the gift and art of command'.[12]

Military theories of all stripes would soon be put to the test as never before, as the carnage continued on an unprecedented scale. General Joffre's instructions to his commanders at the Marne, reversing the retreat, would be long recalled: 'The hour has come to advance at all costs and to die where you stand.'[13] And so they did.

With the German advance on Paris stalled, on 14 September the German Army's 66-year-old Chief of Staff, General Helmuth von Moltke, was replaced by a younger and more vigorous successor, the 53-year-old career soldier General Erich von Falkenhayn. The new Chief of Staff launched his armies on a series of battles designed to outflank the enemy resistance, only to come up against hastily dug trenches at every turn (the best defence against machine guns and shrapnel from shells),[14] obliging his own men to dig in.

For the French, things were now so desperate that General Joffre felt obliged to strip men and guns from those sectors where little appeared to be happening, including, most particularly, the forts around the town of Verdun, which sat astride the River Meuse, 140 miles east of Paris. The French held, and the Germans kept trying to outflank to the north. In the path of the German flood in late September lay a very small hamlet on the slope of a small rise, strung out for three-quarters of a mile alongside the road between the towns of Amiens and Bapaume. That windmill at Pozières was among the first structures to be destroyed as the German Army rolled through on 27 September, on its way to taking over the adjacent village of Thiepval.

Blocked by the French just a mile to the west, the Germans tried to attack on their right flank, only to be blocked again, occasioning the invaders to try again, further still on the right flank. And so a similar process went on and on, the front slowly extending towards the English Channel.

As both sides had machine guns and artillery, the only way to survive and hold ground was to dig *still more* trenches, and the only way to stop being outflanked was to dig a trench that went further than your enemy's. In this area, the Germans were to dig two trench systems that would incorporate the captured villages of Thiepval and Pozières. They then turned them into 'fortress villages', with many of their houses fortified with Lille concrete and their cellars linked to form underground warrens.

—

Further north still, the Germans had very nearly overwhelmed the French at Arras, only for General Foch to inspire his men with the command 'No retirement; every man to the battle'.[15]

Again the Germans were blocked, and again they tried to outflank to the north. The famed 'Race to the Sea' was now well underway as the

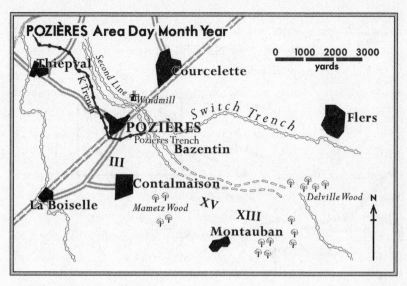

Pozières area at the end of 1914

two sides continued their furious efforts to outflank the other, with the parallel trenches of *die Westfront*, as the Germans called it (the Western Front), snaking north for what would be a scar on the landscape 470 miles long, from Alsace at the Swiss frontier with France to the North Sea, separated by a No-Man's Land that continued to kill most of those who ventured into it. For with no further chance to outflank the enemy, the only choice for those who wished to attack was to do so front-on, straight at their guns, across open ground. Thousands more were killed and the need for reinforcements was more urgent than ever.

And for the tiny village of Fromelles – just ten miles west of the huge concrete-manufacturing and wool-processing centre of Lille, with its major rail junction – it was the beginning of the end.

Fromelles was a typical village in the poppy fields of Flanders, where a thousand citizens lived in red-roofed houses amid a whole ocean of farmlands. They built their lives around the church and the market, proud of the height of its fourteenth-century steeple and the quality of its corn and vegetables in equal measure. Of course, *tout le monde* knew *tout le monde* and all of their *enfants* besides, the cobblestoned streets were deserted from midday for two hours as all of the population was at home for lunch and a nap, and in the evenings the strains of violins

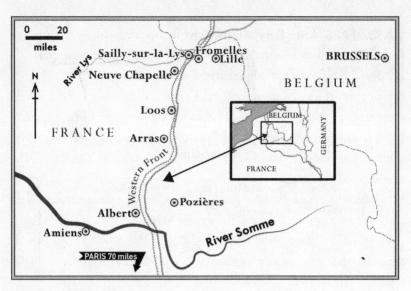

Fromelles in relation to Pozières

and accordions could be heard unusually late as just this very year the arrival of electricity lines had allowed the people to more easily press on into the night.

Modernity? It was just some weird movement among Parisian artists, and nothing to the people of Fromelles, whose horizons extended not much further than they could actually see – though, admittedly, as their settlement was perched atop a tiny ridge, that was further than most in the area.

The fertile soil, heavily worked by the industrious folk, was a rich quilt-work of colourful squares – here a freshly ploughed field, there a crop of corn, next to it a paddock of lucerne and beside it again a field as red as blood, filled with poppies in the warmer months.

And in the end, for Fromelles, it was exactly as had happened to hundreds of other French towns that lay in the path of the German advance. The experience really was like seeing the approach of a terrible storm that you just know is going to devastate you but against which you are powerless.

First the sky turned dark and they could hear the sound of distant gunfire, and even see flashes of artillery fire streaking across the dark night. Then the thunder was closer still, and a stream of refugees from nearby towns came racing through, with shocking stories of murder and rape, and then they could hear rifle and machine-gun fire and . . . after a flurry of bloodied remnants of French soldiers, finally the first of the German troops came, initially as a grim trickle and then as a fierce and fearsome flood, engulfing all before it. And then the British pushed back, retaking the town for a brief period, before the flood of German soldiers came once more, this time securing it, from 21 October 1914 onwards.

Those who could get away quickly did so, loading wheelbarrows and carts before pushing west. All those who remained had to witness the devastation. Food was devoured by the German soldiers, cellars raided, weapons and ammunition confiscated. The order was given that all weapons must be handed in at the town hall (*la mairie*) on pain of their owners being shot. The French flag in front of *la mairie* was hauled down, and the German flag began to flutter. The clocks in the town were put forward an hour to German time, and those men who had not fled were soon dragooned into a labour force working for the German Army. And, as with other occupied villages, Fromelles was given its very own German name, Petzstadt ('town of Petz', after Friedrich Petz, the newly installed regimental commander), while Aubers became Buchheim and even a patch of previously unnamed woods just below Fromelles was called Fasanen-Wäldchen ('Little Pheasant Wood', as it was here where the pheasants flocked).

In no more than a few days, the peaceful village was under occupation. All residents were issued with new identification passes that they had to carry with them at all times. They now had to live under German rule with 11 million other Belgian and French citizens, for this was now *German* territory, run as a military state, and any *Schweinehund* who resisted that notion . . . risked being shot. Others – no fewer than 60,000 Belgians and 3000 French – were sent to German concentration camps.

And, yes, there was great distress among the local populations – most particularly about being obliged to eat the German *Kriegsbrot*, 'war bread', which had 'an exterior like a rock and a soft, slimy interior'[16]

– but, at Fromelles in particular, no real surprise. For invasions by soldiers in this part of the world were like bad droughts in other areas: they simply came with the territory and always had done, since the Romans, led by none other than Julius Caesar, had arrived in 55 bc. The Hundred Years War was fought in these parts from 1337, as was the Thirty Years War from 1618. The Battle of Agincourt was fought nearby in 1415, as was the Battle of Waterloo in 1815, 70 miles east of Fromelles. Indeed, this part of Flanders had only become French after Louis XIV had successfully waged war against the Spanish Netherlands from 1667.

For the moment, however, both Fromelles and Pozières remained in relatively quiet sectors, and most of the killing took place in other areas, where both sides sent sally after sally across No-Man's Land, only to be killed in great numbers and for the contours of the trenches to barely change from one week to the next. 'I don't know what is to be done,' Great Britain's Secretary of State for War, Lord Kitchener, said in the face of this dreadfully static battle. 'This isn't war.'[17]

All up, it meant that, by early November 1914, at the German Oberste Heeresleitung (Supreme Army Command), a key decision had to be taken. With Germany's resources increasingly required against the Russians in the East, and the Allies continuing to get stronger in the West, it was clear that further German advances in France were simply not realistic if they kept going in the same way. After seven infantry divisions and one cavalry division were diverted from the West and dispatched with all possible speed to the East, Falkenhayn felt he had no choice. Following the first, failed Battle of Ypres on 17 November 1914, he made the decision to 'act purely on the defensive in France, with the most careful application of every imaginable technical device'.[18]

The key tactical innovation was to have defence in depth, with specific German GHQ regulations ordering that 'several lines connected with one another [are] to be instituted, with two or several positions one behind the other'.[19] In this manner, even if the enemy did break through the first line, there would be enough defence behind that to contain the outbreak and then counter-attack. 'The garrisons in the front line,' Falkenhayn further insisted, 'are indeed to be kept as small as possible in order to avoid losses by artillery fire. But they have to hold out at all costs until the reinforcements stationed in the rear-lines can come up to give what support they can.'[20]

The route of that system of trenches, while broadly determined by the points at which the attackers' forces were roughly equalled by the defenders', was influenced by many other factors.

A key one was the value to the Germans of each piece of captured French territory, in terms of providing the raw resources, industrial output and skilled workers to keep their war machine fuelled, humming and productive. A clear case in point was the 250,000-strong town of Lille, surrounded by rich agricultural land and an industrial centre that, among other things, produced millions of tons of concrete annually – something that would be in high demand as the Germans built concrete machine-gun emplacements and artillery shelters all along the front. It had to be held, whatever the cost.

Another factor was the directive by von Falkenhayn to his generals to secure the high ground – with good observation and a distinct tactical advantage over those who would attack them uphill – and nowhere was that more important than in the remarkably flat country just to the west of Lille. For just as 'in the kingdom of the blind, the one-eyed man is king', so too, militarily, on an otherwise pancake-flat terrain even a small ridge is priceless. And Aubers Ridge happened to be exactly that: a small swell of land that rose just above sea level – by just how much depended on whether the tide was in or out in *La Manche*, the English Channel, just 55 miles to the west – upon which the villages of Fromelles and nearby Aubers were nestled.

Any move by the British to retake Lille meant they would have to take this ridge, so the Germans put enormous efforts into protecting it. The starting point was the construction of a front-line trench system, Stellung I – two parallel trenches, Front and Support, 200 yards apart – placed a thousand yards or so from the foot of the high ground, supported by concrete dugouts capable of withstanding even direct hits by small shells. Then a second trench system, Stellung II, was constructed a mile further back on the high ground. If the enemy got through Stellung I, they'd be too weak to also capture Stellung II, and it was from Stellung II that counter-attacks would be launched. Here they would be safer from shelling yet still close enough to move quickly to the front-lines if necessary. It was even hoped that Germany's new western border across France would have a third line when completed, Stellung III. Observation posts would occupy the high ground, with artillery stationed on the far side of the ridge from the enemy. Together, that artillery and those observers would be able to rain down hell on all those who would seek to attack that first line.

As the Pozières windmill also stood near the top of a ridge – in fact, both the windmill and Fromelles village (40 miles north of Pozières) occupied the highest ground for miles around – it too was heavily entrenched.

The British defenders did not have the luxury of building their trenches to exploit the terrain. As the most noted Fromelles historian, Peter Barton, would observe, the British were imbued with the doctrine that the offensive was the soul of defence: 'regardless of tactical, topographical or sanitary suitability, the order went out: the troops were to hold the positions from which the last German attack had been repulsed'.[21] At Fromelles, this put them in the squalid and marshy flatlands before Aubers Ridge. At Pozières, it similarly subjugated them beneath the eponymous ridge.

For the Commander-in-Chief of the British Expeditionary Force Sir John French was firm: 'As much pressure as possible'[22] must be brought to bear upon the enemy. Not an inch of territory was to be conceded. And if that meant trying to build trenches in soggy mud, beneath the gaze of the Germans lobbing shells onto them from on high, well, so be it.

By the end of 1914, there were almost 3,000,000 men on the Western Front: 60,000 Belgians, 200,000 British, 1,200,000 French and 1,500,000 Germans. The British, at this point, were holding 40 miles of the 450-mile-long Front, from the Belgian town of Ypres in the north to La Bassée, France, in the south, and . . .

And it is an officer of the Royal Irish Rifles who distinctly hears it first:

Stille Nacht . . . heilige Nacht
Alles schläft . . . einsam wacht

The Germans have the same Christmas carols as us? Who knew?

But, of course, it was not long before soldiers on the British side of the line were joining in, and the two sides were singing together, their voices mingling high over No-Man's Land and drifting off into the night sky:

Schlaf in himmlischer . . . Ruh!
Sleep in heavenly . . . peace!

'They sang and played to us several of their own tunes,' a British soldier recorded, 'and some of ours, such as "Home, Sweet Home", "Tipperary", &c., while we did the same for them.'[23]

Further down the line, at a spot just a few miles north-east of the village of Neuve Chapelle and a similar distance north-west of Fromelles, a cry from the German side came out: 'English soldier, English soldier, a merry Christmas, a merry Christmas!'

'Come out, English soldier; come out here to us.'

For a time, the English soldiers were cautious and did not even answer, their officers ordering the men to be silent. But then English shouts were heard up and down the line. 'Merry Christmas, German soldiers!'[24]

On Christmas Day, Major Robert Fellowes of the Rifle Brigade inspected his trenches in front of the nearby village of Fromelles: 'An armistice was on and the whole of the neutral ground between our trenches and the Germans was covered with men . . . It was a weird sight, English and Germans all hobnobbing together, perfectly friendly.'[25]

With similar fraternisation between British and German soldiers along much of the line, there was hell to pay. Once General Sir Horace

Smith-Dorrien, commander of the British II Corps, learned of the consorting, he instantly issued 'strictest orders, that on no account is intercourse to be allowed between the opposing troops. To finish this war quickly, we must keep up the fighting spirit and do all we can to discourage friendly intercourse.'[26]

When the *Daily Mirror* published an image of the truce on the front page – 'Exclusive. The First Photographs from the Unofficial Xmas Truce' – all the authorities could do was prevent distribution to the Western Front. Similar silence was ordered by *dem Kaiserreich*, the Kaiser's government, for the same reasons. The French did not need any kind of censorship, as they had already printed their version of events, that 'When the Germans started singing, the brave French yelled, *"Maul halten, deutsche Schweine!* Shut up, German pigs!"'[27]

In General Sir Douglas Haig's First Army Headquarters, mean-while, all the talk was on how to retake Lille by unleashing four divisions – 80,000 soldiers in all – at the German lines around Neuve Chapelle, which lay five miles south-west of the village of Fromelles, on an important crossroads. It would be the first major British attack against entrenched German positions of the war, and the intent was to stop containing the brutes and start pushing them back. After they took Aubers Ridge, they would press on to Lille.

One obvious place to start was the relatively lightly defended sector in front of Fromelles. The major obstacle was the Germans occupying Aubers Ridge, which – running through the villages of Fromelles and Aubers – was the key 'high ground' geographical feature of the area. Added to this, the simultaneous attacks would threaten from north and south the rail, road and canal junction of La Bassée, cutting the major German supply line to the German front further south.

And so, at 7.30 on the morning of 10 March 1915, it began. For 35 minutes, no fewer than 530 British guns poured a total of 40,000 shells of hell on Neuve Chapelle, on both front-line and reserve German positions, with an intensity the British had never remotely approached before in the history of their empire. (In fact, as it would be noted, more artillery shells fell over the next four days, 216,000 in total, than

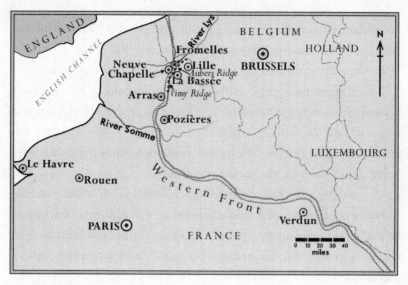

Northern France

had been expended in the Second Boer War – an indication of how far the science of war, the industrialisation of the act of slaughtering your enemies, had advanced. In this new warfare, you could be killed not just from in front but also from on high, from either side, from behind and from below.)

Outnumbering the German defenders by a factor of five, 40,000 British and Indian soldiers charged forward across a 4000-yard front, only for many of them to be gunned down by German soldiers emerging from reinforced dugouts left substantially untouched by the bombardment. In the confusion of battle, little of this was apparent to the senior officers at HQ. The Middlesex Regiment, for example, was thought to have stormed through, 'for not a man came back to report otherwise'.[28]

Yet not all the British casualties had fallen to German fire. In fact, many of the attacking soldiers had fallen to their *own* bombardment, which was of insufficient accuracy.

Four days after it began, the battle was over, with the British managing to hold on to just one square mile of formerly enemy territory at Neuve Chapelle for all the lives lost and lamed – 11,652 casualties in all.

———

'Consider the casualties,' the aghast former British Prime Minister Arthur Balfour said to Secretary of State for War Lord Kitchener. 'There must have been nearly 10,000 men lost in these engagements.'

'Eight thousand seven hundred at Neuve Chapelle,' Kitchener confirmed. 'But it isn't the men I mind. I can replace the men at once, but I can't replace the shells so easily.'[29]

As a matter of fact, worthy replacements for some of those men were being formed in Australia at that very time . . .

General Haig looked on the bright side. A GHQ memorandum recorded for posterity the wonderful lesson that had been learned, if only it could be properly applied! 'In spite of wire and trenches,' he wrote, 'we can break the enemy's line, given adequate numbers and preparations.'[30]

But the Germans, too, had learned some hard lessons from the fact that they had lost control of Neuve Chapelle. The first and most important thing: they needed more men in this part of the Western Front, and so the entire 6th Bavarian Reserve Division, which had been rushed there during the battle from Lille, was ordered to return and stay permanently. ('Reserve' here indicated that it was predominantly made up of reservists – men who already had some military training and could be called up in the event of war.)

Front and centre in the lower ranks of the newly arrived 16th Bavarian Reserve Infantry Regiment (RIR) was the just-promoted Corporal Adolf Hitler. The one time infantryman now became a *Meldegänger*, messenger, for the 16th Bavarian Reserve Regiment HQ, whose job in the midst of battle was to brave the bullets and run messages. With his comrades, he marched through the village of Fromelles for the first time deep in the night of 17 March 1915.

Met by Prussian non-commissioned officers (NCOs) who were there to guide them to their positions, the men marched down the slight slope to the trenches that awaited a mile north-west of the village. They awoke the next morning to look out on a ravaged vista across No-Man's Land of 'British trenches, meadows, brooks, drainage canals, occasional trees, and a small forest in the distance'.[31]

There was a strong sense of being in the middle of a once beautiful painting, now slashed. In the words of the chaplain of the 6th Bavarian Division, 'We find ourselves in a magnificent area . . . We are surrounded by *einem lieblichen Hügelland*, lovely rolling hills, with many small towns and villages, as well as numerous castles in magnificent parks . . . Naturally not everything remains in its ideal condition. The villages and castles are sad ruins, the parks are laid waste in parts. Everything speaks of former grandeur and lost glory.'[32]

But quiet? Yes, at that moment. So quiet that the key concern of the military authorities was to remind the newly installed Bavarians 'that on Belgian and French railroads the platforms are usually on the left'.[33]

Ran an die Arbeit! But to work! For in the wake of the recent battle, it was clear that the German line had to be reinforced, and so Adolf Hitler and his comrades set about building ever more secure fortifications. With a water table that was only 18 inches below the surface, 'breastworks' were built up (rather than trenches dug down), and the Germans piled their existing parapets ever higher and wider. In the space of just a week, fortifications went from four feet high and five feet wide to seven feet high and as much as 20 feet across.

Extra tangles of heavy-gauge barbed wire – up to five feet high in places and as much as 15 yards wide, with a few gaps left for men to venture through – were installed just forward of the front trenches. Even more barbed wire was secreted in the breastwork earth excavations – 'borrow pits' made directly in front of the parapets, invisible from those in the flatlands opposite. High-powered pumps were installed so, below the surface, the Germans could construct secure concrete shelters in which to take refuge from enemy bombardment. The shelters increased in size, depth and purpose the further back from the front-line they were built.

Machine-gun emplacements in heavy hardwood boxes were positioned 20 yards apart in the breastworks so their arcs of fire perfectly interlocked – with all parts of No-Man's Land exposed to front-on and flanking fire from *both* sides. Wooden bridges were constructed to cross the deep drainage ditches that lay all around. In No-Man's Land itself, there was one ditch in particular, ten feet wide and three feet deep, Laies creek, known by the French as La Rivière Laies and the Germans as Leierbach, that went all the way through No-Man's Land and cut through the British front-line, forming a natural impediment. Meanwhile, front-line living quarters for soldiers and officers were improved in terms of both comfort and safety. Everything possible was done to protect the front-line troops from a barrage, allowing them to survive . . . so they could slaughter all those enemies foolish enough to venture forward.

Nowhere was more energy devoted to strengthening the defences than on a particular spot on the plain just a thousand yards west of Fromelles. This particular part of Fritz's line jutted forward in a deliberate salient – meaning defenders who manned it could shoot both forward and along the channels either side of No-Man's Land. If it could be held, it would be a perfect defensive point, and the Germans made sure that all of its machine-gun emplacements were in working order. British soldiers soon called this low-slung defensive structure the 'Sugar-loaf', as, from the air, it resembled the shape of the loaves of sugar being sold at the time, with a wide, round base and rising to a narrower rounded top.

Some 100 yards wide, it jutted out at the point of a wider salient of about 1500 yards, and was constructed in such a manner that machine guns could fire as easily from its sides as from its front, meaning that, no matter from what angle it was attacked, the German soldiers would be able to bring massive firepower to bear – including on those trying to pass on either side anywhere within 600 yards.

And even then, it was only a beginning to the defences in the area.

Above ground, low-lying structures were built, acting as an as yet uncompleted second line of defence, about half a mile back from the front-line (between the first German trench system on the flatland and the second trench system on Aubers Ridge). Many buildings, such as farm houses, barns and churches, were taken over and given extra concrete superstructures, in case the enemy broke through and the Germans had to fall back. One particular structure was an unfinished, concealed German strongpoint called the Grashof.

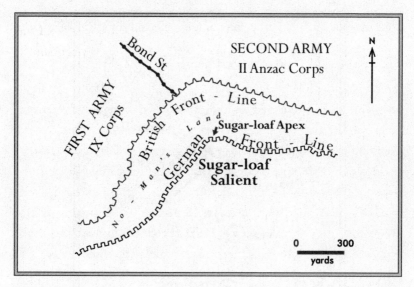

Sugar-loaf

If the Germans were working particularly assiduously, as if their lives depended on it, it was because they did. If the defences were weak, it was they personally who would suffer, because – unlike the British and French – they didn't rotate often. And because they were no longer trying to take over France, it made sense that these defences be supreme. The German attitude was that this rich slice of France and Belgium was now theirs. As one writer would put it, the Germans viewed their defences 'as the borders of the new, greater Germany. Thus they were designed and built to fortress standard, constructed on a scale and quality unmatched by their opponents.'[34]

That acute observer the official Australian War Correspondent Charles Bean would much later note, 'The German staff and troops, unlike the British, pursued a policy of extreme economy, and spared no pains to protect the trench-garrison from such avoidable losses, a difference of practice which had important consequences, and of which the roots lay deep in the respective national characters.'[35]

The Germans also increased their firepower, both in terms of machine guns and artillery.

Which was propitious.

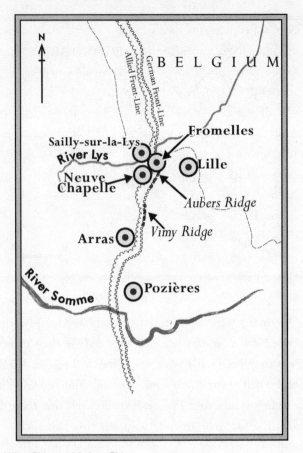

Location of Vimy Ridge and Aubers Ridge

For, at 5 am on Sunday 9 May 1915, the improved defences were tested when a second major battle was launched in the same area. While the French Tenth Army attacked Vimy Ridge 18 miles to the south, General Sir Douglas Haig's First Army, comprising six divisions, carried out a pincer movement against German positions to the north-east and south-west of Neuve Chapelle, attacking once more towards Aubers Ridge. The northern claw, comprising two British brigades advancing on a front of just 1400 yards, was aimed right at Fromelles.

A 40-minute bombardment – which, as Second-Lieutenant K. H. E. Moore of 1/7 Middlesex, 23rd Brigade put it, meant 'the ground simply shook like a jelly'[36] – failed to damage the well-secured Germans in their dugouts. Haig sent his forces over open ground at an enemy dug into entrenched positions, with enough ammunition stockpiled to sink a battleship. It all meant the subsequent catastrophe had Haig's name in the bottom right-hand corner.

The experience of soldiers such as Lance-Corporal William Prouse of the Royal Berkshire Regiment, as recounted to a friend, appeared near universal: 'The bombardment started . . . and there were about a thousand guns on the go until 5.45. I thought the Germans' front line trench would have been filled with their dead, but at the order to advance the Germans were still in their front trench, and what a murderous fire they put into us!'[37]

And it was just the same a little further back, as detailed by *Times* Special Correspondent to his readers in London, in his report of the battle: 'The enemy's infantry was massed in great force on their second line and had suffered little from our shells. These trenches were deep and reinforced with concrete, with under-ground galleries, giving almost complete immunity from shell fire. When our bombardment ceased and our infantry began the advance the enemy issued from these subterranean shelters, manned their battered surface trenches, and turned upon our advancing troops the concentrated fire of massed machine guns.'[38]

Nowhere was the casualty list heavier than among the troops under the command of now Major-General Richard Haking's 1st Division. After just one hour, they had lost 2135 men, without having gained a yard. Nevertheless, a man of principle, the 53-year-old Haking stayed true to the view he had published in his textbook *Company Training*. In that book, after fondly endorsing the attacking tactics of the Confederates in the American Civil War half a century earlier in 1861, and going through some of the other wars since, he exulted in the virtues of the 'paralysing breath of an attack . . . vigorously maintained and continued to the final assault. We shall find it again in the next great war. Put any army we like against the other, put what we think is the stronger on the defensive, and imbue it with the defensive spirit, and the weaker on the offensive, and the [attackers] will win as sure as there is a sun in the heavens.'[39]

Was there a sun in the heavens on this day? There certainly was, shining brightly, and no matter that this meant the attackers were perfectly visible to snipers, machine-gunners and artillery observers – nor that the ubiquity and power of high-powered rifles, machine guns and artillery had increased many times over since Haking had first formed his theory.

For Haking had attacked *again*, an hour later, following a bombardment that did most damage to the wounded still lying on the field from the first assault. This second attack had failed too, and so, at 4 pm, with encouragement from General Haig, Haking sent his reserves forth for King and Country, for God and Honour, for . . . exactly the same result.

Haking's solution? Attack, AGAIN, over the same ground, against an enemy so far entirely untroubled by the first three attacks. This time, mercifully, Haking's most senior officers nearly mutinied. Appalled at such wanton waste of life, Brigadier Sir Cecil Lowther of the Guards and Brigadier Harold R. Davies of 3rd Brigade tell Haking to his face, 'We have had enough of this reckless waste of life . . . To send troops forward yet again into the teeth of such machine gun fire would be a criminal squandering of brave men . . . Another attempt would be pointless and disastrous.'[40]

With his Brigadiers saying it would amount to 'a criminal undertaking',[41] the attack was called off, but no fewer than 3968 of Haking's men had gone down.

When the smoke had cleared, just 24 hours after the battle had begun, no fewer than 11,500 British and Indian soldiers lay dead or wounded.

The Germans? From their secure, well-entrenched positions, the Germans suffered just 1551 casualties.

Ground gained by the attackers?

None. Not a yard.

Where they had broken into the German lines at one point, it was only to be quickly driven out again.

Still, it seemed a valuable lesson had been learned – by some. Without first destroying the defensive infrastructure and the defenders with artillery, mass attacks against entrenched German positions were suicidal. This time, even General Sir Douglas Haig was clear. 'The [German] defences in our front are so carefully and strongly made,' he noted in his diary, 'and mutual support with machine-guns is so complete, that in order to demolish them a long methodical bombardment will be necessary by heavy artillery before infantry are sent forward to attack.'[42]

Nothing like that had happened on this occasion, and *thousands* of British women were now widows, yet the editorial of *The Times* substantially spared Haig from blame. He was, after all, following the orders of his Commanding Officer, Sir John French. Instead, the writer pointed an accusatory finger in a different direction: 'British soldiers died in vain on the Aubers Ridge on Sunday because more shells were needed. The Government, who have so seriously failed to organize adequately our national resources, must bear their share of the grave responsibility. Even now they will not fully face the situation.'[43] Among other causes, no fewer than 3000 shells that had been earmarked for the Aubers Ridge battle had been diverted to Gallipoli to support the Anzacs.

And yet, as successful as the German defences had been, still German High Command was unhappy that many of the shelters protecting its soldiers from shells were too weak for the task. German engineers now oversaw the construction of still stronger dugouts, with yet *more* reinforced concrete, further protected by more earth piled on top.

Even the house of God, the Fromelles church, was converted to the cause of German defence, becoming 'a solid cube of concrete, except for a stair so narrow that only with difficulty could a normally built man ascend . . . It terminated in a loophole for an observer who with a telescope could, with perfect safety to himself, count every sentry in our lines. He also had an extensive view across our back areas, and could at once detect any preparation for attack.'[44]

To increase German firepower, specially protected emplacements were constructed just 200 yards behind the front-lines for the *Minenwerfer* – mine throwers or trench mortars, capable of hurling 200-pound shells right onto the British lines.

On the British side, little changed in terms of approach. Allow almost all of Belgium and a fifth of France to remain German? Out of the question! Have High Command hold individual commanders accountable, then, for the wanton waste of the lives of their men, even long after it was obvious that continuing would see their certain massacre? No. And certainly not when the officers in question were friends and allies, such as Major-General Richard Haking, who had attended the British Army Staff College for officers, Camberley, with Haig and risen through the ranks with him from there, as Haig is only a year older. (Haig had failed mathematics in the entrance exam, only narrowly escaping rejection, while Haking had gone on to become no less than a Professor of tactics.)

Still, not only was Haking not held to account for the loss of so many men – as the overall plan had not been of his making, and the lack of adequate artillery support not his fault – but he was also promoted shortly afterwards to Lieutenant-General to command XI Corps, thus placing him in charge of three divisions, totalling 60,000 soldiers in the line.

And so, on 25 September 1915, just ten miles south of Aubers Ridge, at the Battle of Loos, 'The Big Push' began. Using classic nine-teenth-century military thinking against twentieth-century military technology, at Loos the British soldiers walked in formation straight into a blizzard of machine-gun bullets and lost over 2000 men, killed, in the first hour. And yet, this was just the opening stanza of a battle that was still far from reaching its crescendo of slaughter.

Author Robert Graves, who related his First World War experiences in his book *Goodbye to All That*, described how in the 2nd Battalion of the Royal Welch Fusiliers one officer charged forward and called for his men to join him . . . only to receive no immediate response.

'*You bloody cowards*,' he roared, 'are you leaving me to go on alone?'

'Not cowards, sir,' his wounded sergeant gasped back. 'Willing enough. But they're all fucking dead!'[45]

They had been felled by a single burst of a German machine gun at the moment they had charged forward.

After a delayed four-mile march, General Haking's XI Corps arrived too late at the firing line on the first day to make any impact. The sole, limited involvement came at 3 pm, when two of the 21st's battalions were as quickly ordered forward as they were annihilated.

At 11 the following morning, 26 September, Haking, chipper, ordered the remainder of his men to attack with force, and huge offensive spirit, the heavily defended enemy second line. That line, Haking told his senior officers, would be like 'a crust of pie – one thrust and it will be broken'.[46] Noting the scepticism in the faces of the veterans, Haking had followed up with an insistent, 'I don't tell you this to cheer you up. I tell you because I really believe it.'[47]

That scepticism among the hard nuts was heightened by their observation that the pre-assault barrage had failed to destroy the German wire, waist high and five yards deep. Still they and Haking's 14,000 sleep-deprived fledglings obeyed his orders and advanced across open fields in blinding daylight straight towards German machine guns. Tragically, as it happened, this particular pie crust proved to be made of solid steel, which the bombardment hadn't even dented, and so shambolic was the attack that, beneath a barrage of shells and machine-gun fire from both flanks, the soldiers were slaughtered for their trouble.

In just a single day, Haking lost 8229 of his men: 4051 from the 21st and 4178 from the 24th – over 50 per cent of those committed to battle from the two divisions. The area became known as 'the corpse field'.[48] The Germans, meanwhile, were prospering. All they needed to do was to ensure that their machine guns were pointed in the right direction – somewhere into the broad mass of men coming their way – keep the ammunition up to them, and keep the trigger pressed. On the final day of the battle, Lieutenant-General Haking's XI Corps lost another 7122 men – with 20,000 men now killed and wounded on his watch over the last six months – for the final gain of a few football fields of German-held territory.

Most of his men had been in France barely a month, with no experience of real war before this battle had begun. Which was precisely as Haking wanted. 'I had it from the XI Corps Commander himself,' a fellow officer would recall of his conversation with Haking before the battle, 'that . . . not having previously been engaged in this way, they would go into action for the first time full of esprit and élan, and being ignorant of the effects of fire and the intensity of it, would go forward irresistibly and do great things.'[49]

And yet, not for the first time, Haking's theories had not remotely worked. As one of the British correspondents, Philip Gibbs, would say of the British forces to Charles Bean, 'They simply broke and came back in pieces . . . column after column coming past dejected, hangdog, disgraced – they knew it, almost ready to weep on the mention of the disaster – a beaten ashamed army . . . It never got into the papers but there was a real row about it.'[50]

By battle's end at Loos, Britain had suffered 59,247 casualties, of which one was the son of Rudyard Kipling – prompting the famed poet to come up with the line 'Known unto God' to be put on the headstones of the graves of unknown soldiers.

To some, this high rate of casualties represented abject failure on Haking's part. To others, it showed he was that most prized of military men, a 'thruster',[51] a man not afraid to put his troops in harm's way in order to achieve the definitive breakthrough.

No, it had not quite worked this time, but it might next time. And he quickly started planning for it – a scheme he was very passionate about. It would see his forces straighten out the salient in the German lines around Fromelles and take Aubers Ridge before marching on Lille. He was convinced it could be done and a great victory recorded against his name.

Haking, in fact, would be knighted within months, his military career blossoming at least on paper, notwithstanding the fact he was personally detested by most who knew him well. In the words of Lieutenant-Colonel Philip Game, a future governor of New South Wales, who served under him, Haking was 'really impossible, untruthful and a bully and not to be trusted'. In a letter to his wife, he warmed to the theme. 'We are all very angry with the Corps Commander,' he wrote. 'I shall not be sorry to pass from his ken, he is a bad man.'[52]

Yet, even beyond the fact that he was a thruster, and a friend of Haig's, Haking had another thing going for him. That is, he was Haig's ally in bringing down Sir John French, the Commander of the British Expeditionary Force. Well connected, Haking had told King George V quietly when the latter visited France a month after the Battle of Loos that Sir John French was manifestly unsuited for the role he was filling.

Another British Army commander to speak on this matter to his Sovereign was Hubert Gough of 1st Corps, who would later recall, 'I would not pretend that Sir John [French] was fitted for the responsibilities he had, and the King was surprised by the examples I gave him of the C-in-C's failings.'[53] French's failings had been a rather enduring problem.

As long before as November 1914, Lord Kitchener had wanted to replace French with Sir Ian Hamilton – who had soon gone off instead to run the Dardanelles campaign – but the power of incumbency had seen French remain. After the disasters of Neuve Chapelle and Aubers, Loos had been General French's last chance to show he had what it took to run an army of 60 divisions instead of the six he had started with, and this time there would be no forgiveness.

Grateful for the preliminary work done by the likes of Gough and Haking, Haig also had the King's ear, and he was strong in his remarks to his Sovereign on the subject, even if it was certain His Majesty needed little convincing. In fact, on a visit to the front, it had been the King himself who had raised the subject in a private conversation in Haig's writing room, and who had spoken 'a great deal about a paper which Winston Churchill had written and given to the Cabinet, criticising the operations in France, and arriving at the conclusion that nothing had been achieved!'.[54]

Privately, Haig was of the view that 'Winston's head is gone from taking drugs', but on the subject of the failings of General French, he was eager to expand.[55]

'I therefore think strongly,' Haig concluded with George V, 'that, for the sake of the Empire, French ought to be removed. I, personally, am ready to do my duty in any capacity, and of course would serve under anyone who was chosen for his military skill to be C. in C.'[56]

Of course, there was never any doubt as to whom Haig truly had in mind to fill the position.

And so begins the tale proper . . .

PART ONE

THE BATTLE KNELL IS NIGH

Under the level winter sky
I saw a thousand Christs go by.
They sang an idle song and free
As they went up to calvary.

Careless of eye and coarse of lip,
They marched in holiest fellowship.
That heaven might heal the world, they gave
Their earth-born dreams to deck the grave.

With souls unpurged and steadfast breath
They supped the sacrament of death.
And for each one, far off, apart,
Seven swords have rent a woman's heart.
'Marching Men', by Marjorie Pickthall

Chapter One

THE DRUMS OF WAR

Well Dad, that finishes with the Peninsula where we showed
the world that Australians, with all their faults, are not
quitters. What is in store for us in the future remains to be
seen, but I don't think it will be any worse than what we went
through at Gallipoli, anyway we can only do our duty.[1]
Sergeant Richard Job Gardiner, 7th Battalion,
1st AIF, early January 1916

The first Anzac 'die-hards' arrived . . . and marched along
a road a mile long between lines of cheering troops. Very
proud they looked as the men cheered. None can forget
those strained, exhausted, dauntless faces. Their only
casualties were three sprained ankles. The troops were as
full of fight as ever, and will yet win some great battle.[2]
The Argus reports from Lemnos, 22 January 1916

Goodbye homeland and farewell to the many happy
hours of carefree youth! Farewell to the land we loved
so well and to those we held near and dear; before us lay
active service abroad on some foreign soil, privations,
hardships, dangers and perhaps even death itself.[3]
Private Harry Hartnett, 2nd Battalion, 1st AIF, writing
of the departure from Australia in January 1916

20 DECEMBER 1915, GALLIPOLI ASTERN, LEMNOS HARBOUR AHEAD

And here is Lemnos!

Through the boom that lies across the entrance of the harbour, the ships make their way, the surrounding hills that had been so lush with greenery when they had arrived in the spring now devoid of all vegetation in the winter. And now before them is a forest of masts and funnels rising from the most 'motley an assemblage of ships as ever came together'.[4]

And oh, the cheering when, at midday, the mighty 'Die Hards' – the last bastards to leave Anzac Cove – arrive. Disgorged from their ships, they march into camp down a route lined by men who had left Gallipoli earlier. They are led by the band of a Scottish regiment based on Lemnos, who are blowing their bagpipes as if there is no tomorrow. Then comes a portly brigade major, and now the Die Hards themselves.[5]

Look at them! Dirty ragamuffins the lot of them, with torn clothes, filthy faces, scraggy beards and boots that have more holes than leather. And how exhausted they are, 'a weary lot of men with heavy packs'.[6] Ah, but how we, their now rested comrades, cheer them 'all the way' with our 'good hearty lungs'.[7]

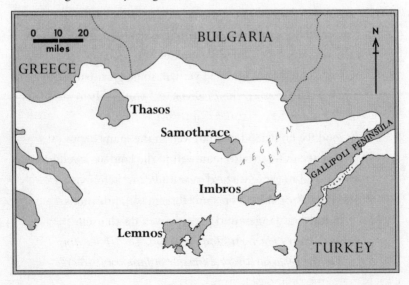

Lemnos

Most are young men, but all have old eyes, while one youngish officer is seen to have an amazing shock of white hair, likely for what he has seen and done. They march past like Guardsmen in front of Buckingham Palace, on parade for the King himself!

'Australians have made their name at Gallipoli,' Goldy Raws enthusiastically writes to his brother, 'and you should see the way the English officers (with all their smart clothes and tan belts, and we in our much worn out breeches and tunics) look up to us. I don't believe there is one that would not rather have been an Australian and one of the heroes at Anzac.'[8]

22 DECEMBER 1915, PASSING THE MARMALADE

They're a fine body of young Australian men, marching as to war. Clear of eye, straight of back, intent in purpose, marching in perfect rhythm – *leeeeft, leeeeft, left, right, leeeeft* – from Casula Camp on the northern banks of Sydney's sparkling Georges River. They are now heading down the thick red dust of the slight incline that leads into Liverpool Railway Station – where they are to board a train for a final musketry test at Long Bay Rifle Range.

The good citizens of Liverpool are beaming just to see them. The people stop in their tracks, pause in their paths, nudge each other. There they go, the reinforcement contingents destined for many AIF battalions.

And the soldiers themselves share their awe. After weeks heading into months of hard training, they *feel* like soldiers, feel like a body of fighting men, ready to take on whatever the world in general and the Huns and the Turks in particular can throw at them.

As they march by, not absolutely *everyone* is impressed, however. As a matter of fact, one snotty-nosed kid playing by the road only has to look up before he gives his own instant summation. '*Garn*,' he yells, 'you're only a lot of poofters anyway!'

Merry laughter rings through the ranks, as they continue marching. Again, though, not everyone is quite with it.

'What's a poofter?' Ray Bishop whispers to his cousin Bert, who, as ever, is marching right beside him.[9]

Just as quietly, Bert confesses he has no clue. It is hardly surprising, as the two 18-year-olds, fresh from the area south of Sydney around the towns of Milton and Ulladulla, have led fairly sheltered lives to this point. And in any case, this very naivety has stood them in good stead. Back in early September, when Ray and Bert had first arrived at Holsworthy Barracks – with service numbers 3761 and 3762 respectively – the two had just been having a bit of a natter when they were approached by two older blokes.

'Have you two any mates here you want to stick with?' one of them asked.

'No. We want to stick to ourselves.'

'That's good. We're trying to get a tentful of chaps together to pounce on a tent. You two would give us the twelve wanted. How about it?'

'Why pick on us?' Ray demanded.

'A tentful of decent, clean, good-living men makes a happy home, while even one or two misfits can spoil home life.'

'How do you know we are what you want?'

'It's written all over you. You've not lived long enough to become anything else. You aren't much more than babies.'

And that's how Private Herb Hodges and Private Tom Roberts – what else but 'Hodgy' and 'Robbo'[10] – had become not just Ray and Bert's tent-mates but also their best mates. A 24-year-old dairyman originally from Gloucester in England and a 32-year-old labourer from Sydney would surely know what 'poofters' were, and why everyone else felt it so funny to be called that. For now, keep marching, get on the train. Who knows what the day might bring?

And sure enough, 12 hours later, as they return from Long Bay Rifle Range and disembark on the platform at Liverpool, it is to see newsboys running hither and thither selling the afternoon paper. The edition contains such extraordinary news that people are throwing a penny a pop at the lads and grabbing copies. For have yers heard? Gallipoli! They've got all of the Anzacs out, and lost nary *a man*. *The Sydney Morning Herald* soon carries the banner headline:

DARDANELLES
Anzac and Suvla Troops Withdrawn
FINE MILITARY FEAT

The paper says the whole thing was accomplished with 'insignificant casualties' and, if you can believe it, 'without the knowledge of the Turks'. In London, it reports, 'the abandonment of Anzac and Suvla is the sensation of the day'.[11]

And it certainly is here, too. It seems extraordinary that, with two armies engaged in such a death grip, one of them would be able to slip away, but there you have it. And while some of these new soldiers greet the news with a sinking feeling, wrestling with the fact that their dearest desire – to tread the sacred shores of Gallipoli and fight the Turks – must now remain unfulfilled, others such as Bert and Ray are more optimistic. Yes, Gallipoli appears to be over, but surely there will be some war left for them, if they can just get there in time . . .

It is true that when Bert had finally manoeuvred his father into the position that, if his widowed Aunt Alice had let his cousin Ray go, then his father, the editor of *The Milton Times*, had to let him go too, that good man had snarled, 'You're just a young idiot without the slightest idea of what you are letting yourself in for.'[12] But in some ways that was the point. Joining the army and going to war might be just the thing to make a young idiot a strong man.

And Ray feels much the same. Beyond being cousins, the two are great mates and always have been. They have grown up together, gone on adventures in the bush together, and are now embarked on the biggest adventure of their lives. And yes, it might be difficult, and they don't know what the world might throw at them, but whatever happens they know they will stick together, as their whole life starts to move to the rhythm of the bugle.

For now, as 'Marmalades'[13] – the camp vernacular for new recruits, named for the universal dislike for the army's ubiquitous watery version of the spread (when these same recruits are not being even less kindly referred to as the 'white feather horde')[14] – the greatest challenge is to get through all the training. This is particularly true for Bert, who is unused to hard physical exercise. Since leaving school, he had worked only in the sunless printing workroom of his father's paper, *The Milton Times*. The sweat pours from his pimply face and it is all he can do to stay upright on some of the route marches. But Ray, born and bred on the farm, is able to help him through, as are Hodgy and Robbo – and their other seven tent-mates, described by Bert Bishop as 'all tip-top fellows'[15] – as, bit by bit, Bert starts to toughen up.

After training finishes – mercifully, at 4 'pip-emma', as they learn to call it in this man's army – there is time to wash up before an early dinner, and there are usually concerts and singalongs and lectures to keep the men entertained. First, though, at sunset, there is yet one more bugle call, the 'Retreat', a long, low, haunting tune that is played as a tribute to the fallen. As one, they stand to attention to face the setting sun and take a moment to respectfully reflect on those who gave their lives under the British flag.

Finally, when it is time for getting some kip, they retire to their red-dirt-floor tents. Sure, it is uncomfortable at first, as they don't have bunks, only swags, but after Hodgy and Robbo show the young'uns how to scrape out a hollow in the dirt for their hips so they can happily lie on their sides, they are soon able to sleep the sleep of the dead and the dead exhausted. Sometimes, on weekends, as a mass, they head to the city on leave, telling the overwhelmed railway officials to 'Book our fares to Lord Kitchener',[16] before raising hell in Sydney Town. (On one occasion, when the stationmaster orders the engine driver and fireman to get off the train, to prevent it leaving with these khaki yahoos, two soldiers who followed that profession in civilian life step forward and drive the train themselves!)

CHRISTMAS DAY 1915, KAISER'S PALACE, PUTTING THE SWORD TO ENGLAND'S BEST SWORD

Now, whether the Chief of the German General Staff General Erich

von Falkenhayn is a brilliant military strategist or merely a confident one is not yet obvious, but in this *Denkschrift zu Weihnachten*, Christmas Day memo to Kaiser Wilhelm II, he at least projects an air of both. It is his view that while all of France, Italy and Russia are exhausted, Great Britain remains a most formidable enemy, the only country that still really wants to continue the war and the least likely to negotiate a peace, because of its '*Vernichtungswille*', will to annihilate.

Von Falkenhayn is passionate in his belief that if the Germans are clever, it will be possible to knock 'England's best sword'[17] out of its hand, by destroying the French Army, which has already suffered 2,000,000 casualties, a quarter of them dead. And here is his brilliance. The battles of 1915 had demonstrated that, in this war, decisive breakthroughs are not really possible, and that in any conflict the advantage lies with the defender. If they could just pick the right target to attack and partially take, von Falkenhayn maintains, the French leadership might throw every last man at getting it all back:

> Should they do this, then the forces of France will bleed to
> death for there is no retreat, regardless if we ourselves reach
> the target or not.[18]

Yes, that is the way forward. In the late winter, when the snow starts to thaw, they must strike a precise, controlled blow to the most psychologically vulnerable part of the whole country. And von Falkenhayn already has a shrewd idea of where that is: a place that has been a Gallic stronghold for 2500 years, that was captured by the Prussians in 1792 and was the last French fortress to surrender to the same enemy in 1870. It has a place in the heart of every true Frenchman. They would rather die than give it up again.

Ja, kein Zweifel, yes, no doubt about it . . . 'The objectives of which I am speaking now are Belfort and Verdun . . . yet the preference must be given to Verdun.'[19]

29 DECEMBER 1915, *À CHANTILLY, LA CRÈME DE LA CRÈME DES MILITAIRES*

Could there be anywhere better in the world to have a meeting?

And typical of the French to install their GHQ in such a grand establishment as the Hotel du Grand Condé at Chantilly – some 40 miles north of Paris – all chandeliers, shining brass, deep mahogany and deeper bows from hovering waiters at ten paces. All that and a sense of history, for the hotel is named, of course, for Louis de Bourbon, Prince of Condé, the great French general of the 1600s who had dominated all before him. If only they, and their armies, can somehow manage to do the same . . .

For this is far more than just a gathering of seven men around a table in this grand Chantilly establishment, and more still than a meeting of minds. When those men are Commander-in-Chief of the French Army General Joseph Joffre, together with French President Raymond Poincaré, Prime Minister Aristide Briand, Minister of War General Joseph Gallieni, and the Generals Auguste Dubail, Fernand de Langle de Cary and Ferdinand Foch, and their principal focus is on the newly installed Commander-in-Chief of the British Expeditionary Force (BEF) General Sir Douglas Haig . . . whole empires hang in the balance.

Most pointedly, the subject of their discussion is the Dual Alliance's (the German and Austro-Hungarian Empires') incursion into France, Russia and Italy, and how best to push it back again. In his rolling cadences, quickly turned into English by a hovering translator, General Joffre is very firm.

The obvious need is for the Allies to launch 'co-ordinated offensives'[20] in the summer of 1916, around June or July. While the Russians with their new conscripts thrust forward on the Eastern Front, the Italians will attack their enemies in the Alps, even as the English and French will jointly aim a dagger right at German lines on the Western Front, along the postcard-perfect Somme Valley.

With this in mind, Joffre desires for the British to immediately relieve the French 10th Army and begin the planning for this combined

Franco-British offensive on a 60-mile front, with the valley of the Somme as its principal focus. If all goes well, the French can put 40 Divisions into the offensive, if the British can commit . . . about 20? He is also keen that the British engage in some *batailles d'usure*, battles designed specifically to wear out the Germans in the area where they will subsequently attack. The important thing is that the French keep themselves fresh so they can deliver the decisive blow at the end.

Haig, as is his wont, listens calmly, exuding the confidence for which Winston Churchill would say of him, 'The esteem of his military colleagues found a healthy counterpart in his own self-confidence . . . He was as sure of himself at the head of the British army as a country gentleman on the soil which his ancestors had trod for generations and to whose cultivation he had devoted his life.'[21]

Haig is a man of the Old School, and his great military passion is the cavalry. He is convinced that soldiers on horseback will be able to charge through whatever breaches are made on the Western Front and create mayhem behind enemy lines. For now, he agrees that the ever-growing BEF will extend their front, taking over the trenches of the French 10th Army around Lens. He will consider launching a British battle around the Somme and come back to General Joffre – whom he regards, he will tell his wife, as a 'dear old boy'[22] – in due course.

It is not obvious to him why this is such a brilliant scheme, particularly because behind the German lines in those parts there are few things of great sensitivity, crucial to the Boche's war effort, that his cavalry could strike at. But Haig is, typically, careful in the way he speaks to the French General. At the time that Lord Kitchener had appointed the Scot to this post, he had specifically told him, 'You must keep friendly with the French. General Joffre should be looked upon as the Commander-in-Chief in France as of course he knows the country and general situation well. It is different elsewhere, like the Balkans and Egypt, etc. But in France we must do all we can to meet the French Commander-in-Chief's wishes whatever may be our personal feelings about the French Army and its Commanders.'[23]

MID-JANUARY 1916, TEL-EL-KEBIR, MEANWHILE, BACK AT THE CAMP

Cairo it ain't.

I mean, really? After all these months of fighting in Gallipoli, of dreaming of getting back to the fleshpots of Cairo, of going back to the Wazza, this, *this*, is to be their new digs?

To the amazement of the Die Hards, after being taken by ship from Lemnos to Alexandria, instead of heading to the Egyptian capital they've long been dreaming of, the heroes of Anzac have been hauled across the desert for seven hours in open sheep railway trucks to this spot. What is it called again? Tel-el-Kebir – described by one soldier as an 'immense camp, acres and acres and acres of tents and guns and transport vehicles and lines of horses, and everywhere Australian soldiers. We have heard there were 40,000 men.'[24]

Built on either side of the railway line, this slight mound in the desert bakes in the sun, just beyond the eastern edge of the Nile Delta and right on the edge of the Eastern Desert. It is 30 miles south-west of the core of the Suez Canal's defensive focus, which is around that 'picturesque little village'[25] of Ismaïlia. The location is judged perfect for the Australians, as this 'Concentration Camp',[26] as it is known, will keep them out of trouble in Cairo, some 70 miles to the south, while patches in the desert nearby have a hard surface, so it is perfect for setting up camp and doing hard marching. The orders from London are that the Anzacs are now in the category of a strategic reserve, which can be sent anywhere. So, yes, they must be in position to defend the canal, but they also must be reconstituted, re-equipped, restored, refreshed and retrained so they can be sent wherever required.

The place even has a grand military history to it, as it is right by the famous battlefield of 1882 where the forces of Great Britain's General Garnet Wolseley put paid to Arabi Pasha's men, who had rallied to the cry of 'Egypt for the Egyptians'.[27] From then on, it would be 'Egypt for whatever Great Britain *says* it is for'.

'This is a very miserable and lonely spot,' a 4th Battalion Digger writes. 'We all wonder how long we are to be kept in this dismal place . . .'[28]

(A curiosity of the dogs in these parts, they reckon, is that the few mangy mutts around don't usually lift a hind leg, rather they squat, because the poor little bastards have never seen a tree to pee on. The best they can do on occasion is a few gravestones for some of the British soldiers, in the cemetery down in a depression by the railway.)

One bloke, however, who resolves to make the best of it is Lieutenant Goldy Raws of the 23rd Battalion. Though he has, like many Australian officers on Lemnos, recently fallen 'very much in love'[29] with one of the Canadian nurses, at the moment anything that doesn't look like Gallipoli, where he had been fighting for the last four months, looks good to him.

As far as Cairo is concerned – which so many of the other soldiers are lusting after – he can take it or leave it. Never a man to go to red-light districts such as the Wazza, Goldy doesn't even like going to the military camps there, as he finds it is 'the home of the "cold-footed" men who by all kinds of devices get out of going into the danger zone'.[30]

For himself, like all of his deeply religious family, he abhors killing and violence of all kinds, but in this case, as he writes to his father in Adelaide, the Reverend John Garrard Raws of the Baptist faith, there is an overriding factor. He knows that by fighting for Australia in the cause of the British Empire, he is 'following the call which Christ voiced – the call is, and always must be, to the human heart, "For whoever wants to save their life will lose it, but whoever loses their life for me will find it."'[31]

MID-JANUARY 1916, BIGGER BREASTWORKS FOR FROMELLES

It has been, of course, for each German division to interpret the instructions from Oberste Heeresleitung (Supreme Army Command) as it sees fit. In the area in front of Aubers Ridge at Fromelles, given the fact that it has already been so heavily attacked and is in such an important area, the defences are as formidable as they are intricate, with the front-line breastwork walls built eight feet high and six feet wide. In just the 1500-yard section held by 16th Bavarian RIR, there are no fewer than

75 machine-gun emplacements – an average of one every 20 yards.

The Germans' MG08 machine guns are capable of spitting out 500 rounds a minute to 2000 yards effective range, and as much as 3000 yards maximum range with a 500-yard lateral arc. Typically, a German regiment has about 20 machine guns, with a dozen in use at any one time and the rest in reserve. And, of course, the engineers have constructed defences with multiple slits in the concrete walls, so the machine-gun crews can quickly change places during an attack, depending on where it is coming from.

Some ten yards back from the front-lines, a series of concrete dugouts are built, sunk into the ground to a depth of four feet for the soldiers to take shelter from enemy artillery. Each one is designed to hold between three and five men. Ten yards further back again, concrete dugouts are built for officers, as much as ten yards below ground level, requiring pumps to keep the water out but secure against even direct hits from above, and well lit, powered by the electricity network of Lille, as are the searchlights. Alarms are carefully installed, so that should the company be taking shelter in the dugouts, the observers can quickly alert them to the oncoming attack. Once it has been confirmed that the barrage has lifted and the attackers are on their way, the German infantry can immediately react and take to their posts on the front-line.

To allow war materiel to be moved forward, a tramway network is built, extending from the French railway system in Lille. The cargo is ultimately transferred to small trundle carriages and pushed the last 1600 yards or so by the soldiers directly to the front-lines.

And, of course, the German artillery is situated just behind Aubers Ridge, far enough back that the artillery crews are beyond the range of rifles and machine guns but still close enough to be able to rain down hell upon their enemies on the low-lying flatlands, their shells guided by the front-line observers with whom they are in communication.

Always, the emphasis in the construction is on heavy protection for the defenders, so as to keep casualties to a minimum.

19–20 JANUARY 1916, *RUNIC II* TURNS HEADS AT SYDNEY HARBOUR

Young Bert Bishop's eyes shine just to look at it. It is the White Star liner SS *Runic II*, built a decade and a half ago by the same mob in Belfast who built RMS *Titanic*, which . . . well, never mind.

Now converted to a His Majesty's Australian Transport (HMAT), why *thar she blows*, bobbing about at Pyrmont and nearly shipshape to take on board 1500 men before heading for Egypt.

She is a beauty: black hull, white from the deck up, all 12,000 tons of her. And for Bert – as it is for many thousands of Australian recruits – she represents the fulfilment of a dream, a big ship on which to travel the world. For now, though, as the worthy tugboats tow her over to Wharf 6 at Woolloomooloo, he, Ray, Robbo, Hodgy and a couple of others must get to work, doing the last bit of hard yakka necessary so the ship can receive not just their 19th Battalion reinforcements but also the reinforcements for other battalions of the 5th Brigade, who are due to come on board the next day. Much of their time in the interim is spent getting big piles of hammocks and blankets at the top of the stairs and kicking them to the bottom – 'It's better than rolling stones down a mountain . . .'[32] – before setting them all up in the different berths throughout the vessel.

Come the time for the arrival of the troops aboard the grand ship, on the early morning of 20 January, Bert Bishop is beside himself, as he records in a letter: 'At last the long talked of, much longed for, day has arrived, the day on which we set out on our journey to Egypt to join the Australian troops who have gone before, and to help them in their fight for the good old British Empire.'[33]

Even this short time in the army has changed Bert, his pimples now gone, a certain muscularity now apparent where all had been string bean in character. And, most of all, he has a sense of community, membership of a brotherhood he has never previously experienced.

These men now approaching the wharves – after having marched triumphantly through the roaring crowds down Macquarie Street – are like his brothers, and Bert is proud to guide them to their quarters, show them where to stow their kit, and ensure that all is as it should be when HMAT SS *Runic* finally makes ready to depart in the mid-morning.

Oh, the tears . . .

'Mothers, fathers, sisters, brothers, sweethearts, friends are there in hundreds to see the last of their soldier boys,' Bert would describe it in a letter. 'It was magnificent the way they turned out that morning to see us leave.'[34]

Crowded onto the wharf beneath leaden skies, all the loved ones wave and cry, as the soldiers throw down the streamers they have been issued in a rare example of army empathy. And now the rain bursts upon them, but no one leaves or goes for shelter. The loved ones simply grab the other end of those streamers as best they can and grip all the more eagerly as, with a blast of its horn, at eight bells, the ship at last pulls away from the quay, backing out into the harbour with its propellers churning. The streamers pull taut and then break, just as the hearts of those on ship and shore are breaking.

Goodbye! Goodbye! Goodbye!

And now the soldiers start to sing the old classic, beloved by them all:

Goodbye Sydney Town,
Sydney Town goodbye
I am leaving you today
For a country far away.
Though today I'm stony-broke
Without a single brown,
When I make a fortune I'll come back
And spend it in dear old Sydney Town. [35]

Soon after leaving the Sydney Heads and turning right, some of them must spend some time hurling their stomachs up, over the sides of the ship. For the first few hours, they're afraid they're going to die. For the next few hours, they're afraid they're *not* going to die.[36] Most, though, are just happy and joyful to at last be Suez bound, and on such a ship as this. As one bloke says to Bert Bishop, 'Fancy getting five bob a day to act the millionaire like this!'[37]

27 JANUARY 1916, GERMAN GHQ, IN SPA, BELGIUM, VON FALKENHAYN PUSHES HIS PLAN

And so, von Falkenhayn has confirmed, the attack on Verdun will go ahead. But let him repeat: this is *not* to be simply another mass of men charging forward, hoping to overwhelm by their sheer numbers whatever machine guns and artillery are ranged against them.

That, von Falkenhayn is convinced, is unwise in the extreme. For he is one of the first senior officers on either side who has come to appreciate that the dynamics of twentieth-century artillery have changed warfare forever. True, quick-firing, hydraulic-recoil artillery has been around for 20 years, but – just like the modern machine guns – never on this massive a scale, and never with this degree of deadly efficiency.

'The lessons to be deduced from the failure of our enemies' mass attacks,' he tells his senior officers, 'are decisive against any imitation of their battle methods. Attempts at a mass break-through, even with an extreme accumulation of men and material, cannot be regarded as holding out prospects of success against a well-armed enemy, whose *morale* is sound and who is not seriously inferior in numbers. The defender has usually succeeded in closing the gaps.'[38]

If the enemy wishes to '*ANGRIFF! AAANGRIFF!* Attack, attack, *attack!*' so be it. But to get them to attack you where you want, you first have to capture something they will attack foolishly to try to get back: Verdun. As the Chinese strategist Sun Tzu put it 2500 years ago, 'Seize what the enemy holds dear, then he will be amenable to your will.'[39]

Exactly!

Falkenhayn believes Germany has 'succeeded in shaking England severely – the best proof of that is her imminent adoption of universal military service. But that is also a proof of the sacrifices England is prepared to make to attain her end . . . Germany can expect no mercy from this enemy.'[40] If it comes to it, the British can be expected to continue to make terrible sacrifices by launching mass attacks at the Germans.

Von Falkenhayn is insistent the attack on Verdun will proceed under strict conditions. The German infantry is to advance only after a massive shelling of the enemy positions, a shelling far more intense than anything before seen in this or any other war. When the guns lengthen range, then, and only then, will the soldiers burst forth, but they are *not* to go beyond the previously held enemy trenches. Only after the artillery is brought forward to do the same again are they to go forward again.

And yet, the speed of that artillery coming forward is also essential, for, as von Falkenhayn issues his order on this day, 'It is of vital importance for the Verdun operations as a whole, that the attack is never permitted to come to a standstill, so that the French are given no opportunity to settle themselves again in rearward positions, and to organize resistance again after it has once been broken.'[41]

Once sufficient ground has been taken, Falkenhayn plans to halt the attack and let the French bleed to death attempting to recover what they have lost.

5 FEBRUARY 1916, ISMAÏLIA, THE CONCEPT OF AN AUSTRALIAN ARMY HAS BEAN

Such a relief. Having travelled down the English Channel from the port of Folkestone and followed the west coast of France and then Spain before turning to port and entering the Mediterranean through the Straits of Gibraltar en route to Egypt, Charles Bean had been afraid the whole way of 'being submarined',[42] but at last he has arrived in Port Said safely and . . .

And where are the Australian troops he is expecting to find here? Nowhere to be seen. There are Tommy soldiers everywhere, and no one seems to be sure exactly where the Australians are, so he has barely landed before he is on the train to Cairo to find them and . . .

And here they are!

Having travelled 50 miles south of Port Said, Bean's train pulls into the settlement of Ismaïlia, on the west bank of the Suez Canal. Suddenly he can see slouch hats everywhere and that distinct, rather ambling gait that marks the Australian soldier. Quickly disembarking, Bean is not long in getting the lie of the land and working out just how it is the men come to be here.

For the evacuation of the Allies from the Dardanelles had released not only them from duty there but also about 200,000 Turkish soldiers. The British Secretary of War, Lord Kitchener, is convinced the greatest danger now is that the Turks will send them across the Sinai Desert once more – as had happened the year before – to strike the Suez Canal at this spot. It will likely happen within just weeks. Reports have come through that the Turks have been massing at Beersheba, a possible prelude to another attack being mounted on the Canal. So, where better to base the bulk of the Australians than here at Tel-el-Kebir – where the ground is hard enough for them to do their training without perpetually sinking into soft sand and from where they can easily rotate a sufficient number of battalions to guard the 30 miles of Suez Canal from Ferry Post in the north to Serapeum in the south.

General Sir Archibald Murray, the Commander of all British forces

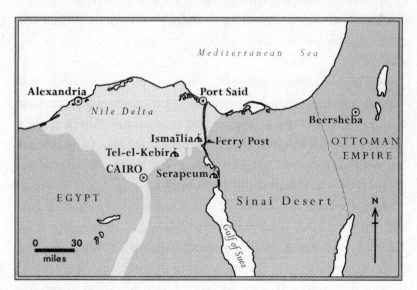

British camps around the Suez Canal

in Egypt – a bristling and bewhiskered veteran of no less than the Zulu uprising of 1888 and General of the Old School like they don't make them anymore – is appalled by the 'extreme indiscipline and inordinate vanity of the Australians'.[43]

Fights, insubordination, drunkenness.

And that's just the officers . . .

As a body, he finds all the Australians untidy in their dress, worse still in their manners and disrespectful of military hierarchy. The failure of these oft-lounging louts to salute him as he passes in his staff car is 'felt almost as a whiplash by the Commander-in-Chief', Bean records.[44]

And Sir Archibald is not alone. 'The British staff here hate the Australians pretty badly,' Bean notes. 'It is the English common people who like us; with the exception of those British officers who have fought with us, the British officer does not generally like us. The Australian doesn't salute him – as a general rule; also he is jealous of the praise we get as soldiers and he probably also quite honestly fails to understand our discipline.[45]

Perhaps the lack of deference is just in the Australian blood? British writer John Masefield would later record that when a British officer told off an Australian for not saluting him, the friendly Australian reached out, gave him a pat on the shoulder and said, 'Young man, when you go home, you tell your mother that today you've seen a real bloody soldier.'[46]

While it had been one thing to keep recruits under control back when they had first arrived in Egypt a little over a year earlier, it is quite another to do the same to grizzled Gallipoli veterans. After all, when they have faced off against the Turks firing from trenches above and just ten yards away, what do they care for mere British Military Police, not good enough to be real soldiers themselves?

And, of course, it is not just the veterans from Gallipoli who are here but also the 30,000 reinforcements who have arrived in Egypt from Australia in recent months. For the glory of Gallipoli has had a marked effect on recruitment in Australia, as has the news that the Western Front is not going well, with men falling over themselves to join up, to have the honour of serving their country and doing what had to be done to stop the Boche. Enlistments, which had been just 6250 in the month of the Gallipoli landing, had risen nearly six-fold in just the following three months.

All up, there are now some 60,000 Australian and New Zealand soldiers gathered in two camps in the Egyptian desert. The most exciting thing of all? There has been talk that, given the Anzacs had done so well at Gallipoli and there are now so many troops arriving, they might even be formed into their own 'army' – that is, two corps of Anzacs under almost exclusively Australian and New Zealander officers, with General Birdwood, who had commanded the ANZACs at Gallipoli, unofficially retaining overall command.

For Charles Bean, his passion for this whole growing idea of a separate Australasian army is an indication of just how far he, and the entire Australian political and military leadership, have come since the opening days of the war.[47] Back then, it had seemed quite obvious that the role of Australian soldiers was to bolster British forces in whatever manner London required – as the man who would become Prime Minister, Andrew Fisher, had put it, 'to the last man and the last shilling'.[48] But not now.

Like many Australians who had come into close contact with the British military at Gallipoli for the first time, Bean's views had changed. The assumption that the British officers and British soldiers were likely to be better than their Australian counterparts, just on principle, had been proven false. The Australian officers were at least as good, and undoubtedly more careful with the lives of their men.

Put together, it simply makes sense that an exclusively Australasian army should be formed, just as the British had four such armies in France, with each composed of nine or ten divisions of 18,000 men. Bean has witnessed with his own eyes, and documented, this rising sense of 'Australian-ness' among these soldiers, who had previously defined themselves as being from New South Wales, Queensland, Victoria and all the rest. They had joined the army to fight for the British Empire but are now fighting for something much more personal – their own country. And just as those men have evolved, so has he, coming to a view much closer to that of his friend and colleague Keith Murdoch, who 'makes a religion'[49] of this new nationalism.

'He is wholly Australian,' Bean had noted admiringly in his diary, 'and nothing except Australian. I never realised the qualities of this type before but there's a great deal more in it than I was wont to give Murdoch credit for. These young Australians aren't afraid of any other creed and they'll go a long way . . . They think the world would be better for being Australian and they tell it so whenever they can.'[50]

And yet, whatever the Australians think of themselves, one problem in them having leadership of their own is that 'British staff here hate the Australians pretty badly . . . the British officer generally does not like us'.[51]

That wide British view notwithstanding, the logic of independence is so compelling that, from Cairo, the Commander-in-Chief of the Mediterranean Expeditionary Force, Sir Archibald Murray, has even sent his recommendation:

I FIND WE NOW HAVE A VERY LARGE ACCUMULATION OF AUSTRALIAN AND NEW ZEALAND REINFORCEMENTS HERE, WHICH CANNOT BE ABSORBED IN EXISTING ORGANISATIONS . . . I STRONGLY RECOMMEND THAT THESE BE FORMED AT ONCE INTO AN AUSTRALIAN AND NEW ZEALAND ARMY OF TWO CORPS UNDER BIRDWOOD.[52]

But, back in London, the Chief of the Imperial General Staff, Lieutenant-General Sir William Robertson, is robust in his refusal. 'He didn't see it served a useful purpose,' the deeply disappointed Bean would write, 'and the fact that we were a nation and wanted to fight and carve our history as a nation didn't go for anything with him.'[53]

Beyond everything else, an Australasian army could only muster seven divisions at best, while all the British armies on the Western Front boasted a minimum of nine divisions. More pertinently, if you allowed the Australasians an army of their own, there'd be little choice but to allow the Canadians and other colonials their own army too, which would soon make the British subject to *their* suggestions, recommendations and so forth on how best to conduct one's wars. Already, the BEF has had to suffer the indignity of heeding the Australian Government's presumptuous insistence that they not execute deserting Australians. If they allowed the formation of an Australasian army, where might it end? No, much easier to maintain a command structure that gives you the greatest control. There will simply be a new version of the old model: I Anzac Corp, composed of the 1st and 2nd Australian Divisions, will be under the command of Englishman General Sir William Birdwood, while II Anzac Corps will consist of the newly arrived 4th and 5th Australian Divisions and be under Birdwood's colleague, Englishman General Alexander Godley.

The news is not well received by the Australian soldiers and officers, and no one is more annoyed than Lieutenant-Colonel Harold Edward 'Pompey' Elliott DCM, of the 1st Brigade, who is well acquainted with Godley's performance in the field at Anzac. 'We are now the 2nd Anzac [Corps] under General Godley an Englishman who came out with the New Zealanders and became so unpopular with them that he came over to us,' the 37-year-old decorated Boer War veteran and one-time top-line Melbourne barrister writes to a friend. 'Another example of the things that are done here . . . This is a great compliment to Australians after what we did in Anzac – we are not considered to be fit to command our own men. Yet in the newspapers we are wonders – supermen marvels – what you will – according to Birdwood and Hamilton our Idols – yet when it comes to reward or promotion – not for beastly colonials – don't you know. This has gone so far that in 2nd Anzac Staff the word has gone forth, if any job on this staff is vacant – "No Australian need apply".'[54]

And there is another problem. As the first 16 Anzac battalions of the 1st, 2nd, 3rd and 4th AIF Brigades have seen serious action at Gallipoli, while the 2nd Division arrived late and was in no major battles, and the

4th and 5th Divisions are completely green, it means that the two corps are totally unbalanced when it comes to veterans. General Birdwood's solution is simple.

Each experienced battalion, he has decided, will be split down the middle. One half of each battalion will be transferred to a 'daughter' battalion, thus ensuring a leavening of veterans in both I and II Anzac Corps – the 50 per cent troop deficit in either being made up with fresh reinforcements.

12 FEBRUARY 1916, AT GHQ, GOOD KNIGHT, MY LORD . . .

In talking to the Secretary of State for War at GHQ, on the outskirts of Calais, Sir Douglas Haig is more than ever aware that this Kitchener is not the same supreme figure who had started the war, the military man whose word was law to the British Government. No, as the losses have mounted – in terms of both soldiers and battles, not least in the Dardanelles – so has his influence waned to the point that many in government now want him out of it completely. And even Kitchener has started to doubt himself.

He is, in person, a curious mix of the defiant and the defeated. 'Rightly or wrongly, the *people* believe in me,' he says at one point to Sir Douglas, before adding morosely, 'Probably quite wrongly. [But] in any case it is not *me* that the politicians are afraid of, but what the people would say to them if I were to go . . .'[55]

In London, Lord Kitchener says, the politicians are constantly intriguing against one another and often ask him to join them against Prime Minister Asquith, which he always declines, as he believes that Asquith is the best man for the job. But there is no doubt that all of them, the military and political leaders of Great Britain, need a big victory in the war and they need it some time soon. On that subject, Haig is under pressure from the French to commence planning for attacks on the German lines before the end of April, even before the big offensive that is planned for the summer. In the words of General Joffre, they want the British to 'wear out' the German reserves in a *bataille d'usure* whereby, while the French rest, their cross-Channel allies will keep attacking, soaking up the German reserves until they are all gone. Haig has managed to put them off so far. For what he is in fact beginning to warm to is the plan to launch a very big attack astride the Somme River, as originally suggested by Joffre himself.

If it all works, they could break through the German line somewhere around the high ground of Pozières and then strike north-east, 'rolling up' the German line from there, going *up* their trenches, instead of straight *at* them.

12–17 FEBRUARY 1916, BY THE SUEZ CANAL, WHEN THE PENNY DROPS

The Commanding Officer of each battalion comes up with his own method of splitting his men in two. In the 12th Battalion, Lieutenant-Colonel John Gellibrand first divides his senior officers into two lots and then invites them all into the Officers' Mess, before taking a penny from his pocket.

Now let's be clear, men. If it comes up heads, this half on my right will stay here by the Canal with the 12th Battalion of the 1st Division, awaiting reinforcements to bring us back to full strength. If it's tails, this same half will go back to Tel-el-Kebir to join the new recruits soon to arrive from Cairo and form up together to become the 52nd Battalion of the newly formed 4th Division.

With no emotion attached to the result, there can surely be no complaint.

Ah, but of all the men, in all the world, there is no group of men more expert in the vagaries of the game of two-up. These men know more than any how whole fortunes can change on how the penny lands. Most are even of the passionate view that the best coin to use is 'Old Baldy', boasting King Edward VII, 1901 to 1910. See, because of the King's bald head, these pennies are considered to be much better balanced than the Victoria-head penny or the George V head. They lean in close.

With a flick upwards, the penny spins and spins and spins, reaching its zenith near Gellibrand's eyes, and then descends.

Gellibrand's right hand flashes out, snatches the coin and whips it onto the back of his left hand. His senior officers lean forward and gaze upon it.

Heads.

In that instant, the odds shift for hundreds of women in Australia, who now look destined to be widows, with their men off to the wild Western front any day now – while hundreds of others still have the gift of time, and the faint chance to live full and happy lives with their husbands.

What the brass base wallahs don't seem to properly appreciate is that those men who have served together from day dot are intimately bound to one another. They take great solace in one another's company and simply don't want to have a forced association with those who *weren't there*. Most offended are the original men of the old battalions, who have been with it from the beginning, 'as they had to leave old friends and start afresh with a new Battalion which has no records'.[56]

Sergeant 'Darkie' Kenyan of the mighty 9th Battalion (half of which is now announced to become the new 49th Battalion) expresses it for them all:

> *Goodbye, Colonel Robbie,*
> *Farewell Salisbury, too,*
> *Ever since we left Australia,*
> *We've been messed about by you.*
> *Digging is a failure,*
> *Ceremonial is a farce,*
> *You can stick the 49th A.I.F.*
> *Right up your [bloody arse].*[57]

For complex reasons, the 14th Battalion is already part of the 4th Division, and pretty much the entire job of choosing who goes where in its D Company falls to the most revered man in the AIF, the first winner of the Victoria Cross at Gallipoli, Sergeant-Major Bert Jacka. Brother is to be separated from brother on his whim, and rumour spreads he is going to keep all of his cobbers with him in the 14th – together with his own younger brother, Bill – and send all the ne'er do wells to the daughter battalion of the 46th.

The 14th Battalion is drawn up on the parade ground, and Jacka – his heels set tightly together, steeling himself to do what has to be done – calls out.

'The following men fall out on the right: Banyard, Twomey . . .'

'By gum, Bert, but this is a bit of all right!' Private Twomey roars.[58] 'No more soldiering for me! You can make out a sick report, because I'm off to hospital. To think that a man has never left the battalion and been in every stunt, and now he's to be chucked out like this. Bah – I thought you were a cobber of mine!'[59]

Sergeant Banyard feels the same and, as noted by one of his comrades, his 'language would need recording on asbestos'.

But those bastards can protest all they like. At the limit, Bert Jacka might take it from the Sergeants – he will deal with them later – but no one of any lower rank dares utter a peep. Unmoved, Jacka reads out the Corporals who are to go to the right, then the Lance-Corporals and then the privates.

Those who remain unannounced are to stay with the 14th Battalion, with Jacka – who is not going anywhere – while all those named must prepare, within hours, to march off to join their new battalion, the 46th. 'There were feelings of consternation among all ranks at the news,' one soldier writes. 'The thought of leaving the old battalions whose names we had helped to make famous, during the Gallipoli Campaign, was a very bitter pill to swallow. Also most of us were leaving old friends behind.'[60]

'I felt,' one officer would later tell Charles Bean, 'as though I were having a limb amputated without any anaesthetic.'[61] A soldier quite agrees. 'It hurt I can tell you,' he writes home, 'when they ripped the old green and white stripe off our arms as already we were proud to be in such a battalion . . . Now we don't care what is going to happen to us.'[62]

As the losing half of the 6th Battalion marches out to join the 58th Battalion, they are farewelled by the remaining half with cheers, good wishes and claps on the back. On cue, those marching unveil a tune penned and memorised overnight, sung to the melody of the well-loved ditty 'I Didn't Want to Do It' and renamed 'We Didn't Want to Leave You'.

Half a battalion of reinforcements arrive to join the foundation half, and new bonds immediately start to form, notwithstanding the fact that it is noticed by the old hands that 'there is a lot of difference between those who are coming now and those who came before, some of them don't even know how to load and use a rifle'.[63]

One veteran of the 14th Battalion who watches the new arrivals closely – wryly amused at the open-mouthed awe with which they greet the news they are to join the famous 'Jacka's mob' – is Eddie Rule, a 28-year-old railway foreman from Cobar. Though himself a man of the world, who before joining up had worked as a foreman on the Panama Canal project and toured through both North and South America, Eddie does not feel superior for their awe. For Eddie had been exactly the same the year before when he had arrived at Gallipoli in September with other reinforcements posted to find – can you believe it, Dig? – they were with *Jacka's* 14th Battalion. All of them had had just one question to each other in the few days after their arrival on the sacred shores: 'Have you seen him yet?'[64]

Ah, Albert Jacka, the timber-worker from Victoria who had been awarded the first Victoria Cross of the First World War for Australia for his heroism in taking on and killing a big gang of Turks in the early hours of 19 May 1915 back at Anzac. He had captured all of Australia's imagination, and of course all of the new recruits had been elated to have been posted to Jacka's mob, as the battalion was enviously referred to by other battalions. True, he is not a huge man, but there is massive power in his lithe limbs, a glint in his eyes, and he has 'a determined face with crooked nose. His feat of polishing off six Turks single-handed certainly took some beating.'[65]

And look at that .45 Colt revolver he carries in his holster, which makes him look like a figure from the Wild West. Course it's not the regulation army-issue Webley revolver, but too bad. Jacka prefers the Colt, 'cos it's single action, which means you can fan the hammer with your left hand to fire off quick and accurate shots, better than the Webley. And in this man's army, who is going to tell Jacka he can't have it?

Still, with his own men, Jacka has an even more potent weapon. If any bastard plays up – gets drunk, assaults someone, goes Absent Without Leave (AWL) or the like – instead of reporting them to higher officers, Jacka would say, 'I won't "crime" you, I'll give you a punch on the bloody nose.'[66]

(Rarely, but sometimes, it goes the other way, where it is the veterans who are impressed with one of the Marmalades – as in when the veterans of the 58th Battalion realise they have alongside them none other than George Challis, the heir to Fred 'Pompey' Elliott as the star of the Carlton team, who had guided the Blues to a 33-point win over Collingwood in the 1915 Grand Final. There had been much mirth that the army had initially rejected him because one of his toes curled over the one next to it, but in the end, on Challis's insistence, the army had to concede that he was 'medically fit'. Even the grizzled veterans are charmed by this gentle bloke who never stops smiling, and concede that he is a 'good bastard'.)

For the most part, however, there is early tension between these veterans and the latecomers, these 'Heavy Ponderers'[67] who had not joined up immediately like those in the 1st Australian Division, and not as quickly as the 'Dinkum Australians' of the 2nd Australian Division. No, they have joined up only after Heavy Pondering indeed. 'You're here at last,' a gnarled Gallipoli veteran of the 4th Battalion sneers at a group of Heavy Ponderers who have just marched into Tel-el-Kebir, 'only 18 months too long in coming. You've been a bloody long while making up yer minds to come.'

Oh, really? 'You came away and thought you was coming to a picnic,' one of the incoming Ponderers says, with some dignity. 'We didn't.'[68]

A lot of the new coots have never even *held* a rifle, let alone fired one, and have to be taught from the beginning. Digging trenches? No bloody idea! Lack of fitness is also a problem, and things are not helped by the fact that the heavy woollen uniforms all of them are wearing are totally unsuited for heat, and that the only respite at 'Smoke-Oh'[69] – also called 'emma emma esses', from the signal alphabet 'MMS', as in 'Men May Smoke' – is to sit down on the burning hot sand in the same hot woollen clothes. Could it be that the only thing that seems more out of place in this scorching desert are the 'mass of sea shells and water-worn pebbles'[70] that are everywhere you look? How the hell did they get here? How the hell did *we* get here? And when will it end?

Well, on that very subject, rumours are circulating that they might be sent to France: the Western Front. They reckon we're going to be heading that way soon!

Much of their training is done on the old battlefield, still littered with spent cartridges, shattered trenches and even bones – a fair reminder of the consequences of being on the losing side.

At day's end, the troops fall in once more to march back to camp, sometimes led by regimental bands playing everything from the usual martial tunes to 'Waltzing Matilda' and 'Advance Australia Fair'. And of course the troops have their own favourite songs, which have grown in popularity as the months have passed. Sing it with them as they march in the falling dusk, this fine body of Australian men, proud of their cause and buoying themselves up with a great sense of fun:

My mother told me
That she would buy me
A rubber dolly,
A rubber dolly,
But when I told her
I loved a . . . soldier
She would not buy me
A rubber dolly . . .[71]

Back in the camp in time for tea in the mess huts, a new and more pleasant world starts to emerge for these Australians so far from home as the shadows of the evening move towards each other, and, as Charles Bean would describe it, 'the beauty of the twilight pass[es] swiftly into darkness. Then hundreds of lights would twinkle through the night, the booths of the natives would flare with torches, and the men would wander through the lines, visiting and being visited, making new friendships and renewing old ones, or filing away in hundreds to some picture theatre or boxing match.'[72]

The only way that the 1st and 2nd Divisions can depart for France with the number of required artillery batteries (increased from nine to 15) is to immediately transfer to them the batteries of the 4th and 5th Divisions, even though they have just begun their own training. True, this will leave the 4th and 5th having to start from scratch, but they will have to make do.

Not everyone thinks it can be done so quickly. 'Artillery officers,' Captain Frederick Biddle, who had commanded a battery of the 1st Australian Division at Gallipoli, would note, 'are not produced by turning a handle. [Infantry officers] require mainly personality and pluck without technical qualifications [but] the work of artillery officers is increasingly technical.'[73]

7.15 AM, 21 FEBRUARY 1916, VERDUN, 20 MILES FROM THE GUNS OF HELL TO THE HOUSE OF GOD

It is just one of 1200 guns that the Germans have brought forward for this barrage, which is planned to go for the next ten hours today and for as many days afterwards as the French continue to put soldiers in the way. The Germans call it Dicke Bertha, Big Bertha. With a flash and a massive roar, the shell, which weighs almost a ton, roars forth and soars skyward, tracing a perfect arc across the heavens towards Verdun before coming to earth with a shattering explosion 20 miles away in the . . . Bishop's Palace, right by its legendary sculptured mural depictions of the River Meuse.

'These decorations,' a *New York Times* correspondent would report, 'have been literally hashed to pieces by violent shelling, as if some burlesque Hercules has used a giant hammer to crush these exquisitely delicate bits of sculpture.'

Almost the next to be hit is Verdun's famed fifteenth-century cathedral, all but destroyed. 'Even the huge mosaic paving stones are wrenched into masses of débris. Columns and pillars are broken into fragments, rich candelabra and lustres reduced to bits, and the carved pulpit and sculptured railing around the chancel are lying in shapeless piles.'[74]

The Battle of Verdun has begun, as has a new phase in warfare – with guns firing masses of powerful shells from so far away they can't even be seen by those in the target zone.

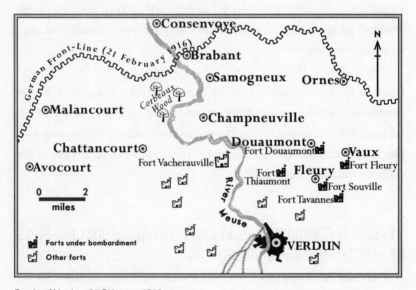

Battle of Verdun, 21 February 1916

Strangely, for the French defenders of Verdun, the most terrifying thing on this freezing morning is not the shells themselves, it is their sound. Some whistle, others howl, still others moan. 'All uniting in one infernal roar,' one French soldier would recall. 'From time to time, an aerial torpedo passes, making a noise like a gigantic motor car. With a tremendous explosion, a giant shell bursts quite close to our observation post, breaking the telephone wire and interrupting all communication with our batteries.'[75]

The attack codenamed by the Germans *Unternehmen Gericht*, Operation Judgement, has begun. Following the strict timetable set out by General von Falkenhayn, the German artillery starts to pour the first of what will be 2.5 million shells on the French positions, in the first week of the battle. They come from a front of eight miles, landing on what is roughly a 100-acre rectangle. 'Men were squashed,' one French soldier would recount. 'Cut in two or divided from top to bottom. Blown into showers; bellies turned inside out; skulls forced into the chest as if by a blow from a club.'[76]

Only when those French positions are completely shattered and nearly all of their soldiers dead or gone – late in the afternoon of the first day – do the first of the 140,000 German soldiers in position move forward along a six-mile front. Their numbers include an entirely different group of soldiers, the *Sturmtrupp*, stormtroopers. Their job is to storm enemy trenches en masse straight after the prolonged artillery barrage has lifted and to quell what resistance remains.

In one particular part of the battle, the Commanding Officer of the 33rd Battalion's 10th Company, Captain Charles de Gaulle, finds that he and his men are surrounded, under attack from bayonets, short-fused grenades and swarms of Germans coming from all sides. In such pressing circumstances, there is no room to shoot for fear of killing your own, but de Gaulle is able to rally a few men to him for *la patrie*, to lead a charge out of the enemy ring and . . .

And isn't that so often the way? Though the charge succeeds, it is the leader who pays the highest price, as 'a bayonet pierced his thigh and the battle swept over him'.[77]

A short time later, as de Gaulle comes to, he finds himself on a stretcher being carried back to a German emergency dressing station to stop his bleeding. And one of the men carrying him with such care is the same one who had wielded the bayonet. They are ferocious, these Germans, but there can be decency to them. (For de Gaulle, some three years of being a prisoner of war awaits.)

Back in the thick of the battle, it is probably the dead French soldiers and those like de Gaulle – safely taken prisoner – who are the lucky ones. For just when the few valiant Gauls who remain think there is nothing left in this hell on earth that they haven't seen, the Germans unleash, for the first time on a mass scale, their latest weapon.

Called *der Flammenwerfer*, the flamethrower, it comes in different sizes. The largest one is operated by three men – one directing the nozzle, another supporting the pipe attached to the gas cylinder and the third wheeling the cylinder around – and is capable of throwing a flame 30 yards, right into the artillery shelters and dugouts still held by the last of the French.

For the defenders, all they hear is a sudden hissing sound before a crimson glare washes over them, and then they are on FIRE.

Screams.

Flaming human *torches*.

Horror on a scale rarely seen before in warfare.

As described by one shocked stretcher-bearer, 'Some grenadiers returned with ghastly wounds: hair and eyebrows singed, almost not human anymore, black creatures with bewildered eyes . . .'[78]

For most, though, it is just the ongoing explosions, hour after hour after hour, on all sides of them that they must face. 'When you hear the whistling in the distance,' one French soldier would recall, 'your entire body preventively crunches together to prepare for the enormous explosions. Every new explosion is a new attack, a new fatigue, a new affliction. Even nerves of the hardest of steel, are not capable of dealing with this kind of pressure. The moment comes when the blood rushes to your head, the fever burns inside your body and the nerves, numbed with tiredness, are not capable of reacting to anything anymore. It is as if you are tied to a pole and threatened by a man with a hammer. First the hammer is swung backwards in order to hit hard, then it is swung forwards, only missing your scull by an inch, into the splintering pole. In the end you just surrender. Even the strength to guard yourself from splinters now fails you. There is even hardly enough strength left to pray to God . . .'[79]

Oh, the *horror*.

A horror ever hungry for fresh forces.

Chapter Two

REINSTOUSHMENTS TO THE FORE

One's thoughts fly back over many months of gloom and
anxiety to those days of March, 1916, when the thousands
of care-free young Australians assembled at Tel-el-Kebir
and launched the Division on its proud and terrible voyage
into history. How is it possible for any pen to describe
in fitting terms the sufferings and the dangers that it
endured, the sacrifices that it cheerfully rendered . . .?[1]
Alex Ellis, The Story of the Fifth Australian Division

8 AM, 22 FEBRUARY 1916, *RUNIC II*, SUEZ, TOMMY SHOUTS

And now *Runic II* drops anchor just off Suez, bobbing about in the
stream, before finally entering the Canal at dusk the following day,
heading for disembarkation at Alexandria. Of course, in the night
little can be seen, but come the dawn the Australian soldiers crowd on
deck and up the rigging to have a gander at all the interesting sights.
What is most obvious is that they have come a lot closer to the war. All
along the eastern bank of the Canal they can see Tommy soldiers manning massive fortifications that are bristling with guns and stacks of
ammunition. Sunshine glints off vicious-looking rolls of barbed wire.
More fortifications are being built. Army trucks patrol back and forth

on the dusty tracks, as do English and French warships in the Canal, while from above comes the endless drone of British planes – for many Australian soldiers, the first planes they've ever seen in their lives – on the lookout for enemy activity. Yes, just a short time before, the perfidious Turks had been forced back from the Canal, but there is no telling when they will try again.

Further up the Canal as *Runic* continues, huge working parties of Egyptians, under the command of shouting Tommy officers, are building more fortifications. A certain chill passes over the Australian soldiers just to see it all. To this point, their only real contact with the possibility of a violent death has been the practice, every sundown, of the bugler playing the 'Retreat'[2], when they are obliged to stand to attention and face the sinking orb as a mark of respect for those who have lost their lives in the service of the British Empire. But that had been just sorta *nice*, the right thing to do.

This, however, is starting to look *serious* – well away from such ceremonies, and all their chiacking and carrying-on and playing cricket on the deck and singalongs into the night – like there is a real war going on here and men are going to die. Some of *them* are going to die, once they get to action. Maybe a lot of them . . .

In preparation for possible attack, 500 rounds of ball cartridge are handed out to each of the Machine Gun Sections, while those with rifles are also issued ammunition. They pile up bags of sand on the starboard side of the bridge, as protection against any snipers who might be lurking in the desert as they go through the Suez Canal.

25 FEBRUARY 1916, VERDUN, A CHOICE BETWEEN RUIN AND REASON

After just four days of the battle, the Germans have killed some 10,000 French soldiers and taken the same number of prisoners. The French resistance has been patchy: in parts very strong; in other spots nearly non-existent. Most surprising has been Douaumont Fort, just five miles from Verdun, which was thought to be close to impregnable.

Instead, the Germans have taken it easily, as it was manned only by 56 elderly gunners.

Who can France turn to in its hour of need? General Joffre has no hesitation, and as none other than Charles de Gaulle would later note, 'On the day they had to choose between ruin and reason, Pétain was promoted . . .'[3]

France indeed needs its General with the most famous piercing blue eyes in the land, Henri-Phillipe Pétain. He is a 59-year-old veteran of great distinction. But where is he? A series of cables fails to rouse him, as it appears he has slipped away from his HQ during a lull in the fighting in northern France, leaving no contact point.

But his long-time aide-de-camp knows how to find him all right and, as the fate of France hangs in the balance, goes after him. Reckoning Pétain will have gone to Paris, and guessing the purpose, the aide heads south, getting off at the nearest major Parisian station, the Gare du Nord, before prowling the corridors of the Hotel Terminus attached to the station. The practice of the time is for guests to leave their boots outside for polishing overnight, but the aide is not just looking for any set of boots.

There! Outside one room is indeed a set of massive army boots, right beside the delicate shoes of a lady. He examines the boots closely. They are the General's!

Bursting through the door after a quick knock, the aide tells the General that the call has been put out by General Joffre himself. Verdun is teetering on the edge, and he must come.

It is the stuff of legend that Pétain replies he has urgent business he must first attend to here, but he will indeed be ready to leave on the first train at dawn. *Bon nuit!*

When Pétain does arrive at Verdun the next day, it is immediately obvious to him that while courageous soldiers are one thing, far more important is the need for his forces to have strong artillery themselves. Before the war, his constant cry when lecturing at the École de Guerre had been '*le feu tue!*', firepower kills,[4] and here is the tragic example. The situation in Verdun is as devastating as it is desperate. 'My heart leapt as I saw our youths of twenty going into the furnace of Verdun,' he would recount. 'But . . . when they returned . . . their expressions . . . seemed frozen by a vision of terror; their gait . . . betrayed a total dejection; they sagged beneath the weight of horrifying memories.'[5]

Pétain's first instruction is to cancel the mass counter-attacks of French soldiers that had been planned. There is no point when all that is going to happen is their being shot down. Instead, the emphasis must be placed on massed artillery to stop the Germans, with the soldiers used only once the artillery has done its work. As the Germans have penetrated on such a narrow front, they are vulnerable to artillery attacks from the flanks.

And supply is clearly crucial. There is just one road into Verdun from the French side, so it must be protected at all costs. Most urgent, however, is manpower, as Pétain calls forth reserve division after reserve division – including those earmarked for the forthcoming attack on the Somme – to contain the situation. It is inconceivable that Verdun can fall, whatever the cost! Slowly, under his command, the situation at Verdun comes back from the edge of the abyss.

26 FEBRUARY 1916, EGYPT, AUSTRALIANS TO TAKE FRENCH LEAVE

In the wake of the news out of Verdun, there is an urgent need for fresh units of soldiers to man the Western Front.

It is with this in mind that, on this day, in his Ferry Post HQ, the Commander of the Egyptian Expeditionary Force, General Sir Archibald Murray, receives from the Chief of the Imperial General Staff, General Sir William Robertson, in London a 'clear the line' telegram, one that must be sent ahead of all other telegrams:

WE FIND IT NECESSARY THAT WE SHOULD GIVE THE FRENCH EARLY PROOF OF OUR INTENTION TO SUPPORT THEM IN EVERY VISIBLE WAY.[6]

Sir Archibald quickly replies that he can send three British divisions: the 31st, followed by the 29th and 11th.

But Robertson demurs, saying they need five or six divisions:

THINGS AT VERDUN GOING NONE TOO
WELL . . . WE MUST ACCORDINGLY BE
PREPARED TO RISK SOMETHING IN EGYPT
. . . DO NOT ALLOW IDEA OF FORMING AN
AUSTRALIAN ARMY TO INFLUENCE MATTERS
AS THAT CANNOT MATERIALISE IN ANY CASE
FOR MONTHS, AND YOU SHOULD GENERALLY
WORK ON THE PRINCIPLE THAT THREE
AUSTRALIAN DIVISIONS IN FRANCE IN
APRIL MAY BE WORTH SIX AT A LATER
DATE . . .[7]

In short, even though it goes against the grain for Sir Archibald to denude Egypt of divisions under his command that are not yet fully trained, Sir Douglas Haig has also made it clear to him that time is of the essence in France. An ill-prepared division *now* is still better than a prepared division *later*.

Besides, there is no denying that, with winter now just about done, the spasmodic desert rains will soon disappear, meaning that the chances of the Turks even attempting to cross the Sinai Desert and attack the Canal have already all but disappeared. So Egypt actually can spare two Australian divisions, even though Murray is strongly of the view they are not sufficiently trained for the Western Front.

For his part, General Robertson appears to have no doubts:

IT WILL BE A GOOD THING FOR THE
AUSTRALIANS TO GET TO FRANCE. IT IS
AN EXCELLENT TRAINING SCHOOL AND THE
GERMANS WILL SOON PUT THEM IN ORDER.[8]

In response, Murray commits to sending the six divisions, AS FAST AS THE ADMIRALTY CAN PROVIDE SHIPS.

Murray has no hesitation in deciding which divisions of the AIF should go. The ones in the best shape right now, though still not good, are the 1st and 2nd Divisions – while the 3rd Divvie is still forming in Australia, and the 4th Divvie should be ready in a few weeks. The 5th Divvie, alas, is nowhere near well-enough trained yet and will have to be held back till late June, at the earliest. In the meantime, however, they could also send in a month or so the New Zealand Division to make up I Anzac Corps in France.

General Sir Archibald Murray tells fellow General Birdwood that the 1st and 2nd Australian Divisions must be ready to go within a fortnight. Truly? When it comes to the Australians, Murray will be glad to see the back of the bally brutes.

26–27 FEBRUARY 1916, EGYPT, POMPEY ERUPTS

By the morning of 26 February, *Runic* is moored at a wharf in Alexandria Harbour. The Australians are able to disembark and by midnight are sitting on hard wooden seats in a carriage on their way to Cairo. There they are quickly dispatched to the Aerodrome Camp at Heliopolis, about an hour's hard march outside the teeming Egyptian capital.

Suddenly among 95,000 other Australian soldiers, Bert and Ray Bishop have arrived at a time of great flux. Throughout all the AIF divisions there are opportunities for promotion as never before, as double the officers are needed to cope with the doubling of divisions. Where can the new officers come from? At the top level, Birdwood is insistent that there are no Australian officers of sufficient calibre to take over the 4th and 5th Divisions, so they must bring over British officers from the British and Indian Armies – an idea that sits so badly with the Australian Government and particularly Defence Minister George Pearce, who expresses his 'surprise and disappointment'[9], that it is instantly shelved.

A compromise sees Major-General Sir Herbert Cox, the Englishman 'whose Indian brigade had done such good work at Gallipoli',[10] as Birdwood put it, become the Commanding Officer of the 4th Division and Major-General James Whiteside McCay, the one-time Australian Defence Minister turned military officer, who had been in charge of the 2nd Brigade at the Gallipoli landing, placed in command of the 5th Division. (This notwithstanding the fact that McCay's five-week-long Gallipoli experience had been his only time spent on an actual battlefield. And, by now, it has been substantially forgotten that on the day of the landing McCay had been 'completely lost',[11] only pulling himself together when a 'coldly contemptuous'[12] General Sir William Bridges had spoken to him sharply.)

And Cox and McCay are not the only ones to gain major promotion, as across the board Corporals find themselves Sergeants, Lieutenants become Captains, Colonels are suddenly Brigadiers, and so forth. Lieutenant-Colonel Harold 'Pompey' Elliott, who had been in charge of the 7th Battalion at the Gallipoli landing, and then the 1st Brigade, now moves up a rank to Brigadier-General and is given charge of the 15th Brigade. Originally nicknamed after 'Pompey' Elliott the famous Carlton captain, he is also a man of volcanic temperament, in a manner to bury old Pompeii when he blows.

As it happens, however, rarely has this temper been on more volcanic display than now, as he finds foisted upon him any number of 'officers', sent to him by General Birdwood and Birdwood's Chief of Staff, Brigadier-General Cyril Brudenell White (the mastermind behind the successful evacuation at Gallipoli), whom he quickly determines are not remotely satisfactory. Back in Australia, when first forming up the 7th Battalion, he had been allowed to choose his own officers, and the result, if he does say so himself – as well as in a letter to a friend – was 'a Battalion whose name I think outshines all the others in Camp as in the Field'.[13] And now, at brigade level, they want to force upon him all the officers from 2nd Brigade whom 'no one else wanted, as a way of getting rid of them without unpleasantness', and expected him to roll over like General Irving had done with the 14th Brigade?

Not bloody likely!

'Do you want an efficient brigade or will any old thing do?' he thunders to General Birdwood in writing, after confronting him in person. 'I am willing to obey either way but my instructions should be plain. If you imagine I will be willing to tolerate inefficiency for the sake of maintaining a comfortable position, you are mistaken and rather than do that I will ask to be returned to Australia . . . The lives of 4,000 men in my Brigade depend upon me. How can I discharge that trust with officers like these to depend upon?'[14]

However, Birdwood will not back down and Elliott is firmly informed that the new officers 'must remain [as] their reputations are sacred'.

'The lives of my men are more sacred!'[15]

Whatever else they might say of Pompey Elliott, his care for the welfare of his men is as well known as his temper.

One of Birdwood's staff officers is sent to give Elliott the rounds of the kitchen about how his mutinous communications are entirely out of line. 'However,' Pompey delights in telling his friend, '[Birdwood's staff officer] was an Australian and he could not do it.'

True. It is one thing for an Englishman to be high and mighty and lay down the law to a colonial but quite another for an Australian to try such a stunt, most particularly on a matter so key to the welfare of Australian troops. So, after the Australian officer has faithfully said his piece, as he has been ordered to do, he takes his cue from the look of disgust on Pompey's face, softens and tells the General straight, Australian to Australian. 'I know you are [upset],' says the staff officer, 'but if you object any more it is you who will be moved, not they.'[16]

In short, pull your bloody head in, Pompey. Whatever you might think of the Pommy officers, you bloody well have to fit in on this if you really want to look after your men.

In the end, Pompey rescinds his notion of returning to Australia but will have to polish his boots when it comes to military protocol and toeing the line. For General Elliott has decided on a different scheme. That is, he will humiliate, in front of their men, all those officers he considers unworthy, using language that is 'far from saintly'.[17]

Some resign, some break down, some begin to improve. One way or another, Elliott's stamp is put on the surviving officers and he is also able to bring in some of the officers that he wants as replacements, ones 'I can fully trust and rely upon to keep discipline'.[18]

The Victorian is particularly pleased that Captain Geoff McCrae, scion of a Melbourne artistic family – and himself a noted poet and budding architect – who had been with him in the 7th Battalion at Gallipoli is able to join them, initially as second-in-command of the 60th Battalion but soon promoted to Major and made Commanding Officer. 'He is,' Elliott enthuses of the good-looking young officer, just 26 years old, who is forever writing loving letters to his young wife, Maude, 'a great favourite with everybody, officers and men'.[19]

Another in the same battalion is Lieutenant Tom Elliott – no kin – who is something of a special case. While most officers, like McCrae, tend to be as high-born as they are highly educated from an early age, the good-looking six-footer is the beloved son of a Sydney labourer, who had been in the second intake at the Royal Military College at Duntroon – the only tertiary institution in the country that would educate him for free – and he had prospered like no other. After serving with distinction with the 7th Light Horse at Gallipoli, young Tom is in turn taken with General Elliott from the first time he meets him – a senior officer like no other, who clearly doesn't care what an officer's social ranking is so long as they can perform. And so Tom Elliott signs on and is soon promoted to the rank of Major, becoming, at the age of just 21, the second-in-command to the also recently promoted Major Geoff McCrae.

For, from the first, Major Tom Elliott is different. Charles Bean, for one, had always noted a distinction between the British and Australian officers. 'It is the secret of the British Army system that officers should be as unlike to and different from their men as possible,' he would note in his diary.'[20] '[Britain has] a race of gentlemen who can command and a race of Tommies who are to receive commands and who wouldn't dream of disputing that order of things.'[21] But the Australian officer is not like that. He wants 'his men [to] follow him for what he knows and what he does – and sometimes for what he is; not because he is of a superior social caste'.[22]

And Tom Elliott has those qualities in spades. He really is *of* the men he commands. They follow him for what he knows, for what he does, for what he is – a fine man, and natural leader. (A man who, by the by, is desperately in love with a gorgeous young woman from Sydney, Alice Thurlow, but that is another story . . .)

In the other brigades, things are far more established from the first. Moving up to take their posts as Commanding Officers of the new battalions are such men as Lieutenant-Colonel Walter Cass, now commanding the 54th Battalion – a 40-year-old veteran from Albury, twice wounded at Gallipoli.

As to the common run of soldiers, like Bert and Ray Bishop, together with Hodgy and Robbo, one important factor in their training now is to prepare themselves for fighting cheek by jowl, by towel, by bayonet, alongside the British. Though this happened a little at the Dardanelles, most particularly in the 2nd Battle of Krithia, for the most part, at Anzac Cove, the two groups had run their own races. Now, it seems, the Australians will be constantly under direct British command and alongside British officers, and so must get used to their way of doing things.

In short, and most importantly, the Australians must get used to *saluting*. Oh, they salute in the AIF, of course, but rarely with enthusiasm, and *never* by deferential instinct. Charles Bean puts his finger on it: 'Men of the AIF were never in the least convinced by the explanation generally given of the need for saluting – that it was "an honour paid to the King's uniform" . . . The British regulations, however, insisted upon this observance between soldiers and officers, wherever met, to a degree which was not enforced in all armies – in the French, for example – and which to Australians appeared humiliating.'[23]

Bean was born in Bathurst, New South Wales, where he spent his first ten years, but he was raised from the age of ten in various towns across England and substantially educated in England, including at Oxford. So he is well equipped to appreciate the difference in approach of the two countries. 'At the time of the Great War, the political system of England, though democratic in form, was still largely feudal in practice and tradition. Forms of military subordination, such as saluting, therefore came more easily to English soldiers, the majority of whom had been brought up to consider themselves inferior, socially and mentally, to their officers.'[24]

But Australian soldiers – raised in a land where a vogue saying, from the days of Eureka Stockade, is that 'Jack is as good as his master, and in many cases better'[25] – simply don't believe in that kind of bloody nonsense.

And not even the Australian officers themselves are too fussed. 'We [officers] may be a bit to blame on the score of saluting,' one of them would record in a letter, 'but it goes against our grain to make these fine fellows salute us when they somehow feel it demeans them to do so. And so we never pull them up . . .'[26]

So they will all have to be taught.

The 3rd Battalion even goes so far as to have hour-long 'saluting drill',[27] while the 5th Brigade adopts a 'saluting scheme',[28] whereby a Captain walks through town followed by a Sergeant who takes the names of all those who do not salute him, and who are subsequently punished for their trouble.

Perhaps in a growing sign of Bean's own sense of 'Australian-ness', the correspondent decides that in his own case he detests being saluted, despite his rank as Captain. 'I also suffer,' he will soon write in his diary, 'because though many of the men salute me through courtesy (and one is particularly anxious not to offend them by not answering it) many do not and there is no earthly reason why they should. One doesn't like to appear to look for a salute, *I hate it* . . .'[29]

This interaction between the English way and the Australian way really can be a cause of friction. At Tel-el-Kebir at one point, a battalion of Australian soldiers is put on parade to be informed that the General Officer Commanding, an Englishman, desires the use of bad language to be cut out, most specifically the words 'fuck' and 'c–nt', as in any case he understands that these two words are not used in Australia.

At this point, a voice rings out from the back of the parade: 'The fucking c—t has never been there.'[30]

27 FEBRUARY 1916, ON THE WESTERN FRONT, DEATH AFTER DISHONOUR

Lieutenant-Colonel Frank Crozier, Commander of the 9th Royal Irish Rifles, orders the firing squad to form up on one side of the wall of a villa, while the condemned man is dragged forth. This Irish teenager, Private James Crozier (no relation), had gone missing a fortnight earlier in a fearful battle close to Serre before turning up a few hours later at a nearby field hospital, saying he had not known what he was doing when he made off, only that he had been 'in a daze at the time and suffering from pains throughout his body'.[31]

On the examining doctor's conclusion that young Crozier was fit in mind and body, Lieutenant-Colonel Crozier promptly had him court-martialled for cowardice. Found guilty as charged, the young soldier had been stripped of all insignia, as he was no longer a member of the 9th Irish Rifles.

And today he must pay the piper.

The wretch is dragged forward by the guards. Nearly insensible with the drink he has been plied with through the night, he is hauled before the execution post. 'There are hooks on the post,' Lieutenant-Colonel Crozier will later describe it. 'We always do things thoroughly in the Rifles. He is hooked on like dead meat in a butcher's shop.'[32]

'Take aim . . .' the officer in charge of the firing squad calls to his men, raising his sword high above his head.

Heartbeats raised as one, they bring their rifles to their shoulders and take aim at the poor private's chest.

In one sharp movement, the officer brings the sword down.

'A volley rings out – a nervous ragged volley it is true, yet a volley.'[33]

Private Crozier slumps.

Lieutenant-Colonel Crozier nods to the regiment's doctor, who steps forward to discover that Private Crozier's heart still has a light beat. The firing squad has not had its heart in its work, or perhaps too much heart to do the job properly.

The young officer in charge of the firing squad strides forward, pistol drawn, and – after the doctor steps back from both the post and his Hippocratic Oath – fires a final shot into young Crozier's head.

'Life is now extinct . . .'

The regiment marches back to stomach breakfast, leaving behind the men of Private Crozier's company to pay their final respects.

Lieutenant-Colonel Crozier has no sympathy for what has happened. 'This is war.'[34]

LATE FEBRUARY 1916, CAIRO, THE NAKED TRUTH AND DONKEY-BOYS

Saaay, Bert and Ray?

Hodgy and Robbo want to show the young'uns a part of Cairo they're familiar with from their early days in the British Army. 'We'll be your guides, and your teachers,' they tell them.[35]

Which is as well, because shortly thereafter the youngsters are lost in the labyrinthine back streets of Cairo, beset by an onslaught of sights, sounds and smells they have never even imagined, let alone experienced. And blokes and sheilas from all parts! Persians, Syrians, Sudanese, Armenians, Turks, Italians, Greeks, Arabs and French, all with something to buy or sell – including their bodies. Hawkers and peddlers of all kinds see the Australians coming and react instantly – as the Australians are known to be the best-paid soldiers – imploring them to try their wares: *'Australi very good, very nice . . . Plenty money, Australi . . .'*[36]

Those with nothing to sell but their knowledge of the city try that, promising to act as guides despite their lack of English, and even producing references from other soldiers. Another Digger will later recount how one such reference, written by a fellow Australian, was nothing if not frank: *"To whom it may concern – This is to certify that the Bearer – Abdul – is the greatest thief North of the Equator.'*[37]

A couple of hours into this tour of the Wazza, young Bert and Ray get the shock of their lives, on the second floor of a ramshackle stone building, after following Hodgy and Robbo. 'Have a look in here,' Robbo says, pointing through a massive doorway.[38]

Bert, particularly, nearly falls over, he is so stunned.

For there she is.

Standing up, looking at him, right next to an inviting, low, cushioned couch is 'a perfectly nude brownish-black woman', the first naked woman the two young men from down Milton way have ever seen in their lives. And now what?

She's turning for them! Slowly pirouetting! Smilingly showing off her ample wares, so they can see her voluptuous breasts and buttocks from all angles! It is as if she is saying, 'Would you like to have a go?'

No, Bert bloody wouldn't. And neither would Ray. When Bert looks over, he sees that his cousin has this kind of glazed look about him, like he's been hit in the head too many times and is now punch-drunk.

Hodgy and Robbo? They're just grinning like mad things.

Bert closes his eyes and opens them again, hoping he is imagining the whole thing. But no, she's still there, still showing off her wares, still asking with her eyes if he wants to buy.

Finally, Robbo takes mercy on them. 'Come on,' he says, ushering them away.[39]

Ah, still, how Hodgy and Robbo laugh and laugh, just to see the expressions on the young'uns' faces! And those expressions become even more contorted when, in other parts of the building, they pay a few piastres to see some sex shows of indescribable vulgarity. In the last of these shows, two naked girls and two naked 'donkey-boys'[40] – don't ask – are going at it right in the middle of a roaring crowd, and it is getting very close to the, um, climactic moment when someone throws a burning, scrunched-up copy of *The Egyptian Times* right into the middle of them!

Bedlam. Complete bedlam. The girls scream, the donkey-boys yell, fighting breaks out around the bloke who threw the burning paper that has ruined the show, and nude women and their nude patrons are running everywhere as the fire takes partial hold.

Hodgy and Robbo get the boys out – pausing only so Ray can be violently ill in the courtyard – and they laugh their way home at everything that has happened.

The young'uns are a long way from home, ain't they? Such are their lives right now, the older blokes showing them the ropes, shocking them but still looking after them.

EARLY MARCH 1916, VIA THE RED SEA TO SUEZ AND A SEA OF RED

At last! The word has come through. The 1st and 2nd Divvies will shortly have to leave the Canal and head back to Serapeum and Moascar to catch trains.

Lieutenant Goldy Raws of the 23rd Battalion, for one, is delighted. They are leaving. They must pack up and get ready to move out within days. 'We are to be ready to leave Egypt,' he writes to his mother, 'and go to . . .? That is the question. France is first favourite, direct to Marseilles; next is England for re-shipment to France; third is Salonica, and fourth is some new landing. I'll tell you when we get there!'[41]

On 5 and 6 March, both divisions start moving in from the desert to congregate at Moascar and Serapeum. To bolster the divisions that must replace them, a flood of reinstoushments, as they are known,[42] starts arriving from Cairo, including Bert and Ray Bishop.

Put in a long line of open, flat-top rail trucks, they pass through an enormous camp at – what is the name of this place, up on the siding sign? – **Tel-el-Kebir**. The train stops, and suddenly they are surrounded by their fellow Australians, firing questions at them.

'Where are you going?'

'Are you heading for France?'[43]

Buggered if we know, Blue. But France certainly does seem to be the word on everyone's lips. There is obviously a big push to the Western Front, and Bert and Ray hope to be there sooner rather than later, so they can at last take part in a 'real war'.[44] However, they shortly settle in Ismaïlia, where they are distinctly underwhelmed. 'Of all the God-forsaken holes that human beings were ever expected to live in,' Bert writes home, 'I think this takes the prize. Sand, sand everywhere, terrible heat and flies in millions . . .'[45]

And training. Lots of training, with soldiers learning the mechanics of killing on the various forms of weaponry provided to them, and the officers learning the stratagems for doing it most effectively. For, apart from everything else, Ismaïlia is the training centre to beat them all, with its bomb-throwing school being a specialty, as well as its machine-gun school. The troops are taught all about modern warfare, by British veterans who have *actually fought* on the fabled Western Front in France and have been invalided to these posts.

None of them, true, wants to go back there ever again – 'You go and do your whack, and get knocked out, and see if you want to go back there,' one of them says, with a faraway look in his eyes[46] – but they are more than happy to pass on to the soldiers and officers what they have learned, and then give them exams at the end of the week.

Most interesting to many of the officers who take such courses is instruction in how best to use the much-fabled 'Mills bomb'. It is an invention that makes the 'jam-tin bombs' they used in Gallipoli, with fuses lit by a smouldering piece of rope hanging off your belt, look positively primitive. No, these are state-of-the-art bombs, though some call them 'grenades' and those who must learn how to throw them 'grenadiers'.[47] The key breakthrough is that these are detonated by first removing the safety pin and then holding down a striker lever. While that lever is held down, you're safe. But once you throw it, thus releasing the lever, you have seven seconds before it explodes.

About the size and shape of a big egg, the grenade is nevertheless very heavy due to the fact that its high explosive is encased in grooved cast iron, designed, once it detonates, to erratically shatter along those very grooves and send furious fragments of scything hot metal into the soft flesh and hard noggins of your enemy.

How to throw it? Well, this is where the men of the British Empire have a distinct advantage over Fritz, as we know how to throw cricket balls a long way and it is much the same action. As a matter of fact, for maximum distance, it has been proven that an action just like bowling a ball is best – except you're standing still. (At Gallipoli, no one, they reckoned, could throw a grenade further and with more accuracy than

the great Australian fast bowler 'Tibby' Cotter, known to English sup-
porters as 'Terror' Cotter, in part because he had once beaned no less
than W. G. Grace with a full toss. *Legend.*)

13 MARCH 1916, ISMAÏLIA, I ANZAC CORPS IS NEEDLED

Movement at the station, by the light of the desert moon. Company
by company, 36 men to every flat-bed railway truck, the soldiers of
Australia's 2nd Division – the first half of the mighty I Anzac Corps –
make ready to leave.

If some of the departing soldiers are feeling denuded at this time, it
is only natural. Although the men of the artillery batteries are travelling
with their horses and all their harnesses, their actual guns have been
left behind for use in Egypt by the remaining divisions. Similarly, the
transport section have left their wagons behind. Both wagons and guns,
apparently, will be waiting for them wherever it is that they are going.

The 1st Division will follow in a week's time, and once the New
Zealand Division joins them in early April, that will be I Anzac Corps
gone.

Of course, Sergeant Leslie Newton of the 12th Battalion notes, the
move entails yet another round of big needles. 'The medical officer,'
he would record, 'to cheer us up, decided to inoculate us. It was either
for typhoid, diphtheria, para-typhoid or something. They seemed to
inoculate us for everything except gun-shot wounds.'[48] (A pity.)

The men of II Anzac Corps – the 4th and 5th Divisions – watch
them go with real regret. Lucky bastards, heading off, no doubt, to
fight on the Western Front, although nothing has been confirmed as
yet. But where else would they be going? Of course it is the Western
Front. 'We have not had any fighting yet,' an envious Digger from the
5th Division's 32nd Battalion writes home on this very day. 'I think
they must be keeping us to look pretty, they seem to be frightened to
knock the paint off us.'[49]

Which is as maybe, but at least disciplining the men of the 4th and
5th Divisions will become easier from this point, as for any soldier,

company or battalion that misbehaves or underperforms the clear threat is they will not be allowed to follow the 1st and 2nd Division to France, to fight on the Western Front – the dearest wish of everyone.

———

All aboooooard! Toot, toot!

With a grunt of effort, the Australian soldiers of the 2nd Division, by now burned dark brown by the Egyptian sun, haul their kit onto the open, flat-top rail trucks and place their packs and rifles in a line right down the centre, just as instructed. Then they lie down on either side, using their packs as a pillow, in two rows of 18 soldiers. No matter that it is as uncomfortable as kissing Great-Auntie Doris . . . they are all soon asleep to the rocking rhythm of the railway.

This first contingent of the 2nd Divvie, the 7th Brigade, wake at dawn to find that the desert has been long left behind and they are now in the richly fertilised fields of the Valley of the Nile – with green crops as far as the eye can see – before the fields give way to more and more buildings and the next thing they know their puffing steam train is pulling them to the docks by Alexandria Harbour, where massive troopships await them.

In their absence, of course, II Anzac Corps must take over many of the duties of I Anzac Corps, including their defence of 25 miles of the Canal, from Ferry Post to Serapeum. The Anzac Mounted Division is holding the fort in the interim, but it does not have enough numbers to do it for more than a fortnight or so.

But how to get the replacements there, these soldiers of the 4th and 5th Divisions, when all the railway cars available are now being used by I Anzac Corps to get to Alexandria? Major-General Herbert Cox, who commands the 4th Division, is in no doubt. Recognising it would be madness to have his men marching through the desert with the full weight of their packs, he arranges for them to have camels – those mighty ships of the desert – to bear much of the load.

The Commanding Officer of the 5th Division, however, Major-General

James McCay, has other ideas. The notoriously strict disciplinarian is, in Digger parlance – and not to put too fine a point on it – 'a prick'. Even in the more sober assessment of Bean, he is a man who 'talks far too much',[50] and one who believes that, just as cleanliness is next to godliness, tough training is next to manliness. This in turn makes great soldiers, and though reluctant at first to get his men there by foot, he now intends to use the whole thing as a serious training exercise.

His soldiers, by God, will *march* there in full kit – including rifle, extra ammunition, bombs, blanket, sleeping swag, great coat, entrenching tool, water bottle, mess tin, mug, rifle, bayonet *and* 120 rounds of ammunition for good measure. All up, they will be carrying 70 pounds on their three-day trek. Now, some might think this a tad on the foolhardy side of things, as it is a distance of over 50 miles and it is generally considered that a mile's march on the desert is worth two miles anywhere else. But McCay is insistent. And nor does he care that many of the men have just been inoculated against typhoid and are feeling lower than a snake's belly button – just about as crook as Rookwood. He has only just arrived from Australia following his evacuation home to Melbourne after being wounded at Gallipoli, and this is his perfect chance to make his mark on the 5th Division and show them just who is in charge: *him.*

Yes, there are complaints, but for McCay that's too damn bad. He is one whose eyebrows are almost as thick and luxurious as his moustache, and no one is ever in the least doubt when he is upset – the eyebrows glare on their own. This is just such an occasion. He insists it must happen exactly as he has ordered and puts some serious early work in now for the title that *The Bulletin* will later accord him: 'the most detested officer in the AIF'.[51]

THIRD WEEK OF MARCH 1916, ZEITOUN, FORWARD THE LIGHT HORSE, WAS THERE A MAN DISMAYED?

Paraaaaaade! Attennnnnn-*shun!*

Men, the Camp Commander has a few words he wants to say to you. Now, men, this is a bit difficult because you are all obviously proud of being a part of the Australian Light Horse, but there is no escaping one central fact.

'The Light Horse Regiments are over double strength in men and officers, and as the Light Horse would not be wanted much more in this war, and [as we desperately need men for the artillery] it is therefore proposed to form two more Divisions of Artillery here in Egypt out of the Light Horse surplus.'[52]

A groan goes through the men, and more than a murmur of anger. After everything they have done to get into the mighty Light Horse, all the training they have already done, now they're being asked to *leave it all behind?* Few are more distressed than one Norm Nicolson, a garrulous Queenslander who has been with the Light Horse for the last six *years*, the last four of those as a Second-Lieutenant. 'A nice douche of cold water this,' he records in his diary, 'for us who had all tried so hard to get away as Light Horse!'[53]

Against that, the logic really is compelling. The Light Horse had achieved great things in Gallipoli, but only as 'horseless-horsemen', as 'beetle-crushers', not on their mighty mounts. And every word out of the Western Front in France – which they eagerly devour – is all about infantry, machine guns and artillery, with nary a mention of cavalry. If this is their best chance to see some action, to get involved in some 'stunts', then so be it.

It really is something to think about, and all the more so when, three days later, they are formed into a hollow square to await a big black motor car that pulls up, only to disgorge artillery officers and recruiting sergeants who proceed to give them what the men call 'kid-stakes', otherwise known as flattering bullshit.

But it works all right, and in short order there are 850 volunteers, 420 of them coming from just one regiment, the 5th Light Horse – and one of them is Norm. 'We are told we will have to make good inside of two months,' he writes to a friend, 'an almost impossible thing, but I'll have a try at it.'[54]

For indeed, speed is the key. With the original artillery units of the 4th and 5th Divisions now on their way to France with the artillery of the 1st and 2nd Divvies, it is a matter of urgency that they quickly learn the many things they need to. Before they know it, thus, the artillery volunteers are on their way to Ismaïlia and embarked on a seemingly endless round of lectures.

Can we start from the beginning? There are basically two types of artillery: field guns and howitzers. Field guns fire on a fairly low trajectory, while howitzers use a much higher trajectory. Field guns such as the 18-pounders – named for the weight of the shell they fire – are direct-line-of-sight weapons and are at their most devastating when targets are visible and you can bring a sustained barrage on a selected point. For example, on the barbed wire before enemy trenches, or just ahead of an infantry advance. If the battery is practised enough, the range can even lengthen as the troops move forward.

The 18-pounders – with a firing crew of six, and four more to handle the ammunition – have a maximum range of just over 10,000 yards, when the elevation of the barrel is set to its maximum 37 degrees. They unleash around four shells a minute. But if you're attacking something on, say, the lee side of a hill, or a trench on flat ground, then field guns just aren't going to be able to do as much damage, and you need howitzers, which can elevate their barrels to as high as 45 degrees. This means the shells come from a much higher trajectory, so you can drop a shell right on Fritz's square head, even when he's right down a trench.

In the AIF, the standard is to use 18-pounder field guns and 4.5-inch howitzers, the latter of which requires a crew of six.

We also have heavy artillery, 60-pounder guns and some 8-inch, 9.2-inch and even 12-inch howitzers, all of which can fire shells at least 12,000 yards. As a matter of fact, the 12-inch 'rail howitzer', so called because it is mounted on a railway flat-bed carriage and can easily be transported on specially built rail lines, can send massive 750-pound high-explosive shells as far as 15,000 yards – nearly nine miles!

Now, when it comes to the choice of shell, there are two basic types. The 18-pound shrapnel shells are ever so tightly packed with 374 small metal balls. The shells are designed so that the nose blows off just above the ground, releasing the balls to blow out like a shotgun blast to kill and wound men within a radius of as much as 300 yards from the burst. High-explosive shells, though, are for destroying trenches, with both the explosive power and the fragmentation of the projectile casing doing the damage – in this case, the casualties are just a bonus. Understand what we are trying to do here, most particularly when it comes to supporting our advancing infantry.

It is in the handbook you've all been given:

The object of the preliminary bombardment
   1. Overpower enemy artillery
   2. Physical and moral reduction of the enemy's
infantry
   3. The destruction of material obstacles to
the advance of the attacking infantry and other
defences.

Now, when it comes to more detailed information, the recruits are soon put on a series of specific courses, including battery tactics, calibration, camouflage and drill order. The officers also do map reading, meteorology, gun registration and how to read photographs of enemy trenches taken from your own reconnaissance aircraft.

The last subject is particularly interesting and a sign of just how far the art of artillery has come. No more do cannons lob shells at random into enemy territory. Now, with aircraft taking photos, and accurate maps being made from those photos, you can see exactly where their trenches are, fire accordingly and, most importantly, provide artillery support for raids.

LATE MARCH 1916, UPON THE SUNNY MEDITERRANEAN, BOUND FOR MARSEILLES

How good is this?

Goldy Raws and the men of the 2nd Division's 23rd Battalion could not be more pleased. After endless stuffing around, all 943 soldiers of the battalion are at last on their way to France, aboard the good ships SS *City of Edinburgh*, *Caledonia* and *Lake Michigan*. He is still thrilled that, in their last few days in the desert, his 6th Brigade had been the first Australian brigade to receive the colossal honour of being inspected by HRH the Prince of Wales, accompanied by General Birdwood. Not only that but he, personally, Lieutenant Goldy Raws, had had the honour of roaring to his men in the march past, 'EYYYES ROIGHT!'[55] and then giving the salute, which the Prince of Wales had returned – even if it had taken two or three nudges from General Birdwood to get him to do so. But now the 23rd are away, among the last of the 2nd Division to be on the high seas. The first of the 1st Division have already left Alexandria, and when all are away, General Birdwood and the officers of I Anzac HQ, together with a collection of reinforcement troops for each battalion in I Anzac Corps, will follow.

Also crossing the Mediterranean at this time with his mates from the 1st Battalion, 1st Brigade, 1st Division is Private Archie Barwick, a farmer and Gallipoli veteran originally from Tasmania, as short as a gate-post and every bit as tough and strong, often to be found scribbling in his diary when he has a moment free. Just like he is now . . . He has only one real complaint, apart from the execrable food: 'We had a severe injection into our arms & it stung us properly, our arms were sore & swollen; they dug the needle in properly, I don't know how many times this made us but we have had plenty of it, there were 2 doctors on the job & they did not take long over it; the very thought of being inoculated makes some chaps sick, they turn quite yellow yet these same chaps will stand up to bullets & bombs with the best of them, & think nothing of wounds. I have seen strong men faint when they have been inoculated . . .'[56]

Getting 'butchered', the boys call it.[57]

Did someone say it? They're a weird mob.

Landing at Marseilles in the rain, the men are 'told to get our things ready to move off that night as we had a journey of 3 days in the train before us.'[58]

Not all the men catch the train, however. One of them, 22-year-old Russell Bosisto – a notably good-looking six-footer, with his hair as black as his eyes are piercing blue – a baker from Hindmarsh, who never saw a bit of trouble that he didn't want to gravitate to, up to and including Gallipoli – has to go straight to Marseilles Hospital to be treated for venereal disease.

Look, it is not necessarily, to use the vernacular, that Russell would 'root a pile of hair on a barber's floor', but he has certainly been as careless with whom he shares his physical affections as he has been reluctant to wear condoms. And now he must pay the price.

His many comrades in A Company of the 27th Battalion are not surprised. Yes, 'Boss' is immediately missed, but for one thing it is a rare circumstance that in this case he is away *with* permission, as usually he just takes off. There are those in this war who go Missing in Action. Boss usually goes missing to get some action. A few days like that, living high off the hog, and then he turns up, gets arrested and does his punishment, without complaint.

This time, it might be taking a bit longer.

27–29 MARCH 1916, 16 MILES NORTH OF SAILLY, 'HE'S A FINE LOOKING MAN, MOTHER'

Oh, the honour that is done these first Australian troops to arrive, a little back from the Western Front. Just to think that, in the space of two days, two of the most powerful British military men in the world – General Sir Douglas Alexander Haig and Secretary of War Lord Horatio Kitchener – take the time to inspect two bodies of the freshly arrived Australian troops. It really is something.

And both of these elite military men are impressed, in turn. 'The men were looking splendid,' Sir Douglas writes in his diary after inspecting three battalions of the AIF's 7th Brigade, drawn up beside the Morbecque-Hazebrouck road. 'Fine physique, very hard and determined looking . . . The Australians are mad keen to kill Germans, and to start doing it at once . . . The Australians are now taking over a fairly quiet front of the line . . . near Armentières, where I hope they may be able to do some winning!'[59]

Some of the Australians are equally impressed at the vision of Haig, with one, Lieutenant James Aitken, writing home, 'He's a fine looking man, Mother.'[60]

Lord Kitchener's review of the 5th and 6th Brigades takes place on a bright morning two days later, near Aire. The old man – for, somehow, he really does look old now, and certainly much older than he appeared in the famous posters – walks slowly along the ranks, his practised eyes flickering up and down, back and forth, along this fine body of Antipodean manhood. 'Well, boys,' Kitchener finally gives his summation to the Australians, 'I am glad to welcome you in France. If you uphold your reputation gained on Gallipoli you will be liked by everyone but the Germans.'[61]

Oh, the honour!

And, exhausted as Kitchener is, weighed down by the military matters of the world being on his shoulders for so long, the arrival of the Australian 2nd Division in France really does lift him a little.

Just two days earlier, at a conference of the Allied military leaders in Paris, the Secretary of War had been quite shocked to hear the oft-repeated entreaty from the French, 'They had lost severely in men, and it was now time for the British to play their part . . .'[62] Meaning, of course, they want the soldiers of the British Empire to do the job. And these men from Australia are clearly of the finest order.

Which is as well, for only a short time later a meeting of the War Council in London finally will give its formal assent for the joint British and French attack on the Somme to proceed. Churchill calls it 'á cheval sur la Somme', referring to the gambling expression 'á cheval', astride a horse, when two bets are placed on adjoining numbers. In this case, the two gambles are either side of the Somme, with France responsible for south of the river and Britain the north.[63]

A LATE MARCH IN LATE MARCH 1916, WITH THE 5TH DIVISION IN EGYPT

'The air,' Captain Geoff McCrae describes it in a letter home, 'has been like the mouth of a brick kiln . . .'[64]

And it is time for the 4th and 5th Divisions to take their place guarding the Suez Canal, some 40 miles away from Tel-el-Kebir.

The most sensible method is embraced by the 8th Brigade, commanded by the oldest and most experienced senior officer in the 5th Division, Brigadier-General Edwin Tivey. Already called the 'Bloodless 8th',[65] for the fact they had missed Gallipoli, they now earn the new nicknames 'Tivey's Gentlemen of the Desert' and 'Tivey's Chocolate Soldiers', for *taking the train*.

Brigadier-General Godfrey H. Irving's 14th Brigade, on the other hand, do exactly as ordered and march across the desert in the full heat of the day. 'The desert for some distance was shingly and undulating,' one soldier of the 14th Brigade would recount of the first day. 'But by 10 a.m. we had got into country where the sand was very soft.'[66]

So soft that their boots frequently sink down to their tops, and so hot that the sun does not merely shine, it *beats*. The 14th Brigade soon begins to break apart, as hands steal to water bottles and drain them dry. Onwards they press to a camp that sits somewhere beyond the burning, shimmering and sizzling horizon that refuses to come forward to meet and comfort the men. They are tortured by the fact that 'a fresh water canal runs along a little distance from the route', from which they are 'forbidden to drink, bath or even wash in it as it is found to be contaminated by all sorts of disease germs, the natives being filthy in their habits and all drainage going into the canal'.[67]

The sweat pours out of them, their trousers chafe their thighs, and as soon as the fine sand works its way into their socks and boots, each step is a severe irritation of the skin and spirit.

'All along the route one could see the articles thrown out by the boys,' one Digger would recount. 'The boys lagged and lagged behind, hundreds needing the doctor's attention, and many fainting. Many begged and begged for water.'[68] Some men revisit the technique they learned in the freshwater-deprived trenches of Anzac during the previous year, and futilely suck on a pebble (if they can find one).

'Every hill was a painful scene,' a soldier from the 14th Brigade's Field Ambulance records in his diary. 'Naturally what water the men had was soon finished so there they were – begging most painfully for just a mouthful. Our ambulance men were running here & there all over the field but we only had our little drop of water. This however only went to the very serious cases but I'm sorry to say that they were too often serious. Men were groaning in agony, some offering all the money they possessed for a mouthful of water while others were almost lifeless on the sand foaming at the mouth. It was a treat to hear these words from some who were truly bad: 'Yes, mate keep it for worse cases than mine – there are plenty of them.'[69]

When their route takes them up and down sandhills, they only just manage to keep going, with the heat in the hollows like a furnace. Those few who have water left sip it, only to find it makes their lips drier! Before long, that water becomes so hot they cannot even bring it to their lips. And now stronger blokes start to carry the rifles of weaker blokes, who appear about to drop in their sandy tracks. 'We were . . . foaming at the mouth like mad dogs,' Harold Williams would record, 'with tongues swollen, breath gripping our throats with agonizing pain, and legs buckling under us.'[70]

All this, and there's General Irving, prancing around on his high black horse, with his staff officer also mounted by his side, trying to *order* them to keep in formation. That bastard.

—

On a different route, Pompey Elliott's men of the 15th Brigade are in relatively better shape, because he has deliberately started their march in the comparative cool of the late afternoon. Still, when one soldier drops out to sit in a rare bit of shade, Elliott is outraged and insists he gets up and keeps moving.

The soldier refuses.

'I will blow your brains out if you don't fall in at once,' Elliott declares, pointing his revolver right at him.[71]

'When the lads saw the drawn revolver,' one soldier would record in his diary, 'many quietly placed a cartridge in the chamber and waited.'[72]

Finally, the soldier returns to the march, but it is a near-run thing. And some of the tension remains. 'Get off your bloody horse and carry a pack yourself,' some exhausted men of the 15th later shout as Elliott rides past.[73]

They are *Australians*. They will go on with this military malarkey to a point, and do the odd salute and even a 'Yes, Sir' and a 'No, Sir' . . . but don't *push* 'em, mate.

In an instant, Elliott wheels his horse around and rides in among his men, scattering them like confetti. At 5 foot 11 inches for 15 stone and small change, a champion footballer and shot-putter, with a chin like a clenched fist, this decorated veteran will back himself in a fight against any man-jack among them.

This time, there is not a peep.

As their march continues, the men get used to the conditions, and the column actually grows stronger. By the time they reach Ferry Post, 'the Brigade looked very well and General McCay was delighted with it. Of the 146 who fell out all but four [soon] rejoined.'[74]

Not that Ferry Post is much of an oasis. 'This place is the abomination of desolation,' Geoff McCrae would note. 'I never thought such a God-forsaken hole could possibly exist. My eyeballs are like flames of fire after the continuing glare of the shining sand.'[75]

———

By three o'clock, the heat is so intense, and the water in their bottles so depleted, that the soldiers of the 14th Brigade start collapsing in their dozens. 'At each halt we looked back,' one 14th Brigade private would recall. 'Away to the skyline, we could see forms of men lying huddled in the sand, as though machine-guns had swept the columns. As we looked, some would rise and totter a few paces, to collapse again.'[76]

The first man of the 14th Brigade to arrive at Moascar is challenged by a sentry. 'Who goes there?'

The exhausted Australian soldier drops his pack with relief, stretches and replies, 'I'm Burke and bleedin' Wills.'[77]

———

At Moascar, Bert and Ray Bishop are resting in their tents after a long day's training when suddenly there is movement outside, and the sound of running and shouting. What is going on?

'Every man out!' the roar goes up. 'Bring your dixies, water-bottles, buckets, anything to hold water, fill them up.'[78]

Quickly, the word spreads. A brigade of Australian soldiers has been ordered to march the 31 miles from Tel-el-Kebir to Moascar, through the hot desert sands at an incredible 140 degrees Fahrenheit, and has neglected to take enough water with them. They're still out there, and they are dropping like flies.[79] Come quickly!

And so Bert and his comrades do, forging out into the desert to find the column broken up into small clumps, each just trying to move forward however they can. From the first clump, they hear something of the story. At one point, the men had come to a lake of salt water. Some, driven mad with thirst, had jumped into the lake to cool down and then taken huge gulps of the salt water, at which point they had been driven madder still. One poor bastard had been seen to jump around like a kangaroo bitten by a bee, while laughing like a jackass.

Those who have had the discipline not to drink the salty water have managed to move on, and it is the first of these men that Bert and Ray Bishop get to, at the place near the railway line designated as their bivouac spot. By definition, though, as shattered as these men are, they are the ones who are okay. 'Don't worry about these fellows,' an officer yells. 'Get going out in the *desert!* Men are mad and dying out there!'[80]

The rescue party finds them by simply following the tracks through the still-burning sands. Many have dropped, unable to go on. Bert and Ray are able to get some water into them by lifting their heads, though often they have to pull the bottles away as their charges start gulping. 'That's all you need,' the distressed men are told. 'Rest a little while, you're almost in.'[81]

Those who cannot be revived are left where they lie – after having at least some water trickled into their open mouths – to soon be picked up and carried in by the ambulance men.

And then Bert and Ray move on, looking for the next lot. It takes a good couple of hours in the now cooling desert air, but at last it is done, and the worst of disasters is averted. All up, just 38 men of the 750 men of the 56th Battalion – the worst affected of the 14th Brigade – are able to get in unaided, while the rest straggle in through the course of the night, 'like the remnant of a broken army'.[82]

The one upside of the whole thing is that Bert and Ray soon realise that the 54th Battalion – also badly stricken – boasts another of their cousins, Billy Bishop, from up Casino way on the north coast of New South Wales. As they know he is in B Company, they are able to find him before long, in one of the tents at the bivouac spot. He is alive, though without water.

'You're Ray and Bert,' he croaks. 'Letters told me to watch out for you. I can't get up to shake hands.'

Don't bother, Billy. Ray still has just a little water left in his bottle, and – blood being thicker than water, but water more to the point on this occasion – offers it to his long-lost cousin, who is four or five years older than the both of them. He is Uncle Ed and Auntie Maud's lad. It is the measure of the man that Billy takes only one sip before passing it to a mate who he is sure needs it more.

It is time once more for the second-greatest Australian restorative of all – hot tea – which is soon being passed out. Bert and Ray go and get some and return to Billy's tent to gently serve it to their cousin and his mates.

Billy drinks it slowly, treasuring every blessed drop. 'That's the most delicious drink of my life,' he says.

How the hell did this happen, his cousins want to know.

'Don't ask him,' one of Billy's mates says. 'He's a lance corporal hoping to become a general, and must be careful of what he says.'

'Well, you tell us.'

Bit by bit, the yarn comes out. But a furphy soon arises that a couple of blokes from another brigade are meant to have died. At this statement, one of Billy's mates begs to differ. 'They didn't "die",' he spits out. 'They were *murdered*.'[83]

The furphies grow, and ever more catastrophic stories circulate. 'Seven men, it is said, died en route,' one Digger records, 'and a Captain disgusted with the treatment of the troops shot himself . . .'[84] Another Digger from the 32nd Battalion reckons it's even worse. 'Heard of the terrible march of the men of the 14th Brigade from Tel-el-Kebir,' he writes. '9 men died on the way and one shot himself.'[85]

Disgust is widespread. 'They call this getting men fit,' an ambulanceman from the 14th Brigade records that night. 'Why, men from Gallipoli said that they would rather face Turkish shells & bullets, than to even attempt a march like this again.'[86]

McCay is not long in expressing his views. Words cannot quite encompass just how badly let down he feels, but he still gives it a fair shake, in a memo to General Irving:

```
I am compelled to say plainly that today's
failure in soldierliness of the 14th Brigade . . .
has been a great disappointment to me, and that
the blame rests largely with regimental officers
as well as NCOs and the men themselves. The
Brigade must pull itself together and every man
must remember he is part of a regiment and not
merely an individual, if I am to hope to take it
into battle . . . until a great improvement takes
place I shall not be able to report the 14th
Brigade as fit for active service.[87]
```

While McCay is disappointed, Pompey Elliott is *enraged* when he finds out that his men have been sent to bivouac in a spot where no water is provided. He telephones McCay, who promises to see that a temporary pipeline is laid immediately. And yet, when by 11 that night still no water has come, Elliott cables McCay to inform him, UNLESS WATER IS SENT I WILL MARCH THE BRIGADE BACK TO WATER 2 MILES AWAY AND LEAVE MY POST AND TAKE THE CONSEQUENCES.[88]

Elliott is soon promised that the water will flow by 5.30 in the morning, and in the meantime he personally goes to General Irving's 14th Brigade camp and returns with a water-cart filled with 200 gallons to get his men through the night.

When, at 5.30 am, still no water has come through, Elliott does the obvious. He rouses the bleary-eyed officer concerned and shouts at him: 'Is it a case of can't or won't? If the former, I am going in to see General Godley. If won't – I am going to order up a firing party for you in half an hour.'[89]

And, yes, eventually the water flows, and, yes, there is hell to pay, with McCay rebuking Elliott for sending such a mutinous cable and for his carry-on afterwards. 'Now,' Elliott writes to a friend who'd had two sons in his battalion at Gallipoli, 'you have the real secret of Suvla and Anzac and Helles. Downright glorified incompetence beginning middle and end of the whole thing.'[90]

The following morning, the 14th Brigade's General Irving arrives in the lines on horseback, in the company of none other than the young Prince of Wales. The men no sooner see Irving than they begin 'a disgraceful outburst of hooting. The Prince of Wales's horse reared and nearly threw him. It must have been an awful experience for General Irving in front of the Prince of Wales and other high army commanders.'[91]

McCay, who believes that Irving's 'arrangements for the march were . . . very defective',[92] relieves him of his command and replaces him with the popular Colonel Harold Pope, who has been commanding the 16th Battalion of the 4th Brigade. A distinguished veteran of Gallipoli – for whom Pope's Hill on that battlefield was named, after he and his troops took and held it on the day of the landing – the 42-year-old

Pope has a notably kind approach (for an officer) and is known to be solicitous of the welfare of his men. He has a cleft chin that you could lose a shilling in and just looks like one who is born to lead.

As for the 14th Brigade, from now on it must undertake a daily march of two hours, in full kit, in circles in the desert, to toughen itself up. Never liked at the best of times, McCay is now actively detested, while Elliott remains disgusted by the whole exercise. 'All other Brigadiers have been made Brigadier Generals . . .' he writes to a friend. 'I, because I dared make a fuss, have not been made a Brigadier General and still stand temporarily in Command of the 15th Brigade. This is an example of General Birdwood the "Idol of Anzac" as the papers call him.'[93]

Chapter Three

MOI AUSSIE

We sighted the shores of France. Everyone was excited
and in the best of spirits; we were all thinking that at last
we had arrived in the country that was foremost in our
minds when we enlisted. For us the war was in France
and Belgium, and although Gallipoli did, and always
would, mean much to us . . . all other campaigns were of
a subsidiary nature to that in the great Western theatre.[1]
L. M. Newton, The Story of the Twelfth

During the trip which took over sixty hours the train
stopped at different centres . . . where for the first
time [we] came in contact with the French people,
who gave us coffee, wine and fruit. At each halt
we received a wonderful reception from the warm
hearted people, who made us feel that they and
their beautiful country were worth fighting for.[2]
Lance-Corporal Harry Preston of the 9th Battalion

We have Australians against us, daring
fellows, who want watching.[3]
The commander of the 27th (Saxon) Division in his diary

2 APRIL 1916, ABOARD *TRANSYLVANIA* IN THE MIDDLE OF THE MEDITERRANEAN

Whatever else – now that they have been told their destination really is the Western Front – it is comforting to know that God is on their side. On this sparkling morning, aboard the 14,000-ton transport *Transylvania* – which had departed Alexandria three days earlier and is now well on its way to the French port of Marseilles – a one-time parson, now officer, from Tasmania, Second-Lieutenant Frank Pogson Bethune, takes a spot high on the bridge, looks down upon a rough third of the 3500 soldiers on board, drawn from the 1st and 2nd Divisions, and gives a brief service. As Charles Bean is on friendly terms with Bethune – who had been studying theology at Cambridge while Bean's brother Jack had been studying medicine – he takes more than a passing interest in Bethune's sermon for the ages concerning the rightness of their cause and the fact that God will be with them whatever they are facing on the Western Front.

Upon completion of the sermon, there is a hymn, and the service is over. The men return to their allotted deck space or head off to relieve those posted on the machine guns at the bow, stern, and port and starboard sides, on the lookout around the clock for the German U-boats known to be prowling these waters. As further precautions, *Transylvania* is being escorted by two British warships, and everyone on board, from the Captain down, wears a lifebelt at all times. But they have not seen a submarine yet.

The sea has been wonderfully calm and the weather temperate all the way. The same sunshine that had been near driving them mad in Egypt is now being served along with a delightful spring breeze. All up, it is good to be alive.

3 APRIL 1916, CROSSING THE SUEZ CANAL, DON'T PAY THE FERRYMAN

It is quite a moment in the life of Bert and Ray Bishop, their mates Hodgy and Robbo, and all these newly arriving reinforcements of the

5th Division. Having crossed the Suez Canal in small lots by virtue of a singularly hard-working ferry that claws its way across by gripping at a sunken wire rope, the troops form up on the other side and then must scramble with some difficulty up a steep sandhill.

And there it is!

The Sinai Desert.

Wisps of wind come scudding off it, contemptuously blowing sand in their faces.

And here now is the one-time Cootamundra kid, accountant turned soldier, the soon to be 30-year-old Lieutenant-Colonel (Temporary) David McConaghy – a veteran of Gallipoli who had led his 3rd Battalion through Lone Pine with distinction and was appointed to the Order of St Michael and St George as a result. He and his senior staff are welcomed to the 55th Battalion of the 14th Brigade, 5th Division. After this, they are marched off to the few dozen tents allotted them, mere specks in what seems like *millions* of them, arrayed in perfect symmetry upon the desert sands and filled with thousands of Tommies, Kiwis, West Indians and, of course, their fellow Australians. For they all, too, are here to defend the Canal, while all around them an enormous 90-mile trench is being constructed by Egyptian labour gangs.

And so the question has to be answered: which job to try for? Bert and Ray Bishop discuss it in the tent, as ever with their older mates, Hodgy and Robbo, soon to be Lance-Corporal Hodgy and *Corporal* Robbo, if you please. (Bert and Ray know enough by now to understand this makes them non-commissioned officers, NCOs, whereas commissioned officers, those who receive a commission from the King, start at Second-Lieutenant – in Digger slang, 'artists', short for 'one-star artists' – and upwards.) 'Try for nothing,' Robbo says firmly. 'You'll get all you want and more without sticking your heads out. I'll go where I'm pushed.'[4]

Bert and Ray are not particularly fussed either way, so long as they can stay together. Still, as Ray has a bit of an interest in machine guns, he puts his hand up to be part of a Lewis gun section, and as Robbo is in fact pushed in exactly that direction, he does too. Hodgy goes for transport and is accepted. Bert stays a simple soldier. This war is going to need a lot of them.

Ray 'n' Robbo, for their part, are soon assigned to one of the battalion's 16 five-man teams (one per platoon of 50 to 60 men) to operate the brand-new, air-cooled Lewis guns they will be allotted. While two men are responsible for working the gun, another three men use leather panniers to keep carrying 200 rounds of ammunition a time, to keep it fed. Heavy training begins for all of them.

Among Bert and Ray Bishop and their mates, much of the chiacking stops. For this is suddenly starting to seem more serious. 'It all looked as if we were really getting near a war at last,' Bert would recount. 'Up to date it had all been more like travelling and sightseeing, and we were all boys, mischievous, full of fun and nonsense. The fun part was ending, the serious part beginning.'[5]

And with that serious part, they now find themselves alongside the serious men, the other half of this battalion they have just joined – the Gallipoli veterans. You can tell them immediately by a certain haunted *hardness* about them – the wizened look that can only come from having done it tough for months on that sacred shore and having survived. None of them is more arresting than Captain Norman Gibbins, a 35-year-old man, educated at the Ipswich Boys' Grammar School and son of a highly regarded Queensland family, with a father who was one of Australia's pioneer engineers. 'Gibb' had started the war as a private and quickly ascended to Captain.

What truly stands out about Gibb, though, is not his air of quiet authority. Oh, no. It is that he is one of the biggest bastards in the Battalion. No, *really* one of the biggest bastards. At over six feet, he is described by Bean as 'a gaunt, brave, humorous, cool-headed Australian . . . older than most company officers, but an athlete, promoted from the ranks at Anzac'.[6] He is a huge man who, if he farted in your last pound of flour, would leave you with nothing but a spluttering white face. But he is strangely sensitive too. He never goes *anywhere*, they say, without a little book of pressed Australian flowers, which his treasured younger sister Violet gave him before leaving Australian shores. (Yes, those who know him best say that the bachelor is estranged from the rest of his family for some reason – his outraged eldest brother maintains it is caused by him doing something with his life that is 'to be deplored'[7] – but he remains very close to a younger sister. And he'd had those flowers with him when he had landed on the shores of Gallipoli on 25 April 1915 – when he'd taken savage wounds to his thighs, courtesy of Turkish bullets.) Strange cove. Good man.

Now, you see that fellow over there, with the amazing shock of white hair on such an otherwise young man? Well, that's Captain Percy Woods, a bloke from Sydney, and that white hair tells a story. For they reckon that on the morning of 6 August last year at Anzac Cove, at which point he was still a Lieutenant, his hair was dark brown. But after just one night leading his platoon in the attack on Lone Pine, for which work he was mentioned in dispatches, it turned white! Didn't stop him none, though, and he stayed at Gallipoli till the end, overseeing the evacuation. But he's still here, still going strong, is Captain Percy.

And, of course, not just the officers. All the rest of these veterans have seen and done things the newcomers can only imagine, already proved themselves. They're usually found moving only with other Gallipoli veterans, often with a bemused look on their faces at all these wet-behind-the-ears poddy calves just arrived from Australia who dare to call themselves – if you can believe it, Bluey – *soldiers*. There are plenty more where they came from, arriving in a constant stream from home, and constantly being organised into the whole new series of battalions, brigades and divisions that are being created.

It is decided that only one battalion of each brigade needs to stand guard on the Canal on any given day, while the other three can train. All together, in all their different sections, they start their serious training to become a real working battalion. After reveille every morning, at 5 'ack-emma' – as they have learned to call 'am' – they go on parade at 6 ack-emma, and after a quick breakfast begin their marching, their drills, their weapons training, their fitness exercises, their endless inspections.

It's manageable, sort of, when they can rest in their tents, but it's hard yakka when they spend their first night 'on outpost, living some of the time in trenches & dugouts on the watch for Turks & Arabs', as Bert Bishop describes it in a letter home. 'The place was crawling with lice & vermin. After one night I spent in a dugout I think it would have been hard to find a square inch on me anywhere that hadn't a flea-bite mark on it. There were also rats, mice & flies in galore. I'm absolutely sick of the desert life . . . It's awful, & I never want it again. The work here is very stiff, though I haven't done any yet, being too crook.'[8]

Meantime, back at Tel-el-Kebir, most busy are the new artillery lads as the 5th Division essays to replace the highly skilled personnel it has lost to the 1st and 2nd Divvies, by training up 2500 new recruits – with each infantry battalion contributing 100 men and the many Australian Light Horse Regiments also raided for replacements. In such an environment, even a little knowledge has to go a long way, and all too frequently Captains and Lieutenants who have been given instruction on one aspect of artillery for just a few hours in the morning have to teach their men – the bulk of whom are starting from near scratch – the same thing in the afternoon.

'I don't suppose there are more than 10% old artillerymen [left] in these Brigades,' one grizzled veteran writes in his diary, 'so . . . they will take a good deal of training to become efficient.'[9]

Day after day, Second-Lieutenant Norm Nicolson and his mates – all now in the 52nd Field Artillery Battery – move out into the desert, the horses dragging the heavy artillery with them. They set up at a spot specifically selected by the Captain to provide some protection from imagined enemy fire while still allowing them to easily advance if the attack is successful. But careful, the guns must be sufficiently spread out, at least ten yards apart, so the whole lot doesn't go up if one enemy shell hits us. So too the ammunition dumps, which must be well protected and far enough back that if a shell hits them, the explosion will not hit the artillery crew, but close enough that the ammunition can be quickly carried forward.

And now using two field guns to get the precise range, Norm and his fellow new artillerymen focus on the selected target, those dunes over yonder with the tuft of bushes. Firing accurately, the men soon learn, is a painstaking process, requiring a good deal of time and extraordinary expertise. There is actually not a lot of luck in it. Each time they fire, the Observing Officer in the forward position determines exactly where the shells have landed in relation to the target, transmitting back the coordinates on the map.

One shell lands 150 yards too far, so that gun must be adjusted accordingly. 'Drop 150,' the Battery Commander orders, and the elevation is dropped a degree. The sight clinometer is set at the range ordered and adjusted until the bubble is levelled.

The shell of the other gun is 200 yards short. 'Lift 200!' and it too is adjusted. And so it goes. Slowly, carefully. Always the emphasis is that true accuracy comes at the end of deliberate preparations. By tightening the bracket of distance each time – down to 100, 50 or even 25 yards – they should be able to ensure that everything within that bracket will be plastered.

'But,' Norm Nicolson records, 'great accuracy isn't so necessary with shrapnel, which bursts and spreads all over the place. Shrapnel can be timed to explode in the air at any height, or upon the groundline, and if the burst obscures the target, well, one knows it is short, and if the burst is behind, the target shows up white on the background of the smoke of the burst.'[10]

Day after day, they keep at it, trying to first learn the ropes and then tie them together in such a fashion, with enough fencing wire and elbow grease, that they might *look* like an artillery battery if not yet quite actually be one. 'I have yet a tremendous lot to learn,' Norm Nicolson writes in a letter, 'tho' I would not be frightened to go straight into action with my men, provided I did not have to find the Battery Angle when firing from behind cover, or what is known as Indirect Firing, which I must confess still puzzles me dreadfully.'[11]

One who had been impressed before his departure for France is Charles Bean, who would go on to record his view that the creation of the 4th and 5th Division's artillery corps is 'unparalleled in British experience'. He is stunned by 'the speed with which Australians could be trained'.[12]

A quick lunch of greasy stew, bread and whatever jam they can get in their mouths before the flies have pinched it, washed down by weak tea, and then they are back at it until 4 pm, when it is at last time to knock off. But it is for very good reason that the old artillerymen say, 'It always takes longer to tidy up a mess than to make one.' Because it really bloody does. A battery, after a day's training, has equipment, spent brass cartridge cases and signal wire scattered everywhere, which all has to be cleaned up before they can leave.

But finally they get to the favourite part of the day for so many of these Australian soldiers still training in Egypt. That is to trek for a mile across to the Canal to go for a quick dip in its cooling waters, always with one eye to the south. For it is from that direction that come the most hoped for things of all: upper decks, funnel and masts of a big ship that looks like it is sailing to them from across the sandhills but is, of course, on the waters. And every now and then the most wonderful thing happens. For the shout goes up: 'She's from Aussie!'

Hoooo-ray, and up she rises!

For, oh, the excitement! At this point, all those on the shores run like mad things to the water's edge, dive in and swim towards this vessel from home, always moseying along at the standard four knots.

'How's Aussie?' they shout to the amazed figures on the deck.

'How's Sydney?'

'Got a gumleaf?'[13]

In return, they usually reap a harvest from heaven, as packets of Australian cigarettes, or a tin of Mareeba Fine Cut Tobacco, are thrown into whatever small boats are handy, together with tins of fruit, cans of condensed milk, bottles of soft drink and *Aussie beer* – quite unlike the dog piss they serve up in Egypt – not to mention packets of sweets and lots of fresh fruit. Oh, but it's grand to be an Aussie, and wonderful to feel like a 'veteran', on the strength of having been here for *a month*, while these wet-behind-the-ears recruits haven't set foot here.

The ship keeps sailing on, of course, while the Australian soldiers in the Canal swim back to shore with their treasures, and the poor bastard work crews sweating by the Canal 'looked enviously at their comrades in the water, or beguiled the tedium of their work by chanting weird and unprintable verses in imitation of the natives' hymns to Allah'.[14]

As the ship continues north, it gets smaller and smaller, and usually the last thing they can hear of it is a fading '*coooo-eeeeee . . .*' coming from its stern.

These are grand days, and, so far for the new recruits, it is a grand war.

MORNING, 4 APRIL 1916, MARSEILLES HARBOUR, *TRANSYLVANIA* ARRIVES

It is the cry of the sailor since time immemorial: 'Land! Land! Land ahoy!'

And so it is on this hot morning for the soldiers aboard *Transylvania*. Straight ahead over the bow of their ship, but impossibly high up in the clouds, they first see the mountains that tower around Marseilles Harbour and, presently, the harbour itself. And look there, cobber, the lovely red-roofed homes clinging to the sides of those mountains, for all the world as if they are trying to climb up to the summits, already clearly claimed by massive churches and monasteries, all with huge crosses starkly silhouetted against the pristine blue sky.

To some, perhaps, the vision of those crosses is a reminder that the men have arrived in a civilised land that worships the crucifixion of a man for a higher cause, while others, including a much later arrival, will remember it more simply as nothing less than 'a glimpse of paradise'.[15]

And yet here is a funny thing. As *Transylvania* docks, the Australians can't help but notice that French soldiers – all of them in the same bright-red trousers, navy tunics and red caps that had made them such perfect targets in the first months of the war – are guarding the entrances to the quay, armed with ancient rifles that have two-foot-long bayonets affixed. Just *who* are they expecting to attack?

Oh.

Now the new arrivals realise. The old French soldiers – for, on close inspection, most of them are old enough to remember when the Dead Sea was only sick – are not keeping others out; they're keeping the

Australians *in*. The reputation of *les Australiens* does precede them, and the French authorities are clearly nervous that all is kept under control.

That notwithstanding, as the Australians form up to march through the streets to Marseille–Saint-Charles railway station, the reception is entirely different, as they are cheered to the echo by the people, including many beautiful young women.

'*Bienvenue, les Australiens! Merci! Merci!*' Welcome, you Australians, and thank you!

Old men remove their hats and stand to attention as they pass.

Then, as they arrive at the station, there is good news and bad news. The good news is that even the most beautiful of the young French women, the most voluptuous, throw their fragrant arms around the Australian soldiers and kiss them on both cheeks, breathing into their ears, several more times for good measure, '*Merci, merci!*' The bad news is that so too do even the most gnarled and sweaty of men, and their breath stinks of garlic or worse. This time, it is the Australians who say it: 'Mercy! Mercy!'

It is the most unheard of thing *les Aussies* wish they'd never heard of, and they are not happy about it. (At least, however, there is no snotty-nosed kid sitting in the gutter and crying out, 'Garn, you're only a lot of poofters anyway!')[16]

All aboooooooard!

The Diggers extricate themselves slowly from the French women and with remarkable speed from the men, as, with their kit still in tow, they pile into the railway carriages and are soon under way.

Well, some would call it a carriage. 'The thing that struck us most forcibly was the notices on the cattle trucks (as they are called in Victoria),' one Digger notes. 'Each one bore a notice stating that 6 *chevaux* or 40 *hommes* could be packed into the trucks. I think that 6 horses would have more comfort in them than 40 men.'[17]

Soon enough, whatever you want to call it, they are on their way.

'For sixty hours,' Eddie Rule would record, 'we forgot that we were on a deadly mission, and in imagination lived within the pages of Grimm's fairy-tales. Mansions nestling into the folds of hills, and old castles perched on crags, overlooked the verdant valleys, while the beautiful River Rhône was never out of the picture in the early stages of the journey. The farms were the envy of us all. Everything was so peaceful that the existence of a state of war was almost incredible.'[18]

Here and there, they can see German prisoners, under French guard, doing work around and about the railway stations – and they certainly look like a fine breed of strong men – but, all up, they are far from the major point of interest.

For look there, Dig!

Way to the east, far over and above the green fields and gorgeous orchards in full bloom in this early spring, far higher than the tops of the lazy columns of smoke rising against the pristine sky from the scattered red-roofed farmhouses, you can see in the glorious sunshine the snowy tops of the Alps!

If this is not heaven, I don't know what heaven looks like.

At every stop – Lyons, Mâcon, Les Laumes, Laroche, Montereau, Juvisy, Melun – the soldiers are plied with 'coffee, vino and fruit' from the ever-grateful and warm-hearted French people, who, as one Digger, Lance-Corporal Harry Preston of the 9th Battalion, records, 'made us feel that they and their beautiful country were worth fighting for'.[19] (On the platform at Lyons, the warm-hearted crowd even cry '*Vive l'Australie!*'.)[20]

This vision splendid of rivers, streams, green fields and endless avenues of trees continues all the way north, as the Diggers gaze with wonder at this extraordinary country they have come to, with seemingly every window frame on their rattling carriages containing picture-postcard shots. The castles! The cathedrals! The gorgeous fields of scarlet poppies and wild marguerites!

Can there really be a *war* on, somewhere here?

Oui.

For the temperature has turned much colder and wetter as the train approaches Calais on the third day, and the soldiers can suddenly see the distinctive uniforms of the Tommies, wearing their new invention, these steel helmets – also called 'battle-bowlers', as in bowler hat – that a lot of coves are talking about. Yes, the British soldiers are here in abundance, as well as whole rivers of heavily laden lorries charging back and forth. Time and again, their train is stopped to make way for other trains heading to the front, laden down with munitions.

At last, however, after their train turns east it slows down and eventually comes to a halt in the town of Hazebrouck, at which point they must gather up their kit once more, form up into platoons and then companies, and begin their march to the places where they are being billeted in the local farms and villages.

As they march, they can hear in the distance, far to their east, a regular *whump . . . whump . . . whump.*

Guns. Big guns.

As the sun fades and twilight falls, the eastern horizon shows endless flashes of light through the trees. Crosses above village churches are silhouetted against this most unnatural of lights. High in the sky, rockets rise, burst into light, and white flares lazily fall.

The Western Front.

Just over there, Blue.

Christ.

They keep marching.

> *Far and near and low and louder*
> *On the roads of earth go by,*
> *Dear to friends and food for powder,*
> *Soldiers marching, all to die.*[21]

Christ on a cross.

But at least they are comfortable for the moment. For his part, Lieutenant Goldy Raws finds his company split up among four farms dotted around 'a pretty little village behind the firing line', with 'a platoon occupying the barn and hay loft and each farm house giving accommodation to one officer'.[22]

Wonderfully, he is that officer. 'I am in the house a royal person,' he writes to his father. 'I have what I should think the best bedroom, and

I also have the use of a large sitting room. I understand I have to pay something myself for the sitting room, but as the farmer's wife is very old and very dense, and cannot understand my attempts at French, I have to wait until the interpreter comes round to complete the deal.'[23]

'Tomorrow we move forward,' he recounts excitedly, 'and the following day we shall be "in it", and shall have the bullets "piffing" round us once more.

'I have got myself pretty right now, and I don't feel the nervousness that I first felt when I landed at Gallipoli. We hear the artillery booming away night and day. I guess it will be a bit louder tomorrow night.'[24]

The common soldiers are also settling into their barns with mixed fortunes, with many having to argue the toss with pigs, geese and chooks as to who the primary residents of said barn are, but they make do.

4 APRIL 1916, MONTREUIL-SUR-MER, OF WHISKY AND TIN TACKS IN THE NURSERY

The sentries salute. The papers are in order. The British staff car sweeps down the driveway between the blooming poplar trees and pulls up at the bottom of the stairs of a gracious French château, tucked well away from the main road.

'Our new HQ [at Montreuil] is certainly much pleasanter than St Omer,' Haig's Chief Intelligence Officer had noted of this place when he arrived. 'The town itself stands on a hill. There is an old wall with distinct evidence of ancient war around it, and a very picturesque old citadel. In peacetime artists congregate here . . .'[25]

As General Sir William Birdwood alights from his car, casually returning the salute of the junior officer who has glided forward to open the door for him, the faint boom of artillery from the Western Front, some 30 miles to the east, wafts past. But the most prevalent sound is that of the birds singing, cows mooing and junior officers cooing as they usher him inside. It is hard to believe that he has arrived at Sir Douglas Haig's GHQ, the nerve centre of the largest army Great

Britain has ever assembled, holding a front-line of just on 80 miles that lies on the northern end of the Western Front.

From this château, General Haig commands no fewer than 41 British divisions, three Canadian divisions, plus three British and two Indian cavalry divisions, as well as, now, two Australian divisions, with the New Zealand division soon to be on its way there from Egypt – 1.263 million troops in all. They are organised into four separate armies, with 300,000 soldiers in each army. And another army, General Hubert Gough's Reserve Corps, is soon to move from that reserve bench to become the Reserve Army, later renamed the Fifth Army.

South of the Somme, the French have 111 divisions, defending 370 miles of the Western Front. Against the 160-odd divisions the Allies are putting into the line, the Germans have 120 divisions – plus state-of-the-art, carefully thought out and constructed defences.

The quiet is in part because that is just the way Haig likes to do things, and also because such quiet goes with the oft remote nature of command in modern warfare. Though the battles themselves have never been noisier, twentieth-century communications mean that Generals can run battles from enormous distances and there is far less need for bugles, for messengers rushing back and forth on galloping steeds.

As a matter of fact, for those in the highest echelons of military power, there is not only no need for any discomfort but also the opportunity to enjoy luxury of the highest order. That much is obvious as General Birdwood is escorted by a Staff Officer past the hovering lackeys, down the long corridor, beneath the vaulting portraits of French family members long gone, and finally into the presence of the great man himself, General Sir Douglas Haig.

Ah, yes. Birdwood. Do come in.

Possessed, of course, of the kind of glorious moustache without which few officers can hope to rise high in the British Army, Haig is an affable Scot born of the Haig Whisky family, who, despite being in his mid-50s, still projects a certain animal vitality above all. At both Clifton School and Oxford University, he had been 'more conspicuous for his muscle than for his learning',[26] and so it had always been with his aggressive military approach. It is an approach that has served him well, through all of the conflict in Sudan and the Boer War. He has risen in the army since, most particularly through his sterling service in India, and not least because of his patronage by the King of England, George V.

Hence, perhaps, a little of his stiffness with Birdwood, who is known as a 'Kitchener man', another 'Easterner' who believed the war could be won in other ways than killing Germans right here on the Western Front, which is what Haig has believed from day dot.

Sir Douglas immediately gets down to tin tacks. In his clipped tones, he informs Birdwood that the 55,000 soldiers of I Anzac Corps will join the Second Army under Sir Herbert Plumer and form a crucial part of the 1.2 million soldiers of the British Empire defending the Western Front in France and Belgium.

The job of his I Anzac Corps when they all arrive – that is, the 1st and 2nd Divisions, together with the New Zealand Division – will be to defend nine miles of the front, from the salient around a mile west of the village of Fromelles to the River Lys's southern bank, slightly east of Armentières.

Birdwood is delighted and, as he would later recount, 'could have wished for nothing better'.[27]

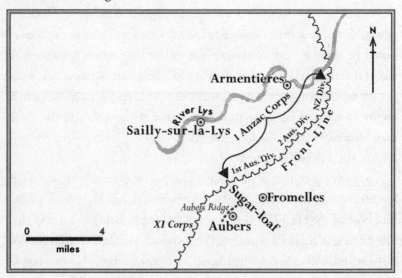

The Nursery, 1916

Plumer he knows to be a fine chap – they had served together in the Second Boer War – and this section of the front is known to be a 'nursery', a quiet area where the newcomers will be able to find their feet and learn the ropes, all without risking much in the way of full-blown attacks. These days, the focus of German firepower is on Verdun, while in these parts they are really only lobbing the odd shell over just for practice. There has been little action there since the battle of Aubers Ridge on 9 May the previous year, so it should be a good place for the Anzacs to start out until, hopefully, they can be assigned something more interesting.

Thank you, Birdwood. That will be all.

Haig gets back to his paperwork, and is upbeat. He looks forward to the joint British and French offensive against the Germans and is in agreement with the view put just a few days earlier by the Chief of the Imperial General Staff, General Sir William Robertson, to the War Committee asserting, 'Everything leads to the general belief that if the general offensive which the coalition has decided to take shortly is successful, a happy ending of the war will quickly follow.'[28]

General Haig has no reason to believe otherwise, and there is a possibility that he is receiving help from powers far greater than himself. He, for one, has a deep and abiding faith that the Lord is with him. (And, for her part, his sister Henrietta is so convinced that he is being helped by their late brother, George – who is getting advice from, among others, the equally late, great . . . Napoleon Bonaparte – that she sends him constant updates on what George and Napoleon think is best now. George's messages to his living brother are almost always upbeat: *'So tell Douglas with my love and blessing to go on as he is doing trusting to the mighty power above to shew him the way and tell him he will not ask in vain.'*)[29]

BEGINNING APRIL 1916, NEAR THE WESTERN FRONT, WINE OF THE GODS, WHINE OF THE SHELLS

General Birdwood quickly finds himself installed at I Anzac Corps Headquarters at the grandiose Château de la Motte aux Bois – a well-heeled historic establishment of nearly a thousand years old. From here, the front-line is just 17 miles away. For the moment, however, Birdwood and his senior officers give in to the warm bosom of hospitality provided by *la châtelaine*, the venerable Madame la Baronne de la Grange, and dine that evening on the sumptuous fare at her table, savour her fine wines and turn in to grand rooms where four-poster beds have freshly laundered *sheets*. He and his Australian troops have come a long, long, way from their miserable dugouts at the Dardanelles.

For that same evening, the delighted Australian soldiers, usually in batches of 50 or so, are settling into their own billets, in farmhouses and barns dotted around the villages, about half a dozen miles back from the front.

It has all been organised by Sergeants and the like, who have come as part of an advance guard to mark with a piece of chalk who is to billet where – '*II Pltn*'. Each inscription on each door, however, has come only at the end of a long negotiation with the village women. For whereas an officer billet earned the women five francs, a private delivered only one franc, so all the women wanted officers. The women would thus offer the billeting Sergeant all kinds of inducements to get

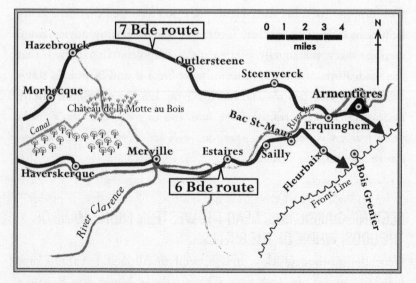

2nd Division routes to the front-line

the most lucrative deals. The haggling could be fierce. 'I've dealt with Indians and sundry Asiatics, with Sicilian curio sellers and others,' one Sergeant would record, 'but never have I met anyone to compare with a Frenchwoman when it comes to a bargain.'[30]

For Goldy Raws and the rest of the first lot of the AIF's 5th, 6th and 7th Brigades of the 2nd Division, now slowly moving forward on growling lorries and old London buses, their introduction to the Western Front is nothing if not gentle.

See, even though they know there are hostilities going on no more than a few miles ahead, right here, right now, French life goes on. Crops are growing in the fields, children are running about, laughing, on their way to school, housewives are doing their morning shopping, and the front is just up there.

More slowly now, as the traffic thickens, the lorries continue to rock, rattle and roar along the cobbled roads, passing through the tiny village of Croix du Bac and then, a mile further on, crossing a brimming stream signposted as **Rivière Lys**.

And now, more villages: Sailly-sur-la-Lys, Bac St Maur and Erquinghem. They are getting so close to the front that many of the windows on the eastern side of the houses have sandbags stacked in front, against possible wayward shells landing.

Okay, everybody out. No lorries allowed within three miles of the front. And no marching in big groups, either. We can't risk one shell from Fritz taking out 100 men bunched together, what? In the company of your British guides in the lead, just push forward now in small, unformed groups, no more than five in each, a hundred yards apart. Yes, the German observers on yonder ridge will be able to see you, but experience has shown that if no more than five soldiers are clustered, the dynamics of death in these parts means they're unlikely to bother wasting a shell on such a small haul. Shells aren't cheap, and the Germans much prefer killing *en masse*, which is far more efficient.

Walking now through the devastated village of Fleurbaix past the church ruin at the crossroads, where rumour has it the Germans burned a pile of their dead in 1914, this advance group of Australians sees huge mounds of earth in tight pods in the fields, which, the men are told, protect the emplacements of artillery that lie in their centre. The farms from here on in are untended, and for good reason. 'We could see the shell-smoke behind the trees,' one soldier would record of his first experience in the area, 'and hear the swift whine of the shells — 77's, or, as they call them here, "whizz-bangs".'[31]

But even here some of the French are holding on. 'It is extraordinary to see little children – golden-haired – running about the farm buildings when a farm only one or two fields away is being shelled – but there it is.'[32]

Seemingly, the sole concession of these kids and their families to the fact that a million men whose aim is to subjugate them are encamped just a few hundred yards away is the gas helmets that are tied loosely around their waists, ready to be whipped on should the alarm sound.

And now the Australians descend into the first of the communication trenches that lead to the front-lines . . . 'The officers and men of the advance parties, almost all of whom had fought at Anzac,' one chronicler of the times recorded, 'came to this new front like boys who go from a small school to a greater, with their eyes wide open, intending to learn all they could . . .'[33]

Of course, they look through their periscopes across No-Man's Land – an untidy stretch of ground, rather like the blowy bit on the edge of Australian garbage dumps – at the menacing lump of German breastworks, above which can be seen the roofs of the two villages that lie on Aubers Ridge. Way to their right is Aubers, the map says. Right in front is the village of Fromelles with its ruined church tower. The German front-line is across a few hundred yards of flat, wet land from them. There are fortified positions beyond that, and a third line can be seen along the top of the ridge. The job of I Anzac Corps, specifically the 2nd Division when all units have arrived, is to relieve Great Britain's 34th Division – made up of Pals' Battalions such as the 10th Lincolns, known as 'The Grimsby Chums' – and man four miles of trench just south-west of the town of the Mademoiselle from Armentières.

And for this advance guard, there really is much to learn. The first and most obvious thing about fighting here, compared with Gallipoli, is the luxurious space of No-Man's Land. In one place at Anzac, the Turkish trenches had been just 15 or so yards away. Here, it varies, but the gap is usually at least 100 yards and sometimes as much as 400 yards. True, that extra distance might be a problem should ever they need to charge – particularly as most of it is little more than a marshy swamp, with huge puddles everywhere – but for the moment there are no plans for such a charge. For now, the fact that the Germans are so far away bestows a certain sense of security, as if life can go on without constant fear of enemy raids. They are amused to note that, the shambolic nature of the key communication trenches notwithstanding, they all have rather grand names, such as the ones at Fromelles called 'VC Avenue', 'Bond Street', 'Brompton Road' and 'Pinney's Avenue'.

At Gallipoli, the soldiers had mostly named their trenches for Australian officers and soldiers, so this must be a bit of a Tommy thing – and they wouldn't dream of changing names already bestowed by the Brits, whose empire they are proud to belong to. But, of course, the differences don't stop there.

In the Dardanelles, they constantly lacked water. Here, it is *everywhere*: falling from the sky, flowing in the brooks, drenching the ground and causing vast puddles in No-Man's Land. (Sadly, though, the water is not suitable for human consumption. It eventually stagnates on top of the clayey ground, bringing flies in – at times, in plague proportions.) And it's flat here. Gallipoli was a campaign of rugged hills, but if 'flat as Flanders' is not an expression, it ought to be.

At Anzac Cove, all supplies had to be brought forward by a combination of donkeys and Shanks' pony – your own two legs. By contrast, many of these trenches are supplied by actual tramways, laid down to connect to the supply dumps in the back areas, which the lorries are supplying every night.

At Anzac Cove, artillery was a fact of life, but it was rarely overwhelming, and you always had a fair clue where it was positioned, and hence some chance of knocking it out. Not here. The newly arrived Diggers, of the advance guard, have already realised that plentiful

German artillery is positioned on the lee side of yonder ridge, making it – what is that technical term again? – bloody impossible to attack. See, the Boche can pour fire onto them on these low, marshy flatlands, aided by observers who can easily inform the gunners as to accuracy, but it is something else to try to put shells on their noggins in return.

Anyway, the bulk of the Diggers of the 2nd Division, who are now not far behind them, will just have to do what they have long done under difficult circumstances – the best they can.

EVENING, 7 APRIL 1916, SAILLY-SUR-LA-LYS, THE AUSTRALIANS MOVE IN, SO WATCH OUT

Australian soldiers marching. Straight of back. Clear of eye. Sore of foot. Buggered to buggery and back.

They are the 8000 infantry of the AIF 2nd Division's 6th and 7th Brigades, who left their digs to the east at Roquetoire and Morbecque three days before and have been marching ever since. Hence the problem. Their feet are used to the desert sands of Egypt and now must tread the cobbled streets of the Romans. Ankles turn, blisters burst and burn; they continue to limp along on close to will alone – all of it compounded by the fact that their army boots, like all Quartermaster's issue, only come in two sizes: 'too bloody big' and 'too bloody small'. Many soon find it difficult to continue carrying their packs and rifles.

'On such occasions,' Harry Hartnett of the 2nd Battalion, a country lad from south of Tumut, would note, 'one witnessed many striking examples of comradeship [though] we preferred to call it "mateship". Portions of the equipment of a weary man were divided amongst his fitter mates, many of them just staggering along themselves but who were unwilling to fall out or see a good pal in difficulties.'[34]

Every battalion of every brigade of this, the AIF's 2nd Division, is followed by its wagons and travelling kitchens, all of which have the cooks with them preparing the next lot of grub, even while rolling, and their chimney stacks leave thin trails of smoke drifting away into the pristine blue sky. On today's menu from the babblers (short for 'babbling brooks', as in Digger rhyming slang for the cooks): brown stew and beef tea, followed by milk-biscuit pud. Tomorrow, milk-biscuit pud following brown stew and beef tea. And so too the day after.

Don't complain. Worse where there's none, and better than a poke in the eye with a burned stick. Birds are singing, a light wind of spring is rustling through the branches of the endless elm trees that line their route, and they are marching to the Western Front, cobber, don't you know?

All of the picturesque villages of Haverskerque, Estaires and Sailly-sur-la-Lys, Outtersteene, Steenwerck and Erquinghem fall to their respective treads, 'a great khaki snake winding its way over the hills', as one Australian Warrant Officer would later describe the vision.[35]

But careful now, as they are getting close and must pause half a dozen miles from the front.

Companyyyy, halt!

Form up, fall in, for the handout. See the Quartermaster Sergeants for your steel helmets, and you must give him your felt hats and your personal effects, which will be kept until you return. Hopefully . . . It's 'battle order', lads, so your packs will stay here. Now, you must also ensure that whatever you currently lack in live ammunition, field dressings and rations, such as bully beef and biscuits – the last oft-known as 'concrete macaroons' – are made good and in your haversack before we move off.

Like all such thoroughfares in these parts, their road to hell is paved with the good intentions of the French, but also with flinty, uneven cobblestones, making it hell on earth to march on . . . but the Australians persist.

By nightfall at around 9 pm, the first of the Australian troops – the soldiers of the 21st Infantry Battalion of the 6th Brigade – approach their destination. The unaccustomed weight of their steel helmets make them feel as though their necks 'had been driven down deep into our chests'.[36] (Previous fears that the helmets would make a man 'go soft' have been lost, as it is realised it takes a strong man just to wear the bloody things.)

Though this causes their heads to naturally bend down, lift them they must as they approach the front-lines. As they do so, their awe-struck faces are lit by the endless, arcing 'Verey light' flares up ahead – which they still must learn about – even as their ears are assaulted by the rolling thunder of their own and the enemy's artillery. 'Indicating the position of the front-line trenches,' one Australian soldier would record of this experience, 'the sharp rat-tat-tat of machine-guns, the loud crack of rifles and the crash of bursting artillery shells echoed all around us.'[37]

Branching off to the right of the main road, they move through the devastated village of Fleurbaix. All the roofs of the houses have been blown apart, and what walls are left standing reel drunkenly. The people of this village have long since fled. The soldiers keep going and, as one would recall, 'as we marched along the stone-flagged streets; the iron toe and heel plates on our heavy boots sent eerie echoes through the dark, deserted buildings'.[38]

And now, the start of a communication trench opens up before them, leading to the front-lines, and they are soon swallowed whole . . . 'A sense of fear momentarily transcended all other emotions; our hearts began to thump violently and a strained contraction gripped our muscles. The crash of an exploding shell, even though some distance away, sent a queer feeling down one's spine. No doubt every man, no matter how fearless, experiences these same emotions when he comes in contact with the realities of war for the first time.'[39]

As they arrive on this first cold night, pushing forward to the front-lines, there is no joking. Frankly, it is more a matter of *crunching*, as, by the light of those flares, they encounter in the trenches 'rats nearly as big as kittens – ugly soft beasts which gave up the ghost with sickening squelch under the feet of the men marching up . . .'[40]

A couple of hours after dusk, the Australian soldiers of the 21st Infantry Battalion are taking over the positions of the 10th Lincolnshire in the trenches in front of Fleurbaix, opposite the German-occupied village of Fromelles. The 27th and 28th Battalions quickly follow them, relieving the 20th and 21st Northumberland

Fusiliers. Over the next few days, the Australian soldiers of the 2nd Division become established, defending their sector and getting their bearings night and day.

For some, from a distance, it looks and sounds a bit like cracker night at home, for the endlessly flowering and fading light provided by a series of Verey light flares gives a surreal aspect to the whole scene. Not for nothing would the joke run that 'Germany holds the contract to light up the Western Front'.[41]

In the daylight, getting their bearings, it is the Gallipoli veterans such as Goldy Raws in the 23rd Battalion who look upon the trenches with most interest, for, truth be told, they are really 'trenches' in name only. With the high water table, the British have made only a shallow trench line in the ground itself, and then built above ground.

'[The] breastworks,' a Digger explains in a letter to his mother, '[are] made of millions of tightly-made sand-bags laid one upon the other, packed well together.

'Every eight yards there is . . . a great mound of earth and sand-bags . . . round which the trench winds. This is to localise the explosion of shells or prevent an enemy who might reach the flank being able to pour fire right down the length of the trench.'[42]

Against the front of the breastworks – which are about five yards wide at the base, tapering to two yards wide at the top – is constructed a firing step, about two feet high, upon which men stand to shoot.

'When there is a bombardment nearly everyone gets under this step, close in against the side.'[43]

At the back is another sandbag wall, as protection against any shell that lobs behind. The bottom of the trenches is covered in wooden walkways called 'duckboards', to keep boots out of the mud. These duckboards are a little like upside-down wooden railway tracks, with six-feet long beams joined by short pieces of timber going crossways, sometimes covered in wire netting to provide extra traction.

The two on-duty battalions of each brigade will be defending about 650 yards apiece of the front-line, while the other two battalions will be billeted in nearby villages, on a six-day rotation.

And the truth of it? Even when you're on duty in the front-line, it is sometimes not too bad. Back in Gallipoli, Goldy Raws had noted in a letter home how extraordinarily cosy one could feel in one's dugout, tucked in against the sandbags as the bullets whizz by harmlessly overhead, later listening in silent watch of the night as the iron wheels of carts clatter over nearby cobblestone roads, bringing supplies forward.

Others, however, take a dimmer view . . . 'I look round me,' one soldier writes home, 'at my damp rat-hole, the sides and roof of which are lined with sandbags, which, by the way, are not filled with sand but clay . . . The lower bags are green with mildew and the upper ones near the sun and air are sprouting grass. Half-way up in the corner a cluster of poisoned mushrooms . . .'[44]

Not home sweet home, perhaps, but at least home . . . until they can be relieved.

Meantime, always remember, you men in the front-line, you are being watched, from high points in German-controlled territory, such as church towers, and from German planes with observers – dozens of times more than the veterans ever saw at Gallipoli – and the observation 'sausage balloons' the enemy have positioned just back from the front-lines, beyond machine-gun range. These balloons are manned by German soldiers with binoculars and a telephone connection to the ground, who take notes of all they see, from troop movements and trench works to shell fire and the locations to which the troops are ferrying materiel, the likely position of ammunition dumps.

One thing those on the ground will not lack is Mills bombs. No fewer than 52,000 of these lethal grenades are allocated to every division as it approaches the front-line. The way things are structured here, it is necessary for 30 men in every company to receive expert instruction in how to throw them and achieve maximum effect. (Now, while those who throw them had until *recently* been known as 'grenadiers', this had stopped once the Grenadier Guards had officially complained to the King that this word belonged to them – and His Majesty had personally intervened to insist that all those trained in the throwing of grenades would henceforth be called 'bombers'.)

And yet, despite the abundance of bombs and the vastly improved supply lines, many of the Gallipoli veterans look upon these new trenches with a gimlet eye and are far from satisfied.[45] To begin with, it is obvious that 'the majority of the communication avenues shown on the trench maps had become waterlogged and impassable, while even those in use were often quite inadequate, a passenger through them being, in some parts of his journey, exposed from the waist upwards to the enemy's view'.[46]

One wonders, in passing, how those in divisional HQs can possibly do proper planning when the maps don't necessarily reflect reality – and a very grim reality it is. As Private Archie Barwick would note in his diary, 'The English left this part of the line in a most disgraceful state: nearly all the duckboards were under water & slush, the parapets & dugouts were in a shocking state, & as for communications & reserve trenches, well they simply didn't exist for all the use they would have been if ever the Germans made an attack.'[47]

Not all the tramways are working, and much of the inner support line has also caved in, due to being waterlogged. The British have constructed nothing in the way of deep dugouts where soldiers can take shelter from heavy bombardment – as the odd German prisoner has revealed that the Boche have on their side. It's not just that members of the BEF, which had originally defended this sector, are thin on the ground; it's that they are mostly in the ground. And the vast majority of the British soldiers who have rotated through since have been of the New Army – that is, ordinary citizens recruited by Kitchener's famous 'YOUR COUNTRY NEEDS YOU' posters, who are inexperienced and have managed to build little in terms of serious defences.

Most dissatisfying to the Australians is that the barbed-wire entanglement at the bottom of the breastworks would struggle to stop a dog, let alone an enemy soldier, while the earthen parapet facing No-Man's Land is barely thick enough to stop a bullet. And nor is it high enough, requiring a tall man to stoop to gain protection. And nor does it have enough sniper and observation posts, found to be so crucial in the Dardanelles.

Some of the springs for such lassitude are found in the attitude of the Tommy officers. For, as they explain to their Australian counterparts, their view has been it is best not to stir the Germans up. In the Digger argot, these are 'cushy trenches', so soft that, according to the Tommies, a French *mademoiselle* recently came along flogging chocolates. 'If you leave the Boche alone here he will leave you alone,' they say firmly. 'Keep watch, strengthen your positions, but don't get too lively.'[48]

They said that. They really said that.

An English General, Lord Gleichen, will later tell the story of touring the trenches at Fromelles before the Australians arrived and asking a soldier whether he had taken any shots at the Germans. The soldier replied that there was an elderly gentleman with a bald head and a long beard who often showed himself over the parapet.

'Well, why didn't you shoot him?'

'*Shoot* him?' said the soldier, completely amazed. 'Why, Lor' bless you, sir, 'e's never done *me* no 'arm!'[49]

And there is a lot of that languor about. 'Oh dear!' Brigadier-General John Monash would write to his wife. 'Compared with Anzac, the people here don't know what war is.'[50]

That is not the view of the Australians, as they are eager to get to grips with Fritz immediately. But they know they must improve the trenches first – focusing on building the breastworks higher and thicker for more protection so they can actually stop shrapnel, getting more barbed wire and digging the dugouts deeper.

One troubling thing the Tommies had referred to as the Australians had relieved them was a 'barrage', and while not even the Gallipoli veterans are clear what that is, they figure that it 'resembles a curtain, or fence, which, when they [the British] attack might be dropped at any time' immediately behind their advancing line. 'When once the barrage fell, everything on the forward side of it [the curtain] is cut off and hidden' from its support (e.g. ambulances, reserves, supplies) in the rear until it is raised once more.'[51]

Odd. Perhaps they will find out.

At the moment, the Hun is not firing many bullets or shells in these parts. Nor is he launching any raids to speak of. But there is no telling how long that will last. The companies are thus immediately set to work to improve those defences across the board. They must make deeper many of the communication trenches that lead to the front-line. And let us put some doglegs in these trenches, so that if the bastards take one section of it, they can't just fire machine guns along it to wipe us all out – and they will also limit the damage of any shells or bombs that land here. True, blokes who've just arrived tend to get lost in the endless maze of trenches and it can be very difficult to get your bearings, particularly at night, but after a week or two they learn the lie of the land only too well, and in the meantime the work goes on.

'It's wonderful the improvements that have been effected even in so short a time,' Archie Barwick writes in his diary two days after arriving. 'We have built 2 more new communication trenches, numerous saps, besides improving all other things out of sight. The Tommies would scarcely know this part of the line now if they were to return.'[52]

In fact, getting to know the whole layout of the trenches, even in the dark, is another thing the freshly arrived Diggers realise is crucial. On his second night there, Lieutenant Goldy Raws goes out on his first patrol, just before three o'clock in the morning, and becomes more aware of that than most. He is crawling along on his hands and knees, having a close look at the British barbed-wire entanglements, when, every 30 seconds or so, the German flares light the whole of No-Man's Land nearly as bright as day.

'If you can see the flare just as it is going up,' he explains to his father, 'it is best to let your limbs just sink under you and drop flat. If you can't you just stand absolutely still. It is fatal to move. It's a pretty risky business, this patrol work, and really I'm not keen on going out. It gives you a horribly lonely feeling out there, and it's a horribly long way to get back if you're shot. You see, you have to get back through your own barbed wire and other entanglements, and that isn't too easy in the dark.'

Generally, Raws, like all of them, is very pleased at how much easier things are here than at Gallipoli, how 'there is not anything of the strain of close proximity to the enemy. We get only long distance bombs.'[53] Which isn't to say there is no danger, and only shortly after arriving a senior Australian officer had insisted to him 'that officers as well as men should wear the steel helmets'.[54]

Ah, the steel helmets. Whatever the initial reluctance of the officers to wear them – fearing they would be showing un-officer-like fear by doing so – GHQ is quick to insist that the whole issue of wearing your steel helmet in the front-line is to be taken seriously. So seriously, in fact, that the commanders of each company are under strict orders that the report on every wounded man sent to hospital for treatment must state whether he was wearing his steel helmet when hit. The man may lose his pension if wounded while without.

What to do when one fellow has to go to hospital for treatment for syphilis? The Commanding Officer does not hesitate, dutifully writing on the report, '*He was not wearing his steel helmet at the time.*'[55]

Meanwhile, it is necessary to get serious training underway for those first Australians to arrive on the Western Front not used to trench war-fare – which is to say the vast majority of them. And even the Gallipoli veterans must prepare for an entirely different kind of warfare to what they had known at the Dardanelles, using a vast array of different equipment – steel helmets, flamethrowers, Lewis guns, to name a few – not to mention being in close proximity to difficult English officers. (By the by, beyond their wizened looks, you can tell the Gallipoli veterans by the iron hooks positioned just under their bayonet handles. They're designed to catch the enemy's bayonets and disarm them with a sharp twist. Only issued in the Dardanelles, they are a sign of a fighter's status as a Gallipoli veteran.)

Beyond the usual long route marches, and inevitable instructions on how to use a bayonet in hand-to-hand combat, the Diggers also start receiving daily lectures on how to counter gas warfare. Gas masks are issued, and all the troops are obliged to walk through a trench filled with lethal chlorine gas. Yes, back in Gallipoli they had also had gas masks, but there they had mostly been used to ward off the overpowering stench of dead comrades. Here, they are used to ensure you don't *become* a dead comrade. After walking through the chlorine trench, if they fall down dead or gasping, they fail the test.

Poison gas is not the only thing they have to worry about. Of late, the Germans have also been launching canisters of a gas formerly called 'lachrymatory agent' and now called 'tear gas', which renders its victims temporarily blind and incapable of sighting along their rifles for hours.

Or worse. For despite the initial roughness of the appearance of this Western Front, the Diggers soon learn that the defensive system is actually far more sophisticated than at Gallipoli, and . . . exponentially more lethal. While at Anzac Cove, there had certainly been artillery, it had been more patchwork than pervasive, more 'needs must' than nous. Here, every sector of the front is covered by a pod of artillery batteries behind, which are connected by telephone. At any time, the Commanding Officer of every company could, if under attack, call in an SOS, together with the number of his sector, and a 'barrage' (there's that word again, only this time their own) would be laid on the enemy's parapet to catch any German soldiers venturing forth – before the barrage would move back, to lay down a 'curtain' of shrapnel in front of this threatened sector. Absolute trust in one's own artillery is essential as it draws its barrage back to cover immediately in front of its own front-line; any miscalculation may well result in death from one's own short-falling shells.

By night, one of the rockets kept handy at every Company HQ could be fired, and the subsequent green flare in the night sky would in turn be an indication of where the barrage was required to land in front of.

To ensure constant readiness, the Commanding Officer could call for a single shot to be fired, and it has been 'ordered that the time taken by the artillery in answering this call should be reported to divisional headquarters'.[56] So too could a rocket be fired and the time measured before the response. An artillery officer in the front-line is attached to each battalion, and it is for him to observe the accuracy and effectiveness of the fire – ideally keeping in constant telephone contact with his artillery battery situated well behind the front-line.

Oh, and one thing is as important as it is top-secret. Each brigade is issued with two Stokes mortars – an extraordinarily portable trench mortar capable of rapid-fire devastation of enemy trenches at a distance of as much as 800 yards, using just a four-man crew with observers up front. The key to this state-of-the-art weapon is that the charge that launches it is attached to the mortar round itself. Drop her down the tube and thar she blows! A trained crew with a plentiful supply of mortars can fire no fewer than 22 shells a minute – a previously unheard of rate. (The first British trench mortars of the war could manage only three rounds a minute, on a good day, when the wind was howling from the south.)

Whatever happens, the Australians are told, 'on no account are any Stokes mortars to be left in the front-line at night',[57] as they cannot allow this invaluable military weaponry to fall into German hands, for fear it would quickly be copied and the Stokes mortar rounds would be coming right back at them.

And another thing. All infantry brigades must train in how to survive 'liquid fire' projectors, *Flammenwerfer*, the devil's own weapon that the Germans have been using of late to great effect. Now, men, though horrifying, if ever you are attacked in this manner, the way to survive is 'simply to lie down in the trench and wait for the intruder, with the flame passing over [you]'.[58]

From one extreme to the other, the Australians are also lectured in how to prevent frostbite – something in which the men of Gallipoli, sadly, are already expert.

Bit by bit, they all start to get the hang of it. The two most important times of the day are the two hours either side of dawn and the two hours either side of dusk, when every man in the front-line must 'stand to arms'. That is, they must actually stand on the fire-step – another plank built into the wall, about two feet off the ground – and point their rifles at the enemy trenches. After sun-up, there is an almost symbolic exchange of shell fire as both sides wish the other 'good morning' until an hour later they may stand down.

The day is then filled with working on trenches and checking weaponry and munitions until sundown, when again they must stand to, with a few more shells wishing them *'gute Nacht'*. An hour later, the order comes once more that all bar the night sentries may stand down, after an officer has inspected their weapons for cleanliness. (At night-time, the stand-down order is also the signal for the distribution of their rum rations, particularly welcome when it is cold and wet.)

Meanwhile, the night sentries – thinned out to the point where they are placed only in every second bay – regularly pop their heads up to gaze into the darkness, straining with every fibre of their being to identify all strange sounds, even over the ongoing roar of artillery, ready to alert the others at the first sign of attack.

There!

Uh . . . no. Just scurrying rats again, squeaking to each other as they tear past.

The rats, one soldier would recall, 'were cunning and hard to shoot. If one was killed by a bullet, other rats pounced on his carcass to drag it out of sight and devour it.'[59] Oh, and one more thing the soldiers soon learn from the old hands: 'After an action [the rats] grow fat on ghastly banquets of the mouldering flesh of the corpses.'[60]

Ah, but back to the sentries now. Is it dangerous for them to put their heads above the parapet? Yes, and with tragic regularity a sniper's bullet shatters their skulls. But someone must do it, and so it is done. You can tell the veterans, because they have a singular way of doing it. With your helmet well down over your brow – get it, mate? – you push your head way back and squint down your nose. Small target, savvy?

'In the front-line trenches,' the 2nd Battalion's Harry Hartnett would recount, 'the veterans took charge of the new arrivals, protecting them like hens caring for their broods, advising them what to do and what not to do. Each man on coming into action with his section or platoon for the first time, found himself a member of a brotherhood, the like of which did not exist in any other walk of life.'[61]

But careful now, you lot who are on night sentry duty. If you fall asleep on the job, you will be court-martialled for endangering the lives of the battalion, and one precaution against that is to have you fire a dozen rounds at the enemy for every two-hour stint. We take this measure so seriously that when you are relieved, the platoon sergeant will count the spent cartridges at your feet. And there bloody well *better* be a dozen of them, sport.

Now, another thing. You have to understand the flares. If the Germans send up a red one right in front of you, it means some of their mob are pissed off with the shells they have been taking, or they think we are about to attack them, or both. That red flare means they want their own artillery to plaster us, and a pound to a penny says that somewhere, two miles back, a German officer is looking at all the little squares on his map and then instructing his battery to 'turn handles, squirt out wonderful little instruments giving levels and directions, and then, pipe in mouth, just press a button or pull a string, and away comes a little token across the sky to us'.[62]

Meantime, you'll note there is always an officer on duty whose job it is to keep firing his Verey light pistol, regularly sending up our own brilliant white flares. You'll see the flares go up hundreds of feet, trailing sparks all the way and then 'burst into a brilliant white star, which falls gracefully, brilliantly illuminating the area for at least a quarter of a mile around, until the star lies smothered in the grass of No-Man's Land'.[63]

And careful now! As that flare goes up, it will throw shadows everywhere, making 'the whole landscape appear to move, and it is not easy to distinguish men from lifeless objects, so long as they stay perfectly still'.[64] A part of your job is to work out just who in that swirling maelstrom of shadows are actually advancing Germans. And if you see the bastards, tell our officer, who will send up our own red flares as a signal to the artillery to attack *them*.

Good luck!

In the daylight hours, the sentries use periscopes – turning their back on the enemy to look through the two acutely angled mirrors in a wooden box some four feet long, the top mirror just above the parapet – but at night-time there is insufficient light for those periscopes to work.

In the daytime, after a usual breakfast of a slice of lukewarm bacon – known as 'lance-corporal bacon' for its one line of lean amid the fat

– 'on bread, or biscuit, with hot tea drunk from their mess-tins',[65] those not on sentry duty or having a kip to recover from night duty must work on the breastworks. They fill endless sandbags and place them so that, ideally, with every passing day, they are more secure against the German shells and raids.

For those going about their business in the front-lines, old hands tell them that the key to escaping the attentions of the German snipers with their telescopic sights is to do things irregularly, for predictability can be fatal. An example is Lieutenant Robert Hunter of the 2nd Battalion, who is in the habit, first thing every morning, of taking a quick look above the parapet, *always at the same spot.* One morning, he does so only to fall down dead with a sniper's bullet through his forehead. To impress upon the new fellows just what dangers they face, the veterans regularly put a steel helmet on a stick and poke it above the parapet. Usually it is only a matter of seconds before a shot rings out and the helmet is sent flying. Sometimes they can hear a cheer from the Germans, in the mistaken belief that someone has gone down.

Bastards.

(The Brits, on the other hand, had gone to extraordinary efforts in this field, building papier-mâché dummies designed to lure snipers into revealing their positions. A senior British officer, Major Hesketh Hesketh-Pritchard – yes, really – would recount, 'Some of those who wanted to give the dummy a particularly lifelike appearance, placed a cigarette in its mouth, and smoked it through a rubber tube. It is a curious sensation to have the head through which you are smoking a cigarette suddenly shot with a Mauser bullet.'[66] And, of course, it is not just the British who embrace the practice. The story would be told of an English soldier running all the way across No-Man's Land to savagely attack with his shovel – oh dear – a puppet, before running back. Ah, how they'd laughed.)

In the meantime, whatever else, for those in the front-lines there is work to be done. To this point, the reckoning has been that as bullets from the Germans' 7.92-mm Mauser rifle and 7.92-mm MG08 machine gun can penetrate about two feet of sand, or 18 inches of hard clay, the most crucial thing is that all sandbag walls – filled with dirt and clay from their diggings – be that thick. But walls like that are no defence against a direct hit from a German shell, and so the Australians put it right, adding endless sandbags night after night, following the order put out by General Brudenell White:

> . . . To ensure immediate security, the front
> breastwork must at once be strengthened until
> it [is] at least seven feet in height and twelve
> in breadth throughout.[67]

And another thing is to build the back part of the trench – the parados – higher than the front part – the parapet – facing No-Man's Land. That way, if your melon pops above the parapet, it doesn't form a perfect silhouette against daylight to help Fritz blow it off for you.

This activity does not go unnoticed by the enemy. '*Der Feind*, the enemy, builds up his parapet very well,' a 21st Bavarian RIR observer records, 'and by increasing the height of his breastwork gradually obtains even better observation over our position than heretofore.'[68]

For all of the newly arrived Australians, though, the most wonderful time is when they can retreat to their billets in nearby villages. Here, life can actually be *enjoyed* – even if they do need to have their equipment 'all rolled up and ready to be moved at a moment's notice, if they should shell our billet'.[69] For, to the troops' stunned amazement, after you have clocked off from your time on duty, you can walk through the most picturesque countryside, past the prettiest of girls, into the most wonderful villages, where your billets await, usually across the puddles of the farmyard, past the well – hold your nose as you pass the manure pit – and into the barn. There, you drop your swag and settle down with another dozen blokes or so, often even more. For they must always follow the dictates of the Great Britain War Office's *Field Service Pocket Book 1914* and its instructions on securing 'quarters' for the troops:

> Tactical considerations have precedence over
> considerations of comfort. As many men and animals
> as possible are billeted, and the remainder
> bivouac.[70]

The luckiest of the officers are able to sleep in the beds in the farmhouse left by the brothers, sons and husbands who have gone off to join the French Army – and too often have already been killed.

In this second week of April, the Australians settle in to their billets, usually half a dozen miles or so back from the front-lines. At night, when sound travels best, the *whump* of shells landing to their east becomes much more of a WHUMP, and they can even feel the tremor in the earth.

And, of course, just as the butchers, bakers and candlestick makers look with a critical eye on how their French counterparts go about the same thing, so do the farmers among the Australian soldiers look carefully at how the Froggy farmers go about it. For the most part, the Australians are impressed, as the French fields are well cultivated, the crops flourishing, and the hedges and stone walls that separate the fields a delight to behold. Other things, however, they don't get, such as having piles of manure in the farm courtyard, right next to the bloody well that they are all drinking out of. What are these foreigners thinking? And sometimes the French have dogs drawing their carts.

And the latrine system no more than a stinking hole in the ground that would make a brown dog weep, frequently in full view of members of the opposite sex? Don't get them started.

Some things, however, are very much to their liking, and one of these is the newly formed institution of the estaminet – based on the word '*staminet*', meaning 'cowshed'. For, in just such small shelters, many of the French farmers, strapped for cash and now playing host to many men who are earning a colossal six shillings (150 francs) daily, have set up what amounts to a small, shabby cafe cum bar. It is a place where, at base level, the Madame and her children serve piping-hot tea, *vin blanc* – inevitably referred to by the Diggers as

'Point Blank'[71] – watery beer and delicious food from Madame's kitchen, including eggs and chips, for less than one penny (just one and a half francs). Most of these establishments have someone playing the accordion, while many of the more elaborate ones actually run to dancing girls, who for a few francs dance up a storm as one of them bangs out a tune on an old piano. And there are *thousands* of them, on both sides of the Western Front.

Ah, these French girls, they are something else again. 'The mademoiselles are very wide awake to the soldier's flattery,' one soldier records. 'Their stock answer to ardent love makers is après la guerre . . .'[72]

Not that they are prudes for all that. Far from it! '[They] have no mock modesty,' he notes, 'and will discuss subjects that would make an Australian Miss blush with shame. Obscene postcards are sold . . . and girls will take filthy cards out of a box to show a soldier, if he wants to buy such cards.'[73]

The truth? Many of the girls are selling more than just obscene cards, and a lot of the estaminets run to more than even dancing girls, with one British soldier, Corporal George Ashurst of 1st Battalion, Lancashire Fusiliers, noting in his diary, 'We were drinking vin blanc in the estaminet and it was absolutely crowded. There were five women in there, and it was five francs – just 2½ pence! – to go up the stairs and into the bedrooms with them. The stairs leading up to the bedrooms were full; there was a man on every step, waiting his turn to go in with a woman.' And it is happening right there! The women grab the money, undo the men's flies and squeeze their genitals to see if any pus emerges. If not, up they go!

'I was sat at a table with my friend, Tom, when the padre came in. He dressed us all down. "Have none of you any mothers? Have none of you any sisters?"'[74]

Yes, but that is hardly the issue right now. Many Australian soldiers – aware that, whatever the pastors might say, it would be a sad thing if they died virgins – partake, and business flourishes. After all, where better to take 'French leave'[75] – that is, just go, without permission, and deal with the consequences later – if not right here?

It is for a very good reason that a popular song among the local French translates to:

After the war is over
Australian Soldiers go away
Mademoiselles of Roguetour stay & weep
And nurse the babies.[76]

For their part, the Australian soldiers sing a different tune:

Après la guerre fini
Australie soldats parti
Mademoiselle in the family way
NOT bloody born to me.[77]

Oft times, there is not even a pretence at affection. 'Prostitution is very rife,' one Australian officer notes. 'Most decent people have left, one is assailed by little boy touts who run up, "You want mam'selle?", "I show you officer's place" – and so on. Called in at a shop . . . to buy a shirt but mademoiselle wanted 16 francs for it and another appeared and were prepared for amorous dalliance.'[78]

Of course, many of these women suffer from venereal disease, but in some cases that can actually be an attraction to the soldiers. For the diary entry of one officer even records how some soldiers 'deliberately risked contracting one of the two diseases, hoping by this "self-inflicted wound" to win a respite from the trenches'.[79] Such women, it is said, can even cost more to sleep with than the clean ones.

Either way, it can be a very grim life. How do the women cope? For many . . . only just. As one postcard on sale in the shops attests, for some the answer is drugs. The card shows a very lightly clad, pretty girl injecting morphine into her leg, above a subject title of 'Consolation'. 'This drug habit is very widespread among the demimonde,' one officer comments. 'While talking to a girl she will make some excuse and furtively glancing round, sniff vigorously at a small bottle in her handkerchief – sniffing cocaine . . . An instance of the wrecks it makes was seen by us at Cairo – a shrieking naked maniac locked up in a vomit strewn room.'[80]

Beyond the working women, however, the local *mademoiselles* 'appear to be very decent and preserve their chastity to all appearances'.[81] In such instances, real love can grow. One example is the young and exquisitely beautiful Marie, who tends an estaminet at Erquinghem, just three miles back from the front-line, with her mother – 'Ma' to the men.

'Marie ruled as a queen,' one Digger of the 2nd Division's 18th Battalion would record. 'A glance of her deep-blue eyes commanded more reverence than the storming or strutting of a Cleopatra. To use a phrase of O. Henry, "to see her was to love her, to speak to her was to conceive a wild desire to give her board and lodging for life". Marie was eighteen. She had the bluest of eyes, the softest of skins, the merriest of laughs, and the trimmest of ankles . . .

'To men coming from out of the filth and vermin of the front line, Marie was a tonic. Her tinkling laugh put new life into one. Petite, arch, winsome as a kitten, Marie was adored by the company. Amidst the mud and blood and sandbags she was an alluring memory. In her mother's cosy estaminet she was a glorious reality.'[82]

As to the rather more sordid contacts between Australian soldiers and French women, the British authorities, of course, could have shut it all down, but as the French themselves are quite relaxed about their own soldiers using such establishments, it would almost have been rude. Still, the Secretary of State for War, Lord Kitchener – who has never married and keeps extraordinarily close company with his aide-de-camp, with whom he has shared living quarters for the last ten years – does put out a leaflet for distribution, warning soldiers to keep constantly on your guard against any excesses. In this new experience you may find temptations both in wine and women. You must entirely resist both.

The official Australian view is more bemused than outraged: 'Whether we like the idea or not, and whether or not it was helpful to the real cause of the nation, the fact remains that many women, not inherently "abandoned", surrendered themselves partly in the belief that the loosening of sexual relations promoted the winning of the war, or was, in a way, a patriotic act . . . The most striking feature for the V.D. problem in the War was the rise to prominence of the "amateur" prostitute.'[83]

Yeah, yeah, yeah. 'Prostitutes' to some, and a danger to the war effort to others, but to many of the Diggers, they are no more and no less than beautiful young French women, who are the delight of their lives. And can you really wag a finger of opprobrium when so many men risk going to the 'stiff's paddock' – as the Diggers call the cemetery – as virgins? And so it goes on, with one young private, William Roworth, who is still only 15 – having lied about his age to enlist – losing his virginity on exactly that reckoning, even recording that the experience was just like 'pulling your thing, but you have some one to talk to'.[84]

And on the other side of the Western Front? The Germans in the 6th Bavarian Division are no better. One *Offizier der Kommandantur* says of the women of Lille, *'Alle Frauen hier sind Dirnen.* All the women here are harlots.'[85] One of their own, Pastor Hermann Münderlein, has already written a scathing report on the soldiers of the 16th Bavarian RIR, which is rotten with problems of *'Alkohol, Unkeuschheit, Streitsucht und liebloses Kritisieren, Diebstahl, Ungehorsam, Materialismus, Versinken in Gleichgültigkeit und Stumpfsinn'*[86] – which is to say 'alcohol, promiscuity, aggression and unkind criticism, theft, disobedience, materialism, descent into indifference, and apathy.'[87]

The officers are no better. Bad enough that they display 'antisocial behaviour towards the men', they also consume *'exzessiv Alkohol* and were just as lecherous and *sexuell promisk* as the troops'.[88]

Of course, the List soldiers have their own version of estaminets, and their troops flock to them, with inevitable results. In villages such as Fromelles, there are notices, in German, pasted everywhere, warning on the perils of V.D.:

Warnung. Soldaten! Wahret Eure Gesundheit,
alle Dirnen, Kellnerinnen
und schlechten Frauen sind krank.[89]

Warning: Soldiers!
Protect your health!
All prostitutes, waitresses,
And loose women are infected![90]

Rumours swirl that some of the French doctors are declining to treat the women with V.D. on the grounds that the more German soldiers they infect, the better, and even that one woman is boasting she has personally brought down more German soldiers than 'many French soldiers at the front'.[91]

Which is as maybe. One German soldier who is never at risk of being brought down by such women is Corporal Adolf Hitler, sometimes referred to as '*der Streber*', as in 'a bit of a conch'. For he wants

A sketch by Adolf Hitler labelled 'Flanders, January 1916', with his signature in the bottom right-hand corner

no part of such things and is 'a committed teetotaller'.[92] Truly, Hitler doesn't even like engaging in the wildly popular low-brow activities of his comrades, such as reading the semi-pornographic wartime novels '*Kriegsbräute* (War Brides), *Die Schwester des Franktireurs* (The Sister of the Franc-Tireur), *Deutsche Hiebe, Deutsche Liebe* (German Thrashing, German Loving)'.[93] No, he much prefers going for long walks with his dog, *Fuchsl*, Fox, going to Lille's *Theatre de l'Opera*, where he can see plays put on by *Deutsches Theater Lille* and, sometimes, doing what he had done before the war, sketching street scenes or heading out into the countryside to paint landscapes, while softly singing.

A strange fellow is Adolf: *'ein unscheinbarer, blasser Soldat*, a homely, pale soldier'.[94]

Chapter Four

AUX ARMES AUSTRALIENS, FORMEZ VOS BATAILLONS!

How many times, at Fromelles, during the first world war, I've studied my dog Foxl . . . I used to watch him as if he'd been a man – the progressive stages of his anger, of the bile that took possession of him. He was a fine creature . . .[1]

Adolf Hitler, reminiscing about his time on the Western Front

The English suddenly became aware of a new kind of man, unlike any usually seen here. These strangers were not Europeans; they were not Americans. They seemed to be of one race, for all of them had something of the same bearing, and something of the same look of humorous, swift decision. On the whole they were taller, broader, better looking, and more graceful in their movements than other races. Yet, in spite of so much power and beauty, they were very friendly people, easy to get on with, most helpful, kind and hospitable. Though they were all in uniform, like the rest of Europe . . . they did not always salute; they did not see the use of it: they did from time to time fling parts of Cairo down the Nile. Then came stories of their prowess in war.[2]

John Masefield, 1933

SECOND WEEK OF APRIL 1916, FRANCE, BEAN ARRIVES

It has always been a curious feature of rail travel that despite the clatter of steel wheels rolling over lengths of rail, the gentle swaying of the carriages can be enough to lull one to sleep just as though you are back in the crib. But on this day, Charles Bean does not feel it at all. Despite his long trip across the English Channel, and then from Calais aboard this train, he is wide awake and excited as the train pulls ever closer to the area where he knows the Australians of the I Anzac Corps are situated. And, sure enough, shortly before the train arrives at Hazebrouck, he spots in the distance that curiously shambling amble of the Australian soldier . . . as he has a bit of a natter with mates . . . goes for a bit of a gander . . . rides Shanks' pony down to the village . . . and it is not long before the countryside is teeming with them.

'After that,' Bean records in his diary, 'outside every farmhouse were Australians, sitting in the garden cooking, gathering round the estaminet, walking through the fields in twos, sometimes a hundred or two on parade outside a barn. The country seemed populated with them.'[3]

It is a part of a foreign field that is, for this time . . . Australian.

14–15 APRIL 1916, AT THE WAR OFFICE, LONDON, OF WAR AND . . . GOLF

Now in the middle of spring, with summer just up ahead, it is time for Sir Douglas Haig to get down to tin tacks on the coming major offensive against the Germans, and there can be no better time than now. On a quick trip back to London, he has arrived this morning for his reluctant meeting with the Secretary of State for War, Lord Kitchener, to find the Chief of the Imperial General Staff, General Sir William Robertson, there as well. And so Haig asks them directly.

'Does His Majesty's Government approve of my combining with the French in a general offensive during the summer?'[4]

It most certainly does.

At this point of the campaign, Kitchener and Robertson agree, the entire Cabinet has come to the exceedingly difficult conclusion,

'The war [can] only be ended by fighting,' and what is needed now, more than ever, is a definite, large victory over German arms.

'I explained to Lord K,' Haig confides to his diary that night, 'my general plan.'[5]

Thirteen British divisions will attack north of the River Somme on the first day and, hopefully, secure 26,000 yards of the German front-line to a depth of 2000–4000 yards – including, crucially, 7000 yards of the German second line from Serre to Pozières.

The French, meanwhile, will attack predominantly south of the Somme.

In their own attack, the British will rely on an overwhelming artillery bombardment of almost 1,700,000 shells, fired over a week, before the infantry emerges to advance. After the first objectives are captured, there will be a pause, likely of several days, to bring forward guns, ammunition and the fresh troops of the further dozen divisions on hand – then they will drive forward a further 4000 yards, repeating the dose as necessary. Even if they don't break through at this point of the Western Front, which would be the best case – at which point the cavalry would run *riot* – the Germans would have to call off their thrust at Verdun so as to parry the British and French thrust on the Somme, which would be victory enough in itself.

The following morning, at Kitchener's behest, Haig turns up at 10 Downing Street for a meeting of both military officers and senior politicians to discuss how to get more men under arms to the front-lines as quickly as possible. 'For the first hour of the meeting,' Haig would recount, 'the "Civilians" and the "Military" wrangled over certain figures. This really did not interest me, and I felt that the real issue of the war in the "Civilians'" minds was votes, and not the destruction of the German military party.'[6]

This sense is exacerbated in the early afternoon when none other than Prime Minister Asquith arrives, 'dressed for golf and evidently anxious to get away for his weekend',[7] and a brief discussion ensues about how to recruit the soldiers they would need to maintain the British Army on the Western Front over the summer and, perhaps even more importantly, how to pay for them. For, as it has transpired recently, it is Britain itself that is bearing most of the expense for the Allies, with France simply unable to pay its share, and even asking to borrow money from *les Anglais*.

Hence the problem. In order to keep the war going, Great Britain has to help pay for its allies too, and in order to provide the money for this, whatever else happens, Great Britain's trade must not be impaired. 'With this object in view,' the Prime Minister says, whatever is done in terms of recruitment, and conscription, 'it is of vital importance not to interfere with the labour market.'

The meeting breaks up just ten minutes after the Prime Minister has arrived, so he can indeed get to his golf game on time. 'I felt . . . sad,' the stunned Haig would write in his diary that night, 'at the sight of the inner Cabinet of this great Empire being so wanting in decision and public spirit. Real war and the basic principles of success seemed to hardly enter into the calculations of these "politicians" . . .'[8]

The labour market! *Golf!*

———

No time for golf for the Australians of the 2nd Division's 22nd Battalion, as they continue to take over the positions around Fromelles. All is hustle and bustle in the mud, mixed now with no little fussing as, on the night of 14 April, no less than General Birdwood arrives on a visit. He even stops to talk for a minute or two to the men, as they stand to arms in the sullen rain, and he walks along inspecting them, before returning to his château.

For the soldiers, it looks likely to be a long night, and they have 'all kinds of garb in readiness . . . all wearing cap comforters turban like, heavy greatcoats and their waterproof sheet shawlwise over their shoulders.'[9] The worst of it? 'The whole place is infested with rats,' one appalled young soldier records in his diary, 'and in the hours of darkness you can hear the broods of young ones round the sandbag walls whimpering . . . Filthy.'[10]

21 APRIL 1916, FERRY POST, EGYPT, NORM GOES FROM CARRYING THE STRETCHERS TO FILLING THEM

The artillery training goes on, and ever more recruits keep joining . . . and struggling. For it is no easy thing for soldiers such as Norm Pearce of New South Wales, just transferred from the 5th Field Ambulance, where he had come through remarkably unscathed at Gallipoli, to now work out how best to inflict the damage on other blokes, so German stretcher-bearers can go through the same hell he did. 'We are going to practice firing next week,' he writes in his diary. 'I'm afraid it will be an awful showing as very few know anything about the gun.'[11]

Things don't get better very quickly, as he notes a few days later. 'We are going to try some practical work today with the guns and on Tuesday we will have some proper target practice. Our ranging turned out fairly well but the signallers couldn't get our messages through. The 14th Brigade had some target practice today but the shooting was abominable. I hope we can do better at any rate.'[12]

23 APRIL 1916, FROMELLES, FRONT TRENCHES, WORSHIPPING TWO BASTARDS ON BIKES

What the *blazes* is that?

On the parapet opposite the AIF's 2nd Battalion, a flashing light suddenly appears. And for most of the soldiers it is exactly that – just a flashing light. But not for the 'spooks', the signallers, it isn't. For they instantly recognise it as Morse Code and have no trouble reading the messages coming from the Germans. Quickly, the signallers write it down:

AUSTRALIANS GO HOME.
GO . . . IN MORNING.
YOU WILL BE DEAD IN THE MORNING.

Charmed, they are sure. Still, why not reply? No matter that the English officers of GHQ severely discourage any communication with the enemy, a signaller of the 2nd Battalion cannot resist, and flashes back:

WHY?

A minute later, the rather feeble German answer comes:

WE ARE GOOD.[13]

That remains to be seen . . .

In the meantime, the Australian artillery would like to practise their skills a little more, but this is not possible as, when it comes to shells, they must exercise 'the strictest economy in view of the vast supply required for the coming offensive on the Somme'.[14] Their resultant lack of practice can be a real problem. When, at one point, an observer of the 22nd Battalion spots German helmets bobbing about in some kind of trench offshoot into No-Man's Land, he is quick to advise artillery, to see if they can bring a shell down on their noggins. But because of various mistakes made, 'the shell lands half-a-mile to the left!'[15]

Still, the Diggers of the Australian artillery manage to keep busy and, among other things, play a lot of their favourite game: two-up – something that arouses a great deal of curiosity among the French. One old fellow in a beret becomes convinced that it is a religious ceremony. 'The High Priest takes the shining coins and tosses them in the air,' he explains to another Frenchman. 'And now watch as all eyes reverently follow the flight of the coins. When they land on the ground one worshipper steps forward and says in a loud voice, "Two bastards on Bikes!"'[16]

In other words, two 'tails' have landed!

Both in the front-lines and in the billets, Bean finds happy Australians, and perhaps even happier French. 'From these first days in France,' he would later note, 'it was obvious that the Australian soldier, in whom natural friendliness was untrammelled by any consciousness of social distinctions, was much nearer to the mass of the French people than the shyer and less expansive men of the British Army'.[17]

Against that, there is no doubt that the French take some getting used to for those born beneath the Southern Cross. At one billet in a French farmhouse, the Diggers notice 'a large wooden contraption resembling a huge wheel, about eight feet high by one foot wide, revolving at high speed at times each day'.[18]

What the *devil* is that?

Upon investigation, they find a small dog inside, running for his life and in the process turning the wheel as a treadmill. Of course, they set the dog free . . . and don't they catch hell from Madame? In a mixture of French and English and international sign language for 'If you ever do that again, I will wear your balls for earrings', she makes them understand that the wheel the dog is turning is operating a churn inside the kitchen with which she is making butter. And so, back the dog goes, running hard as the wheel turns and the butter churns. The Diggers do not interfere any further. (Still, the only thing busier than that dog seems to be an 80-year-old grandmother on a nearby farm who, one Digger notices, 'makes dresses from morning till night, and they are all black'.)[19]

The language problems are oft a source of great amusement. One day, a few Australian soldiers from the 2nd Battalion are standing outside a small shop with their money burning a hole in their pockets, wondering both what they are going to buy and more particularly just how they are going to get the people inside to understand what they want, when their problem is solved. For along comes a rather loud kind of bloke from A Company who grandly informs them he is a master of the French language and would be delighted to do all the translations. Ripper! As one, they head into the shop, whereupon it is decided that biscuits would be the very thing to hit the spot, if you please, Mr A Company . . .

Right you are. Approaching the very fetching young *mademoiselle*, he gives it his best shot. 'You! You!' he roars. ''Ere! *Compre Biscoota!*'

Mademoiselle looks him coolly up and down and then replies with a clarity of expression that would do an Oxford don proud, 'Do you want some biscuits?'[20]

Oui. Oui do.

Inevitably, French words quickly enter a Digger dialect already boasting many words and phrases incorporated in Egypt. Though they struggle to say '*très bon*' for 'very good', the brand name of a bully beef can, 'Fray Bentos', fills in nicely. '*Monsieur*' becomes 'manure'. 'Madam-you-smell' does the trick for '*mademoiselle*'.

Still, it is not all one-way traffic. Not long after the Australians arrive, one small French boy is overheard telling another, 'You bastard, you *compree* dat?'[21]

The French kids, generally, warm to the Australian soldiers and have a particular love of the game the Diggers introduce them to: French cricket!

24 APRIL 1916, ARMENTIÈRES, A SIGH TO HIGH IN THE SKY

Look there!

It is one of the English planes heading in over the German lines, a sight that the Australians have come to greatly enjoy in their brief time here. Whereas planes in Gallipoli had appeared infrequently, and then mostly in the role of observers, in these parts both English and German planes are constant visitors over the front-lines and – most spectacularly – frequently engage in 'dogfights' with each other. True, it is against orders to look up – because, if a whole body of troops did so, it would appear 'as a white sheet to the airman [observer] with obvious consequences'[22] – but such orders are routinely ignored.

On a lazy afternoon, the soldiers on both sides of the trenches often watch spellbound as planes or squadrons of planes – the French Farman Experimental 2s on one side; the German Fokkers on the other – go at each other, wheeling, cavorting, doing loop-the-loops, diving at each other from out of the sun as they try to blast their opponents from the sky. When, high in the sky, a Fokker suddenly explodes or trails black smoke before plummeting earthwards, a cheer goes up from the Australians, just as they groan when the same happens to a British plane.

On this day, however, this particular English plane comes in remarkably low, no more than 2000 feet up, allowing the airmen to make close observation of the German trenches below and the enemy's anti-aircraft guns to fire 'Archie', the 'Ack-Ack' gun, as if there is no tomorrow. And it is staggering. As this plane goes back and forth along the German lines, its course is marked by an endless series of angry black puffs from the German Ack-Ack as the brutes try to bring it down. Each puff represents a spray of shrapnel, which, as one Australian soldier would inform his mother in a letter, 'has a spread of 300 yards by 30 yards when it bursts'.[23] The shrapnel spreads out and smudges after a while, though at first it stands out as a brilliant pinhead against a clear background, and so machines that escape – most of them do if they keep high up – leave a trail of spreading smoke-spots behind them.

Always, just above or below or beside this particular plane, there is the puff, sometimes close enough to make it rock, but the shrapnel never quite hits, as the Australians cheer it on. At least 150 shells are exploded, but all miss. 'They may get any of the others,' one of the Australian soldiers drawls, 'but I'd be dead sick if they got him.'

The others agree.

'Well, I haven't got his "guts"!' says another. 'That chap clean beats me.'[24]

As it turns out, they meet the pilot later on, when he pops by to visit the artillery. They're not surprised to find that he is known as the 'Mad Major' – so called because of his penchant for flying under bridges – nor that he regards his job of roaring around in that fashion, taking on the Germans in the air as well as on the ground as 'the only sport on earth'.[25] The Australian troops come to love the Mad Major for the way he flies 'long and low over Fritz's lines through a veritable curtain of anti-aircraft shell-bursts, [and] his appearance was looked forward to daily'.[26]

24 APRIL 1916, WESTERN FRONT, SOUTH-EAST OF ARMENTIÈRES, AT THE GOING DOWN OF THE SUN, AND IN THE MORNING . . .

An ear cocked to the wind. A flash of red hair, by the light of exploding shells. It is, of course, the intrepid official Australian War

Correspondent Charles Bean, come to observe the Australians of the 1st Brigade, who had recently relieved the 104th British Brigade of the 35th Division from responsibility for holding this Petillon sector near Armentières. (The introduction of the 1st had been difficult, as on their first day, 'despite warnings not to advertise their presence, the troops demonstrated a distinct lack of discipline, and the Germans pounced, shelling their billets'.[27] The tragic result had been 24 soldiers of the 9th Battalion killed, the AIF's first battle losses in France.)

Though not a talkative type by nature, Bean has an enormous admiration for Australian soldiers and can chat to them easily. And on this night, of all nights, on the eve of the first anniversary of the landing at Gallipoli, he is interested to learn that, of the soldiers in these two battalions, the 1st and the 2nd, about a quarter of them are Gallipoli veterans. Of course, he is soon reminiscing with those very few who had been the most esteemed breed of all, the 'original Anzacs' who'd been there from the first, about what it had been like that extraordinary dawn a year ago as they approached the fatal shores.

Do you remember how it was? The soft moonlight? The convoy, slowly arrowing its way through the phosphorescent waters of the Aegean? The first scattered sounds of rifle fire coming from the Turkish shore? The first deaths?

They remember.

And now, here they are, in this place, against a different enemy.

Strange – back then it had all been terrifying, but now they can talk of it with something very close to nostalgia. There had been just something about Anzac that had got to them all – and Bean, particularly, hopes it will always be remembered as the place Australia and Australians came of age.

The following evening, Bean is still in the mood for commemoration of the anniversary of Gallipoli, and so, in the company of a friend, he wanders back from the front-lines to a nearby estaminet, where they partake of a wonderful dinner and, over two bottles of champagne, drink to 'the health of all Anzacs'.[28]

Later that night, back in his billet, Bean tries to work, but it is no good. Too many memories of Gallipoli. Too many good men gone to their graves, or crippled, or mentally shattered. And how many more, here, to go the same way? How many families yet to be bereaved? He rises and goes to the door. In the distance, on the horizon, coming from near Richebourg or perhaps Neuve Chapelle, he can see the gloomy flashes from the artillery reflected on the low clouds, followed several seconds later by the boom of dirty thunder rolling to him through the damp night air. A soft mist is starting to rise. Somewhere, in or near some of the trenches, friend or foe, a shell has just landed and several or many men may very well have been blown apart. Devastating. Appalling. Depressing.

And what is that he can hear now?

. . .

There it is again.

It is a nightingale singing! A series of perfect, high-pitched notes, each one with a different intonation, snatches of a different song. The first nightingale of the season!

And now, other nightingales in the wooded night answer the first'un, entirely untroubled by the artillery and machine-gun fire coming from the north. Somehow, despite it all, life goes on. On this same day, Bean has heard the first cuckoo. The birds have adapted to the destruction all around and are intent on singing regardless. He turns away from the soft night air and returns to his writing.

There is much to report. At least, for the moment, the Australian troops have not been in harm's way, as this part of the Western Front is relatively calm, and that is something.

25 APRIL 1916, ACROSS EGYPT AND THE WESTERN WORLD, THE LITTLE DIGGER DIGS DEEP FOR HIS DIGGERS

Dawn.

For so many veterans of that extraordinary sunrise one year ago, it is hard to believe that the first anniversary of the Gallipoli landing is already upon them. And yet none are in doubt. It is a day for commemoration, for remembrance, for bowing your heads to pray for the souls of dear departed comrades. At Moascar, Ismaïlia, Ferry Post, Tel-el-Kebir and in Cairo, church parades are held 'to commemorate the landing and the lads who fell on the Peninsula'.[29]

All those Diggers who were at the landing on the day have a red ribbon hanging from above the left breast pocket, while those who had seen service in the Dardanelles are entitled to a blue ribbon worn above the left breast pocket. With the services completed, the troops are given the rest of the day off from training to participate in sporting events and enjoy concerts.

The grandest commemoration, however, is in London, on a balmy day, where a memorial service is held in Westminster Abbey, attended by 3000 people. These include none other than the Australian Prime Minister, Billy Hughes, known as the 'Little Digger' for his endless championing of their lot, Australia's High Commissioner to Great Britain, the Right Honourable Andrew Fisher, and some 2000 'Knights of Gallipoli', as the newspaper refers to the 1300 Australian and 700 New Zealand veterans who march from Aldwych in full ceremonial dress for the occasion, through streets lined a dozen deep.

The able-bodied sit on the right side of the Abbey, while those on crutches or in wheelchairs, and those carried in on stretchers – 'some of them but wrecks of the strong men who left their homes in October two years ago'[30] – are on the left. The blind sit with the only man in the gathering who does not stand when 'God Save the King' is played: King George V. With him are Queen Mary, Lord Kitchener, General Sir William Robertson, General Sir Ian Hamilton, General Sir William Birdwood – a man inclined to attend the opening of a wound, let alone something as august as this – and Mrs Asquith, the wife of the Prime Minister, among many other notables.

As one man sitting in the nose-bleed section records, 'I looked down on the floor of the Abbey. It was filled in every nook and cranny. "Anzacs" clung to the pedestals of the mighty dead whose monuments recall the glories of our history. They crowded every foot of standing room . . .'[31]

It is an ocean of khaki and black, the latter worn by the many grieving widows in attendance. At the conclusion of the magnificent service, marked by a haunting rendition of 'The Last Post' by 16 trumpeters, many of the Australian soldiers are invited back to the Hotel Cecil, where their Prime Minister addresses them in a speech for the ages:

'Soldiers of Australia . . . on this day, called Anzac, one short year ago, the Australasian soldier leapt unheralded into the arena of war, and by a display of courage, dash, endurance and unquenchable spirit, proved himself worthy of kinship with those heroic men who throughout the history of our race have walked unafraid into the jaws of death, thinking it glorious to die for their country . . . I feel that the spirits of those dauntless men whose bodies now lie on the Peninsula are not far from us on this day of Anzac, urging us to press on, and ever on to victory. They gave up their lives for their country and their liberties. Their deathless deeds will yet be sung in sagas to generations of Australians to the end of time.'[32]

And so it goes on and on *and* on. It is, nevertheless, an enthusiasm not necessarily matched in all quarters. Though similar services are held around Australia on the day, they tend to have a theme of encouraging other men to enlist, with many returned veterans pledging to secure at least one new soldier at events held afterwards. 'Many answered the call, but many still held back,' the *Herald* reports.

In Sydney's Martin Place, one veteran who is missing an arm does his best to attract interest. 'Australia was there!' he cries, waving around his stump, almost by way of proof. 'Look at me. I have lost an arm and can fight no more, but I tell you what, boys – if I had my arm back I'd be over there again. Now I want someone to take my place – who will volunteer?'

No one answers. Not one of the many men streaming past even looks him in the eye. Tears come into the soldier's eyes.

'No one?' he asks, plaintively.[33]

On this day, for him, no one.

At least many are already on their way . . .

26 APRIL 1916, ON THE WAY TO TEL-EL-KEBIR, LOOKING FOR GOLDY

It has been a long trip for the second-eldest son of the Reverend John Garrard Raws and his wife, Mary, but at last Lieutenant Alec Raws is on to the next leg. Having landed at Suez the day before, Alec knows he must be getting closer to his younger brother, and the youngest in the family, Goldy. Had things gone differently, they might have been together from the first, but while Goldy had easily met all the physical requirements, the 32-year-old Alec had been rejected for being too short, at just five foot five inches – an inch under requirements.

As the war had chewed through ever more men, things had loosened, and when he had applied again in July of 1915, the medical officer had asked, 'Do you want to go?' Alec had replied, 'Yes,' and the preliminary papers had been signed.[34]

Though he had no wife to protest, there remained the continued resistance of his Reverend father and mother Mary to overcome before formally committing. Reverend Raws, a very peaceable man of the Lord, had written an impassioned letter to him, *begging* him not to do this. Alec had replied, trying to address his father's fears, 'I do not think that I was ever a great man for heroics, but I do believe that there are some things worth more than life . . . I hope that you will be proud to think that you have two sons, who were never fighting men, who abhor the sight of blood and cruelty and suffering of any kind, but who are yet game to go out bravely to a war forced upon them.'[35]

And yes, of course he is risking the most terrible fate imaginable. But on the other hand . . . 'Death does not matter. If it comes through this agency earlier to me than it otherwise would have done, it can bring me the nearer to you, my mother and father. You, after all, are the only two people in the world that I have really loved.'[36]

And so he had resigned from his high-powered job as lead writer of the parliamentary reporting staff for Melbourne's *Argus* paper, put down his quill, abandoned his typewriter, *left his dingy little office . . . and the language uninviting of the gutter children fighting . . .* to take up arms instead.

For now, what he really wants to do is find Goldy. He has come across some officers who think he has already gone to France, but whether he has or not is anyone's guess. Alec cannot wait to reach him.

26 APRIL 1916, THREE AND A HALF MILES NORTH-WEST OF FROMELLES, IN A CORNER OF A FOREIGN FIELD, A LETTER HOME

Sitting outside his dugout as the sun starts to wane, with his back to the firing line, Goldy Raws takes the opportunity of a rare break to write to his beloved father, in their home of 'Gwenholm', 76 Cheltenham Street, Malvern, Adelaide. Yes, the odd bullet is whizzing by and there is the occasional thunder of artillery, but it is amazing how, in war, you can barely blink at what, in peacetime, you would hurl yourself to the ground over. After three days' rain, the soldiers have had a perfect afternoon, the trenches and their clothes are drying, and before Goldy now is what would have been a *vision splendid of a grassy plain extended* but is in fact now the ruins of what was a place of God, a convent.

'A few odd pieces of wall here and there, a chimney perhaps left from some house which has escaped the shells,' he writes, 'the trees all bare and lifeless – it is "Dead Man's Land", in truth, for 1000 yds . . .

'The bullets whizz harmlessly overhead; towards dusk the firing always gets brisk; many bullets hit the convent wall at the back, and you can judge how high they are up from that.

'The most curious thing that would strike you, were you to spend a day here, would be that the shells all go over our head. Practically never do they shell our breast-works. It is apparent with heavy guns, in an hour's bombardment they would smash up our breast-works; but they don't – why? Well, if they started to do so, we should immediately open on their breast-works, and what would be the result? There would be a mess-up. They could not charge until they had broken down all our wire entanglements and other obstacles, and it is practically proved at a tremendous cost that infantry can't advance against artillery – that artillery must first be silenced, or partly silenced . . . So by tacit understanding we don't fire heavy artillery at the first line trenches.'[37]

As to what it is all about, Goldy is clear. 'The general idea is that we . . . be ready for the grand offensive which is to be made . . . The difficulties of a big offensive move are tremendous. If the war could be won without it, I am certain it would not be made. The man who orders the attack signs the death warrant of not thousands, but hundreds of thousands . . .'[38]

LATE APRIL 1916, MONTREUIL, GENERAL HAIG SENDS FOR ALL THE KING'S HORSES AND ALL THE KING'S MEN

The difficulties of a big offensive are tremendous, but General Haig is really starting to feel he is getting there, as the plans for the joint attack in the summer continue to take shape, with Sir Douglas's thumbprints on every part of them.

No matter that General Henry Seymour Rawlinson, G.C.B., G.C.S.I., G.C.V.O., K.C.M.G., has been of the strong view that his Fourth Army only has sufficient troops and artillery to attack over a width of 20,000 yards, and to a depth of 2000 yards, with the artillery knocking out the first German line and then being moved up to knock out the second a few days later. General Haig is a man of *ambition*, a man who wishes to crush the Germans, not merely hurt them. 'I think we can do better than this,' he had told Rawlinson after first viewing what he saw as the latter's rather timid plans. 'It is usually wiser to act boldly and secure at the outset positions of tactical value. The first advance should be pushed as far as the furthest possible objectives of tactical value that we can reasonably hope to retain after capturing . . . The zone to be prepared by the artillery should be as deep as possible.'[39]

Haig has insisted that the attack must be wider – going to 26,000 yards – and wants none of this 'two steps' business. No, once the infantry have taken the first trenches, they must immediately push on to exploit the German shambles. And *cavalry*! A former cavalry officer himself, he insists that men on horseback still have a place in modern warfare, capable of capitalising on the gains made by pouring through a gap in the front to wreak havoc. 'In order to shorten the war, and reap the fruits of any success,' he says firmly, 'we must make use of the mobility of the Cavalry.'[40] (Not for nothing would Charles Bean soon write of him, 'I suppose Haig is one of those British soldiers – old-fashioned simple gentlemen to the backbone – who abide till their deaths in the beliefs which they learnt at their mother's knee.')[41]

For Haig's desire is clear. He wants to break through and get 'as large a combined force of British and French [as possible] across the Somme and fighting the enemy in the open!'[42]

For his part, General Rawlinson does not think it feasible to make a quick breakthrough in the line to let those horses through. A student of military history and tactics, he had made it his business in the mid-1890s to visit both Germany and France to study their military methods, and noted most particularly that the German concept of warfare was to have all of infantry, artillery and cavalry working tightly together – a concept foreign to the British Army. In the Boer War's Siege of Ladysmith in 1899–1900, Rawlinson had realised that the Boers' skill with artillery entirely left behind the British gunners, who 'think too much of their horses and not enough of their guns'.[43]

And now, for this attack, Rawlinson wishes to bring all his theories to bear at once. He wants to just 'bite and hold', as he puts it. He believes that the way to advance is like a pack of rugby forwards: collectively, slowly and surely, and only a foot at a time if necessary. But Haig will not hear of it! Too conservative. Too slow. He wants a breakthrough, don't you understand? Like a rugby centre, making a break, and isolated from support if necessary. But *gloriously*! Through the first line and on to the second line all in one go, and then with the cavalry out into open country, sowing havoc everywhere! And if you then have to spread your limited shells over two lines, not just one, then we will just have to make do with that, old chap!

It took time, but General Rawlinson had reluctantly ceded to General Haig's insistence. 'It still seems to me that an attempt to attain more distance objectives,' he had written to Haig on 19 April, 'that is to say the enemy's second line system, under the conditions above described, involves considerable risks. I however fully realise that it may be necessary to incur these risks in view of the importance of the object to be attained. This will, no doubt, be decided by the Commander-in-Chief, and definite instruction be sent to me in due course.[44]

Indeed. When Haig had replied, it was to make it clear that he was sticking to his guns, and he wanted the shells from those guns to be spread across all two lines of trenches, 'continued until the attacking units are satisfied that the obstacles to their advance have been adequately destroyed'.[45]

With Haig's basic plan agreed upon, General Rawlinson and his Fourth Army staff – in their HQ at Querrieu, near Amiens – get down to tin tacks, nuts and bolts, bullets and bombs, shells and shrapnel. Depending how well the first phase of the 'Big Push' goes, provisions are also made for a second and third push, perhaps a week or two later.

What is not remotely in dispute is the importance of gaining the high ground now occupied by the Germans, most particularly the ridge that lies just above the village of Pozières. With that taken, the British will be able to place artillery observers on the ridge, who can call down accurate fire on German positions within an eight-mile radius – effectively the entire German line that they are attacking. It must be secured by the end of the first day.

27 APRIL 1916, SHORTLY BEFORE 10 AM, NEAR BOIS GRENIER, THE 2ND DIVISION SMELLS A RAT

That odour! Hyacinth. It is unmistakable.

Clearly they are under a devastating new kind of attack – just as, they know, the Brits around Armentières had been the previous night. God help them all. Scrambling from his dugout – praying that just one of his oft too wet matches will work – an officer of the AIF's 1st Battalion manages to do it. With shaking hand, he gets the flaming match to the fuse of a signal rocket, which soon roars up to burst against the night sky, to indicate they are under a gas attack.

Quickly!

Now, just as they have been trained to do, the AIF's 5th Field

Artillery Brigade brings down a flurry of fire on the enemy's front-lines, the theory being that 'the bursting shells would help to dissipate the cloud'.[46]

Mercifully, this time it proves to be a false alarm, and there is an additional bonus. To the seeming amazement of the 2nd Division infantry, they see an artillery attack put up by their own mob, and it more or less seems to work. The enemy parapet starts blowing up before their very eyes. True, there is hell to pay, as the enemy artillery soon replies – for the Australians have broken the tacit agreement – and shells start to rain down upon them, but it is really something. 'At least we didn't hit our own trenches,' Brigadier-General George Johnston, the commander of the 2nd Division's artillery, tells Charles Bean. 'I suppose that's something.'[47]

It is a more than merely sobering assessment. The vastly experienced Johnston clearly knows, better than anyone, just how far from capable these men are.

LATE APRIL 1916, VERDUN NOT SO WELL DONE, AS THE GERMANS ARE CANED

The French living in German-occupied France who have observed General von Falkenhayn closely at this time have noticed a couple of curious things. The first is his passion for long, lonely walks around his GHQ at Charleville. The second is the way he carries his cane. For it proves to be a barometer for the way the war is going for Germany. 'When he carried it in his right hand, his face beamed . . . If the stick was in his left hand, the General seemed annoyed.'[48]

Lately, they are very pleased to see that the cane has been in his left hand.

For while von Falkenhayn's notion that the French would stop at nothing to keep Verdun in French hands has been proved correct, and they have indeed been 'bled white', so too have the Germans. Just nine weeks into the battle, no fewer than 120,000 German soldiers have become casualties, against 133,000 French soldiers. Falkenhayn is shocked. His plan was meant to bleed only *France* white, not Germany also.

But yes, the French, too, are suffering. Though the now wildly popular General Pétain had indeed stabilised things, General Joffre had grown impatient at Pétain's reluctance to counter-attack and so had promoted him away from direct control of the front-lines, replacing him with the thrusting General Robert Nivelle. But, as a result, again the casualty rate among the French has soared to such a shocking extent that, as April wanes, General Joffre feels obliged to inform General Haig that instead of the originally planned 40 divisions to contribute to the Somme offensive, the French, *je regrette*, will now only be able to spare 30.

EARLY MAY 1916, TEL-EL-KEBIR, NOTHING BUT SAND, HEAT AND FLIES

Such events in faraway France, of course, mean that the War Office looks with ever more covetous eyes to the two remaining Australian divisions in Egypt. Perhaps their training, enhanced by the Gallipoli veterans among them, has proceeded to the point where they are now fighting fit and ready to go?

But, in Cairo, Sir Archibald Murray is firm in response to General Sir William Robertson's query:

IT IS HARDLY CORRECT . . . I KNOW THIS IS A THEORY OF BIRDWOOD'S, BUT AS A MATTER OF FACT I JUDGED FROM PERSONAL INSPECTION AND OBSERVATION THAT THE INFANTRY OF THE 4TH AND 5TH DIVISIONS IS DECIDEDLY INFERIOR, BOTH AS REGARDS PHYSIQUE, TRAINING, AND OFFICERS, TO THAT OF THE FIRST TWO DIVISIONS . . .[49]

Look, they might be ready in a month, but even then it will be another month again before the 4th and 5th Divisions' artillery is in shape. You could rush it and have them complete their training in France itself, but that would obviously not be advisable.

Very well then. Sir William passes the views on to General Plumer of the Second Army in France, doubting whether the 4th and 5th will be 'sufficiently trained to justify their employment in offensive operations on a large scale during the next few months'.[50] And so the training for the 4th and 5th Divisions goes on unabated.

'It's nothing but sand, heat, flies and thousands of other discomforts here,' an exhausted corporal of the 55th Battalion, Rupert Campbell, writes home. 'Everyone is as black as a nigger, you have no idea of what they look like; we are all in fairly good condition but trudging for miles through this loose sand with full packs up is breaking our hearts. It's not training men, it's killing them. We are out at the trenches at present and for the last couple of days the temperature has been 130 degrees in the shade and 170 degrees in the sun. Where they got this from I don't know, probably the shade represented the inside of a sandbag dugout, at any rate . . .'[51]

When will this agony end? When they get to France – which is the chief hope of them all. 'They have been telling us for some time that we will be leaving for France in 3 weeks. A military 3 weeks is a very indefinite period, it is nearly as bad as a military mile and a half,' writes Campbell.[52]

Of course, in such an arid environment as the desert, it is only the hardiest of creatures that will survive, let alone prosper. Beyond the soldiers of the 4th and 5th Divisions, the occasional hare and gazelle are seen scampering in the distance, and more particularly snakes and scorpions.

The snakes, of course, have a famous history in Egypt – with Cleopatra so legendarily clasping one to her breast to take her own life – and even though most of them are no more than a foot in length, the better part of their slithery forms must be taken up by their lungs to judge from their 'extraordinarily powerful hiss which would have done credit to the vocal apparatus of a fully grown boa constrictor'.[53]

Curiously, the creature the soldiers take most interest in is the hardy scarab beetle – once revered in these parts as a symbol of life – though this is less a matter of empathy or admiration than the fact they can make money from it . . .

That massive roar in the distance? Go closer. See how dozens of Australian soldiers of the 5th Division are standing in a circle around a scarab beetle that has been placed in a small ring of heaped-up dirt? Within that ring have been left small openings through which the beetle can escape, and the soldiers are furiously betting on which one he will choose.

Ah, how they roar, and oh, how amusing to see the little beetle, so valiantly scrabbling across the sand, butting up again and again against the sand barrier only to eventually find a way through.

4–6 MAY 1916, THE AIF 1ST DIVISION'S 5TH BRIGADE GOES HIGHER, EVER HIGHER

Higher, higher still! As the AIF 1st and 2nd Divisions continue to settle in to their new digs on their section of the Western Front, the most basic drive remains to get their own sand-barrier parapets higher and thicker. In the face of continuous German shelling and raids, that barrier is the best thing to keep the brutes back. Sometimes they manage to make themselves a lot more secure; sometimes they're just getting going when a shell comes to destroy their work – and the survivors must start again.

Of course, as it goes on, the Australian artillery is doing its best to give Fritz some of his own back, albeit with only mixed results. Oddly enough, the most devastating batteries on the Australian side are also the least popular. They are the Stokes mortar boys, the keepers of this new, top-secret weapon everyone is whispering about. Officers have even been known to shoo the mortarmen away by advising them, 'You'll find a much better possie if you head down to A Company's trench.'

And here they are now. Just watch these bastards on the late morning of 4 May, hauling their two Stokes mortars forward along the duckboards. 'The Shoot and Scatter Mob',[54] we call 'em, or even the 'Imshi Artillery', after the Digger fondness for the Arabic word *imshi*, meaning 'bugger off'.[55] It takes them only a matter of minutes to set up the mortars – large pipe barrels – on an angle, so that the bombs will land right on Fritz's blond curls.

Ready?

Ready.

Christ. Hold your ears, boys – as these mongrels are capable of firing off a mortar bomb every three seconds or so – and watch through the periscope as the mortar bombs land, sending duckboards, sandbags and sometimes Germans flying high into the air. And now the inevitable result. For the Stokes mortar boys break new records in how quickly they dismantle the whole thing and shoot through like a Bondi tram, leaving us 'PBIs (Poor Bloody Infantry) to take the consequences'.[56]

For of course the German artillery quickly draws a bead on where the firing is coming from and starts raining shells on us as never before, causing us to huddle in our bays, knowing that the next second on Earth may be our last and just praying we can survive. And now that we have, we can stop sucking mud and spend the rest of the afternoon repairing all the damage that has been done, all the sandbag walls that have been blown down, carrying away the wounded, gathering the body parts, burying the dead.

Somehow, what is even more frightening is when our own heavy artillery starts dropping seven or eight shells just 30 yards to the rear of us! Mercifully, they are all duds, but still. One theory is that 'the ground is so soft here that the big shells often don't get enough resistance to make them explode and become duds'. Another theory, wholly untested yet circulating among the men who are astounded by the sheer number of duds, is that '50,000 of the American shells have been found filled with sawdust'.[57]

Either way, how bad must our own artillery be when it is so scattergun as to nearly drop the shells on us, *and* the shells are all duds? 'This puts the wind up the mob who respectively get out of the line of fire for half an hour,' Corporal Dudley Jackson records, 'as we did not want to be killed by our own side. None of our artillery would own up that they had done any firing.'[58]

But it is still as nothing compared with what is to come on the morrow. For, from first light on 5 May, the Germans – by way of saying *'Guten Morgen'* – fire a few shells upon the Australians of the 5th Brigade's 20th Battalion of the 2nd Division, who respond in kind – and here's a 'Gidday' to you – sending over a few rounds from our Stokes mortars. And we might even have stung Fritz this time, because he comes back with such a furious artillery attack on our northern sector it is as though he is *angry*, and many of his planes roar overhead, clearly spotting just how effective their fire is.

Still, as the afternoon begins to wane and the twilight falls, so does the fire from both sides, until there is barely a shot fired in anger. It seems we are agreed. That is enough for the day, and the night, until we exchange a couple of wake-up shells early on the morrow. Until then . . . *'Gute Nacht'*.

But no.

At precisely 7.40 pm,[59] just as it finally falls dark, the German artillery opens up on the Australians of the 20th Battalion in the lines at the Bridoux Salient.

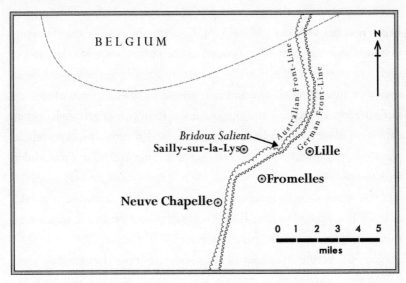

The Bridoux Salient

It is an attack so severe that even at 'The White City', the sandbag shelter 600 yards to the rear of the front-line that is 20th Battalion HQ, the concussion of the shells three times extinguishes the acetylene lamp. What the *devil* is going on?

It is an artillery barrage the likes of which the Australians haven't seen before – a concentrated, very precise artillery attack with a very specific purpose. Unknown to the Australians, it is all part of a German raid, ordered nine days before by their HQ and minutely planned and trained for thereafter. Having noticed a new enemy formation moving in, the Germans have set out to capture prisoners and learn more about them.

With typical Teutonic efficiency, the raid goes like clockwork, and this barrage is just the preliminary.

But what a preliminary!

When the officers step outside at 20th Battalion HQ, they can see that just forward, the shells are bursting on their men in the front-lines with such devastating hurricane force that 'the air seemed alive with whining fragments of metal . . .'[60]

Good Gawd, if it is this bad back here, what must it be like for the men in the front-lines?

At the moment that the company of Captain Arthur Ferguson is being relieved by Major Harold Paul's company – with the relieving platoons making their way forward in the communication trenches – their world goes suddenly crazy. A roaring rumble to their south-west rises to a shattering climax and is followed by a fearful whistling . . . building to a screech . . . and then no fewer than two-dozen shells begin exploding close to them in as many seconds. The ground jumps, whole platoons are slaughtered, and men scream. The Australians are under ferocious attack.

'The whole thing is indescribable,' one 20th Battalion soldier would note. 'It is supposed to have been the severest bombardment seen along this part of the line for eighteen months.'[61]

Captain Ferguson, realising that such a barrage must mean they will soon be victims of an infantry raid, runs towards the SOS rockets, which are just ten yards from him. Once their green colour explodes in the night sky, it will be a signal for the artillery to focus on the German parapet. But so intense is the barrage that Ferguson is knocked over three times before he can get to the rockets. And it is not just here in the front-lines that the shells are exploding. With extraordinary accuracy, the German shells are also falling on the support lines and communication trenches called 'Safety Alley' and 'Queer Street', preventing the front-line Australians getting any support.

'A shocking bombardment [saw] hell let loose . . .' Corporal Arthur Thomas of Toorak will describe it in a letter home. 'It seemed as though every gun the enemy possessed was ranged against us and then when our own artillery got going behind us it was God darn awful.'[62]

Yes, the Australian artillery makes reply, but it takes fully 13 minutes to do so, their own shells trying to both extinguish the German artillery wherever it is situated and punish the German soldiers in the front-line. But it is like using a water pistol against a fire-hose. The German artillerymen are as experienced as they are expert, using state-of-the-art guns. The Australians reply with what amounts to little more than angry shots in the dark, lobbing shells where they think it might hurt and hoping they are not duds. Some of the shells do explode, though for the most part 'high and to the rear',[63] and even those that find their mark in the front-lines do little damage, courtesy of the fact the German dugouts are so strongly constructed, with concrete reinforcements. And, the 50 German soldiers of the I/230th RIR who are to do the raid have been kept well back from the front-lines for the moment.

There is no doubt, meantime, that the German shells find their mark, roaring from a well-organised artillery force composed of 'the supporting batteries [which were] two of heavy field-howitzers, two of light field-howitzers, and four of field-guns . . . also supported by three heavy trench-mortars . . . four medium, and eleven light trench-mortars, and six bomb-throwers'[64] – some 70 guns in all, plus 20 mortars.

Crouched behind the parapet with four mates, Corporal Jackson would note that the shells come so thick and so fast they make 'one continual whooshing scream and roar as they skimmed our parapet. The wind of the shells lifted sandbags off the top, blew men's tin hats, packs and any loose gear for yards. It was cold before they started but before long we were sweating like anything. The concussion of the bursting shells made our bodies sway like being hit by a giant hand, and the noise made our ears ring . . . The ground shook in waves just as though an earthquake was on.'[65]

And in the end, it is a measure of just how experienced one of the soldiers, Private Barney Meechan,[66] is that he rises to the occasion and yells at the others over the roar that a watch should be put up top to look out for raiders.

He must be bloody joking!

None of them moves.

So Meechan himself pokes his head above the parapet to peer into the gloom for any German soldiers rushing their way, only to feel a 'shell skin his head'.[67] He decides on the instant 'that a watch should not be kept, by him at any rate'.[68]

All they can do is stay crouched down, hoping not to take a direct hit, their extreme discomfort exacerbated by the fact that many near misses throw water and mud all over them. And then one piece of shrapnel hits Sergeant Charles Coglan in the shoulder, which sees him go down as a screaming mess – though the wound is not mortal. (Which is no surprise to old soldiers, who know that a 'badly hit man never yells'.)[69] And now a shell hits the parapet right in front of them, sending sandbags flying everywhere.

In all the screams and confusion, Jackson feels two more violent bumps, which prove to be Privates Barney Meechan and Monty Parnell rushing along to another part of the trench where the parapet is still intact, while the wounded and terror-stricken Coglan, 'in a voice that vibrated called everyone cowards and prayed to all and sundry not to desert him'.[70]

And where is Jackson's other mate, Little Joe Hughes? Buried under the sandbags! Jackson can hear his amazingly calm calls and proceeds to dig him out, alive and remarkably intact.

Other bays have experienced similar results. 'What surprised me,' Jackson would note, 'was that anyone was still alive, it seemed a miracle.'[71]

Deutsche Pünktlichkeit. German clockwork. At *Punkt acht Uhr fünfzehn*, precisely 8.15 pm – a time when there is light for the Germans to see their immediate surroundings but insufficient for their shadowy forms to be seen at a great distance, as in from the Australian lines – the raiders move forward from their deep dugouts. Beyond their pistols and rifles, they all carry daggers, six bombs each and these new-fangled flashlights, which – if you can believe it – allow them to shine a discrete beam of light in the darkness. None of them carries any identification – and most certainly not the 230 they have in elegant red stitching on their epaulettes signifying their regiment – in order that, if killed or captured, they can give no information away.

All are now ready to attack and so, as agreed, the radio signal is sent back to HQ: '*Rationen verteilt*, rations distributed.'[72]

And now, at exactly 8.20 pm, upon the signal of their leader, Captain Richard Volkmann, all of the German raiders leap the parapet and charge forward into No-Man's Land. As they do so, the German shelling on the trenches they are charging towards stops, and it moves back to a 'box formation'. That is, from pounding just the narrow section of the front-line trenches they are attacking, it suddenly lifts, while remaining on the front-line immediately to the left and right, in the manner of a three-sided box. This carved-out barrage box should afford the attacking troops the room to penetrate, while at the same time trapping in their trenches those poor sods who may remain alive.

The instant the artillery fire lifts, the Australian NCOs know what's coming next.

'Up, get up!' they roar. 'Look to your front, look to your front!'

It takes but a matter of seconds.

'The Germans set up a cheering and a shouting the like I have never heard before and charged us in mass formation . . .' Corporal Arthur Thomas of Toorak would recount. 'They reached our left flank and got in among our fellows. It was fearful yet awe-inspiring, for the first few

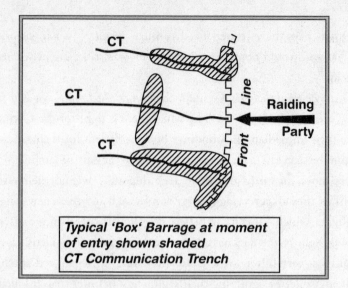

Diagram of a 'box formation' barrage, after a map by Charles Bean in *Official History of Australia in the War of 1914–1918*, Vol. III, p. 214

minutes I felt sick, then as steady as a rock. I was right in the line of fire . . . some fellows' nerves gave way & they became gibbering idiots, Sergeants & all sorts, god it was little wonder for fighting here is just simply massacre.'[73]

The Germans manage to get to within 50 yards of the Australian lines before they come under fire from the surviving Australian infantry. Five of their own are hit, but, just as they have long trained for, they succeed in bringing their own precise fire, together with their hurled bombs, upon the defenders, before crossing the spot where their artillery has blown the barbed wire apart.

Like clockwork still, one section of raiders – an even more heavily armed 'blocking party' – departs to the right, while another blocking party positions itself to the left to shield the raiders against Australian counteroffensives from the flanks, while the main body gets to work. The key purpose of the raid is to determine whether the Australians are doing any tunnelling towards the Germans, and, if so, to blow the entrances to those tunnels apart. They also wish to seize whatever prisoners they can, and whatever *Beute*, booty, from weaponry to letters and diaries that might contain key information.

Making their way past the comparatively large number of dead Australians in the front trenches – there are *dozens* of them – these German raiders from hell move forward, overwhelming whatever resistance they come across, which includes throwing grenades into dugouts. Screams, angry shouts, explosions and shots fill the night. Those Australians who do not resist, who put their hands into the air in surrender, are led back across No-Man's Land.

Out to the right of the attack, two German *Musketiere*, infantry privates, Göpfert and Mai, come across two interesting-looking trench mortars of a type they have never seen before, clearly all set up ready to fire. Perfect booty! The mortars are thrown back over the parapet and quickly carried to German lines.

The bulk of the raiders are about to push even further forward into the Australian second line when the shout goes up, '*Die Pioniere lassen eine Miene hochgehen!* The Pioneers are exploding a mine!'[74]

Hauptmann Volkmann quickly orders retirement, and the raiders – less the Pioneer section, whose job it is to blow up enemy infrastructure – steal back across No-Man's Land. By 8.40 pm, just 20 minutes after the raid had been launched, Volkmann is able to report that he and his men are back safely. At 9.10 pm, after a huge explosion lights the enemy lines, most of the Pioneers also reappear. All up, the German raiders have lost just four men killed and 15 wounded, while capturing 11 Australian prisoners, whom Intelligence will be able to closely question for information.

—

The following morning, the Australian captives – many still peppered with shot and shell – are feeling ghastly. Even though they have been carefully tended to by German Army doctors, their loss of blood has left them weak. Or is it the prospect of many long months, and maybe even years, as prisoners of war in some German camp?

Either way, it is a very dejected group of Australian soldiers from the 20th Battalion who are now traipsing slowly, under heavy guard, behind German lines towards Lille on this misty morning. But, now, what's this? As they make their way through the streets of the village of Haubourdin, suddenly they are rushed by French villagers, who are trying to press upon them cigarettes and food – *croissants, saucissons, fromage!*

Zurück! Zurück! Get back! Get back!

Understandably, the grim-faced German guards take a very dim view of the men they have legitimately conquered being treated as conquering heroes by the French, and they lay about them with fists, feet and rifles used as clubs.

But it is no use. The word has spread among the French villagers, and now more of them pour out of their homes, shouting out, '*Vive l'Australie! Vive l'Australie! Vive l'Australie! VIVE L'AUSTRALIE!*'[75]

By the time the mob gets to Lille's central railway station – the Australians on their way to Douai for interrogation by German Intelligence – the enthusiasm of the French is so great for the Australian prisoners that the German guards have to turn a fire-hose on them, to keep them back. (Later, when one of these Australians is asked by his German interrogator *why* he is fighting, the Digger's reply is swift: 'To prevent Germany conquering the world, and Australia in particular.'[76] This, the German notes, is a typical Australian response.)

———

Back in the Australian lines, now that the smoke has cleared and they have made it through the terrible night, it is time to assess the damage. '20th Battalion,' as Charles Bean would chronicle, 'lost four officers and 91 men killed or wounded, [while] in neighbouring units, 25 men were killed or wounded.'[77]

Even more troubling than that is the fact that a couple of Stokes mortars have gone missing, obviously captured by the Germans. There will be hell to pay. For instructions had been explicit: On no account are any Stokes Mortars to be left in the front line at night.[78] But they had been all right, and this is the result.

At the Second Army HQ, General Plumer and his senior officers are shocked and appalled to find out about it, via reading the translation of the German daily communiqué:

> Western Theatre of War. - To the south-east and south of Armentires some operations carried out by our patrols were successful. Some prisoners were captured and two machine-guns and two mine-throwers were taken.[79]

Can this *possibly* be true? Two Stokes mortars taken, and General Plumer's HQ has not been so informed? A flurry of cables is soon sent back and forth between the Generals Plumer and Birdwood, with the latter forced to concede that, though he had not himself been so informed, it appears that the worst has happened, and the enemy is now indeed in possession of some of their most prized weapons.

General Birdwood's subsequent report on the matter to General Plumer does not mince words:

> I much regret what I cannot help considering to be the unsatisfactory results of this attack by the Germans, and I cannot sufficiently express regret for the loss of the two Stokes mortars, which is inexcusable.[80]

Plumer could not agree more, stapling to Birdwood's report a letter he sends to Commander-in-Chief Haig, noting:

> The loss of the two Stokes Mortars is, as stated by the Corps Commander, inexcusable . . . The two officers who were in charge of the mortars . . . will be brought before a court-martial.[81]

Making everything so much worse is that the Germans appear to have got away with this daring raid without losing a *single* soldier. No fresh German dead are visible in No-Man's Land in the area of the raid, none suspended on the wires, not even the sign of freshly spilled blood. Nothing! Oh, how the Germans must be *schneerink* at them, or however it is those bastards say 'sneering'.

The upshot is that, in their first military action on the Western Front, the Australians have not performed well. And that is certainly the view of Sir Douglas Haig, when he shortly afterwards writes a letter to none other than His Majesty the King. 'I inspected the Australian and New Zealand Divisions,' he informs His Majesty in his careful though slightly pinched hand. 'They are undoubtedly a fine body of men, but their officers and leaders as a whole have a good deal to learn . . . A portion of their front was shelled last Thursday night and a small party of Germans entered their trenches. I understand that the severity and accuracy of enemy's artillery fire was a revelation to them!'[82]

8 MAY 1916, L'HÔPITAL DE MARSEILLE, *IL N'EST PAS LÀ*

Où est l'Australien?

Le patient, le soldat avec la gonorrhée, a disparu!

And that's just the way Russell Bosisto is. In family life, the 19-year-old is a warm and loving fellow, writing letters to his parents every week, together with a postcard to each of his five sisters. And they all adore him in turn, having sent him away with a beautiful fountain pen that he always has on him so he can write those missives, and a handcrafted and engraved identity disc, which he treasures.

But in this man's army, he is a wild'un, and after six weeks' treatment he just gets bored one night, does a runner and goes out on the town. Has the time of his life *avec les filles françaises*. Gets arrested. He is taken back to *l'hôpital*, whereupon he is handed over to the Australian authorities the next day and – 'mercy bowcup' – released into their care. They give him 12 days of Field Punishment No. 2 – basically heavy labour – and then he can head off to join his 27th Battalion again. Russell don't care.

16 MAY 1916, IN THE DESERT OUTSIDE TEL-EL-KEBIR, ALEC WRITES

God help him, mother.

Never in Alec Raws' life has he survived such a hot day, and even then, only just. So hot that it was 113 degrees Fahrenheit in the shade early in the day at Cairo, 117 degrees outside the Tel-el-Kebir hospital, and it would have been somewhere between 120 degrees and 130 degrees in the shade in the desert where he is . . . if there had been any shade to begin with. But there is none.

At its worst, the only way Alec – and the other members of his company – had been able to survive was to 'lay naked in my tent . . . for two hours just gasping'. And even now, in the 'cool' of the evening, it is not comfortable, at probably just over 100 degrees. When he had sat outside that same tent, at 6.45 pm, just before sunset, to write to his mother, there had been no wind. But within seconds, he tells his mother, 'a hurricane of sand, burning hot, is blowing across the encampment'.

But, no matter. For things are on the up and up! 'I have great news. I've been warned to be ready to move overseas with a number of other officers at a moment's notice, and I've been transferred to Goldy's battalion, the 23rd. Of course we go to France. I am overjoyed because life here in all this heat is impossible. I shall try to get a cable away to you tomorrow.'[83]

And sure enough, three days later, Alec and his comrades, all bound for France as reinforcements for the divisions already in place, are on their way. As their carriage starts to gently rock upon departure from Tel-el-Kebir station, so joyous do many of them feel to at last be on their way that, with high hilarity, they start to yell to their farewellers that they have 'cold feet'! 'Sometimes those on the platform retorted in kind,' Alec tells his sister, 'but mostly they just laughed. It struck me as so much like those romantic and cheering departures of troops for the front that one reads about, but never sees.'[84]

They're on their way to France!

Chapter Five

WITH GOD ON OUR SIDE

Nothing could prevent him from showing himself, as he
really was, the fresh, gay, modern counter-part of the old
Stuart cavalier, enjoying life to the full, always ready to take
a chance either for himself or a friend, whether behind the
lines or in action, and in both cases with that easy natural
manner by which he could invariably be recognised even on
the farthest sky-line when advancing against the enemy.[1]
Bean on the Australian soldier in France

Men get into the spirit of the game, gain confidence in
themselves. It is part of that strange process through which men
unconsciously go which enables them to kill men without being
murderers. When this reaches its perfection, soldiers become men
of the chase. They take delight in battle and kill without hatred.[2]
Herbert McBride, A Rifleman Went to War: Twenty
First Battalion Canadian Expeditionary Force

SUNDAY 21 MAY 1916, CHÂTEAU DE BEAUREPAIRE, ON THE OUTSKIRTS OF MONTREUIL, HAIG CALLS ON THE LORD, BEFORE JOFFRE CALLS ON HAIG . . .

It is the kind of thing that General Haig likes to do now and then:
gather different officer chappies and various characters to join him for

a meal, to ensure that their part in the coming battle fits in with his own plans. In this case, he has invited a large number of 'devil dodgers', otherwise known as army chaplains, to lunch, and he is most insistent on one thing in particular: 'You shall preach to [the troops] about the objects of Great Britain in carrying on this war. We have no selfish motive, but are fighting for the good of humanity.'[3]

In any case, it is good to have God on their side, as within hours General Joffre will inform Haig that the number of divisions *La France* can spare for the forthcoming Somme offensive is now down to 25.

EVENING, 21 MAY 1916, FORT ROMPU, SIX MILES NORTH OF FROMELLES, PUTTING THE KNIFE IN

It is the way of these things.

Having taken a week's course at a School of Instruction for bayonet fighting, Goldy Raws is now the Bayonet Fighting Instructor for the whole battalion. The nature of his lessons is as far from Goldy the man as it is possible to get. For 'Guiding Rule Number 8' of the *British Army Manual* does not mince words so much as the enemy: '*Vulnerable parts of the body*. If possible, the point of the bayonet should be directed against an opponent's throat . . . as the point will enter easily and make a fatal wound on penetrating a few inches and, being near the eyes, makes an opponent flinch. Other vulnerable and usually exposed parts are the face, chest, lower abdomen and thighs, and the region of the kidneys when the back is turned. Four to six inches' penetration is sufficient to incapacitate and allow for a quick withdrawal, whereas if a bayonet is driven home too far it is often impossible to withdraw it. In such cases a round should be fired to break up the obstruction.'[4]

There is more, much more, including the advice from an old Major that the best way to make sure your bayonet doesn't get stuck in a man is to twist it as you withdraw, thus allowing air in to break the seal. (The German instruction is to avoid the ribs altogether for that very reason and to go for the stomach, from which there is never a problem with extraction – most particularly if you give them a kick *in den Bauch*, in the guts, as you pull it out.)

Meantime, heed the words of General Alexander Suvorov, so beloved by all bayonet instructors: 'Never forget, men, the bullet misses, the bayonet doesn't. The bullet's an idiot, the bayonet's a fine chap.'[5]

It is grisly stuff, particularly for as naturally gentle a man as Goldy Raws, but, whatever else, he finds he is surprisingly good at it. 'I like the work,' he writes to his mother, 'and it keeps you in good nick – also it brings your name well to the fore in the battalion . . . The best compliment was given by the OC when [after seeing my lesson] he told me "it was horrible" . . .!'[6]

Plus, there is something else lifting Goldy's mood these days.

A word, Major . . .?

Yes, Lieutenant Raws, what can I do for you?

As Goldy Raws notes in a letter to his father, he and his fellow officers of the 6th Brigade 'are all billeted pretty close together, and among the officers there is always a good feeling, except when there isn't, and then there's a row'.[7] But there's unlikely to be a row between these two. The always conscientious Lieutenant Goldy Raws really is one of the more popular men in his 23rd battalion, and Major Leslie Matthews, the second-in-command of 22nd Battalion, is not far off that as well.

So, what can I do you for, Goldy?

'It's my brother Alec, sir. He is in charge of the 11th Reinforcements that have recently arrived in France. A new order has just come in for four extra Lieutenants to be allowed to each battalion, and they will be drawn from Reinforcements coming forward. I was hoping Alec could be one of the ones selected for the 23rd battalion?'[8]

Yes, Lieutenant, of course.

Wonderful!

(Against that, the sad thing is that the need for reinforcements in recent times has been substantial as, through the month of May, the I Anzac Corps in the nominal 'nursery' sector has been losing no fewer than 20 men per day killed and wounded.)

24 MAY 1916, CHÂTEAU DE LA MOTTE AUX BOIS, FOREST OF NIEPPE, A CLOUD OF PESSIMISM IN THE GLOOM

There is no man in the Australian Army – and certainly not in the British – whom Charles Bean admires as much as he does General Cyril Brudenell White, the gentle and assiduous Victorian who, among other things, had been the architect of the successful evacuation of the Dardanelles. The two are close, with Bean particularly appreciating the fact that Brudenell White talks to him openly and honestly, without fear that the journalist will betray his confidence by putting his words into print.

And on this day, as the two talk at I Anzac Corps HQ in Château de la Motte aux Bois, General Brudenell White is frank: 'I wonder whether we're going to win this war, Bean. You know, I'm a bit doubtful of all this talk that's going on.'

Talk? What talk?

'They're manoeuvring as to who shall offer to enter into negotiations first – that's the meaning of it. We could win the war if we organised, I have no doubt of it. But I wonder if we are ready to do it. I don't know that we are.'[9]

Bean knows what he means. White is referring to 'total war', as advocated by the Australian Prime Minister, Billy Hughes – for conscription; severe censorship and rationing; forced re-tooling of factories to make munitions; tight regulation of wages and hours; everything for all-out war; for victory at all costs; for doing everything possible to destroy Germany once and for all. And this was the same Hughes who as recently as October last year had said in the House of Representatives, on the possibility of a conscription referendum, 'The Government would not put [a question] certainly of that kind, to the people.'[10]

Well, he's not talking like that anymore. Things are grim across the board and Hughes knows it, just as Brudenell White knows it, just as Bean knows it. Rather than fierce resolution, a quiet pessimism has taken hold. 'Everyone here knows,' Bean confides to his diary, 'that our great offensive may not necessarily succeed – if it indeed comes off . . .'[11]

26 MAY 1916, HAIG HQ AT MONTREUIL, NOT QUITE A MEETING OF MINDS

It was ever thus, it is now, and so it will always be.

When a Frenchman meets an Englishman to try to reach agreement on a given issue, it is more than likely that, rather than there being merely two strongly opposing opinions, there will be three . . . *non, monsieur, quatre!* So it most certainly is on this occasion.

The French commander, General Joseph Joffre, has come to see General Douglas Haig on something of a mission. For this English ally *must* understand. 'For three months, we French have supported alone the whole weight of the German attacks at Verdun . . . If this goes on, the French Army will be ruined! I am therefore of the opinion that 1 July is the *latest* date for the combined offensive of *les Britanniques et les Français.*'[12]

General Haig chooses his words carefully, only in part because he must enunciate clearly . . . and pause . . . regularly . . . so that his meaning is clear. 'Before fixing the date,' this highest of British officers says, in fluent French, 'I would like to indicate the state of preparedness of the British Army on certain dates and compare its condition. Let us look at 1st and 15th July, and 1st and 15th August . . .'

Joffre explodes the instant that Haig gives the date for the attack commencing as the middle of August. His face turns red, his mouth opens, there is a volcanic rumbling, and then out it bursts. '*L'Armée Français* will cease to exist,' he roars, 'if you do nothing till then!'

Du calme, General Joffre, *du calme*. 'The 15th August remains the most favourable date for the British Army to take action,' General Haig says. 'Yet, in view of what you have said regarding the unfortunate condition of the French Army, I am prepared to commence operations on the 1st July or thereabouts.'[13]

With such a promise, Joffre immediately does indeed calm down, and the meeting resumes. It is finally agreed their joint battle will begin against the German lines around the date of 1 July, unless one side gives the other three weeks' notice of a change in the date of the attack.

One problem that the British will just have to learn to live with,

Joffre sadly informs them, is that because the battle at Verdun continues to chew through so many French divisions, France will not be able to contribute as many men as previously hoped for to the Somme offensive. In fact, against the 40 divisions originally planned – and, in Haig's view, *promised* – after yet further reduction, the French can now commit only . . . 16 divisions, which is fewer than 200,000 infantry soldiers. With that reduced number, it seems apparent that the chances of completely destroying the German Army in France are fading, and the best the British can hope for is to at least relieve the pressure on Verdun. *Merde.*

General Haig watches the French officers take their leave, with some relief. 'They are, indeed,' he writes in his diary that night, 'difficult Allies to deal with!'[14]

But at least it is all confirmed. The offensive will begin around 1 July, the precise date dependent on the weather. From the British side of the Somme, the central thrust, Haig has decided, will be delivered by the Fourth Army, under General Sir Henry Rawlinson. In the time that remains, there is much to organise, and in short order Haig issues a stream of key orders, most pertinently including the directive that all of his units along the Western Front must conduct as many raids as possible, both so that German attention is distracted from Rawlinson's preparations north of the Somme and so the German defences can be worn down.

Another imperative at Haig's GHQ is to gather the manpower they will need to not only launch the major attack on the Somme but also hold the rest of the front while it is done. And at a time when beggars can't be choosers, that also means calling on divisions that are not yet fully trained or equipped. All but immediately, the two remaining Australian divisions in Egypt are ordered to leave for France within a fortnight.

General Sir Archibald Murray, the Commander-in-Chief of all the Egyptian Expeditionary Forces, takes the opportunity to give Chief of the Imperial General Staff General Sir William Robertson his assessment:

```
I think it is desirable to give you some idea of
the degree of efficiency which these divisions
will be found to have attained . . . As regards the
artillery, which is the most backward arm, further
training is undoubtedly required to enable the
batteries to take their place in the line with a
reasonable standard of efficiency . . .¹⁵
```

Of course, such machinations are kept secret from the soldiers of the 4th and 5th Divisions themselves, but still it doesn't take long for the men of the 4th Division to work things out, as they are the first to be sent on their way. 'When we took the train for Alexandria our hearts beat almost to suffocation,' Corporal Hugh Knyvett of the 15th Battalion would record, 'and it was only when the troop-ship cleared the harbor, and eager eyes watching the compass saw her course was set N.W., that we gave a cheer, feeling that at last we might have a chance to show our mettle with the Canadians and Tommies, where the biggest fight was raging.'¹⁶

They must be on their way to France!

And even those left behind, the men of the 5th Division, now have a fair clue. 'The impression was gaining ground that the Division would soon be shipped to France,' the Official History of the 5th Division would record. 'It was known that the 1st and 2nd Australian Divisions had already arrived there, the 4th was reported to be on the way, and the training that the Division was now undergoing seemed to be especially directed to fitting it for the conditions of the Western Front. Much importance was attached to gas training and officers received instruction on billeting troops in villages . . .'¹⁷

31 MAY–1 JUNE 1916, AT VIEUX-BERQUIN, DIGGING IN FOR AUSTRALIA

They don't call them 'Diggers' for nothing. On this night, the men of A Company, 2nd Battalion, 1st AIF, whose motto is *'Nulli Secundus'*, second to none, are set to work digging yet more communication trenches in the VC Avenue area of Fromelles, freeing up passage between the front and support lines. It is back-breaking work, first to make the shallow indent in the cloying, muddy field, and then to fill the sandbags to build up the walls on either side of the trenches. And yet these soldiers – many of whom are coalminers drawn from Newcastle, Maitland and the Hunter Valley – are nothing if not experienced. In Digger slang, they are 'swinging the banjo', as the most common argot for a shovel is a 'banjo'.

At around 4 am, after 16 hours' hard slog, they throw down their shovels and return to their billets, only to be told by the orderly sergeant that, after orders from on high, 'every man in the battalion is to fall in . . . in full marching order before 8 am'.[18] Apparently, somebody important is going to inspect them.

The cursing would curl hair, but no matter how exhausted they are, sure enough, at 8 am there they are. Fix that collar, tighten that rifle sling, push that chest out, pull that gut in! Only when everything is to the complete satisfaction of their officers is the order given, and the entire battalion is directed to march in the direction of Vieux-Berquin, where, in a deserted orchard, they join the three other battalions of the 1st Infantry Brigade to form a hollow square. The men are standing at rigid attention, but nothing happens, as the minutes and then half-hours and then hours crawl by. There is to be no standing at ease, no breaking of ranks, no sitting down. They are not even allowed to remove their heavy packs, weighing all of 70 pounds.

Where the *hell* is this important visitor?

—

Look, it is a tad on the difficult side, because the men are all waiting, but what can General Haig do? Billy Hughes is the Prime Minister of a country of the British Empire that is providing no fewer than five divisions of first-class soldiers – actually six divisions, if you include the Light Horse in Palestine. So when he is staying at your HQ and does not come down for breakfast at 8.30 am as expected – because he 'suffers from nerves [and] sleeps badly'[19] – everyone simply must wait. The previous night at dinner, this strangely 'magnetic little man, not great in any sense, but magnetic to an extraordinary degree', as Haig's Chief Intelligence Officer describes him,[20] had been equally late, without apology.

Finally, the irascible Prime Minister emerges for breakfast at Haig's GHQ at 9.30, and he and Haig are able to talk, seriously. On many subjects, they are in complete agreement, and none more than for the British to pursue a policy of 'total war', irrespective of the costs. 'No one could be more determined than he [Hughes] is that we must endure all things for victory in the field. He is frankly scornful of the [British] Cabinet, calls them a lot of old women, and says they should have but one aim and purpose – to back up the soldiers and sailors.'[21]

Where they disagree is on how the Australian forces in France should be organised. Though the War Office had not seen fit to even advise the Australian Prime Minister and Cabinet back in January that there had been a push from General Birdwood to have the Australians and Kiwis form an army of their own under his leadership, and had simply rejected it outright, now that Hughes is fully apprised, he thinks it would be a good idea.

Haig chooses his words carefully in reply, begging to point out, 'Australasian soldiers fall short of what is necessary for an Army, and that it would therefore disarrange our plans to treat them as such. Even if you put six Divisions into the field that force would not be large enough to admit of "an Australian Army" being formed'.[22]

Haig resents that the Hughes Government will not allow him to have any Australian soldiers shot for desertion or cowardice – on the grounds that it is 'necessary to make an example to prevent cowardice in the face of the enemy as far as possible'[23] – as he does for all the other troops under his command.[24] And the worst of it is that the Australian troops themselves have become infected with the same infernal spirit of independence. At one point, when an Australian soldier of the 5th Division is about to be court-martialled, the English officer presiding begins by asking politely, 'Do you object to being tried by myself as President or any other member of this Court?'

'Certainly I do,' the Australian answers immediately.

'What is your objection?' the President inquires curiously.

'Well, to start off with,' says the Digger, 'you're all Tommies! In fact, I've never clapped eyes on such a pack of duds in all my life!'[25]

Outrageous!

'Nearly one Australian in every hundred men is in prison,' Haig would much later note in his diary. 'This is greatly due to the fact that the Australian government refused to allow capital punishment to be awarded to any Australian.'[26]

But these rather more delicate issues must await discussion another time. For now, the Australian troops await them . . .'[27]

—

Yes, he's nearly two hours late, but the crunch of gravel on the dark drive that leads up to General Birdwood's Château de la Motte aux Bois presages the 'Little Digger' himself.

Nearing midday, he alights from his car. To Bean's eyes, he looks 'rather white and worn', but that is to be expected from a man who, in the last week, has made no fewer than '14 speeches in the Midlands in 4 days'.[28]

On this gloriously bright day – as, to their near east, shells continue to burst around 'aeroplanes in the blue sky, making it mottled with a hundred little fleecy shrapnel clouds'[29] – he is travelling with an entourage. Accompanying him is former Prime Minister Andrew Fisher – now the High Commissioner to Great Britain – together with Generals Birdwood, Brudenell White, MacLagan and Walker, and many 'swank, pretty staff boys',[30] as one Digger puts it. Hovering near are such luminaries of the press as Charles Bean and Keith Murdoch, while one of General Haig's aide-de-camps is also here, ensuring that all is as it should be. (Extraordinary the transformation in Murdoch, from one-time mere journalist to now confidant of Prime Ministers, Princes and Kings. His 'Gallipoli letter' really has changed everything for him.)

'Why have you not written to me, Bean?' the Prime Minister immediately says to Bean with some warmth. 'Why did you not visit me
when you were in London?'[31]

The two talk, Bean amazed at the Prime Minister's obvious personal
regard for his humble self. '[H]is one idea now,' Bean would record in
his diary, 'is to beat Germany, hip and thigh, to fight her and organise
against her not for the present merely, but for the trade rivalry that will
follow the war. He has no idea of compromise, which I am sure British
statesmen have in the back of their heads.'[32]

'Well, have you got it?' Andrew Fisher asks Bean.

'What?'

'Your thing – your camera,' Fisher replies, referring to Bean being
cleared by the British War Office to use his camera. 'They said they'd
write ahead and tell headquarters here to let you have your camera.'

'I have no letter.'

'Well, it's disgusting! Disgusting! They're just fooling us – it's
disgusting that they can't treat us [better],'[33] says the man who once
pledged Australia would defend the Mother Country 'to the last man
and the last shilling'.

Finally the group turns its attention to the Australian troops assembled in a field next to the estate's orchard for the past four hours. The
boom of the guns in the near distance occasionally drowns out the
tune of 'Advance Australia Fair' being banged out by the brigade band
to welcome Mr Hughes. The bayonets of the 4000 Australian soldiers
glint in the sun as Hughes slowly walks along, inspecting their ranks.
They are in great fighting trim and a credit to the nation. Hughes – still
'looking ill'[34] – stands on the back of a lorry to deliver a stirring speech,
crisp with his pride in them.

'I wish to tell you how Australia appreciates what you have done,
what you are doing, and what you are going to do,' he says. 'I am proud
to be a fellow countryman. I wish you well. I hope to acclaim you to
your native country as the victors in the greatest war the world has seen.
We believe there is no peace for the world till Germany is crushed.
I am one of those who believe that a compromise at this juncture

would prove infinitely more destructive of civilisation than if we had at the outset failed to come into the war. There can be no comparison between might and right.'[35]

With only a little prompting from General Birdwood, the men give Prime Minister Hughes three rousing cheers, and with a little more prompting also give three cheers for General Birdwood. A little later, exhibitions are given of rifle-firing, grenade-hurling, bayonet drill and trench-catapult firing. This latter is a massive catapult just like the Diggers had first developed at Gallipoli, with arms six feet high shaped into a 'V' from which very strong elastic can be wound back by a winch. In the middle of it is a leather sack, ideally suited to hold small bombs and grenades. Let 'er rip, Bluey, and show the Prime Minister how it works! The Prime Minister will say to reporters that this experience had been 'the most inspiring of my life, and I only wish the war conditions were such as to allow this splendid body of fighters to make a headlong charge at the enemy in the open'.[36]

Truthfully? The Australian soldiers are not all equally impressed with him. 'Inspection by Fisher and Hughes such as it was,' Private Lionel McCrae would note in his diary. 'It was nothing too much, a couple of miles and then to hear nothing.'[37]

———

Two days after Hughes departs, Birdwood and Brudenell White are called to a meeting with General Sir Richard Haking at his XI Corps HQ at Hinges, to discuss a plan of his . . .

Still consumed with taking Aubers Ridge, which has been denied him in the previous year, General Haking wishes to 'discuss a combined possible operation . . .'[38] He proposes that his own XI Corps combine with Birdwood's I Anzac Corps under his own command and attack the Germans at the point where the two armies – the Second Army and First Army – meet, directly opposite the German strongpoint called the Sugar-loaf. If the combined forces could overwhelm that, Aubers Ridge from Aubers to Fromelles would be theirs, and after that the reconquest of Lille would be a real possibility.

It is much the same scheme that Haking had prepared 'during last winter in cooperation with the GOC III Corps, for the capture of the German front and support line of trenches', around Fromelles.[39] That had not come off. But here, now, is the chance to dust it off, re-present it, and see whether others might at last recognise the virtue in what he – the one-time Professor of Tactics at the British Army Staff College – has come up with.

EARLY JUNE 1916, IN THE ARC OF ARMENTIÈRES, ALEC ARRIVES

The figure making his way through the thick shadows of the forest on this late afternoon is small but strong, ragged with exhaustion but resilient, determined but a little downcast. After a long journey from Alexandria across the Mediterranean, and then by train to north-eastern France, only to go into immediate heavy training, Alec Raws is not his usual sunny self. Covered with the mud and perspiration of a long day's drilling, he is walking back to his billeted digs . . . when suddenly the track is filled with a man on a horse that thunders straight at him. It is all he can do to leap out of the way in time, though the horse itself, complete with startled English officer, must veer into the bush.

'Why the devil didn't you get out of the way?' the officer roars at him, once the two have gathered themselves once more.[40]

Alec takes pause. As one who has started military life as a private, he retains an ingrained fear of officers, even though he has himself now risen to the rank of a Second-Lieutenant. On the other hand, this baby-faced officer can be no older than 19 and is addressing him as if he is a 'lowborn dog'.[41] He will be damned if he will take it . . . 'Why the hell should I get out of the way?' he roars back in turn. 'Isn't there enough bloody road for you without having to ride over me?'[42]

And now the Englishman explodes, threatening to arrest Alec and have him put in the nearest guard tent.

Now, while Alec doesn't like English officers at the best of times, mostly he lets it pass. But *this* kind of insolence? Not him. 'Well, you better do the thing properly,' Alec replies evenly, 'and report it to Joffre.'

And so the confrontation would have gone on, but as Alec can see men approaching, he decides to spare the young man, informing the Englishman that he is an officer too.

Astride his horse, the English officer examines Alec more closely, raises his eyebrows and says, 'Oh, an Australian of course,' before riding off, muttering, 'Impossible . . .'[43]

Alec pushes on.

Perhaps the whole thing is not surprising. After all, the French officers he has seen since arriving a few days earlier 'seem to have all colours of the rainbow joined up together by a Bond Street tailor',[44] which would 'need a woman's tongue to describe', so there is never any mistaking them. And the English officers in all of their finery always 'appear to be absurdly mincing and effeminate, and have an extraordinary desire to look foppish'.[45] But the Australian officers, in their 'sombre and less shapely khaki', have as their 'only distinction [as officers] the little star on the shoulder, that can't be seen far off'.[46]

Sigh.

The good news, since Alec arrived in France just a few days earlier, is that there was a letter from his brother Goldy awaiting him, and it seems likely that it won't be long before he will be able to join Goldy's battalion. He has even been able to hear more recent news of Goldy from men coming back from the trenches. They are not far away from each other!

—

Speaking of that 'little star on the shoulder', Private Russell Bosisto – now substantially recovered from his venereal disease and reunited with his comrades of the 27th Battalion positioned at Fromelles – has discovered something wonderful. For it is not only in the realms of physics and mathematics that genius can strike . . .

He has managed to procure such a star – don't ask – the classic insignia of a Lieutenant, which he now keeps in his pocket. And when on leave – French or otherwise – he simply whacks it on to impress the girls and even get into Officer's Clubs that would otherwise deny him.

Magic!

5 JUNE 1916, THIEPVAL WOOD, JUST ANOTHER DEATH OR DOZEN ON THE WESTERN FRONT

Thiepval is a German stronghold of unusual significance, overlooking the valley of the Ancre, where the British are entrenched. As described by Charles Bean, 'in German hands, [Thiepval] operated as a solid buttress or gate-post, narrowing the intended breach in the German line'.[47]

Two miles beyond Thiepval, just behind the village of Pozières, is the highest ground of all, Pozières Ridge, upon which the windmill stands. He who controls the ridge can shell the visible enemy for miles. This whole hush-hush 'big push' on the Somme is coming up in a matter of weeks, and for the British, beyond widening their front, taking Thiepval is the stepping stone to the ridge – which is why the suspicious Germans are shelling the British forces so unmercifully. Perhaps it is not as hush-hush as one would like to think . . .

The 9th Battalion of the Royal Irish Rifles, under the command of Lieutenant-Colonel Frank Crozier, is holding on for dear life as the Germans send down barrage after barrage of heavy field-gun and howitzer fire.

Typically, in these parts, the crisscrossing trenches and sunken roads are named after places in the United Kingdom familiar to the battalions holding the line, such as Gordon Castle, Elgin Avenue and Speyside. Somehow, in all the strange ferocity of their surroundings, where the Angel of Death bears wings of steel, and scything shrapnel buzzes like bees on a busy summer's day, such familiar names give comfort. And yet it is a comfort not immediately apparent to newcomers, who need more than nice words to acclimatise. On this morning, as a case in point, an old school friend of Crozier's, who is now a battalion commander, has just arrived on the Western Front and come for a – WHAT THE HELL WAS *THAT!* – visit.

For while Crozier barely blinks at shells that land further than 75 yards away, his old school chum quivers with every blast, nervously looking around him and wondering whether the whistle of every incoming shell is to signal his last moment on Earth. Unperturbed, Crozier takes his friend on a walk up the main communication trench of Elgin Avenue, towards the front-lines, and . . .

And *hulloa*, here is a rifleman coming the other way, carrying something that looks suspicious – a sandbag. With so many thefts of rations lately, it is as well to check.

'What have you got in that bag?' Crozier challenges him.

'Rifleman Gundy,' the fellow replies.[48] Alas, a shell had exploded right on him, and in that tiny bag are Gundy's only mortal remains, being carried back for as Christian a burial as can be managed.

Crozier's school chum, with no experience in such barbarous bloodshed, turns green, but in these parts there is no relief. Some 50 yards further on, at the junction of Elgin Avenue and the fire trench, they come across another soldier, carrying a severed human arm, the bloody stump still gushing blood.

'Whose is that?' Crozier asks mildly, though he is clearly genuinely interested.

'Rifleman Broderick's, sir,' the fellow replies, just as he might have answered 'Paris' if asked what the capital of France was.

'Where's Broderick?'

'Up there, sir,' the fellow says, pointing to the highest reaches of the shattered trunk of an oak tree, where the dripping, shattered trunk of a soldier has come to rest.

'I give it up,' his friend says wanly, a little later. 'This is no place for a white man.'

'Of course it isn't,' Crozier agrees firmly. 'All the world knows that, but mankind put us here, and there's only one way out, through that part of mankind over there.'

With these words, the British officer points in the direction of the German-held Thiepval village, and his point is made.

What is certain is that, with this shocking rate of attrition, the

British are going to be needing a lot more men very quickly to feed into these trenches.

6 JUNE 1916, NEAR ARMENTIÈRES, EIGHT MILES NORTH OF FROMELLES, LITTLE LOSS FOR FOSS

It is time.

A week earlier, Sir Douglas Haig had issued an order for the First, Second and Third Armies to 'take steps to deceive the enemy as to the real front of the attack, [including] raids, by night, of the strength of a company and upwards . . .'[49] And so, on this night, 66 men from the 26th and 28th Battalions of the AIF's 2nd Division prepare to head out into No-Man's Land under the command of the young but deeply experienced Gallipoli veteran Captain Cecil Maitland Foss. Born and raised in the Aboriginal community of Arrino in Western Australia, Foss is a 24-year-old mountain of a man and former farmer. He is described by the foremost newspaper in his home state, *The West Australian*, as 'a very promising young officer of exceptionally fine physique'[50] who had started the war as a private and risen on ability alone.

The raiding party have been intensively trained by a group of Canadian soldiers – 'inspired, perhaps, by Red Indian personnel'[51] – who have initiated trench raids in this area and since perfected the dark art of night-time raids. Having been taken into the backblocks well away from the front-lines, the Australians have practised again and again, dashing across No-Man's Land in the dark, partially cutting their way through the rolls of barbed wire, before quietly breaking through the rest of the way by hand to avoid that telltale clicking sound of the wire-cutters, and then getting into replica trenches that have been constructed from aerial shots of the German ones opposite – the very trenches they are about to raid now, just before midnight.

Fully armed with revolvers, bombs, knives and clubs, their faces blackened with burned cork – an item of which there is never a shortage in France – and wearing clothing with pockets emptied of all papers, and with no identifying marks elsewhere, they move out, silent black phantoms of the night, flitting through the shadows as quickly as their legs will carry them. Just as the Canadians have taught them – for this raiding business is a fine art of life and death – all of them wear white armbands covered with black cloth, that cloth to be ripped off once the attack proper begins, so they can identify each other in the gloom. Their Australian uniforms have been abandoned in favour of British ones with no identification marks, against the possibility they are killed or captured, and they have neither hats nor helmets but dark woollen caps. Even their bayonets, which usually gleam, have been blackened with paint for the occasion. All their sandshoes are equally blackened with boot polish, and padded for silence.

Not that, in the final stages, they will have to be *that* silent. The previous evening, they had tried the 'silent method'[52] – hoping to overwhelm the enemy with surprise, first of all – but as the Brigade History would record, 'scouts coming upon an occupied listening post . . . raiding party were withdrawn and raid postponed'.[53] The scouts had seen the sentry's *Pickelhaube*, spiked helmet, poking above the parapet of his listening post from far enough away that he had neither heard nor observed them, which had saved their bacon.

So tonight they are going in again, in a different manner. After passing through gaps in their own wire at 10.30 pm, they creep as close as they dare – well back from the offending listening post of last night – and now lie doggo until 11.15 pm when, sure enough, their field artillery unleashes 'a comparatively short and light bombardment' from behind them.[54]

The Australians' minutely calibrated plan is that, once they are in the German trenches, their own field artillery will unleash a 'box barrage', just as the Germans had done to them in the first of their successful raids back in May.

Exactly as planned, the 60-pound shells now pound the German front-lines, forcing most of the soldiers to take cover, with those shells hopefully blowing the barbed-wire defences of their trenches to ribbons. At 11.35 pm, the scouts push forward and come back to report that there is a clear passage to the German trenches. Everyone up, and go!

It all happens so quickly it is staggering. Still expecting at any moment to be machine-gunned, the Australians are in fact able to charge forward and get through with barely a shot in their direction. They are soon enough up and over the German parapets. Yes, there is some shock when the trenches don't look exactly as they have trained for – the aerial photographs can be confusing – and as it happens there is no back set of breastworks as they expected, but the rest is good.

It is with a great deal of satisfaction that Foss, the first man to the top of the parapet, looks ahead to see in the flickering light of the ongoing explosions – right on time – the box barrage of the Australian artillery exploding just 100 yards in front, and off to the left and right. And now as he looks down into the trenches they are attacking . . . it is to find them all but deserted. Nevertheless, exactly as trained, they throw Mills bombs down into the trenches and, the instant after they explode, follow up hard.

Foss, all six foot four of him, and strong as a Mallee bull, is among the first into the German trench and promptly grabs the first enemy soldier he sees, a stripling of a lad whom he decides not to kill. Instead, with seeming superhuman strength, he bodily lifts the wailing lad and hurls him back over his head towards the rest of his men to be taken prisoner.

'There's number one!' cries he.[55]

Selected men move off to the left and right to act as blocking parties for any counter-attacks, including any coming from the communication trenches – and they roll bombs into whatever dugouts they find as they go along. 'Enemy troops were not in evidence,' their history would record, 'but two Germans marched along the trench in the darkness and were promptly bayoneted.'[56]

A few other Germans are quickly either taken prisoner or shot – six are killed in the process.[57] With the box barrage still doing its work for a few minutes, they know they have the enemy trenches to themselves, so they continue to search for enemy soldiers, weaponry, ammunition and anything else that might be of use.

And yet one key mistake is made. On this, their first raid, they stay just a tad too long. After the allotted seven minutes, Foss fires a green flare into the sky to signal everyone must return immediately, while also blowing his whistle, and yet even then some men are not alerted. And this really is an art of life or death. For while those who had immediately crossed back by following the luminous tape left out by the scouts are okay, those who have lagged are still making their way back across No-Man's Land – with Foss bringing up the rear, making sure all are accounted for – when the ground in front of them suddenly explodes from German artillery fire. There is nothing they can do but run for their lives, and so they do, alas losing six of their number in the process, while a stray shell also causes some 20 casualties in the trenches they are running to. Back in those trenches, it is time to go through their booty and have some of the German documents translated.

Oh dear.

One of them is a letter taken from the breast-pocket of a German soldier they have just killed. It is a loving missive from his wife, telling her husband how much she is missing him and, 'I have been sending you butter and cakes. Do not worry about me. But I am wondering why I have not heard from you for two days?'[58]

Christ. Such a love they must have had that, though he is in the trenches, and on the Western Front, they have been writing to each other *every day*.

For his heroism in so successfully leading this first major Australian raid on enemy lines, on no less than Birdwood's recommendation, Captain Foss would be awarded the Military Cross.

General Birdwood even cables Foss personally, congratulating him for the COMPLETE AND DETAILED ARRANGEMENTS OF EVERY SORT (THAT) HAD BEEN MADE BEFOREHAND . . .[59]

The principle that any operation must be as well prepared as it is detailed in planning is now a well-established one. As the old stagers say, 'sweat saves blood'.[60]

11 JUNE 1916, TEL-EL-KEBIR, EGYPT, THE STRAINING, THE TRAINING

And still the artillery training goes on. After 14 weeks of it now, the 52nd Field Artillery battery has at least a basic proficiency, but it is not enough for General McCay.

Having become very dissatisfied with the way the men marched in after training this morning, he has ordered them to go out on 'another route march at 4 o'clock the next morning'.

'Oh!' Norm Nicolson writes home. 'What joy the announcement caused you can imagine. [McCay] was already famed – and hated – for his stern discipline when a Brigade Commander in Egypt, before the days of the Peninsula, and there he kept it up till he was shot, and rumour says strange things about where that shot came from.'[61]

12 JUNE 1916, WEST OF LE BRIDOUX, 'ME COME, *KAMERAD!*'

And now it is the turn of the Victorians of the 1st Divvie's 6th Battalion to launch a raid of their own – the first major raid by any unit of the 1st Division. After careful observation over the last fortnight, it has been determined that a part of the Germans' defences west of Le Bridoux, between two strongpoints, 'the Lozenge' and 'the Angle' – some two miles north of Fromelles – is manned about as thinly as the barbed wire in front. But, careful now. Though the obvious thing is to lay down a barrage on such wire as there is, and follow that up with a protective barrage around the trench they intend to raid, much has been learned in the preceding couple of months. Though two such barrages are planned, similar barrages also attack the other German strongholds in the neighbourhood, so as not to forewarn those in the real target area that we Australians will be coming for this very spot.

Thus, at 5 pm, just as the trench mortars start destroying the wire in front of Le Bridoux, so too do an equal number of shells start landing all along the line. This goes on until shortly after midnight, when that man from Tumut, Private Harry Hartnett, in the front-line with his A Company, sees the soldiers of the raiding party start to assemble just back from the front-line he is manning.

In truth, raiding parties are generally a queer-looking lot – in the words of Eddie Rule, 'more like pirates than soldiers'.[62] Like those in the raiding party the week before, both their person and their apparel is as black as their weaponry, and this lot are carrying revolvers as well, while still others have 'knobkerries' – small, lethal, pick-handles tipped with cast-iron cogs on the end, capable of cracking a skull with even a light blow.

All present and accounted for at 12.30 am, with the barrage still underway, the raiding party follows the lead of Lieutenants Albert Hyde and Austin 'Lockie' Laughlin. Some 50 Australian soldiers of the 6th – the best of the best, whittled down from the 400 men of the battalion who had volunteered – steal forward over the parapet and through the sally ports left in the wire, with another 22 men in support protecting the rear and flanks. Just like the previous raiding party, they have trained extensively for this exercise 'and practised on a facsimile of the enemy's trenches, which had been reproduced, eight feet deep, at the divisional bomb-school'.[63]

Across the muddy field, 'neath the dim light thrown by a setting moon, the party stealthily moves, now following their Intelligence Officer, Lieutenant John Rogers, who takes the lead, compass in hand. Their eyes try to pick out the obstacles in their way through the drizzle of cold rain that has just begun, from shell holes and abandoned farm equipment to the dead bodies of men who had previously tried to cross this expanse. Right behind Rogers, ready to surge forward, are the bomb parties, whose job it is to quell initial resistance before the trench parties move in to capture prisoners. Behind them trails the support party, who will secure the portals to No-Man's Land – guarding the flanks, looking to stop counter-attacks cold – and last are the signallers, with one of them, Gallipoli veteran Corporal James 'Mutt' Barker, in turn trailing a telephone wire so they can keep in touch with the artillery (which makes it a state-of-the-art raid indeed, this being a first for an Australian venture). The man in charge of the whole raid is Captain Percy Moncur, who stays at the back of the main group.

About halfway across the 220 yards, still undetected, they pause to take shelter behind a small lip of dirt thrown up by a shell crater. Just ahead, they can hear a German working party right in front of The Angle, hammering in stakes for some purpose or other, likely to support wire entanglements.

Well, they likely won't be there long. Lieutenant Hyde confirms their exact position, gives the order over the telephone and, sure enough, at exactly 12.50 am, a heavy artillery barrage coming from the batteries of the 1st and 2nd AIF Divisions starts raining down on the wire and trenches right in front of them, and the hammering stops and . . .

And bloody hell. Some of those shells are landing short, just to the right flank of the raiding party – throwing mud and detritus all over them. This time, mercifully, no one is badly injured, and the raiders are able to steal forward once more.

Their advance is carefully timed so that, at precisely 1 am, when the box barrage begins, the raiding party is positioned to attack.

Suddenly, alas, just before the enemy parapet, their way is barred once more by another belt of barbed wire that had previously gone undetected as it lies just in front of the German lines 'in a wide ditch . . . from which earth had originally been taken in order to cover the front slope of the breastwork'.[64]

Most dangerously now, the raiding party, previously spread out for safety's sake, bunches against it, as the men with wire-cutters come to the fore and snip their way through, while German flares start to go up on either flank. And now here is a German soldier come to investigate the strange noises, his silhouette rising from the trenches. A shot rings out and Lieutenant Laughlin staggers, shot in the leg, before whipping out his Webley revolver and killing the sentry with a single barked reply.

And now, just as they have minutely planned, four soldiers move forward carrying cricket mats for this stickiest of wickets, which they throw over the last of the wire to allow the others to get over the last barrier without trouble. They're in! Now the bomb-throwing party hurl their Mills bombs all at once, ideally to land right on the noggins of the Boche, an instant before the other soldiers charge forward.

Following Lance-Corporal Josiah Fogarty, 'a bayonet man',[65] a soldier who'd sooner a fight than a feed – and one who on this night has the honour of being the first into the German trenches – the rest rush forward. And it is like a miracle. For their Intelligence Officer, young Rogers, has landed them bang on the money, in the very part of the trenches that they have trained for on replicas. They know every twist and turn of the way and can move through, even in darkness, as if they were in their own homes. But if only their own homes could be as clean and well organised as these trenches.

For as the raiding party charges forward, they are stunned at just how carefully constructed the German trenches are, all of them 'floored with boards like a house, and noticeably clean and dry',[66] and this one even has electric lighting and telephones.

Defenders are remarkably scarce for the moment – many having taken shelter from the drizzle on what had seemed like a quiet night – with just one retreating in the distance as the Australians arrive. As the Australians move back, however, to the dugouts and superbly constructed sleeping quarters, the pickings are more promising, and they soon find a leg coming from a bed. When they pull roughly on it, a German soldier emerges: 'Mercy, *Kamerad*! Me come, *Kamerad*!'[67] He is quickly bundled backward until he gets to the party before the parapets specifically charged with taking prisoners back, and they do so immediately.

And now look at this, Bluey! The German trenches have highly sophisticated, superbly engineered bombardment shelters, where soldiers under heavy shelling can secrete themselves and pull a heavy metal door across behind them! When one is pulled back, the Australians quickly have another prisoner. And now two Germans charge forward out of the darkness, both quickly killed by Sergeant William Fullerton, who shoots one and hits the other with his heavy 'knobkerrie'. Corporal Fogarty is equally quick to dispatch one German with a bayonet, before taking another prisoner.

Now, far on the left flank, another steel door is opened and a light shines out . . . a bomb is hurled in.

The raiding party gather what booty they can in the time that remains, amazed that they are seeing so few Germans and that a counter-attack is not already underway. Soon enough, the word comes from the raid commander, Captain Moncur – who has stayed on the enemy parapet, trying to keep a grasp on all that is happening from this forward position – that he wishes them to return. Meantime, he orders the Australian artillery to shorten the range, his words being transmitted by Private Hubert Higgs, who manages to ignore, for the moment, that he has been shot in the head, and send Captain Moncur's order in the right code – 'Hooray'[68] – for shelling to resume on the enemy's front-line.

Yes, sir.

Quickly now.

The withdrawal of the raiding party is not a minute too soon. For now, as German flares soar above and start descending right upon them, they are suddenly exposed to heavy Hun fire and must make a run for it. Mercifully, the Germans firing are at just enough distance that the running Australians tend to have bullets flicking the rain from the wet grass at their feet, rather than slamming into their heads and torsos, and apart from three wounded in the course of the attack, and the deep scratches many of them bear from the barbed wire, the raiding party is able to get away scot-free. They have killed around a dozen of the enemy while over there and have even come back with six German prisoners – *and* brought back a heavy German machine gun, weighing over 150 pounds. (And that's one in the eye for the two Stokes mortars taken by the Germans the month before.)

Private Hartnett is relieved to see them all so intact and victorious but suspects what will follow. For, sure enough, that raiding party has soon disappeared back towards Fleurbaix, while Hartnett and his companions are subject to a furious fusillade of shells. The Australians have broken the tacit agreement – for they have dropped no fewer than an extraordinary 2500 shells on the German lines – and now must pay the price. It wounds several men on the Australian side but, mercifully, there are no deaths.

All up, the exercise has been a stunning success, and, as a reward, all members of the raiding party are given ten days' leave, to *London*, can you imagine? 'All sorts of congratulatory messages arriving from Generals Plunkett and Birdwood, drawn up and congratulated by latter,' one raider records. 'We marched back in the morning with our faces still blackened.'[69]

Their raid has been well led, superbly organised and long trained for, and its success has proved the virtues and necessity of all three factors.

—

Two days later, on 14 June, with the provisional date for the launch of the Battle of the Somme set as 29 June, subject to the weather, Haig's HQ issues the order: 'As many raids as possible should be undertaken between June 20th and 25th.' Shortly thereafter, however, an amendment adds that there should be, if possible, 'between the 20th and 30th of June . . . a raid each night on the corps front . . .'[70]

On the same day, General Sir Charles Monro calls together his First Army Corps Commanders, informing them that 'the reason I am holding the conference in the first place is so I might tell you what I know about the proposed offensive operations, while at the same time emphasising the importance of the occasion and the necessity for everyone to do their utmost act up to the spirit of the GHQ instructions. Everyone must be strained up to the highest pitch of efficiency and energy with a view to harassing the enemy, containing his reserves and giving him no rest day or night.'[71]

In the subsequent discussion, the key question arises of whether or not, after conducting a raid, they might actually hold on to it. 'It depends on what GHQ desires,' Haking replies. 'From the point of view of containing the enemy's reserves there is no doubt that holding portions of the hostile trenches would be by far the most efficacious method. It would make the enemy counter-attack and spend ammunition.'

'I will ascertain from the Commander-in-Chief to see what he wants,' Sir Charles says. 'But I do agree that the holding of the enemy's trenches would be by far the most effective method of fulfilling the spirit of the GHQ instructions.'[72]

All up, Haig's order is well received by the armies north of the Somme, with General Birdwood suggesting to his Second Army commander Plumer, DURING THE LATTER PART OF THE PERIOD NAMED WE MIGHT TRY A RAID ON A BROADER FRONT – SAY THAT OF A COMPANY.[73]

At last!

For Haking, such an order is manna from heaven. True, his men had been heavily involved in the previous year's Battle of Aubers Ridge and Battle of Loos, and between both battles cumulatively he has lost 20,000 men. But, completely undeterred and seemingly untroubled by those losses, he is more than eager to try again. So eager, in fact, that within two days he puts forward to General Sir Charles Monro, Commander of the First Army, a list of 13 possible raids he would like to pursue. The list includes two operations that are in fact full-blown attacks on two salients in his area – effectively, bumps in the line that jut towards the British and are always problematic because of their proximity to British lines and their capacity to send enfilading fire down No-Man's Land. One is known as the Boar's Head; the other the Sugar-loaf . . .

At Boar's Head, Haking wishes to attack the bulge in the German line, while at the Sugar-loaf in front of Fromelles, his idea – which he had broached with Birdwood and White a fortnight earlier, and actually planned for the first time the previous winter – is to launch an attack with a view to 'capturing and holding permanently 2,100 yards of the enemy's trenches . . .'[74]

For the moment, although the proposals are well received by General Monro, no further action is pursued.

15 JUNE 1916, BEF HQ, MONTREUIL, HAIG SETS HIS SIGHTS ON POZIÈRES

General Haig is just back from London, where he had been when the most stunning news had broken. On 5 June, Lord Kitchener had perished aboard HMS *Hampshire*, one of 650 fatalities from the crew of 655 and seven passengers, after the ship struck a German mine off the Orkneys and soon sank by the bows. He was on his way to Russia.

At least Kitchener had no children to mourn for him.

For his part, Haig had been overjoyed to at last manage to be reunited with his wife, Doris, and two young daughters, and have what could have been a wonderfully anonymous few hours sitting on a beach in Kent with his beloved, while the girls gambolled about. Here, the war seems so far away it is delightful. Alas, noticing that he was still attracting a great deal of attention from other beach-goers, he and Doris turned around to find the girls had written in large letters on the rock face behind them:

THIS IS SIR DOUGLAS HAIG.[75]

While in London, Haig had attended a meeting of the War Council at 10 Downing Street to make clear what his needs would be for the coming offensive and receive their thoughts in turn.

And that is why now, a fortnight before the attack begins in earnest, he has called to Montreuil all of his principal army commanders in France, the Generals Henry Rawlinson, Hubert Gough, Sir Edmund Allenby, Sir Charles Monro and Sir Herbert Plumer – listed in rough order of the luxuriance of their moustaches. They of course arrive with their most senior cadres of officers, whose facial hair is, appropriately, a little more modest. (When it comes to girth, however, Sir Charles Monro is the clear leader, with Haig once having recorded that he regarded him as 'rather fat'.)[76]

On a few points now, Haig is very clear: 'The length of each bound forward by the infantry depends on the area which has been prepared by the artillery . . .

'The advance of *isolated detachments* [except for reconnoitring purposes] shall be avoided. They lead to loss of the boldest and best without result: Enemy can concentrate on these detachments. Advance shall be uniform. Discipline and the power of subordinate Commanders shall be exercised in order to prevent troops getting out of hand.'[77]

The Commander-in-Chief of the BEF emphasises how important it is that the Fourth Army, under the command of Rawlinson, achieves its objective, on which much of the fate of the campaign will rest. 'Firstly,' he says, directing his remarks straight at Rawlinson, 'you must gain the line of the Pozières heights, organise good observation posts, and consolidate a strong position.'[78]

For those heights of Pozières lie right in the middle of the British area of attack and are the highest point of the battlefield – the particular summit is marked by the ruins of a windmill and lies 500 yards north-east of the village. It won't be easy, as the Germans have heavily fortified all their positions and have defended it staunchly from the beginning. That much is verified by the fact that behind the front-line series of two trenches is a second series of trenches, known as the old German lines, and they are also heavily manned.

Haig goes on: 'If the Enemy's defence is strong and fighting continues for many days, as soon as Pozières heights are gained, the position should be consolidated, and improved . . .'[79]

Another point to cover, and Haig is particularly strong on it, is that 'reserves must not be wasted in impossible frontal attacks against strong places – they should rather be thrown in between these strong places . . .'[80]

Finally the meeting is over. The staff cars arrive once more and the Generals and their 'bumbrushers' (as the Diggers refer to their batmen, as ubiquitous as they are obsequious) return to their own HQs to conduct their own briefings to their own mid-ranking officers, who in turn can brief their men.

One of those so briefed is of course General Birdwood, who of course has much food for thought. The way things are turning out, it looks a real possibility that his men of I Anzac Corps will themselves be thrown into this coming Battle of the Somme. He has already been told, a fortnight earlier, that they should be prepared to move to another part of the front, and the Somme is the obvious choice.

So it is that even the newly arrived divisions must be battle-prepared, and it is with this in mind that on this same day Birdwood orders that the first troops of the 4th Division, which had arrived in Bailleul on 10 June, be blooded on the front-line as soon as possible.

16 JUNE 1916, CHÂTEAU DE LA MOTTE AUX BOIS, A CHAT WITH BRUDENELL WHITE

It is the same for all journalists, whatever the subject matter. Always within any organisation, there are fonts of wisdom and information that you can rely on – and fountains of foolery that you are wasting your time in even talking to.

For Charles Bean, the I Anzac Corps Chief of Staff General Brudenell White is definitely of the former variety. And as the Chief of Staff is visiting Birdwood's HQ at Château de la Motte aux Bois on this afternoon, Bean takes the time to catch up with him in his quarters.

The conversation turns to a particular missive Keith Murdoch has sent to Bean, asserting gross incompetence on the part of the British authorities, both political and military. 'You know my opinion, Bean,' breaks in Brudenell White, with enough warmth to turn his face red. 'I think [Asquith, Kitchener et al.] ought to have been put on . . . trial for undertaking that [Dardanelles] expedition. I do honestly. Hamilton may not have been a success but we know that if he had had the help which these Generals here have – the ammunition and guns and so on – if they had backed him up as they back up other Generals, he would have got through.'[81]

It is a staggering comment. This time last year, it would have been unthinkable for this most senior of Australian officers to have expressed a disloyal opinion about the British command. But now things are different. More and more of the senior Australian leadership are becoming wary of their British military superiors – and never more so than when it comes to those British dealing with Australian soldiers.

—

As it happens, many Australian officers have problems with many English officers, and none more so than Albury's Lieutenant-Colonel Walter Cass, of the 54th Battalion. For Colonel Cass is in love with a Canadian officer, one Helena Holmes, a native of Truro, Nova Scotia, who is trying to decide whether her own love resides with him or with an English officer by the name of Sam McInerney.

The passionate Cass thinks of Helena as 'a beautiful queen with a "touch-me-not" air' about her,[82] and it wasn't quite that their ships had passed in the night so much as, five years ago, they had been on the same ship crossing the Indian Ocean going from India to Perth, and Cass had wooed her and pursued her ever since by His Majesty's mail service, without ever actually seeing her again. Though he has never even kissed her, he certainly *wants* to, and is distressed to hear in a letter from her just how far she has progressed with the said McInerney.

'Sorry to hear you have been making love to another man, even if his name is McInerney,' he writes to her on this day. 'You see, dear, you will be so expert and I such a novice that I should be quite out of it and comparisons are odious. So don't please be too expecting when we meet or I shall run and run away to practice on someone else. You don't know how you harrow my feelings when you tell me of all these conquests. And if I flirted with a nurse here, I could hardly be blamed, could I . . .? As for pretty halfwits like the English subaltern – well if we swapped our knowledge of soldiering and their table manners we might be farther ahead in this war (for he is such a fool). Now dear that subject makes me feel ill and I shall say no more of the English officer . . .?'[83]

Chapter Six

'ON THE ROAD TO ROUEN'

Blessed be those happy ages that were strangers to the
dreadful fury of these devilish instruments of artillery,
whose inventor I am satisfied is now in hell.[1]
Miguel de Cervantes, Don Quixote

[Haig] wore down alike the manhood and the guns
of the British army almost to destruction.[2]
Winston Churchill, The World Crisis

16–17 JUNE 1916, MOASCAR, THE 5TH DIVISION PACKS UP, HEADS OUT, MOVES ON

After four solid months in the land of the Pharaohs, at long last the 5th
Division has got the word. They are to march from the Canal back to
Moascar, where a train awaits them.

True, the march is only five miles, but even that is enough. 'Our
packs,' a comrade of Bert and Ray Bishop's in the 55th Battalion writes,
'are packed that way that we could not even get an extra toothbrush in
and in addition to this load we have to carry our blankets and waterproof and 24 hours rations. Even in this short march we were fairly
fagged out, for after all it is an unnatural load for a human being to
carry – in all it must weigh over 100 lbs.'[3]

And speaking of unnatural loads, the open railway trucks waiting for them at Moascar are clearly designed for carrying tons of coal, or perhaps timber, but no matter. For, of course, the soldiers of the 5th Division climb on board as ordered, and are no sooner settled than the swarming 'Gyppos' are crowding around, offering their wares: 'Eggs-a-cook, tomatoes, doughnuts, o-rang-gas, very good, very cheap, *upta* . . .!'[4]

Tell you what, cobber, after months of bread topped with fly jam, and stew that would not just kill a brown dog but very likely *is* a brown dog, the Gyppos' fresh fare looks good, don't it? It does. And no matter that we haven't had a pay day for weeks. That just means that the obvious must happen . . .

In only the time it takes to say 'Come 'ere, you bloody Gyppo!' something like 2000 men have jumped off the train and simply helped themselves, entirely ignoring the howls of outrage from the hawkers. Shouts, screams, Arabic imprecations. The Gyppos do what they can to defend their wares, but they would have had more chance of keeping fresh sausages from 2000 starving dingoes. Within two minutes, all the soldiers are back on the carriages, with eggs, doughnuts, tomatoes and every bit of fruit they can carry, leaving behind many still dazed and bleeding hawkers.

The Australian officers do what they can, throwing whatever 'disasters' – piastres – they have at the outraged locals, but it is little enough. The Australian troops have committed whatever the evening equivalent of daylight robbery is.

'*Maleesh*.' You know, Digger slang – appropriated from Arabic – for 'It doesn't really bloody matter'.

The train gets underway, just as the dusk of the desert starts to close in, and they are soon rolling and rocking through the moonlit landscape on this spectacularly starry night, gorging on their fresh food the way Ali Baba and his 40 thieves likely once did in these parts. Sated, they fall asleep, well pleased with the world.

Dawn brings them into Alexandria Harbour and the sure vision that, at last, their ships have come in. For there, tied to the wharves and waiting for them, are a number of the 14 troopships that have been earmarked to take the 18,000 Australian soldiers of the 5th Division across the Mediterranean.

Among them are Brigadier-General Pompey Elliott and his men of the 15th Brigade. The last few months have been tumultuous, and there have been many frustrations, but Elliott has been generally pleased with the development of his men as fighting soldiers ready for battle, and with none more so than his pride and joy: the 60th Battalion under Major Geoff McCrae and his second-in-command, Major Tom Elliott. They are 'both magnificent young officers',[5] with the one qualification being, as Pompey would later note of Major McCrae, 'The only fault I have ever had to find with him was that he was too gentle & kindly & hated to *tell off* those who thoroughly deserved it but this fault (if fault it was) was rapidly being remedied as he grew older & more experienced.'[6]

However, Major Tom Elliott – no relation to Pompey Elliott – has proved to be something else again. This son of a Sydney labourer is nothing less than the most extraordinary young officer that Pompey has ever come across in his long career. A complete package of intellect, work ethic, decisiveness, charisma and character, young Elliott has displayed from the first the capacity to speak to the men on their own level, and amazingly enough has also excelled on the administrative side, with paperwork. Pompey has developed a near filial regard for him.

'He was immediately placed in command of a company of the 60th Battalion consisting of raw, and in many cases, unpromising material,' Pompey, the notoriously hard marker of his junior officers, would later recount of Tom Elliott's early period with the battalion. 'His personality was of such sterling value that . . . the company speedily became a well disciplined and trained fighting unit. Men considered incorrigible were unable to resist his authority and generally became good soldiers.'[7]

And now, after all these months of training, not only has the 5th Division's ship come in, but it has also gone out again, with them on it – the finest battalion in the 15th Brigade – and it now ploughs north, the men eager to join their fellow Diggers already in France.

Four days behind Pompey Elliott comes the rest of his brigade, most of the rest of the 5th Division and . . .

And, oh, how the mighty have fallen.

Back in the day, *Caledonia* was a luxury passenger liner of great repute. No less than 500 feet long, with two storeys of white on the upper deck, adorned by two great black, cylindrical funnels, she plied her plush trade back and forth across the mighty Atlantic between Glasgow and New York City, accommodating 250 First Class passengers, 350 Second Class and 850 steerage, which is to say Third Class. But, seriously, it was all about First Class passengers, who could feast in her First Class dining saloon on eight-course meals – Sweetbreads à la Dreux, followed by Roast Prime Beef with Horseradish, anybody? – before adjourning to her magnificent Music Hall, and, after a nightcap in either the Ladies' Boudoir or the Gents' Smoking Rooms, retire to floral wallpapered cabins from where they could summon a steward by virtue of electric bell . . .

But not anymore, cobber! Now she is a troopship that can squeeze in well over 3500 of us soldiers of the 5th Division and over 200 of our horses and lug us across the Mediterranean. Now it's all canvas cots stacked tightly up against the cabin walls and all throughout the ship, the Music Hall now being one massive dormitory.

After a wretched train ride through the Egyptian desert going all through the night, Bert and Ray Bishop have no sooner stowed their kit below decks than they head off to find their other cousin, Billy Bishop, who they have found out is on board. To get to him, they must make their way through a torrent of sweaty Diggers coming their way, going their way, and heading every other way. 'Crammed like sheep,' one of their fellow Diggers notes. 'Don't know how we shall sleep down below, everyone looked as if they had had a Turkish bath . . .'[8]

Another member of the 55th Battalion is equally unimpressed: 'Bad food [and] damned little of it. No issue of cigarettes & no money to buy anything with such is being a soldier & dying for your country . . .'[9]

These would prove to be merely their opening remarks. For, after a coupla days of laying up in Alexandria's outer harbour, at eight bells on this crystal Mediterranean morning, slowly and with some fanfare, the final convoy of five transport ships that includes *Caledonia* weighs anchor and gets underway, starting the journey north.

They are escorted by four destroyers riding shotgun and are bound for Marseilles, where a train for the Western Front awaits. It is, of course, stinking hot – *as hot as Hay, Hell and Booligal* – and it is hard to either eat or sleep. 'Our mess room a fearful disgrace not fit to feed pigs in,' one of Bert and Ray's fellow soldiers notes in his diary. 'Half the men sit down with only shorts on & the sweat streams out of them if it was not that we are always so hungry could never stand the odour of their bodies. feet etc. A Soldier's life is about the lowest going & curse the day I ever was fool enough to take it on, writing this the perspiration is dripping off me & I am soaked through, food very poor so far.'[10]

And, of course, the rest of the 5th Division are moving out in their own ships. Aboard *Ivernia*, Lieutenant Norm Nicolson settles in with the 52nd Field Artillery Battery, to find themselves on there with several companies of 'Tivey's Gentlemen of the Desert', the 8th Infantry Brigade. Nicolson records in a letter, 'They are looked down upon by the other men who have been on the Peninsula because they were not. They are pining for a fight in order to stop the Gallipoli Brigades poking it at them and calling them the "Bloodless 8th" . . .'[11]

God forbid.

Among those members of the 8th is Corporal Theodor Pflaum, a 19-year-old, and his 18-year-old brother Ray. Two blue-eyed brothers from the South Australian town of Blumberg – renamed 'Birdwood' the previous year, as it just won't do to have a town named after a Bavarian province (where the Pflaums had emigrated from) – they had signed up on the same day, trained together all the way through, and been mainstays of their 32nd Battalion. As they had gone off to war, the one solace for their worried parents was that they would be able to stick together and look after each other. The older and more protective brother, Theodor, intends to, even if he has just left the 32nd to join the 8th Machine Gun Company – his new unit is still part of the same brigade as the 32nd.

20 JUNE 1916, NIEPPE, HAKING AND PLUMER TALK TO A LITTLE BIRDIE

Another day, another meeting. On this occasion, however, it is Haking and Plumer who visit Birdwood, in his Château de la Motte aux Bois in the Forest of Nieppe. The distinguished visitors wish to discuss, as Birdie would recount in his diary, 'possible co-operation between us & XIth Corps'.

With Birdie making no objection, the next day Monro gives Haking permission to liaise directly with Plumer 'as regards offensive operations on my extreme left flank'.[12] Plumer is amenable, agreeing to all that Haking suggests, and asks him to put his scheme of attack in writing.

The bee in Haking's bonnet, to attack Aubers Ridge around Fromelles, is now buzzing as never before.

23 JUNE 1916, MONTREUIL, SIR DOUGLAS IS SATISFIED THAT THE WAR CAN BE WON

At Montreuil-sur-Mer GHQ, the officers rule without question. A story would ever after be told about the strictly enforced rule at the Officers' Club that says no one is allowed to smoke before 8.20 pm, and how it was breached by a General who pulled out a big cigar at 8 pm. The Sergeant-Major knew immediately what to do. 'Bringing in a ladder, he mounted it to the mess clock and set it to 8.20 pm. A General was smoking, therefore it must be 8.20.'[13]

When it comes to the Commander-in-Chief of the entire BEF, the same rule applies, only it is to everything. If he says something is a good idea, then it is an *excellent* idea. And at his Montreuil château, Haig can look at his maps with some satisfaction. For just as the broad thrust of the plan for the coming battle is his, so is much of the fine detail.

All is now in readiness for the greatest artillery barrage the British Army has ever attempted, to begin on the morrow – five days before the planned infantry attack. No fewer than 1450 guns and 1,700,000 shells – which is to say about 150,000 tons of ammunition – have been moved forward under the cover of darkness, ideally to keep the

Germans unaware of what is about to happen to them. Those shells are due to fall on both the German front-lines and secondary lines, before the real Battle of the Somme, the much vaunted 'Big Push', can begin.

And yet, while all this secrecy is all very well, the truth is that both the British and French papers are *publicising* the coming offensive, with even *The Times* helpfully pointing out, the week before, 'the absence of infantry actions at Verdun since Monday probably means that preparations are being made for the fresh "gigantic effort" which our Paris Correspondent predicted'.[14]

In America, *The Washington Post* would soon have a headline and story beginning:

ALLIED DRIVE BEGINS

Signs Point to Real Opening of Superoffensive.

ACTIVITY ON ALL FRONTS

London . . . Every surface indication pointed to the beginning of the long-expected superoffensive of the allies . . .[15]

And isn't that the truth?

After a long day holed up with a poisoned heel, writing summaries of what the Australian soldiers have been doing in April and May, Charles Bean is sitting behind a tightly shuttered window relaxing a little, reading Ian Hay's book *The Right Stuff*, a comic novel about the adventures of a wee Scottish farmer in London. (By the by, though Bean does not know it, the author is then and there serving with the Argyll and Sutherland Highlanders, just ten miles from where Bean sits.) The book is compelling, but still he cannot help but notice the ceaseless tramp of soldiers' feet, together with the clip-clop of horses and the squeak of the wheels of gun-carriages heading east. Yes, as an informed journalist, he has a fair idea of where they are going and what is soon to start, but still.

As ever, he notes what interests him in his diary. 'I can still hear that distant faint rattle – ten or fifteen minutes after it has passed – along the distant cobbled road through the forest – just as you could have heard it in Napoleon's time or Caesar's for that matter . . .'[16]

On and on and on, through the night . . . night after night after night.

And so it goes.

Dear to friends and food for powder,
Soldiers marching, all to die.[17]

24 JUNE 1916, SOMME VALLEY, 'WHITE PUFFS, BLACK PUFFS, BROWN PUFFS AND GREY'

Outside his dugout on this day at 2 pm at the Western Front near Pozières, on the northern reaches of the British Somme offensive, a German *Leutnant* by the name of Ernst Jünger is sitting at his table, on a break, reading Rudolf Herzog's *Die Burgkinder*. The novel has been sent to him by his family, who, like everyone else at home, has been encouraged to post highbrow books to the soldiers at the front, to impress the enemy should they be captured. Suddenly, in the near distance, a powerful boom bursts forth.

An instant later, the lookout screams, *'Achtung!* Shell!'[18]

Jünger jumps so quickly from his chair that he gets tangled up in it, and finally manages to leap into the dugout without his *Mütze*, cap. He is only just in time as '30–40 heavy shells'[19] land in quick succession with a shattering roar as shrapnel flies, men scream and all is engulfed with dust.

—

The Battle of the Somme has begun, as the British guns unleash what is intended to be five days of solid bombardment, even before the battle proper begins. If all goes well for the Allies, the infantry attack will begin on the early morning of 29 June, the date agreed on by the Generals Haig and Joffre.

On a hill overlooking the German positions under attack, around La Boisselle, Lieutenant William Bloor, of the Royal Field Artillery, watches the unfolding carnage below with some satisfaction. 'White puffs, black puffs, brown puffs and grey,' he describes it. 'Puffs which start as small downy balls and spread sideways and upwards till they dwarf the woods. Darts of flame and smoke – black smoke these last which shoots high and into the air like a giant poplar tree. These are the [high explosives].'[20]

What it must be like under such devastating attack, he can barely imagine.

—

Hölle auf Erden! Hell on Earth.

It is like being right in the middle of a thunderstorm, with a constant roaring fury going on all around you, regularly striking dead those closest. The best they can, Jünger and his comrades start to fire back with their *Minenwerfern*, trench mortars, but whatever damage they are doing, they know they don't have the range to hurt the Tommy artillery, as the shells continue to rain upon them. Jünger roars at a newly arrived soldier by the name of Wasmann to keep his eyes on No-Man's Land to warn them if any enemy soldiers are storming towards them.

Wasmann, shaking, does not move. Jünger shouts the order again. And again and again. Paralysed with fear, Wasmann is incapable of movement. And now the enemy artillery have clearly got their range in, as shells that were falling in front and behind are now falling on their trenches and wreaking catastrophic losses. Jünger is hit with a few small steel splinters but manages to keep going.

By now, there are so many shells it is obvious that a man's primary duty is just to survive. Jünger and most of his comrades retreat to secure dugouts, leaving only a skeleton crew of observers – just one man per platoon on the top side – ready to call them up if there is any general advance.[21]

———

With great malice aforethought, the British artillery continues to inflict as much damage as possible. After high-explosive shells pound villages where the Germans are most heavily quartered, then comes heavy artillery firing shrapnel shells – timed to explode at that point above the ground where the radius of shrapnel will be at its widest and most devastating, hopefully 'to destroy any men who might then be exposed like ants upon a disturbed ant-heap'.[22]

At other times, the artillery focuses on destroying enemy batteries, and then communication trenches. Most heavily hit of all are front-line trenches and the barbed-wire entanglements that protect them from ground attack, in the hope that a passage can be forced. And yet, the intensity of those attacks is inevitably diluted by General Haig's desire that the second line is also hit. Still, together, a hurricane of hell descends: 'The field-guns placing a whirlwind of shrapnel on the enemy's front-line, while the 6-inch howitzers fired on targets farther back and the 8-and-9-inch howitzers on a line more distant still, the whole artillery thus creating a barrage of 800 yards in depth.'[23]

Along the line, particular German strongholds such as Pozières and Thiepval are pulverised unmercifully. At regular intervals, box artillery patterns are put on the Germans exactly as will be used on the day of the real attack, by way of rehearsing and also to conceal the infantry attack from Fritz when that time comes.[24]

Are they doing enough damage? One close observer is Charles Bean, and he is under no doubt that 'the earthern walls of the enemy's forward trenches were practically everywhere blown or shaken down and the area immediately around the front turned into something like a sea of shell-craters'.[25]

The question they all have, however, is whether the German dugouts holding their soldiers remain fundamentally intact.

—

In his concrete-reinforced dugout at La Boisselle, alongside the Albert–Bapaume road, *Leutnant* Wilhelm Geiger of the 111th RIR has just put his head on the sandbag he is using for a pillow after a long night on duty at the signals desk and is pulling his greatcoat up around him for a blanket when all hell breaks loose in the dugout. The lights go out and there are shouts in the darkness and choking dust . . . but they are alive. At least, most of them are. The man who had taken Geiger's spot at the desk, *Leutnant* Jansen, slumps forward, dead, *mit einem Splitter im Kopf*, with a splinter of steel in his head. 'His hand,' Geiger would recount, 'still held the pencil that he was using to write a letter to his wife. It was, I believe, his sixth wedding anniversary.'[26]

Elsewhere in the dugout, some beams have come down but the fact remains: despite the hits it is taking, most of the structure is holding, and the men will live to fight on.

A little to the north, on the other side of the Ancre River, in a deep dugout at Beaumont Hamel, *Landwehr Leutnant* M. Gerster, of the 119th Bavarian RIR, would report that though the artillery fire was 'nerve shattering', he and his comrades, 'tired and indifferent to everything', were able to 'sit it out on wooden benches, staring into the darkness when the tallow lights were extinguished by the explosions . . . Whose heart was not in his mouth at times during this appalling storm of steel? All longed for it to end one way or another . . . A searing rage against the enemy burned in our minds.'[27]

And so it goes.

When it turns dark after the first day's barrage, and the blizzard of shells landing on them seems to ease somewhat, *Leutnant* Ernst Jünger and his comrades emerge from their deep dugouts. They are shaken, but alive. 'All came out of the earthy holes,' Jünger would write, 'pleased about being so well prepared [to survive such an attack].'[28]

At his GHQ, General von Falkenhayn is not remotely surprised that the barrage has descended, as the Germans have expected exactly this for some time. So be it. All that can be done to protect their soldiers has been done, all requests of the Second Army for reinforcements in that particular area been met as much as possible, and he is as confident that the vast majority of his soldiers will survive in their dugouts as he is that they will be ready for the British infantry charging forward, whenever that occurs.

Von Falkenhayn does not fear it, and, in fact, in his memoirs describes it as 'the long-expected and hoped-for enemy offensive'.[29] His only surprise is that it appears to be falling here, on the Somme, instead of where he has predicted, up around Lille.

25 JUNE 1916, ABOVE THE SOMME, ATTACK OF THE BALLOON BUSTERS

Moving in packs, the British Airco DH.2s and French Nieuports diving on the German observation balloons are like a flock of angry hawks attacking so many defenceless, fat pigeons. And, yes, the German Ack-Ack roars with rage as it tries to defend the balloons, but the planes are so numerous and the attack so well executed, using incendiary bullets designed to turn them into flaming hydrogen horrors, that in just a matter of minutes the German observation balloons are no more.

The barrage on the German lines, meanwhile, goes on.

Deep in his concrete dugout just south of Thiepval, Private Eversmann of the German Army's 26th Reserve Division is struggling, as the pounding makes the beams on his ceiling descend by as much as four inches. Like all the others, he has no choice but to hold on. 'The barrage has now lasted thirty-six hours,' he writes in his diary. 'How long will it go on? In twelve hours shelling they estimate that 60,000 shells have fallen on our battalion sector. Every communication with the rear has been cut, only the telephone is working. When will they attack – tomorrow or the day after? Who knows?'[30]

MORNING, 25 JUNE 1916, ABOARD *CALEDONIA*, A MALTESE CROSSING TO HOME

An uncanny stillness suddenly permeates the ship. The engines have stopped.

After three days of pushing north across the glassy sea, those below decks aboard *Caledonia* and its accompanying ships suddenly realise they have come to a halt. Rushing up to the top deck, near noon, they find themselves at anchor in Malta's fine St Paul's Bay – about halfway to Marseilles. (A German submarine sighting on the route ahead means they have had to divert to a safe harbour.)

They have come to an ancient land, with the shores of the harbour lined with crumbling fortifications 'built up in a succession of walls',[31] which, back in 1565, had allowed no less than the Knights of St John to hold off the Ottomans in the Great Siege of Malta. And yet, they are close enough to the port to see something of the inhabitants and establish, as one Digger puts it, that 'they seem to be a clean class of people for a dark race'.[32]

One who knows that better than any of them is an Australian soldier who was born and raised here before emigrating, and who can now see his childhood home across the waters. 'My people, my mumma, my poppa, they live just there!' he tells his mates in his thickly accented English, pointing with a mixture of excitement and frustration to a small pod of white cottages that lie right by the ancient fortifications.

'Swim for it!' one bloke encourages.

'No, no, too far,' he says in near tears. 'I poor swimmer, and ship might go.'

Still, he has been overheard by an officer, who ducks away and minutes later returns with the 55th's Commanding Officer, Lieutenant-Colonel David McConaghy, and a high-ranking officer of the ship. 'We're not getting under way till dark,' the ship's officer tells the Maltese-born man. 'If you wish, it is O.K. as far as the ship is concerned.'[33]

McConaghy gives his orders and it is done. A four-man crew with a longboat is provided, a ship's ladder thrown over the sides, and this son of Malta is quickly on his way, to the cheers of his mates. He may spend one hour ashore, and not a minute more, and must immediately return to the ship. And there he goes – beside himself with excitement – as the longboat wends its way through the other ships.

The Diggers who remain are given permission to swim in the cool water. Ah, the sunbathed frolics of these young men as they swan-dive like kids from the upper decks, duck each other, splash water into each other's faces, race from ship's side to ship's side and chiack around. Yes, the dangers of the Western Front lie ahead, and that is a worry, but for now they can do one of those things that Australians have always done remarkably well: fool around in the sea! (Another of their talents, of course, is fighting, and one or two of the more educated Diggers are able to point out the curious eight-pointed Maltese Crosses seen atop the churches on shore. This is the cross that the most coveted bravery award of them all, the Victoria Cross, was supposed to be based on. Who knows which one of them might be awarded it one day?)

A couple of hours before sundown, as promised, here comes their Maltese mate, beaming from ear to ear. He scrambles aboard *Caledonia* amid great cheering and excitedly tells his cobbers that he'd seen his family, soaked up their love and joy, and drenched them with his. Watching it all, a fellow turns to Bert Bishop and reflects, 'Wasn't that a wonderful thing to happen? Humanity isn't completely dead.'[34]

Not yet anyway.

That night, when they are under way once more – with all a little nervous owing to the rumour that now *seven* Austrian submarines are stalking convoys and have already sunk a ship called the *City of Mexico*[35] – the moon rises above the shimmering ripples of the Mediterranean. Those moonbeams manage to just illuminate three men speaking softly on the foredeck of *Caledonia*. They have a manner, a way of having their heads close to each other, that makes it obvious they are either the tightest of friends, or family.

In this case, they are the tightest of both. The cousins Ray, Bert and Billy Bishop are talking of their time just gone in Egypt and what likely lies ahead in France, at the Western Front, when Billy suddenly starts talking of what they will all do when they get home, how they will properly celebrate their safe arrival back among kith and kin. The three argue passionately, each coming up with different ways to celebrate their safe return, and the only thing they can agree on is that they would all go on a holiday together. And then, all at once, just as they're about to plan the details of their joint holiday, much the same thought strikes all three, as the shadow of the Valley of Death passes over them. 'A cold, clammy feeling came into the air,' Bert would record. 'It was difficult to describe. The joy and fun disappeared, we all remained silent for some minutes.'

With nary a word spoken, but all of them knowing what they are thinking, they gather their blankets and head off to their sleeping berths on the mess decks below. The holiday is never referred to again.

NIGHT OF 25/26 JUNE 1916, BOIS GRENIER, BILLY GIVES A HAND FOR HIS COUNTRY

Another night, another raid, this one right on midnight. With the attack on the Somme Valley now only days away, it is more important than ever that the Germans be kept guessing as to where the Allies' focus is. On this night, nine officers and 73 volunteer soldiers of lower ranks drawn from the 17th, 18th, 19th and 20th Battalions from the 2nd Division head out, among them an 18-year-old, Private William Jackson, who hails from the tiny town of Gunbar in the Riverina. Known as 'Billy' to his family and 'Jacko' to his mates, the previous year he had successfully lied about his age by 12 months to join up, courtesy of his solid build and imposing height. He is now a veteran not only of Gallipoli in general but also of the famed 'Battle of Hill 60' in that campaign. Which is to say, he has been under heavy fire before and, to his surprise, is not too troubled by it.

Still, on this night – his heart in his mouth, his hand on his rifle and his bayonet handy – he is with the foremost group of 'scouts', charged with reconnoitring the enemy defences, particularly their listening posts. It is important to know where these shallow, disguised positions in No-Man's Land are placed, and they are proceeding carefully.

'It was pitch dark,' Jackson would later recount. 'It suited me. I see well in the dark.'[36]

An instant after a box barrage of artillery comes down, the raiding party comes under furious fire from the now alerted Germans in the front-lines. And yet, after replying in kind, they are able to neutralise the defenders to the point where, in seemingly no time at all, the entire party has been able to cover the 400 yards of No-Man's Land and enter the enemy's trenches. Quickly now, the Australian engineers place their sticks of dynamite in those parts of the ammunition dumps and bomb stores where they are guaranteed to take the whole lot with them when they blow, and then trail their electrical wires and plungers back a safe distance.

The others, meanwhile, quell whatever resistance remains and essay to capture prisoners for interrogation, as ordered. Of course, the inevitable occurs. Once the German Divisional HQ realise that their front trenches have been taken, they bring down heavy artillery fire from their closest batteries, meaning that the Australians must withdraw – pausing only for an engineer to press the plunger and blow the lot sky-high.

And *that* should give Fritz the shits.

They make their way back across No-Man's Land with shells exploding all around, and many of them are inevitably hit.

After escorting a German soldier he has taken prisoner back to Australian lines, young Jackson hears that some injured comrades have been left behind. 'But I didn't like leaving any wounded men out there,' he would later recount.[37] So he heads back out. After indeed bringing a wounded man in, even though the shelling and machine-gun fire is heavier than ever, *again* he goes out to bring in another. It takes some doing, but with the help of the 19th Battalion's Sergeant Hugh Camden, Billy Jackson is able to get yet one more wounded comrade, Private Alfred Robinson, on his shoulders. He is staggering back to the Australian line, with Robinson's blood pouring down his back, when a shell explodes nearby and a piece of shrapnel 'blew my right hand clean off . . . a pretty clean job'.[38] It also knocks Sergeant Camden unconscious and wounds Robinson further for his trouble.

Jackson, knowing he can no longer carry the wounded man unless he stops the blood gushing from his stump, returns for help, has a tourniquet applied by use of a string and stick, and returns once more in an effort to bring the sergeant and the wounded man back in. He stays out there for a further 30 minutes until satisfied that no wounded man has been left behind.

No Australian is killed on the night, though 14 are wounded. The Germans suffer *dreißig tote Soldaten*, 30 soldiers killed.

Though Jackson does not know it yet, his actions will earn him the first Victoria Cross to be awarded to an Australian on the Western Front – the youngest man born beneath the Southern Cross ever to be given the honour, and invested by King George V himself, at Buckingham Palace.

A small parenthesis here. Over a year later, young Jackson, accompanied by Sergeant Camden, arrives in Hay, a town in the Riverina still glorying in the fact that the first Australian winner of the VC at the Western Front had come from nearby Gunbar. The huge crowd gather to meet him at the railway station, desperate just to 'get a sight of Private Jackson', and it includes many of the people he had grown up with, together with many more that he has never seen before in his life. They cheer him three times through, and three times more for luck, and then the two soldiers are officially welcomed in front of the Post Office, with Hay's Deputy Mayor, Mr Butterworth (the Mayor being out of town), reflecting on Hay's reflected glory in this region having raised such a son that they could all be proud of. Now, though young William Jackson – stunned at his reception in this proud country town, which had always seemed so huge when he was growing up – is not much of a speaker, he does ask Sergeant Camden to speak on his behalf, and that gentleman does the occasion justice. 'Bill was not looking for a VC that night,' he declares, 'he was looking for a cobber.'[39]

And even now the festivities are only just beginning, as Tattersall's

Hotel that evening hosts a dinner for their guests of honour, where many toasts are raised, drinks drunk, and a splendid meal consumed at a table covered with the Union Jack and festooned with table-napkins done to resemble military tents. Such a night! Close parentheses.

LATE JUNE 1916, FROMELLES, THE GERMANS HAVE TO STRAIGHTEN UP, *SCHNELL*!

Sergeant Dominikus Dauner of the 6th Bavarian Reserve Division is annoyed. There is a slovenliness to this lot unworthy of a regiment fighting for the Fatherland, and this company in particular. Not Adolf Hitler, for he remains dedicated to the cause, but others!

'*Ihr taugt nichts*,' Sergeant Dauner shouts this morning at two soldiers who had joined the company earlier in the year. 'You are useless . . . If you . . . were good for anything, you would have a commendation. You fit in well with the regiment. It is full of shirkers and good-for-nothings. You are scallywags. You haven't suffered anything yet.'[40]

But perhaps they will soon. For days now, they have heard the sounds of the fearful bombardment occurring at the Somme, some 50 miles to their south. Already it is clear that a massive battle is under way, and there is a strong likelihood that their regiment, or other regiments in this quiet area, will be drawn into it.

As a member of Regiment HQ – now based at the small village of Fournes, some three miles back from the front-lines of Fromelles, loved by the soldiers for the fact that it feels so *Bavarian* – Hitler and his fellow dispatch runners have their own room, with bunks, in a former estaminet. 'Every one of us in the trench would have given his eye teeth to swap with . . . Hitler even just for eight days,' Josef Stettner, a fellow soldier, later writes in an article.[41] And, indeed, life for the messengers is much better than for those in the very front-lines, as one of Hitler's few friends, Alois Schnelldorfer, had reported to his parents in a letter: 'Everything in our vegetable garden is growing beautifully. I can't wait to taste the first radish.'[42]

However much the others might be jealous of the messengers, at least Hitler and Schnelldorfer have each other, and a few others, for solace. The same cannot be said for another German soldier, positioned well to the south in the German defensive lines of the Valley of the Somme.

Fähnrich (Cadet) Parl is 'Der liebe, kleine Kerl'; the kind, little fellow', with a club foot. His presence among the more robust troops is testament to how desperate the German Army is now for manpower – they will even accept the likes of him. And still, Cadet Parl professes himself eager to take part in a real battle and fidgets with impatience 'um den Zauber mitzumachen, to join the magic . . . to get into the Schützengraben [trench]'.[43]

We'll see how he goes when the shooting starts. The others are less than kind, and make fun of him.

To their north, the German soldiers around Serre take pause in the eventide. For there it is again. A bugler on the other side, an Englishman, is playing a pleasant tune, and for the soldiers on both sides of No-Man's Land it is their favourite time of day – a time to dream of being in more civilised circumstances, where music is just a normal part of life.

Not like here, where their every hour is devoted to working out how best to kill those on the other side, or how best to not be killed by them.

Play on, young man, play on. Das ist gute Musik!

29 JUNE 1916, BOAR'S HEAD, LOWTHER HAS SOME LITTLE LAMBS

Today has, of course, been intended as the day to start the whole Battle of the Somme, but there has been a problem as, in tandem with the shells falling, so has the rain. And the more it has poured down, the thicker the mud has become, deadening the impact of the shells, which were meant to be destroying the rolls of barbed wire in front of the German fortifications. They have been landing with huge THUDS rather than with blasts of shattering shrapnel. The dismal weather has also made it impossible for the observers to register the guns.

In fact, so heavy had the rain been over three days that the British decided to delay the attack until 1 July, extending the bombardment by two days, although inevitably slackening that bombardment in intensity to save shells.

Fortunately, however, there is no reason to stop the raids, and today there is to be a big one. For now is the time for Brigadier-General Richard Haking to prove the truth of his published theory: 'There is one rule which can never be departed from and which will alone lead to success, and that is always to push forward, always to attack.'[44]

It is true that the theory failed at Aubers and Loos, with 28,000 casualties out of 100,000 men thrown in, but this time, *this* time, it will surely work.

Of the 13 proposals for diversionary raids he had put forward a fortnight before, the first one to be approved had been for the salient of Boar's Head, just two miles south-west of the Sugar-loaf Salient, which he also has ambitions to attack. Both lie before Aubers Ridge, which has been an enduring passion of Haking's to take, having been denied twice the previous year in attacks on it.

For this attack, Haking has decided to unleash the 3000 men of the 116th Brigade of the 39th Division. The Brigade includes three 'Pals' Battalions' – Kitchener's idea having been that men who join up as 'pals', drawn from the same town, or calling, or sporting association, will fight as pals and fight better because of it. In this case, the battalions are the 11th, 12th and 13th of the Royal Sussex Regiment, known locally in Sussex as 'Lowther's Lambs', after the Lieutenant-Colonel, Claude Lowther MP, who had raised them in 1914. Having arrived in France only the previous month, they are still really yet to find their feet in terms of trench warfare, but Haking is confident they will be up for the task he has set them.

While one battalion is kept in reserve, two battalions will attack, charging across the 250 yards of No-Man's Land in the wee hours to 'bite off the Boar's Head salient'.[45] Once the attackers enter those trenches, they will clear out whatever German resistance there is and then push on to the support trenches to do the same. There, they will establish a new front-line. If all goes well, this diversionary attack will first confuse the enemy and then soak up some of their precious reserves that might otherwise be sent to the Somme when the battle there starts in two days' time.

All good?

NO!

As it happens, the Officer Commanding 11th Battalion – which has been selected to lead the charge – Lieutenant-Colonel Harman Grisewood, is appalled at the whole idea of sending virgin troops 250 yards over open ground they are entirely unfamiliar with, straight at heavily entrenched German positions. It is his passionate view that the whole thing is bound to fail, as the preparations have been hopelessly hurried and conducted in full view of the enemy; they have been without adequate preliminary bombardment and now have insufficient artillery support; they have no proper intelligence on enemy defences and no element of surprise, using insufficiently trained troops . . .

And he simply wants no part of it.

'I am not,' he tells his Brigade Commander, 'sacrificing my men as cannon-fodder!'[46]

Lieutenant-Colonel Grisewood is, for his trouble, relieved of his command – leaving the front on the eve of the battle – and as further 'punishment', his 11th Battalion loses its prime position in the attack, becoming the Reserve Battalion only, while the 13th Battalion is now in the prow.

For all that, Haking remains confident that they might still be able to surprise the Germans, and that the furious 15-minute barrage he has ordered will break the spirit of what few Germans it does not kill.

However, on the morning of 29 June – under 24 hours before the attack is due to go in – the Sussex men are appalled to see that the Germans have erected signboards on their parapets overnight, reading:

When are you coming over Tommy?[47]

The Germans' guns are primed, their ammunition plentiful, and most of their soldiers secure in their underground dugouts. They are just waiting for the call.

—

That call comes just after 3 am, when the German flares illuminate 2000 men charging at them across *Niemandsland*, No-Man's Land.

Schneller! Schneller!

Faster! Faster!

In fact, the German observers first alert the soldiers sheltering in the dugouts to come forward and man their posts, and then send up red flares – a signal for their artillery to bring down massive fire upon the stretch of No-Man's Land in front of them.

There is no contest. The German soldiers are easily in position before the Sussex men are even halfway across, and a devastating blizzard of bullets and shrapnel gives Death a bountiful harvest of brave youth as never before seen in these parts.

And now the German soldiers don't even need to take shelter behind their parapets but can climb to the top and with perfect observation pick off those few brave Brits who have survived to get even close to the enemy line.

'*Komm*, come on, Sussex!' they roar, encouraging the brave British soldiers to come even closer to their guns.[48]

With much of the first two battalions cut down quickly, the situation is desperate. And yet the carrying party is sent forward as planned, to support those who are still alive, only to be promptly shot down in No-Man's Land – and all but entirely wiped out. Among the dead is Second-Lieutenant Francis Grisewood – who had been running the cattle station he'd bought in Western Australia before returning home to England to join up when the war began – the younger brother of the same Lieutenant-Colonel Grisewood who had been dismissed for predicting this very result. Out in No-Man's Land, with the Pals' Battalions, another six sets of brothers lie dead, while one family, the Pannell family from Worthing, have three sons killed in the action and another taken prisoner.

Of 2000 British soldiers who went over the top at Boar's Head, no fewer than 1153 become casualties, and just under 400 are killed. Not for nothing would it be known in the regimental history as 'The Day Sussex Died'.[49]

It is another slaughter of men under Haking, just like at Aubers and Loos – only this time *full* responsibility lies dead at his feet. General Haking's official report, nevertheless, is positive, insisting that it was 'a successful raid . . .'[50] Not for the raid itself, you see, but for what it accomplished for Sussex, which had previously not 'shown much offensive spirit'. But now look at them. 'I consider that this operation,' Haking reports to his superiors, 'has greatly improved the fighting value of the Division.'[51]

All that notwithstanding, General Haking is quick to sack Brigadier-General Robert Dawson, the Commanding Officer of the 39th Division. And yet the view that Dawson alone is to blame is far from universal. 'The Divisional general was ungummed,' one of the officers present would chronicle, 'but it seemed to us that there were others [like Haking] who were responsible, and, if they had lost their commands after this failure, possibly greater disasters might have been avoided, for a similar experiment was made a little later on with two divisions and the result was exactly the same.'[52]

The survivors of the 39th Division, for their part, are embittered, with one by the name of Edmund Blunden commenting that the only reason the battle had been launched in the first place was that 'Boar's Head . . . was to be "bitten off", no doubt to render the maps in the chateaux of the mighty more symmetrical'.[53]

Just after the war, at least one officer, Major Neville Lytton of the Royal Sussex Regiment, would get his views into print: 'The conception of the attack was so futile that nothing but failure could have resulted. Then as a diversion to the Somme offensive where some forty divisions were concentrated it was absurd to do a show where only one brigade was involved.'[54]

DAWN, 29–30 JUNE 1916, *EN MARSEILLES, FORMEZ VOS BATAILLONS*

There it is! As the rays of the rising sun burn off the mist, and the sea-gulls screech all around, the men of the 5th Division's 55th Battalion can see, off the starboard quarter of *Caledonia*, the shores and town surrounding the very Marseilles Harbour they had dropped anchor in the night before. Soaring cliffs, *green* fields – the first they've seen since leaving Australia – and the rusty red roofs of stone houses. And now, in boats coming their way, the Australian soldiers can see the most wondrous thing of all . . .

Girls.

French girls.

Gorgeous young women, not covered by veils or long dresses or the pox like the women always are in Egypt, but come-hither girls, who come alongside in boats and look at them – I'm telling you, Macca – *appraisingly.*

'*Bienvenue!*' they call. '*BIENVENUE!*'

This is apparently Froggy speak for 'welcome'. Most frustratingly, however, the Diggers have already been told that, although *Caledonia* will be berthed at the wharf by 5 pm, they won't be able to leave the ship till the next day, and all they can do is blow the women kisses.

Do they know where they are going to from here? Not specifically, though certainly they overhear things of interest, as had happened with the 53rd Battalion, when their Commander, Colonel Ignatius Norris, had been heard saying, 'From Marseilles we proceed to Paris and Rouen.'

Upon the burst of laughter, he had quickly followed up with, 'Oh, I don't mean what you think. I am referring to a town [Rouen, not ruin].'[55]

The following morning, sure enough, the men of the 55th are roused at 5 am, and then have to wait . . . . before at last getting onto the wharf at 9.30 am, and then marching the quarter-mile to the railway station to wait . . . . . . for the train. (The one bit of excitement along the way had been when the 55th Battalion band struck up the tune to 'La

Marseillaise', at which point 'the few people who were there nearly went mad. They seem to be a very excitable race of people.')[56]

'In the Train at last,' one Digger writes. 'Have been standing & marching for about 3 Hours with all our gear on Puts you in mind of an old woman getting up at 5 . . . to catch the 11 o' clock Train. These officers would break the heart of an iron monkey always want you ready about 4 hours before time. The Lord only knows how they will lead us or command us at the Front.'[57]

But at least, now, they get to see more French girls. They're on the streets and at the station, and after the soldiers tumble onto the train – eight to a compartment – they strain forward for a better gander. And yet, once they start to rumble through the French countryside – dreamy green fields with neatly trimmed hedges as dividers, filled with poppies, daisies and buttercups – it is a surprisingly close-run thing as to whether it is those fields or the French girls that is the most stunning. At one point, when the train stops beside such a field, the young Australians spontaneously jump off to roll around in all the wonderful *green*-ness of it, to smell the flowers, pick them, chase the bees, laugh like kids and wrestle each other to the fragrant fecundity of, oh, *sweet Mother Earth*.

But then they really do see the French girls up close and the issue is settled. For beside another green expanse – look there, cobber – suddenly comes the vision splendid, on that sunlit field extended, of *dozens* of French girls carrying baskets of luscious strawberries and apples. A very few of the soldiers are able to negotiate with these Gallic girls of awe to part with their fare in exchange for the few local coins they have in their pockets, while the rest must content themselves with just gazing longingly at these luscious lovelies . . . and the strawberries and apples as well.

But now, the most wonderful thing. For just before the train is due to leave, the girls come forward and, for no money, put strawberries and apples into each outstretched hand. It seems to be their way of saying *bienvenue* to France and *merci* for fighting, and even dying, for our country. With their baskets soon empty, they still stand and wave and smile and gaily laugh as those outstretched hands now turn into furiously waving hands in reply.

With everything happening, the spirits on the train are very high, and many of the soldiers sing together a song that has been a favourite among them of late, 'Australia Will Be There'. Ah, sing it, lads, as the glorious French countryside whips past us in the sunshine, and we soak it all up:

> *Rally 'round the banner of your country,*
> *Take the field with brothers o'er the foam;*
> *On land or sea, wherever you be,*
> *Keep your eye on Germany.*
> *But England, home and beauty have no cause to fear,*
> *Should Auld acquaintance be forgot,*
> *No! No! No! No! No! Australia will be there,*
> *Australia will be there.*[58]

The song is in fact so popular among Australian troops that French newspapers have already translated the words, telling their readers it boils down to *'Australie sera la'*.

Northward, ever northward, they push. One officer who is particularly enjoying the view is the man from Albury with the luxurious moustache, Colonel Walter Cass, the Commanding Officer of the 54th Battalion. From his rattling rail-carriage, he pens another letter to the woman he loves, Helena Holmes: '[France is] a glorious country. One could live in it and really enjoy life. After Egypt this place is Paradise. The valley of the Rhone is unequalled even by Canada . . .'[59]

—

At I Anzac Corps HQ at la Motte aux Bois, and II Anzac Corps HQ at Blaringhem, the Generals Birdwood and Godley are relieved to hear that these last of the Australian troops have safely made it across the Mediterranean. For Birdwood, it comes at a significant time. He has just been officially informed that his I Anzac Corps 'should be held ready for sending south at any moment'.[60]

If the Battle of the Somme goes well for the British forces, they will need extra troops to follow up and consolidate the gains. If it goes badly, they will need extra troops to replace those who have been killed. Such is the way of this murderous war. Whatever happens, good or bad, extra troops are always needed to feed into the military machine. French General Charles Mangin had put it best in 1915: 'Whatever you do, you lose a lot of men.'[61]

EVENING, 30 JUNE 1916, CHÂTEAU VALVION, LIKE A PIANIST AT HIS KEYS, SHELLS PLAY ON THE HORIZON OF THE NIGHT SKY

Now at his advanced headquarters at Château Valvion, 15 miles west of the front, General Sir Douglas Haig is writing his own letters on this eve of the battle that he knows will define his career. 'The attack is to go in tomorrow morning at 7.30 am,' he tells his wife, Doris. 'I feel that everything possible for us to do to achieve success has been done. But whether or not we are successful lies in the Power above. But I do feel that in my plans I have been helped by a Power that is not my own. So I am easy in my mind and ready to do my best what ever happens tomorrow.'[62]

As he had already written to King George V, two days earlier: 'Everywhere I found the troops in great spirits, and full of confidence of their ability to smash the Enemy when the moment for action arrives. Several officers have said to me that they have never known troops in such enthusiastic spirits. We must, I think, in fairness, give a good deal of credit for this to the Parsons . . .'[63]

Haig shares the confidence of those troops, of course. And as backup, just in case things *don't* go exactly as planned, he has responded to yet one more appeal from Joffre, and put in place 'a scheme . . . for the withdrawal of fresh formations' from other parts of his front that will allow, whatever happens, for the Battle of the Somme to be prosecuted 'with such vigour as will force the enemy to abandon his attacks on

Verdun'.[64] On this very day, Haig has arranged for I Anzac Corps – all of 1st, 2nd and 4th Divisions – to be placed on standby, ready to be sent south to the Somme.

EVENING, 30 JUNE 1916, AMIENS, THE PRESS PRESS FORWARD

Ever and always, before a major event, there is a conviviality between the men of the press, a sense of shared excitement, of privilege, even of exclusivity – an awareness that they are the envy of all their colleagues back at their home newspapers. Sure, the others all want to be here, but it is *we* who are the chosen ones, we who on this day have pushed past the endless convoys of motor transports and horse-drawn guns and marching soldiers all heading east, to get to this place, at this time.

So it is with the gathered war correspondents at Amiens, just 20-odd miles from the Western Front, as, in the darkness, they gaze to the east. Though their accommodation at the Hotel Belfort in Amiens is close enough to hear the constant explosions like thunder in the distance – rumbling balls of menace that can rattle the soul of those nearby – for them it is like a world away, and they are able to settle down in complete comfort to discuss the events of the day. They are not aware exactly of when the offensive will begin, but they know it is imminent, and all the talk is of what form it will take.

In the midst of the throng, the Australian correspondent Charles Bean settles back into one of the Hotel Belfort's more comfortable lounge chairs. For him, the fact that through the floral patterns of the curtain he can see the constant throbbing anger of the distant battle front brings forth rare whimsy. For it really is a strange thing to see the explosions of those British shells 'playing up and down the distant skyline, running over it from end to end, as a player might run the fingers of one hand lightly over the piano keys. There were three or four flashes every second, here or there in that horizon.'[65]

'Bloody Bosch wont stop until we're beaten into total submission,' says *Times* correspondent John Buchan, the 'natty little Oxford chap of the British civil servant type' and author of *The 39 Steps*, who has just popped up at Bean's elbow.[66]

Bean agrees but remains hopeful that the British Empire is about to beat Germany into total submission itself, starting with this coming offensive in the Somme Valley, which will see, as he had put it in his diary a couple of days earlier, 'the biggest battle that the Empire has ever been engaged in – the last great effort, very likely'.[67]

On this evening, Buchan – who, like Rudyard Kipling, Arthur Conan Doyle and John Masefield, also writes for the War Propaganda Bureau and is supremely well connected within the Establishment – divulges lightly that in this coming offensive, 'the British High Command is prepared to sacrifice as many as half a million men'.

'That is all right for *them*,' one of the other pressmen notes drily, 'but what about the half million?'[68]

PART TWO

HELL'S BELLS IN FROMELLES

'Good-morning, good-morning!' the General said
When we met him last week on our way to the line.
Now the soldiers he smiled at are most of 'em dead,
And we're cursing his staff for incompetent swine.
'He's a cheery old card,' grunted Harry to Jack
As they slogged up to Arras with rifle and pack.

. . . .

But he did for them both by his plan of attack.[1]
Siegfried Sassoon, 'The General'

Chapter Seven

THE BATTLE OF THE SOMME

Once more unto the breach, dear friends, once more,
Or close the wall up with our English dead.
William Shakespeare, Henry V, Act 3, Scene 1

Now strap on your sword, my son,
Go willingly into the field!
God willing, you'll come home a victor.
If not, you'll die a hero,
For our beloved precious Fatherland,
And as a reward I'll tell you:
You were, you are, and you'll always be,
A brave German son.[1]
Poem written by the father of Karl Naundorf, a 24-year-old comrade of Adolf Hitler's in the 16th Bavarian RIR

DAWN, 1 JULY 1916, IN THE VALLEY OF THE SOMME, FIE THE CANNONS' ROAR

This morning begins with what Haig describes as a propitious early 'mist in the hollows that concealed the concentration of our troops'[2] and develops into the conditions that the Germans call *windstill*, where the sun comes out, the birds sing, the butterflies prance from poppy to poppy undistracted by even the tiniest breeze, otherwise delirious delights of the summery Somme Valley, the sun has also risen on two armed camps totalling over one million men, separated by nationality, philosophy, loyalties and a No-Man's Land that threatens to kill all who attempt to cross it. And yet, only one of the assembled armies is planning to do that, which is why, on the side of the Allies, there is now so much activity, preparation and . . . trepidation. Today is the day.

In one and a half hour's time, at precisely 6.25 am, the barrage upon the German's front-lines will start once more. It will go for a broad hour before, from 7.25 to 7.30 am, intensifying with five minutes of intensely rapid 'hurricane fire'. Right in the middle of that hurricane fire, at 7.28 am, four mines will be exploded at La Boisselle, right by the Bapaume road on the approaches to the village of Pozières. As the largest two have 40,000 pounds and 60,000 pounds of explosive respectively, they should wipe out German defenders and leave a crater that will both shield the attackers from crossfire and give them an obvious spot to occupy.

As the attack opens, no fewer than 120,000 British infantry, drawn from 13 British divisions, will launch themselves across a 16-mile front, all of them backed by a total of over a thousand heavy and field guns, which have already fired 1.5 million shells at the Squareheads.

The point of the British arrow is to thrust along the Albert–Bapaume road, which has the village of Thiepval on its left and the village of Pozières strung along it. Both of those villages, on high points of the landscape, are crucial. Thiepval is the key to taking the first line and Pozières the key to the second line. Once they are taken, the windmill ruins on Pozières Ridge can be taken, and their own observers installed on the highest point of the battlefield, able to give precise instructions to the artillery further down the slope. From there, ideally, the British might be able to get all the way to Bapaume and so secure a large town, with significant resources and skills to aid the Allied war effort, including a large and well-resourced hospital. The town also encompasses the key road and railway junctions in the area behind German lines.

South of the Somme, five French divisions – comprising 60,000 men – will be attacking across a six-mile front, with six more in reserve.

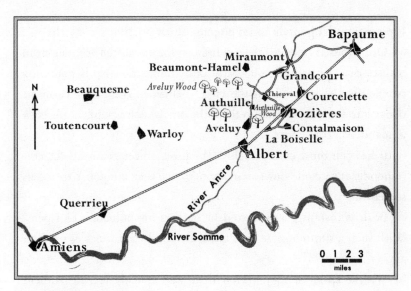

Pozières and surrounds

In the thick copse of oak and birch trees covered with vines and shrubs that is Aveluy Wood, on the British side of the line immediately west of Thiepval, the first sound of the morning is blackbirds singing. For once, there is no rumble of artillery in the near or far distance, no crack of rifle or staccato of machine-gun fire. Just the melodious song of the birds.

First up are the cooks, aware that an army fights on its stomach and today is to be the fight of their lives. Around and about them in the growing light, soldiers are rising, stretching, gazing to the German lines that they know they must soon attack. The officers, being officers and knowing they must look the part, take the time to shave.

Among them, in the lines before Thiepval, is the Commanding Officer of the 9th Irish Rifles of the 36th Ulster Division, Lieutenant-Colonel Crozier. It is with some satisfaction that he notes how the British shells, just as they have been doing spasmodically through the night, are regularly pounding the German positions, preliminary to the pounding proper, due to start at 6.30 am. The artillery pounds and it pounds and it pounds.

—

It pounds and it pounds and it pounds. What is it?

Oh. Aroused from his deep slumbers, the exhausted Charles Bean realises that, even though it is still only 5 am, someone is pounding on the door of his room at the Hotel Belfort in Amiens. Blearily he opens it to find his Kiwi equivalent, the official correspondent for New Zealand, Malcolm Ross.

Bean, you must come quickly. The press officers want all the correspondents to come downstairs by 5.30, as 'they are going to tell us something'.[3]

Bean is instantly awake, and he gathers his notebook and pens. With such a summons, at such an hour, clearly the attack is on after all.

Within minutes, they are on their way, quickly leaving Amiens and heading through many tiny villages chock-a-block with battered British soldiers fresh from battle, and then down into a long valley where they can soon see the red-roofed town of Albert before them – a hub of hospitals, warehouses, roads and railways, crucial to the British cause this close to the front.

As Bean and his fellow members of the press head down Albert's main street towards that front – now just six miles away – they find themselves 'neath the stricken figure of the Virgin Mary leaning out at an impossible angle from the top of the red-brick church tower of Notre-Dame-de-Brebières. She looks, to Bean's eyes, as if she is prostrate with grief at the sheer tragedy of what is happening to her children . . . but in fact she was put that way by a German shell in the early part of the war. (At least, most people think so. Corporal Arthur Thomas of Australia's 6th Battalion records in his diary a different theory: 'It was pushed over by the French as it was too much of a target for the town, glittering as it did in the sun.')[4]

———

It pounds and it pounds and it pounds. The British shelling on their positions is terrifying. Most of the front-line German soldiers, however, remain secure in their specially built dugouts, often as much as 30 feet below the surface, leaving just a bare minimum of sentries and observers in the trenches – ready to call them up the instant the barrage ceases and it is clear the British are beginning their infantry attack.

It is with satisfaction of their own that those observers note the shelling is doing very little to disturb the massive rolls of barbed wire that lie in front of their trenches, most of them suspended on stakes. Because the shells only detonate when they hit the ground, the actual explosion is occurring several feet into the dirt, and it mostly just hurls the wire about without destroying it. Many other British shells are defective, and just over a quarter of them don't explode at all.

———

At 6.40 am, Lieutenant-Colonel Crozier gives the order. His men, as trained, start to 'fall in, in fours', assembling themselves in a four-wide marching formation. His companies are now lined up, as ordered, along the Hamel–Albert road, safe from German view.

All along the British and French lines, other soldiers are equally either moving up or already in position, depending on which of the four waves they are designated to be in. Mercifully, Crozier and his men are due to advance in the follow-up attack, starting at 8.05 am, which is hopefully going to be a bit easier than being in the first wave. If all goes well, the six battalions of the first attack in their sector will take the first German line, while Crozier's men, in the follow-up attack of four battalions, will take the Germans' second line.

All are coming face to face with the possibility of their imminent violent death or agonising mutilation. As they nestle in their trenches, and German shells fall all around, they can still distinctly hear the *whut-whut-whut* of German bullets firing through the barbed wire, which has lanes that they must presently make their way through to even *begin* their charge on No-Man's Land.

'I made up my mind that I was going to be killed,' one of the British soldiers would recount.[5] 'I was to be in the third wave. While I was waiting, during the last half-hour, I kept saying to myself: "In half an hour you will be dead." "In twenty-five minutes you will be dead." "In twenty minutes you will be dead." "In a quarter of an hour you will be dead." I wondered what it would feel like to be dead. I thought of all the people I liked, and the things I wanted to do, and told myself that that was all over, that I had done with that; but I was sick with sorrow all the same. Sorrow isn't the word either: it is an ache and anger and longing to be alive. There was a terrific noise and confusion, but I kept thinking that I heard a lark; I think a lark had been singing there before the shelling increased. A rat dodged down the trench among the men, and the men hit at it, but it got away. I felt very fond of all my men . . .

'Then I thought, "When I start I must keep a clear head. I must remember this and this and this." Then I thought again, "In about five minutes now I shall be dead." I envied people whom I had seen in billets two nights before. I thought, "They will be alive at dinner-time to-day, and to-night they'll be snug in bed; but where shall I be? My body will be out there in No-Man's-Land; but where shall I be? What is done to people when they die? The time seemed to drag like hours and at the same to race. The noise became a perfect hell of noise, and the barrage came down on us . . ."[6]

Now Crozier and his men move forward across the River Ancre into Thiepval Wood, just a short time before what seems to be a massive earthquake wrapped in mighty thunder suddenly detonates ahead of them as the ground roars, the air bursts, and everything within a mile shakes. It is exactly 7.28 am, and the four mines have gone off. The air is rent, the concussive force momentarily cleaves the trees, and the combined blast is so overwhelming it rattles windows even in Kent, across the English Channel, just on 100 miles away.

Across the 16 miles of British front now, the soldiers grapple with their ladders and, with a throaty roar, start to climb up and over the parapets. Some are trembling with fear. A few have already been rendered 'silly' by the German barrage that has been falling among them – one man has taken all his clothes off and is giggling – while others display extraordinary sangfroid and even humour. As one soldier slips on the ladder, he is heard to mutter, 'The damned thing. I'll miss the bloody train.'[7]

As one now, the first wave charges forward, beneath the stunning blue skies of a bright summer's morning, out into No-Man's Land, described by one chronicler of the attack as 'a strip of earth without life, made smoky, dusty, and dim by explosions which came out of the air upon it, and left black, curling, slowly fading, dust and smoke-devils behind them'.[8]

Some trip on the wire. Some are cut down in a fusillade of bullets before they have taken a step forward.

'I suppose machine gun fire had caught them suddenly like a great scythe . . .' one observer would note of such fire. 'The result is very strange. They sink onto their knees and topple gently forward and remain hunched up in this position . . . of a Mohammedan at prayer. [People think] when a man is shot, he flings himself up in some dramatic action . . . In reality he stoops gently for the earth to receive him.'[9]

As to the still upright survivors, they continue 'into the darkness of death, cheering each other with cries that could be heard above the roaring and the crashing of the battle'.[10]

But careful!

Even in this situation, a full-on charge is out of the question, as for this particular sector the British embrace the new tactic of a 'creeping barrage' – a system whereby a curtain of artillery shells continues to land in front of them, advancing at the rate of some 50 yards a minute. Ideally, it will pass over the enemy front-line trenches just seconds before the attackers rush in, not giving the defenders a chance to gather themselves and their weapons.

Ahead of Crozier's men of the 9th Royal Irish Rifles, 107th Brigade, 36th (Ulster) Division, it is the men of the 108th and 109th Brigades who constitute the first wave. Now, cognisant that this is the 226th anniversary of the Battle of the Boyne – who could forget? – and the inspiring victory of the Protestants over the Catholics, they charge forward shouting 'Remember the Boyne!',[11] only to be cut all to pieces.

In the German trenches, their NCOs now roar to their men, *'Sehen Sie nach vorn!* Look to your front! *Schießen Sie tief.* Fire low! *Verschwenden Sie keine Munition.* Don't waste ammunition.'

And so they do.

'We just had to load and reload,' one German machine-gunner would recall. 'They went down in their hundreds. You didn't have to aim, we just fired into them. If only they had run, they would have overwhelmed us.'

And, of course, it is not just the machine guns doing the damage. *Unteroffizier* Sergeant Felix Kirchner of the German Army in the 26th Field Artillery Regiment is with a fellow artillery observer high in the Pozières church tower, watching with amazement as their comrades pour shell after shell onto the advancing soldiers, tearing them to pieces. The shells fire on all things bar one. 'We could clearly see the tower of the Cathedral in Albert, with the Virgin's statue hanging over,' he would recount. 'Through our telescopes we could even see British observers at work there, their binoculars gleaming in the sun. But we refused to fire on the tower; we had a superstition that the nation which shot down the Virgin would be vanquished.'[12]

The British artillery does not return the favour, and brings such fire to bear on the Pozières church that much of it starts to topple. 'Literally at the last second', the Germans inside 'slid down the ropes of the bells and were saved'.[13]

Down at ground level, the carnage against the British goes on. 'There were so many of them,' German soldier Wilhelm Lange of the 99th Reserve Regiment would note, 'they were like trees in a wood.'[14] And the Germans indiscriminately fire directly into the thick of them.

At least the British artillery is making more of an impact up around Serre, where *Unteroffizier* Otto Lais of the 169th Infanterie Regiment watches closely, trying to work out, among other things, whether he is going to live or die. 'All around us was the rushing, whistling and roaring of a storm,' he would record, 'a hurricane, as the destructive British shells rushed towards our artillery which was firing courageously, our reserves and our rear areas . . .'[15]

—

From atop a hill just north-east of Albert on this morning, Charles Bean and the other war correspondents stand gathered at the spot to which they have been taken by the British press officers and watch carefully. Before them, as the cacophonous sound of the endless big guns rolls over them, lies a spectacular plain of absurdly pretty mustard flowers. And now look there!

Less than a mile away, they can see a line of British infantrymen marching over the crest of a small rise and disappearing from view. As the war correspondents strain for their next sight of the British infantry, whole minutes pass until . . . there they are again!

On a dim and distant hillside, midst shrouds of smoke and dust, the men are visible once more. At least, some of them are. For, clearly, many have been struck down, and, as the newsmen continue to watch, many more are falling.

The English correspondent John Masefield is colourful in his description: 'Perhaps not many of all those thousands knew what was happening even quite close at hand, for in those times all souls are shaken, and the air was dim, and the tumult terrible . . . [We saw] promising swarms of men dropping in twos or threes, till the rush was only a few men, who went on until they fell like the others and lay in little heaps in their tracks. Within a few minutes, the second and third waves were following on the first, not knowing, in that darkness of dust and tumult, what success had been won, if any.'[16]

And so too, across the front of the attack, are many other British soldiers playing the game, but the result is no less disastrous for all that. For the tragic truth is that the British artillery is too thinly spread across the front they are attacking, and little damage has been done to the German wire or machine guns. It means . . . massacre.

And all too often it is the massacre of those who simply don't understand the horror of what they are facing: industrialised slaughter on a scale the world has never seen. A case in point is Captain Wilfred

Nevill, a dashing young officer of the 8th East Surreys, popular among the men for his charming insolence towards the Germans, frequently jumping on the fire-step in the evenings to shout amusing insults at them. For this big day, he unveils something else he hopes will amuse the men: a soccer ball for himself and one for each of his platoons, with a cash prize offered to the first platoon to kick their ball into the German trench. On one of the balls is written:

The Great European Cup-Tie Final
East Surreys v. Bavarians
Kick off at Zero[17]

While, to indicate 'anything goes', another is marked:

No referee

Now leading his men over the parapet, he gives the ball a mighty kick towards the German line, as the men let out a cheer. They understand. It is for them to advance, and so they do. Though the East Surreys in fact are one of the rare units that take their objective on the day, Nevill can neither congratulate nor pay them, as he is killed.

At Serre, just three miles north-west of Crozier's soldiers, a 720-man battalion of the East Lancashire Regiment, composed of Accrington Pals, loses no fewer than 584 killed, wounded or missing by 8 am.

Meanwhile, Crozier and his men, with the Lieutenant-Colonel himself in the lead, are also advancing. The fire upon them is just starting to become withering, with some men going down – with usually something between a scream and a soft moan – when Crozier glances to his right. He sees, first, the 10th Rifles, and beyond them . . . the rest of the 32nd Division, or at least what used to be that division. For it is, effectively, no more. What had been a fine body of 7000 – two brigades of infantry – is clearly either on its last legs or has already had those legs shot from under it.

For these men are now all but universally horizontal in No-Man's Land. There they lie on the ground, dead, dying, grievously wounded or taking shelter from the machine-gun fire, with just a few still upright, including some officers trying to urge their men onwards. As obvious targets for the gunners, these brave officers don't last long and are soon hit.

Obviously, Thiepval village has not fallen, for that is where most of the fire is coming from. With the clock now close to 8 am, it should have been in British hands 15 minutes earlier. It means Crozier's own flank will soon be totally exposed, but still he decides to keep his men pushing forward. Soon enough, through the trees, he sees the village itself, complete with 'masses of British corpses suspended on the German wire in front of the Thiepval stronghold, while live men rush forward in orderly procession to swell the weight of numbers in the spider's web. Will the last available and previously detailed man soon appear to do his futile duty unto death on the altar of sacrifice?'[18] Very likely.

It is not quite the shadow of the Valley of Death, but it is not far off. Marching along the narrow track that has been cut through the forest for their passage, Crozier and his troops focus on the light at the end of their leafy tunnel, which is where, in expectation of their arrival, German shells are falling at the rate of six a minute. Crozier and his men are coming to the end of their deep cover and must now emerge into the open. Their task is to follow up on the first wave provided by the 107th, 108th and 109th Brigades, and be the second wave that leapfrogs their hard-won positions.

'This way to eternity!' a cry from one wag goes up.

And he is not wrong. For just before they emerge from the forest, a German shell lands 30 yards in front of them and explodes.

One piece of shrapnel flies past Crozier's shoulder and an instant later slices open the leg of a soldier behind, who drops to the ground and crawls out of the way of the oncoming ranks.

There is no sympathy for him – only envy. 'Lucky bastard,' one of his mates says. 'You're well out of it, Jimmy, good luck to you, give 'em our love, see you later.'[19]

One officer in Crozier's battalion, Major George Horner Gaffikin, even has the wherewithal to take off his orange sash, wave it above his head and roar, 'Come on boys, no surrender!'[20] With which, dozens of men follow his lead and are off into No-Man's Land.

'Good-bye, sir, good luck,' Gaffikin shouts cheerily to Crozier, *en passant*. 'Tell them I died a teetotaller, put it on the stone if you find me.'

'Good luck, George,' Crozier replies. 'Don't talk rot, anyhow you played the game!'

Gaffikin has less than 60 seconds to live, as, just 50 yards later, Crozier walks past his corpse – which is missing the best part of its head.

They push on.

Withering enfilading fire from Thiepval village itself on their right flank, together with shells coming from field guns that lie directly in

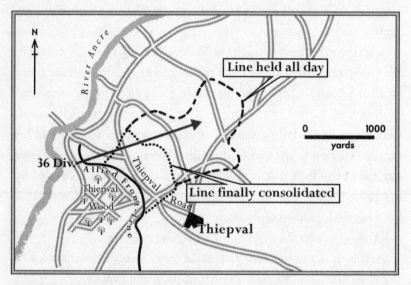

The advance of the 36th Division, 1 July 1916

front, cuts them to pieces. Clearly the 32nd Division, to their right, *still* have not taken Thiepval, as had been hoped.

The German machine guns and artillery now open up in earnest on Crozier and his men, leaving 50 of them killed and 70 wounded, but

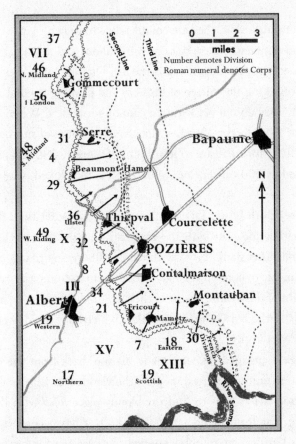

Battle of the Somme, attack divisions, 1 July 1916

as he will record, 'The dead no longer count. War has no use for dead men. With luck they will be buried later; the wounded try to crawl back to our lines. Some are hit again in so doing, but the majority lie out all day, sun-baked, parched, uncared for, often delirious and at any rate in great pain. My immediate duty is to look after the situation and not bother about wounded men.'[21]

And the view of GHQ on the whole disaster? The failure to take the strategic keypoint of Thiepval.

By this time, it is clear that there is going to be no major breakthrough on this first day, and the Commander of the Fourth Army, General Rawlinson, records in his journal, 'There is of course no hope of getting the cavalry through today.'[22] The cavalry are stood down.

A few hours after that, they are completely withdrawn.

All too frequently, it is the bravest battalions and divisions who are hit the hardest. Most devastated is the 8th Division, who had been set the task of taking the village of Pozières and pushing beyond it to the windmill. They do not get within a cannon's roar of it. When they are relieved at 7 pm by the 12th Division, the headcount of survivors does not take long, for there are so few. From 9600 men who had attacked, they have lost 200 officers and 4908 other ranks, killed, wounded or missing.

Crozier's 36th Ulster Division have advanced better than the divisions on either side – the 29th and the 32nd – but that fact has left them exposed on either flank. Now, with nearly 5000 casualties for the day, they are unable to hold on against furious German counter-attacks, and by the light of dusk must return to their original trenches – apart from 800 yards of the old German front-line, which they hand over to the relieving West Yorks.

Crozier is appalled. Having made his way back from the carnage among his men to the deep dugout in the woods that is to serve as his battle headquarters, it is to find the bloody place *filled* with the dead and dying. Far from being a Battalion HQ, it has become a refuge. Worse, as Crozier enters, the wounded men cry out for his help, for water, for food, for bandages, for *mercy* in the name of Jesus Christ. Crozier will have none of it and orders their immediate removal from his domain – a miserable task, carried out by harassed stretcher-bearers with haunted eyes, but it is at last accomplished.

Back to the business of the battle. Climbing quickly to an observation point, he sees everything is as bad as he feared: 'The attack on the right has come to a standstill; the last detailed man has sacrificed himself on the German wire to the God of War. Thiepval village is masked with a wall of corpses.'[23] And beyond that wall, Thiepval is still firmly in the hands of the Germans, making the occupation of the ridge an extremely difficult task.

Crozier's friend Colonel Bernard, commander of the 10th Royal Irish Rifles in the 109th Brigade, is killed, he soon hears, together with half his men. And now, in the last gasp of the twilight, what's this? Off to Crozier's right, a large bunch of British soldiers is retreating from the German fire.

Before Crozier can do anything, a young officer charges up to them and orders them to turn back to the front. They refuse to stop. The officer draws his revolver and gives them fair warning: turn back, or I will shoot you dead myself.

They push past.

The crack of his pistol rings out, and a British soldier falls dead at the officer's feet.

The retreating soldiers instantly turn back to the front-lines.

9 PM, 1 JULY 1916, DOUCHY, ALL QUIET IN THE CRYPT

In the small, German-occupied French town of Douchy, just back from the front-line at the Somme, the 21-year-old German *Leutnant* Ernst Jünger has endured a terrifying day in the trenches, and now enters the village church on this evening for a specific purpose, his head bowed. For there, in the crypt, are 39 hastily constructed wooden coffins, inside which are his dead comrades. Somehow, he is still alive after this day, and they are not. Beneath the carefully stacked coffins, a large lake of congealed blood has formed.

An old German priest is there, watching over the bodies. '*Sie haben einen guten Kampf getan*,' he says to Jünger. 'They have done a good fight.'

Jünger nods, *ja*, but does not speak – in fact, cannot speak.

'*Gibraltar, das ist euer Zeichen und fürwahr, ihr habt gestanden wie der Fels am Meer*,' the priest offers. 'Gibraltar, that is your sign, and indeed you have stood like the rock in the ocean.'

Ja.

It is his *Oberleutnant* who sums it up best, a little later. 'The men had been too brave, thus that many losses.'[24]

One of those losses, it would soon transpire, is Fähnrich Parl, the very man his fellow soldiers had doubted, but who, as it would turn out, fought like a tiger to the end. It is with that in mind that his Commanding Officer would stand over the roughly hewn grave where his coffin lies – along with the coffins of nine other soldiers and officers – to reflect on how strange it all is. 'Yesterday still so young and happy,' Jünger writes in his diary, 'today in this little house. The dear, little fellow . . . Made fun of and not fully respected by many, he died in a trench the death of a whole man, and many who have made his life difficult, are not worthy of standing at his pit . . .'[25]

For all that, they have defended well, and the one Englishman who had made it to the German wire had been immediately grabbed by the throat by *Leutnant* Brecht, who – courtesy of having lived in America – shouted at him in English, 'Come here, you son of a bitch!'[26]

On the British side of the line, the burial crews are busier than at any time in the history of the British Empire. Through the darkness, small groups of soldiers – many of them weeping – work through the night, gathering up what bodies they can from No-Man's Land, wrapping them in sheets or blankets before placing them on stretchers and bringing them back for burial.

Often, when there has been a direct hit on a platoon in a trench, it is not possible to easily match which body part goes with which torso, but they simply piece it all together as a rough approximation – this arm likely going with that arm, as they are the same length, and I think with this head.

Most of the wrapped bodies are placed together in mass graves – usually an abandoned trench or shell hole – without coffins, because there are just so many to bury. After a brief service, the army chaplains refer to the tags given to them by the burial crew and carefully note down, as instructed, just who has been buried where, and what identifying features there are near to the gravesite – all to be passed on to both the Commanding Officer of the battalion and the Graves Registration Unit, with a view to possible future exhumation and reburial in military cemeteries. As a further precaution, grave markers are placed on top of the site, using whatever is available, often put in the shape of a cross.

One of the worst hit regiments, out of the many contenders, is the Cavan Ulster Volunteers. From 600 men who went over the top, only 64 returned. This night, one of them – 17-year-old Private Herbert Beattie – writes home to Belfast, finishing his letter thus:

Mother if god spers me to get home safe i will have something uful to tell you if hell is any wores i would not like to go to it Mother let me here from you soone as you can . . .
This is all I can say at present from your loving son Herbie.
Mother xxxxxxxxxxxxxxxxxxxxxx
Father xxxxxxxxxxxxxxxxxxxxxxx[27]

10 PM, 1 JULY 1916, IN THE WOODS BEYOND THIEPVAL, NO-MAN'S LAND GROANS AS ONE: WAS EVER THERE SUCH A DAY?

No matter that Crozier had previously banned dead and dying men from his HQ dugout, they are now back with a vengeance – particularly the dead, who now litter the ground all around. Of the 700 soldiers and officers of Crozier's battalion who had started the attack that morning, there are now just 70 left with him unscathed – physically, at least.

Crozier smokes through the night. 'The birds have gone, nature has been supplanted. The wood itself has disappeared; was ever there such a day?' he would write in his memoir, *A Brass Hat*.[28] Heading out into the near-darkness of No-Man's Land to see how the recovery of the wounded is proceeding, he finds 'about seven hundred dead and wounded . . . in an area of perhaps a quarter of a mile square'.[29]

Heading out to the left, the Ulsterman is suddenly confronted by the shadowy figure of a German sentry. Crozier whips out his revolver and fires . . . but misses. Is his last moment on Earth now upon him?

Suddenly, there is a roar, a flash of light, a wave of heat . . .

The head of the German sentry before him is blown clean off his shoulders.

It is Crozier's orderly who has fired the shot, from the only weapon he has with him: a Verey light pistol.

—

After eight solid days of barrage, followed by this day-long attack, *Unteroffizier* Otto Lais is with the 'exhausted, half-starved, thirst-suffering, but incomparable German infantry' of his 169th Regiment at Serre, and would chronicle, 'Evening falls. The attack is dead! Our own casualties are severe; the enemy casualties are unimaginable. In front of our divisional sector lie the British in companies, in battalions; mowed down in rows and swept away. From No-Man's-Land comes one great groan. The battle dies away; it seems to be paralysed at so much utter misery and despair.'[30]

It is true.

British machine-gunner George Coppard would report of his first vision at dawn the next morning, 'Hundreds of dead were strung out like wreckage washed up to a high water-mark. Quite as many died on the enemy wire as on the ground, like fish caught in the net. They hung there in grotesque postures. Some looked as if they were praying; they had died on their knees and the wire had prevented their fall. Machine gun fire had done its terrible work.'[31]

Just out in front, a British medical team with many stretcher-bearers appears, under the flag of the Red Cross. Not only are they not shot at by the Germans, but, as *Unteroffizier* Lais records, 'Where to start!? On almost every square metre whimpers come towards them. Our own first aiders . . . go forward to bandage the wounded and deliver the enemy carefully to their own people . . .'[32]

The same kind of thing is happening elsewhere. Many local armistices are arranged – with one rider. They don't tell their Divisional Commands, for fear they will refuse permission. 'During the night I was approached by an officer of [the 1st London Rifle Brigade],' one German officer would recount. 'He had a white flag and asked if he could remove the wounded. I could speak English and told him I would put his request to my *leutnant*. My officer gave permission but he only informed the troops on either side, not the H.Q. in the rear. We helped the English to find their wounded. Sometimes we carried them over to their own side, sometimes the English laid a white tape to the wounded men so that their stretcher-bearers could find them in the dark.'[33]

Many such impromptu truces are arranged, allowing both sides to reclaim their wounded from No-Man's Land. In some measure, the spirit of Christmas Eve 1914 lives on.

—

The next morning, at his advanced HQ at Beauquesne, eight miles behind the lines, General Haig is beginning to get to grips with the situation. South of the Somme, the French have done extremely well. By using 900 heavy guns along just six miles of the first German trench – taking depth of field of firing into consideration, a heavy gun for every 21 yards of trench attacked – they have taken over most of the German front-line in their sector and captured some 4000 enemy soldiers, all while incurring only a comparatively light 7000 casualties.

Alas, for Haig's own British forces, the news is not so good. Ignoring General Rawlinson's request to use the French tactics, Haig had insisted the fire of their own 400 heavy guns be spread over two German lines, across a width of 16 miles – a heavy gun for only every 58 yards of German trench attacked. And the results are there for all to see. Only in the bottom third of the British front had there been significant advances, while in the northern two-thirds there had been dents only. And of the 120,000 British infantry that went over the top, some 57,500 had fallen to a bullet or a piece of shrapnel, or – and this was a frequent occurrence – simply ceased to exist after being directly hit by a German shell. Of those casualties, some 19,240 had been killed outright. And now those bodies lie festering, bloating, rotting in the sunshine, as the 'disgusting smell of the vapour of warm human blood heated by the sun'[34] rises from all parts.

If there is a lesson out of the battle, it is that artillery really is everything. Use enough of it, like the French, and you'll do well. Don't and you won't.

For all that, General Haig is not particularly concerned.

In the manner of General Hunter Weston, the 'Butcher of Cape Helles', who had once expostulated in response to a concerned query about how many casualties he was suffering, 'Casualties? What do I care about casualties?'[35] the good General is nothing if not insouciant, as he writes in his diary of the figure of 40,000 – for this is the preliminary estimate he has received – *This cannot be considered severe in view of the numbers engaged, and the length of front attacked.*[36]

(Others, when the true picture emerged, would be less forgiving, noting that Rawlinson really had been right and that bombarding both lines had been tactically misguided, meaning that on two-thirds of the front there had been no advance at all, and in sum total, for 19,000 deaths, just four square miles of enemy territory had been gained.)

On the German side, the death and destruction had been comparatively light, as it is they who have had the obvious advantage of staying securely in their trenches while ruthlessly shooting down all those who would try to cross No-Man's Land. They have lost around 8000 men killed and wounded and 4000 taken prisoner against 64,000 British and French casualties. But if the loss to both sides on the British front alone is counted, then seven British were hit for every one German.[37]

Far more importantly, Haig must now wrestle with the next step his forces will take. For the fact that the Germans have held on to the ridge-line on both sides of Thiepval, including the crucial Pozières Ridge, means they are still menacing the very narrow breach in the line the British have made to the south. Though General Joffre is eager that the British renew their frontal attack on Thiepval and Pozières – and at a meeting the following day is even presumptuous enough to *order* Haig to do it – the British General rejects this outright.

'When Joffre got out of breath, I quietly explained what my position is as regards him as the "Generalissimo". I am solely responsible [to the British Government] for the action of the British Army; and I had approved the plan, and must modify it to suit the changing situation as the fight progresses.'[38]

Joffre calms and tries to cajole him, saying, 'France expects great things of you.'[39]

Which is *merveilleux*, but Haig still won't do it. For the moment, the instinct of Sir Douglas is to reinforce what little success the British have had, and continue to push forward where they have advanced best: south of the Albert–Bapaume road. They will get to the harder part in due course, ideally rolling up the second German line from the south. If all goes well, they can push forward there, *then* take Pozières, and *then* push north to come at the crucial Thiepval from the rear, via a spot known as Mouquet Farm. Yes, it will take ever more men, but that is already happening as reserves are rushed forward.

Exit stage left, General Joffre.

EARLY JULY 1916, WESTERN FRONT WEEPING, AS FRANCE TAKES THE FIFTH

The further north to the Western Front the newly arrived Australians of the 5th Division go, the less gay the mood. In the south, they had seen young men in the fields, but not now. Now it is only old men, and old women, and young women, some with children, and many of the women are wearing dresses as black as their sorrowful expressions.

'It was a common sight,' Bert Bishop tells the folks at home, 'to see an old grey-headed lady wiping the tears from her eyes with her apron in one hand and waving to us God-speed with the other.'[40]

'Another thing that impressed me greatly,' another Digger records, 'was the admirable way in which the female sex are helping their [absent] husbands, sons and brothers on every farm. The girls are to be seen bringing in the harvests and working the farms generally. And at every station along the way the girls are doing porters work and the elderly women working the signals.'[41]

The steam train keeps pulling them on as Lyons, Chalon and then the outskirts of Paris – there is the Eiffel Tower! – arise on their northern horizon before slowly falling to their south. (True, there is always some disappointment for all the Australian soldiers as the Eiffel Tower has no sooner appeared than it sinks below the horizon once more, as their train skirts the city, but they have seen it all right.)

But they keep moving, and soon the country is even *more* spectacular. 'The wild flowers on the country side were a sight,' Theodor Pflaum writes. 'The crops were thick with poppies and corn flowers and apart from those; buttercups, foxgloves, candytuft, canterbury bells and miniature scotch thistles . . . were very numerous.'[42] For many of the Diggers, though, it is the poppies that truly get them. They're everywhere! And they're beautiful.

At midday on Sunday 2 July, the train bearing the 55th Battalion pulls into the station at Amiens, right beside a Red Cross train on the other platform, heading in the opposite direction. The Red Cross train is as full as a Bourke Street tram with wounded British soldiers. But it is not just their wounds – the bandages, slings and crutches, and the *stench* of some of those open wounds! – that draw the attention of the Australian soldiers; it is also the strange, unworldly, haunted look in their eyes, 'a look that spoke of suffering and of sadness, and of an expectation to meet more of both'.[43]

It makes Bert Bishop immediately think of that strange night on *Caledonia*, when he and Ray and Billy had been talking about what they'd do when they got home . . . only to suddenly realise that all three of them were unlikely to make it. For the truth, of course, is that to this point the war had been fun. But there is a change just up ahead, and the eyes of those British soldiers – 'that indescribable something . . . that tired grey look, that soulful sadness'[44] – says it is going to be grimmer even than their worst imaginings.

The 5th Division keeps moving and, just as the sun sinks that evening at around 9 pm, they catch a glimpse on the left-hand side of their carriages of the English Channel. By midnight, they are at Calais, and all the rough-house bantering, the laughter and the chiacking have stopped. This is not simply because many of them are now asleep but because those many who are awake know that getting to Calais means they are indeed close to the Western Front.

Sure enough, the following morning, after their journey takes them through the most verdant fields, fair ablaze with red poppies, blue corn-flowers and stunning white marguerites with yellow centres, their train lurches to a halt at a town called – *what does it say on the platform sign, Bluey?* – '**Hazebrouck**', and they are ordered to get off with their kit. A short march of ten miles through wonderfully picturesque agricultural country brings them to the tiny village of Thiennes, and as dusk falls they find themselves being steered towards massive barns to bunk down for the night on sweet-smelling hay.

But what is that?

What?

That.

Oh, yes. Now everyone can hear it. Far to their east, they can hear a distant rumble a little like thunder – except there are no breaks between each clap, just a perpetual *throbbing*. Could that really be the Western Front they have heard so much about, a place where the shells never truly stop falling?

Must be. After all, just before dark, you'll remember, we saw those odd-looking observation balloons far to the east, and they obviously overlook the whole shebang. You could also tell because that is where the British planes were, with those puffs of black smoke going off all around them, which they reckon was coming from the German anti-aircraft guns firing at them.

The men of the 5th Division settle down to sleep, but the rumbling takes no pause. They are no more than a dozen miles from the notorious Western Front.

3 JULY 1916, THE NEWS BREAKS, THE GERMANS ARE BROKEN

The news from the Western Front is excellent! Look there, the headline in *The Times*:

EVERYTHING HAS GONE WELL[45]

John Irvine of the *Daily Express* could not have agreed more, telling his readers, 'It may be taken as certain that our men entered into the grand assault in the true spirit of a sane and cheerful manliness . . . Non-combatants, of course, were not permitted to witness this spectacle, but I am informed that the vigour and eagerness of the first assault were worthy of the best tradition of the British Army . . . We had not to wait long for news, and it was wholly satisfactory and encouraging. The message received at ten o'clock ran something like this: "On a front of twenty miles north and south of the Somme, we and our French allies have advanced and taken the German first line of trenches. We are attacking vigorously Fricourt, La Boiselle and Mametz. German prisoners are surrendering freely, and a good many already fallen into our hands."[46]

The *Daily Chronicle*? 'The British troops have already occupied the German front-line. Many prisoners have already fallen into our hands, and as far as can be ascertained our casualties have not been heavy.'[47]

Another report in the same edition of *The Times* is exultant: 'Our troops have successfully carried out their missions, all counter-attacks have been repulsed and large numbers of prisoners taken.'[48]

And, yes, some British soldiers have died, but even then there is a certain magnificence about it, as reported by the *Daily Mail*: 'The very attitudes of the dead fallen eagerly forwards, have a look of expectant hope. You would say that they died with the light of expectant victory in their eyes.'[49]

Perhaps.

In truth, of course, it is the Germans who have emerged the closest to triumphant in the face of the British attack, though not against the French, where they have lost nearly ten miles of their front-line. (Von Falkenhayn's presumption that the French would not be able to mount a serious attack because of the pressure they are under at Verdun – allowing him to thin the line here at the Somme accordingly – has been proved disastrous.)

General Fritz von Below is under no illusions, and on this day issues an order that is read out to all of his troops, by all of his command-ers: 'The decisive issue of the war depends on the victory of the 2nd

Army on the Somme. We must win this battle in spite of the enemy's temporary superiority in artillery and infantry. The important ground lost in certain places will be recaptured by our attack after the arrival of reinforcements. The vital thing is to hold on to our present positions at all costs and to improve them. The voluntary evacuation of trenches *ist strikt verboten*. The will to stand firm must be impressed on every man in the army. The enemy should have to carve his way over heaps of corpses.'[50]

It is all part of General von Falkenhayn's broad principle of '*keinen Fußbreit Boden*' – not one inch of ground to be given up – and yet, very quietly, both General von Below and Crown Prince Rupprecht are furious at their Supreme Commander. Both had insisted that the British/French attack would fall precisely where it did, and the fact that von Falkenhayn had overruled them to insist that it would be likely up near Lille meant there now had to be *ein wildes Gerangel*, a mad scramble, to bring troops from elsewhere to hold the line. Meantime, von Falkenhayn's whole concept of bleeding France to death at Verdun is also being shown up. No country bleeding to death could possibly have unleashed the punch it just has.

In the words of one German observer, 'for Falkenhayn, a very dangerous discontent spread out within the high commands of the Western Front as well as in the general staff'.[51] Clearly, the General's career is now riding on what happens over the next month on the Somme.

The common German soldiers, meantime? They know little of General von Falkenhayn, one way or another, and simply focus on keeping their enemies at bay.

Amid one group of Germans, however, there is real regret for one enemy in particular. Every evening now, *Unteroffizier* Otto Lais and the men of the 169th Regiment, posted around Serre, hope to hear the strains of a trumpet coming to them across *Niemandsland*, but . . . there is nothing. Before the bombardment had begun in late June, a young English trumpeter would entertain both sides of the line around dusk, playing many tunes from his vast repertoire. The Germans actively looked forward to his performances and could even see him blowing away on his trumpet. But now, *Feldwebel* Karl Stumpf would recount, 'there was nothing to be heard and we all hoped that nothing had happened to him'.[52]

3 JULY 1916, A GODLEY MAN TAKES OVER

With the arrival of the 5th Division, II Anzac Corps is complete, meaning that their commander, General Godley, can now take the place of General Birdwood at La Motte aux Bois, while II Anzac Corps itself takes over from I Anzac Corps in the Nursery. The latter are on their way to Bailleul, ten miles back from the front-lines, to catch the trains that will take them the first part of that haul south to the Somme, before they march the rest. With this mass exchange of soldiers in his area of control, Godley is busy, certainly, but his very presence as head of an Australian corps is not pleasing to all.

'I didn't realise,' Bean notes in his diary, 'what the army meant to us until I see Godley, with his all-British staff, and practically on an equality with White and Birdwood as far as two divisions of Australians are concerned. Somehow the idea is one I can't reconcile myself to in the very least.'[53]

For now, Godley's first order is for the 4th Division to take up their positions in the front-lines in the Armentières sector in front of Fromelles on Aubers Ridge, while the 5th Division continues to train in preparation for going onto the line in a week or so. Then the 4th Division's infantry can go south, leaving behind just their inexperienced artillery batteries, which are regarded as not up to the task of fighting in the Battle of the Somme. It is better they stay quietly in this nursery, while learning the tricks of the trade.

The 5th is settling in well, with one soldier of the 54th Battalion reporting to his family at home that his billet is in a 'beautiful country village' and that, 'even if our own country's interests were out of the question then it would still be worth our nation's manhood, and it would still be our duty as human beings of this 20th century to assist in defending such homes as these and such occupants from the onslaughts of such a detestable scourge as the "Boches". You should only see the country and its people to appreciate this.'[54]

The Diggers *love* these people and this place, as they settle in to their temporary digs around Hazebrouck. The greenery! The girls! The grog! The best thing about the beer, decides one private from the 29th Battalion, Bill Barry, is that for the equivalent of just a penny a glass at the estaminets 'you could drink a ship load and it would not take any effect'.[55] Which is no small thing for Barry. He's one of those blokes whose face in repose is just grim, with piercing eyes, pursed lips, and an expression of distaste . . . and beer bucks him up for a bit. As do the other drinks: 'We could get "Bombard" or champagne for four and sixpence a bottle and on a pay day, or as we called it "When the Lord fed his lambs", we celebrated some big event and had a bottle or two.'[56]

This is the life!

And now that the two weeks' tutelage of the 4th Division artillery under the 2nd Division artillery is supposedly complete, the next morning they laboriously haul their guns forward, in relief of their mentor batteries. By sundown, the batteries of the 4th Division artillery are all installed in the front of Fromelles, as their counterparts of the 2nd Division make their way south. Somehow, 3000-odd men who just three months before barely knew which end of the field gun the 'bang!' came from – and certainly not how to load, aim and fire it – are now responsible for the artillery defence of 7000 yards of the Western Front. Of course, what they most need is experience. Alas, on the day that they arrive, General Plumer issues an order to all of his corps commanders that, for the sake of the Somme Offensive, strict economy in ammunition is necessary – so extra practice for the newly arrived artillery is now out of the question.

4 JULY 1916, ALEC IS MIGHTILY ANNOYED IN THE BACKBLOCKS OF ARMENTIÈRES

Alec Raws has been in France for over a month now and *still* he has not been able to join up with his brother, Goldy. Stuck in this back area, not far from Armentières, doing his training and awaiting his orders, his frustration only grows as he constantly hears talk of Goldy from officers who have come from the front-line and know him well. But his posting to join him simply has not come through.

And what a scurvy bunch he is stuck with back here! 'This depot,' he writes to his sister, 'is the home of the Cold Feet. Those who are making their last struggle to avoid the actual fighting front catch hold of soft jobs here and hang on . . . keeping always a wary eye open for the chance to step on one side in a comfortable but honourable position, allowing the brave, but foolish, to crowd past them to fight and suffer and perhaps die . . .

'God forgive them, my sister, for we do not. They save their lives but lose their souls. And we shall remember them when we return. Of course, they are not so bad as those who never left Australia.'[57]

There is only one upside to the whole wretched thing . . . 'All the women, except the poorest working fisher women and peasants, are singularly charming and vivacious, quick witted and with a sort of frank immodesty – that is not the word, but I search in vain for the right one at the moment. They have not, somehow, the puritanic modesty of we English, and they carry off, without a blush, situations which find even coarsened soldiers embarrassed. There is a charming little girl in the picture – she will have to wait for another letter . . .'[58]

Oui, Alec has found *l'amour* . . .

5 JULY 1916, ADVANCED GHQ, VAL VION CHÂTEAU, HAIG SEEKS TO STOP THE COWS FROM MILKING

Oh goodness. Intelligence reports have just come in confirming the arrival in the German line, right opposite where the British forces are attacking in the Somme Valley, of the 13th Jägerbataillon – which is usually based up on the northern end of the British section of the Western Front, somewhere around Armentières. It is not the single battalion that worries Haig – it is that, on past patterns, the 13th Jäger is likely part of at least one division also arriving.

Something must be done, and it must be done quickly.

The key now, in the view of General Haig, is to prevent the wretched Germans from 'milking' formations on other parts of the Western Front, and among the urgent orders he and his staff send out are clear-the-line ones to his Generals in that region: The First and Second Armies should each select a front on which to attempt to make a break in the enemy's lines, and to widen it subsequently . . .[59]

With just one small break, the Germans will have to stop milking. With a big breakthrough, the Allies might launch a pincer movement with the expected breakthrough on the Somme, and it 'might turn the retreat on the Somme into a general retreat'.[60]

Haig needs something to fall his way. As further casualty lists have been compiled, and fiercely added to, it is clear that, including 1 July, nigh on 80,000 of his men have gone down. It is carnage on a previously unimaginable scale.

FIRST WEEK OF JULY 1916, AROUND HAZEBROUCK, FOR THE 5TH DIVISION, TIME FOR LE COQ-A-DOODLE-DO

Everyone up!

Up! *Up!* UP!

At 3 am on 8 July, the 8th and 15th Brigades of the 5th Division[61] are suddenly roused in their billets and ordered to be 'in full marching order by six am'.[62] Suddenly in the night, lanterns are lit, households roused, orders shouted, dogs startled from their slumber and – *Christ*, all this noise! – hangovers from the night before in the estaminet . . . bitterly regretted. All is hustle and bustle, movement and mayhem, in the military manner. They are to be in full kit, including being issued with 150 cartridges for their rifles, a day's rations, two blankets and a waterproof sheet. All put together, they are loaded up to the Plimsoll line, the whole thing weighing nigh on 80 pounds – like having half a bloke on your back. And, yes, they are ready by 6 am, as ordered, but, of bloody course, they now must wait around for a couple of hours before anything happens. Hurry up and wait: that's the army for you.

In Private Bill Barry's 29th Battalion, it is the Commanding Officer, Lieutenant-Colonel Bennett, who addresses them first. 'Your holidays are over,' he tells the men in grave tones, 'and your work is about to start. We have come to France to kill or be killed and the more prisoners that you take, the more food will be required to feed them.'[63]

Look, he doesn't quite say that the more prisoners they take, the less food they'll eat, but Barry and his mates get the drift. 'You can rest assured,' he would recount, 'we did not intend to take prisoners if it could be helped.'[64]

And then they are off, marching out of their billets in Hazebrouck, soon passing through the village of Morbecque and heading east towards the town of Merville. As ever, the cobblestone roads play hell with the troops' feet, and soon enough blokes are seen to drop out, take their boots off and be rewarded with 'French women with pieces of soap, rubbing the chaps' socks and their feet'.[65] Most of them, though, simply must press on, now towards Estaires.

True, this environment provides much more wondrous scenery than back in Egypt, but one thing doesn't change. As they march along, they must suffer the Commanding Officer of the 5th Division, Major-General James McCay, cruising up and down the columns in his motor car, exhorting them to keep formation and march faster! Even when they get to Estaires, McCay decides they 'haven't done enough for the day',[66] and sends them out on a route march.

Still McCay is not happy, and the next morning, after Battalion Orders are read out, as recorded by Private Bill Barry, McCay tells them that he is 'disgusted at the way the men marched and if in the future any man falls out while he [is] on the march, he is liable to be immediately shot . . .'[67]

The anger among his troops at such treatment is palpable, and McCay is regarded as so mean he wouldn't show his blind grandma a short-cut to the shitter on a dark night. 'It was all very well for anybody on horse back or sitting back in a motor car to talk like that,' Barry notes, 'but it is another for the men on foot and our Commanding Officer was thought no more of for issuing such instructions.'[68]

There is just something about McCay that grates on the men, perhaps a sense that his career as an officer is more important than their welfare as soldiers. Stupid bastard.

As the 5th Division prepares to march towards the Western Front, General McCay returns to his HQ at Blaringhem, where he receives a directive from General Godley to all units of the II Anzac Corps:

> It is imperative that raids and all possible
> offensives should be undertaken at once by
> both divisions of the corps in order to make a
> certainty of holding on our front such German
> troops as may now be there . . . in order to give
> help to our comrades fighting desperately in
> the south . . .[69]

McCay is ecstatic, and he wastes no time in instructing Lieutenant-Colonel Walter Cass of the 54th Battalion 'to do a raid tomorrow night'.[70]

What? Cass can barely believe McCay is serious. Do a *raid?* When the 54th Battalion has not even *seen* the front-line? No one in the 5th Division has.

McCay does not care for such negative talk, insisting that the raid has 'got to be done and could be done all right'.[71] After all, the further words of Godley – 'however little we may be ready, or however difficult it may be, we should never forgive ourselves if we did not make the necessary effort, and, if necessary, sacrifice, to help them'[72] – resound with him. *He* is quite prepared for his men to make that sacrifice.

Mercifully, at this point Colonel Harold Pope and Brigadier-General Edwin Tivey, the commanders of the 14th and 8th Brigades, and Brigadier-General Pompey Elliott of the 15th Brigade, all intervene and, *in extremis*, manage to persuade McCay that it would be murderous folly to send their troops forward on such a raid, when they have neither training nor even base-level familiarity with the terrain they would be raiding across.

McCay appears to take it personally for all that. He *wants* to see his men in action.

—

Meanwhile, the Second Army's General Plumer and his senior staff have come to a significant conclusion. It is their belief that the German defences opposite the southern end of the Second Army's sector, where it joins the northern end of the First Army's sector, is more thinly held than elsewhere. If they must attack, this would seem to be the obvious spot. Perhaps a joint operation between the Second and First Armies would do the trick here? It is the Second Army's General Plumer who suggests it:

```
Dear Monro,
... the only place I can attempt to 'make a
break' would be somewhere on my right - in
conjunction with your left. If it should happen
that your left was the place you chose, we might
make a joint arrangement ...
Yours very sincerely,
Herbert Plumer73
```

You can see the point he's talking about on the trench map, that unsightly bulge they call the Sugar-loaf. Plumer's only reservation is that, because I Anzac Corps is about to leave for the Somme, he can spare only one of his divisions, the Australian 5th Division . . .

General Monro, a man whose face in repose looks naturally disapproving at the best of times, as his mouth curves downwards, nevertheless likes the idea. But who can plan and lead it? Who is the northernmost commander in his sector? Ah, yes, General Richard

Haking, the Commanding Officer of the XI Corps.

At a conference the next morning, on 8 July, Monro requests Haking to revisit the plan he had first floated a month before, for an attack on that very spot. And, Monro tells Haking, he may count on Plumer contributing one of the Second Army's divisions to mount the joint attack.

Haking is delighted. This, *this,* is precisely the chance he has been waiting for. His previous grievous failures at Aubers Ridge – *losing 4000 men in an hour for no ground gained* – and Boar's Head – *with 1200 casualties from 2000 starters in fewer than five hours* – have demonstrated, in the parlance of General Haig, that Haking is one who is prepared to pay the price of victory. Haking's view is that mass casualties go with war . . . the way another might characterise flies as going with summer, shivering as going with winter, and discipline problems as going with Australians. It is not pleasant, but you have to make the best of it. It is what is expected.

This time, Haking is confident, it will be different. The key will be to display the very attacking spirit he has always so championed, albeit with a ruse.

8 JULY 1916, II ANZAC CORPS HQ, LA MOTTE AUX BOIS, TIME TO . . . SAY GOODBYE

It's always like this. A few conversations at GHQ, a couple of slashes on a notebook, several cables, a change in the diagram on the pin-up board . . . and in short order 10,000 men go one way, 10,000 men go another, and another 10,000 still another!

On this occasion, I Anzac Corps' General Birdwood and II Anzac Corps' General Godley – in consultation with General Haig's GHQ – put the finishing touches to their plan. Once the 5th Division completes the 20-mile march forward from its current position around Sailly-sur-la-Lys, it can take the position of the 4th Division in the line, allowing the 4th – less its artillery – to join the 1st and 2nd Divvies at the Somme.

With the 4th Division's 14th Battalion (Jacka's mob) one night just before they head south, Private Eddie Rule stands watching as the white flares from the German line soar high into the sky. With him is a bloke by the name of Private Leslie Schaper,[74] a cove who is as Aussie as you please but has a curious background. For not simply is his father German-born but, just a few months before the outbreak of war, his father had gone back to Germany to see his folks and had been dragooned into the German Army. His father had tried everything to get out of it but, as a German citizen, at a time of conscription, there had been no escape.

Hence the odd look on Schaper's face now. 'Well,' he says to Eddie, quite casually, while gazing at the German lines. 'I wonder if my old pop is over there; it would be interesting to meet him.'[75]

9 JULY 1916, CHOCQUES, SIR RICHARD HAKING'S PLAN IS PRESENTED TO MONRO

And that, of course, is the other thing. Neither the messengers who dart back and forth from HQs to front-line positions nor the motor-cycle couriers who frequently roar between all the corps, divisional and battalion HQs and GHQ have any idea of the content of their missives – even though their portent can seal the fate of tens of thousands of men.

On this morning, a particular courier reports, as requested, to Sir Richard Haking's XI Corps HQ at Hinges, and is quickly loading his leather satchel with the 50 pages of summaries, orders, maps and charts. He slings it over his shoulder and is soon roaring to General Monro's HQ in the 'grimy village'[76] of Chocques. Within two hours, the courier arrives, hands the document over to a junior Staff Officer, who signs for it, and then roars off again.

It is done. Within the hour, General Monro is reading the plan of Haking's dreams, the latest incarnation of his long-held passion to take Aubers Ridge. To achieve this goal, Haking plans to commit two divisions – one from his XI Corps, the 61st, and a division loaned from the Second Army – to attack 4200 yards of German trenches after a three- to four-hour bombardment. The targets will 'include the two main tactical localities on the ridge, the high ground around Fromelles and the village of Aubers'.[77]

Here, even Monro must step in, as Haking is clearly trying to do what General Haig always wants him to – break through – even when it is just not feasible. The capture of Aubers Ridge is not contemplated, Monro tells Haking flatly. Such an exercise would only be worthwhile pursuing if executed as a preliminary to 'a big combined attack of the left of the First Army and the right of the Second Army'.[78]

For the moment, Haking cedes, while insisting that his *pièce de résistance* is really something for the fact that it will surely kill off all German resistance. It is a military manoeuvre traditionally known as a 'Chinese attack':

```
The man-killing portion of the scheme will
be carried out as follows. After an intense
bombardment all along the line lasting some
ten minutes, the guns will suddenly lift,
and the infantry will make a show of getting
over the parapet, the enemy will come out of
his shelters and man his parapets, and the
guns will drop again to the front parapet
and support line. This will be repeated three
or four times with intense bombardments in
between.[79]
```

General Monro is a little interested, but no more than that. After ensuring that a copy is sent to GHQ, he has the document filed.

9 JULY 1916, THIENNES–ESTAIRES, THE 14TH BRIGADE OF THE 5TH DIVISION ON THE ROAD AGAIN

We're moving, you Bishop boys, and your mates. Like the newly popular song says, *pack up your troubles in your old kit bag, and smile, smile, smile.* Roll up the swag too, pack up the kit, grab your rifle, and fall in. Late morning on this Sunday, the entire 14th Brigade is soon thereafter marching through the nearby town of Merville, as many of the locals crowd in close for a look. In their honour, Lieutenant-Colonel McConaghy has the 55th Battalion band strike up 'La Marseillaise', and the effect is all but instantaneous. From everywhere, they come! Old men, old women, young kids, lots of little girls grabbing the soldiers' hands and marching with them, and, yes . . . some rather more shapely girls, whose hands are even more welcome.

'*Allez!*' they cry.

'*Merci!*'

'*Allez les Australiens!*'

'*Merci, les Australiens!*'

All up, it is a reminder of what they are here for. Not just to kill the Germans but also to save these wonderful French people, who are clearly so appreciative of their having come to this faraway country to fight for them. Soon, though, the girls and the kids and the old folk fall behind and they are marching through the glorious French countryside, through the neat green fields and swarms of butterflies. In fact, they keep marching for the rest of the day, the sound of the artillery getting louder all the time, until they reach the small village of Estaires, where they are billeted for the night. Oh, how far they've come from those dreadful days of tramping through the desert on their way to Ismaïlia, three months earlier.

The two other brigades of the 5th Division – the 8th and the 15th – are arriving at their own billets nearby, where their reception is not always what they might have hoped for. At Erquinghem, some seven miles to the north-east, the first of the 8th Brigade, 'Tivey's Darlings' – those coves who never fired a shot at Gallipoli, and who took the train when the other brigades were on that desert march from hell – are *not* embraced as brothers in arms. For don't the other Australians let them have it.

In an estaminet, a gnarled veteran of Gallipoli about to head south with I Anzac Corps spots the shoulder patch of the newly arrived 8th Brigade soldier and is quick to unload. 'So yer 'ere are yer?' he says. 'G'struth, fancy seeing you blokes where there's any bullets!'

The 8th Brigade man rises to the insult. 'We didn't get pushed off Gallipoli anyway!'

'No,' replies the Gallipoli veteran, 'and we didn't get pushed out of Australia by the womenfolk!'[80]

It stings.

'Officers and men of the 8th Brigade were . . . animated,' Charles Bean notes, with some understatement, 'from the brigadier to the last reinforcement, by one chief desire – to show themselves in their first action not inferior to the older troops who had fought at Gallipoli . . .'[81] Their only hope, now that they are here at last on the Western Front, is that they will soon have the opportunity.

'Went to Bde HdQu billet near ERQUINGHAM,' General Tivey writes in his diary the next day. 'Afterwards spent the afternoon with Gen MONASH. Arranged for taking over from the 4th Brigade, and had a long conference on the Scheme of Defence etc.'[82]

It is useful to be able to ease one's way into such an important role.

11 JULY 1916, TOO MUCH SECOND CLASS TRAVEL IN A ROUNDABOUT WAY FOR THE 2ND DIVISION

Nearly there now. It has been a wretched week of seemingly endless route marching, training at Steenwerck, five miles to the west of Armentières, route marching some more – as their feet throb and their blisters burst – and then finally catching a train from Wizernes to Saleux, of course going way off-track, via the coast, calling in at Calais and Boulogne before turning back inland and proceeding through Amiens. And now, after marching the rest of the way, Lieutenant Goldy Raws and the men of the 2nd Division's 23rd Battalion are at last approaching the Somme battlefield. The plan for now is for the 1st and 2nd Divvies to congregate in the villages to the north of Amiens and the neighbouring town of Vignacourt, some 15 to 20 miles west of the front, so they can move up as and when required.

Their feet and lower legs continue to ache from the effect of the wretched cobblestones, their forms slump from the weight of carrying their packs, but at least they know they are not far away now – to judge from the endless booms of artillery rolling their way and getting progressively louder as they march through village after village.

'They all look very peaceful on the map,' Goldy advises his father this evening in a letter, 'but over their line a few hundred yards in depth that runs all along between the Huns and us, there has been enough blood spilt to blot out all the maps that have ever been drawn in the world . . .'

Oh, and one more thing . . . 'An officer has just come in to say 5 reinforcement officers are to join us in the morning. Alec will most likely be amongst them. I would rather he would not, for he will find we are just going into severe action for a novice.'[83]

The most extraordinary thing, as ever, is that despite the endless rumbles of artillery rolling over them and the flashes of light on the eastern horizon, the delights of the town of Amiens are manifest – the theatres, cafes, shops and estaminets – and they can avail themselves in full.

Eat, drink, and be merry, for tomorrow we die – or at least *fight* at last.

Chapter Eight

DRIFTING TO A DECISION

In the lead-up to the [Battle of Fromelles] the solitary
constant among the fog of high-placed indecisiveness was
Haking's vigorous advocacy. Amid uncertainty about
whether there should be an artillery demonstration, a
combined onslaught involving infantry and artillery,
or no operation at all, Haking's blustering optimism
brushed aside the waverers and the sceptics.[1]
Ross McMullin, Wartime, 2004

When the bloody war is over,
No more soldiering for me,
When I get my civvy clothes on,
Oh how happy I shall be,
No more going in the trenches,
No more asking for a pass,
You can tell the sergeant-major,
To stick his passes up his arse![2]
Anonymous, popular Western Front song

10–11 JULY 1916, SAILLY-SUR-LA-LYS, FEEL THE CANNON'S ROAR

And so it begins.

On this afternoon and into the evening, the 12,000 Australian infantry in the three brigades of the 5th Division start their march forward to begin to take over the positions of the 4th Division in the front-line before Fromelles. Specifically, Brigadier-General Edwin Tivey's 8th Brigade, Colonel Harold Pope's 14th Brigade and Brigadier-General Pompey Elliott's 15th Brigade replace the 4th Brigade, 12th Brigade and 13th Brigade respectively.

For most of the men of the 5th, it is sobering. The closer they get to the front-line, the fewer in the fields, the more vacant the villages. Now, all around them is the artillery, some of it belonging to the 5th Division, constantly firing.

By dawn of 11 July, half of the 5th Division infantry is in position, and half the 4th Division infantry consequently relieved, able to head south to the 'big show' at the Somme Valley. That afternoon, the men of the 55th Battalion of the 14th Brigade make ready to move from their billets and bivouacs around Sailly-sur-la-Lys.

One way or another, Bert never likes to be away from Ray for too long, and on this afternoon he goes off to find him in the barn where the machine-gunners are billeted. The two chat, and Bert can tell instantly that something is wrong. This is his cousin, a man he has grown up with and, under the intense circumstances of the last year or so, has come to know better than anyone in the world. And though Ray chats about how happy he is with the Lewis guns, he is avoiding eye contact and too easily drifting off into moody silences. Clearly, the whole battle business is weighing heavily on him. He is asking himself the questions so many soldiers ask themselves at this time: am I now in the last hours of my life? Are you? How will I perform? Will I let my cobbers down? Am I a coward or a hero? Will I do my family proud? Will I add honour to our name?

A war, mate, a real *war*. After all the training, all the travelling, chiacking and carrying on, we are actually about to be in the front-lines.

And, of course, it is not just Ray feeling it at this time. For within just a few minutes, Robbo and Hodgy pop by for what should have been a happy meeting of mates – all together after too long apart – but it is far from that. For now they all know that something is up, that things are on the move, and very fast at that. Hodgy is with the transport section and so has been among the first to get the orders. Transport has to be ready to take the men forward *tonight*.

Already from outside comes the rumble of heavy trucks getting into position. Confirmation arrives soon after. The falling-in orders begin to go out, and the 5th Division is due to complete its replacement of the last of the 4th Division along the established 7000-yard front from east of Bois Grenier in the north to the Sugar-loaf in the south around midnight tonight – the usual time for a changeover, when the Germans will be least alert.

As the 55th Battalion prepares to move forward, Bert Bishop takes the time to register just how he is feeling at this point. It seems kind of unreal. He, too, can barely believe it, but it is actually happening. He is, really, about to go to *war*. And, yes, he is fearful of it, because his life is about to be placed in grave danger and it is all but certain that either he or his mates will die or be fearfully wounded. But against that he is also strangely fascinated. An adventurer by nature, this is sort of why he joined up, to experience real danger, to prove himself man enough to take it – and under no circumstances does he want to miss it. This is the greatest war in the history of the world, and he is going to be a part of it, going into it with his mates.

Quietly, Ray walks back with Bert to where his platoon is billeted. The two talk of everything but the coming battle: they chat of their mums and dads, their brothers and sisters, their friends, the things they used to do, the fun they used to have, the time they spent living in each other's pockets.

One of those times that Bert often thinks of, but doesn't raise now, is when he'd been staying over at his friend Margaret's place and had gone out with his pea-rifle to shoot rabbits. By pure happenstance, afar through the dense bush, he had seen Margaret and Ray sitting before a log by the river. Ray had been using the log to rest his back against. Margaret had her head on Ray's shoulder and Bert had rounded the corner just as they had started to kiss. As he would think of it afterwards,

'I was no Arab, I had no tent to fold, but I silently stole away.' Margaret had declared her love for Ray.

And, of course, there was that other time, when he'd gone home, to the small spread his parents kept on the edge of Milton, for his final four days' leave before departing for the war. On one of those days, he'd gone on a picnic to the lovely, pure-white-sanded beach by the river that ran through Margaret's family property 'Tyrone' with some of the gorgeous girls he'd grown up with – so clean, so lovely and fresh. All together, they had frolicked among the cascading water over the rocks, swum through the lagoon and cavorted on the sandhills, before lunching under the bottlebrush trees on that wonderful summer's day, and he had then realised just how sweet this life was, this life that he was leaving behind.

Two days later, when the service car had come to pick him up to take him to the station – to return to barracks, to go to the wharves, to get on the ship to come to this war – he had been overwhelmed with such sadness he had almost burst into tears. Sensing this, Dolly, the pony on which he had learned to ride, had come up to nuzzle his shoulder and snort in her old way. And then Timmy the old cat had jumped from the fence post onto his shoulders to rub her head against the side of his face, and purr and meow her goodbye. And then, of course, his family – his father, his mother, his two sisters and younger brother.

His father, who initially had been so harsh about his decision to go to war, had barely been able to stop beaming with pride. My son, the soldier, off to war.

And then, Bert had been still so emotional he had barely been able to get out his goodbyes, and so had got in the car, leaving them all behind to go to the station.

Would he ever see his home again?

LATE AFTERNOON, 11 JULY 1916, THE I ANZAC CORPS DIGGERS ARRIVE WHERE THE POPPIES GROW

It has been a fair haul, over 50-odd miles. But after being pulled out of their 'nurseries' around Fromelles and travelling for three days in

Australian 1st and 2nd Divisions west of the front-line of the Somme

ever-decreasing circles, the first troops of the 1st Division of the AIF at last arrive in their billets within coo-ee or right in the heart of the picturesque towns of Vignacourt and Amiens, some 20-odd miles back from the front-line of the Somme. They quickly settle in to their neighbouring towns and villages, like birds to a tree, dogs to a porch and sailors home from the sea.

The beauty of this place! Amiens, as Charles Bean would describe it, is 'a miniature Paris, far beyond shell-range, practically undamaged, the important streets and boulevards thronged with a bright population not visibly affected by the war; hotels, shops, cafes, cabarets, and newspaper kiosks carried on a brisk trade, the light blue uniforms of the French brightening the sombre crowds of black-coated civilians and khaki-clad British.'[3]

Vignacourt is a much smaller version thereof, if positioned in a much more rustic setting, with the green, rolling hills and misty valleys from which the spires of the village churches peak providing a great and welcome contrast with the flat, marshy lowlands of Fromelles, whence they have come. In these parts, the farmers tend to live in the villages and communes, with their farms either within walking distance or, more commonly, starting in their backyards with orchards.

The AIF's 2nd Division is just a day behind the 1st, and is due to begin arriving the next afternoon. But careful, you men settling in around Vignacourt. I must tell you that just a few miles to the west of here is a French count who lives 'in a large chateau, surrounded by a forest full of deer, which he keeps for his own private pleasure'.[4] That forest is out of bounds, and anyone caught trespassing in it will be severely dealt with. Are we clear?

Yes, sir. Of course, sir.

However, late that afternoon, as the suns starts to wane and the twilight to creep forward, several Australian soldiers head that way with their .303s at the ready. Some time later, several shots ring out. That evening, for the first time in many moons, the delicious aroma of roast venison wafts over Vignacourt.

11 JULY 1916, GERMAN 5TH ARMY HQ, STENAY-SUR-MEUSE, VON FALKENHAYN ORDERS UP *STRIKTE DEFENSIVE* FOR VERDUN

Rarely has the countenance of General Erich von Falkenhayn been so variously thunderous, anxious and sad. And never has his cane, in this war, been so firmly ensconced in his left hand as now.

Ja, die Sommeschlacht, yes, the first part of the Battle of the Somme has been good for his own forces and the *englischen Schweinehunde* have made little advance despite suffering great losses. But his more skilled opponents, the French, are the greater concern. He needs more forces to counter their ongoing thrust, and there are only a couple of places fresh men can come from: Verdun, where the heaviest concentration of German soldiers in France continues to press, and up around Lille/ Fromelles, where things are quiet. His confident prediction to the

Kaiser last Christmas that, should they attack at Verdun, '*so werden sich Frankreichs Kräfte verbluten*,[5] the forces of France will bleed to death . . .'[6] has been proved false. In fact, far from bleeding to death, it is the French divisions astride and south of the Somme who really have penetrated, forcing his men into a humiliating retreat, desperately defending their second line.

In the extremity of the situation, von Falkenhayn knows he has no choice and orders the *Armeeoberkommando 5*, Army High Command 5, in charge of the attack on Verdun, to move to '*strikte Defensive*', so that resources may be diverted to the Somme.[7] One way or another, his Verdun *Blutpumpe*, blood pump – the very one on which he has bet his military career – must be turned off.

Within three days, Haig's Chief Intelligence Officer (aka 'Haig's evil counsellor'),[8] Brigadier-General John Charteris – an eternal optimist who insists on starting every day with a brandy and soda – is able to exult to his wife in a letter, 'We have already accomplished one thing; the attack on Verdun is over, or practically over. All their available troops are being sent here.'[9]

11 JULY 1916, HINGES, HAKING'S PLAN DOESN'T GO TO PLAN

For General Haking, it had all been so exciting, only to so suddenly fizzle out. As requested by Monro, he had provided the plan – the very one he had been effectively working on 'since last winter'[10] – to first attack around the Sugar-loaf, and then go beyond it.

Attack! Attack! Attack! Just like the good book – his book – has always proclaimed. For, after subduing the Sugar-loaf, he wants his forces to push on, to capture the village of Fromelles and all of Aubers Ridge, which lies a mile beyond the German front-line. Lille would be at their mercy, and they would be able to accomplish the task they had first attempted over a year before.

However, as has been made clear in the First Army briefing document regarding potential sites for 'subsidiary operations', while Aubers Ridge possesses the 'most suitable terrain if we are short of heavy guns' – which, given the amount of heavy guns being required for the Somme, is most certainly now the case – it is 'however not suitable for a general advance . . .'[11]

Monro has rejected a general advance as now being rather beside the point. When the goal is to stop the Germans from milking battalions and sending them south, there is no need to risk so much in taking Aubers Ridge. (It would only make sense if it was done as a follow-up to a breakthrough on the Somme, perhaps launching a pincer movement south on retreating German forces – 'crushing the intervening Germans as between the jaws of a nut-cracker'[12] – but that currently appears unlikely.)

So Haking's plan has been reduced to being merely a feint, an artillery-only demonstration, not a full-on attack, which would suck in their own precious resources, better devoted to the main thrust along the valley of the Somme. Perhaps, then, the way forward is to take that basic concept of an attack in those parts but do it with artillery only, to spare the troops? For Haig knows more than most the difficulties of attacking that particular heavily entrenched fortification.

The previous year in May, of course, Sir Douglas had been General Officer Commanding the First Army when it had attacked Aubers Ridge – the northern part of his attack encompassing almost exactly the same sector that Haking wishes to attack now – only to suffer complete failure. The attack had been foiled by areas of uncut wire, undamaged German breastworks and well-sited German machine guns. Those parts of the German front-line initially penetrated by the British had been quickly isolated and the attackers destroyed. Under Haig, they had suffered 11,000 casualties in just a day, the greater number within a few yards of their own trenches. Mile for mile, division for division, this was one of the highest rates of loss for the British during the entire war. No ground was taken. For generations to come, that attack on Aubers Ridge would stand as the most classic example of how *not* to do an attack. Sir Richard Haking, who had been commanding 1st Division, had contributed just under 4000 of those casualties.

And while the survivors of that attack had gone on to many assignments, the defenders now were the defenders then: the 6th Bavarian Reserve Division. And its men had been industriously developing their defences ever since, even though those defences had been formidable at the time!

After the first attack, Haig had concluded in his diary, 'The defences in our front are so carefully and strongly made, and mutual support with machine-guns is so complete, that in order to demolish them, a long methodical bombardment will be necessary by heavy artillery (guns and howitzers) before infantry are sent forward to attack.'[13]

Haig's GHQ, together with Monro, comes to the conclusion that the answer is to make 'an artillery demonstration [to] form a useful diversion and help the southern operations'.[14] After all, with the help of the artillery of the 4th Division, which had been left behind, Haking will actually have 288 field guns and 72 howitzers on call – five divisions' worth of artillery[15] – able to bring fire on the connecting point between the German 6th and 2nd Armies.

All put together with the ammunition available, the British could fire across a front of 15,000 yards for as many as three days in the manner of a pre-attack barrage, and if they mixed that with several raids, the similarity with the bombardment prior to the Somme would not be lost on the Germans, and they would surely be convinced that such an attack was imminent. Ideally, this artillery demonstration could commence tomorrow, when the second major offensive on the Somme is due to begin, at a time 'when it becomes evident that this front is likely to be milked'.[16]

It is true, this proposal is quite different to what Haking had originally proposed, as this is now a brassy and bold bombardment, with no particular infantry attack planned – whereas Haking's plan had been typical of him, involving thousands of soldiers charging forward to seize a ridge. But GHQ does ask Haking to devise a new scheme for an infantry advance to Aubers Ridge, just on the chance it becomes 'advisable at a later stage'.[17]

8.30 PM, 11 JULY 1916, SMACK BANG IN THE MIDDLE OF THE NURSERY, THE GOGGLE-EYED BOOGER GETS ON THE TIT

Falling in at dusk, the 55th Battalion of the 14th Brigade of the 5th Division can barely believe it.[18] Yes, the lot of them are laughing and joking, if perhaps a little self-consciously, but they are also hiding an obvious nervousness as, at long last, they are about to take up actual positions on the front-lines of the Western Front, before Aubers Ridge.

Leaving Sailly-sur-la-Lys, they head out onto the roadway, their Australian-made Blundstone boots – all of which have small, rectangular nails on the soles and a metal plate on the heel, to reduce wear on the leather – making that curious *clomp-clomp-clomp* on the ancient cobblestones, their faces illuminated by the endless flares and star-shells exploding just a couple of miles away.

No more than an hour and four miles later, marching due east through the moonlight and towards the front-line, the men of the 55th Battalion come to a long, deep communication trench, Bouteillerie Avenue, and are just descending into it when suddenly explosions break out. Some men instinctively throw themselves to the ground, knowing they are under attack, but no . . .

This is just their own artillery, firing at the Germans.

'If you get so scared of our own artillery,' one corporal laughs, 'what will you do when we get Fritz's?'[19]

It is a fair point, even if, in Bert Bishop's view, every salvo from their own artillery sounds 'like the crack of doom'.[20] But it is made all the more pertinent when the horizon ahead suddenly explodes into life, with streaks of flame shooting skyward, and then real enemy shells start exploding nearby with roars that make the previous explosions look puny by comparison. 'Don't worry,' yells one soldier to Bert Bishop, 'each side is giving the other's front-line a pounding, so you don't have to worry at all.'[21]

It is a curious logic, but still somehow comforting, as the pounding continues for the next 30 minutes. Mercifully, the shells are not landing close to the Australians, despite them getting closer and closer to the front-line. Wide-eyed, they keep marching, before shedding some of their men at the support line, to replace those leaving. The rest of the battalion marches on until they get to a gas alarm post, where another soldier of the 4th Division is waiting to be relieved.

'Here, Bishop, you're nearest,' says the sergeant. 'You take this job.'[22]

And so, as the rest of the 55th Battalion marches on, Bert is left in his sentry box between the front and the support lines, his duty very simple. Before him is the empty case of an 18-pound shell hanging from a piece of rope, the top end of which is tied around a plank driven into the sandbag wall. In Bert's hand is an iron bar. Up ahead in the front-lines, another man is stationed beside much the same implement. At the first sign of a 'greenish, yellow cloud rolling along the ground out in front',[23] with an odour 'not unlike that of hyacinth',[24] the first man must beat his bell shell, pell-mell, to warn of a poison-gas attack. Then Bert is to sound his own alarm as if

Gas helmet, in *The Illustrated News*, 1915

there is no tomorrow – which there won't be if he falls asleep and the cloud engulfs them all. As German poison gas is heavier than air, the danger is that it will drift across and find its way into the trenches and dugouts where the men are sleeping.

On hearing the warning, the men are trained to put on their gas masks – essentially a peculiarly shaped grey bag made out of cloth that you put over your head and tuck inside your tunic collar. Sewn into the bag are two eyeglasses to see through, while a tube goes into your mouth. Known to the Poms as – wait for it – 'the goggle-eyed booger with the tit',[25] a complication is that, for it to work, you can only breathe in via your nose, through a piece of cloth soaked in some mysterious chemical, and out through a valve held in your teeth. With one of these gas masks, you can last as long as five hours. But you have to be quick in getting it on, as the troops are told that 'the gas travels about 25 yards a second with a favourable wind'.[26]

Now, as Bert doesn't actually have to go on duty for another two hours, and as dawn has come, he asks the NCO who has come back to give him his breakfast of porridge if he can accompany him forward to have a quick squiz at the front-line itself. That worthy agrees, and Bert, his heart in his mouth, his rifle on his back, steals forward, only to find . . . a stranger world than he had ever imagined.

Instead of a long series of parallel trenches, what he finds on their own side is a kind of elongated village of soldiers in the shadow of a huge breastworks – an enormous man-made mound that just goes on and on, disappearing into the distance left and right. In fact, it is two man-made mounds of sandbags, the one fronting No-Man's Land being about four yards thick. In the back wall of sandbags, at regular intervals of every ten yards or so, are fire bays – small indents in which there are firing steps for the soldiers to stand on when firing – and 'behind the bays were rows of dugouts, each housing two men'.[27] These dugouts are made of more small walls, using the back of the mound as one wall, and are covered with odd scraps wood and sheets of tin that will keep the rain out. Dotted along the tops of the parapets are toy aeroplanes or broad arrows on sticks, to show wind direction – the point being that when the plane or arrow is pointing at you, you must be doubly alert for a gas attack.

A series of cook-houses lies close to the dugouts, and uncomfortably close to them are also latrines: a small piece of hessian strung around four poles, with a door that opens onto a stench that will outlast the stars. Inside, about knee high, is a horizontal pole on which you can sit over a pit. Luxurious latrines have two parallel poles, on which you can take your perch more easily, with less chance of falling in.

At the point that Bert has come to, there is a sign tacked onto the latrine saying *Ladies Only*, while just a little along is another latrine marked with a notice of its own: *Officers' Powder Room*.

Bert starts wandering around, stunned at this new environment. Dotted here and there are the wonky crosses of the graves of English soldiers, the dates of the deaths recorded in a fading scrawl, '*December, 1914*', '*February*', '*May*', '*October, 1915*'.[28]

Arriving at one particular fire bay, he comes across a lone Australian soldier looking very bored. 'What's the idea?' the bloke asks. 'What are you doing here?'

Bert's answer, that he is just having a stickybeak, stuns the bloke. 'You're missing out on sleep just to admire our front-line? You're not nuts are you?'

'I hope not. What are you supposed to be doing? You can't see anything.'[29]

With this, the soldier grabs a recently crafted home-made periscope and pops the top of it above the breastworks. 'Get up here beside me,' he tells Bert, before giving him instruction on how the periscope works.

Carefully, Bert does as he is told and then peers through the bottom mirror, which shows the reflection from the top mirror of No-Man's Land right before him. Instead of fire and brimstone, raining shells and whizzing bullets, all is quiet on the Western Front. There is no action whatsoever, and all he can see, some 200 yards away, are the ramparts of the German breastworks, encompassing what look to be a few concrete fortifications. The whole space between resembles a garbage tip, with overgrown, foot-high summer grass poking through, and 'weeds and rubbish everywhere, masses of rusted barbed wire sprawling in front of both our own and the German line'.

And nothing is moving.

'This is the world-renowned Western Front,' Bert says to his companion, 'and there's no war at all.'

All along the line, other men of the 5th Division are taking up their places, many of which are not so quiet. Out on the far-right flank, men are just moving into their positions when a furious fusillade of machine-gun bullets rips into the sandbags at the top of their parapet, spraying sand over those below. 'That's Parapet Joe,' a 4th Division Corporal helpfully explains to one of the newcomers. 'He can play a tune with his bloody gun.'[30]

And not a very nice tune at that, as it sweeps back and forth along the line, seeking out any new soldier who just might be stupid enough to poke his head up at the wrong moment. Mercifully, few are *that* stupid, and they prefer the periscopes, where they gaze intently across the pockmarked wastelands to where they can see the brooding, menacing bulk of the German lines – with spasmodic flashes along it indicating the positions of the rifles and machine guns firing at them.

For most men, the very sight of the enemy's fortifications puts a chill in their hearts, a sense for the first time of just what they are up against. But not all of them. One tall bloke from the back o' Bourke can stand it no longer and, rising well above the parapet, fires off a burst of ten rounds. 'Thank God,' he says, 'I have had a crack at something at last.'

Just a few seconds later, the clear sound of a horn comes to them from the German lines.

'You're lucky,' a 4th Division Sergeant offers to the tall'un. 'That's Fritz's casualty horn. You must have winged somebody.'

But the tall private will have none of it. 'Winged?' he snorts. 'I hope I blew his bleedin' head off.'[31]

Around and about, it is easy to spot which soldiers of the newly arrived battalions have fought in Gallipoli and which are new to battlefields. For the new arrivals are seen to gag at the overwhelming stench.

What *is it*? Tragically, the Old Originals of the battalion know it only too well. That, son, is the smell of dead men rotting. It is exactly the same sickly sweet smell that dead animals make in the midday sun a week after being shot, and it is what they lived with at Gallipoli, praying that some day soon it would not be *them* out in No-Man's Land with spilling guts, glazed eyes and a mortal coil long unwound.

In vain, the new men try to settle into this new world, instinctively ducking as a spray of German bullets hits the top sandbag – or, worse, throwing themselves to the ground, while the veterans laugh. There is no escaping a sense of the power of those guns. Many a soldier shudders just to think of it – what would it be like to be out in the open, without the protection of the parapets, and have those machine guns mowing you down?

Christ, what a place. The 5th Division has arrived in the trenches of Hell. And, of course, it doesn't stop at night-time either, as from dusk to dawn the extraordinarily beautiful German flares go up, exploding as high as 700 yards above No-Man's Land before gently floating down on tiny parachutes. As they do so, they illuminate the terrain between the trenches with the most exquisite coloured light for over 30 seconds. Just let any patrol be caught out there beneath one of those flares and they will be massacred just as neatly as if it were broad daylight.

And now it is time for the newly formed Light Trench Mortar Brigade of the 5th Division to have their first go, lobbing a few mortars the way of the Hun. It is with a fair degree of cynicism that the front-line soldiers watch the brigade make their preparations and then – exactly as instructed – fire off ten quick rounds, before quickly disassembling their weaponry and scrambling back.

'They issued Fritz his ration,' one 5th Division infantryman would comment wryly. 'Ten in the air and they were half-way down Pinneys Avenue before the first one burst. Then Fritz issued *his* ration and *we* got it!'

A comparison between their artillery and that of the Germans? There really is none. 'We were obliged to admit,' one Digger would recollect, 'that the enemy fireworks were superior to our own . . .'[32]

General confidence is little improved for those in the front-lines of the 5th Division's 15th Brigade when they follow that most traditional of military commands and turn *'Eyes . . . right!'*. For there on their right flank lie the British soldiers of the 61st Division, a second-tier volunteer unit of the Territorial Army composed of home-service men who have been on the home front for all bar the last six weeks of their existence. The training of its three infantry brigades – the 182nd, 183rd and 184th – has been limited due to 'lack of arms and equipment',[33] and as a distinctly underwhelmed General Pompey Elliott would note of his near-neighbours, they had 'just arrived from England [and] had been milked of their best men to replace casualties on the Somme'.[34]

The contrast in experience, thus, is not encouraging. For while a third of the 15th Brigade are veterans of Gallipoli (around 1300 men) – overall, some 30,000 such veterans are now spread among an AIF force 100,000 to the good – very few of the soldiers in the 61st have seen any action at all, bar the odd pub brawl . . . and even then.

This low opinion of the capacity of the 61st is one shared by its own soldiers and officers, with one of the latter, Lieutenant Christopher Gallagher, informing his family by letter that he has been '*Posted to the 61st. We call it the sixty worst.*'[35]

Comprising factory workers from industrial Birmingham and Coventry, and farm labourers from the likes of Gloucestershire, Buckinghamshire and Berkshire in the south, the three brigades of the 61st Division contain 12 battalions that have been in training for only a month longer than the 5th Division. And, yes, the British 61st are more experienced as a division than the Australian 5th, having engaged in eight raids in that time, but those raids – all without significant result – have exhausted what little fighting spirit they had in them to begin with.

And many of them, having witnessed up close what had happened at Boar's Head, or at least heard about it from witnesses, are skittish about being under the command of Sir Richard Haking. 'We understand,' one of them would chronicle, 'that part of this force reached its objective and was isolated by the enemy's Barrage and gradually exterminated, while the remainder were exterminated on the way over. We were told that the casualties of the two Battalions were between

1100 and 1200 . . . a truly disastrous enterprise [and] our own troops could only be demoralised by such handling.'[36]

Their Commanding Officer, General Colin Mackenzie, a Scottish aristocrat from a famous military family, has served in half a dozen colonial wars, but his only active service in this war has not gone well. Arriving on the nascent Western Front in October 1914, to take over the 3rd Division following the death in action of its Commanding Officer, he had, in effect, been sacked after just a fortnight, though nominally 'invalided' home. 'General Mackenzie went home this morning,' one of his Brigade Majors of the Rifle Brigade had recorded. 'I presume owing to the mess made of the attack [at La Bassée] . . . Mackenzie was, I thought, not of great merit . . . He was not physically fit.'[37]

Normally, such a humiliation would mark the end of a Commander's career. But these are desperate times, and needs must, so he had been able to make his way back to this front-line command – though no fitter. Whether he is wiser remains to be seen. In short, with a certain aged weariness to his 55-year-old swagger, it is for very good reason that Mackenzie has found his way to such a lowly division – it is thought he is not up for much else.

But to grips. On the morning of 12 July, it is time for the artillerymen of the 4th Division to show the newly arrived 5th Division the ropes. No, it is not quite the blind leading the blind, but certainly it is those who are still wet behind the ears trying to give instruction to those drenched behind the ears. The very reason the 4th Division artillery is still here is that they have been judged as not up to fighting in the Battle of the Somme, though at least they have fired a few shots in anger – something entirely beyond the 5th Division artillerymen.

It is with great satisfaction, meantime, that General McCay, at noon on this day, takes over from General Cox of the 4th Division in the Sailly Château, which has been the HQ for this part of the Western Front and assumes responsibility for the sector. Within hours, all of the 4th Division, less their artillery that they are leaving behind, will be on their way south, to join the 1st and 2nd Divisions as they prepare to enter the Battle of the Somme.

12 JULY 1916, FRONT-LINE, FROMELLES, MINNIE MOANS, WITH FALSE TEETH

Among the Australians of the 5th Division settling in to the front-lines on this night, there is no little trepidation. As the Germans are aware by observation that a new division has entered the fray, they have indeed unleashed the shells of hell upon them, in an effort to break their spirit.

Those 'two red stars hovering in the night'[38] over the Australian lines? These, they are told by the old hands, are an SOS. It seems that one part of No-Man's Land is alive with raids, with the Germans coming over No-Man's Land. Meantime, a quick peep over the parapet shows the chaos caused by the *Minenwerfern* as they hurl their 200-pound 'moaning Minnies',[39] so called because they tumble and moan through the air like the Grim Reaper with a bellyache, trailing 'lines of sparks criss-crossing in the gloom, swerving just before they fell, confounding, dreadful, abhorred far more than shells, killing by their very concussion, destroying all within many yards'.[40]

Bastards of things, they are. They only go about 1000 feet in the air, come down on you nearly vertically and then blast a crater as big as a large room!

The Germans also improvise bombs and hurl, via a huge mortar resembling a medieval siege gun, two-gallon drums filled with high-explosive and whatever scrap metal they can find. When the Diggers dissect one bomb that hasn't exploded, they find nuts, bolts, screws, 'the cog-wheels of a clock and half a set of false teeth'.[41] (Yes, there is General Rawlinson's military tactic known as 'bite and hold', but this, as a Welshman might say, is *fookin' ridiculous*.)

Most of the Minnies, alas, *do* go off, sounding like the 'Day of Judgement'[42] has arrived.

Willkommen an der Westfront, Ihr Australier! Welcome to the Western Front, you Australians!

And a stinging welcome it is too.

'Took over command from Gen. Monash at 6 a.m.,' General Tivey of the 8th Brigade writes in his diary this evening. 'Visited 29th Battn in the trenches. Two men of the 29th Battn killed, two wounded. The first men killed in action of 8th Brigade.'[43]

It is a bitter blow, and both the battalion and the brigade take it hard. But, as Tivey is wont to say, 'this is war'.[44]

13 JULY 1916, VIGNACOURT, POUND FOR POUND, POZIÈRES BOUND

Today is the day. The order has come through. The 1st Brigade of the Australian 1st Division must move out towards some place called Pozières, to take it off the Germans. Time to pack up and move, Dig. The 2nd and 4th Divisions will soon be following us.

Charles Bean is there as they march out, and he will choose his words to describe the scene carefully. 'There was,' he writes, 'a perceptible sadness among many of the inhabitants, who of late had watched many similar units march away, to return a week or two later lacking a large proportion of the familiar jolly faces.'[45]

The other brigades of the 1st Division are also under way on the same day, thickening the traffic in areas all around them. Their movement makes things a little slower than General Sir Douglas Haig would like as, on this day – the eve of the second big push on the Somme – he visits his key Generals. Of course, when the other traffic sees the three-car convoy with Haig's personal pennant front and centre on the bonnet of the first car, and the lone figure in the back seat, they try to get out of the way, but it is still all slow enough.

Having started the day at his base at advanced GHQ, Château Valvion, Haig has first visited General Rawlinson at Château de Quierrieu, and now Major-General Pulteney at Château de Montigny, as he continues to make his way along the main line of the action on the Western Front, including navigating through huge masses of Australians on the roads around Vignacourt.

Alas, it is soon after sitting down with General Pulteney that Sir Douglas receives confirmation of a troubling and most credible report. Pulteney informs him that, by interrogating captured soldiers and taking identifying badges from dead ones, III Corps intelligence has just discovered that some of the Germans facing them here astride the Albert–Bapaume road had until recently been up around Lille. A week ago, there had been the report of just one battalion moved from that relatively quiet area to the Somme battlefield, where they were more urgently needed. But now – curiouser and curiouser – the word is that the Germans from *nine* battalions previously in the north are now here in the south.

Clearly, this must be stopped, and as raiding alone has been ineffective in making the Germans feel they have to leave their battalions there, then obviously the British will have to be more aggressive. Maybe Monro's recently proposed artillery demonstration is not going to do the job o'work that needs to be done. Perhaps a full-on, all-in, everyone-out infantry attack is the thing?

Yes, that is it. In Haig's words, when it comes to Crown Prince Rupprecht's 6th Army, which he knows is opposing them up around Lille, he is coming to the conclusion the best thing will be 'to tap on Rupprecht's front, to see if it [is] hollow'.[46]

That afternoon, back at GHQ, General Haig discusses the situation with his Chief of Staff, Brigadier-General Sir Launcelot Kiggell, and his Chief Intelligence Officer, Brigadier-General John Charteris. It is not just that German soldiers of nine new battalions from the north have been confirmed – it is that they come from two divisions. Does this mean two whole divisions, encompassing 24 battalions, are present at the Somme, or just elements of them?

What is clear is that they must beef up the Fromelles attack in the north in the area from which the battalions are being taken. Perhaps it is time to give that plan – that infantry attack Haking had proposed on Aubers Ridge – another look.

Ah yes, here it is. One of Haig's senior staff officers retrieves the proposal.

Haking had suggested that his XI Corps could attack the Sugarloaf salient, the bulge in the German line, and thereafter take the two main tactical localities on the ridge, the high ground around Fromelles and the village of Aubers.[47]

As time is of the essence, Major-General Butler – in the company of Major Harry Howard of the General Staff – is sent north that very afternoon to visit First Army HQ in their château outside the town of Chocques. In conference with, first, Sir Charles Monro and, second, the two Chiefs of Staff of the First and Second Armies, something of an accord is reached.

The artillery demonstration can become a three-day preliminary bombardment, at which point they will send in an infantry attack limited to taking the German front-line at Fromelles and its support trenches. That attack, added to the limited bombardment, should surely do the trick of stopping the milking.

Now, if that bombardment starts on the morrow, more or less coinciding with the second push at the Somme, the attack could go in as soon as 11 am on 17 July. Upon consultation between Monro and Plumer, it is decided that Haking can have not two but *three* divisions – the Australian 5th Division borrowed from the Second Army, and two divisions of the First Army, namely the 61st and the 31st.

Under the overall command of Haking, they can attack at the Sugar-loaf, which is the spot that marks the boundary between the First Army and the Second Army. (This reasoning, of course, is remarkably similar to the way the Somme Valley had been chosen as the location of the joint attack between the British and French Armies.)

Agreed?

Agreed.

Major-General Butler quickly confirms the arrangement with an official note:

```
The role of the First Army is to fully occupy
the enemy on its front and prevent the
detachment of hostile forces towards the south.
This role has hitherto been fulfilled by
constant raids . . . along the whole front. Some
more incisive operation, however, is required
. . . and for this purpose the attack on the
```

```
left of XI Corps assisted by troops from the
Second Army, under General Haking, has been
projected.⁴⁸
```

With this, General Butler and Major Howard are soon on their way to confer with the Generals Plumer and Godley at II Anzac headquarters at La Motte aux Bois.

Do General Godley and his all-British staff make any protest at the *very idea* of throwing inexperienced Australian troops of the 5th Division, who have been on the ground for just days, in against well-entrenched German positions, under the command of a British officer with a tragic track record of suffering huge casualties for no ground gained?

They do not.

British officers to British officers, this administrative matter is all quickly locked down with a crisp official order from GHQ:

```
The First Army will carry out an offensive
operation as early as possible . . .⁴⁹
```

When Monro briefs Haking at 6.30 pm at Chocques, Monro is firm. Knowing the Commander of XI Corps is still desperate to make the huge breakthrough, Monro tells him that he must not try it on this occasion. No, when the attack goes in, they must go for no more than the support trench in the first German line of defence and not overextend themselves. Are we clear?

Clear, sir.

In the meantime, it is agreed that the artillery already in position can start the bombardment first thing on the morrow, while the other guns required can be moved forward. Late that night – *upon a midnight dreary, as he ponders, weak and weary* – General Godley sends for the 5th Division's General McCay to come and see him at his château, La Motte aux Bois.

McCay is promptly informed that, because his 5th Division is the southernmost divvie in the Second Army, it is to be part of a joint attack with the two northernmost divisions of the First Army of General Monro, the 61st and 31st Divisions – with the whole attack under the control of Sir Richard Haking, who commands the XI Corps of the First Army, where the two other divisions are drawn from. Their task will be to take 6000 yards of the German front-line.

General McCay's dearest wishes, thus, have been realised, and he greets the news with 'much gratification'.[50] It is really something to think that his division, the last of the lot to arrive in France, is nevertheless going to be the first unit of Australian forces to be thrown into serious action. And no matter for him, either, that six of his battalions have not even laid eyes on the front-line, and the other six battalions have only been there for two or three days. He is confident they will be able to adapt.

Godley explains something of Haking's plan. It will be for the 5th Division of the AIF and the British 31st Division of Haking's XI Corps to capture 4000 yards of German trenches eastward from the Sugar-loaf, while the British 61st Division of Haking's XI Corps will do the same, for 2000 yards of trenches from the Sugar-loaf to the south-west. They will attack at 11 am on 17 July, just four days hence.

DAWN, 14 JULY 1916, SOUTH OF POZIÈRES, BITING AND HOLDING GERMAN NUTS

A fortnight after the first British attacks have gone in, Pozières Ridge is still firmly in enemy hands and continues to be what the Germans see as *eine harte Nuss zu knacken*, a hard nut to crack – the archetype of defence in depth.

On 1 July, the only success had been south of the Albert–Bapaume road, where, true, a large bite had been taken out of the first of the three Hun trench systems. But even there, at Bazentin, south-east of Pozières, the second trench system, with a 30-yard-deep belt of wire in front of it, remained as intact as it ever was, bristling with intent across a 200-yard-wide No-Man's Land. And two miles behind that again is the unfinished but still formidable third trench system.

All of the trenches in the first two trench systems are equipped with concreted-roof dugouts, about 40 feet deep, and most have multiple exits. Worse, tunnels have been dug between the basements of most of the buildings still standing (and those not), and many of them have been converted into fortified strongholds, with reinforced concrete and bristling guns.

This time, however, there is a change in tactics. Though Haig certainly does not lower himself to acknowledging that he had been wrong and General Rawlinson right when it came to artillery tactics, there is no doubt that Haig's ideas had not triumphed on 1 July. On this occasion, thus, Rawlinson's idea, which is to 'bite and hold' – as in 'Bite off a piece of the enemy's line, like Neuve Chapelle, and hold it against counter-attack' – is the guiding force of the artillery.

'The bite can be made without much loss,' Rawlinson has long maintained, 'and, if we choose the right place and make every preparation to put it quickly into a state of defence, there ought to be no difficulty in holding it against the enemy's counter-attacks, and in inflicting on him at least twice the loss that we have suffered in making the bite. This policy, I think, we should adopt all along the line.'[51]

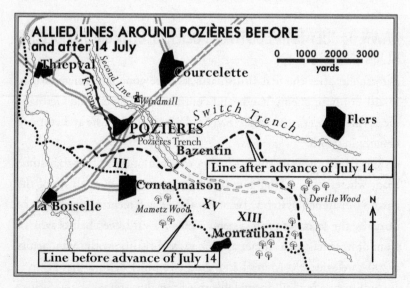

British lines around Pozières before and after 14 July 1916

While the forces of General Hubert Gough's Reserve Army[52] attack Thiepval, it is Rawlinson's Fourth Army that attacks from south of the Albert–Bapaume road. And this time, after getting into position in the wee hours, they go in at the crack of dawn.

It works. At the end of an intensive barrage on the German front-line that has gone on for two days – finishing with five minutes' hurricane fire – and an expertly timed rush, two miles of the second German trench system south of Pozières is indeed secured by just before 10 am, albeit at the cost of 7000 casualties.

In sum, even though the village of Pozières has not been secured, and the troublesome part of the second trench system that runs along the ridge-line by the windmill remains in German hands, General Haig cannot help but be delighted by such positive results, at a time when there are precious few that answer that description. Perhaps one more big attack might do it, and so put in British hands the highest point on the whole Somme battlefield.

Who can do the job?

Perhaps the highly accomplished Australian 1st Division. Already in the process of moving, battalion by battalion, from billets east of Vignacourt to billets closer to the front-line around Allonville, they had done well in the Dardanelles, have gained experience of French conditions up around Fromelles, and have proved themselves adept at raids. They are the answer. Haig makes preliminary arrangements to put them under General Hubert Gough's Reserve Army, which has carriage of the coming attack at Pozières.[53]

Ah yes, Gough. It would be noted, 'The key element in Hubert Gough's character was impetuosity . . . [He was as] inclined to be reckless of danger . . . in war as he was in the hunting or sporting fields.'[54] In war, this had infamously resulted in a debacle at Blood River Poort during the Second Boer war, where he had been captured by the Boers with 240 of his men, while 22 were killed and 25 wounded, all because they had proceeded in their attack with insufficient intelligence.

But, whatever else, he is a 'thruster', and that is what Haig feels is necessary to take Thiepval – even if it does result in mass casualties. It is just a part of war, what?

9.45 AM ON 14 JULY 1916, XI CORPS HQ, HINGES, HAKING SWAGGERS AND WAGERS

In an atmosphere of barely restrained excitement from at least two of the participants in this meeting, Haking outlines his amended plan for the coming attack to General McCay of the 5th Division and the 61st Division's General Colin Mackenzie. Outside his study as he speaks comes the sound of many footsteps, and doors being opened and closed, as his personal staff pack up in readiness to move General Haking and his most senior officers to his forward battle HQ at Sailly-sur-la-Lys.

And yet, beyond the excitement, to Haking's great frustration, things have changed from first conception. Overnight, he has found out that, instead of 300,000 shells for his field guns and 30,000 shells for his heavy guns, upon which he had been counting, problems with supply mean that he will have to make do with just 200,000 and 15,000 shells respectively. Worse, at 2 am, the Second Army advised that they would *not* be able to provide one of their mooted divisional artillery units, upon which he had been banking for their deep experience. This will leave him relying substantially on the entirely inexperienced and not yet fully trained artillery of the Australian 4th and 5th Divisions, men who until just a few months ago had been common infantry and light horsemen. (Some of them, in the words of Pompey Elliott, 'had barely fired a shot in France'.)[55] The Australian 5th Division artillery, Haking has found out, lack trained trench-mortar personnel – something now regarded as crucial in mounting any serious attack.

Because of this lack of expert artillery and sufficient shells, Haking has, on this occasion, realised the obvious: he no longer has enough artillery for a three-division attack. And so they now must make do with just two: the 5th Division and the 61st.

Now, as he puts it in his written instructions: [Each] Division will attack with 3 Brigades in line, each brigade with 2 assaulting battalions, and each battalion on a front of assault of about 350 yards.[56] Thus, instead of an already narrow front of 6000 yards as he had planned, the attack will go in on an even narrower front of just 4000 yards.

Now, to the wall map. Using his 'swagger stick' – a polished, straight piece of dark wood, boasting an ornate silver top embossed with the symbol of his original regiment, the Hampshires – he points out what he wants, regularly tapping the map with the tip.

—

In his HQ just behind his brigade on this same morning, Pompey Elliott is settling into his digs, a habitation of sandbag walls and wooden rafter roof, in turn layered over with yet more sandbags, positioned two miles back from the front-line.

From 6 am, it had been he and his men of the 15th Brigade who had taken responsibility for defending nigh on a mile of the front.

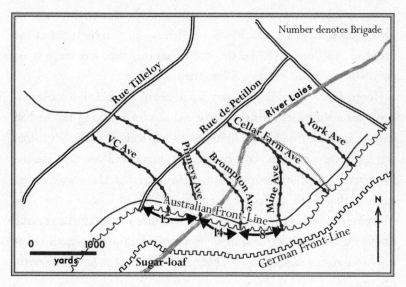

The Australian front-line, Fromelles, 19 July 1916

As he quickly learns by consulting the rough maps at his disposal, the sections to be defended by the three brigades are connected to the front-line by five communication trenches, with the 15th relying on 'Pinneys Avenue' and 'VC Avenue' to move troops back and forth, and supplies forward. The 14th has 'Brompton Avenue', and the 8th has 'Cellar Farm Avenue' and 'Mine Avenue'.

To their immediate right, the men of Britain's 61st Division are equally defending 2000 yards of the front, having also squeezed sideways left towards the 5th Division. They are not much to look at, the men of the 61st, particularly not in comparison with Elliott's own men. For while the men of Australia's 15th Brigade tend to be tall, strapping and still bronzed from the sun of Egypt, the 61st men are closer to human versions of what Cornish coalminers call 'pasties', small white things with sparse amounts of meat, drawn from the impoverished South Midlands of England. And they are clearly still a little shell-shocked to find themselves actually defending a front-line position on the Western Front. For they are, in fact, only 'Territorials' – men who had volunteered for 'home service only' – and were never intended for such a task.

'I don't want Territorials,' Kitchener had remarked when the possibility of sending such units to the Western Front had been raised, 'I want soldiers.'[57] Even Haig had regarded them as 'untrained for the field',[58] and yet so desperate is Great Britain for manpower after the dreadful attrition of the Battle of the Somme, they feel there is no choice but to throw these men into the fray.

Immediately preceding the attack will be an extremely intense seven-hour bombardment, with the particular aim of breaking the barbed wire, destroying the machine-gun posts – particularly in the Sugar-loaf – and making sure Fritz keeps his bloody square head down. In the last three hours, that bombardment will intensify and, as the written orders instruct, include four 'lifts' for the planned Chinese attacks – the tactic whereby the soldiers in the front-line will show their bayonets above the parapet and in some cases lift up papier-mâché dummies and stuffed sacks, just as officers will whistle and shout orders.[59]

This time, there will be no 'creeping barrage', as had happened on the first day of the Somme battle. Experience has taught the Germans to emerge as soon as the shells stop falling on their front-lines, so a new method will be tried. Now, the shells will continue to rain down upon the enemy front-line, which varies in distance from 400 yards from the trenches to be occupied by the 15th Brigade on the right down to 200 yards for the 14th Brigade and further down to just 100 yards for the 8th Brigade on the far left. It will be the job of the troops to get as close to those trenches as they can while the shells are still falling. Then, and only then, will the barrage lift, enabling the forward troops to rush forward and take the trenches at the point of the bayonet.

Now, one obvious complication is that the dividing line between the two divisions is right near the most formidable defence they will have to overcome: the Sugar-loaf. It juts out into No-Man's Land, and the heavily reinforced though mostly sunken machine-gun posts therein are capable of first shooting at all comers before enfilading *both sides* on ground so flat that the guns are able to execute devastating 'grazing fire' – so called because it chops the tops off long grass like grazing cows – for hundreds of yards. If they don't hit a man in 50 yards, there'd be every chance of hitting one at 75 yards, 100 yards, 125 yards and so forth . . . all the way to 400 yards away. Most devastatingly, after cutting the British and Australian soldiers down at the knees, there is every chance of hitting them again, as they fall through the line of fire.

That means it is *doubly* important that the Sugar-loaf is quelled, and Haking gives carriage of that task to the 61st Division. Now, once they have taken the enemy's front-line, they are to immediately push on and take the support line as well, and endeavour to hold that position.

Attack, attack, attack!

Chapter Nine

THE HORROR OF POMPEY

A General should possess a perfect knowledge of
the locality in which he is conducting a war.[1]
Niccolò Machiavelli, The Discourses, Chapter XII, 1517

Failure of the first duty of a commander
– personal reconnaissance – resulting in
selection of unsuitable ground . . .[2]
*General Pompey Elliott later listed what went wrong
at Fromelles, and this was his first point*

The precise forms of discipline suited for a nation imbued
with the feudal tradition were not found to be, in their
entirety, well suited for such people as Australians, among
whom the sharp social distinctions and inequalities
of the older nations are practically non-existent.[3]
*Charles Bean, Official History of Australia in
the War of 1914–1918, Vol. III*

14 JULY 1916, SAILLY-SUR-LA-LYS, A WRETCHED, HYBRID SCHEME

Just a few hours after General McCay has been briefed by Haking,
the Commanding Officer of the 5th Division briefs the commanders

of his three brigades: General Elliott of the 15th Brigade, Colonel Harold Pope of the 14th Brigade, and General Edwin Tivey of the 8th Brigade.

Pompey Elliott listens closely and, caught between stupefaction and horror, quickly surges towards anger instead. Try as he might, he can barely bring himself to believe that they are serious.

But they are.

As serious as premeditated murder.

He listens with rising fury as this ludicrous mishmash of ideas, with different guiding philosophies – 'a wretched, hybrid scheme, which might well be termed a "tactical abortion"'[4] – is fleshed out by McCay, in his insufferably pompous manner.

McCay, clearly pleased that the 5th is at last to be blooded, goes on. The men will be a yard apart, charging forward, with the two assaulting battalions from each brigade providing four waves of some 200 men a time. The first two waves are to be ready in the front-line trenches three hours before, and the next two waves are to be ready to move forward, positioning themselves in the support lines 300 yards back.

As ordered by General Haking, the bombardment will begin at 4 am on 17 July and continue for seven hours, at which point the attack will go in at 11 am. The key will be for the first and second waves to go out into No-Man's Land while the bombardment is under way, and then lie down 'about 100 yards in front of the enemy parapet, during the last fifteen minutes of the artillery bombardment'.[5] They must be ready to attack the instant the bombardment lifts, as per the tactical notes provided by GHQ, which is the bible for how everything should be done on the Western Front: The assault must follow absolutely on the heels of the lift . . . This is a matter of seconds.[6]

The next waves will follow them out with an interval of 100 yards between.

Meanwhile, the third and fourth battalions of each of the three brigades are designated 'Reserve Battalions' – though they are 'reserve' only in the sense of not being involved in the initial assault. The third battalion is intended to be particularly active. As soon as the last of the assault waves depart, half of the third battalion will move forward to garrison their front-lines, support lines and 300-yard lines against the possibility of a German counter-attack. The other half is to provide 'carrying parties', loaded with ammunition and supplies, ready to move forward once the German trenches have been secured and they have received a signal from the assault battalions.

The fourth battalion of each brigade, meanwhile, goes into 'Divisional Reserve', to stay a mile and a half back, ready to move forward in support once given permission from McCay.

Once the attack has begun, those forward elements must mark their positions with red flags to let our artillery know where they are, while flares should also be fired so the planes overhead can spot them. It will then be for working parties of each third battalion to provide the manpower to help their respective Field Engineer Companies dig two communication trenches apiece across No-Man's Land, so that supplies can go more safely forward, and the wounded and captured can be brought back.[7]

Now, this is important. It concerns the Vickers machine guns and the Stokes mortars. They cannot be lost to the enemy, so they can only be brought forward 'when it is fairly clear that we hold practically all these trenches'.[8]

The way McCay speaks about it, the plan is all fairly straightforward, and he sketches a scenario whereby few things can go wrong. But Elliott, for one, remains both stunned and outraged. In front of his 15th Brigade, No-Man's Land extends for *400 yards*. And his brigade has to cover *that* distance, against *entrenched* positions, with *untested* troops who have only *just* arrived? Straight across the face of the all but *impregnable* Sugar-loaf, in broad *daylight*?

And not just that, but that 'formidable bastion' is dead-on the meeting point of the right of the 5th Division and the left of the 61st Division, meaning it is not the sole responsibility of one or the other brigade commander.

A man who has continued to study military history with the same assiduity with which he had studied the law, it is obvious to Elliott – or at least as he will later express it – that such a target should 'have been entrusted to a complete unit – battalion, brigade or division'.[9] And yet, against all reason, they must go in, backed by an inexperienced artillery conducting an 'insufficient artillery preparation'[10] that will lay down a barrage of just seven hours?

Most problematic of all, of course – for any fool can see it – is that the whole scheme lacks 'the supreme element in war . . .'[11]

Surprise.

For instead of coming at the Germans when and where they least expect it, this attack will give them three days' warning . . .

Still other things worry Elliott. He is firmly convinced that 'the first duty of a commander [is] personal reconnaissance', and yet though Haking and Monro might have been previously familiar with the area, they have not visited the site before this major attack, and this has resulted 'in selection of unsuitable ground commanded everywhere by enemy observation and fire'.[12] All this and 'hurried and insufficient preparations resulting in mistakes by inexperienced junior staff officers'[13] are happening before his eyes.

It is extraordinary.

But the meeting must break up quickly as there is so much to do in the precious time that remains to bring the 10,000 attacking infantrymen of the Australian 5th Division forward and into position, together with artillery and ammunition. First, those few battalions of the 5th Division that are already in position must be withdrawn and replaced with British troops so that the 5th will be fresh and rested when it enters the line to make the attack.

Inevitably, rumours of the plans leak to many other officers and soldiers of the 5th Division, who, for the most part, do not share Pompey's pessimism that, as he expressed it to a friend, the attack is 'doomed to failure', that it would be nothing less than the notorious Battle of the Nek 'on a tenfold scale'.[14] Second-Lieutenant Waldo Zander of the 8th Brigade's 30th Battalion is a case in point. 'A stunt!' he would recall as his battalion's primary reaction. 'We knew little of what it meant, but to us it seemed something wonderfully new and exciting – a chance for a chap to win his laurels and make good.'[15]

And, yes, they are also told 'Secrecy must be strictly observed', but it just doesn't work like that. 'In every estaminet in the neighbourhood there was nothing else to be heard but the "stunt". Even the mademoiselles asked when it was coming off.'[16]

———

Just a few hours later, Pompey Elliott's anger is so focused he realises he must do everything in his power to change the order. For it has been issued by officers who see things on maps, who surely cannot see what he can see – that this will be something perilously close to a mass suicide, carnage on an unimaginable scale. He *must* get someone from GHQ to see what he can see!

Luckily, Major Harry Howard has returned to the area of the proposed attack on this day to confirm arrangements of the previous day and to work out some details with the Chiefs of Staff of the First and Second Armies. Elliott takes the opportunity, once the meeting is over, to persuade Howard to come for a visit, to survey the ground on this melancholy afternoon. He steers him towards a spot known as VC Corner, just to the east of the Sugar-loaf.

Do you see, Major Howard?

To get to it, to even *begin* to attack it, his men will have to cover 400 yards of open ground, under fire from shot and shell, shattered by shrapnel. Among the obstacles is what the maps have marked down as 'the River Laies', though it is not really a river but just the deep drainage canal that slashes right across No-Man's Land in front of them. It is fordable, not formidable, but still an awkward barrier to get across. More to the point is that, once they get across it, they will still have to breach, under heavy fire, the rolls of barbed wire, the ten-feet-high parapet and the dozens of reinforced concrete shelters.

And now the Australian plays his ace. Brandishing the little booklet issued by General Haig's own GHQ, containing the distilled essence of what the French and British staff had learned about fighting on the Western Front, Elliott points out what is written under the key heading of:

```
Trench to trench attack
Such an attack cannot possibly succeed if the
enemy's front-line trench is distant more than
200 yards from the 'hop-off'.[17]
```

Voilà. It is Elliott's strong view that the attack as planned does not have 'an earthly chance of success'.[18] And surely this experienced British officer, who has the ear of none other than General Haig, must realise that! 'Major,' Elliott says firmly, 'you have read my plan of attack and the orders thereon and have approved of them. I want you now to tell me as man to man, in view of the fact that you have had nearly two years experience in this fighting as against my ten days, whether this attack can succeed, for according to the axioms laid down in this pamphlet which your staff has issued to us we *cannot* succeed.'[19]

Major Howard is, frankly, a little stunned. This is *not* the way things are done in the British Army. One does not speak 'man to man'. One speaks by rank, and is sniffingly superior or cloyingly deferential, accordingly. What to do? The Englishman pauses, and turns a deep shade of red. But then he gathers himself. 'Sir,' he says carefully to General Elliott, 'since you have put it to me in that way I must answer, but I expect the result to be "a bloody holocaust".'[20]

Honoured by the frankness, the Australian officer urges him to go back to Haig and tell him so. Howard promises he will do exactly that.

In the meantime, when it comes to the sickly Mackenzie, Commander of the 61st Division, Elliott also has dire misgivings and is not at all sure he is up to the task set him in the coming battle. For one thing, Mackenzie's division have followed Haking's direct orders and cut sally ports in their parapet – dug by the engineers to within a few inches of the other side – as a way of getting their men out into No-Man's Land. Elliott and all the other Australian brigade commanders know this to be most unwise – they all refuse to do it. Such an act, in Elliott's view, 'advertised the intended attack, and at the same time, weakened their parapet to a great extent'.[21]

And, of course, Elliott – who never saw an ear he didn't want to bend – tells his views to both Mackenzie and Brigadier-General Charles Herbert Carter, who commands 184th Brigade, pointing out that 'a single man getting shot in the sally port would spoil the whole attack'.[22] But it seems to have no effect.

Now, the 52-year-old Welshman Carter – who, like Mackenzie, has recently been promoted from a desk job in Great Britain – is a man with a supremely grim countenance at the best of times, courtesy of a bullet that had taken out an eye 16 years earlier during the 'Relief of Kumasi' in West Africa, but on this occasion his words are even grimmer. 'I am going to try that way anyhow,' he replies flatly, 'and if it fails, I will send the men over the top.'[23]

Pompey Elliott persists in trying to change Carter's mind, convinced as he is that, 'Such a plan is bound to fail. You cannot rearrange your plans in a moment.'[24]

Mackenzie ultimately defers to Carter.

The problem for Pompey Elliott, of course, is that it is not just the lives of Mackenzie's men that are at stake. Given that the 61st have been given the task of attacking the Sugar-loaf and subduing its machine guns, if they fail to do it, it is his own men of the 15th Brigade whose right battalion must stream past it on the left of 61st Division, and who will also be devastated by enfilading fire.

Mackenzie has decided that the 2/1st Buckinghamshire Battalion will be at the head of the attack, specifically given the task of attacking the Sugar-loaf. They must go in hard after a special effort to neutralise the German strongpoint with artillery. Just like the Australian attack, the 2/1st Bucks will form up on a two-company front and go at the Sugar-loaf in four waves.

The fact that Haking wants them to attack in this spot, right by Aubers Ridge, comes as no surprise to any of them. 'Gen. Haking, bless him,' one of the Brigade Majors in the 184th would later recall,

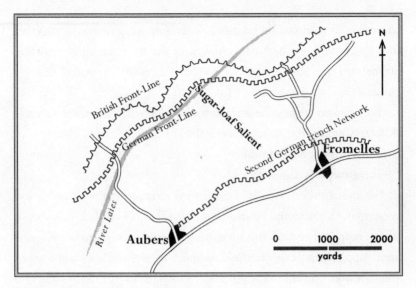

Aubers and Fromelles relative to the front

'was always very keen to take the Aubers Ridge and always told us if we behaved ourselves we should be allowed to attack it.'[25]

EVENING, 14 JULY 1916, KNIGHTS, BISHOPS, ROOKIES AND PAWNS DEFEND THE KING

The word is out among us blokes of the 55th. We, and the rest of the 14th Brigade, are being rotated out. We are being temporarily relieved. Some new coves are coming in to take our spot, even though we've only been in the line for three days.[26]

The good news for Bert, Ray, Hodgy and Robbo is that, in their whole time there, the 55th Battalion has not suffered a single casualty and . . .

And, oh dear. With their high observation points and constant vigilance, the Germans are instantly aware of the changeover and so send artillery shells raining down just back from the front-lines, onto where they know the communication trenches to be, resulting in 'a man in D Company being killed and several others wounded'.[27]

It is sad, but that night in the wee hours, at least Bert and the boys are safely in their billets in the tiny village of Bac St Maur. And it is safety they should savour, because, by the following morning, together with the singing of the birds, something else is in the lightly rustling summer breeze. 'Rumour was everywhere,' Bert Bishop would recount, 'about a stunt we were booked for.'[28]

They reckon we're to be thrown back into the line soon, and not just to hold it, either. But to attack *their* line!

Is it a furphy, or dinkum?

This time, it is dinkum.

For shortly thereafter, it is confirmed that something is going on, as company after company from other battalions is called up to begin taking supplies forward. It is, of course, a logistical nightmare. Wagons from supply dumps as far afield as those by the railhead some seven miles away are loaded to the gills, taken forward to rear dumps just two miles from the line and then taken on Shanks' pony from there to the forward positions.

In the 8th Brigade, General Tivey decides that the position of honour – the assault battalions to go over the top first – will be his 31st and 32nd Battalions, commanded by Lieutenant-Colonels Frederick Toll and Donald Coghill, respectively, with the 30th and 29th as his third and fourth battalions.

In the 14th Brigade, Colonel Pope deems the 53rd and the 54th will do the task, while the 55th will be the third battalion and the 56th the fourth battalion.

In the 15th Brigade, as the 57th and 58th Battalions are already in the front-line, preparing to 'hop the bags' as the assault battalions, and the 59th is billeted in Sailly-sur-la-Lys, the carrying duties fall to Major Geoff McCrae's 60th Battalion.

Among them all, of course, is George Challis, perhaps the most popular man in the 58th Battalion, and not just because he is the champion who had led Carlton to victory in the Grand Final at the MCG the previous year. There is just something *about* George, the way he never stops smiling, pitching in and looking after anyone who is struggling. And today he is in it with the best of them, right there in the front-lines, trepidatious like everyone else, and no doubt fearful as huge

German shells start to explode around them – but trying not to show it, and to settle those around him. As the eldest of six kids, who was always looking after his brothers and sisters at home, such care comes naturally to him. It is just what you must do in such situations – like leaving the glory of being an Aussie Rules champion to join the army as a soldier, because your country needs you – and George does it.

All through the day and night, the carrying goes on, and into the next days and nights, as exhausted men – often using a couple of empty sandbags for shoulder padding – ferry supplies forward, including 'rifle and machine-gun ammunition, hand-grenades, trench-mortar bombs, sandbags, more than a thousand picks and shovels, and a large quantity of engineering stores for use in the captured trenches'.[29] (The Gallipoli veterans know to sharpen those shovels as, in hand-to-hand battles, they can do more widespread damage than a bayonet, and never more so than when chopping at the enemy's neck.) They also carry light bridges, needed to get them over the creek, and lots of scaling ladders to climb up and over the ten-feet-high German parapets in the first place.

No fewer than 57,000 rounds required for the 18-pounder field guns, for example, have to be brought forward by teams of horses, whose horseshoes send sparks flying as they strike the cobblestone roads.

The carrying continues and the men, pawns of the wider scheme, in the service of the King, get progressively more exhausted . . .

Just to the 5th Division's right, the 61st Division is also setting up for its own attack, with one officer of the 2/1st Bucks recording, 'the troops were practically engaged every night in the line or on working parties . . . and practically none of the troops detailed for the attack had a decent night's rest for . . . a clear week before the attack'.[30]

There are many problems, including the fact that one of the 61st's own horses, 'Old Tom',[31] has previously been in service hauling a milk cart and insists on stopping at every farm gate he sees.

From those observation points dotted around Aubers Ridge, including from high in the tower of L'Église de Fromelles, German observers are under no illusions. Everywhere they look, they can see four times the normal traffic of men, trucks and horse-drawn vehicles streaming forward. And meanwhile, though the barrage has not yet begun, a higher than usual rain of British shells keeps falling upon them. Strangely, as the German War Correspondent George Querl notes, 'on the projectiles stood again and again the pious word "Bethlehem Steel Works" – 18-pounder, 60-pounder, heavy howitzer projectiles of 23.4 cm, also 30.5, always gifts from Bethlehem. One studied the duds zealously: Thank *Gott*, there were many of them.'[32]

But, duds and all, they continue to rain down.

'The issue,' Querl would recount, 'looked serious and one was on alert.'[33]

Whereas previously it seemed likely that the barrage was just 'an answer to the previous night's raid',[34] it is now obviously something far more significant. The long-expected attack must be upon them.

The Commander-in-Chief of the 6th Bavarian Reserve Division, General Gustav von Scanzoni, does not hesitate. In response, he orders his own reserve troops forward, and makes sure the dumps of grenades and ammunition in the front-line are full to capacity.

Schnell! Schnell! SCHNELL!

(One thing, however, confuses them. The Germans already know something of who opposes them but cannot quite believe they could already have aggressive intent: It remains to be seen whether the 5th Australian Division has taken over the entire sector from the 1st Australian Division. The 5th Australian Division was only formed a few months ago in Egypt, where it underwent training. It would be a departure from previous British practice if the Division were to take over the whole sector without at least some measure of prior 'acclimatisation'.[35] Surely, they wouldn't be such *Dummköpfe?*)

———

Far to the north on this same evening, at his headquarters in the French town of Charleville, on the Meuse River, General Erich von Falkenhayn is caught between devastation and desolation. The news throughout the day has become progressively worse, most particularly when it comes to one noted area of the campaign.

With colleagues Major-General Gerhard Tappen and General Adolf Wild von Hohenborn, he goes through report after report detailing setback after setback at Verdun. 'Probably never before,' the Reichskriegsministerium, the German Reich's Ministry of War, would later document in its *Official History*, 'the responsibility that he had taken on with the attempt of the attack on France's strongest fortification, had laid so heavily on him as in this moment, as he had to admit for good the failure of the whole endeavour.'[36]

And it does not get any better the next day, when yet more bad news comes in, from both Verdun and the whole Battle of the Somme. 'The evening conversation,' von Hohenborn would record, 'was very serious. It is not comprehensible to us yet that our troops there crumble away and lose village by village, forest by forest . . . Falkenhayn's nerves are pretty shot and . . . he threw his Flint rifle into the field altogether'[37] (as the common German expression goes – just as soldiers did back in the old days in the early 1600s, to escape more quickly from their enemy pursuers. Their British counterparts, curiously, on such occasions, would continue to throw in the towel. But not on Sir Douglas Haig's watch, they won't. Never!).

AFTERNOON, 15 JULY 1916, 14 FURLONGS BACK FROM THE FROMELLES FRONT-LINE, THE WHIZZ-BANGS WHIZZ AND BANG

For Second-Lieutenant Norm Nicolson, whose battery was transferred just a week earlier and now joins the men of the 25th Field Brigade of the 5th Division artillery, it is finally time to put everything they have trained for into practice. After being hauled forward by their horses, they have positioned their guns behind a hedge – which has holes cut into it for the barrels – loaded them and primed them once more, ready to go.

What is more, their Major has climbed a high tree some 300 yards away to a position where he can observe and adjust the fire on their target: the German wire. He now gleefully gives the signal.

They fire!

And fire!

And fire again!

And . . . wh . . . what is that sound?

What sound?

That whizzzzzzing sound.

The big one or the little one?

The little one.

That little '"whizz whizz" sort of sound'[38] proves to be bullets, which is tough enough, even if it does cause the gnarled Gallipoli veterans to grin at the evident shock of the Marmalades. The larger *whizzzzz* sound is, however, a lot more problematic.

'"BANG!" a German 5.9 inch high explosive shell burst a bit beyond the Battery,' Nicolson confides to his diary. 'But before its smoke disappeared another landed just in front of a gun-pit . . . For an hour the Germans shelled the position, putting in 62 rounds of high explosive shells weighing nearly 60 pounds each.'[39]

Shrapnel flies, men go down, one gun and crew are completely obliterated by a direct hit, and the cook-house is shattered. This is not like firing out in the desert, where the dunes don't fire back. This is terrifying!

15 JULY 1916, 5TH DIVISION HQ, SAILLY-SUR-LA-LYS, NO WORD ON THE 'HOLOCAUST'

Of her Prime Minister William Ewart Gladstone, Queen Victoria had once said, 'He speaks to me as if I were a public meeting . . .'[40] and General McCay, a former Australian Minister for Defence, is a lot like that. 'Clearly understand,' McCay is lecturing his brigadiers on this afternoon, 'that each wave, so soon as it has cleared of enemy the work it gets into, goes on to the prescribed limit of attack, [as in] the rearmost enemy work,' estimated to be 100 yards or so beyond the front-line.[41]

Australian soldiers walk along a duckboard track on their way to the front-line trenches near Fromelles in northern France, 5 June 1916. Breastworks reinforced with timber and sandbags can be seen behind the line of men. (AWM EZ0048)

An old Frenchwoman serves coffee to soldiers at an estaminet in her village, within 800 yards of the trenches. (AWM EZ0032)

A group of Australian soldiers lean out of a shelter, well protected by sandbags, in a part of the front-line rebuilt by troops in the Bois Grenier sector south of Armentières. (AWM EZ0053)

Soldiers walk along a path beside the row of front-line trenches, Fleurbaix, France. (AWM P00437.017)

Two gunners sit beside a 4.5-inch howitzer Mark I in a gun pit of the 102nd
Australian Howitzer Battery in northern France. Each man is holding a shell.
(AWM C01409)

A soldier stands beside a crater made by a German *Minenwerfer* (trench mortar)
that fell just behind the front-line trench of the 11th Battalion near Cordonnerie
Farm during the bombardment that preceded a German raid. About 40 men were
killed and 60 wounded in the bombardment of this short section of front-line.
(AWM EZ0057)

Men of the 53rd Battalion wait to don their equipment for the attack on Fromelles, 19 July 1916. Only three of the men shown here will come out of the action alive, and those three will be wounded. (AWM A03042)

Two men of the 53rd Battalion minutes before the launching of the attack. (AWM H16396)

Australian and German bodies lie in a portion of the German second line held throughout the night by the 5th Australian Division during the Battle of Fromelles. (AWM A01558)

The body of an Australian soldier killed in the German second line. The photograph was taken on the morning of 20 July, after the Germans had reoccupied their trenches. (AWM A015660)

Unfinished defensive works in the German front-line during the Battle of Fromelles. (AWM A01564)

The remains of a German pillbox that formed part of the defences in the Sugar-loaf Salient, covered with snow and overgrown grass. The view is from the south side, looking north across No-Man's Land. (AWM E05793)

A two-storey concrete observation post built up inside an old house on the Fromelles–Le Maisnil Ridge. From this position the enemy could discern the movements of the 5th Division in preparation for the attack on Fromelles. Enemy intelligence papers that were obtained subsequently stated that the actual moment of attack was known some considerable time beforehand. (AWM E04040)

Captured Australians arriving at the German collecting station on the morning of 20 July. (AWM A01552)

The church of Fromelles in May 1915, drawn by the artist Otto Ammann. 'Ghostly the ruins of the church tower rise into the dim dark of the moonlit night,' one of the Bavarian soldiers new to Fromelles would recall.

A young Adolf Hitler serving as a regimental message runner on the Western Front, including during the Battle of Fromelles.

Hitler visiting one of the Fromelles trenches he served in during the First World War, 1940.

British Lieutenant-General Sir Richard Haking. His overly optimistic view of Fromelles as a point of attack, despite the topographical disadvantage, would lead to a horrific number of Australian casualties.

Field Marshal Sir Douglas Haig, Commander-in-Chief of the Expeditionary Forces in France and Belgium from 1915 to 1919. (AWM A03713)

Major-General James McCay, Commander of the 5th Australian Division. Note the A on his sleeve, indicating service on the Gallipoli Peninsula. (AWM A03729)

Lieutenant-Colonel Walter Cass, 2nd Infantry Brigade. (AWM 01470)

The original grave and cross of Gallipoli veteran Captain Norman Gibbins, 55th Battalion, killed in action on 20 July 1916. The message on the plaque from his sister reads, 'With my soul's homage and my heart's utmost love to my beloved and deeply mourned brother. Violet Gibbins.' (AWM P03788.003)

Brigadier-General Pompey Elliott. He tried in vain to convince his superiors that the attack on Fromelles was doomed to fail, and wept as he met survivors coming out of the line. (AWM A03084)

Raymond Bishop of the 55th Battalion.

Gunners of the Australian Siege Artillery Brigade ramming home a shell in a 9.2-inch breech-loading howitzer on a hot summer's day. The batteries of this brigade were among those that supported the I Anzac Corps at Pozières. (AWM EZ0145)

Eight Australian officers having breakfast in a shell hole in Sausage Valley in the forward area near Pozières. They are using wooden food crates for a table, but they have crockery and a teapot. (AWM EZ0075)

A view of the heavily shelled old Pozières cemetery. (AWM E00001)

An Australian fatigue party from the 7th Brigade (far left) carrying piles of empty sandbags to the front-line through the devastated area near Pozières. The structure on their right is the remains of the concrete German observation post nicknamed 'Gibraltar' by the Australians, which stood on the western end of the village. (AWM EZ0098)

The village of Pozières and the road to Bapaume, as it stood on 25 August 1914. (AWM G015341)

The village of Pozières some months after the battle. The view is from the southern side of the main road, looking southwards. The lone grave is that of Captain Ivor Stephen Margetts of Wynyard, Tasmania, who served in the 12th Battalion and was killed in action on 24 July 1916. (AWM E00532)

A group of four Australian artillery men with one of the battery of 8-inch mortar guns that fired on the Pozières Windmill. (AWM C00450)

The Windmill site at Pozières Ridge, with the 2nd Australian Division Memorial Cross. (AWM H16941)

The Basilica of Notre Dame de Brebières, showing the leaning statue of the Virgin, later destroyed by shell fire. The peasants in this area held the superstition that war would end when the Madonna fell. It collapsed, however, at the time of the operations in the spring of 1918. (AWM E02068)

General Birdwood addressing soldiers of the 2nd Australian Infantry Brigade in Vadencourt Wood after their first tour of duty at Pozières. Between 23 July and early September 1916, as part of the Somme offensive, the 1st, 2nd and 4th Divisions between them launched 19 attacks on German positions in and around the ruins of Pozières. (AWM EZ0085)

Captain Albert Jacka VC MC and Bar, 14th Battalion. Captain Jacka was awarded the Victoria Cross as a Lance-Corporal for 'conspicuous bravery' on the Gallipoli Peninsula, becoming the first Australian recipient of the Victoria Cross in the First World War. He would be awarded the Military Cross for his actions at Pozières. (AWM P02939.001)

Bronze statue by Peter Corlett (the Cobbers Memorial) in the Fromelles Australian Memorial Park, Fromelles, France. (Photo: Maurice Savage/Alamy)

And now, as he gives his detailed instructions, this is particularly important . . . 'The mode of taking the trenches should be as follows,' McCay says, and subsequently puts it down as a formal order. 'The first wave must clear enemy out of the first row of enemy trenches in which any enemy are, whether they resist or not. Then advance further. Meanwhile the second wave must pass the first wave to next enemy row . . . and so on till the works of the enemy's first line system, which in most places extends about 100 yards behind their front parapet, are taken.'[42]

True, this idea for the assault waves to keep leapfrogging each other until the final target trench is reached is consistent with the GHQ orthodoxy. What is neglected in McCay's instructions, however, is another key part of that orthodoxy, which is to leave a garrison in the first of the trenches that are captured, to ensure that they can be held.

In the meantime, Pompey Elliott has still had no word back from Major Howard about his warning that a catastrophe awaits if the plan goes ahead, and so has taken up the issue with others. 'Pompey,' Captain John Schroder, his Signal Officer, would recall, 'was dead against it, and had several sharp exchanges with Generals Birdwood and McCay, but he was overruled.'[43]

Just like Colonel Grisewood before the battle of Boar's Head a fortnight earlier, Elliott is consumed with a fatalistic frustration. He can see what is coming and is doing everything he can to put a stop to it, but nothing is working. And his most immediate superior officer is complicit. For the life of him, Pompey just cannot understand why the GOC of the 5th Division doesn't raise hell at the very prospect of what his men have been asked to do. 'McCay was [terribly] anxious that it shouldn't be stopped,' Pompey would later recount, 'and made no mention of the difficulties facing us.'[44]

It is Elliott's later recorded view that McCay is blinded by what he sees as the glory of being the Commander of the first Australians to make a big attack in France, 'and so get a big splash.'[45] As to the sharp exchanges Pompey Elliott has with Birdwood and Brudenell White, the latter is not surprised. 'Summing up Elliott's capacity and character,' he would later say, 'the two c's that count – I should say that he had most of the attributes of a great soldier but just lacked an appreciation of the knowledge of the defects of his qualities and the will power to . . . control them.'[46]

In fact, though General Sir William Birdwood is firm that they all simply must do as ordered from on high by Haking and General Sir Douglas Haig, and that Elliott is borderline insolent in his protests, quietly both Birdwood and Brudenell White also are in daily contact with Haig's GHQ, and both men make 'no secret of their adverse opinion'[47] for what Brudenell White will later characterise as 'a most undesirable operation'.[48]

Does it have an effect?

Perhaps. As does Howard making his own report to Haig . . .

For now that the time comes for Haig to sign off on the whole attack going ahead, the Commander-in-Chief of the BEF formally notes at the foot of the report detailing how the attack will go in:

Approved, except that infantry should not be sent in unless an adequate supply of guns and ammunition for counter-battery work is provided. This depends partly on what guns enemy shows.
D.H.
15 July '16.[49]

In short, Haig is giving Haking an easy 'out' to stop the attack if he wants, and is perhaps even hinting that he wants that to happen.

—

No matter that the 60th Battalion is not to be one of the two assaulting battalions in the 15th Brigade, on this day the Commanding Officer of the 60th, Major Geoff McCrae, and his second-in-command, young Major Tom Elliott, push forward to have a closer look at the lie of the land, which they have only seen spasmodically over the last few days when taking their men forward on fatigues, digging and filling sandbags, carrying ammunition and the like.

Notwithstanding the fact that Major McCrae is the superior officer of Major Elliott, there is an easy friendship between the two, a mutual respect. There is nothing of resentment from McCrae for the brilliant rise of Elliott – which likely presages the younger man leapfrogging him in the future – and nothing from Elliott in turn that is resistant to McCrae's leadership. They agree on most things, and perhaps never more so than now. One look at the distance they and their men must traverse, against entrenched positions, across difficult ground, and neither are under any illusions about what they are up against. They come away more quietly than they arrive, with much to reflect on.

McCrae has been a little out of sorts lately, and this doesn't help. 'I had a letter from Helen with samples of the wallpaper,' he writes around this time to a friend. 'How I wish I could be within the walls they clothe once again . . . I am feeling fearfully homesick. I suppose it is owing to worry.'[50]

———

Frantically busy in his HQ, ensuring that everything that can be done is done, General Pompey Elliott feels ever more desperate. Is there no hope? When a member of General Haig's own staff acknowledges that a 'bloody holocaust' is the certain result of an attack and promises to bring it to Haig's attention, surely there will be a change in plans?

But there is nothing. Instead of the penny dropping, it is only ever more German shells – and right on their noggins at that.

'I confess I have very grave doubts as to whether the attack can be a success,' Pompey confides in his diary. This 'trench warfare needs very careful preparation and not hastily improvised as in this case'.[51]

On this night of 15 July, a devastatingly accurate and concentrated German bombardment falls upon A and B Companies of the 58th Battalion in the front-lines, just instants before an enormous German raid succeeds in penetrating their line, creating havoc and causing no fewer than 140 casualties – and the taking of 'three members of an Australian Lewis-gun team with their gun',[52] as prisoners.

'I saw one huge hole made by a shell, that you could put the kiddies' playhouse in,' Pompey Elliott informs his wife in a letter, 'being fully 15 feet deep and about the same square. So you may judge what a man is like when one of these hits him. About 20 we could not find at all.'[53]

Even before the assault is launched, thus, one of the 15th Brigade's two assaulting battalions is already seriously damaged.

And it is not just the 15th Brigade that has taken terrible punishment. That same night, Bill Barry of the 8th Brigade's 29th Battalion is just moving along a communication trench to the front-line trenches when he sees a chap coming the other way, carrying something wrapped up in a blanket. 'What's that?' asks Bill, blithely.

'This,' the chap replies, 'is all that we could find of George Challis, the Carlton champion footballer.'[54]

SUNDAY 16 JULY 1916, FIRST ARMY HQ, A SHOCK AT CHOCQUES

It is the way of such things. The more calculatedly violent an act, involving death and destruction on an industrial scale, the more sit-down meetings it takes, with maps, secretaries and note-taking, and this morning sees another one.

It has been hurriedly arranged by Butler as, on behalf of Haig, he requires an urgent conference with Generals Monro, Plumer and Haking. For, you see, GHQ has just received some intelligence that changes everything! It seems the Germans are *not* removing their divisions from these parts and sending them south to the Somme after all.

Butler also advises the Generals that Haig has serious reservations about whether Haking has enough artillery and ammunition to first subdue the German line and then, crucially, hold it, should they be able to take over the German trenches.

Finally, a marked success in the Battle of Bazentin Ridge on the Somme, in which the British have broken open the second German line, has provided some relief and further throws into question whether an attack at Fromelles is necessary. Everyone at GHQ, he now tells them, is asking whether Fromelles has become surplus to requirements. After all . . .

The main object of the operation was to prevent the Germans from withdrawing troops from this part of the line, and our information at the present time 'does not impose the necessity for the attack to take place to-morrow . . . as originally considered desirable'.[55] Perhaps, thus, it might be better to keep 'the troops and guns ready to carry out the operation later, if there are better indications of the Germans withdrawing troops, [or even] cancelling the operation . . .'[56]

Haking's brow blackens. The attack not take place? *His* attack? The one he has conceived and thereafter planned? Please, no. 'I am,' Haking says emphatically, 'quite satisfied with the resources at our disposal. I am quite confident of the success of the operation. I consider that the ammunition at our disposal is ample to put the infantry in and keep them there.'[57]

So persuasive an argument does he mount, so passionate is he about the chances of success, that Major-General Butler allows that, all right, they might have the wherewithal to mount the attack. But still Butler persists. Given that it is now *not* urgent that they go ahead, would it not be better postponed or cancelled and perhaps undertaken later, 'if the necessity arose'?[58]

Again, an outcry from the three commanders, Haking, Monro and Plumer, who are unanimously against a postponement. Such a decision would hit the men hard. 'The troops are worked up to it,' all the commanders, with Haking at their lead, insist. '[They] are ready and anxious to do it, and they consider that any cancellation or change of plan would have a bad effect on the troops now.'[59]

The way Haking tells it, the troops *want* to charge 400 yards across open ground at entrenched machine guns. Haking is the rock, the one man absolutely sure of his plans, convinced that they will work. And this helps to allay Butler's concerns. Haking is fully backed by Monro, as they both make the case, 'Unless it is to the advantage of the main battle that this operation should not take place we consider that the orders should hold good . . .'[60]

Now that the question has been put to him in this manner, Butler considers it. 'There is nothing in the general situation to prevent the operation taking place . . .' he reluctantly allows.

Well, then!

In the face of such insistence, Butler backs down. They are the local commanders, and they are insistent that the operation should go ahead. He finally cedes and agrees that 'the operation should continue'.[61]

At last given the go-ahead, Haking follows up hard, seeking – one more time – to pursue the goal that has been his passion for well over a year. 'In the event of great success,' he asks, 'might we push on to Aubers Ridge?'

This time Butler *is* firm. '*No*,' he says with some force. 'The objective was to be a strictly limited one, and the Commander-in-Chief does not intend to embark in more extended operations, however inviting.'[62]

And so it is agreed. The bombardment will start the next day at 4 am, and the attack will go in at 11 am. True, there are many of these senior officers who quietly think this is crazy, as there is so much rain and mist around that it will be impossible for the artillery observers to spot their targets and properly do their registration, but Haking insists.

—

Despite the previous discussion, *still* Major-General Butler cannot leave it. Deeply troubled by those who are saying this will be a catastrophe – and cognisant of what had happened at Boar's Head just three weeks before under the same commander – in the afternoon he returns once more to Monro's First Army HQ in Chocques, encouraged by the fact that heavy rain is now falling.

And he is insistent.

'If the weather, or any other cause, renders a postponement desirable,' he tells Monro's senior staff hopefully, while gazing pointedly out the window at the pouring rain, 'it is to be clearly understood that it is in the power of the Army Commander to postpone or cancel the operation at his discretion.'[63]

In other words, on your head be it. It is *you* of the First Army who have carriage of this operation, not us.

Understood. Understood.

With still no wavering from the commanders on the ground, Butler takes his leave, encouraged only by the weather, which continues to deteriorate, with rain now falling just heavily enough to make it impossible for the heavy guns to 'register' . . .

Butler returns to GHQ and, in the company of two other senior officers, holds a discussion with Haig. The Battle of Fromelles – only ever planned as a diversion – is barely discussed, if at all. Instead, all of the focus is on the actual Battle of the Somme. Haig is insistent on three particular objects, the last of which he writes with a particularly heavy hand in his diary that night:

3. Take Pozières village.[64]

Preparations to do exactly that are now well under way.

—

The heavens weep, making it hell on earth for the Diggers at Fromelles, who continue to ferry supplies forward, desperately racing against the clock to be ready in time.

By now, most of the shells for the artillery are in their dumps, and the most crucial thing is bringing forward rifle and machine-gun ammunition, together with the exceedingly precious Lewis guns – which in one swoop can double the firepower a platoon can put out.

No one works harder than the purposefully selected huge men of the 4th Division Ammunition Column, whose job is to bring the shells for their artillery forward, with each man delivering an approximate three tons on the day – the equivalent of moving 150 bags of cement weighing 44 pounds each a distance of 50 yards. All up, they are under such pressure that at one point they even lose count of the number of rounds issued . . .

'It is a most pitiful thing to see them all,' one veteran officer notes in a letter dashed off to his fiancée, 'going about, happy and ignorant of the fact that a matter of hours will see many of them dead; but as the French say – *c'est la guerre*.'[65]

Meanwhile, the second-in-command of the 60th Battalion, Major Tom Elliott, has suddenly found himself called to General Pompey Elliott's 15th Brigade HQ on an urgent matter.

As all around him senior staff are consulting maps, drafting orders and giving instructions to underlings, Pompey Elliott, with no preludes, tells the young man the news. Major Tom is to leave his position as second-in-command of the 60th, effective immediately, and join Pompey as a senior member of his staff. True, this means that the young man won't be with the 60th should they go into action – they are currently the carrying battalion, which will likely see them in plenty of action – but there is no way around it.

A small parenthesis here. Quietly, privately, this is *precisely* the reason that Pompey Elliott has made the move. He has come to the view that young Elliott, 'a splendid boy', is a priceless officer, a fellow whose 'blood is worth bottling', to use the Digger parlance. In fact, Pompey says of him that he has the potential to be nothing less than an Australian Kitchener, and it is for the greater good that he be kept from an attack that is going to be more than merely dangerous. No, by bringing forward a decision to have him transfer to the 15th Brigade HQ, which Pompey was going to do anyway, he gains a great asset for his staff, and also keeps Major Tom 'out of the fight'.[66] Close parenthesis.

For his part, Tom Elliott is equally quietly torn. On the one hand, he is of course honoured by what is effectively an extremely early promotion, and the opportunity of working closely with a General he admires as much as Pompey is a great one. On the other, having worked so hard to get the soldiers of the 60th to battle-readiness, he does not wish to leave them now that the battle is right upon them. And nor does he wish to leave Major McCrae, to whom he has grown close.

Nevertheless, in this man's army, he is not asked for his opinion. That will be all, Major.

—

Through the night, the ferrying of materiel to the front-line goes on, and into the dusk, and then the night. Once it is at last done, and the compulsion of duty lifts off them, the inevitable happens . . .

'Men got in dead flagged,' one Digger would recount. 'Some dropped down and went to sleep on reaching the trench.'[67] A Lieutenant of the 60th Battalion records that when his own lot finally dropped, it was to have their 'first [sleep] for 48 hours'.[68]

Beyond mere exhaustion, there is growing trepidation as the realisation sets in of just what they are likely facing. 'Day spent in preparing for attack on enemy lines,' Lieutenant-Colonel James Stewart, Commanding Officer of the 57th Battalion, had written at the beginning of this long night. 'Had no sleep for 2 nights now and looks like another. Well we are in for a real scrap this time and I don't know, it seems as though things have been bustled too much but I suppose it will pan out alright but a hell of a number of people are going to get shelled.'[69]

But . . . let the war do its worst. They simply must rest.

It has taken an extraordinary effort, but both the 5th and the 61st Division are now in position to launch the attack. But with the rain so heavy, can the attack go in? Perhaps, but it is not just the rain that is the problem. Even as the artillery crews stand to, ready to fire their big guns at dawn, no one can help noticing that dawn itself is not going to make it to the rendezvous on time. For the mist is so thick, those first glimmers of the rising sun are lost somewhere high above, leaving those below in enduring, deathly darkness.

17 JULY 1916, CATS AND DOGS SAVE THE DAY, FOR TODAY

From the rain alone, Haking had already felt he had no choice. At 3.45 am, he had reluctantly made the decision – unbeknownst to most of the infantry in the front-lines – to put the beginning of the artillery barrage back from 4 am to 8 am, with the attack itself now due to go in at 3 pm. Two hours later, at 6 am on 17 July, with still no sign of the mist lifting, Haking – now installed in his advance HQ at Sailly-sur-la-Lys – decides to put the beginning of the barrage back to 11 am, the original hour that the attack had been meant to go in. The news is greeted 'with intense relief by both divisions'.[70]

Finally, at 8 am, when neither the mist nor the rain has abated, General Haking, with 'extreme reluctance',[71] comes to the inevitable conclusion and writes of his decision to postpone the attack to General Monro. He adds, in the manner of a man who has himself come to his senses and so realised the folly of the entire exercise, his desire that the whole thing be called off:[72]

> The infantry and field artillery, who are to carry out the attack, are not fully trained and G.H.Q., from what was said at your conference yesterday, do not appear to be very anxious for the attack to be delivered . . . I should be glad to know if you wish me to carry it out tomorrow on the same programme. It is important, with these new troops that this information should be given to me as early as possible so I can issue such instructions as will minimise any loss of morale owing to postponement.[73]

Even Haking, it seems, has given up the ghost on this whole murderous plan.

—

One of the officers whose morale is *lifted* the moment he hears the attack has not gone on is Brudenell White. He is greatly relieved to hear it from Bean himself, but, as the *Sydney Morning Herald*'s War

Correspondent would note, he is also 'very anxious to know [if it was off for good] or whether it was merely postponed'.[74]

For Brudenell White makes no bones about it. 'I hate these unprepared shows, Bean,' the architect of the superbly well organised evacuation of Gallipoli would tell him with extraordinarily trusting frankness, 'and that is what it is. I am quite in favour of having a push at [the Germans] up north but not just there. I think it would be quite a good thing to try and push where we thought we could go forward with a force sufficient to go forward and really do something. But I hate these unprepared little shows. What do we do?

'[Here] we may deceive the enemy for two days and after that he knows perfectly well it is not a big attack and that we are not in earnest there. We don't get anything that does us any good – the trenches are hard to keep and it would mean the breaking up of two divisions. It would cost two divisions. No, I am all against these little half-baked attacks.'[75]

Even while they speak, however, the question of whether or not this particular unprepared little half-baked attack is indeed cancelled or just postponed is being settled. Mercifully, despite Monro having been an ardent proponent of the battle just the day before, he now decides on a change of plans. Monro sends a personal cable to Haig, requesting permission to tell Plumer the operation will not be proceeding – noting simply that, under the circumstances, I DO NOT INTEND TO CARRY OUT THE OPERATION.[76]

This time, astonishingly, it is Haig who insists. Overnight, GHQ has received fresh intelligence that the Germans are about to put on a big show at the Somme and may well be about to shift divisions from around Aubers Ridge. Haig, thus, wants the attack at Fromelles to go ahead, with one rider. Monro will have to make the final decision himself:

THE COMMANDER-IN-CHIEF WISHES THE
SPECIAL OPERATION . . . TO BE CARRIED
OUT AS SOON AS POSSIBLE, WEATHER

PERMITTING, PROVIDED ALWAYS THAT
GENERAL SIR CHARLES MONRO IS SATISFIED
THAT THE CONDITIONS ARE FAVOURABLE,
AND THAT THE RESOURCES AT HIS
DISPOSAL, INCLUDING AMMUNITION, ARE
ADEQUATE BOTH FOR THE PREPARATION AND
THE EXECUTION OF THE ENTERPRISE.[77]

'The form of [Haig's] telegram,' Bean would comment, 'was obviously determined by his principle of standing to a decision already given. As Monro had already given his opinion that the resources were sufficient, it was a foregone conclusion that the operation would now take place.'[78]

Is it?

Monro has already said he wants to cancel it, and Haig has now given him the authority to do so. With one signature, on one order, Monro can stop the whole thing. An added reason to do so is the partial success of the German attack on the night of 15 July, which has not only shown up the 5th Division artillery's lack of skill in retaliating but has also taken out some of his men – with 50 dead, 100 wounded and, most worryingly of all, three captured. What if those soldiers have talked and divulged their plans?

There are many reasons to call it off, starting with sanity, but it is also true that the only way GHQ has given him to stop it is to acknowledge that what he has been saying to this point – that everything is fine and they have everything they need to go ahead – is false. Monro chooses not to tell Haig any such thing. He bows to his betters and agrees the operation can go ahead.

Yes, sir. Very good, sir. As you say, sir.

The final decision is now locked in.

As ever, Bean would later summarise the evolution of the plan for the Battle of Fromelles astutely, and with understatement: 'Suggested first by Haking as a feint-attack; then by Plumer as part of a victorious advance; rejected by Monro in favour of attack elsewhere; put forward again by G.H.Q. as a "purely artillery" demonstration; ordered as a demonstration but with an infantry operation added, according to Haking's plan and through his emphatic advocacy; almost cancelled – through weather and the doubts of G.H.Q. – and finally reinstated by Haig, apparently as an urgent demonstration – such were the changes of form through which the plans of this . . . operation had successively passed.'[79]

Not that Bean knows anything of this at the time.

There will be a two-day delay to allow the weather to clear, but the attack is now back on. Haking takes control once more and arranges for an intense seven-hour bombardment to begin at 11 am on Wednesday 19 July, with the main infantry attack to go in at 6 pm.

Not that the soldiers know anything more about it than Bean.

'The day wore on,' one Digger would note of that Monday. 'No orders came through – very little firing on either side – no news; night – and still no definite orders.'[80]

At least, none that the soldiers know of. In the higher echelons, of course, orders are flying back and forth like winged arrows – crisp and clean and powerful, a beauty to behold. And, of course, if all goes well, they will call devastation to their intended targets.

With two days' reprieve – enough for his men to at least get some rest – Pompey Elliott decides to make some key changes to his assault battalions. Though it had been the 57th and 58th that would have gone over the top if the attack had gone in on the morning of 17 July, he now decides to swap them with the much fresher 59th and 60th. Which raises another point. He still has before him the request of McCrae, an officer for whom he has the highest regard, that the officer for whom he has an even higher regard, Major Tom Elliott, be returned to him as his second-in-command. Now Major McCrae is even more insistent. Young Elliott is the best organiser in the battalion, and they now have just 48 hours to get themselves organised on an assault footing. He *must* have him back.

18 JULY 1916, IN THE FACE OF FROMELLES, THE HEAVENS CRY

Dawn breaks, but the weather does not. It is as bad as it had been the previous day. At least by dusk, however, the rain stops to give way to a lovely evening just the way mother used to make. There appears every chance that the morrow will be dry and warm, perfect for launching an attack. Haking gives the order for preparations to be made for the Battle of Fromelles to finally begin the following night, just before 6 pm.

('G.H.Q. said "do it as soon as you can",' Haking will blatantly lie, as to why he gave the order to go ahead. For, yes, Haig had given distant approval to attack, but that's it. The battle is proceeding because of Haking's insistence over GHQ's reluctance, not the other way around. There is no necessity for the attack with regards to the current situation on the Somme.)

Supplies continue to move forward accordingly, often observed by the Germans, who note a particular preponderance of men carrying boxes – likely holding Mills bombs – and strange rolls of material.

In the meantime, Haking commands that his orders be conveyed to each company commander:

> Don't let the position go when you have once
> got it . . . A counter-stroke across the open
> you can easily repel with rifle and machine
> gun fire and with your Artillery. Get your
> communications across to the new line as
> rapidly as possible in the early part of the
> night, and have a good fire position along the
> whole front ready by daylight on 20th. Have
> this order conveyed to all ranks.[81]

Haking also asks for some of his words of encouragement to be read specifically to the assaulting troops, albeit with the strict admonition that you will arrange for ALL COPIES OF IT TO BE DESTROYED DIRECTLY IT HAS BEEN READ so that no copy is taken forward with the attacking troops. What he most wishes for the assaulting troops is for them to bear in mind one thing:

> I know you will do your best, for the sake of
> our lads who are fighting hard down South.[82]

—

Down south, the second push of the Battle of the Somme is going a lot better. German counter-attacks have been hurled back in baths of blood, and gains south of Pozières are now so strongly held that, slowly and surely, if once again bloodily – for it has taken no fewer than five full-blown attacks, the first on the opening day of battle and the last four in the last four days – the British have been able to edge within 1000 yards of Pozières. The time is ripe to bring forward fresh troops and at last capture the village, no matter that it is ringed by hastily built German trenches, with a two-storey concrete blockhouse – nicknamed 'Gibraltar' by the British troops – standing at the closest end. Once the village is secured, they must take the second line of German trenches, running past the ruins of a windmill at the highest point for miles around, and the real prize, the high ground there, will be accessible.

And so, *once more unto the breach, dear friends, once more* . . .

Haig orders General Gough of the Reserve Army to take Pozières 'with as little delay as possible'.[83]

General Hubert Gough is a man whose modus operandi belies his appearance. Though the heavy bags beneath his watery blue eyes reveal his growing exhaustion and give him a rather sad, hound-dog appearance, in military matters he has never moved like a hound-dog. No – a proven 'thruster' from way back, and loved by Haig because of it – he always moves quickly. And even if with each promotion those bags turn a shade darker and a smidgeon heavier, and he is more hound-dog than ever – as if he stored the full weight of responsibility not on his shoulders but stuffed into those small bags beneath his eyes – still he gets even quicker as the war goes on.

On this occasion, no sooner has he received the order on this afternoon of 18 July than he sends for the just arrived General Harold Walker, Commander of the AIF's 1st Division, to visit him at his HQ in the village of Daours seven miles east of Amiens, on the north bank of the once picturesque Somme River – now cursed with the bodies of dead soldiers and horses, which regularly come bobbing down it.

Within minutes of his arrival, General Walker – who is accompanied by his Chief of Staff, Colonel Thomas Blamey – is told by Gough straight up, 'I want you to go into the line and attack Pozières tomorrow night!'[84]

You want *what?* To attack a line in a little over 24 hours that my men have not even seen yet? Can you be serious?

He is.

Well, so is General Harold 'Hooky' Walker. He is an old-timer, a 'fighting soldier' for the last 32 years, including service in the Sudan. The Dervishes hadn't intimidated him there back in 1884, and General Gough has no chance of doing so now. He has been in charge of the Australian 1st Division since the tragic death of General Sir William Bridges at Gallipoli, and is known as an officer solicitous of the welfare of his men, not one to follow orders just because they are exactly that.

In this case, Walker – notably, one of the key officers who spoke to Keith Murdoch at Gallipoli, where he had expressed his displeasure at British command – is simply gobsmacked at the order. And this turns to something very close to anger when he continues to talk to Gough – who, it turns out, hasn't even personally gazed from afar upon the positions he is ordering them to attack. (It will later be said that one reason Gough has not found the time is that, just as General Haig loves nothing more than going horse-riding every day, Gough – an ex-cavalryman himself and former polo player – loves to go boar-hunting and has been doing a great deal of late.)

In the end, Walker all but 'argues desperately for a postponement'.[85] His men will need at least another 48 hours, he implores, as it will take that long to get their artillery into position, let alone the men.

The ever-impetuous Gough, however, is reluctant to delay. But, when Birdwood and Brudenell White lend their considerable weight to the argument – as the 1st Division are, after all, their men – Gough backs down. The Australians, he reluctantly concedes, can have until the night of 21–22 July, when they can attack Pozières in concert with the British 48th Division attacking on their left, while to their right the Australians will be relying on the British 1st Division to ensure they do not take fire from that flank when they push forward.

—

Back near Fromelles, settling down for the night in 8th Brigade HQ is Colonel Harold Pope, whose notably kindly eyes are now bloodshot through lack of sleep, as he has worked himself to a standstill over the last three days and nights.

Have done everything possible that I know of for tomorrow,[86] the man with the most famous cleft chin in the 5th Division writes in his diary, before turning in. Alas, as shells near and far continue to pound, as the light of flares continue to throw grotesque shadows across his humble, sandbagged abode, sleep comes hard, if at all. So many things to worry about. He thinks everything has been done, but has it? Is there anything more he can do to prevent what he fears will happen, just as Elliott and Tivey fear: that their men are about to be *slaughtered*?

His key hope remains – which is the same key hope to which all the brigade and battalion commanders are clinging. Maybe, just maybe, their attack on the German lines can be something of a surprise, and maybe their artillery will clear the way. For if the Germans know they are coming, or if the artillery fails in its task, then the consequences could only be carnage on an unimaginable scale . . .

Chapter Ten

THE BATTLE OF FROMELLES

We thought we knew something of the horrors
of war, but we were mere recruits, and have
had our full education in one day.[1]
*Lieutenant Ronald McInnis from Mackay, a Gallipoli veteran of the
53rd Battalion, in his diary at the Battle of Fromelles, 19 July 1916*

The romance of battle had been replaced by horror. The
enthusiasm gradually cooled and the exuberant joy was
stifled by mortal fear. The time came when every man
had to struggle between the instinct of self-preservation
and the admonitions of duty. I, too, was not spared by
this struggle. Always when Death was on the hunt, a
vague something tried to revolt, strove to represent itself
to the weak body as reason, yet it was only cowardice,
which in such disguises tried to ensnare the individual.[2]
*Hitler, concerning his time at the Western
Front with the 16th Bavarian RIR*

To throw away men's lives where there is no reasonable
chance of advantage is criminal . . . the real indictment
of leadership arises when attacks that are inherently
vain are ordered merely because if they succeed they
would be useful. For such manslaughter, whether

it springs from ignorance, a false conception of
war, or a want of moral courage, commanders
should be held accountable to the nation.[3]

General Pompey Elliott quoting historian Basil Liddell Hart
in Elliott's 1930 critique of the Battle of Fromelles

DAWN, 19 JULY 1916, FROMELLES BATTLEFRONT, A SIGN OF THE TIMES

What the *blazes* is that?

Keen observers in the Australian lines – always on the lookout for any change in the enemy's defences – notice it taking shape from first light. It is a large rectangular shape, positioned right in front of the German ramparts. It is a . . . a . . . oh, it is another sign. There is large black writing on it. What does it say? Some 20 minutes after the first lustre of dawn, they can at last make out the words on a sign in front of the German trenches:

WHY SO LONG?
YOU ARE TWENTY FOUR HOURS LATE.[4]

As luck would have it, the day dawns bright, with nary a cloud in the sky. The birds, bees and butterflies are out in force, and it is obviously going to be a clear-as-crystal summer's day. It is all so perfect that soldiers such as Private Walter 'Jimmy' Downing and his mates of the 57th Battalion, waking up in a mill on the outskirts of Sailly-sur-la-Lys, are reminded of the magpies back home in Australia . . .

Well, not quite magpies . . .

'Here were only twitterings under the eaves,' Downing would record, 'but at least it was a cheerful sound, pleasant on a lazy summer morning when the ripening corn was splashed with poppies, and the clover was pink, and the cornflowers blue under the hedges.'[5]

And so, up and at them. Clearly, with weather like this, the 'big show' of two days before – the 'stunt' that had been delayed – will be back on.

For his part, Jimmy Downing is just glad to be here. Eight times, he had been rejected by the recruitment officers for being too short, only to be accepted on the ninth occasion after – and he swears this is true to anyone who asks! – his mates had 'stretched' him. (Don't ask.)

And so to the day proper, starting with an unaccustomedly large breakfast of egg and chips, courtesy of McCay's specific order that the troops be given two good meals before the attack goes in.

As Jimmy Downing and his mates begin their preparations, many other Australian soldiers and officers are dashing off letters to loved ones. One such is Pompey Elliott, who, despite regularly erupting with righteous rage at those above and below who have not met his expectations, actually has a tender side. In fact, he regards his men as family, to be protected – and they know it. (As one Lieutenant serving under him later put it, 'his bark was worse than his bite and most of his incipient victims became his devoted admirers'.)[6] But when it comes to his actual family, he is beyond tender, and Pompey now writes in his careful hand to his wife Kate:

> I am writing this in the morning, and about 6 o'clock this evening we will start a battle. Nothing like what is going on down on the Somme but in other wars it would be a very considerable battle indeed. I have taken every precaution that I can think of to help my boys along and am now awaiting the signal which will launch so many of my poor boys to their death . . . If mischance comes I can only say God bless and keep you my dear wife and helpmate and may our little ones comfort you always . . . My will is in the safe at the office.[7]

In Bac St Maur, the 35-year-old Commander of the 53rd Battalion, Lieutenant-Colonel Ignatius Bertram Norris – a Sydney barrister in civilian life and former member of the New South Wales Legislative Council – has his head bowed and is on his knees before both his battalion padre, Father John Kennedy, and his men, receiving Holy

Communion. A realist, he knows there is a good chance he will die, leaving behind his beloved wife and infant son, and if that happens, he wants to be at peace with his Lord.

He takes onto his tongue the proffered piece of bread – the body of the Lord – and swallows before sipping red wine, the blood of Christ. Crossing himself, he now rises, feeling cleansed and spiritually renewed.

'Thanks be to God,' Father Kennedy intones as, in the distance, the roar of artillery fire from both sides continues.

In the 60th Battalion, young Henry Williams of Collingwood, a 19-year-old private who only joined the AIF in January, has already written to his beloved mother, and has the letter in his pocket:

> The time is near at hand for a great offensive and, should I fall, I will be proud to know I did so in the cause of Righteousness and Justice . . . This will be a great blow to you, but cheer up . . . Mum! I have kept your wishes, neither smoked nor taken liquor. Give my regards to all the boys and girls. So good-bye for a short time . . .[8]

In his own elegant hand, Major Geoff McCrae, the 26-year-old Commanding Officer of the 60th Battalion, who had been specifically pursued to fill that role by Pompey Elliott, the youngest of six children, with singularly devoted parents, writes to his family:

> Today I lead my battalion in an assault on the German lines and I pray God that I may come through alright and bring honour to our name. If not I will at least have laid down my life for you and my country, which is the greatest privilege one can ask for. Farewell dear people, the hour approacheth . . .[9]

Nearby, Major Tom Elliott is thrilled. For the last two days, he and Major McCrae have been lobbying General Pompey Elliott for permission to join the attack, and that had at last been granted the day before.

'Elliott himself was anxious to go,' Pompey would record, 'so at last with great reluctance I let him go.'[10] It was no small achievement. Tom Elliott is deeply satisfied to know he will have the honour of being in command of the 60th's second wave. (True, there is no doubt that such a command lessens his chances of getting safely back to Australia, to be with his family, particularly his devoted mother, and to see Alice, the young woman he has loved most in this world, but he does not hesitate.)

And now, he and McCrae must head off for a last meeting with McCay, at 10 am, to go over final arrangements.

Emerging from the meeting, the Majors Tom Elliott and Geoff McCrae have a quiet moment together. The bombardment is due to start in just minutes. Within hours, the 60th will be in the thick of it, and they will be at the fore. They both know that they may have only hours to live. Whatever happens, their regard for each other could not be higher, and the two now warmly shake hands and wish each other well.

In the time that remains, Tom dashes off a note to his beloved sibling, Emily:

My Darling Sister,
Just a line to let you know all well . . . Some operations
are pending so must cut this short.
Your loving Brother,
Tom
. . . N.B. Don't worry about me I'll be alright.[11]

Another young Duntroon graduate of equal brilliance to Elliott – in fact, they were near rivals, in the same class of 35 students, and both graduating in November 1914, after just three years of the fast-tracked four-year course – also preparing on this day is the 21-year-old Major Arthur Hutchinson. The softly spoken son of a Tasmanian clergyman, he is described by Charles Bean as a man 'of the finest type that his country produces'.[12] Among his men at their billets in Sailly-sur-la-Lys on this morning, as they ready themselves to march out at 2.30 this afternoon, Major Hutchinson is in charge of the two companies of the 58th being held in reserve and, like Elliott, is eager to see action.

And then there is Lieutenant-Colonel Frederick Toll of the 8th Brigade's 31st Battalion, which will be entering the battle one battalion in from the extreme left of the 5th Division's assault. A natural leader of men, who had shone as a rugby player at Brisbane Grammar School just as he had as a marksman and athlete, this 43-year-old favourite son of Charters Towers knows more than most the devastation of what they might be about to face, even though he has only been in France for a fortnight.

A man with the curious combination of being only slight of figure while also physically powerful, he is a Boer War veteran who had been mentioned in dispatches for gallantry and seen a great deal of action. When this Great War had broken out, he had been among the first to volunteer for overseas service, despite being embarked on his happy second marriage. And yes, too, he knows more than most of the agony a war can visit on a man, having lost his first son from his first marriage at Gallipoli. Now, on this morning, Toll moves among his men, offering an encouraging word here and a pat on the back there, checking that all of them are in the right frame of mind for what awaits.

Lieutenant-Colonel Toll's equivalent in the 54th Battalion is of course the Albury native with the luxurious moustache and proud, square jawbone, Lieutenant-Colonel Walter Cass. He too is busy with his men. The 54th is due to go over the top at 5.45 pm, as the left flank of the 14th Brigade, and yet there is little doubt that some of his thoughts remain with the Canadian officer he is in love with. 'If I get out of this war in one piece and alive,' he has written to Nursing Sister Helena Holmes a week earlier, 'you are to marry me, so do please make up your mind to it . . .'[13]

No reply as yet. She, as far as he knows, is with her unit in England, where she is nursing in a hospital.

In a nearby billet at the village of Rae St Naur, the commander of the 55th Battalion's B Company, Captain Norman Gibbins – the biggest man in the unit – is making ready in the room he is sharing with the battalion's chaplain, Reverend James Green. They talk quietly. Gibbins is under no illusions as to what kind of day this might be, having faced similar at Gallipoli with the 3rd Battalion, where he had been so badly wounded he had had to be sent to an English hospital for five months, before returning. 'It was quite evident,' the Reverend would later recount, 'that he had faced the situation and there was no doubt in his mind about doing his share, at all costs.'[14]

—

True, on the Australian side of the lines, the morning has not started well, with reports coming in from patrols that had been sent out into No-Man's Land overnight that while the bombardment had indeed cut swathes through the rolls of wire in front of the 8th Brigade, there was no such luck with the German defences in front of the 14th Brigade. And it is impossible to say what the situation is with the defence in front of the 15th Brigade because the patrols had not even been able to get close. Anyone getting within even two coo-ees of the Sugar-loaf comes under immediate fire, so there is no doubt it is intact and its soldiers alert. Hopefully, the main bombardment to come will fix the Sugar-loaf. It'd want to, because the consequences of attacking it over open ground if everything is operational would be catastrophic.

In the meantime, there is much to be done. Those men with luminous compasses are seen to take them out and expose the open face to the sun. All else being equal, they will need those compasses to be glowing all night long tonight, as it would be an unimaginable horror to be out in No-Man's Land without any idea which direction to head in.

MORNING, 19 JULY 1916, THE 1ST DIVISION APPROACHES THE SOMME

While the 5th Division readies itself to attack Fromelles, it is time for the first battalions of the 1st AIF, some 50 miles to the south, to move forward from the village of Warloy, 14 miles north of Amiens, to Pozières.

Late this morning, the men of the 1st Battalion – who are the first to leave – march into the shattered town of Albert, just one and a half miles back from the line, to see that 'Fanny', aka the Virgin Mary, is now even more supplicatory than she was the last time, praying for the Lord to stop this war. 'You could readily imagine,' one Australian officer will write, 'that she had purposely leaned down over the street to bless the thousands of soldiers who pass and re-pass day by day and going to and returning from the battle line . . .'[15]

Local lore has it that when 'the Virgin falls into the street, the war will end'.[16] Hearing it, a British soldier has suggested to his mates, 'Let's knock it down now . . .'[17] – but neither happens.

Soon enough, alas, Albert falls behind and the men are confronted for the first time with harbingers of horror. For as they approach this part of the Western Front – 'singing as we swung along, little reckoning of what lay before us and wishful of impressing the Tommies with our martial ardour . . .'[18] – they see more and more shell craters, abandoned equipment, shattered farm buildings and, yes, now dead bodies here and there.

Further on, they experience even worse than that, as the ground underfoot in the trenches seems strangely . . . spongy?

How could that be? It's not even muddy, so that can't be the answer. It takes a while but they finally understand. 'That which we took to be spongy ground, that we were walking over,' recalls Private Dick Roberts, whose 3rd Battalion marches through Albert and the front-line that afternoon, 'was the bodies of dead soldiers.'[19]

Gasping, gagging from the putrescent gases the weight of their feet sometimes releases from those bodies, they keep moving. 'Good Christ! The place was packed with dead! They were lying 2 and 3 deep, all along the parapets, on the barbed wire, and out in the open. Where there had been a deep communication trench, in the first place, it had been blown in on top of hundreds of killed and wounded Germans and Tommys.'[20]

Jesus, Joseph and Mary, pray for me.
O God, have mercy on me, a sinner.

As they come still closer to the front-lines and start to pass the gaunt and ghostly figures of the British soldiers coming out, one scarecrow of a man says to a group of Diggers with Doug Horton of the 1st Battalion, 'If you Anzacs can take and hold Pozières, we'll believe all we've heard about you.'[21]

'We'll both take it and hold,' replies one of the Diggers, only to be laughingly told by his mates to stop being a skite, and to wait and see how we'll be when we come out.

And, on that subject, only a few hundred yards further on, they pass another scattered, shattered group of British soldiers with haunted eyes, gathered before a Sergeant-Major forlornly reading out names, with just the occasional 'Present, Sergeant-Major' being called back. Clearly, this is their first roll call after an attack.

'That's all that's left of [that] Brigade,' a British officer remarks.

'That sounds healthy . . .' a Digger dryly replies.[22]

They keep moving and finally arrive at a place called Gordon's Dump, positioned right beside the beginning of the communication sap (a tunnel dug forward from an existing trench) that leads to the front-lines.

Shortly afterwards, Private Giles Eyre of the Kings Royal Rifle Corps drops in on some of the men of the Australian 1st Division in the company of a mate, in the hope of swapping German hats, helmets and brass eagles for some wine they feel sure the new arrivals will have with them. They find them down in a spot they know as Mash Valley.

'Fine looking men, tall, lean, bronzed and keen, busy settling down,' Eyre would later write. 'We made our way to their transport lines and Carpenter began his quest after juice . . . Our souvenirs were disposed of quickly. Money we didn't want, and somehow or another four bottles of *vin rouge* materialised.

'"Come on you lads!" said a Colonial in a hearty voice. "You'd better have some tucker with us" and led us to where a cook was busy frying steak and onions.

"'Ha!' said Carpenter sniffing appreciatively. "You fellows know how to live all right.'"[23]

LATE MORNING, 19 JULY 1916, FROMELLES, A BELLOWING, THROATY ROAR

Fifty miles north at Fromelles, among the Germans of the 6th Bavarian Reserve Division, there is movement.

After collating the intelligence and observer reports that have come in from those atop Aubers Ridge – including in the tower of Fromelles church and in observation balloons – all of them reporting the signs that in recent days and nights there has been a flood of vehicles, men and horses moving towards the lines in front of Fromelles, Colonel Julius Ritter von Braun, a career army officer of enormous experience and no little ability, has no doubt. An attack upon their positions will shortly be launched. In preparation for it, he crisply orders one of the two battalions in Divisional Reserve, the I/20th Bavarian RIR, to move forward to a position just three miles back from the front-lines, ready to move quickly when needed, to help his III Battalion 21st Brigade, which is directly opposite the Australian 5th Division's 14th Brigade. Meticulous in his manner, confident in the way he carries himself, he also assigns two reserve battalions to ferry even more ammunition forward than previously carried, on the grounds that it looks as though the attack will be bigger than previously thought.

—

And, sure enough, at 11 am a throaty roar bellows across No-Man's Land, and some three seconds later a massive geyser of mud and maybe blood spurts high above the German lines. And then another! And another and another and another! The planned-for seven-hour bombardment has begun, as the divisional artilleries begin some fresh registration and step it up from there, gradually increasing in intensity with every passing quarter-hour. In short order, all the British and

Australian crews manning the heavy artillery three miles from the German line, the field artillery a mile away and the mortars in the front trenches are working themselves into a lather of sweat. It is all part of the plan that will see all the guns getting registered over the first two hours and 'the field-artillery then beginning to cut wire and practically all guns bombarding from 3 o'clock onwards'.[24]

All up, on the British side, no fewer than 296 field guns and 78 heavier pieces, served by 9000 gunners – about as many men as are in the attacking battalions – are being brought to bear along the 4000-yard front, of which 140 guns are Australian. It is to be hoped this mass of artillery is now destroying the enemy defensive posts, cutting the wire and killing the enemy soldiers.

(Not as many as they'd like. In response to the bombardment, the Bavarian officers in the front-lines around Fromelles give the order for most of their men to retreat to their semi-secure timber, steel or concrete-reinforced dugouts beneath the breastworks, and their two-man cubbyholes dotted in the breastworks, while the officers head to their even more secure dugouts 20 yards behind the front-line. Left behind are only the sentries, who must 'continue the observation under all circumstances and keep oneself ready for the defence of an imminent attack'.[25] Those brave sentries are soon engulfed as a whistling, roaring artillery storm breaks upon them.)

Even then, the barrage is only beginning to warm up. From its beginning, machine-gun sergeant Les Martin would write to his brother, 'there was not a space of a second's duration when some of our guns were not firing, the row was deafening. I put my wadding in my ears while we were down in the supports waiting to go forward and take our place in the fighting.'[26]

There remains a problem, however, and it is a deadly one. Through all of the bombardment, the drifting palls of smoke and dust, it is clear that while damage is being done to the German breastwork, the Sugar-loaf is displaying just about no visible effect. Far from being destroyed, it practically appears to be glowering in reply: *Nur zu. Ich hab' schon auf Euch gewartet.* Go ahead. I've already been waiting for you . . .

It looks mostly undamaged, as are the visible rolls of barbed wire, most particularly right in front of where the 15th Brigade is to attack. (And, in fact, it will later be verified that of the 75 concrete shelters that just the 16th Bavarian Reserve Regiment are operating from, no fewer than 60 remain entirely functional throughout the day.)

Haking's firm promise that the bombardment will cut all the wire, destroy all the enemy's machine-gun emplacements, knock down most of his parapets, kill a large proportion of the enemy, and thoroughly frighten the remainder[27] is obviously not happening right along the line.

What to do?

There is nothing they can do, other than Haking's artillery commander giving the order for more rounds to be fired at the Sugar-loaf. And this is done. Perhaps continued deadly accurate shell fire might still be able to quell it, but accuracy is in very short supply. 'Some of the guns were undoubtedly firing erratically,' Bean would later chronicle, 'and, with artillery so new to its work, the error could not readily be traced or prevented. The defect was the direct outcome of the rapidity with which this artillery had been raised in Egypt.'[28]

Things are looking grim, and yet there is still the crucial hope that Haking's Chinese attack will convince the Germans that the Australians are charging, to draw them out of their dugouts to be killed off, but this seems far from sure.

As a further move to bring pressure to bear on the German defence, Pompey Elliott has placed serious firepower at a key juncture. Because the angles of attack of Australia's 15th Brigade and the British 184th Brigade on the Sugar-loaf are different, there is actually a 300-yard gap between their starting points, and in this gap on the Australian parapet four 15th Brigade Vickers machine guns and five Lewis guns are placed, set the task of sweeping the Sugar-loaf until the Australian and British soldiers begin to converge on it.

—

Among the Australian artillery are Second-Lieutenant Norm Nicolson and the 52nd Field Artillery battery. Despite all his training, Norm is shocked. 'Such a noise! Guns everywhere! The field guns barking and the big English Howitzers coughing and banging; and down on the front there's a fearful and dreadful noise of bursting shells and trench mortars. The Germans too are pouring it on, and our and their mortars are adding to the din and slaughter. How awful to think of the poor infantry catching it.'

For they are all catching it. 'As shells burst just in front and behind of the 52nd, while the communication trenches in our front seem to be getting particular Hell.'[29]

A particular Hell indeed, as both the communication trenches and the front-line trenches where the attacking battalions of the 5th Division are congregating are now subject to horrifying German shelling. Right from the opening of the barrage, wounded soldiers have been coming back past the 52nd, 'some walking, many carried on stretchers in ever increasing numbers. Some of the poor chaps on the stretchers have ghastly white faces as tho' every drop of blood is being drained out of them.'

Meanwhile, going the other way are the men of Tivey's 8th Brigade. 'All morning and much of the afternoon a long line of men are streaming in single file, in small parties with intervals between them on the opposite side of the road towards the Front. We see them pass by and they are absorbed into the haze ahead.'[30] Whatever else anyone will say about them, it seems unlikely that they will be Tivey's 'Bloodless 8th' much longer.

The gunners keep going, in a frenzy of fire. 'The earth quaked with the roar,' one of them would recall, 'and before long the smoke of discharging guns lay thick over the whole area, revealing through interstices the half naked bodies of perspiring gunners.'[31]

Not everyone is worried. A couple of miles back from the front-line where the Australians are about to go into action, some of the men, most particularly in the reserve battalions, are doing the obvious. Why, of course, they're at their local estaminet, drinking up a storm. Eat, drink, and be merry, *cherie*, for tomorrow we die. Or maybe tonight. Or maybe not at all. After all, they have seen with their own eyes – even if from a distance – the kind of devastation being wrought on the German front-lines by artillery. 'The forward area was shrouded in a pall of dust and smoke and shell-bursts,' Corporal Harold ('Dick' to his mates) Williams of the 56th Battalion's A Company would recount, 'and we believed that no man could live in such an inferno.'[32]

In the time before the parade for the attack, Williams ducks into his favourite estaminet, only to find it as full as a sailor on shore leave in Marseilles. As he would recount, 'Madame and her assistants were hard pressed to cope with the rush. The men were in the best of spirits and looked forward to the attack as if it were a football match.'[33] Instead of the roar of the crowd, however, in the near distance they can hear the roar of the guns, constantly bellowing their fury as they fire their endless rounds.

Drink up, cobber. *Your* round.

———

The German soldiers are not drinking.

Rather, in the face of the barrage falling on their front-lines, they are meticulously following set orders. Among the soldiers of the 3rd Battalion, 16th Regiment – positioned in and either side of the Sugar-loaf salient – it is their Commanding Officer, Hauptmann Hans Gebhardt, who takes the lead. Over the roar of the barrage, he tells his men he is now more convinced than ever that '*der Engländer* wants to shoot our position *stürmreif,* [so that we are] ripe-to-be-stormed'.[34]

There is little concern.

'Our men,' German War Correspondent George Querl would recount, 'were looking forward to [the attack] . . . They were sick and tired of always lying there quietly; they were brave men, who did not fear a fight nor a wrestle of the bloody kind.'[35]

Had things been different, those German soldiers held in reserve could have congregated in the support lines just back from the front trenches, but the truth is, despite the grand plans to have these fully established, after early progress the trenches had been effectively abandoned, and for the moment they are little more than watery ditches.

—

The most amazing thing, as the individual companies of the 15th Brigade form up on this glorious day, is the sheer normalcy of everything around them, at least as far as the French are concerned. No matter that the shelling just three miles away makes the ground vibrate like an earthquake that just won't stop – here at the old flour mill by the Lys River, old women and small girls are selling gingerbread and sweets laced with cognac.

As the 57th heads off at 1.45 pm on the three-and-a-half-mile march just to get to the front, Downing notices how, just as ever, the French farm labourers are hoeing away in the fields, keeping the weeds down. 'Stooping men and women watched the Australians pass, without ceasing their work. It may have been courage, or stolidity, or the numbness of the peasant bound to the soil, or else necessity, that held the sad tenacious people here in such an hour of portent. Their old faces were inscrutable. They tilled the fields on the edge of the flames, under the arching trajectory of shells.

'Bees hummed in the clear and drowsy sunshine. There was little smoke about the cottages, where the creepers were green. The road curved between grass which was like two green waves poised on either side.'[36]

The first waves have been ordered to move across No-Man's Land laterally, while subsequent movements will go in single file – for a line is best for an attack formation, and single file is best for manoeuvring.

Meanwhile, other units of the 5th Division are receiving their own instructions, as runners from all the brigade HQs charge hither and thither with orders for the different battalions, who in turn send runners to different companies and platoons.

It is with some disappointment that Bert Bishop's platoon learn they are not to be in the first wave to go over the top with the 14th Brigade. Their job will be to wait till the first trenches are taken and then carry water and ammunition to them across No-Man's Land. In the meantime, they are to go to VC Corner, just 300 yards from the spot in front of the Sugar-loaf where an attack is to go in on the pointy ends of the bayonets borne by Pompey Elliott's mighty 15th Brigade. 'There was a feeling of suspense,' Bert Bishop would chronicle, 'of something unpleasant about to happen, over everything.'[37]

The 54th Battalion of Billy Bishop – Bert and Ray's cousin – is being mustered on parade in a huge cobblestoned yard, right by the factory where Bert's mob has been billeted, and even in his own busyness to get ready, Bert pauses to admire 'what a splendid-looking lot of men they are'.[38] Straight of back, clear of eye. Strong young men, the finest sons of places such as Gulargambone, Walcha and Moree. And how they can march! At their Sergeant-Major's command, they move like a military machine, gliding across the courtyard, wheeling and lining up in perfect synchronicity, the sound of their boots on the cobblestones making a martial beat.

And now Lieutenant-Colonel Walter Cass takes his place in front of them. He is impeccably turned out, and it is not his moustache alone that bristles. The man is a tightly coiled spring, just holding himself in, aware that the moment for his battalion has come, and it is for him to give them their last words before the battle begins.

Tonight, he explains to them in his militarily clipped tones, at 1730 hours, the 5th Division will be attacking the German line in front of Fromelles. It is our battalion, together with the 53rd, which will have the honour of leading the attack for the 14th Brigade.

And *now* comes the warmth, as his tone changes, as he starts to talk to them not as soldiers taking orders but as his men. 'Remember,' Lieutenant-Colonel Cass says, in intimate, inclusive tones, 'each one of us, that this is the first A.I.F. battle in France. We must achieve success. Our orders are that the ground we win must be held at all cost. We will be the centre brigade of our division. We have to take two lines of German trenches and we must hold them. Good luck to all of us.'[39]

And then it is done. The Colonel finishes, nods to the Sergeant-Major, who roars '*Atten . . . shun!*', and in short order Billy's battalion marches out to take up its position near the firing line, ready to leap forward on command. Bert watches the men go, his eyes focused on Billy the whole while, a lump in his throat. And then he can't see Billy anymore, and all that is left of his battalion in this yard is the sound of retreating feet, marching, marching, marching away.

In the distance, the roar of the British artillery pounding the German front and second lines is getting ever louder. 'That's to let them know we're coming,' Bert's mate Nugget growls, 'and give them time to get ready.'[40]

—

The German soldiers and their artillery are exactly that. Ready, as never before.

Now convinced by the sustained British bombardment and observed movement forward of so many troops and so many supplies that an attack upon them really is imminent, the Commander-in-Chief of the 6th Bavarian Reserve Division, General Gustav von Scanzoni, has ordered 'the garrisons of the second line . . . to stand to arms'.[41] They are, henceforth, on '*erhöhter Bereitschaft*, heightened alert'.[42]

Most importantly, however, General von Scanzoni has given the order for his artillery to 'open fire on sight of a red signal flare',[43] and at 2.30 pm they see that flare suddenly burst red against the impossibly blue sky! The heavens themselves are now bleeding – and Fritz opens fire accordingly. Both sides of the Western Front around Fromelles are now roaring at each other, with the Germans lobbing the bulk of their shells onto the assault trenches in the front-lines where the attacking troops are seen to be massing and also the communication trenches leading to them. If, as they suspect from past experience, they are facing an early-evening attack, this is the time when all those trenches should be at their busiest.

Now, though the Germans at this point have less than one-third of the artillery opposing them on the other side of the line – they have just 102 guns in all – they more than make up for this in experience. Most of their artillerymen have been trained in the deadly art since before the war began, and are part of the Royal Bavarian Artillery, which has a history, a tradition and a pride dating from its formation on 12 October 1682. Many of the officers and NCOs have been artillerymen for ten years or more, and have been in this sector for 18 months. They are intimately familiar with the landscape before them, as are their observers on high. As if that is not enough, so sophisticated is the German response that they also put up two aircraft that are able to guide the fire of their guns. Most of those guns, in turn, have been registered on such obvious targets as VC Corner many months earlier.

(The first of the German bombardment descends on all posts where it is presumed the enemy's artillery observers lie, in the hope that the British artillery will be shooting all but totally blind.)

The Australian guns have been on site for only a matter of days, and the results are still far from certain. Yes, the Australian artillerymen have come a long way since their formation in Egypt on 18 February 1916, but the 5th Division Artillery has been in the area for a little over a week, the 4th Division Artillery two weeks, while even the British 61st Division Artillery has only been on site since mid-June. This compared with the 6th Bavarian Reserve Division's 18 months with which to precision-register their guns. They know precisely what they're doing, and are able to extract a terrible toll.

Speaking of which . . .

Those now of the view that everything that could go wrong has gone wrong are now proven demonstrably . . . wrong, as a German shell hits the 31st's ammunition dump. It not only blows the whole thing up but wounds many men with it, including Lieutenant-Colonel Toll, who takes several pellets to the face, and is soon bleeding profusely.

'[It] went off with a terrible explosion,' Sapper William Smith of the 14th Brigade would recount, 'and sent up a large column of gaseous smoke – evidently a direct hit from a shell or a "Minnie". This was a serious loss as the ammunition had taken three days to carry to the line, and it could not be replaced. All along the line the stretcher-bearers were busy picking up the wounded. Their numbers were hopelessly inadequate to cope with the casualties, but their spirit was fine, and they did magnificent work.[44]

—

The troops of the 15th Brigade get closer to the front-line. Here now a dead man on a duckboard, just lying there, a big fellow with a bald dome, a red moustache and a red vest from all the blood he has lost. This part of the trench has taken a direct hit and is effectively no more. The only way to get across the gap is to make a mad dash, hoping not to be hit by shrapnel.

And here now another man, who has clearly been weeping, sitting by a dead man with a shattered head, his blood and brains oozing into the mud. The man looks up. 'Sniper,' he explains. 'My brother – keep under the parapet.'[45]

At least those in the 15th Brigade can largely make their way to the front-line while still in the cover of the communication trenches. Those of the 14th Brigade are not so fortunate, as there are insufficient communication trenches to accommodate its third and fourth waves. For them to get to the front-lines, they must make their way over the 300 yards of open ground that separates the support line from the front-lines. Of course, German artillery observers instantly spot them and rain down fire upon them, and they are extremely lucky not to lose more than the scattering of soldiers they do.

Once they arrive in their designated positions, almost unbelievably, it gets worse, as these front-line trenches are being completely overwhelmed with shells. 'Our breastwork, which was a wonderful target, was blown to pieces in places,' Sapper William Smith would record, 'dugouts were destroyed and timber was sent skywards. Large enemy guns gave us a bad time with enfilade fire. Every gun had been previously registered, and had our position accurately. One could not imagine a more nerve-racking ordeal. There were no deep dugouts; the ground being water-logged – and yet the Diggers – most of them raw troops – faced this fierce bombardment; crunched against the breast-work watching their comrades being killed or wounded beside them; grimly waiting for the time to "hop the bags".[46]

And there really is nothing they can do but wait.

'For the first time in the war,' it would be noted by Bean, 'an Australian attacking force was actually meeting the contingency most dreaded by commanders: its intentions had been discovered, and the enemy barrage was crashing upon its assembly position with the object of destroying the attack.'[47]

The German volleys are like the fingers of an angry blind man, groping for the eyes of an opponent before moving to other sensitive parts. *Herr Blind Man* doesn't know exactly where the Australians are, but is fairly sure he can feel his way well enough to do damage. And so he does . . .

AFTERNOON, 19 JULY 1916, POZIÈRES-BOUND, AS FAST FALLS THE EVENTIDE

On this same afternoon, around Warloy, the men of I Anzac Corps – and specifically the 1st and 3rd Brigades of Walker's 1st Division – are just about to move on Pozières, not that most of them know it yet.

But first, many of them must make time for something precious, as several hundred soldiers of the 2nd Battalion gather for a church service.

And now let us pray.

The Church of England padre asks them to bow their heads, before, among other things, assuring them of God's love, and His forgive-ness. 'Many of you,' he says carefully, 'are attending your last church parade.'[48]

Indeed . . .?

For most of them, it is the first clue they have that they are about to go into battle.

The padre then invites Major McKenzie, better known as 'Fighting Mac', the Salvation Army chaplain of the 1st Brigade, to address them.

Now, Fighting Mac is a beloved figure to the Australian soldiers, well known for his fiery sermons, his humour and for the fact that, in their days in Cairo, he would go into brothels in the Wazza and physically drag drunken Diggers out and put them on trams back to camp. (Many a man has he saved from ruin, from having a dishonourable discharge, in both senses of the word, by actually wrestling them from the clutches of fallen women.) And then there was his bravery at Lone Pine, when, just before the men had gone over the top, he had turned up and told them straight, 'Boys, I've preached to you, and I've prayed with you, do you think I'm afraid to die with you? I'd be ashamed to funk it when you're up against it right here.'[49]

No, as a man of God, he wouldn't fight, but he was there all right – onward Christian soldiers – at Lone Pine, with an upturned shovel in front of his face his only protection.

On this afternoon, as ever, he begins with the gathering of soldiers singing hymns to draw in others within coo-ee, including 'Abide with Me', 'Lead, Kindly Light' and 'God Be with You'.[50]

All together, sing!

Abide with me; fast falls the eventide;
The darkness deepens; Lord, with me abide;
When other helpers fail and comforts flee,
Help of the helpless, oh, abide with me . . .

A few soldiers stop and join in, singing the well-loved words with a reverent gusto:

I fear no foe, with Thee at hand to bless;
Ills have no weight, and tears no bitterness;
Where is death's sting? Where, grave, thy victory?
I triumph still, if Thou abide with me.

And, yes, *hundreds* more soldiers are soon attracted by the now roaring but still resonant voices:

Hold Thou Thy cross before my closing eyes;
Shine through the gloom and point me to the skies;
Heav'n's morning breaks, and earth's vain shadows flee;
In life, in death, O Lord, abide with me.[51]

Within minutes, there is well over a thousand soldiers, all straining to hear the words of their dearly beloved Fighting Mac.

But what was that about this being, for many of them, their last church service? It would seem so. For once they return to their billets, all men are issued with the usual array of battle necessities and are checked by their officers to ensure they are carrying basic medical kits (most importantly including a small bottle of iodine together with a bandage to dress wounds) as well as their gas masks and their identity discs – the men call them 'dead meat tickets' – in case of death.

All their haversacks are looked at, too, to make sure they are carrying all their regulation kit, while those things they don't wish to carry are put away in their packs, tagged, and put into storage against the time they come back. *If* they come back.

Just like those in the 5th Division, all of them are given two Mills grenades – even though it is only those in the bombing parties who have received instruction on how to arm and throw them. They will just have to make do and receive rough instruction from those who know. See, first you pull out the pin, making sure you keep the lever pressed down until you are ready to hoik the bastard . . .[52]

Now fall in!

And so the 1st Brigade does, standing there in serried ranks, receiving their last instructions. On their backs and shoulders, all have pink squares, issued to them that morning, which they have attached using their standard-issue sewing kit of needle, thread and buttons, known as 'a housewife'. They are wearing their back patches so that, in the frenzied fury of the battle to come, they will be able to instantly identify each other and, most importantly, not be shot by their own riflemen and machine-gunners from behind. The patches on the shoulders are there, Lance-Corporal Ben Champion of the 1st

Battalion records in his diary, 'for aeroplane observation, so that they could spot the front line'.[53]

They are going to those front-lines around the stray French hamlet of Pozières, these sons of the stray Australian hamlets of Walcha, Glen Innes, Inverell, Dungog and the like, as well as a big crop in the 1st Battalion from Sydney itself.

> *Theirs not to reason why,*
> *Theirs but to do and die.*[54]

All right, men, move out.

The more they march, the louder the artillery becomes, and the more frequent its explosions. There they are, 'battery after battery of heavy artillery – six- and eight-inch howitzers, all in position with stacks of ammunition close to each gun. It was an encouraging and heartening sight . . .'[55]

And now, what is this they see far ahead in the distance, every time they are on high enough ground?

Is it a broken windmill?

No.

It is something more moving still. For, as they approach the tiny town of Albert – long since abandoned by its 7000 residents and now populated by British soldiers – they can see more clearly the town's famous red-brick Catholic Church, Notre-Dame-de-Brebières, atop which there is a statue of Madonna and child, dubbed the 'Golden Virgin'. Alas, Our Lady has been hit by German artillery shells, has keeled over to an alarming angle and now lies prostrate, parallel to the ground. It is as if she is weeping, praying, supplicating the heavens to end this war.

'As we marched past the ruined building and gazed up at the mournful figure hanging with outstretched arms high above us,' Australian 1st Division soldier Harry Hartnett would record, 'we realised how much the French people must have been profoundly affected by this tragic sight.'[56]

With typical irreverence, the Australians nickname her 'Fanny', after Fanny Durack, the famed Australian Olympic swimmer who had won the gold medal for the 100 metres at the 1912 Stockholm Olympics, because, to a certain extent, it looks as though Mother Mary is diving forward.[57]

She is leaning far enough over the street that her shadow falls upon the slightly scarred face – courtesy of his experience at Gallipoli – of 19-year-old Lance-Corporal Ben Champion. 'This march through Albert was very eerie,' the Sydney man records, 'the houses being shattered and often the cobbled road full of shell holes. We were picked up by guides from the English Regiments and went forward over shell-stricken country until we reached a large valley, the sides of which were packed with guns. They seemed almost locked wheel to wheel, 18 [pounders], howitzers and huge guns were everywhere. The ground we crossed was most difficult and often as we passed, the guns would roar out, nearly knocking us over with the noise of their discharge. Through this valley and on through winding, chalky communication trenches, and we realised that at last we were in a war.'[58]

It is confronting. 'Soon we came to an area with the sickly smell of dead bodies, and half-buried men, mules and horses . . .'[59] and for the first time they can see the ruined village of Pozières up ahead.

Clearly, whoever attacks across that No-Man's Land is going to lose a lot of men. Equally clearly, it is the Australian 1st Division that is going to be the next to try.

Oh, Christ. Abide with me.

—

Charles Bean feels strong. On this beautiful afternoon, he is being driven south from Fromelles through the idyllic French countryside to join the three Australian divisions, where they are preparing to attack Pozières. As this is to be the first major attack by the AIF in France, of course this is where he must be, and though he doesn't wish to see any of his fellow Australians killed, it really will be exciting to see them in action again for the first time since Gallipoli.

Yes, it had been mooted that the 5th Division would be thrown in against the Germans at Fromelles even before this attack, but there have been so many twists and turns along the way that it is anyone's guess what will happen and, more importantly for Bean, when it will happen.

And so, now arriving at his destination, Bean settles into his hotel at Contay – 12 miles west of Pozières – right by I Anzac HQ and quickly settles down to the long task of bringing his diary up to date.

MID-AFTERNOON, 19 JULY 1916, CHRIST ON A CROSS, BY THE CROSSROADS

At Fromelles, the German artillery continues to seek out specific targets, ruthlessly moving back and forth, wreaking devastation wherever its explosive fingers start to gouge.

After persuading the British and Australian artillery observers to pull their pointy heads in, the barrage moves to the artillery batteries and their ammunition dumps before targeting the support line and 300 yard line, together with the communication trenches that connect the concentric rings. By 3 pm, the shells are beginning to fall on the front-lines as well, just when the first attacking British and Australian waves are beginning to mass. The German shells exact a particularly heavy toll on the 60th Battalion, which is now moving forward along VC Avenue to its front-line trenches.

The worst affected of all, however, is the Australian 8th Brigade, on the far left, closely followed by the left flank of the 14th Brigade. With the shortest No-Man's Land – where their artillery's margin for error is the smallest – they are getting pasted not only by the German artillery straight in front of them, together with the artillery on their left flank from German batteries not themselves under attack, but also by short-falling shells from their own artillery located well behind their front-line.

—

Battalionnnnnnn, move out!

The men of the 57th Battalion of the 15th Brigade held in 'general reserve' keep marching till they come to the crossroads of Rue Delvas and Rue du Bois, where they must wait by the cornfields, right by a large crucifix that has improbably remained standing in an otherwise badly damaged brick shrine. Private Jimmy Downing can't help noticing the figure of Jesus staring back at him, a being wantonly sacrificed, so the Bible says, for the greater good of mankind.

Christ on a cross.

And now the order comes. The men must move forward, in single file, in small groups some 50 yards apart, and take up their positions, ready for their attack on Fromelles.

—

With little sign of serious damage being done to the German fortifications, while there is no doubt huge destruction is being wrought on their own, things are desperate, but one great hope remains. It is possible that Haking's much vaunted Chinese attack will work.

At 3.25 pm, it is time to unveil it. The elevating wheels on the field guns are wound in clockwise direction to lift the barrels by the requisite degree, and the bombardment landing on the Germans moves back by 100 yards – even as the Australians of the 5th Division and the Britons of the 61st Division in the front trenches shout out like a Collingwood crowd on a bad day. They wave their bayonets above the parapet, and shake dummy figures and helmets on rifles, hoping to appear to the Germans like men who are about to charge, with the eager ones already having sallied forth.

Ready?

Ready.

Now! After two minutes, the field-gun range is suddenly lowered again, except this time the gunners have loaded shrapnel shells rather than high-explosive, in the hope of killing many German soldiers now exposed in their trenches.

Will it work? With the intensity of men who know exactly what is at stake here, the observers watch closely. If the enemy has been taken in by the ruse, there should soon appear German helmet tops and bayonet tips bobbing above the parapets, suddenly coming from their dugouts, out into the open and ready to be killed. The guns roar, the shells explode, the smoke swirls and there is . . . nothing. Stone-cold motherless *nothing*.

In the first report of the British Forward Observation Officer, the enemy did not appear to man his parapets during the 'lift'.[60]

Oh, *Christ*.

—

In their dugouts, most of the German soldiers still sit securely – shaken but not stirred from their posts – as they have not yet heard the alarms that signal they must race to the parapets. And though some of the skeleton crew braving the storm in the parapets do indeed note a sudden diminution in the shells falling on them, together with the waving of the dummies and all the rest, only a very few are taken in by it.

One is German soldier Johann Offensberger, who calls out, '*Jetzt! Sie kemma! Kameraden, sie kemma!* Now! They're comin'! Comrades, they're comin'!'[61] But wiser heads prevail, pointing out it only looks like that. And of course the *Schlauköpfe*, smarty-pants, are proved right. For within a minute or two, the bombardment comes back upon them, and the forest of Australian bayonets disappears again. It is no more than a ruse, and they may settle again, waiting for the main event.

'All were animated by only the one wish,' another *Kriegsberichterstatter*, German Official War Correspondent, *Herr* Wilhelm Scheuermann, would recount, 'that the barrage would stop at last and the enemy would dare to attack.'[62]

—

By 4 pm, the four waves of all three brigades of the 5th Division – or at least the survivors thereof – are in place, with the first two in the front-line trench: one on the firing-step; one in the fire-trench a yard behind them. Both are ready to secretly move forward beyond their own wire into No-Man's Land to reduce the attack distance to the enemy line. The second two waves in the support trenches stand ready to file forward, their eyes agog at the carnage of shell fire up ahead into which they are expected to advance.

At 4.04 pm, it is time to try the Chinese attack again. And this time, the Germans notice – they really notice! At least two sections do, as the 16th Bavarian RIR 3rd Battalion Commander Hauptmann Hans Gebhardt makes his only reference to the ruse of the entire afternoon in this report: the enemy fire lifted to the rear and large numbers of English troops in battle order could be seen in the enemy trenches. Our companies prepared their defences, but then the enemy artillery shortened and began to shell our trenches again.[63]

To his right, *Leutnant* Kleim of 10th Company in the 21st Bavarian RIR – positioned opposite the 31st and 54th Battalions – has much the same short-lived response:

> At about 4pm fixed bayonets were seen
> projecting above the parapet of the enemy front
> trench whereupon the order was given to the
> men in our own trench to also 'Fix bayonets!'
> After a short pause at 4.00 pm, the barrage
> resumed.

With the failure of the ruse for the second time – though two more attempts remain – it seems the last hope for destroying the backbone of the German resistance before emerging into No-Man's Land is gone, and, in Pompey Elliott's worst nightmare, it is the soldiers themselves who will have to accomplish the task.

Though deeply concerned at what he sees, Pompey is of course powerless to stop the military machinery now inexorably rolling forward, shortly to take his soldiers into the maelstrom. All he can do is give his men whatever confidence he can. And, very occasionally, there is something that looks to be very close to a direct hit on enemy lines, with 'wire netting and woodwork . . . observed flying through the air', following a huge explosion across from the 15th Brigade.[64] 'Boys,' Pompey tells those closest to him, sounding far more confident than he actually feels, 'you won't find a German in the trenches when you get there.'[65]

Most of them, soldiers and officers all, who are inevitably keeping their noses to the front wall of the trenches as the shrapnel whirs just above them, must take him at his word. Hopefully, the bombardment really is doing its job. In any case, they will know soon enough.

Observers, however, are far from sure about the damage being done on the Sugar-loaf. For beyond it, regularly disappearing behind ever-larger swathes of smoke, dust, flung mud and, occasionally, hopefully, chunks of concrete, nothing actually changes. Once vision clears, there it is, still brooding and seeming to get angrier all the while.

Meanwhile, there is no doubt that the German artillery has now got the range, as their shells continue to fall on the Australian lines, wreaking terrible devastation, so tightly are the Diggers packed upon each other.

More galling to the Australians still are the shells that continue coming from their *own* side. While there is at least some protection behind the forward breastworks from the German shells in front, there is less protection when their own shells fall short. And it is an important distinction. Those who press their prone bodies tightly into the bottom of the front walls do so because that's the best spot for sheltering from the German shells – but it's the worst for hiding from Australian shells. It is for them, thus, to decide where the greatest danger lies – and for them to live or die on the decision.

As to those short-falling Australian shells, Lieutenant-Colonel Ernest Harris, Commanding Officer of the 59th Battalion, is more than merely aggrieved with the results. His message over the phone to the offending battery commander is nothing if not crisp and to the point. 'We prefer to be killed by the Germans, thank you,' he barks.[66]

The message does not get through.

For, even as he is speaking, another shell from the same battery lands, wounding several men and killing two officers.

This time, Lieutenant-Colonel Harris is clearer. 'If you fire again we will turn our machine guns on to you.'

To make the point, Corporal Hugh Knyvett is sent back carrying one of the dud shells that has mercifully failed to explode. Still the battery commander, a British officer, refuses to believe it. 'You are crazy!' he yells at Knyvett over the roar of the artillery that shakes their very souls. 'You are getting German cross-fire. Our shells are falling two hundred yards in front of you!'[67]

With some aplomb, Knyvett – a one-time Presbyterian missionary from Longreach – brings from out of his pack the dud shell, which clearly has the British markings upon it. 'Have you seen *that* before?' Knyvett asks plaintively.

There is now no denying it, and the artillery officer blanches. 'For God's sake, bury it.'

'No,' Knyvett replies. 'It is going to divisional headquarters. Your little mistake has already cost several lives.'[68]

The artillery officer promises, of course, that his men will be more accurate, but how they can do that is not clear. 'Registering' is only possible when you can clearly observe where your shells land, and this is impossible when so many shells from both sides are landing everywhere. And, yes, it is a mercy for many of the Australian troops that fully a quarter of the shells that mistakenly fall upon them are duds, but it is a serious problem when the same figure applies to the shells falling on the German front-lines – doing 25 per cent less damage than they should. The bitter truth is that, in the wake of Neuve Chapelle, the British armaments industry has been under so much pressure to increase production that most quality control has disappeared and it is anyone's guess which shells will explode and which won't. Similarly, so many of the field guns are so old and worn it is impossible to have them consistently fire upon designated spots.

For the most part, though, it really is the German artillery now doing most of the damage, as their shells continue to roar down upon the British and Australians, bringing blood and devastation with every hit. Surely it must be time for a cup of tea?

Yes, never a better time.

'One of the finest things which I had seen on active service,' one soldier would record, 'was to the credit of the cooks of the 14th Brigade, who, in the height of the bombardment, made some tea in the front lines, and passed the dixies along the bays to the men.'[69]

At 4.45 pm, disaster strikes when short-falling Australian artillery shells begin to descend right on the parapet where the men of the first wave of the 31st Battalion have gathered in readiness to go over the top. Despite Lieutenant-Colonel Frederick Toll's repeated urgent wires requesting the artillery to lengthen, everything just gets worse, as the shells now fall 'behind the whole frontage'[70] held by the 31st. Beyond causing *dozens* of casualties, the shells also wound most of the battalion's signallers and medical staff. ('Of the eight signallers who were organised as runners in event of broken communications six were killed or wounded before we left the support trenches,' Toll would report.)[71]

So many soldiers are lost that Toll, who is able to fight on, is forced to put his third and fourth waves together into one wave. Still, the Colonel is able to gather himself to get his report back to 8th Brigade Commander General Tivey at HQ:

Many of our shells falling short. Flares and ammunition blown up in front dump. Telephone station carried away by a shell.[72]

By now, the German shelling is even more intense and very close to the equal of what is being rained down upon them. And yet, only one side is preparing to send men out into the exposed hell of No-Man's Land.

Even more worrying than the damage being done to the Australians, however, is the lack of damage being done to the Germans. For, to

Lieutenant-Colonel Toll's right, at 5 pm, the second-in-command of the 54th, Major Roy Harrison, sends back to Lieutenant-Colonel Cass the singularly disquieting report: *[the] enemy parapet opposite . . . is not being smashed.*[73]

Against that, the battalion next to Cass, the 53rd, has already reported: *Our artillery very effective and enemy trenches being completely demolished.*[74]

All is confusion, both in the front-lines and at the HQs trying to monitor what is going on. Generally, however, it seems that while there is progress in damaging the Germans to the left of the line, there is little sign of success on the key front: that before the 15th Brigade, where the Sugar-loaf lies.

What is not in any dispute is what the Germans are continuing to do to the Australians, right along the line. 'The Germans started to bombard our line like mad,' John Gotch Ridley of the 14th Brigade's 53rd Battalion, due to go over with the fourth wave, would record. 'The din was terrible, the shells would burst above and then swish, and down came the hail of lead and iron, dealing awful wounds.'[75]

And it is all at a time when the Australian men are more tightly packed than ever. By 5 pm, in the middle of the line, for example, the 55th Battalion has arrived in the trenches beside and behind the men of the 53rd Battalion, ready to take over their positions once they go over the top – and the same thing is happening across the entire front-line at much the same time.

And of course the German soldiers in their own front-lines are taking terrible punishment, but in the face of it, the Commander of the German 21st Bavarian RIR, Colonel Julius Ritter von Braun, for one, remains calm. As the fire on his men positioned opposite the Australians increases to 'the level of drumfire',[76] and enemy aircraft roar back and forth just above rifle range looking for fresh targets, it is more obvious than ever that the attack will soon be upon them.

Das ist gut.

Von Braun, like many of his confident men, has little fear of such an attack. It is simply a matter of getting his companies into position.

With four or five guttural but ever precise commands to his underlings, even above the roar of the exploding shells all around, it is under way.

The support battalion of the 21st Bavarian RIR is soon moving forward, as are six *Meldegänger*, runners, to his own HQ. Whatever happens, he must stay in touch with his forces. And now a report comes through from the observers that the 'enemy are transferring men from their second line into their front-line'.[77] Yet more German reserves are brought forward, while German artillery fire upon the enemy gathering in their trenches intensifies.

And yet, what seems worse to the Australians is that they are *still* getting hit by their own 'Arty'! At 5.10 pm, Lieutenant-Colonel Toll, on the left flank of the Australian attack, sends an urgent wire to General Tivey, 8th Brigade HQ:

> *Please ask artillery A5A to lift another 100 yards on sectors 'A', 'B' and 'C'. Shells falling behind our parapet at 5 p.m. . . . Casualties occurring through our own shrapnel.*

More worrying still, Toll is sorry to report, is the fact that their shells are not hitting their desired targets:

> *Enemy wire . . . not much damaged . . .*[78]

On the right flank, General Pompey Elliott can see for himself much the same thing. For while all the other Brigade Commanders put themselves in their Brigade HQs, safely situated two miles back from the front-lines, Elliott simply cannot bear it. Gripped by the idea that he must do everything possible to help 'my boys', as he always refers to them, he insists on setting up his Advanced HQ on the 300-yard line, hopefully within observation distance of what is actually occurring through the swirling smoke – connected by telephone to his Chief of Staff, Brigade Major George Wieck at Brigade HQ, and to Staff Captain Reginald Legge right in the front-lines.

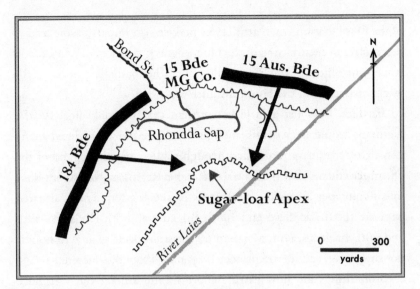

Sugar-loaf showing the 15th Brigade Machine Gun Company

(As close as Elliott is, it still does not sit easily, and no less than General Brudenell White would later say of him, 'The great war did not suit the initiative and valour of a soldier such as Pompey. He should have lived in the time of the Crusades, where leaders led their men from the front, and met face to face, instead of being cooped up in a lousy dugout, waiting for runners to bring tidings of the battle . . .')[79]

It is now that Pompey is handed a message that has come from one of the observers of the 60th Battalion. It seems that the wire on 60th's side of the Sugar-loaf is entirely intact, and at least three of its machine-gun posts are untouched – no doubt meaning that whatever soldiers are manning them are also unaffected.

The same, alas, cannot be said for the 15th Brigade Machine Gun Company, positioned between the soldiers of the 184th and 15th Brigades, right where they hoped they could quell the German machine-gunners in the Sugar-loaf – for they have been wiped out by German artillery.

To the right of the Australians, Great Britain's 61st Division is taking severe punishment, with most battalions losing 100 men even before the attack starts. Most troubling of all, of course, is the failure of the 61st Division's own artillery to make much impact. 'No effective destructive or neutralising of the Hun infantry, Artillery or M.G.s took place,' one officer of the 61st would note. 'The total effect of our artillery preparation on the Hun resistance was nil.'[80]

(In fact, it is just a little better than that but only just. As the Germans would later detail, though they have indeed suffered many casualties, they have more than enough soldiers in reserve, and of the 75 emplacements that the Bavarian Reserve Regiment No. 16 has built into its parapet across its 1800 yards of the Western Front, situated opposite the 61st's 183rd and 184th Brigades and 5th Division's 59th and 60th Brigades, no fewer than 60 are still operative at zero hour – not surprising, as they are protected by a solid foot of concrete.)

Still, things are now getting more frantic among the Germans. The key responsibility for stopping the main thrust of the British and Australian attacks falls to three German officers.

And now, at 5 pm, *Zweiter Leutnant* (Second Lieutenant) Plenge, commanding the 11th Company of the 16th Bavarian RIR located in the apex of the Sugar-loaf, positioned opposite the 2/1st Bucks, reports enemy soldiers moving forward into the Rhondda Sap – so, of course, high-shrapnel shells are immediately organised. *Gruppe Wurm* of the artillery is assigned the task, and within minutes the shelling begins. '*Das Sperrfeuer,* the barrage of our own artillery,' the *Regiment Adjutant* Hauptmann Friedrich Wiedemann records, 'lay well on the enemy trench, especially *auf der Australierstellung,* on the position of the Australians.'[81]

Ah, but the fire on the front-line German trenches has never been more intense, and because by now all telephone lines have been shot to pieces and the signal-lamp stations are unable to flash at each other because of all the smoke, it is now that the brave *Meldegänger,* messengers, such as Adolf Hitler, truly come into their own.

Faithful to the fury, they rush back and forth between HQs and the front, passing on orders and receiving reports. They use their intimate knowledge of the trench system to scout ahead for battalions coming up from the rear to see if the way is clear; and often act as guides, taking the battalions right to their designated positions. On this day, a lot of the messengers return goggle-eyed, bearing reports that the front-line trenches 'lay under the heaviest barrage, that the losses are significant and the damages of the position vast'.[82]

But – and this is the important thing – every single surviving observer is still at his post. As one admiring German War Correspondent would go on to report, 'Where one was injured or fell, without any order the next man jumped into his position, pressed himself at the parapet and stared with burning eyes through the clouds of smoke and dust of the shell across at the gray-brown, hacked-to-pieces by our artillery, strip of land of the enemy position, to not miss the moment in which the first Englishmen started the storm. Every single man . . . withstood *im Sturmgebraus*, the roaring storm [and] was in this moment the embodiment of the German Army at the Western Front.'[83]

And, *mein Gott*, the bravery! The same soldier who had been taken in by the Chinese attack, Johann Offensberger, is twice buried by the soil and debris thrown by massive howitzer shells exploding nearby, and twice his comrades risk their lives to dig him out '*auf Tod und Teufel*, by death and devil. [And each] time he crept onto the parapet, with troublesome breath, bruised and battered – but he did not want to leave his post.'[84]

With soldiers of this calibre, Germany must prevail!

Chapter Eleven

THE BATTLE PROPER

I had read a great deal about a modern bombardment, and what
it was like, but it is beyond imagination and description. At
night it reminded me of a terrific bush-fire in a thunderstorm
without rain, and the wind howling everywhere. The fire
represents the shells bursting, and the smoke the [haze] that is
given off from them. The thunderstorm represents the roar of
the guns, and the wind the shells roaring through the air.[1]
Captain William Bridgeford, a veteran of
the Battle of Fromelles, in a letter

I have nothing to say against the Australians, though I
do not like their faces, nor their eyes. They are strong
fellows – good marksmen – fearful fighters – hard as steel,
but not the sort of people to appeal to Germans.[2]
German War Correspondent George Querl, quoted
in The Ararat Advertiser, 5 August 1916

5.15 PM, 19 JULY 1916, FROMELLES, THE SANDS IN THE HOURGLASS RUN OUT

Every time Elliott looks at his watch, the big hand seems to have leaped
forward, each tick pushing his men to a fate he fears with every fibre of
his being but is completely powerless to stop.

Now the German artillery zeroes in on the 5th and 61st Divisions' front *and* support lines, where they know the attacking troops will be closely massed.

'The first thing that struck you,' one of the 14th Brigade's officers will later tell Charles Bean, 'was that shells were bursting everywhere, mostly high-explosive; and you could see machine-guns knocking bits off the trees in front of the reserve line and sparking against the wire . . . When men looked over the top they saw no-man's-land leaping up everywhere in showers of dust and sand . . . rather confirming our fears that the Germans knew something.'[3]

Are they really going to charge out into that, in broad daylight, across as much as 400 yards, just to get to still intact rolls of barbed wire? Is the plan *really* for them to have more men left over than the Germans have bullets left over, once the artillery has knocked most of the Squareheads' blocks off?

Pretty much, but it is not just a plan; it is an *order*.

Mercifully, most of the attacking soldiers are not looking over the top at the Germans anyway – but are rather doing the sensible thing, which is to huddle as tightly against the breastwork as they can.

———

As it happens, it is the men of the British 61st Division who must face the murderous maelstrom first, as, from 5.31 pm onwards, the 183rd Brigade start to make their way through the sally ports (it has now been 'forbidden to go over the top of the trench . . . by higher authorities'),[4] followed ten minutes later by the 184th Brigade. This last includes the survivors of the 2/1st Bucks, whose job it is to attack and vanquish the apex of the salient, the Sugar-loaf.

In truth, so severe has the German shell fire been upon them to this point that the 184th Brigade has already lost 140 of its men even before emerging. No fewer than 100 of these are from 2/1st Bucks.[5] In fact, the 2/1st Bucks had already lost 78 men the night before when (at least according to Tommy Atkins)[6], yet one more Australian

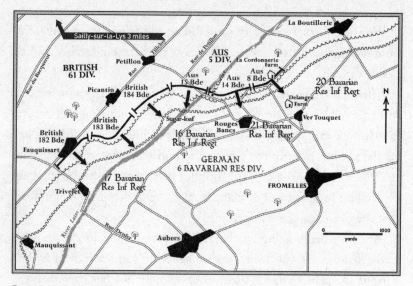

Fromelles, 19 July 1916

short-falling shell 'had burst a gas cylinder in our trenches'.[7]

'It should be said,' one officer of the 2/1st Bucks would note delicately, 'that some of the artillery shooting was bad, notably that of an Australian battery.'[8]

All up, the two assault companies of the 61st's 184th Brigade can now only muster between them 120 soldiers still upright.[9] They now must try to cover 420 yards of open ground straight at entrenched machine guns, hopefully getting within 100 yards or so while the barrage is on, where they will lie down and wait until the barrage lifts.

(That's the plan?

I told you. *That's* the plan.)

Though it is standard policy that the official instructions of the 2/1st Bucks include the demand that they take with them **Large wire cutters - 4 per platoon,**[10] it still seems optimistic to those who think it unlikely they will get within a bull's roar of even the German wire, let alone the Sugar-loaf. Nevertheless, 'deployment commenced as ordered at 5.40 pm'.[11]

Out the sally ports they go!

—

In the German lines, and most particularly to those sentry observers, the vision of these figures appearing at the exit of the sally ports and starting to head through the smoke at them across No-Man's Land, their guns and bayonets thrust forward, arouses not even a flicker of personal alarm.

Rather, this time – now it is confirmed that this is not another Chinese attack – the genuine alarm bell is sounded, and, as recorded by German War Correspondent Wilhelm Scheuermann, 'in a few seconds the whole remainder of the men was out of the shelters and ready for defence. The machine-guns were lifted out of their hiding places and set up freely. At the same time our artillery was contacted and already a few moments later the bloodbath started that in the English history of war will be connected unforgettably with the name Fromelles . . .'[12]

The Sugar-loaf is suddenly filled with machine-gunners of the 11th Company of the 3rd Battalion of the 16th Bavarian RIR – under the command of *Leutnant* Plenge – running to their positions. Once they look out to *Niemandsland* and see the figures emerging from the smoke . . . cheering breaks out among them.

Na endlich! Ihr würdiger Feind versucht es mal. At last! Their worthy enemy is going to have *ein* crack, a go. They even shout out, '*Juhui, sie kemma!* Yee-ha, they're comin'!'[13]

'As they see the enemy in flesh and blood before them,' German War Correspondent George Querl would note, 'they just cannot wait for them to come into range.'[14]

One German soldier even cries out to his comrade, referring to his countrymen's love of taking the highly coveted fine English boots off dead soldiers so they can wear them themselves, '*Schäfer, da kemma deine Schuah!* Schäfer, there're your shoes comin'!'[15] And so they watch carefully as the enemy keeps advancing.

'Their whole demeanour,' Wilhelm Scheuermann would comment on the oncoming soldiers, 'showed that they overestimated the success of their barrage; as our trenches seemed to have been destroyed by their artillery they probably believed also that the men could not defend their own skin anymore.'[16]

So fiercely focused are the machine guns of the Sugar-loaf on the survivors of the 2/1st Bucks that the instant the pitifully thin first wave appears, the worst happens. Just as Pompey Elliott had predicted, after mowing down the first men into No-Man's Land, the machine guns are aimed directly at the sally ports themselves. It means the next men to exit are devastated by a blizzard of bullets, and their bodies block the way for the rest.

In the case of the 2/1st Bucks, there is yet one more last-minute change of plans. The sally ports are abandoned and the troops simply climb over the parapet, sprint forward and enter Rhondda Sap, an unfinished and completely waterlogged trench half-dug across No-Man's Land in previous weeks. This, at least, will provide some protection and bring them some 200 yards closer to the German front. Such is the configuration of the trench network, however, it is only the 2/1st Bucks who have the option, and the other British soldiers must make their way in the open.

'At this point in the operations,' the official report from the Commander of the 2/4 Glosters would run, 'a heavy machine gun fire was opened on D Coy in the open, and the men were driven back on me into the Sally Port of sap 9 where I was standing. This . . . fire was

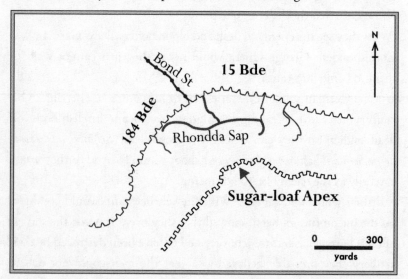

The Sugar-loaf showing Rhondda Sap

particularly heavy and appeared to come from the Front and Right Front from at least 5 or 6 M.Gs.'[17]

It is not, of course, merely the shattered dead bodies now blocking those sally ports; it is the understandable reluctance of the men behind them to push forward and put themselves in the line of the same murderous fire. So they, too, must go over the top, only to be 'met immediately by a very heavy machine-gun fire. The leading platoons were practically wiped out at once and no one could get any further. The other Regiments on our flanks got it worse if anything.'[18]

The men of 2/4th Royal Berkshire – who have been in their position since 9 am, and taking punishment all the while – have also persisted with sally ports, for the same result: annihilation. In sum, in the words of one officer there, the forthcoming attack by the 'Sixty Worst' on the Sugar-loaf is 'more a massacre than a battle',[19] as succeeding waves are 'practically blown back as they went over by machine guns and shrapnel'.[20]

And even those who survive long enough to actually make an advance on the German lines meet their obvious fate. These untested British soldiers are mown down in No-Man's Land by the machine guns of the Sugar-loaf with seemingly as much emotion, and certainly with as much force, as a farmer cuts wheat with a low-swinging scythe, irrespective of their bravery. 'The advance,' one British officer would recount, '[was] magnificent, not a man was seen to waver. The fire brought to bear was annihilating. Hardly a man if any, reached the German parapet.'[21]

And it is not just the machine-gun emplacements in the Sugar-loaf and the like that cut them down. The official report will note the obstacle was also 'machine guns which were worked from the top of the parapet . . . also possibly from Sapheads in NO-MAN'S-LAND'.[22]

The key mission of the 61st Division – to attack and neutralise the Sugar-loaf Salient – does not come close to being accomplished. In the whole attack, just one brave man of the division, Lance-Corporal Arthur Stevens, is reported to have even *got close* to the Sugar-loaf, let alone get to grips with anyone inside.

Though on the far and inconsequential right, where the guns are fewer and the German lines much closer, there is a degree of success as some British soldiers of the 182nd Brigade make their way through the ports, attracting little attention from the distant and mostly destroyed German parapets. The ports of the 183rd and 184th Brigades are all but destroyed.

Watching carefully in the reserve trenches – for he is due to go over with the third wave of the 14th Brigade – Lieutenant-Colonel Walter Cass is deeply worried, and it is not simply for the fact that the No-Man's Land they are about to head into appears to be a murderous maelstrom. It is the damage the men in the forward trenches are taking even before they start.

With just ten minutes to go before the infantry attack of his own battalion is scheduled to begin, Cass sends back a message to 14th Brigade HQ at 5.50 pm:

Enemy are enfilading Brompton Road with shrapnel and trench mortars and [heavy artillery]. Communication blocked for the time. More arty support reqd to check enemy arty as most of their guns are playing on parapet and communications.[23]

Just to Cass's right, John Ridley of the 14th Brigade's 53rd Battalion and his mates are pressing their noses to the front wall of the breastwork as never before. 'The shrapnel fairly whistled through the air,' Ridley would recount. 'Men stood with white still faces and I knew I had to keep a firm hold on myself. The ground in front was being thrown up in all directions by the shells, and the machine guns had commenced to sweep it as the papers says, "like hail falling on a glass-house" and right into and through the inferno we had to charge . . . The sights I saw were terrible, blood and death was everywhere . . .'[24]

At least they are not the only ones copping it, as the bombardment on the German lines at this time reaches its highest intensity, and those who risk gazing across No-Man's Land can now barely even see the

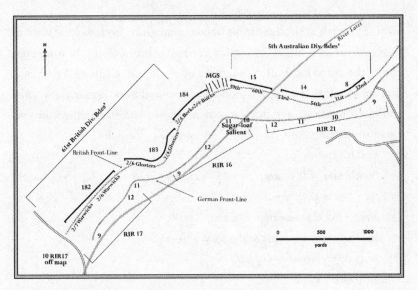

Australian, British and German troop dispositions, 19 July 1916

likes of the Sugar-loaf. Their own shells are roaring down on it, and the air is filled with smoke, dust and the acrid stink of cordite.

Oberst Julius Ritter von Braun's 3rd Battalion, 21st Bavarian RIR sector opposite the Australian 14th and 8th Brigades was, in fact, 'a shambles of blasted sandbags, splintered timber, tangled wire, and dead and wounded comrades'.[25]

It is coming time for the Australians of the 5th Division to enter the fray.

'It is remarkable how discipline can control men at a time like this,' Sapper William Smith of the 14th Brigade would record of his fellow Australian soldiers. 'The majority of the men were new troops, their nerves strung to the utmost tension with shell-fire and inactivity, awaiting the moment when they would mount the parapet and advance to what, for many of them, meant certain death.'

For, as Smith observes, when the time comes to pass the order to move, 'they passed each order along the line more correctly than they would have done on parade. "Five minutes to go!" – those five minutes were the longest of my experience, but at last they were up . . .'[26]

As all look expectantly to their company commanders and the silver whistles they hold in their right hands, many men bow their heads and a certain muffled muttering of prayers can be heard along the line, even above the battering bullets, the roar of exploding shells and that odd grating sound that parapet sandbags penetrated by bullets make as they spill their sand. A lingering last drag on their cigarettes before they toss them underfoot. And then, in many spots all along the line:

Hail Mary, full of grace,
the Lord is with thee;
blessed art thou amongst women,
and blessed is the fruit of thy womb, Jesus.
Holy Mary, Mother of God,
pray for us sinners,
now and at the hour of our death . . .

Meanwhile, some of the cocky ones start to sing a favourite tune:

The bells of hell go ting-aling-aling for you, but not for me
Oh death, where is thy sting-aling-aling, oh grave thy victory . . .[27]

And so it goes.

Many of them know all too well that just ahead lies the German gunner they call 'Parapet Joe', notorious for the fact that he appears to be the most accurate gunner on the Western Front, and more than that besides. Not just a nameless German gunner, this bloke is a distinct individual who can play 'all sorts of jazz rhythms and odd syncopations as he "played' the parapet'.[28] Parapet Joe doesn't just scatter his shots; he has the top of their parapet down to half an inch and can spray sand over your porridge as he likes, the way you could scatter sugar back at home. They all know when he is on duty, and are all too aware that he can catch an unwary head above that parapet in half a second. And now, against such a gunner as this, they have to go over the top and give him a full body shot?

Yes.

Inevitably, inexorably, it must happen. The 'hourglass of eternity', so beloved by General Hamilton back at Gallipoli, drops another tiny grain of sand into 'the lap of time'[29] – this one labelled '5.43 pm'.

And now, as these soldiers of the 14th Brigade watch, mesmerised, an officer climbs the ladder leading over the parapet, blows his whistle, shouts 'Come on, lads!'[30] and goes over the top. Of course, they follow tightly on his heels, these first Australian soldiers to enter the fray, their jaws clenched hard enough that you could strike a match on them, their faces set, their bayonets fixed. 'As they [went over],' Sapper Smith records, 'Fritz opened up with machine-guns and rifles, but on they went, undaunted . . .'[31]

Within seconds, all of them – including Billy Bishop, who is in the first wave – are disappearing into the heavy smoke now lying over No-Man's Land from all the shell fire. Onwards, ever onwards, they push, hopeful of getting to within 100 yards of the German front-line, where they can go to ground until the bombardment lifts at 6 pm.

Just two minutes after the first wave of the 53rd goes over, so too do the first waves of the 59th and 60th Battalions, filled with some of Victoria's finest sons, hailing from Bourke Street, Boort and Bairnsdale, and all the rest – their small bottles of iodine to treat wounds securely in their packs.[32]

Behind them, the men of the second wave take up their positions on the fire-step, getting ready to follow. The machine-gun fire coming at them over the top of the sandbags is now much worse than the scattered shots the first wave had to follow. 'I couldn't describe it, Girlie,' one Digger, amazed to survive, will write to his wife, 'only that if you threw your hat up it would be blown to pieces.'[33]

And now other whistles are heard down the line in this staggered start, dependent on what distance of No-Man's Land there is to cross. The 54th Battalion of the 14th Brigade goes over at 5.50 pm, just before, to its left, the eager men of the 30th and 31st Battalions of the 8th Brigade, at long last, after seven months of waiting, of being derided as 'Tivey's Chocolate Soldiers', get their chance to prove themselves in battle. The 8th have strict orders to ensure that their extreme left flank

– the most vulnerable part of the whole Australian attack, presuming the 61st Division do the same job on the right flank – is heavily barricaded. Whatever trenches they win must be protected from a flanking attack from secure German positions.

With a roar, up and over the first wave of the 8th go, their progress a little helped in the first instance by the planned eruption, forward and off to their left, of 1200 pounds of high-explosive that has been tunnelled in there over the last two months by the 2nd Australian Tunnelling Company. The idea is that the craters made by the mines will provide precious refuge for those soldiers who might need it, 'it being hoped that the upturned edges of its crater would catch some of the machine-gun fire'.[34]

It is something, anyway.

All up, across the Australian line, some 1200 soldiers of the first wave are soon on their way . . . But what is that? High above them now, *die roten Leuchtraketen*, red flares from the German trenches soar skyward.

For the Germans, it is the long-awaited signal, and on the instant their 'light and heavy artillery, which had been continuously engaged in counter-battery work against the enemy artillery since midday, went over immediately to barrage fire . . .'[35]

The day before, the Commander of the 16th Bavarian RIR Artillery batteries had been asked by the Commander of the 16th RIR, *Oberstleutnant* Emil Spatny, 'to concentrate especially heavy fire on the *Australierstellung*, Australians' position, if barrage fire was called for'.[36] Now he proceeds to do exactly that, ordering his men to use shrapnel shells designed to kill men, rather than the high-explosives they have been using to destroy the enemy lines.

From their secure positions just on the far side of Aubers Ridge crest, the German battery crews *pour* fire down onto No-Man's Land where the Australians are attempting to cross, cutting many of them to pieces in the thick smoke that now engulfs them. Most devastating, though, are the Moaning minnies, these *Minenwerfer*, positioned on the close side of the ridge. 'In particular,' the official German report would run, 'where they gathered in groups, the enemy suffered heavy casualties from our [*Minenwerfer*] fire.'[37]

—

At 6.02 pm – a couple of minutes later than planned – the commanders of each artillery battery give the order. In an instant, the section commander of each gun relays the changes in elevation to the rangefinder, who spins the elevating hand-wheel to the right of the breech in a clockwise direction, to lift the barrel by a set degree, meaning the shells firing from them in turn lift and shift to 'barrage lines'. The rain of shells now moves beyond the front-line trenches of the Germans, which the Australians are hopefully about to occupy, to some hundred yards behind, just as, under similar orders, the howitzers target the German communication trenches and crossroads.

Furiously the British and Australian artillery gunners work, ejecting the old shell cases, ramming in the new shells, firing, and then doing it all again. They take heart at the angle of their barrels going up, as it means their infantry *must* be going forward. And now they must paste the Germans even harder!

Regularly the battery crews throw water down the barrels of the guns, followed by a cleaning brush to ensure everything stays clean, and every time they do so huge clouds of steam rise, one Digger says, 'like an overheated car engine after a steep climb'.[38] The only thing more overheated is the gunners themselves, all of them soaked in sweat and working themselves, in relays, to the point of collapse, before having a quick spell and getting back at it.

—

For the men of the 15th Brigade, it hasn't been too bad so far – as those who would shoot them are only now emerging from their dugouts and will need a minute to set up their machine guns. Thus, the Australians of the 60th, particularly, are even able to get to their one precious area of cover, the River Laies, without losing too many of their number, before they traverse it (it is only two feet deep and three feet wide), come up the other side and . . .

And now the Australians of both attacking battalions of the 15th Brigade are hit by thunder and lightning and shells and machine-gun bullets all together! For, in an instant, a blasting blizzard of lead tears across No-Man's Land and into the heads, torsos and legs of the charging Australians of the 59th and 60th Battalions, sweeping across them as 'a hail of bullets in our faces, like a veritable blizzard . . .'[39]

The fire comes not just from directly in front. For as the attack of the 61st Brigade has now fizzled out over on their right, it is a simple matter for *Zweiter Leutnant* Plenge's men in the Sugar-loaf to shift their MG-08 machine guns to a different slot and so help *Zweiter Leutnant* August Bachschneider and his 10th Company 3rd Battalion of the16th Bavarian RIR deal with this neighbouring assault of Elliott's 15th Brigade.

Those Australian soldiers – and there are many – who take a dozen or so machine-gun bullets in their torso are torn in two. One of the

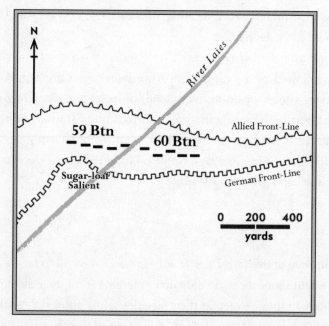

Location of the 59th and 60th Battalions

first men mortally hit is the 60th Battalion's Private Henry Williams of Collingwood – the 18-year-old who had forsworn the temptations of drinking and smoking and chasing wild women – and he falls with a bullet to the breast, his life-blood pouring from him.

Others push on. While, to their left and right, the other battalions who get to within 100 yards of the German line do as planned and lie down, waiting for the barrage to lift, for the 60th that is not possible, as they have no cover at all. Because they are under such heavy fire, with no shelter from any broken ground available, the only choice is to charge forward or back, and they choose to charge forward.

Watching closely, General Pompey Elliott groans. He has seen his men of the 15th Brigade head off with a lump in his throat, and can just hear their roar carried back to him on the wind over the ongoing shell fire from both sides. And what else?

Yes, the staccato bursts of rifle fire and . . . oh, *Christ* . . . is that the rapid *knock-knock-knock-knock* sound of *German* machine guns? It could be either his men or the enemy – or both – firing. It is impossible to say. But if it is German machine guns, it is a very bad sign, as the barrage should have knocked them all out.

All Pompey Elliott can see is wave after wave of men heading into the smoke, and no one returning. What is happening out there? What is *happening* to his men?

And so the men of the first two waves of the 60th are running hard now. Bullets whizzing past, comrades falling near and far, shrapnel bursting overhead. A few are rolling balls of violence just waiting to burst on the first enemy they find. Many are terrified; others are confused – everything seems to be happening so fast it is hard to comprehend. *Many* others, however, experience a certain numbness, almost as if nature is compensating them for the horror they are going through by dulling their senses. Which is as well, for . . .

'They were met,' another Australian soldier would recount, 'with a perfect tornado of machine gun fire. Their own line of fire crossing each other. The machine gunners slowly traversing their gun from left to right swept [them] out of existence . . .'[40]

For those in the oncoming second waves, the fire upon them is intense from the first, like a pelting rain of bullets and shrapnel that spares few. And by now, it is not just German machine-gunners at work, as they have been joined by the soldiers.

'These old Bavarian . . . clay-target shooters,' German War Correspondent George Querl would note, 'laid on the parapets and left none of the English officers who came there alive.'[41] Those officers are easy to spot for the fact they are carrying no rifle and tend to wave their arms about a lot as they give orders. 'It became obvious which were the officers,' the official German account would note, 'and they were immediately shot down.'[42]

They are far from the only ones cut down, however, as the German machine guns open up, each spitting out ten bullets every second, 'swishing in a flat lattice of death'.[43] Those who fall inevitably get hit again on the way to the ground. Still the line keeps going the best it can, though getting thinner with every few yards . . .

Leading the second wave up the ladder, over the parapet and into No-Man's Land is the pride of the battalion, the man whom Pompey Elliott regards as practically his protégé, Major Tom Elliott. Through the high, damp grass they go, Major Tom in the lead, exhorting them forwards, over the ditches, and keep going, men!

Alas, from antiquity on, rocks, arrows and bullets have always had a predilection for cutting down the flower of a nation's youth, and so too on this occasion. For just as Major Elliott is urging his troops forward, a German shell lands right near him, and the explosion lifts the 22-year-old graduate of Duntroon, the man thought to be a future 'Australian Kitchener', high in the air.

'We saw him go down . . .' one of his men, Private Alexander Forbes, would recount. 'Shortly afterwards he stood up and tried to get his tunic off. He got it off after a little and then pitched forward onto his face. He had a big gash in his back, as from high explosive. He remained there all bunched up with his body in the air and his head on the ground as we went past in our wave.'[44]

As that wave presses on, Elliott's faithful batman stays with him, trying his best to stem the blood coming from what proves to be no fewer than six wounds . . . until, finally, mercifully, Tom Elliott . . . the man with the splendid future, and everything to live for, who never needed to be in this attack in the first place . . . dies.

'Major Elliott,' Private Forbes would say of him, 'was one of the best.'[45]

The rest of the wave – inevitably leaving eddying rivulets of blood behind it – rolls on.

The German fire is now more lethal than ever, and Commanding Officer Hauptmann Hans Gebhardt would note in his report, 'A barrage of machine-gun, small-arms and artillery fire mowed down the attacking enemy like a scythe . . .'[46]

As with the 61st Division, when it comes to most of the 15th Brigade, it is much less a battle than a massacre. And, in fact, yes, nothing less than a 'bloody holocaust'. For inside the Sugar-loaf, all is murderous madness as the German machine-gunners keep their four state-of-the-deathly-art MG08 machine guns – two at the apex, one on either flank, all capable of going quickly to different machine-gun slots in the parapet – trained on the charging masses coming at them across *Niemandsland*. The gunners grips tighten around their weapons as cursing, grunting underlings rush back and forth keeping the ammunition up to them.

As some of the attacking soldiers seek sanity, and turn to retreat, the Bavarians shout after them, '*Kommt doch her, kommt doch heran, wenn's Schneid habt!* Come on over, come up close, if you've got the courage!'[47]

Most of them do.

With some admiration, *Regiment Adjutant* Hauptmann Friedrich Wiedemann notes how the 'death-defying [Australian] officers jumped forward with *gezogenem Seitengewehr*, drawn bayonets, take the men with them by their example. They were shot down and the force of the attack *zerflatterte*, fluttered apart into weak advances of singular groups. All those who did not lie, shot or shattered on the ground, tried to crawl back to their own trenches. Again our fire hit into the flooding back rows and brought bloody losses. Those spared by bullets, fell victim to the shrapnel of our barrage. This is how the [Australian] attack in front of the section of the 16th Bavarian Reserve Infantry Regiment was forced down, even before it had properly developed . . .[48]

But, by God, they try.

—

As the 54th Battalion's distance across No-Man's Land is only 200 yards – and it is the machine-gun posts right in front of them and to their left that have mercifully been all but wiped out by the shelling – they arrive at the German trenches at much the same time as the Bavarians who have been sheltering below in their dugouts. After hand-to-hand fighting, they quickly kill or capture them, in the process capturing two German machine guns – which is no small achievement.

Many of the Germans have in fact abandoned their front-line positions opposite the Australian 14th Brigade, and now set themselves in a new line, in a spot known as Rouges Bancs, some 300 yards back. Just let the enemy keep coming and they will pick them off.

Back in the Australian lines, it will soon be time for the third and fourth waves of the 5th Division to go over. These waves, like their predecessors, carry scrambling mats for the wire, small, light bridges for the tiny river, ladders for the far breastworks and 'green canvas bags'[49] of bombs, which should give the Squareheads something to think about, if they can just get close enough to hurl them.

But . . . can they?

—

It is ten minutes since the barrage lifted and the first wave charged forward. Time now for the third wave to hop the bags.

In some parts along the Australian line, the damage caused by the German shelling has been so devastating that this third wave is in fact composed of the survivors of the third and fourth waves. But, such as they are, they make ready. Behind them will come the fourth wave, which generally contains battalion commanders and their staffs, whose job it will be to set up advance Battalion HQs. The intent, of course, is that these first waves will have quelled most of the resistance, thus giving the brain of the battalion, the HQ, the best chance to survive.

The third wave of the 60th Battalion – to the right of the 53rd and 54th – is led by Lieutenant Tom Kerr. Ascending the parapet, his expectation is to see the waves of his comrades ahead. Instead, there is nothing. Not a man standing in front of him in No-Man's Land. Oh yes, there is movement, but it is the horizontal movement of men writhing, and men crawling backward.

And everywhere are totally still lumps of dead men.

What has happened to the first and second waves?

Convinced they must be lying up yonder, or already in the German trench, Lieutenant Kerr takes his men forward, only to come under withering fire. Kerr himself is soon wounded, and he and his surviving men try to take what shelter they can, about 150 yards from the German parapet. From here, Kerr can see the German soldiers practically jostling each other, shoulder high above the parapet, eager to get their shots in. To his eyes, they are 'looking as if they were wondering what was coming next'.[50]

The answer, hopefully, is *hordes* of Australian soldiers, for that is their only chance. As one of the men with him has a Bible, Kerr tears a piece of paper from it and scribbles a note to be sent back: *Here with 4 men, a few yards from parapet. Must have reinforcements. Useless going on without.*[51]

———

And here now comes the 60th Battalion's fourth wave, comprising the Battalion HQ staff and D Company.

Major Geoff McCrae – hand-picked by Pompey Elliott to join him in the 15th Brigade – is only out of the Australian trenches for 60 seconds, shepherding his men and constantly glancing left and right to make sure the wave is in line, when, just 80 yards out, he pauses for a moment. And kneels. The flurry of fire is so strong that all of them – as nature tells them to – make themselves smaller targets. For Major McCrae's part, he must direct operations, and so he indicates with tight hand movements what he wants his men to do.

From the German lines, a rifleman has noted this man so clearly giving orders, so he takes aim, and squeezes the trigger.

Geoff McCrae is still on one knee at the time, peering forward, seeking the best way to proceed. The bullet hits him in the throat and kills him so cleanly – going clear through – that he does not even fall over. The beloved son of Gussie and George McCrae – two parents who have doted on him from day dot – is no more of this earth.

'Hundreds were killed on the parapets,' one soldier would report of the whole of the 60th, 'some reached the stream . . . Wounded crept in shell holes. The Huns bombed them. Others tried to crawl back and they were sniped.'[52]

Extraordinarily, despite it all, some Australian soldiers of the 15th Brigade have actually made it close to the position they were meant to get to, 100 yards from the German breastworks. These include a few soldiers of the 59th Battalion's A Company under Captain Aubrey Liddelow, who tries to take them further. But they come under furious fire that forces them back, Liddelow now with bullets in his shoulder and arm.

Taking shelter in a shell hole, one of Liddelow's soldiers, who has also been badly hit, politely insists that the Captain return with him across No-Man's Land to get medical attention.

Liddelow sends the soldier back but refuses to accompany him, saying simply, 'I'll never walk back into safety and leave the men I have led into such grave danger – we'll wait for reinforcements.'[53]

Those reinforcements are trying to get to them. But . . .

'They were mown down in long lines,' one observer would report. 'Their Lewis gunners rushed from shell hole to shell hole firing short bursts until they were all killed. About 80 wounded men got back. The rest were either bombed or sniped. No living thing could live under such a hell of fire.'[54]

In fact, there are some. The survivors from the 59th Battalion – which has been at the right-hand end of the Australian line, closest to the Sugar-loaf – must go to ground. Others of the 60th Battalion survive only by drifting to the left, away from the Sugar-loaf, and joining up with the soldiers on the far right of the 53rd Battalion's advance, who are actually doing as planned and storming the German trenches. There, at last, they are able to get just a little of their own back.

Liddelow and his men remain in an isolated pocket, without support. That sound? It is the deathly crescendo of a shell descending. It explodes near them – close enough that a piece of shrapnel flies forth and hits Liddelow in the head. He is killed. What is left of his group lie prone, their own heads down, praying that some of the next waves might get to them, that the shooting and shelling might stop. Something, *anything*. Anything but this.

—

By nature, these machine-gunners in the Sugar-loaf are resented by the other soldiers for their privileged lives, the fact they are always spared the hard work of carrying heavy ammunition boxes forward, digging trenches, retrieving bodies and all the rest. But there is no resentment today, as the gunners continue to mow down all the figures charging forward, pausing only an instant in their sweep when an officer is spied and they follow specific orders *diese zuerst zu töten*, to kill these first.

Belt after belt is fired: 250 rounds, 1000 rounds, 3000 rounds. *Mehr! Mehr! Mehr!* More! More! More!

'Pass up the spare barrels!' shouts the *Gewehrführer*, gun commander. The barrels are alternated, so that the firing can be continuous, and soon all the guns are trained once more – 5000 rounds gone now. Though a formidable weapon, the MG08 is prone to overheating as it spits out its eight bullets a second. When fired for just two minutes continuously, which is what is happening now, it can become red hot, even boiling the water used to cool it.

The hands of the machine-gunners are now so badly scorched that the smell of burning skin fills the interior of the Sugar-loaf, but still there is no relief. 'Keep firing!' orders the *Unteroffizier*, just as the boiling water turns to steam.

'*Wo ist Wasser?* Where's the water?' bawls *der Richtschütze*, the gunner.

'*Nichts mehr da, Herr Unteroffizier!* There's none left, *Unteroffizier!*'[55]

Still the waves keep coming from the far trenches, and still the guns must keep mowing them down. From where can the Germans get the cooling water they need? The obvious. They piss into the water container and feed *that* into the system.

The gun is working again!

And now bullets from the enemy are hitting them, and grenades exploding and shrapnel whistling past, and sometimes shards of concrete drive into them, but still the gunners keep going.

Keep firing, or die.

Load!

Forward! Down! Back! (Working parts forward – belt on – working parts back.)

Safety catch to the right. *Fire! Tack! Tack! Tack! Tack!*

One German soldier, Friedrich Hauer, is notable for his extraordinary composure, even as dozens of bullets fly around his head, his two helpers lie dead and his gun is momentarily *kaput*. Calmly, he repairs it, and gets back to it, looking up to find the enemy getting closer. And now a new helper rushes forward to keep the ammo up to him.

'He hummed down his ammunition belt,' the admiring German War Correspondent George Querl would record. 'But he could not equal the neighbour machine gun anymore: there one single shooter had droned down 14,000 bullets until the blood almost spurt out of the squeezing thumb. The tough shooter had a friend *auf Tod und Leben*, a friend for life and death, next to him, who continuously threw hand-grenades as soon as he saw one creeping up. They were two *Würgengel*, destroying angels.'[56]

High pillars of steam rise from all the machine guns, as they all overheat. Soon, skin is hanging in ribbons from the fingers of the burned hands of the German gunners, and the left thumbs that hold down the triggers are swollen lumps of seared flesh, but still they don't relent as they keep their heavily chattering guns firing.

One gunner, shot through the head, falls across his gun and makes the belt jam. But in an instant a replacement has stepped forward, fixed the jam, reloaded, and is now firing once more. And so it happens across the German line. Each time a gunner falls, dead or wounded, another instantly steps forward to take his place. So too those firing rifles. 'Riflemen of the 16th Bavarian R.I.R.,' the official historian would note, 'eagerly awaited the approach of the enemy and shot him down with heavy loss.'[57]

—

Of all the attacking battalions, it is the 53rd and 54th of the 14th Brigade that have been most fortunate, as their artillery bombardment has been most damaging, destroying whole sections of the German parapet occupied by the 11th and 12th RIRs, exacting a high casualty rate and, most importantly, knocking out half a dozen machine guns.

For, there, many of the stunned German soldiers have abandoned their positions – disbelieving that anyone could make it across that human hell of *Niemandsland*, let alone dozens of them. By the time the Australians swarm into the trenches, most of the Germans who remain are found 'cowed and crouching in their dugouts'.[58]

—

In the 53rd Battalion, in the middle of the 14th Brigade attack, Sergeant John Ridley is in charge of a Lewis gun section and is awaiting the time to go forward. A devout Christian, he is praying to his Lord and Saviour, even as he takes out his revolver, checks his ammunition and fingers the whistle he must blow, come the time. And now, his section leader, the hugely respected and really well-liked Captain Harry Paulin

– a six-foot, 200-pound widower with three children at home – gives the word, 'Away you go.'

Sergeant Ridley blows his own whistle, shouts out 'Forward!' to his men and heads over the top with them, Captain Paulin inevitably in the lead. Suddenly, from merely hearing the battle from the safer side of the parapet, they are out in the midst of it, as shells explode, machine guns chatter and men die. Just 50 yards out, Sergeant Ridley gets caught up in barbed wire and is slowed down as bullets start smacking into the ground all around him.

'Oh, God, help me. Oh! Keep me,' he cries,[59] all too aware that his life could be lost or lamed in an instant, just as is happening to so many of the men with him. As the Sergeant, however, he must remain close to the lead and push forward, and so he does, finally extricating himself from the wire to rush forward, as the bullets fall more thickly, and the storm of shrapnel thickens. Suddenly, just up ahead, he spies some kind of trench in No-Man's Land and rushes to it, the way a child might run to the shelter of a tree to get out of the rain. He dives into it, closely followed by many of his surviving men, only to find it packed with a mixture of others doing the same, including wounded men who have crawled back to this point.

Another officer of his company is in there, Lieutenant Henry Briggs, and it is he who now takes command. 'Cool as a cucumber, smoking a cigarette and with a great-coat over his shoulder,' Briggs waves his arm, shouts that it is time to go and leads them out once more. They are running now.

'Bullets spat to the right of me,' Ridley would recall, 'others struck to the left and I knew a machine gun was after me. "God help me, keep me," I prayed as I rushed; when suddenly splash! I was up to my chest in muddy water in a hollow. Dead men and wounded lay about the ditch in all directions; an awful scene of awful war.'[60]

Not all of them make it, however, as there is still fire upon the Australians, and a single shot now hits Captain Paulin right in his guts. He is hurt badly, and no doubt about it, but he asks his men to prop him up so he can at least throw some bombs. It soon becomes obvious, though, that his life is less ebbing from him than *gushing* . . .

Private Charles Doncaster, who is himself wounded and bleeding just a couple of yards away, sees that the Captain is badly hurt and manages to crawl over to him. Both men are experienced enough to know it – there can be no coming back from it, and his death can only be a matter of time. All Doncaster can do is stay with him as he falls into and out of unconsciousness, and give him sips of water when he asks for it. Finally, it is time for him to die, and Captain Paulin seems to recognise it, just managing to get out his last words.

'Give my love to my little girl,' he says, weakly.[61]

> *Abide with me; fast falls the eventide;*
> *The darkness deepens; Lord, with me abide;*
> *When other helpers fail and comforts flee,*
> *Help of the helpless, oh, abide with me . . .*

With a last sigh, Captain Paulin dies.

Amazed to still be alive himself, Sergeant Ridley is nearby in the thick of it when '"crash bang" . . . it felt like receiving a terrible smack from a cricket ball but ten times worse . . . Then the blood rushed out of my mouth and down my face in torrents.'[62]

—

The 8th Brigade, meanwhile, is in a similar position to the 14th Brigade. On the far left, the 31st and 32nd Battalions of the 8th Brigade had been so close to the enemy front trench and had left their own trench so close to the end of the artillery bombardment that there was no sense in lying down, and so they had kept going. And the exploding of the mines and the consequent craters really have helped them, for, although there remains fire upon them, and many 8th Brigade soldiers of the first wave have been cut down, the succeeding waves find the fire thinner. Even that limited shelter allows them to traverse this much narrower No-Man's Land of just 100 yards and make it to the German trenches, against only limited resistance. As they get to the top of the German parapet, they can even see dozens of the enemy running away.

And *that's* what the 8th Brigade can do, when they're thrown into a real stunt. Not bad for Tivey's chocolate soldiers.

———

Now 15 minutes since the Australian assault began, the 8th Brigade's 31st and 32nd Battalions are holding the German front-line on the left, while the 15th Brigade's 59th and 60th Battalions – at least, their survivors – are held up in No-Man's Land on the right.

In the centre, the first German trench has been taken. There, survivors of the first three waves of the 14th Brigade's 53rd Battalion, and Lieutenant-Colonel Cass's men of the 54th, are heartened to be joined by the fourth wave, which includes their Commanding Officer, Lieutenant-Colonel Ignatius Norris, and his senior staff.

Typically, Norris has no sooner caught up with the first wave, vaulting both the first and second German trenches, than he takes the lead – feeling spiritually stronger for the Holy Communion he has taken that morning. 'Come on lads!' this small, bespectacled man with a smaller, still dark moustache roars. 'Only another trench to take.'[63]

Just an instant later, the death rattle of machine-gun fire rings out and, as one private would later recount, Norris is 'shot in the abdomen by a bullet and killed instantly'.[64] As other senior officers are also killed soon afterwards, the command of the 53rd Battalion quickly falls to D Company's Captain Charles Arblaster – a Duntroon graduate in the same class as Major Tom Elliott and Major Arthur Hutchinson, the Tasmanian clergyman's son who, though still young at just 21, has already distinguished himself at Gallipoli with the 9th Light Horse when they lost 50 per cent of their strength at Hill 60 on 27 August the previous year.

Arblaster now finds himself the most senior remaining officer in the 53rd Battalion. Just as happened with the other battalions that have made it across the German front-lines, there is confusion once they begin to look for the second and third trenches that have showed up in the aerial photographs.

For where the hell are they? All that the men can see ahead, once they move beyond the initial breastwork, its adjoining trenches and dugouts, are open fields covered in coarse grass, all of it pockmarked with huge shell holes – with no sign of the second lot of breastworks so clearly marked on their maps. Cautiously, still trying to work it all out, they advance with their rifles at the ready. By one contemporary account, they pushed forward 'through the grass, like sportsmen after quail, occasionally shooting at Germans who had settled in shellholes and who now started up to run farther'.[65] It must be just up ahead!

Every instant, they expect to come under fire from the enemy, who must surely be congregating in the support trench that must surely be just up ahead, hidden by the grass, but there is nothing. And with every passing minute, their advance becomes more scattered. They keep going until they come to the first dismal ditch, which they cross, and then come to the second ditch, some 600 yards behind the first German fire-trench. Similar confusion reigns until the truth of it is realised.

Their maps had been drawn many months before, when those trenches had been serious concerns, but they are now waterlogged and crumbling messes. And, sure, the aerial photographs taken three days ago had shown a distinct line in the ground where that support trench had been, but now, up close, the clearly long-since abandoned trench – or is it a drainage ditch? – can provide very little in the way of protection.

And not just from German machine guns, which start to seek them out. For when they begin to make a stand in the second ditch, it soon proves impossible because the shells from the Australian artillery commence falling on them, from batteries that clearly have no idea that they are here.

Falling back, thus, to the first ditch, about 200 yards on from the initial German line, to make their stand there proves extremely difficult. As they start to dig down, and across – taking the parapet from the side facing No-Man's Land and trying to put it on the German side as protection against their inevitable counter-attack – the wet clay they are trying to fill their sandbags with 'clings to the shovel like an oyster, necessitating removal by hand'.[66]

Still they persist.

Acrid smoke from all the shelling and the exploding ammunition dumps is now rolling over the entire battlefield, heightening the sense of doom and disaster, confusion and catastrophe.

Coming over in the last wave of the 54th, the Commanding Officer, Lieutenant-Colonel Walter Cass, takes pause. His instinct, whatever the orders of McCay – whom he actively dislikes and has little respect for – is to first secure this front-line trench, and he establishes his own HQ for the battalion in a German dugout that is simply stunning for its commodious comfort, including an electric light, a table, chair, stove, bell and *wallpaper*, further 'decorated with gold moulding similar to picture frame moulding'.

With just one look, Cass can see how so many Germans survived the bombardment, if all the dugouts are even half as good as this. 'Thickness of earth on top about 8 feet, depth (below ground level) of about 10 feet,' he would record admiringly, particularly with regard to how deep, well-drained and dry the German dugouts and trenches are. 'It was reached by steps and had a passage or light to a window. It was strongly built and had an upright about 12" x 12" in the centre supporting a rafter of somewhat similar thickness.'[67]

Ammunition and supplies? Try '10 to 20 thousand rounds [small-arms ammunition], many flares, gas helmets . . . Other dugouts in the line were similarly built.'[68]

The situation as he finds it is confusing, as the trenches are not where they are supposed to be, but at least the men of the 54th, as Cass would report, 'had touch on the right with 53rd Bn who stated they were in touch with the 15th Bde. On the left we had touch with the 8th Bde.'[69] If those reports are correct, most particularly the report that has come from the 53rd, that they are in touch with the 60th, who are 'in' to the German trenches, both his flanks are secure.

It comes as no small relief.

Other news for Cass, however, is devastating, as he is not long in finding out that the German tactic of shooting officers first has exacted a terrible toll on his battalion. All four company commanders of the 54th have already been killed, and all their seconds-in-command killed or wounded. The survivors press on.

—

Sergeant Ridley slowly comes to. He is aware that he has been shot in the head, and can *feel* himself to be dying.

It is a strange . . . suspended . . . sensation. A deeply religious man, he wonders what his first view of heaven will be like . . . a calming thought . . . and then comes the jolt. But what of 'Mother and all at home . . . what will they say when they see my name under: "Killed in Action"?'[70] He really wants to *live* . . . but when he next comes to, he finds himself in a dirty, muddy ditch, 'with scarlet round my body'.[71] He is still with his section of men who brought the Lewis gun over, and he pleads not to be left behind, but then realises he has 'no right to keep two of my section back from their work with the guns'.[72]

—

In the forward command post of the 16th Bavarian RIR, Meierhof, the commander, and *Oberstleutnant* Emil Spatny are receiving reports – over the sounds of heavy machine guns firing 'in the whole regiment's section' – from the battalion commander in the front-line:

'*Der Engländer* has broken through on the right at 21st Bavarian Reserve Infantry Regiment and also on the left at 17th Bavarian Reserve Infantry Regiment, and is in the section of 21st Bavarian Reserve Infantry Regiment in the approach of *Grashof* [a concealed German strongpoint].'[73] Quickly now, the 16th Reserve Regiment Battalion Commander Hauptmann Hans Gebhardt gives orders for the men of the 8th, 7th and 6th Companies to begin the counter-attack . . .

Unaware of the major storm that has just been sent in their direction, the Australian soldiers of the 54th and 53rd Battalion who have made it into the trenches fight on. In fact, the 53rd Battalion, on the right, is already taking devastating fire because as well as being shot at from the front, the 53rd soldiers are also taking ever more withering fusillades from their right flank, where the Sugar-loaf lies . . .

It is 6.30 pm, and the 8th and 14th Brigades hold 1200 yards of German trenches. In most places, they also hold the second German trench, 200 yards beyond the first. The survivors of the 15th Brigade, in contrast, have got nowhere. They lie pinned down halfway across No-Man's Land. Back in the Australian front-lines, now that the four waves have gone, the most urgent thing is for each brigade to begin digging communication trenches across No-Man's Land to allow safe passage between their own and German lines – hopefully soon to be Australian lines.

The 55th Battalion's B Company, under the command of Captain Norman Gibbins – the former civil engineer and then Ipswich bank manager who has a heart as huge as his body, and loves his collection of pressed flowers – is waiting in readiness at the 300-yard line for the moment to move forward to help with this exercise. The 14th Brigade's 'Gib' is well loved all right, an officer whose soldiers would follow him through the gates of Hell, which is handy under the circumstances.

For as he leads them forward along the communication trenches in single file, with five-minute gaps between each of the four platoons so as not to be too bunched up, they inevitably pass shockingly wounded men now coming back the other way.

A cold shiver moves up the spine of many who, having spent no more than two days anywhere near the front-line, are now realising the barest beginnings of the reality they are about to face. They push on, only for a German shell to land right in the middle of the front party. Those pushing behind must now go through the grisly remains of men they had been laughing with just 30 minutes before, with one particular man 'blown to pulp, bits of legs and arms . . . scattered about'.[74]

It is horror on a scale previously inconceivable. 'I trod on his head by mistake as I hurried by,' Second-Lieutenant Percy Chapman would recount, 'and it gave under my foot like a sponge – others were lying about moaning and groaning – but all feeling had left me now. I passed dead men without feeling pity or remorse.'[75]

In short order, the survivors of Gibbins's group are in position. Beyond their rifles, which they already have, they are all issued with grenades. Far more importantly, however, for this is their real job of the night, they have with them shovels and 15 sandbags each.

Ready?

Ready.

Just a few minutes after the last wave has gone, B Company is helping the 14th Field Company, which has been charged with the task of digging *like mad things*. No, really. For a course, they follow the contours bravely put out by one of the 14th Company Engineers, Sydney Donnan, who uses a drum of tape to set out 'a zig-zag trench across No-Man's-Land missing a few bumps and utilizing a few hollows'.

'We all simply "dug like hades",' Donnan would recount. 'One man to about six foot of trench.'

Donnan himself goes at it in such frenzy he would describe it as 'a nightmare of hard work and vomiting and now and again comforting

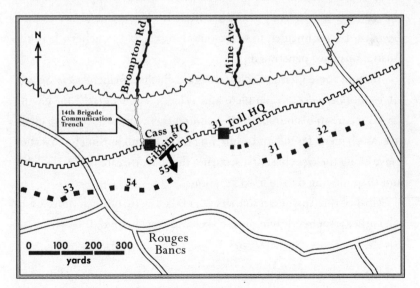

The positions of the 8th and 14th Brigade battalions

some wounded digger'.[76] Another of the digger Diggers, August Band, is certain that his last night on earth has come, that he simply must be killed, but he keeps digging like fury anyway. It is his duty.

On their right, another digging party is also under way, from the 15th Brigade, with the Diggers equally frantic to dig down to give themselves some cover and then forward to push the trench along. But in the 8th Brigade trench, there are . . . problems. There had been plans to use a 'pipe-pusher bomb': a pipe filled with explosive, thrust far forward beneath the surface. Once exploded, ideally it forms long, straight ditches of five or six feet in depth *prêt à marcher* – but it has not worked properly, and the first soldiers assigned to the rough furrow that it created were under constant machine-gun and rifle fire from their left flank, as well as precise German artillery bombardment, before being absorbed into the fight.

And yet, others have taken up the shovels and at least the beginning of the 8th Brigade communication trench is now under way.

Just ahead of them as they dig, in the Old German Lines, young German soldiers are striking back. With the failure of the 183rd Brigade to subdue the Sugar-loaf, the Commander of the 16th Bavarian RIR, Hauptmann Hans Gebhardt, has quickly ordered a couple of dozen of the men therein, most of whom are from 10. Kompanie under *Zweiter Leutnant* Bachschneider, to strike out along the old trenches where the Australians have penetrated.

Though these German soldiers regard Bachschneider as '*ein Schuft, ein ganz miserabler*', a 'complete and utter *Schweinehund*'[77] for having stayed secure in his bunker while sending them out, still they are effective. With grenades in hand – hurtling forward and hurling forth – they move along the trenches, first securing that part threatened by the 60th and then moving on the 53rd's section.

Most of the Australian soldiers who take the first trench move on to take other trenches, leaving just a skeleton crew behind, if that.

—

Bert and Ray Bishop have been waiting separately but quietly – Bert with his carrying party; Ray with the 14th Brigade machine-gunners – knowing their time is soon to come.

And now comes the message. C Company must begin carrying water and ammo across. Loaded up like packhorses – the water in poorly constructed, box-shaped cans known as 'flimsys', the rifle and machine-gun ammunition carried in heavy boxes, with a rope handle held by a staggering soldier on each end – they set off, overland between the 300-yard line and the front-line because there are no communication trenches yet.

The closer they get to that front-line, the more the shells fall near them – for of course the German artillery is now plastering both No-Man's Land and the approaches to the Australian front-line – though mercifully there are no direct hits. Coming the other way now are the first of the wounded, often two hurt Diggers using their combined force to keep going – the bloke with the shattered arm at least able to help the one with the shattered leg. And now, too, the first batch of German prisoners. Bert and Ray look closely at them, the first Germans they've ever seen.

The Boche look . . . well . . . a lot like us Australians, actually. Somehow, not quite the ogres Bert and Ray had imagined, but young men of their common humanity, with a scared look in their eyes, *just like us*. Some of them are hurt, with one big German, stripped to his waist, having a hole in his back you could poke your fist into. But at least he is upright. Behind him are other bloodied messes of German prisoners, crawling along the duckboards, trying to get away from *das Dante-Inferno* that lies behind them.

One of Bert Bishop's mates asks a passing German prisoner, 'Well, Fritz, what do you think of things now?' and is stunned when the German replies in heavily accented but easily understandable English, 'I'm quite happy, but I'm sorry for you poor bastards.'[78]

The Australians are not long in finding out why. When the trench they are marching in starts leading into the front-line Australian trenches, Bert goes numb as he see for the first time, up close, the results of the German shelling and machine-gunning. Everywhere, there are dead bodies, pieces of dead bodies, pulverised bodies, shell-shocked and bleeding men crawling along, some clinging to each other in the ghastly light thrown in the rising dusk by the flares and exploding shells, and crying like babies. And every five seconds or so, another shell lands, causing more bloody carnage.

For the truth of it is that *das Dante-Inferno* is following them still, borne on the wings of the angels of death, as the German artillery continues to search out all the Australian trenches, including these communication trenches, and succeeds in blowing 'great craters along its length as we struggled through, trampling underfoot the dead that cluttered it. All the while we were losing men. Some of the wounded lay in pools staining the water with their blood. Dead men, broken trench-material, shattered duckboards that tripped us as we passed, the smell of the fumes of high explosives, and the unforgettable odour of death made this trench a place of horror.'[79]

Bert Bishop can neither move nor speak as a strange numbness overtakes him, which soon gives way to sheer terror . . . and then . . . disbelief. Can this really be happening? Is the next shell about to end his and Ray's life? Is death upon him? This cannot be true! 'We are supposed to be civilised,' he thinks. 'The most beastly and cruel animals on earth wouldn't do this to each other.'[80]

He feels dazed, his brain trying to move forward through heavy, bloody mud. Maybe he is asleep, having the worst nightmare of his life? That must be it, must be the explanation, must . . .

'Get along there,' a shout intrudes on his reverie. 'What the hell do you think we're here for?'[81]

A tragically good point. They are here to carry water and ammunition to those who are hopefully occupying the German trenches, and they now must get to them. There are the beginnings of a trench now being frantically dug across No-Man's Land – led by good ol' Captain 'Gib', who keeps exhorting his men to dig harder and faster – but so far it goes no more than a dozen yards. The instant the soldiers are out of it, machine-gun bullets swarm all around them like angry bees, getting thicker as they race forward.

'Keep going on top, we've got to get our stuff over!' their officer yells.[82] And they do their best, running for as far as they dare before going to earth again behind whatever cover they can find – usually dead or wounded comrades, or in craters created by the shelling – and then going again.

Other carrying parties are making equally heavy weather of it. One is led by Lieutenant Briggs of the 14th Machine Gun Company. Throwing down his cigarette, he shouts to his party over the roar of battle, 'Are you ready?'

With a wave of his hand, over they go, only to be hit hard by German machine-gun fire from the moment they clear the top of the parapet. Running down the slight slope, the men are soon in a ditch, up to their waists in water, which, though slimy, gives some protection. They follow one soldier as he takes them left and right through crisscrossing ditches, until they get to one that leads straight to the German lines . . . only for him to take a bullet to the neck. He goes down, choking on his own blood. The others do what they can for him, but within minutes that lead gunner is just one of many.

'The ditch,' one of them would recount, 'was full of wounded and dying men – like a butcher's shop – men groaning and crying and shrieking. Ammunition was being carried up by pairs of men, the boxes being carried on sticks. One man would go down, and crash would go the box into the water. Shelling was very heavy.'[83]

Amid all the screaming, and explosions, and death rattles and constant machine-gun fire, some of the carrying party, most particularly the wounded, scramble over to the communication trench being dug by the 14th Field Company, creating havoc for the Diggers as they try to keep going. All is chaos and confusion. Should they abandon? At one point, when someone does suggest retiring, the reaction is immediate.

'What – retreating? Not on your life!'[84]

—

The situation the carrying parties are joining is fluid. The first Australian wave has crossed No-Man's Land and spread out along the front-line German trenches, knocking out whatever pockets of resistance are still there. Subsequent waves are doing as instructed and – after leaving just a few men to establish Lewis gun posts in that first line – pushing on, seeking to subdue the support-line trenches that their sketch maps tell them lie beyond.

'[We] swept on with the intention of capturing the second and third trenches in the first line system,' the 31st Battalion's Lieutenant-Colonel Frederick Toll would recount, 'but we went on and on but no trace could be found of same. It now appeared evident that the information supplied about enemy defences and aerial photographs was incorrect and misleading.'[85]

For now, as machine-gun fire from Grashof up ahead opens up on them, Lieutenant-Colonel Toll decides that the furthest ditch is as good as they are going to get. The surviving officers of the most forward elements of the 8th Brigade – led by Toll, with his head wounds roughly bandaged – order their men to dig in there, fill their sandbags with the muck they get out of the ditches, and position those sandbags on the far side. The best they can hope for now is to hold on to the ground they've won.

Calling for a messenger, Lieutenant-Colonel Toll writes a note for Brigadier-General Edwin Tivey at 8th Brigade HQ – *6.30 p.m. Four waves well over 200 yards beyond enemy's parapets. No enemy works found yet, so am digging in*[86] – and hands it to the waiting man. Rolling the message into a tight roll, the signaller then places it in a tiny canister.

From out of the enclosed wicker basket he has brought with him, the signaller takes an 'umble 'oming pigeon, and attaches the canister to the bird's right leg. Hopefully the pigeon will fly high and quickly, to get above the bullets and shrapnel, and evade both the German fire that the Boche always unleash at the sight of pigeons and the trained hawks they have on the lookout for just such as them. In a similar spirit, albeit with a sweeter distraction, the Germans position bitches on heat to disturb the Allies' messenger dogs. (Pigeons remain the favoured method,

Extract from Intelligence Report: 'Yesterday two of our pigeons failed to return'
(AWM ART02555)

however, and no fewer than half a million such birds will be used in the course of this war, with one of their number even being awarded the *Légion d'honneur*, for its efforts on the fly during the Battle of Verdun.)

If all goes well, Toll's bird will be back in its loft in 17 minutes, at what amounts to 'Pigeon Divisional Headquarters', in Sailly-sur-la-Lys, four miles away as the pigeon flies, where – all else being equal – another signaller will retrieve the message.

Hopefully, it won't be shot by its own forces. After a recent problem in this regard, Army Routine Order No. 132 had gone out to all ranks of the 5th Division clearly stating: No carrier pigeons are to be shot or destroyed . . .[87]

Even as the pigeon takes wing, back at Pompey Elliott's forward battle HQ, 300 yards behind the Australian front-line, the Commander of the 15th Brigade is experiencing a moment of cautious optimism. Though it is impossible to have telephone contact with 5th Division HQ, as all the wires have been smashed, and he still can't see anything for all the smoke from the shells that keep detonating, there is no doubt that for over 15 minutes now the shooting in front of him – in the spot his men of the 15th Brigade have disappeared into – has died away to almost nothing. And artillery observers have actually reported the odd glimpse of the 59th and 60th advancing.

This surely means that his boys have secured the forward German lines, and perhaps even the support lines behind?

He hopes so anyway, and sends a report back to his Chief of Staff at 15th Brigade HQ:

Attack appears to be successful.[88]

In truth, of course, Pompey's men of the 59th and 60th Battalions have been wiped out.

To their left is the much more successful 14th Brigade – far better protected from the machine guns of the Sugar-loaf – and it is here the first small German counter-attacks begin. They are enough to panic one unknown signaller, as at 7.02 pm the staff of the 14th Brigade receive a panicky message: *A Company 53rd wants reinforcements. Can't hold position unless reinforced.*

In the meantime, all those 5th Division troops in far forward positions are doing their best to turn the drain they occupy into a more defensible fire-trench by furiously shovelling its dirt into a parapet on the German side – a project soon helped when the first of the carrying parties arrive with sandbags, shovels and *manpower*, and quickly get to work.

The news from the 15th Brigade of an apparently successful attack is most welcome at 5th Division HQ, but it must be put against another report, that had been sent at 6.23 pm, from the 61st Division's 184th Brigade saying it was 'in', before a follow-up report stating baldly: *Germans holding parapet strongly all along. No sign of our people.*[89]

———

And the Bavarians really are holding strongly. Even in places where they have taken a serious battering, they are beginning to rally.

'The storm [on my front] was repulsed,' one German soldier would record of the mood of the time. 'Everyone had the feeling: they cannot get through. That gave confidence in one's own strength again. Like a tree in the morning after the stormy night defiantly stretched its branches out to the sky, and it, though dishevelled, seems to say: "May many of these storm winds come, I stand fast" – just like so, the regiment stood stronger than before.'[90]

———

Pompey Elliott's confusion as to what is happening, however, does not last long. For suddenly, at 6.40 pm, a senior officer with wild eyes, a deeply shocked countenance and a shattering story to tell appears before him. Coming direct from the fog of war, it is Major Herbert Layh, the second-in-command of the 59th Battalion, which has been attacking on the far-right side of the 15th Brigade. He has been specially sent back by his Commanding Officer, Lieutenant-Colonel Ernest Harris, to tell Elliott that the survivors of the battalion are pinned down by the guns of the Sugar-loaf and have made it no further than just halfway across No-Man's Land.

At least some other reports soon come in from wounded men of the 60th Battalion, just to their left, who are a little more positive – even if bitter Gallipoli experience has taught veteran officers to be wary of the reports of wounded men. For what it's worth, their report has it that away from the worst of the spite of the Sugar-loaf, the 60th has actually taken the first of the German trenches, and even made it to the second line. They even maintain that, further to their left, the 14th Brigade has also secured the enemy front-line trenches and has pushed on.

At 7.06 pm, Elliott receives a message from the remnants of the 59th Battalion informing him that they have not been able to take over the enemy's trenches, that those trenches are still populated by German soldiers, and that the battalion remains under deadly rifle and machine-gun fire, unable to advance unless they receive heavy support.

(In fact, a measure of the desperation of their situation is that, at this very time, no fewer than 35 of a possible 39 officers of the assaulting waves of the 15th Brigade have been wounded or killed, together with most of their Sergeants and Corporals. The furthest advanced of the 59th and 60th Battalions are holding on, 100 yards from the German parapet, in small depressions and agricultural furrows. Behind them, scattered others are taking similar shelter, while hundreds of others are dead or dying.)

The report makes its way to Haking's temporary advanced HQ at Sailly-sur-la-Lys, where it is put with all the rest of the reports as Haking and his senior staff try to make sense of the evolving situation on their large maps. In sum, though neither Elliott nor any of the brigade, divisional or corps commanders know the true situation, instead of the 5th Division and 61st Division being like two closed fists smashing into and breaking the German lines – which was the plan – the right fist has smashed into a brick wall and substantially withdrawn. The left hand, meanwhile, has a broken thumb, leaving only four fingers inserted into the German lines.

And, just like fingers, their penetration is markedly uneven. On the far left, 8th Brigade's 32nd Battalion has advanced some 200 yards forward of the German front-line. On their right is Lieutenant-Colonel Toll's position with his small 31st Battalion garrison. Some 300 yards to Toll's right is Cass's 54th Battalion, with the 53rd to the right again. All up, the 8th and 14th Brigades have taken a bite out of the German positions 1200 yards long and 200 yards deep, encompassing all of their front-line and the second line where they can find it. These two brigades have substantially taken their objective, while 15th Brigade has failed. Now they have to hold it. There are gaps, though, and neither Toll nor Cass can easily communicate with the other. Nor can they easily talk with those in their forward positions, or their Brigade HQs.

—

The only thing crystal clear to Brigadier-General Pompey Elliott at this point in time is that the Sugar-loaf *must* be subdued. While so ever it is functioning, No-Man's Land will always be perilous for all who try to cross the enfilading fire it sends out. And the fact that the Germans are still in the trenches that the 59th was meant to take means they are a danger on the flanks of the other battalions.

Layh, you must return to Colonel Harris and tell him, 'As the rest of the line appears to have succeeded, the 59th must make another attempt.'[91]

And you, Intelligence Officer of the 60th, Lieutenant Dave Doyle? You must follow Layh, see if you can get in touch with Major McCrae of the 60th and tell him the situation – and that we urgently want the 59th to try again . . .

Chapter Twelve

A LAND FOR NO MAN

I'll never forget those early hours of Thursday morning. The
shells were bursting everywhere; now & then one would get
smothered with dirt & mud they threw up, while machine
gun & rifle bullets were whistling round us all the time.[1]

Bert Bishop, in a letter to his cousin, writes of the night of 19/20 July 1916

7.15 PM, 19 JULY 1916, FROMELLES, A MOST HANDSOME FACE AMID THE UGLINESS

The wild-eyed figure in an officer's uniform stumbling out of No-Man's
Land, lit by the flares on high and silhouetted by the shell explosions
behind, has the look about him of one who has just seen Hell on earth
up close and cannot quite believe he is still alive to tell the tale.

Lieutenant Doyle begs to report, General Elliott, sir, he can find
no sign of the 60th Battalion's Major McCrae at all, nor of his second-
in-command, Major Tom Elliott, nor any of his senior officers. The
leadership of that battalion appears to have ceased to exist amid the
'most awful scene of slaughter imaginable'.[2]

On the strength of it, General Elliott sends another message through
to General McCay at 5th Division HQ:

*The 59th cannot advance further. The trenches are full
of the enemy. Every man who rises is shot down. Reports*

from wounded indicate that the attack is failing for want
of support.[3]

Unless they get that support from somewhere, there is no chance the
59th can ever overwhelm the Sugar-loaf. Perhaps McCay will authorise Elliott throwing in another half-battalion in support, but in the
meantime Elliott gives the order that the 59th must dig in and hold the
position they have.

As Colonel Harris has apparently been taken out of action by a shell
bursting shatteringly close to him – rendering him 'incapacitated with
shell shock'[4] – Layh must take command.

—

God help him, what a frightening trip across most of No-Man's Land it
has been so far for Bert Bishop. Inevitably his platoon, in the Australian
centre with the 14th Brigade, has been scattered, with some of them
killed outright, and it has become every man for himself. Seemingly
blessed, Bert has survived as others fell all around and is now able to hurl
himself into a crater just before the German wire. Is there a way through?
Bert thinks so! Working out his path, he rises again and charges forward
as bullets hiss, to race up and over the parapet of the German trench and
down into it, landing full-length on a German body.

It grunts! A long, low groan . . . before it is still. Bert gets off and
is able to stand and look at him. 'His waxen colour meant he had bled
to death,' he'd later recount. 'He was only a boy, his face was the most
handsome I'd ever looked at.'[5]

Bert must be quick. It is one thing to have made it to the German
trenches, but he still must get his water and ammo to the forward
Australian troops who are now, presumably, in the next line of German
trenches, because they certainly aren't here. What is here is a chaotic
shambles of dead and dying men, body parts, spilled intestines, mud,
blood and water. There is no time to try to help any of the wounded; he
and his carrying party must press on. They soon get to a rough kind of

trench, where the survivors of the first Australian waves are fighting for their lives, spread out across a hundred yards.

Bert's Sergeant roars at them over the thunder of battle: 'You lot go along to the left as far as you can, you lot get along to the right.'[6] It does not take long, as eager hands grab the bullets, bombs, water and sandbags they have brought with them. For most of them, it is now time to head back, though many, against orders, decide to stay and fight, taking up the weaponry of those already killed.

While this decision is understandable, the truth is that for every man who disobeys orders and so abandons carrying duties to take up a weapon, the more the supply of ammunition is diminished, and this risks having a disastrous effect. And eagerness to fight is not the only reason they have done this . . .

'We did not mind going forward with our load, and thus face the enemy fire,' one Sergeant from another company would note, of exactly the same situation, 'but the thought of being hit in the back on the return journey was too much for most of us, hence our inclination to remain with the fighting troops.'[7]

Those who do adhere to their ferrying duty, such as Bert Bishop, now have to re-cross a No-Man's Land that is worse than ever, sprayed with machine-gun bullets and shrapnel alike. 'There's nothing for it but to get up top,' an officer roars at Bert and the group he is with. 'Just do the best you can.'[8]

And so, with a roar of their own, they do exactly that, sprinting as fast as they can back to their own lines, bent low, as, on the instant, the German machine-gunners get a bead on them from either flank and start to cut them down. 'We crawled, ran to shell holes, got our breath to run again, bullets zipping around us,' Bishop would later recount. 'A shrapnel shell burst above me. I turned a somersault, for some minutes I could not move.'[9]

With his breath and nerve finally back, Bert charges ahead once more, and makes it back through the barbed wire before tumbling into the original Australian trench. Yes, alive, but with more work to do. For, of course, now that one load of supplies has been delivered, the most urgent thing is to go back to VC Corner and get more, before facing No-Man's Land again.

———

Meanwhile, over to the far left of the 5th Division attack, while his men dig into the furthermost ditch, the 8th Brigade's Lieutenant-Colonel Frederick Toll strides forward once more – at least a little protected by the curtain of their own artillery fire now falling ahead – eager to reconnoitre and see whether there might be a better position, a more worthy objective to secure, than the corpse-filled ditch his men are now making their own.

Beside him is his Intelligence Officer and another messenger with a pigeon basket. Just 200 yards on, they come to a road that shows up on their map as being far beyond the support lines they are looking for, definitively establishing that the miserable ditches must indeed be the nominal targets they were after – the things that looked like support lines on the aerial photographs but in reality are farmers' drainage ditches and half-finished, Fritz-built trenches, long-since abandoned.

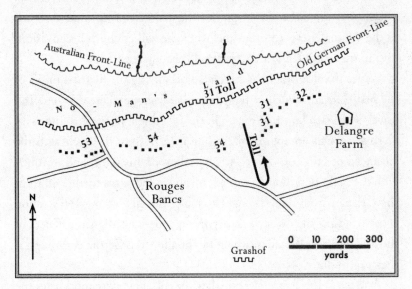

Toll's reconnaissance

A few hundred yards ahead, Toll sees a series of barbed-wire entanglements protecting a German strongpoint and, *over there to the right*, what is it?

Oh. It is a few groups of soldiers from the 14th Brigade making their way forward, through the smoke and thunder. But they have gone too far! Though neither Toll nor any other senior Australian officers are aware of it, no fewer than a hundred men had let their bloodlust trump their orders, and so had pursued fleeing Germans to their Grashof strongpoint, 800 yards beyond the German first trench. Toll's adjutant, Captain Vivian Bernard, is told to recall the men. He promptly moves out towards them, only for . . . a-shot-to-ring-out-and-he-falls-stricken. This son of a banking clerk from Mackay goes down hard, immobilised with a broken left leg – and is soon taken prisoner by the Germans.[10]

Isolated from his wounded officer, Toll returns to his men in the first ditch, where they continue to labour valiantly, but hopelessly, to build a defensive position – as German machine-gun fire and artillery, as well as their own artillery, begin to home in on them. Recognising that they will not be able to accomplish in an hour what the Germans had not managed to do in months – turn the ditch into a defensible position, against the threat of the expected overnight counter-attack – Toll gives the order at 7.14 pm for the majority of his men to return to the original German front-line, where he will establish his advanced HQ to the left of Cass, and try to hold that, at least.

Aware that his order has stipulated occupying the furthest limits of the first German trench system, and unsure about where that lies, Toll leaves 'some two hundred men'[11] in the first ditch, forward of the main German trench, in approximate alignment but not in touch with the advanced position of Cass's 54th Battalion on his right, and in touch with the 32nd Battalion on his left, all about 150 yards further on from the German front-line. Though it is far from his intent, Toll's action actually means there is a weak step in the otherwise aligned defences of the 8th and 14th Brigades, which might allow the Germans through if they can find it.

And so, as the Battle of Fromelles goes on, now two hours after the

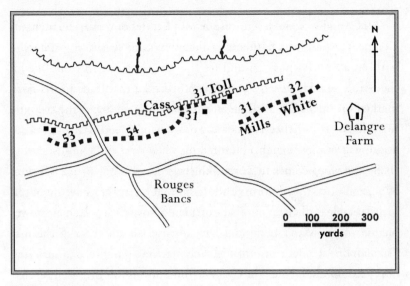

Toll's 'weak step'

men first went over the top, all is a kind of fluid fury as the light starts to wane . . .

The situation is liable to change from one minute to the next, both in reality and perception, but the broad situation of the Australians of the 5th Division is becoming apparent. The survivors of the 15th Brigade's 59th Battalion are pinned down in front of the Sugar-loaf and cannot advance. To their left, most of the 60th Battalion has similarly been forced to find whatever cover it can in shallow depressions – though a few sections that have drifted to the far left to join up with the 53rd Battalion of the 14th Brigade have actually made it into German lines. Against that, both battalions of the 14th Brigade have done remarkably well and have actually moved beyond the German front-line to what used to be their support line, though they must beat off attacks on both their right flank – where it had been hoped the 15th Brigade would be – and their left flank, where a strong pocket of Germans has held out.

Major Croshaw, the second-in-command of the 53rd, has just made his way back to tell McCay that part of the 53rd has dug in 150 yards beyond the first German line. However, the advanced position is cut off from the rest of its battalion occupying the old German front-line in rear and *urgently* needs reinforcements.

McCay also soon learns, from another report, that Lieutenant-Colonel Cass and the 54th are in much the same situation, occupying both an advanced position and part of the old German front-line on the 53rd's left. However, a totally exposed road that leads to the farm marked on their map as 'Rouges Bancs' – elevated above the swampy surrounds – runs between the two battalions, preventing the advanced positions from joining up.

So too word comes from the 8th Brigade, over on the far left. For, by pigeon post, they inform 5th Division HQ that they have managed to get barely sufficient numbers of men across their much narrower section of No-Man's Land and have also seized a section of the first German line. Under constant shell and machine-gun fire, and suffering heavy casualties, Lieutenant-Colonel Toll informs 8th Brigade HQ that his men can hold on 'if reinforcements are sent over urgently'.[12]

In sum, despite it all, the 8th and 14th Brigades have managed to achieve their objectives, with the major problem being that, despite their orders to take the 'German support line', there doesn't actually appear to be one. And beyond denying them the protection that an established trench would, it also denies a neat alignment of the forces, as each company can only just make the best of it, to thinly hold a frequently disconnected advanced line between the 8th and 14th Brigades.

It is only the 15th that, up against the Sugar-loaf, hasn't been able to come even close to taking German lines. All up, the situation is grim but retrievable.

—

The 61st Division's Commanding Officer, Major-General Colin Mackenzie, meantime, is equally trying to make sense of it all. The good news is that, out to his far right, the 2/7th Warwickshire of 182nd Brigade has actually taken over its section of German trenches. In his centre, 183rd Brigade might or might not be in the German trenches – no one is sure – and there is even a report, albeit of dubious veracity, that the 184th Brigade, on Mackenzie's left, has secured a part of the Sugar-loaf.

These scraps are passed on to XI Corps Advanced HQ in a farmhouse at Sailly-sur-la-Lys, where Haking and his senior staff affirm their view that the Sugar-loaf is key. On the reckoning of this one report that General Herbert Carter's men of the 61st Division's 184th Brigade have gained a foothold on it, Haking now sends an order to General Mackenzie to have the 184th attack in that direction once more, to their left, and take over all of the Sugar-loaf, to help the Australians whose right flank has not penetrated because of it.

Upon consultation, General Mackenzie decides to renew the attack with the reserves of his whole division at 9 pm, after a 30-minute bombardment, and so support the footholds he believes the British already have. But to take the Sugar-loaf, it is obvious the 184th will need the help of the Australians – having them attack at the same time, in the hope that a coordinated assault will halve the fire on both of them.

In response to urgent requests from all of his brigade commanders, soon after 7.30 pm General McCay had agreed they could commit their reinforcements and throw in the last half of their third battalions – most of whom are manning the old Australian front-lines, and all of whom are wearing only felt hats, with no steel helmets. It is McCay's hope that such reserves will give the 15th the added *oomph* they need to take the Sugar-loaf, while also allowing the 14th to consolidate. To take the reserves' place in the original front-line, the fourth battalions in those brigades are now ordered to move forward.

Meanwhile, over in the 61st Division trenches at 7.52 pm, the 184th Brigade's General Herbert Carter – having reported 20 minutes earlier that their attack had been unsuccessful – dashes off a message, via General Mackenzie at 61st Division's HQ. It is directed to the 15th Brigade's General Pompey Elliott – the very General whose advice not to use sally ports he had ignored, which has been a significant part of the whole debacle and the reason the 184th need help now: *Am attacking at 9 p.m. Can your right battalion co-operate?*[13]

At 8.13 pm, Elliott – with all his worst fears being so tragically realised – is handed Carter's message. Pompey quickly scribbles a reply in the affirmative. McCay gives authority 'for half of the 58th Battalion to be used to support Elliott's renewed attack and for half of 57th Battalion to be sent to the 300 yards line'.[14] Pompey also asks if Haking could provide reinforcements for the attack, but the Commander of XI Corps declines – he has none to give. The 15th Brigade must do this on their own, with the forces they have left.

For Haking, things are tense, turning grim, and he is disappointed by a report at 8.24 pm that even soldiers of the 2/7th Warwickshire out on the far right – the one 61st Division success of the night – are being *bombed and shelled out of their position, and would require strong reinforcements in order to hold on.*[15]

Compounding the problems with the 61st Division is that 184th Brigade report themselves simply incapable of organising another attack on the Sugar-loaf by 9 pm. Haking agrees that Major-General Mackenzie may hold off during the night, pull back anyone forward of their own front trench – so that when the next barrage rains down, they don't kill their own soldiers – and attack again at dawn, after they have had time to regroup.

Mackenzie, in turn, has no sooner received Haking's message than he messages McCay at 8.30 pm, reporting, `Under instructions from corps commander am withdrawing from captured enemy line after dark.`[16]

And then . . .?

Exactly.

And then . . . nothing.

In the helter-skelter hurly-burly of everything else that is happening, the blood and blizzard of bullets that keep coming and the shells that keep falling amid the billowing smoke, and the constant traffic of mortally wounded men, this crucial message, received at 8.35 pm at 5th Division HQ, is not passed on immediately to the 15th Brigade's HQ, nor to Pompey Elliott's forward HQ, where the Victorian is in his last throes of sending A and B Companies of the 58th Battalion forward in the belief that they will be supported on their right flank by the British soldiers of the 61st Division.

This force of 400 men will go in under the command of the

Tasmanian, the newly promoted Major Arthur Hutchinson, who despite being still only 21 years old already knows something of extreme battle situations. Yet one more graduate of Duntroon, class of 1914, a contemporary, class rival and good friend of Tom Elliott's, Hutchinson is well liked by his men, a softly spoken officer whose courage is displayed quietly, never with bravado. Now, he moves among the men with some words of encouragement and a few specific orders, ensuring that all is as it should be.

We are going in hard and fast, and will be supported on our right by the 184th Brigade. Between us, with a coordinated and synchronised attack, we should be able to overwhelm them.

—

Just 400 yards to Major Hutchinson's right at this time, the men of this said same 184th Brigade are being told of Haking's message to stand down – and are mightily relieved to do so. They can join the other withdrawn troops of the 61st to regroup.

But not the 5th Division. They must 'endeavour to hold and consolidate' the trenches captured 'on its left flank',[17] so that they can assist the 61st when, after they have regrouped, they attack again in the morning. And whatever happens, Haking insists, McCay must *not* 'use additional troops in attempting to make good the unsuccessful assault on his right, but to withdraw any isolated parties from the enemy's trenches on that flank'.[18] This is to ensure that the heavy guns will be able to completely plaster the German trenches when the 61st go in in the morning, without worrying about hitting Australians.

—

Charles Bean, still working away in his Contay hotel room west of Pozières on this night, completely oblivious to what is happening, would later talk to many witnesses and recount the mood of Hutchinson's attacking force in that key period in the lead-up to them hopping the bags: 'The men, as was often the case with Australians, especially when first in action, could be felt straining like greyhounds on the leash, and were not easily restrained from anticipating the word of command.'[19]

Hence, at 9 pm exactly, just as ordered, Major Hutchinson of the 58th Battalion gives that word, and leads his soldiers over the top into the dark to attack the Sugar-loaf. And they're going well! Despite their trepidation, despite the fact that they have to run between the bodies of their dead and dying comrades who have fallen in the previous charges, despite the fact that there is, strangely, a complete absence of attack to their right, from where the 61st Division had been meant to launch, they are able to cover the first 200 yards without losing a man – and never mind seeing the odd flash up ahead from the muzzles of German guns. Never mind Mother Mary, it is the sweet mother of enveloping darkness, deepened by the heavy smoke, that protects them at this distance. (And the red glow from the still burning ammunition dumps, by the by, gives a strong point of reference in the otherwise entirely confusing night to get one's bearings.)

Still, when, from the Sugar-loaf, the German machine-gunners first spot these phantoms coming from the darkness and moving towards them from a distance of some 200 yards, their reaction is not fear so much as a certain detached amazement. STILL . . . *die Engländer*, the English, keep coming?

But the German soldiers are also under orders. They are *not* to fire until the soldiers are close, and even then only on their *Oberleutnant's* orders.

Keep coming . . . keep coming . . . keep coming.

German fingers tighten on their triggers, waiting for the moment.

And now more *von diesen Phantomen*, of these phantoms, are rising up to join the first lot. Unbeknownst to the Germans, it is the surviving hardy souls of the 59th Battalion, now emerging from their pockets of protection to join their brothers in arms of the 58th. And they combine in an oncoming rush, charging at them through the dusky gloom.

Uuuuund . . . jetzt! And . . . now!

Feuer! Fire!

The machine guns chatter in unison, 'unleashing a torrent of fire that sounded like a thousand sheets of calico being rent at once'.[20]

In his advanced position, General Pompey Elliott looks in vain for any sign that the attack of the 184th Brigade that his men have gone in to support is occurring, but there is nothing . . . there is *nothing*.

The shattering roar of the German machine guns simply goes on.

Like a rolling wave that suddenly hits hidden shoals, the line of Australians with Major Hutchinson abruptly falters, changes direction and, a few seconds later, stops, as the surviving Diggers go to ground, taking whatever shelter they can, many of them in a ditch. Men who have been hit are moaning, groaning, screaming or giving out devastating death rattles, even as the 'terrifying din of the machine-gun bullets crack overhead'.[21]

It is Major Hutchinson who not only rises to the occasion but also rises from the ditch, rallying his men as he goes, charging forward once more, in the lead, with a roar of battle fury on his lips.

And with a roar of battle fury he dies . . . as the machine guns have no trouble swivelling onto him, and he is 'riddled with bullets, perished gloriously, close to the German parapet',[22] his body suspended on the first barrier of German wire. Those men who have so bravely risen with him are also cut to pieces. And now, Hutchinson's batman, Private Harry Lyons, risks his life to try to get to this officer he so admires . . . but cannot, as the fire becomes too fierce.

As recorded in the 15th Brigade's War Diary, 'The attack melted into nothingness – passed in a few quivering moments from the realm of man's high endeavour to the record of his deathless failures . . . The ground was covered with [the Brigade's] dead and dying, among whom the wounded dragged themselves painfully, seeking the fearful security of a shell hole or a mound that might give some protection from the machine gun fire that still enveloped them . . . the fruitlessness of further sacrifice was now apparent to all.'[23]

Not for nothing will Bean describe the whole exercise as 'one of the bravest and most hopeless assaults ever undertaken by the Australian Imperial Force'.[24]

It is not that things are all quiet on the Western Front, but by 9.20 pm some two-thirds of the German line – nearly all of the 6th Bavarian Division in front of this attack – has gone silent. And it is for a very simple reason. 'There was no upright standing Englishman anymore in front of the trench,' German War Correspondent George Querl would record. 'They lay dead in thick heaps and among them moaned the injured.'[25]

In another spot, another German correspondent, Wilhelm Scheuermann, notes, 'Approximately 800 dead lay in a width of 250 metres in front of our trench. [Further over] another approximately 250 dead were noticed by our patrols. At this place, beside the rifle and machine gun fire, also our artillery worked exceptionally in the thick gushing masses and fleeing back enemies. Hits were observed where eight to ten men were mowed down by one single *Brennzündergranate*, burning-fuse grenade.'[26] (Not surprisingly. Those grenades weigh a little under two pounds, and the thick iron casing can throw lethal shrapnel up to 100 yards away, let alone right up close in the middle of a charging throng.)

And now that it is clear to the Bavarians that around the Sugar-loaf the battle has been won, the victorious defending soldiers start to express their joy in traditional Bavarian manner. Over the moans of the wounded English and Australian soldiers now can be heard the resounding victors' call, taken up by them all:

'*HURRA! HURRA! HURRA!*'[27]

The feeling among these German soldiers – who have come through the pits of Hell, have held their nerve, survived, and triumphed – is over-whelming. 'All looked at each other with full-to-the-brim glances. Many had to squeeze each other's hands and that did not require a word said.'[28]

The situation, however, is less certain in other parts of the German line, where, despite all the disasters, the 8th and 14th Brigades of *die Australier* still hold 1200 yards of German trench. With the telephone lines shot to pieces, it is the brave *Meldegänger*, messengers, who become even more vital, carrying reports back from the front-lines about where the Australians have penetrated, and then taking messages back about where to counter-attack.

Sometimes they work in pairs, and so it is on this occasion as Corporal Adolf Hitler and his friend *der Infanterist* Balthasar Brandmeyer work in tandem. 'We carried message after message to and from the trenches. Glaring flares lit our way,' Brandmeyer would recount. 'The Australians stormed . . . across the battlefield. I dashed with Hitler to the battle HQ of the 17th Regiment. He scarcely gave me time to get my breath back before we ran on to the 21st Regiment. Grenades chased us through the darkness of the night.'[29]

As a brace of Australian grenades explode behind them, the two dive into a water-filled crater. On the instant, they are soaked to the core, and all is darkness. Brandmeyer's spirits sink, but not his companion's.

The very moment a flare explodes above, and they can orientate themselves, Hitler is on to him. 'Now push on!' Hitler says, leading the way, scrambling up the crater wall. They can only run with great difficulty, as the water pours off them and their boots squelch, but they keep going.

Finally, they arrive before the regimental commander, to deliver the message. 'The envelope and paper we handed the regimental commander were soggy. He was scarcely able to decipher the report.'[30] But he can certainly get the gist of it. The 6th Bavarian Division will soon launch a massive counter-attack, involving the entire division not already engaged. Prepare.

In the meantime, in that third of the Bavarian front where the Australians still hold the enemy trenches, the battle rages on. Localised German counter-attacks are already well under way, despite the Australian artillery attempting to place a box barrage beyond where the most forward of the Australian troops are thought to have advanced to. Ideally, this will give the Australians the time and space necessary for their forward elements to join up into one cohesive new line, and for reinforcements to reach them. And, of course, they urgently need more supplies, so the efforts of the carrying parties must be redoubled.

As Bert Bishop heads back along the extremely crowded communication trenches to get more bombs and bullets for the men in the front-lines, he passes the 55th Battalion machine-gunners slowly going the other way, heading to the front. The fact that two ammunition dumps of the 8th and 14th Brigades have just taken direct hits and exploded, sending smoke billowing across No-Man's Land, has already worsened the confusion that is crowding everything.

But suddenly, by the flickering light of the flares, the two Bishop cousins come face to face, to roughly embrace and even spend a couple of extremely unhappy minutes together. There is something in Ray's eyes that is deeply upsetting to Bert, something that makes him think back to that evening crossing the Mediterranean on *Caledonia* when, of an instant, they had stopped talking about the holiday they would all take together back home . . . on the unspoken recognition that it was highly unlikely they would all *get* back home.

For, yes, Ray's eyes have a terribly sad look to them tonight, almost like he knows he is for it and yet – as a brave and honourable man – is completely powerless to do anything to save himself.

But now, the Sergeant has given the order to move, as section Sergeants have been wont to do since the dawn of time. Time to go, lads. Amid the roar and tumult of battle, each with his own duties to fulfil, the two cousins take their leave of each other.

A short time later, Captain Gibbins of the 55th's B Company – still out in No-Man's Land, digging the sap across it – gets the word. They are no longer mere reserves, available for digging, and they may go and join the fight proper. Gibbins takes out his revolver and barks some orders, and they are soon on their way to help their comrades of the 14th Brigade's 54th Battalion, who urgently need reinforcement.

'Well, Bain,' Captain Gibbins says to the private beside him, as they stride forward, 'you are going into action that will be pretty hot, but if you get out of it alright you will have something to talk about all your life.'[31]

Behind them, others of the reserve – a 56th Battalion company and one of the 5th Pioneers – take over their digging, helping the 14th Field Company. No fewer than 160 soldiers are now digging that crucial trench, with another 40 ferrying duckboards and sandbags.

To their left, the trench of the 8th Brigade also struggles forward, albeit much more slowly for the fact that German shelling upon them is considerably more accurate and continues to pound those who are digging it, constantly blowing apart men and newly dug sections. There are two other problems of great significance. These new trenches keep being blocked by Australian dead – wounded men who crawl to the only shelter they can find, only to breathe their last. And because of that veritable wall of dead Australians, in addition to damage to the drainage system as a result of bombardment, the River Laies – the large irrigation ditch that crosses No-Man's Land, which had been only two feet deep – is now rising fast, lifting the whole water table. 'Many, many wounded,' one Corporal of the 31st Battalion would record, 'were thus drowned, unable to move away from the rising water.'[32]

The Diggers keep digging regardless, their world all mud and blood, as they hurl shovelful after shovelful of the mud and clay to get themselves deeper and make the parapets high enough to protect them from the never-ending guns and artillery. And yet, the tragic truth is that, with the rising of the Laies, the crossing of it becomes ever more confined to certain bridges that traverse it – upon which the Germans now train their machine guns. The dead soon start to pile beside it.

Even more devastating, however, is the now fiercely focused German artillery, which is exacting a far more terrible toll than ever. Far fewer German shells prove to be duds than the British, but, time and again, seeming miracles do occur when a German shell lands among Australian soldiers only to *not* explode. What are the chances?

It is precisely the same luck of the draw as that coin toss back in Egypt four months earlier, which now sees whole swathes of men live or die, depending this time not on their valour or skill but on whether a tired munitions worker in a German factory two months earlier had, or had not, inserted the fuse properly.

———

As Captain Gibbins and his men of the 55th B Company move forward, they are met by a crew from the 53rd Battalion coming back from the old German front-line – now left vacant – with 20 German prisoners in tow. Advised of where Gibbins is taking his men – to help out Lieutenant-Colonel Cass and his men of the 54th – one officer leading wounded men back is frank. 'No good,' he says. 'You can't get up there.'

'The 55th can!' this giant of a man, Captain Gibbins, replies, as he continues to stride forward.[33]

Just behind him is Second-Lieutenant Percy Chapman, who is aghast at what they are seeing. 'Our road,' he would recount, 'was strewn with dead men lying as they had fallen – mostly face downwards and heads towards the enemy – their yellow-white complexions, blue finger nails, and clear staring eyes gazing into vacancy telling that Death had for some time taken his toll.'[34]

Through all the roar of the battle, Cass cannot help but admire his troops. 'The men were simply splendid,' he would recount.[35]

For its part, the Germans' counter-attack is nothing if not passionate. 'Each part of the troop,' the German War Correspondent Wilhelm Scheuermann would exult, 'saw it as a matter of honour to throw the enemy back out of his piece of trench, but also help came from all sides. Whoever was available in a neighbour trench came without prompting to help and threw himself onto the [enemy]. Slowly but irresistibly *die Stoßtruppen*, the storm troops, lumped together against the front and the flank of the enemy. Always more comrades approached voluntarily from the side sections, where the enemy was overcome already . . .'[36]

Inevitably, the brunt of the counter-attack is first felt by the Australians on their left flank, where the Germans know they are most vulnerable. At this time, Captain Frank Krinks of the 30th Battalion – a 22-year-old one-time furniture warehouseman from Hurstville – who has just successfully led his carrying party across No-Man's Land, makes a snap decision. As it is obvious that the 8th Brigade are fighting for their lives on the left, Krinks and his men join the fight.

Krinks personally goes forward with his best men. Using shell holes for shelter, they are able to snipe at the approaching Germans and keep them back. As the battle goes on, and more carrying parties join in, the supply to the 8th Brigade falls accordingly. Things become so desperate that the only way they can keep going is to systematically harvest weaponry and ammunition from their dead comrades. One way or another – using fencing wire, elbow grease, guts and gumption – they are able to keep firing. And it works.

'The effective barrier of fire laid down by the enemy's artillery,' a German chronicler would record, 'and by machine-guns which he had carried forward, the onset of the dark, and heavy losses brought the counter-attack to a stop.'[37]

At least on the left-hand side of the Australian positions.

Over on the right, however, with the advanced section of the 53rd Battalion, as Charles Arblaster looks back to Australian lines, he is shocked to see, silhouetted against the ongoing explosions of shells in No-Man's Land, the distinctive spiked German helmets back in the first German line.

Where the *hell* have they come from?

The Sugar-loaf.

Zweiter Leutnant Bachschneider's forces have begun retaking their old front-line from the thin forces of the right hand of the Australians' 53rd Battalion. And they have gained in strength along the way, picking up elements of the 21st RIR's 12th Company and the remnants of the hard-hit 11th Company.

Revelling in their work, the Bavarian *Bomben und Bajonettmänner*, bomb and bayonet men, of the 11th Company even start singing '*Die Wacht am Rhein*'[38] ('Watch at the Rhine') as they launch themselves into their task, clearing their old front-line of the remnants of the 53rd and anybody else who stands between them and their pride. Just as they have practised for so long, the bombers move forward first, throwing their bombs into the next bay. The instant they explode, the bayonet men rush around the corner and kill anyone who is left. They repeat the process for each fire bay and slowly work their way up the trench.

There are only two ways to stop them. One is to build a trench block of sandbags; the other is to make a stand and throw bombs back at the bombers – causing several periods where a mini No-Man's Land is formed between defenders and attackers – until one side runs out of grenades. Inevitably this is the Australian defenders, and the Bavarians advance once more. Altogether sing!

Zum Rhein, zum Rhein, zum deutschen Rhein,
wer will des Stromes Hüter sein?[39]

The Rhine, the Rhine, our German Rhine,
Who will defend our stream, divine?

Beyond exuberance, such singing is a tactic, allowing soldiers in darkness and the fury of battle to determine friend from foe. As they approach a traverse in a trench, they chant the words – and if the refrain is not spontaneously taken up, they know to lob grenades.

Clearly, the situation for Captain Charles Arblaster and his men is now grim. As the Germans have continued their counter-attack, they are in the process of retaking their old front-line, which, in the 53rd section, has been left all but abandoned behind Arblaster's advanced

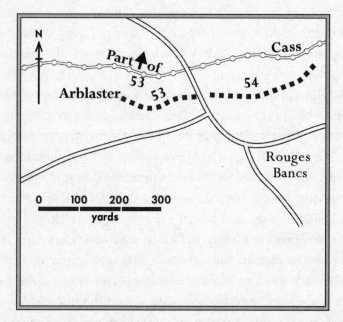

Partial withdrawal of the 53rd Battalion

position. Quickly now, Arblaster – 'who in spite of his youth was show-ing himself a cool and resourceful commander',[40] Bean would comment – sends as many men as he can spare back to support those valiant few who are still resisting the enemy, in the desperate hope they can prevent the Germans from fully taking those lines, and so cutting them off.

The problem Arblaster and his men of the 53rd have is that, as an all but isolated unit, they are taking fire from their front, rear and right flank. At least, just back from Arblaster and to the left, Lieutenant-Colonel Cass's wisdom in securing the 54th Battalion's section of the front-lines is paying off, as he and 200 soldiers he has gathered in – some from neighbouring battalions – try to counter the counter-attack, coming at the Germans from the extreme right rear.

As the bullets and bombs fly, what is obvious most immediately to Cass – the only senior officer of the 54th Battalion still operational, as his second-in-command, Major Roy Harrison, has been killed – is that he urgently needs more men and more bombs to hold on to what they have, as they are very quickly in 'a dickens of a fight'.[41]

—

Though Captain Gibbins has indeed lost some men in the crossing of No-Man's Land, by 9.30 pm, the rest have secured the Old German Lines, to quickly join Lieutenant-Colonel Cass's men from the 54th Battalion occupying a small, muddy trench some 200 yards beyond the German front-line. (Cass remains in his HQ in the German front-line.) To Gibbins's left, the 31st and 32nd Battalions are just holding on.

For Lieutenant-Colonel Toll's men of the 31st Battalion on the old German front-line, things are desperate, and they are taking such heavy fire from front, back and left that – in the absence of sandbags, as the supply has dried up – they stack up dead German soldiers as some protection, and fire their rifles over the corpses.

Gibbins, meantime, quickly writes a note to the 55th's Commanding Officer, advising him of their position, and their needs, in 'the neat clerical hand'[42] of the former bank manager, with no emotion attached:

Have 54th Lewis guns and five of our own under
Sergeant Colless for counter-attack. Each of my
men have three bombs, but require more. Expect a
counter-attack shortly . . .
N. GIBBINS, Capt.,
O.C. 'B' Company[43]

Not long after receiving Gibbins's note, Lieutenant-Colonel David
McConaghy realises he has run out of reserve companies to send
forward. Perfect. Aching to get into the action himself, he decides to
go forward with his deputy Major Robert Cowey and whatever stray
soldiers they can find, bearing fresh supplies for Captain Gibbins and
his men. This accomplished, McConaghy sets up an advanced 55th
Battalion HQ 100 yards to the right of Lieutenant-Colonel Cass's headquarters in the German front-line.

Making contact with Arblaster, they are able to send patrols to
their right, to try to determine just what position the 60th Battalion
are holding. The answer is: the 60th aren't there! Instead they find
Germans holding their own line. Calling on his Gallipoli experience, McConaghy knows to give out orders for sandbags to be pulled
down from either side of the furthest held Australian position of the
old German trenches, and so set up a block against *Zweiter Leutnant*
Bachschneider's soldiers, who are coming towards him.

Through such measures, the situation on the right flank of the
Australian position is also somewhat stabilised, and it means the three
prongs of the German counter-attack are being held off. But for how
long? While it is one thing to have been able to hold the Germans off
in the most forward positions on their left, right and straight in front,
the truth is if the two outer prongs of the Germans meet *behind* the
Australians, then that'll be the end of them.

The 55th Battalion men, meanwhile, are quickly set to work building up the parapets of the flanks of the forward position held by the
54th and 53rd, and the gap between the two is soon closed in by a 'shallow breastwork'.[44] Second-Lieutenant Chapman, meanwhile, busies

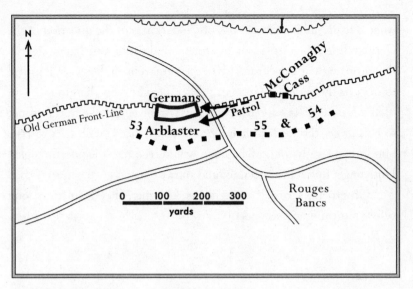

Germans in behind Captain Charles Arblaster

himself organising some of the men to build a special emplacement for the machine-gunners, complete with sandbag walls on three sides, with plentiful ammunition and grenades on hand.

The man running the show on the left, however, remains the towering six-foot figure of Captain Gibbins. He is one of those old-style leaders who never wants to show caution around flying bullets for fear that it might infect the troops, and the risks he takes are outrageous, but still he is not hit, *never* hit. Bit by bit, the parapet of the 55th's sandbag outwork to the right of the 31st's advanced position gets higher. Whatever else, the left flank of the most advanced position of the 14th Brigade will now be protected.

'All night long,' Second-Lieutenant Chapman would note, '[Gibbins] moved up and down his line exposed to the enemy fire, helping and spurring his men on. I have never known a braver or cooler man in action than he.'[45]

And Gib's soldiers agree, with many a man heard to say in the course of the night variations on the theme of 'If ever a man deserved a Victoria Cross for devotion to duty and coolness under fire the Captain does'.[46]

All this, and still the humanity of this giant shines through. For what is *that*? Suddenly, from out of the darkness in the direction of the German lines, the men sense movement, and they immediately tighten their grip on their Lee–Enfields. To their amazement, however, it proves to be a badly bloodied German soldier, crawling on the ground – in itself a feat, as he is only just conscious. Resolved to take him prisoner so he can get the medical help he so urgently needs, Gib tries to take him in hand, only for, as Chapman would recount, 'the poor mangled brute to get up on his knees . . . and start to pray.

'"Oh cruel – Cruel!"' says Gib, as, together, they help him along before returning to their post.[47]

—

The digging of the trenches across No-Man's Land by the 15th, 14th and 8th Field Companies goes on, at 25 yards an hour, as does the battle itself.

The 29th Battalion's Private William Barry has been in the thick of it for an hour now, carrying bombs and ammunition forward, and helping wounded to get back. Now Barry is a man practically born with pursed lips, but never have they been so pursed as right now. Everywhere he looks . . . disaster.

See, here now, right up near the old German parapet is a lad from Barry's platoon with blood gushing from his head, wanting to know how to get back. Barry guides him the first part of the way and is just returning, 'only to meet another poor lad with his arm shattered and he wanted to know if there were any Red Cross men about'.[48]

The short answer is no, and again Barry guides the wounded man back to the wire before returning to the German parapet. 'The enemy was now shelling us unmercifully,' Barry would recount, 'and everybody was running amok with himself, for by the way they were shouting out, there was nobody in charge of the men. The German artillery fire was growing fiercer every minute, in fact it was hellish and their shells were landing with great accuracy and killing the boys like flies.'[49]

As ever, the only way to survive is to get into a trench, and Barry hurls himself into the nearest German one, just a few seconds before a shell hits the parapet right by him. 'Two boys standing alongside of me started to cry for their mother and I told them to cut that out, but pray to God to get them out of this hole. No sooner were the words out of my mouth, when another shell hit the parapet just above my head . . .'[50]

Blackness.

Though Barry is now totally oblivious to it, the battle around the forward elements of the 8th Brigade, still under the command of Lieutenant-Colonel Frederick Toll, goes on. Finding themselves under attack from three sides – and most particularly from three German strongpoints sweeping them with machine-gun fire, while German 'Arty' has now also got their range, and German bombing parties are coming along the trenches from both flanks – the situation of the Australians is dire. Most worrying of all is the German attacks coming along their own original trenches.

Suffering most is the 32nd Battalion on the extreme left, which at 9.40 pm sends back a message to 8th Brigade HQ:

Frontline cannot be held unless strong reinforcements are sent. Enemy's machine-gunners are creeping up. No star shells. The artillery is not giving support. Sandbags required in thousands. Men bringing sandbags are being wounded in the back. Water urgently required.[51]

In all the smoke, confusion and darkness, no one is sure who is where – and the whole shattering shemozzle is compounded by the time it takes communications to get through.

At 10 pm, General Elliott is handed a message addressed to him from General McCay: *9.25 p.m. 61st Division not attacking to-night. General Elliott may withdraw 59th Battalion and its reinforcements if he thinks attack is not likely to succeed.*

A little late for that! Such a message 90 minutes earlier would have had a point. Alas, with no direct telephone lines between Brigade HQs – and all lines within 500 yards of the front trenches blown out by

German artillery anyway – all messages are being sent via Division HQ, the long way round.

As it is, Major Hutchinson and his men of the 58th Battalion – the 'reinforcements' referred to in the message – are long gone, and General Elliott can only hope they have triumphed. For the moment, he just doesn't know. He hopes the 59th are in the German lines, but that is equally unsure, while there have at least been some scattered reports that the 60th Battalion has achieved that goal, but not gone beyond. He has a fair idea, however, that whatever has been achieved, it has come at a large cost, as Major Greenway, one of the engineers supervising the construction of the 15th Brigade's communication trench across No-Man's Land, has told him that 'the losses of the 59th and 60th had been exceedingly heavy'.[52]

Of course, out in the forward trenches, the fierce battle goes on, as the German counter-attack continues to press in from all sides, and the Australians fight back with everything they have – and with everything they can get from the carrying parties, which continue to ferry supplies out to their men.

Theodor Pflaum of the 8th Machine Gun Company has been called forward with his men to take a machine gun across No-Man's Land. He is shocked by how terrible things are, even in the old Australian lines on the edge of No-Man's Land. 'It was already fearfully wrecked and dead and wounded were extremely numerous,' he would recount. 'The shrapnel and high explosives were playing havoc with our chaps, and the groans and wailings were cruel. I felt sick for a moment, but just shut my teeth hard and got my men along to as good a cover as was possible.'[53]

He will never know how he survived the mad dash across the expanse, hauling their gun. 'The ground we covered was one mass of explosions and the shrapnel bursting above us, and flares continually going up lit the whole place up as bright as daylight. Time after time I fell, got hooked up in the barb wire, or fell into a shell hole, but each time managed to scramble together and start again.'[54]

He is just getting his wind in the Old German Lines when something about one of the many wounded men, propped up against the side of a trench, makes him look again. It is his own younger brother, Ray, who has gone over with the first wave of the 32nd Battalion. The 19-year-old is conscious but has taken a bad hit, and is bleeding profusely from a shrapnel wound to the stomach. Theodor makes him as comfortable as he can, getting some help to get him into a sheltered dugout, and then gets him a flask of whisky, a swig of which perks his brother up. Ray is reasonably comfortable lying still and bleeding, but he just can't bear being moved.

Through the roar of battle all around, Theodor Pflaum hears the urgent cry. 'Send a Machine Gun to the left!'[55]

He and his men have the gun they need. He must go. By the flickering light of the ongoing flares and shell explosions above, he farewells his brother with some soft words. He asks a passing bloke he knows from the 32nd Battalion to do his best for him, as he has to keep on keeping on with the battle. A quick pat on the back for his brother, and he is gone. Within minutes, Pflaum is in the fight of his life, against his distant cousins, as a new Bavarian counter-attack begins.

First the flares go up, making things as bright as daylight, and then grenades start landing among them.

'I played the gun on them for all I knew whilst the [others] counter attacked with bombs . . .'

One of his men is killed by a bomb. They fight on . . .

'Riflemen were getting short – ditto ammunition and grenades. My gun was almost out of water, red hot . . .'[56]

Well behind him, at least half-safe in his dugout, Ray Pflaum lies groaning.

Not far away, another severely wounded Australian is lying quietly, knowing he has not long to live. One piece of solace is the small Bible he has carried with him all this way, given to him by his beloved mother when he had gone home to say goodbye to everyone before leaving. And now, though all is going dark, despite the flares that continue to burst overhead, Private Edgar William Parham becomes aware that a German soldier is standing over him, looking down upon him.

With his last gasp, Private Parham takes the Bible and offers it to him. 'Here Fritz . . .' he gasps, 'you'd better . . . take this . . .'[57]

Filled with pity, the German soldier takes it, and moves on.

Private Edgar Parham dies a short time later.

—

Good news!

A report has come in to Haking's XI Corps HQ that a reconnaissance plane has seen flares coming from the pointy end of the Sugar-loaf. And they might be *our* flares. Look, the truth is there are so many flares being fired by both sides, and so many shells exploding, and ammo dumps burning, it is very difficult for anyone 1000 or so feet above to be too sure of anything, but these flares *might* belong to our forces.

On the strength of it, Haking decides on one more change of plans. The attack on the Sugar-loaf, which had been launched, then cancelled, then half-launched, then half-cancelled, is now back on.

The 61st Division, Haking informs its commander, McKenzie, at 11.10 pm, must make 'every possible effort'[58] to carry out this attack on the Sugar-loaf. Once more, the 5th Division must join in, and McCay informs Pompey Elliott that he too is happy to authorise Elliott to send in his last battalion left standing, the 57th, to support the attack.

Could there ever be a better example of the old soldier's saying 'Order, counter-order, disorder'? In the middle of this battle, Pompey knows that this chopping and changing is bound to chop down hundreds, if not thousands, of lives – and so he replies, carefully, that while he believes the 60th might be in the Sugar-loaf, he is sure that the 59th are not:

I cannot guarantee success of attack with 57th as enemy machine gun fire is very hot but will try.[59]

Very well, then. McCay orders Pompey that he must 'take and hold whole of original objectives'.[60]

—

Meanwhile, the blocks put up by Captain Gibbins, and the furious *counter*-counter-attacks he has organised, have worked. By just after 11 pm, the German assault to retake those trenches has stalled.

—

Bert Bishop is exhausted, and this night has been hell. Back and forth across No-Man's Land, he has been going flat out like a lizard drinking since 7 pm, and there is no end in sight, as there become ever fewer carriers still standing, and the need for what they have becomes ever more desperate. But the trip across and back worsens as the German artillery becomes ever more focused on it.

'Once a shell burst over my head, & blew me up into the air, & I couldn't move for a few minutes afterwards,' he would recount, 'while I was often smothered with the dirt & rubbish they kicked up.'

At least with the night properly fallen now, the German machine-gunners must content themselves with firing at flitting shadows, rather than at whole masses of men, but still they have exacted a terrible toll. And every time Bert gets over, the situation becomes worse, with more shells landing, more bullets flying, more dead and wounded comrades, and . . .

And that soldier over there, firing his Lewis gun. The way he moves his head, the contours of his shoulders, the angle he holds his arms at while firing his gun. Bert would know him at a distance of 50 yards on a dark night . . . and here is the proof.

For, of course, it *is* Ray!

To Bert's unspoken amazement, his beloved cousin is still alive, and without a scratch on him. Bert immediately feels a rush of relief for himself and for Ray, of course, but also for his widowed Auntie Alice, who he knows will never recover if anything happens to her beloved son.

Robbo is still going, too, but Robbo is worried all right. Though the Australians now have this part of the trench, they are under strong attack from both flanks as the Germans counter-attack in force. It is obvious that while their own part of the attack has succeeded, the operation as a whole has failed – and they are getting ever more isolated.

'Come on . . .' says Bert's Sergeant, 'back for another load.'[61]

Bert must head off again and, despite himself, is not sorry to do so, as now, beyond the Germans attacking from both sides, shells start shaking the very earth on which they stand. With a quick goodbye to Ray and Robbo, he takes his leave once more. It is at least some solace that the two will be looking out for each other.

—

From the German GHQ at Charleville, meanwhile, General von Falkenhayn makes an exceedingly nervous phone call to the HQ of the 6th Army's Commanding Officer, Crown Prince Rupprecht.

'Is this,' Falkenhayn says, 'the major offensive I have so long forecast will be launched up around Lille?'[62]

Nein, Herr General. This is a small, manageable attack. We can deal with it.

Von Falkenhayn puts the phone down, relieved. Whatever is happening at Fromelles, it is nothing that needs to alter the disposition of his forces. True, it shows he was wrong on his prediction of a major attack around Lille, and that Prince Rupprecht and General von Below had been right all along that the Somme was the enemy's major thrust, but if bad news has to come in the form that the enemy has launched only a minor attack, he'll take it.

Still, as the French locals note, the cane is now *always* in his left hand.

Chapter Thirteen

IN THE MIDNIGHT HOUR

For sixteen hours we worked with blood up to our elbows
on the poor battered wrecks that were brought to us
. . . Men with shattered arms staggered in carrying or
dragging men with battered legs and begged us to attend
to their more unfortunate mates first. Not one of them
murmured or complained. God it made you humble
and brought the tears to your eyes . . . If ever there was
a living Hell, that night and morning was it . . . If there
is a God in Heaven may he strike the bastard Kaiser
and his crew dead. We lost exactly half the battalion.[1]
Alfred Langan, medical officer of the 30th Battalion, to his father

EARLY HOURS, FROMELLES, 20 JULY 1916, HAKING STILL BELIEVES

General Elliott. Another message, sir. This one is from Major Charles
Denehy of the 58th Battalion, and it has come through at 12.30 am:

> The attack of this Bde has completely failed, such men of
> the 60th as actually reached the enemys trench being killed
> or captured, the two coys of 58th mown when close to enemy
> trench . . . Men of all battalions are coming back from
> No-Man's-Land and I expect that they will gradually drift

back to the line. Many men are wounded, many are not. Very many officers are casualties, including Majors McCrae, Elliott and Hutchinson, all of whom are reported dead, and seems impossible to organise . . . Report seems unanimous that not a single man of 15th Brigade has now arrived in enemy's trench, as enemy's flares are coming from the whole of the front allotted to this brigade. I am now organising the defence of our original trenches . . .[2]

Pompey, a strong man to beat them all, slumps. No worst, there is none, no worse message is imaginable. Though he had suspected things were bad, he can barely fathom they are *this* bad. Not a single man from the 15th has reached the enemy trench? Majors McCrae, Elliott and Hutchinson dead, all *dead*? Men 'drifting back' from the line, some of whom are *not* wounded? This last is delicate officer language for 'we have lost control, and some of the men have given into civilian sanity, not wishing to throw their lives away in a battle that can no longer be won'.

The truth is that the 60th Battalion, Pompey's pride and joy, 'had been annihilated as rapidly as any battalion in any army during the whole war.'[3]

In response, the devastated Pompey Elliott has the news passed on to McCay at 5th Division HQ, and asks for instructions.

Major-General McCay bows to the obvious. The 15th Brigade, McCay informs Haking over the telephone, is 'of no further use for attack'.[4]

Haking does not blanch. After all, on the entire Western Front there is *no* officer more experienced than he is at reading reports on the devastating consequences of attacks that he himself has organised. Other officers have read reports listing carnage on a catastrophic scale coming from their battlefront, true. But usually such officers have been fired, or demoted, or shuffled away. Sometimes they have resigned in disgrace, or gone mad with shock and guilt.

But not Haking. Despite the debacles at Aubers Ridge in May 1915, at the Battle of Loos six months later, and at Boar's Head just three weeks earlier, there has never been any sign of self-doubt in him, nor of remorse. And under the patronage of Sir Douglas Haig, there has never been any question of demoting him. Far from it. The upward trajectory of his military career, as a proven 'thruster', has simply given him the capacity to be responsible for ever more men to throw into battle.

So now, in response to the news – which confirms that four of his six brigades have been either wiped out or withdrawn – Haking simply pins his hopes on the two remaining brigades being able to hold on, until the 61st can launch its fresh attack at dawn.

At 1.10 am, meanwhile, McCay orders General Elliott to withdraw his men from whatever forward positions they find themselves in, and get back to the original front-line they had first left eight hours, and 1500 men, ago. On Elliott's orders, the sap being dug by the 15th Brigade is abandoned. There is no point in digging a trench to get to securely held German trenches – though the men working on that are now thrown into digging another trench, to support the 14th – and active operations on the front of the 15th Brigade cease.

Those few men in the 59th and 60th Battalions who are left alive to heed Pompey's orders to withdraw do so immediately, though their situation running back is in turn so desperate that, as Lieutenant Doyle of the 60th would recall, they even had to ignore 'the wounded clutching at you as you passed . . .'[5]

To their right, the 184th Brigade are still active – and, in fact, preparing to follow Haking's further orders to attack the Sugar-loaf. Just minutes before those who are in position are due to attack from Rhondda Sap – Praise the Lord and *stop* passing the ammunition – the 61st Division's Major-General Mackenzie is informed by General Carter that, 'owing to the destruction of [my] communication trenches, the blocking of all avenues of approach with wounded, and the late arrival of the companies for the assault, added to the confusion caused by hostile machine-gun fire and shells, [I am] unable to get [all of] the companies in position before daylight'.[6]

Mackenzie has no choice but to postpone the attack. Haking, however, still insists that it *must* go in at dawn.

For the Germans, it is time to unleash the full force of their focused fury. For the orders of General von Scanzoni, the Commanding Officer of the 6th Bavarian Division, are firm. After calling up his reserves, he now commits no fewer than 6000[7] soldiers against the Australians. After the German counter-attack has staggered along since 7 pm with ill-coordinated actions from different units, it now becomes a centrally organised, serious affair that will prove, perhaps, to be unstoppable.

Its effects are first felt on the extreme right of the 14th Brigade when, at around 1.15 am, *Zweiter Leutnant* Bachschneider and his men are relieved, and a fresh German composite force from 2/16th Bavarian RIR – *alles Freiwillige*, all volunteers – soon joined by another company from 1/16th Bavarian RIR, begin the second major counter-attack. And for them, not weaponry nor ammunition nor grenades are a problem, as they have plenty on hand and none of it has to be ferried forward across No-Man's Land. The result is that, within minutes, Captain Charles Arblaster and his men of the 53rd Battalion are in the fight of their lives, again *for* their lives.

Again and again, the message is passed back from them – 'For God's sake, send us bombs!'[8] – but all to no avail.

And, yes, Arblaster receives the support from nearby companies that he urgently calls for, but the numbers and firepower against them are simply overwhelming. The Germans inexorably move forward, cleaning out pocket after pocket of resistance, including the 'trench blocks' of sandbags that had been set up. In short order, the Hun has fully retaken their old trench behind the 53rd Battalion, cutting off Arblaster and his men in their advanced position.

Meanwhile, fresh German reserves counter-attack from the edges of the 8th Brigade's positions on the left, moving in behind Captain Arthur White (Commander of D Company and now stand-in leader of the 32nd in the field) and his men, now reinforced by the 29th Battalion.

(In moving around in such counter-attacks, the Germans can navigate easily, having become familiar over the last year with every twist and turn, every darkened silhouette and shape on the skyline. The

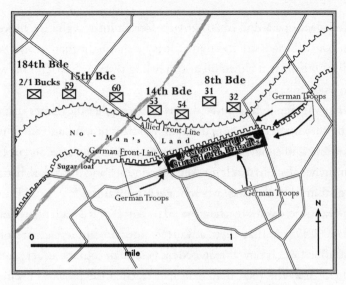

German counter-attack on 8th and 14th Brigade positions, 20 July 1916

Australians, of course, are not similarly blessed. With all the smoke, and all the entanglements, and all the newly dug trenches – and all of it entirely unfamiliar territory – it can all be extremely confusing. At one point, the Commanding Officer of the 32nd Battalion, Lieutenant-Colonel Coghill, with two others, tries to get back across No-Man's Land so he can make a report to General Tivey. After navigating a whole series of wire entanglements and open ground, they at last see a parapet ahead . . . only to find they have arrived back at their starting point. If only the ammunition dumps had still been burning, they might not have got lost.)

Still, some materiel is making its way forward, but, oh Christ help them, the horrific visions that confront them . . .

As one platoon, led by the 30th Battalion's Lieutenant Tom Barbour, make their way over – laden down with ammunition, tools and sand-bags – they see a soldier with two bloody stumps where his legs used to be, crawling towards them. 'Make way, please,' he gurgles as he passes, never to be seen again.[9]

Nearby, Second-Lieutenant Waldo Zander, also of the 30th Battalion, is right there in No-Man's Land right after Fritz sends over some incendiary shells. They explode, throwing sticky, burning material across a radius of 20 yards, before emitting a ghastly, flickering light over all the dead and dying. It is by that light that Zander sees a soldier with an arm blown off also crawling towards him. But his whole body is on fire.

'He was seen to be frantically trying to smother the flames that were eating into his very flesh, tearing up handfuls of mud and earth in his endeavour and agony. His screams could be heard for a second or two – then silence. Fate had at last taken pity on him and had taken him into her arm for that last sleep where there is no waking.'[10]

Meantime, word reaches the 31st Battalion's Lieutenant-Colonel Toll at 2.30 am that their advanced post on the left centre of the Australian front is now threatened by a German counter-attack, coming at them from the road that 'Toll had reached the previous evening'.[11] Toll ignores it, as there have been so many false alarms already, where a nearby row of trees has been mistaken for attacking infantry, but . . .

But what is that?

From the very direction in which the counter-attack is reported, Lieutenant-Colonel Toll can now hear the sound of bombing, getting closer, and closer, the footsteps of hell on the march.

—

Captain Charles Arblaster and the 53rd Battalion are now isolated and running out of ammunition, with German soldiers now reoccupying the old lines between them and safety, while other German soldiers also attack them on both flanks. There remains just one chance for any of them to survive. They are going to have to hurl the few grenades they have left ahead of them and then make a charge back the way they came. Quickly, quietly, by the light of the ongoing flares that continue to give the scene an ethereal feel – like the twilight world is close – Arblaster distributes the grenades they have left to the 150 men he has with him.

Australians all, mates, they have come this far, fought the good fight through the night, and survived it all. And now they're going to make one last charge for their lives.

Ready, men?

Ready.

Now!

With a roar, they hurtle forward, straight at the Germans in the trenches they had so casually abandoned nine hours earlier, and so bitterly fought for since. Alas, the Germans see them coming, and it is a relatively simple matter to bring their guns to bear and take many of the Australians down. In the lead, Arblaster is among the first to fall wounded, shot through both arms. Many of the other Australian soldiers are shot with him, but enough of them make it to the Germans for a furious battle to ensue, with bullets, bayonets and bombs, killing and wounding many on both sides. The duckboards in the trench bottom become sticky and slippery with blood. No quarter is asked for or given.

Some of the Australians make it into No-Man's Land and are able to scramble across it to safety. Others are beaten back to their starting point, managing to drag the heavily bleeding Captain Arblaster with them, while others cross the elevated Rouges Bancs road to join up with the right hand of the 54th's advanced position.

—

Still the ferrying of supplies across No-Man's Land goes on, and Bert Bishop is right in the thick of it. He has lost count of how many times he has been back and forth, and is frankly amazed to still be alive. The wonderful thing is that every time they go over, it gets a little bit easier as the communication trench being dug by the 14th Field Company gets longer. But it's always a wrench, like on this particular trip in the wee hours, when they get to the end of the trench and come to a . . . dead halt.

They are blocked.

Someone has to take the initiative to do what has to be done, and it is their brave officer who does the honours. 'Come out of that sap!' he roars,[12] leading by leaping up and over.

Alas, with a quick, staccato burst of machine-gun fire, that officer falls, riddled with bullets, as dead as a dropped dingo in the desert. And now, an even braver officer charges forth – despite the danger that has just been demonstrated – only to meet the same fate.

Anyone getting out of this sap like that is a dead man.

'And to think,' one of Bert's mates says right beside him, 'I enlisted to have a holiday.'[13]

Despite it all, still some of the men are brave enough to emerge from the sap and try to crawl forward, but they, too, are quickly gunned down. Finally, the order is given, the only one that can be given under the circumstances, as devastating as it is for those Australian soldiers in the forward German trenches – including Ray and Robbo if they're still alive – relying on fresh supplies of ammunition getting to them. 'Get back! Every man for himself.'[14]

They get back. Every man for himself. After a mad dash, Bert tumbles back into the trench, again scarcely daring to believe that he is still alive.

The extension of the sap goes on, with Sydney Donnan and all the others furiously digging the communication trench for the 14th Field Company across No-Man's Land. Personally, Donnan remains

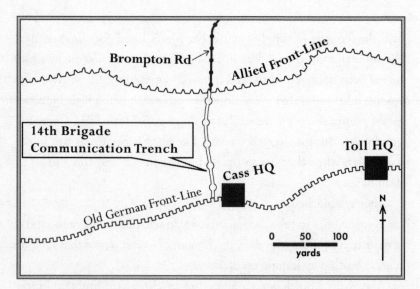

The 14th Brigade's communication trench to the enemy's front-line

stunned that such a job is not under the control of a serious engineer or the like. 'Any undertaking like this,' he would say, 'should have been in the hands of a man who in civil life had been in charge of big undertakings, preferably of a big civil engineering character; a man who in his daily job had encountered difficulties in simple looking tasks and had to make decisions to overcome them.'

But no, there is just them, struggling mightily on their Pat Malone. 'I would say without knowing who was in command at [Fromelles],' Donnan would later note, 'that the action was the result of a mug soldier's fond dream.'[15]

In his 54th Battalion HQ, still in the old German front-lines, Lieutenant-Colonel Walter Cass continues to defend his position with his men, while also monitoring the best he can how the other battalions on either side of him are going – badly, is his general impression, though he has little solid information. What he does know is that to his far right, where he should be seeing the signs of the 15th Brigade, all he can see is German flares.

He consequently sends ever grimmer messages, taken by ever more exhausted, frightened runners back to Colonel Pope at 14th Brigade HQ:

3 a.m.– It is reported to me that the 53rd on my right has given way slightly and that Germans are coming in . . . (350 yards W.S.W. of [my] headquarters).
3.22– Position is serious, as we have no grenades and enemy is preparing to attack . . .[16]

In order to help Cass the best he can, McCay had at 2.40 am asked first the heavy artillery, and half an hour later the field artillery, to bring down a bombardment on Cass's right flank, where the 15th Brigade should have been, and from where more German counter-attacks were likely to develop. Now he sends a message through to Pompey Elliott that as soon as dawn breaks he must have his men ready to fire on that same flank, in order to bring whatever pressure to bear on it they can. It's something, anyway.

The called-for artillery may, possibly, have had some effect on the Germans, but the whole thing is too much for some. 'Our own artillery are shelling us!' Australian troops on the old German front-line cry as the shells land nearby.[17] It is, in fact, something of a siren call, heard along much of the advanced line, together with, 'We have been ordered to retire!'[18] For those of less stout disposition, the siren call is answered immediately. In the case of the 55th's Lieutenant-Colonel McConaghy, who has the support of five officers, it is all he can do to keep all the men he can muster within a 25-yard radius in their positions.

That, alas, does not extend to the men in the advanced position of the 53rd, many of whom now make another charge back to their own line – less Arblaster and others too wounded to move, who will hopefully be cared for by the Germans, and those who hopped the Rouges Bancs road and came in on the right of the 54th forward position. They are seen streaming past Cass's position, bound for home (if not glory). Cass, of course, yells at them to maintain their positions, but, as Bean would note, 'he lacked the influence of their own officers, who had mostly fallen'.[19]

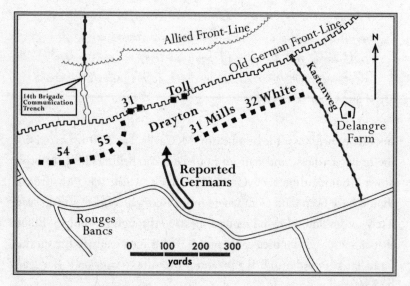

Germans' frontal attack via the 'weak step'

This departure of the last of the 53rd leaves Cass's right flank exposed and shrinking towards the left. Lieutenant-Colonel Cass gets another message away, to 14th Brigade HQ:

3.45 — Position very serious. 53rd are retiring. Enemy behind them and in their old front line . . . (i.e., 480 yards W. of [my] headquarters) and within 100 yards of my right . . .[20]

In fact, the position for Cass and his men is about to get even more serious. For just as to his right the attack of the 15th Brigade has completely failed and the 53rd has now entirely withdrawn, so too has his left flank, where the 8th Brigade, which had been holding the line, has crumbled more than somewhat.

At 3.15 am, the most forward elements of Captain Charles Mills's 31st Battalion had been overwhelmed by a German counter-attacking force. With German soldiers 'all round, bombing, and firing from the hip',[21] Mills himself had been wounded, before being captured. Some of his men had been killed, others captured, while still others had raced back to the old German front trench, only to find it empty, and so had continued back across No-Man's Land. This has left the 31st Battalion's Commanding Officer Lieutenant-Colonel Toll and his HQ staff stranded and alone, in their position in the front-lines.

On the far left, where Captain Arthur White and the survivors of the 32nd Battalion have been most exposed through the night to the withering fire of the Germans on their own left, their position also becomes untenable. For now — after ensuring that the precious machine guns get back first, via a circuitous route that passes mostly through the 14th Brigade lines — White assesses that, as his men are currently being 'taken in front, flank and rear',[22] he has no choice, and begins to organise his men to make a charge back to their own line. As massed German forces now start to emerge from the mist like vengeful phantoms seeking to take their enemies to their graves, it is obvious that Captain White and the roughly 150 Australian soldiers he has with him do not have long to act.

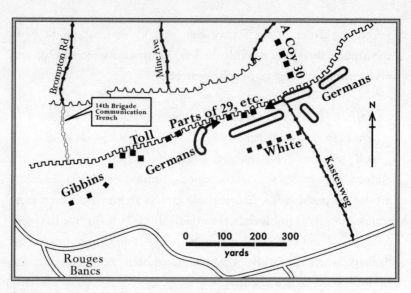

Germans' attack behind White after Mills withdraws

Among them, on the side closest to the German-held flank, is Captain Frank Krinks, with a 1st XI of survivors from his original carrying party of the 30th Battalion, who have also been battling through the night. Just as it had been for Charles Arblaster and his men, it is obvious to them all: it is time to either make a run for it or surrender.

For such a decision, they suddenly stop being a Captain and his men, and revert to being Australians all, on a sticky wicket to beat them all. A quick debate takes place. No one wants to surrender, so that is out. But should they run separately or together? These are men who have fought through the night, shoulder to shoulder, back to back, as brothers in arms and survived against all odds. Again, there can only be one answer: together. But with a solid vow attached, made above the cacophony of battle, even as they eye the Germans coming closer through the fog of war: no one is to be left behind. If one of them falls, the survivors will grab him and *drag* him back.

Agreed?

Agreed.

They further decide that their best chance of staying alive is by fleet of foot, not fire of gun, and so they will leave their weapons behind and simply run like the wind.

Agreed.

Nearby, Theodor Pflaum of the 8th Machine Gun Company, who has not stopped, is feeling faint. He knows he has to go, but still can't bear it. He has tried to get back to where he has left his 19-year-old brother, Ray, in the dugout, but it has not been possible.

Now they just have to . . .

GO!

Heavily laden with their guns, tripods, ammunition boxes and belts, Theodor Pflaum and his men begin their mad charge back, all of it so desperate and dangerous 'that the cries for "help" from the men that fell all round us had to be disregarded'.[23]

Nearby – though not in the same group, nor at exactly the same time – Captains Arthur White and Frank Krinks and their men race across the first 300 yards in nothing flat, and are back in the original German trench before the Germans in there quite know what is happening, as suddenly huge men start flying over their heads. Alas, they are able to react just quickly enough to bring down two of Krinks's men . . . at which point, Krinks and his men turn back.

In similar retreat, White and his men are in much the same kind of fight. It is valiant, but not enough. 'Owing to the lack of grenades,' Captain White would report, 'we were unable to push [Fritz] out so the line was withdrawn to our own trenches.'[24]

They too start to sprint across No-Man's Land, as the machine guns furiously spit death and disaster at them. Mercifully, only 20 yards in, they come to the 8th Brigade's communication trench where it had been abandoned – once it had been established that the Germans controlled the trenches facing it – and are able to gain shelter all the way back to their own lines.

Once Captain Krinks's dirty dozen have liberated their two prisoners, they also run like hares across No-Man's Land. This time, there can be no turning back, as the fire is too vicious. Only Captain Krinks and three others make it back to their own trenches. One man whom they've not been able to get to, though they hope is still alive, is Corporal Sydney Wells, who had been hit, and hurt badly, falling onto the German barbed wire. Last seen, he was suspended on that wire, bleeding badly.

As to Theodor Pflaum, he and his group have also made it, less one man. 'The barb wire gave us a bit of trouble,' Pflaum would record in his diary, 'but we forced our way in spite of our clothes being torn to ribbons.'[25]

Second-Lieutenant Waldo Zander is watching closely what happens to those who have been in isolated pockets, unable to join the charge – most particularly a Lewis gun crew, still caught in the original German trench. 'After all the rest had fallen back they could still be heard firing,' he would write in his diary. 'We could see the Bosche working in along the trench on both their flanks toward them, but they still stuck to their post and the gun kept firing. We saw some stick bombs thrown into their little stronghold – then silence!'[26]

With the exception of Lieutenant-Colonel Toll and his small group in the German front-lines on the right, and a small pocket of 31st men forward of him who continue to fight on in conjunction with Gibbins's 55th, the 8th Brigade no longer holds its objective.

Soon enough, it is time for the last men left standing of the 8th Brigade to make a move or a last stand, as a renewed attack sees the Germans continue to close in on Toll's position in the front-lines, in the process completely cutting him off from Cass and his men on the right. The Germans have plentiful grenades, while Toll and his men are reduced to defending themselves with rifles alone. What's worse, one of the German grenades has destroyed their Vickers machine gun, which had been the core of their defence.

At 4 am,[27] it is Lieutenant-Colonel Toll who takes the decision upon himself. He and his men have followed their orders, done their duty and more, but are now faced with overwhelming numbers of Germans coming at them from their front and left flank, now entirely abandoned by the 32nd. To hold on is to die. 'Well, men,' Toll says heavily, exhausted and likely faint from the loss of blood from his head wound through the night, 'no one could ask you to do more – get back to our lines, but don't bunch up.'[28]

His men don't have to be told twice, and they certainly don't bunch up, but they run as fast as their legs can carry them over the open ground of No-Man's Land. None is as fast as one particular fellow, however. For one soldier, Bill Miles, is running hard, only to be passed about halfway across – as if he *were standing still* – by one of his mates, Harry Littlewood, who, it has to be said, is running as fast as an emu bitten on the bottom by a bee. He is *flying*!

And what is that he is singing over his shoulder as he runs? 'Never knew I won a Stawell Gift did you, Billy?'[29]

No, Billy never knew, but still there is no doubt that Harry is one with a singular ability to run out of sight on a dark night.

Bringing up the rear is Lieutenant-Colonel Toll, all alone bar two wounded men he is shepherding with him 'as he strides back across No-Man's-Land, practically the last of his brigade'.[30]

Now only the 14th Brigade continues to hold any serious length of German trenches – the last finger in the dyke holding back the Bavarian flood. There may have been more lopsided fights in the history of the world, but Lieutenant-Colonel Cass and his 500-odd gathered survivors versus the combined might of the 6th Bavarian Reserve Division would surely run them close.

—

They are nearly there!

After nigh on nine hours of superhuman efforts, the communication trench that had started back in the lines of the 14th Brigade is now close to the Old German Lines. With one last furious hurry and flurry of mud, the men of the 14th Field Company are through to the old German front-line trench, just before 4 am.[31] For the first time, thus, it is at least theoretically possible to get across No-Man's Land from the old lines to the new lines without coming under murderous machine-gun fire – and the whole thing has duckboards along it, with walls four to six feet high. This sap is a thing of beauty, made by mates, for mates – a magic road away from murder.

And none too soon. For, with one look, the exhausted Sydney Donnan can see just how appalling the situation is. 'The front line,' he would report, 'was like a disorderly butcher's shop and there was still a fair barrage over the second line and communication trenches.'[32]

Immediately the trench is through – just next to Lieutenant-Colonel Cass's HQ in the old German front-lines – Cass sends wounded soldiers back along it. He then sets about better defending this crucial section of Old German Line that the trench has entered by ordering groups of his soldiers to take sandbags down from the parapets and set up sandbag walls inside the old line, 50 yards on either side of the junction of the 14th Brigade communication trench with the old German front-line. Whatever happens, this sap has to be defended to the end, for when that end comes – and it surely must, as the Germans continue to press – it will be the only chance he and his men have to get away alive.

Shortly afterwards, Cass looks up to see his grim-faced counterpart from the 55th Battalion, Lieutenant-Colonel McConaghy, approaching. The two know each other well, have fought in Gallipoli together and know this is no time for preamble. McConaghy tells him straight. The German counter-attack is coming so fast towards the entrance to the newly completed communication trench that they have just minutes to stop it. And there is another attack coming from the other direction. 'Unless strong reinforcements are hurried forward,' McConaghy says, 'there is a good chance of the two enemy bombing parties joining forces behind us, and thus cutting us off.'[33]

And Cass can immediately see that McConaghy is right, most particularly when he looks to the right. For as the Germans move along the trenches, they are not only firing flares ahead of them so they can see which Australians to shoot but also holding a signboard above the trenches so that their own artillery and machine-gunners won't kill them by mistake.

The attacks need instant action, and Cass quickly organises it with McConaghy. But it is not the officers who truly shine at this desperate moment. No, it is a bloke from Wagga Wagga way, a gnarled bushie, *tougher* than teak, by the name of Sergeant Frank Stringer, of the 54th

Battalion, who not just steps forward but also steps up onto the parapet. With a cry to his mates to join him, he uses his .303 to devastating effect, firing at every damn German helmet he can see bobbing along, knocking them over like tin ducks at the Wagga Wagga Show. Everybody gets a prize but the Germans. Inspired by his courage, a dozen of his soldiers join him, firing their own rifles and also hoiking their grenades, while trying to dodge the grenades coming back at them.

Stringer leads the way. 'To your left front,' he roars to his men. 'Huns in the trench, five rounds rapid . . .'[34]

The cracks of doom ring out.

Meanwhile, McConaghy, at the urgent behest of Cass, has decided that 'a bayonet charge would be effective'[35] and starts to organise it. Cass gets away another message to Colonel Pope at 4.20 am, noting that the position of him and his men is *almost desperate*.[36] It would have been beyond desperate if not for the fact that, right at the time they most need it, a brave carrying party arrives with more grenades. For now, just as McConaghy is about to send his party of 50 men under Lieutenant Bill Denoon running on both sides of the German breastwork, using bayonets on whoever they come across, they are now given ample grenades too.

Denoon leads the way as he and his men charge forward along the old German front-line, tossing grenades ahead of them into the trenches held by the Germans. There ensues what Charles Bean would describe, from reports he would assemble, as 'a Herculean bomb-fight'.[37] So furious is the battle that one report has it that as many as 12 grenades are in the air at any one time, with one Bavarian later claiming that he had thrown no fewer than 500 himself. And maybe the Bavarians would have done better if their game had been cricket instead of soccer. But whatever else they might say of the Australians, no one would ever say that they couldn't throw things the size of apples extraordinary distances and with great accuracy – and, as Bean would describe it, they did indeed hurl their grenades 'like cricketers throwing at a wicket'.[38]

There are many heroes in the action – not least Bill Denoon, who is shot through the shoulder, meaning he must 'retire hurt' – but perhaps

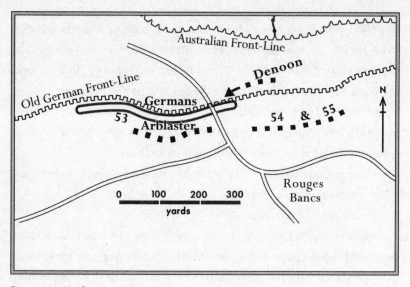

Denoon attacks Germans behind Arblaster

none stand out more than the prematurely white-haired Captain Percy Woods of the 55th Battalion. For now, as they head along beside the German breastwork, that shock of white hair is everywhere, hurling the grenades, exhorting his men, pushing forward, pulling back, going again. It is bravery on a scale beyond, which will later see Woods awarded the Military Cross for displaying 'courage and initiative when officers were fast becoming casualties'.[39]

And it's hot all right, as the Germans throw bombs and fire back at the Australians in turn. But in the end, their ferocity cannot match that of the Australians. The end result is that, at least for the moment, the Australians are able to beat back the most threatening of the German advance in this sector, with this valiant force reclaiming 80 yards of precious trench, even though the Germans continue to push forward in others.

—

Back at 14th Brigade HQ, Cass's message has now come through to Colonel Pope:

4.20 a.m. Position almost desperate. Have got 55th and a few of the 54th together and have temporarily checked enemy. But do get our guns to work at once, please. The 53rd have lost confidence temporarily and will not willingly stand their ground. Some appear to be breaking across No-Man's-Land. If they give way to my right rear, I must withdraw or be surrounded.[40]

Good God Almighty, just how long can Cass hold on?

No one is sure. Only that he must.

Now in receipt of Brigadier-General Edwin Tivey's advice that the last of the 8th Brigade have withdrawn from their position, Colonel Pope sends out a message to Cass informing him that with the withdrawal of the 8th Brigade, and the 15th Brigade's failure, he is exposed on both flanks and will probably be withdrawn. But Pope adds a rider: *Do not retire until you receive word. Machineguns should be brought back.*[41]

With no idea that the entire 8th Brigade has withdrawn, nor that the 14th are only just holding on by their bloodied fingernails, McCay feels bound to leave such men as he has there, in position, on the reckoning that Sir Richard Haking is still insistent that the 61st will make another assault on the Sugar-loaf at dawn. It is something the commander of the whole operation has been emphasising through the night, Haking's instinct guiding him that, in the face of difficulties, the men must still attack, attack, *attack*!

When that comes to pass, having the 14th Brigade, and most particularly Cass's men of the 54th and 55th, in position on the left flank, might prove crucial.

—

For the surviving Australian soldiers back in the front-lines, the shock of what they are seeing, and hearing, as they peer into a No-Man's Land lit by the light of the flares and the endlessly exploding shells takes them beyond horror. As the continuous stream of wounded make their way back, covered in blood and gore, and all too frequently holding their sliced intestines in with their bloodied hands, the survivors all know that hundreds, maybe thousands, of dead and dying men are still out there.

In various hotspots, the survivors can also see that there are small, angry pockets of Australian soldiers 'firing in a careless passion of rage, blazing at the inexorable parapet'. Ever and always, this is 'stopped by a flurry of enemy fire . . . It was a night of horror and doubt.'[42]

Many brave souls head out with the sole purpose of bringing in their wounded comrades, risking their own lives to do so. Every time there is any lull in the artillery and machine-gun fire, the men can hear stricken calls and more coming from their mates, still out there . . .

There! Can you hear that?

It is a clearly delirious Digger, singing one of their marching songs far out in front, the one they had all loved so much back in those carefree days in Egypt:

> *My mother told me*
> *That she would buy me*
> *A rubber dolly,*
> *A rubber dolly,*
> *But when I told her*
> *I loved a—*

The voice is suddenly drowned out by a flurry of grenades exploding out to the left, the fragments 'wailing like Banshees' as they whistle away. And now a burst of machine-gun fire before the wounded soldier takes up again from where he'd been up to . . . when so *rudely* interrupted:

> *But when I told her*
> *I loved a soldier . . .*
> *She would not buy me*
> *A rub—*[43]

Another burst of machine-gun fire and the voice is no more.

Ah, but there are others, including a highly agitated call for 'Bill! . . . Bill! . . .' that goes on and on all night, without Bill ever answering . . . until, finally . . . that voice is stilled too.[44]

Of Bill, there remains no sign.

5 AM, 20 JULY 1916, HAKING'S HQ AT SAILLY-SUR-LA-LYS, TELL THEM I'M NOT IN

At General Sir Richard Haking's HQ at Sailly-sur-la-Lys, some three and a half miles back from the front-line, the first grey streaks of dawn have now passed over No-Man's Land – where a thousand men lie dying – and are just beginning to peer through the curtains of this well-appointed farmhouse, where a meeting is under way.

It is for all the key Generals and their senior staff to 'decide upon the operations for the day',[45] and, specifically, as is viewed most urgent by Haking himself, 'to discuss a fresh attack by the 61st Division'.[46]

Around the table, the Generals McCay and Mackenzie make their reports to Haking and Monro, who is presiding. Major Mackenzie must begin by explaining how all the actions of his division for the previous night had failed, most particularly including the quelling of the Sugar-loaf. On that difficult subject, and the forthcoming attack, he begs to inform that, as a matter of fact, regrettably, it has not been possible during the night to get the companies assigned for the next attack properly into position and provisioned, and . . .

A knock on the door.

Excuse me, sir, a phone call for General McCay.

Put it through.

It is Colonel Wagstaff on the line, McCay's Chief of Staff, who has just been in touch with the 14th Brigade's Colonel Pope, who had in turn just received that message from Lieutenant-Colonel Cass describing his position as 'almost desperate', sent from the German trenches at 4.20 am.

Yes.

Yes . . .

I *see* . . .

It seems the 14th Brigade is still holding on, just. In fact, as Wagstaff now tells McCay, it is even more desperate than Cass knows, because though Wagstaff had told Cass he must hold on, he has subsequently found out that what was left of the 8th Brigade, which was not much at all, has made it back to the Australian lines, meaning Cass and his men are totally isolated, exposed on both their left and right flanks, and merely holding 'a semi-circle' in the German lines.[47]

So this call is to seek instruction. What order should they send to Cass and the remnants of the 14th Brigade who are still out there? 'To hold on with reinforcements or to withdraw?'[48]

Hang on.

McCay puts the question to the meeting.

Perhaps this very question is the slap of reality that is needed to make Monro and all of them face the true situation. Far beyond Haking's neat plans on maps and his endlessly optimistic views, the bitter truth is that despite *thousands* of casualties, the British – well, Australians actually – now hold only one brigade's worth of German trench from the six brigades that attacked, and the hold is far from a secure one.

For once, Monro, who has overall control, does not hesitate, and he gives the order with little consultation: defeat is admitted; the attack of the 61st Division is cancelled; and the remnants of the 5th Division must withdraw. To help Cass and his men get out, an artillery box barrage will be put up around them.

(Back in the Australian artillery lines, as the men continue to fire their guns through the night, all such instructions are earnestly examined as to their meaning. 'We were disappointed,' one gunner with the 13th Field Artillery Brigade would note, 'when we dropped our range – back, back, back – until we were back to our starting point.'[49])

In the meantime, the Commanding Officer of the 14th Brigade, Colonel Pope, acting on his own initiative, has already sent a message to Cass, telling him that they are indeed isolated, as the 8th Brigade have now been driven back to their lines, and that in all likelihood the 14th will also be withdrawn. But, for the moment, they must hold on.

———

For the Germans surrounding Cass and his men in this full daylight of the early morning, there is an eagerness born of the fact that this should be easy pickings. At the end of this long night, with all other brigades withdrawn, there remains only a small group of Australians left in their lines, men who are surely as exhausted as their ammunition supplies.

One of those men is Captain Gibbins, who can see only too well the precariousness of the situation. He now leads the 31st Battalion's Sergeant Francis Law, together with eight of his soldiers, out to the left, to near Toll's previous position. 'I expect enemy attacks from that Quarter,' Captain Gibbins tells Law,[50] pointing to the left flank, before going back to hold his own post and tend to their many wounded.

Gibbins is not long in being proven correct. Sergeant Law and his men are soon under sustained attack from the direction that he had indicated. Seeing what is happening, Captain Gibbins takes action. 'Get as many bombs as you can . . .!' he yells to Second-Lieutenant Chapman.[51] With no bombs left, they simply must trust that Law and his men can hold them off until their own supplies arrive.

A furious battle ensues. As Sergeant Law would recount, the Bavarians make 'five successive attempts to storm along the trench but each, in turn, was met and defeated by the gallantry and resourcefulness of the eight men with me'.[52] Amazingly, they have not taken a single casualty, while also 'inflicting severe loss upon the enemy'.[53] But for how long can they hold on, as the Germans mass once more?

Just before the sixth attack, a thundering of hooves – actually many Australian soldiers at full gallop, a cavalry borne by a pack of Shanks' ponies to the rescue – reveals Gibbins charging back to their aid, just in time, as the canny Germans are now seemingly coming from all sides. 'God knows which way [Fritz] came,' Sergeant Archibald Winter of the 55th Battalion would recall, 'we don't. He appeared to come from every direction. We were unsupported, consequently Fritz could come in on our own flanks. They had snipers everywhere and our own men were falling fast. Then we got into close quarters with the bombs but we were only a handful and Fritz was there in his thousands.'[54]

But 'Fritz', too, is equally shocked by the venom the Australians are *still* able to generate, most particularly one heaving giant of an Australian soldier, who runs from side to side, exhorting his men to beat the bastards back and hurling grenades such distances at them it nearly defies belief.

Yes, Captain Norman Gibbins, in such situations as this, is a force to be reckoned with as he fires and fights and hurls like a mad thing. He is struck by a bullet to the head, but it very much looks as if the bullet has bounced *off* that massive scone of his – his men would not be surprised.

The Germans finally have no choice but to withdraw.

It is really something, but for now the urgent thing is to get the many wounded away. Gibbins orders Law, with his survivors, to hold

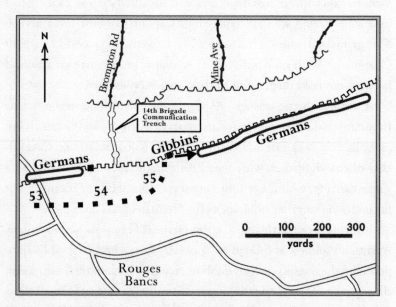

Gibbins rebuffs the German attack along the Old German Line

on for just a bit longer, so the stretcher-bearers will have a chance to evacuate to get them away, and then he will get Law and his men to withdraw.

—

Machineguns should be brought back.

The actual instruction for Cass and his men to withdraw does not leave for the 14th Brigade until 6.30 am – the actual time, as it happens, that Cass receives the news that he and his men are 'to hold on until ordered to withdraw'.[55]

Hold on?

Madness. Absolute madness.

When they are now the only ones out there? Such an order is a death warrant for many men, if not all of them, and Cass knows it. So far gone is the situation now that it is clearly going to be impossible to hold on to the ground they have won at such expense in the long term, and even in the short term the true challenge will be simply to stay *alive*. And the longer they are ordered to stay here, the worse it will be. By this time, they are an isolated island in a rising sea of Germans that must soon engulf them, even though the actions of Gibbins and his men on the left, and Denoon and his men on the right, have given them a temporary respite.

'We've got to save our guns,' Cass, now emerged from his deep dugout to lead the withdrawal, says to his men before pointing out the tops of German helmets that can be seen bobbing their way from the right. 'That group over there is our greatest danger. Will two men volunteer to take bombs and try to hold them back?'[56]

The man with his hand first in the air is Ray Bishop, soon joined by another private. And maybe Robbo could have volunteered to stay with Ray too, but it just hasn't worked out like that. The other bloke has volunteered, and all Robbo can do is hope that Ray will be all right.

Good men. Take these grenades and go for your lives, for *our* lives.

While Cass arranges for the group to carry the precious Lewis guns back, Ray Bishop and his fellow volunteer load themselves up with grenades in their gunny sacks, and start moving to the group of counter-attacking Germans they can see who threaten the passage of the guns.

A shot rings out, and Ray's mate goes down, clearly all but instantly killed. Not pausing for a moment, Ray continues to go at the Germans, only for a second shot to shatter the dawn – just as those with the Lewis guns start to scamper back to the Australian lines.

And now, to Robbo's particular horror, Ray too is hit, and he goes down. Despite blood rushing from his thigh, still he crawls forward, managing to throw grenade after grenade at the Germans. He keeps throwing until every last grenade is hurled, creating havoc among the approaching enemy. The diversion is perfect, and the men with the Lewis guns have been able to take their chances and successfully retreat, while Ray turns and starts to crawl back . . . at which point another shot comes and he is wounded in the other thigh.

Robbo, who has waited for his mate, moves towards him . . .

—

By 7.20 am, when there is still no word back from Colonel Pope at 8th Brigade HQ, Cass sends another message:

> Please arrange artillery to create barrage right around us, as enemy is bombing very heavily. His rifle fire is causing casualties and I cannot get wounded away . . . No order to withdraw yet.[57]

—

It is for good reason that the runners in the AIF wear a large red band on their left arm and always carry the message in their top left pocket. It is so that when you spot a dead runner, you know where to find the undelivered message, to help ensure it reaches its addressee, who is always marked at the top. And yet, while that has worked earlier in the night when there had been enough men going back and forth to look out for dead runners, by now, with Lieutenant-Colonel Cass and his men little more than an isolated pocket, when a runner goes down, that too is the end of the message. And now, with full daylight upon them, no fewer than seven runners come to grief, killed or wounded out in No-Man's Land, or at least tumbled into a shell hole or trench to never emerge.

Does the eighth messenger run fast? As if his life depends on it . . . . . . because it does . . . . . . as bullets kick up mud around his flying feet as he sprints . . . from shell hole to shell hole. (With the communication trench completely clogged with dead and wounded particularly towards the Australian/British front-line end, this is the best choice to get the message there – fast.)

In the wake of the messenger, the Germans are again attacking, and Cass continues to lead his men, roaring orders left and right, and firing and throwing grenades himself. 'I honestly thought,' he would recount, 'that it was certain that I should get hit . . .'[58]

Virtually abandoned, the 14th Brigade must fight as never before. Cass would like to withdraw with his men but, in the absence of an order to do so, feels obliged to stay until that order is received or doomsday descends – whichever comes first.

Still the Germans keep pressing from all sides, and the battle goes on even as, just before 8 am, an exhausted, bloodied runner does make it through to Lieutenant-Colonel Cass. Either way, Cass now has in his hands the message from General McCay containing the decision taken two and a half hours before. Withdraw. Get your men out.

At *last*. Cass has the word spread along the line. We are getting out. Tell the men they are to use the 14th Brigade's communication trench, just by my HQ. In consultation with Lieutenant-Colonel McConaghy, Cass has picked the obvious man to act as a rearguard, holding the old German front-line while the 14th makes good its withdrawal to the Australian front-line. Captain Gibbins, with four other officers and some 50 men, will do the job.

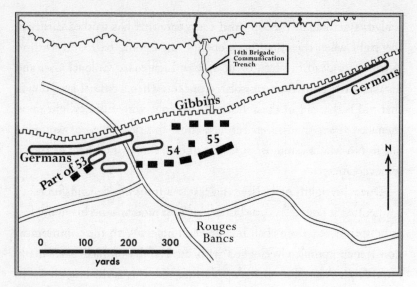

14th Brigade
Communication
Trench

Germans

Gibbins

55

54

Germans

Part of 53

N

Rouges
Bancs

0   100   200   300

yards

Gibbins's rearguard

'You must prepare for an orderly retirement,' Lieutenant-Colonel McConaghy, who has not stopped since first crossing No-Man's Land nearly ten hours before, tells his men. 'We are unprotected on our flanks. Hold the first Hun line until further orders.'[59]

In other parts of the line, however, there is resistance to the order that is passed along. 'Retire be damned!' the word comes back.[60] After everything they have been through, all the lives lost, and they're just going to give it up? Be damned!

Of course, Lieutenant-Colonel Cass insists.

Elsewhere, there is some chaos in parts of the line as soldiers who have received the welcome news that they no longer have to stay in these hell holes of shell holes decide to make an immediate run for it, without the benefit of covering fire or protection of the communication trench. Those back in the Australian lines watch with horror as many of them are picked off.

'We were powerless to assist them, and had to watch them being shot down at point-blank range,' one Digger would recall. 'It seemed an eternity of time until the lucky ones reached our parapets, to be pulled in by willing hands. No sooner was our field of fire clear than we blazed into the Germans who had lined their parapets to punish the retiring troops.'[61]

Hang on, what's *that*? Even as they keep firing, they can see one bloodied Digger crawling back across No-Man's Land. They *will* him forward, to the point where he is now just yards from safety.

Oh, Christ.

That whistling sound?

Oh, Christ.

It is a German shell. The Diggers dive for cover only to find that, miraculously, it doesn't explode! They are saved.

At least, most of them are. Shockingly, the dud shell has hit the crawling Digger amidships, and he is dead a million times over.

What are the chances?

Around his shattered corpse, the mad scramble continues, many of the men equally being shot down within yards of safety. It is as good a lesson as any, for those who remain, that their own withdrawal has to be controlled.

Now, on Cass's signal, Captain Gibbins and his men, who have amassed the ammunition and bombs they need, unleash hell on every Hun head they can see, no matter how far away, while the others rush to the sap of redemption and pile into it. Of course, Gibbins's men receive return fire from the Germans, who continue to press in from all sides, but most of the remaining men of the 14th Brigade are indeed able to make it into the sap . . . followed by the survivors of the rearguard.

The last man standing, the one who makes sure all the others are away and that all wounded who can be assisted have been assisted, is Gibbins. Only when completely satisfied does he himself withdraw, the last man down the sap that he had begun to dig – can it really be that short a time? – 13 hours before.

At the other end of that sap, Lieutenant-Colonel Cass emerges. Miraculously, he has suffered only a 'scratch on the hand and had my sleeve slightly torn in four places'.[62] Now that he can express the emotions that have long been boiling up inside him, he does not hesitate to vent his feeling to his Commanding Officer, Colonel Pope, when they meet 'neath the parapet. 'I tell you,' Cass declares heavily, 'that it was wholesale murder, they have murdered my boys.'

But Pope will have none of it, replying forcefully with the age-old answer, 'Oh, pull yourself together man, *this is war!*'

'This is not war,' Cass insists, just as heatedly. 'They have murdered my boys.'[63]

Sapper William Smith, who overhears the conversation, has no doubt where his sympathies lie. He admires both officers as heroes of Gallipoli, and has served under Cass in the 2nd Battalion for three months, but he is with Cass all the way. They really have been murdered. They have been sent into an impossible situation, with insufficient preparation and not enough skilled artillery, against an implacable foe that has been entrenched in the position for over a year. It was a battle they were never going to win, meaning those who had given their lives had done so uselessly. That amounts to murder.

Watching anxiously as the men come out is Bert Bishop, hoping to see Ray. For the moment, his cousin is not apparent, though everything is so shambolic this is not a worry in itself. What he does notice is the looks on the faces of the others who have just come back across No-Man's Land. 'They all had an ashen grey pallor, and looked years older than when they went in,' he would recount. 'You'd see mates shaking hands with each other in silence, unable to speak, some of them crying, but no words were needed, each understood the feelings in the hearts of the other, feelings which could not be expressed in words. The old Gallipoli men among us all agree that there was nothing on the Peninsula to equal it; not even the landing.'[64]

And now, here at last, the man who – more than most – has been the hero of the night, and certainly the last precious hours: the towering figure of Captain Norman Gibbins. 'Cool as if he were taking his men on to a cricket field, Gibbins lined them out along the German Breastwork, stationed his Lewis gunners, and then covered with their fire this most delicate operation.'[65]

Gibbins calls out to the rest of the rearguard in his sector, 'Come on, all you gunners'[66] and waits until they have gathered their guns, their ammunition, hovering at the sap-head like a mother duck before ducklings. None of them is surprised to see that Gib delays his own departure 'until the last minute, to make certain there were no wounded men left' in his sector before heading off himself.[67]

As Captain Gibbins is the last man down the sap, by the time he comes to the end – just before the Australian parapet – he finds it blocked with many dead and wounded. Of course, Gib does what he has been doing all night. He ignores the danger and climbs out of the sap, to go up and over instead. As he reaches the top of the parapet, however, 'he turns his head round sharply',[68] for one last look back at the German lines, to make sure none of the 14th Brigade men have been left behind – confirmed, he notes with satisfaction – at-which-point-a-single-German-bullet-hits-him-in-the-head-and-kills-him-stone-dead.

'I did not see his body,' Second-Lieutenant Percy Chapman would write to Gib's beloved younger sister, Violet, 'but those who did, say that he <u>died with a smile</u> upon his lips. He is buried near our trenches, with a wooden cross over his grave.'[69]

Meanwhile, in scattered parts beyond the German lines, most particularly where the 8th Brigade had been fighting, some Australian soldiers have become isolated. And though they all continue to ferociously fight for as long as their ammunition holds out, and even for as long as they can wield a bayonet, equally inevitably . . . that resistance finally ends.

As General Monro's Chief of Staff reports to General Haig's GHQ: `Army commander does not consider situation or condition of troops justify continuation of operation, which he has ordered to cease.`[70]

At 9 am, a message from the 21st Bavarian Reserve Regiment, opposite the Australian 14th Brigade, arrives *bei der Gefechtsleitung*, at battle command: 'The last English man has been politely shown out of our positions. Our positions are firmly held by the Division.'[71]

The Battle of Fromelles, going just 15 hours, is over.

'Troops and leadership agree,' German War Correspondent

Scheuermann records, 'that the English could not do us a better favour than wanting to repeat endeavours like the battle of Fromelles more often.'[72]

Chapter Fourteen

THE AFTERMATH

The sandbags were splashed with red, and red
were the firesteps, the duckboards, the bays.
And the stench of stagnant pools of the blood
of heroes is in our nostrils even now.[1]
Private Jimmy Downing, 57th Battalion

MORNING, 20 JULY 1916, FROMELLES, BLISS WAS IT IN THAT DAWN TO BE ALIVE – AND SURPRISING

With the first rays of dawn on this tragic morning, many of those wounded who could still crawl had been at least able to get their bearings – by keeping the rising sun to their right, they must be able to get back to their own trenches – and now, in full light, the flow of men plopping over the parapet back whence they had started early yesterday evening becomes a bloody flood.

There is a groan, a long and agonising moan, an expiration of breath in one last, massive effort and then they heave themselves over the top and tumble down to the floor of the trenches below, inevitably landing on other appallingly wounded men who have preceded them.

And, of course, once the sun had chased away the gentle cloak of night, the true horror of the situation had been revealed for the first time. The battle now well over, hundreds of men still lie there, many missing limbs, some the tops of their skulls, others fearfully shot through the abdomen, with their intestines spilling through their bloodied hands and into the mud. Elsewhere there are simply body parts – an arm, a leg, a head – pieces of soldiers who have been blown to bits by a direct mortar hit the night before.

'The sight of our trenches that next morning is burned into my brain,' Corporal Knyvett would recount. 'Here and there a man could stand upright, but in most places if you did not wish to be exposed to a sniper's bullet you had to progress on hands and knees. In places the parapet was repaired with bodies – bodies that but yesterday had housed the personality of a friend by whom we had warmed ourselves. If you had gathered the stock of a thousand butcher-shops, cut it into small pieces and strewn it about, it would give you a faint conception of the shambles those trenches were.'[2]

Another officer records seeing 'dead bodies lying in all directions, just as they had fallen, some without heads, other bodies torn about minus arms or legs, or pieces cut clean out of them by shells'.[3] Everywhere, men gaze at the living and dead, to determine who of their friends has lived and who has died. 'One did not ask the whereabouts of brother or chum. If we did not see him, then it were best to hope that he were of the dead.'[4]

Oh, the humanity. See now, this white-faced lad, stripped to the waist and with a hole in his side that you could put both fists into. He is being led along the trenches towards some stretcher-bearers – 'body-snatchers' in Digger parlance – who might be able to take him for help when he tells his would-be saviour, 'I think I'll spell a minute, it's all going dark.'[5]

With which, he sits down, and dies.

More fortunate, on another stretcher passing, is Sergeant John Ridley. Despite the terrible shrapnel wound to his head, he has survived the night and been helped from No-Man's Land by three soldiers, only to collapse on the first free stretcher he finds. He is hurt, but will survive.

Others who can still walk make their way back, after the long night, to the rear areas, which sees them walking past the men of the artillery.

'How did you go, mate?' one of them asks one of the soldiers, who looks like he has spent the night in hell.

'You so and sos,' the bloke replies. 'You pasted us all the way there and pasted us all the way back.'[6]

—

The worry now, as German shells start to pound into Australian lines with frightening accuracy, is that Fritz will launch a counter-attack. If he does, the Australians are ill-equipped to stop it, as all of the 5th Division's front is now held by only three half-battalions. One of these, from the 8th Brigade – having been in the worst of the fighting – is reported to be 'absolutely unnerved' and 'unfitted for further resistance'.[7]

The only way to forestall a possible attack is to lay down more artillery on the German lines in turn, and McCay orders exactly that, with both front-lines again taking a fearful pounding.

—

More toast or croissants, *monsieur*?

In the French village of Contay, where Charles Bean is billeted, he is just having his breakfast in the restaurant at his hotel when the English officer beside him comments rather blithely, 'The 5th Division had their little show last night.'[8]

They *what?*

'The 5th Division had their little show' is military jargon for the 5th have launched their attack. Bean is stunned. He *must* get there as quickly as possible, and is at least able to borrow the car and driver of General Brudenell White, the very man who said he 'hated these unprepared little shows'[9] and feared for the consequences.

The correspondent is now filled with dread as he races north through the French countryside, the driver leaning on his horn, trying to clear soldiers, farmers, cows and other traffic out of his way.

—

And now, in the forward trenches at Fromelles, slowly moving among the shattered remnants of the proud unit that the 15th Brigade had been, picking his way through the equally shattered remains of what had been sandbagged trenches but is now just detritus and dead men, is a tall, distinguished figure. Yes, his back is still straight in the military manner, but his shoulders are slumped like one bearing a great weight – responsibility, or grief, or both. It is, of course, Pompey Elliott, and he is beyond being merely devastated, as he has 'a word for a wounded man here, a pat of approbation for a bleary eyed tired digger there',[10] shaking hands with those who still have hands. In truth, the Hun has a barrage on at the time, and both shrapnel and bullets are still whizzing by, but Elliott doesn't flinch. Against what these men have been through overnight, it just wouldn't be right.

Horrified by what he is seeing, haunted that he could have done something more to prevent it – for he had clearly foreseen exactly this catastrophe but had been unequal to the task of persuading the Generals to call it off – he is trying to provide some solace for survivors but is also in the unaccustomed position of pleading for their understanding. 'Don't blame me for this,' he begs soldier after soldier, 'this is wrong, it's not my fault.'[11]

'[I] will always have before my eyes the picture of Pompey, standing at the mouth of VC Avenue, the morning after Fromelles,' one Digger would recall, 'tears streaming down his face, shaking hands with the pitiful remnants of his Brigade.'[12]

He keeps moving, trying to tell as many as he can. '[He] was there with tears running down his face,' one 15th Brigade Lieutenant would recount, 'apologising for the mix up . . . He was very, very upset . . .'[13]

As soon as Elliott comes across Lieutenant Stewart Smith of the 59th, crawling along as he drags his shattered leg behind him, the General insists he receives help from stretcher-bearers. 'There are thousands behind me who can't even crawl,' the ashen-faced Lieutenant Smith replies. 'Let the bearers get them first.'[14]

Spotting an officer friend, Elliott calls out to Captain Bill Trainor of the 57th Battalion, 'Good God, Bill, what's happened to my brigade?'

There is no answer. There can be no answer.

Still, however, Elliott labours for *some* control, and tries not to trip over all the dead and wounded men, keeping his rough composure right up until the moment he gets back to his advanced Brigade HQ in the company of his Signal Officer, Captain John Donald Schroder, at which point there is no further need. No two assault battalions have suffered more in the last 24 hours than the ones he sent in, the 59th and the 60th. Though he does not know it yet, and has only a rough idea of the contours of the catastrophe, the tragic truth is that, of the 1750 men of those two battalions who have gone forward, no fewer than 1452 are dead or wounded.

Have responsibility for that? It would send a man spare.

As Schroder would recount, once arrived, General Elliott, the famed hard man of the 5th Division, 'went straight inside, put his head in his hands, and sobbed his heart out'.[15] Yes, strong man, hard man that Pompey Elliott is, he weeps like a five-year-old who has just witnessed the death of his parents, his huge, racking sobs shaking his whole body. For, somehow, this is worse, as if he has witnessed the death of hundreds of his sons, sons for whom he had been responsible.

Ah, but out in the trenches, Brigadier-General McCay is made of sterner stuff, as he also moves among the troops, with Brigadier-General Tivey. 'They'll get used to it,' McCay says repeatedly, his jaw set.[16]

Spying Major Alexander Murdoch of the 29th Battalion's D Company, Tivey asks him how his men had fared, at which point Murdoch cries out, 'Fall in D Co. along the duckboards!'

Once the men fall in, Major Murdoch can't help but notice one man standing all alone. 'Fall in, fall in,' the exasperated Major cries, 'what are you standing there for?'

'Oh,' the man replies. '*I'm* fifteen platoon.'[17]

The faithful account of one soldier who witnesses this is that, at this point, everybody bursts out laughing. They really *are* a weird mob, these Australians.

—

General Haking? He remains in his farmhouse in Sailly-sur-la-Lys, receiving preliminary reports and, of course, readying to write a report of his own for his superiors, Generals Monro and Haig. Not that he expects any problems. There haven't been any problems for him in the last 20,000 casualties, so why would there be any trouble now? He has no recorded regrets that the operation has gone ahead, and has no doubt where the blame lies.

For, speaking of lies, in the coming official report he would begin by noting that the support supplied by him, Sir Richard Haking, for the assaulting battalions was more than fine, and his plan had been equally good: 'The artillery preparation was adequate. There were sufficient guns and sufficient ammunition. The wire was properly cut, and the assaulting battalions had a clear run into the enemy's trenches.'

And he would further attest that the Australian infantry had been gallant in its attack, but then gets to the nub of it. '[The Australians] were not sufficiently trained,' he insists of a division that had only been in the line for two days, but he had still sent forward 'to consolidate the ground gained'. As to the British soldiers, they were, sadly, much worse. 'The 61st Division,' Haking takes aim, 'were not sufficiently imbued with the offensive spirit to go in like one man at the appointed time.'

All up, he can't help but feel he has been let down. He is convinced the same exercise should be tried again, with much the same resources, just better trained next time. 'From my experience in this attack I am quite convinced that with two good Divisions we can carry and hold the line whenever it is desired. The same number of guns and rounds of ammunition being again used for the purpose.'

After all, everything possible had been done for these two; it is just they weren't up to it. 'With two trained Divisions,' the British General sniffs, 'the position would have been a gift after the artillery bombardment; with these two new divisions there was a good chance of success but they did not attain it.'[18]

In conclusion? 'I think the attack, although it failed, has done both Divisions a great deal of good . . .'

R. Haking
Lieut.-General.
Commanding XIth Corps[19]

Out in No-Man's Land in this aftermath of the battle, the fact that the attack has done the 5th Division, in particular, 'a great deal of good' is not immediately apparent – most particularly out in front of the 15th Brigade's position. There, occasionally, the horrified soldiers in the front-line can see a bloody arm wave in the hope of succour, only to sometimes – but not always – attract furious fire from the Germans, at which point the bodies are riddled with bullets and lie still.

There are *hundreds* of them, 'everywhere raising their limbs in pain or turning hopelessly, hour after hour, from one side to the other'.[20] Eventually, most of the wounded learn to lie absolutely still, as the sun now rises, beats down upon them and begins to suck whatever life remains out of them.

In front of the British brigade's lines, the scene is nearly as devastating. Through the night, trenches have been dug into No-Man's Land in the hope they would act as communication trenches to the new British positions. Needless to say, these trenches are now completely filled with the dead and dying, as the men retreating have inevitably gravitated to them for shelter – while German prisoners also taking shelter have to be kicked out of the way.

—

Where is he? What is happening?

Is someone pulling his leg?

He is Private Bill Barry; he knows that much. And last night, at about 10 pm, he had been in a trench with two soldiers screaming for their mothers as shells had fallen all around, and the next thing he knew everything had gone black. Until now. And even now it is still pretty black, either because he is only just conscious, or it is just dawn, or both – he is not sure.

Oh.

No.

Someone, a German soldier, really *is* pulling his leg, no doubt checking to see if there is any response, if he is dead, still alive, or perhaps just passed out. Barry pretends to be the last, keeping his eyes tightly closed, and in any case soon genuinely passes out once more through loss of blood, before again coming to.

And who is this?

It is some Australian soldiers, shorn of all their weaponry. They have noticed his eyes are open and tell him that they have all been taken prisoner. At least the ones who are still alive.

What the Germans appear to be doing now is working out who is alive and who is dead by bumping them with their rifle butts or, worse, sticking bayonets into their flesh to see if there is any reaction. Those who are dead mostly have their boots removed for the Germans' own future use – before being buried, usually in abandoned trenches or freshly excavated pits. Some Germans 'rat' the bodies of prized items such as wristwatches, binoculars, Woodbines, a flask of whisky.

It is the beginning of a process that will take a week. The way Barry would tell it ever afterward, as soon as one German soldier realised he was alive, the Hun pointed his rifle at him and appeared to want to shoot, only for one of his officers to bark a few guttural commands at him, at which point he went away. It is this officer who tends Barry's wounds, putting a bandage around the terrible gash in his leg before beginning a light interrogation.

How many Australians in France?

Between three and five million, with conscripts yet to come, Barry lies through his teeth.

'You are a . . . volunteer, *korrekt?*'

'Yes.'

And now, for some reason, the officer becomes angry. 'You

Australians are bloody cowards,' he roars, in a curious interpretation of the word. 'We are not at war with you, but you came over here last night and [attacked us] while we always fight a long way off.'[21] The very thought of it so offends the officer that he now rises and barks something at some nearby German soldiers, who proceed to give Barry 'one of the worst beltings it was possible to give a man'.[22]

Again he lapses into unconsciousness.

(Such brutality to Australian prisoners of war, for all that, is rare, with most survivors later reporting that they had been treated exceedingly well. One captured and severely wounded Digger would tell of being evacuated from German lines, under heavy fire, by four German soldiers carrying him on a groundsheet slung between two poles. 'They carried me through a heavy barrage of our machine-gun fire. At places they had to crawl on their hands and knees, but never showed the slightest hesitation. They had "a bit of guts" about them – they were rare plucky men.'[23] The Commander of the 16th Bavarian RIR has seen this kind of thing so much he feels obliged to remind his men that they are only supposed to help their Anglo-Saxon counterparts 'once our own injured soldiers have been taken care of. I also remind you that captured soldiers, rather than the men of the 16th Bavarian Reserve Infantry Regiment, are supposed to carry injured Australian and English soldiers to the rear.')[24]

When he comes to, Barry realises he is 'sitting on the edge of a hole about forty feet long, twenty feet wide and fifteen feet deep and into this hole the dead were being thrown without any fuss or respect'.[25] Mercifully, a quick cry from Bill Barry alerts the Germans that he is alive, and he is rushed to the nearest German medical station.

Meanwhile, the burying of the dead goes on. While the Germans will give their own fallen a Christian burial, in the case of the enemy dead the most important thing – for fear of the stench, and the disease their dead bodies might spread – is to extract what information they can from their discs, papers and so forth, and then just get them beneath the ground and covered up as quickly as possible. Sometimes, this can be done by burying them in abandoned trenches. Other times, whole new pits must be dug. Oberst Julius Ritter von Braun records, 'Plenty of care is needed for the salvation of the fallen and the orderly determining of their identity, so is the recording of their private belongings by officers and by the *Kompanie-Feldwebel*, Company Sergeant Major.'

There is much to be done. 'The large graveyard of Beaucamps must be enlarged significantly again . . . [And] for the fallen enemies, mass graves behind the *Fasanen-Wäldchen*, Little Pheasant Forest [must be] built.'[26] The latter is at a pleasant spot where the pheasants flock, some 1000 yards back from the German lines.

As to those 400 Australian soldiers captured in the battle, the German interrogation goes on, and it is . . .

Sonderbar, sehr sonderbar. Curiouser and curiouser.

For in that interrogation, the Germans have discovered talk of an interesting Australian unit, which had recently been disbanded, or at least many of the captured soldiers had originated in this unit before joining the infantry. It is something called '*die australische leichte Kavallerie*, the Australian Light Horse . . .'[27]

'These people had mastered the art of horsemanship from their early youth,' the intelligence report runs, 'and wait eagerly on the chance of a cavalry charge in the service of their motherland. They are "Bushmen" through and through, and ride only the finest horses.'[28]

The interrogators also work out that, when it comes to '*Gallipolikämpfer*', veterans of the Dardanelles campaign, the 8th Brigade seems to have one in eight, and the 14th Brigade one in four. It is easy to calculate as they have taken 200 prisoners from both brigades, and there is plenty of information. Alas for the 15th Brigade, it is close to impossible to work out, as they shot nearly all of them before they got to the wire, and there have been only two men, both 'dangerously wounded',[29] taken prisoner: Second-Lieutenant John 'Jack' Charles Bowden and Private Henry Hodson. Bowden has already succumbed to his injuries. He had been a married, 35-year-old former bank manager, they will ascertain, while Hodson is a bricklayer, and both are from Victoria.

Hodson – who is shot through both legs, the shoulder and the head, likely from machine-gun fire – is quickly transferred to a clearing station where he can receive expert medical care from German Army doctors.[30] Bowden's body, meanwhile, is searched for information, and all relevant details are recorded, before it is laid aside for mass burials with all the others, while they continue to search other bodies brought in for more information.

Most interestingly of all, despite all the efforts at security, the Germans do find an order on a dead Australian officer:

```
... The objective will be strictly limited to
the enemy's support trenches and no more.
This order is to be read to all troops taking
part in the attack.
R. Haking[31]
```

So much for the loss of so many lives convincing the Germans that this was all part of a full-blown attack.

—

Finally, one man, Private William Miles, a 36-year-old Boer War veteran from the 29th Battalion, can bear the suffering of his mates out there no more. Donning a Red Cross brassard, he heads out into that part of No-Man's Land in front of the 8th Brigade lines not under shell fire, looking for his officer, Captain Kenneth Mortimer, whom he believes lies wounded there. Of course, it is difficult to get far without coming across many other terribly wounded men, whom he helps the best he can, and he is going about his business providing succour where he can, always fearing a German bullet will take him down.

One man who has taken a bullet to the stomach wants water, and Miles has to explain that water would do him more harm than good, but he at least cuts his haversack off. The next man has taken a bullet to the balls, and they have swollen terribly. The fellow borrows Miles's knife to cut his pants open but, even though in horrifying agony, won't let Miles touch him. The private moves on and is soon stunned to see, from the cover of the enemy trenches, a German officer beckoning him to come forth. Carefully, Miles does exactly that.

'What are you supposed to be doing?' the German asks in amazingly good, if heavily accented, English.

'Tending wounded men, giving them a drink and cutting their equipment off so they will lie more comfortable till we can get them in,' Miles replies, evenly.

'You may be laying wires, this is not the "usages" of war.'

'Oh, yes it is, the Red Cross is always allowed to work unmolested.'[32]

'What did you pick up just now?'

'A pair of field glasses.'

'It might have been a bomb.'

'I'll show you.'

'Don't put your hand in your pocket, put your hands above your head.'[33]

As Miles stands there, this officer picks up his field telephone and has an animated conversation in his own language, with the private picking up words here and there – '. . . *der Soldat* . . . *aus Australien* . . . *die Offiziere* . . .' – while other German officers arrive with cameras and proceed to direct Miles to turn every which way while they take photographs.

Finally, the original officer puts the phone down. Before he can speak, Miles asks permission to lower his arms. The officer laughs in a most friendly fashion and says, 'I forgot, your arms must be aching,' before following up with another question. 'What are those decorations you are wearing?'

'*La guerre Afrique*,' Miles replies unthinkingly, which gives the German officer pause.

'Speak English, old chap. You were through the African war, were you?'

'Yes, sir.'

'What is your rank?'

'Only a private, sir.'

'Well, I want you to go back to your lines and ask an officer to come over here and we will have a "parliament" and see if we can arrange about collecting the wounded. Will you come back and let me know what they say?'[34]

Miles wastes no time. It is a chance, a *chance*, for hundreds of his Australians to be saved after all.

As Private Miles approaches his front-line, one of his fellow Diggers fires off a rifle. Miles yells out, 'Tell that bloody fool to stop shooting, I've got to go back yet.'[35]

Hearing this, one of the officers yells at the men, 'I will shoot any man who fires again!'[36] No more shots are fired, and the word is quickly passed down the line to absolutely cease fire. There is a job o' work to be done, and it may save hundreds of their men still out there. Slowly, soldiers and officers poke their heads up over the parapet, to learn the state of play. There is excitement at the news. A chance, a real chance?

But which officer will accompany him back? Major Alexander Murdoch of the 29th Battalion quickly steps forward. Taking the fabric from a red cushion that has, bizarrely, survived in the trenches to this point and attaching it to a wooden board covered with newspapers, Murdoch quickly improvises a Red Cross flag. Then, slowly and surely, he rises and jumps over the top to where Miles is still standing in No-Man's Land, and the pair walk purposefully towards the German lines. Both men are laden with water bottles, which – watched carefully by the soldiers of both sides – they hand out on the way to wounded comrades.

On their arrival at the German lines – still, to their partial amazement, *unshot* – a brief conversation ensues between Major Murdoch and an 'immaculately dressed'[37] Bavarian Lieutenant, the Australian formally asking for a truce. The German replies that he does not have the authority himself, but he is happy to make a phone call to his Divisional HQ.

The Australian troops will be able to come out of their trenches and clear their half of No-Man's Land, while the Germans clear their own half. It is proposed that Murdoch in turn will go to seek official agreement from his own superiors and, if settled, as a measure of good faith, will be taken behind German lines with a blindfold, there to remain until all the wounded are gathered in.

His heart soaring, Major Murdoch instantly agrees to the proposal. The Australians and Germans salute each other, and then Major Murdoch and Private Miles walk back, again handing out whatever water they can to the wounded.

With feverish anticipation, once back in Australian lines, Murdoch lifts the field telephone to talk to General McCay at 5th Divvie HQ.

The answer is quick to come back.

No.

'G.H.Q. orders and all subordinate orders,' McCay will later insist, 'were extremely definite, to the effect that no negotiations of any kind, and on any subject, were to be had with the enemy . . . In view of the definiteness of G.H.Q. orders, as soon as my headquarters became aware of the tentative arrangement, orders were at once sent to put an end to the "truce".'[38]

(And McCay really does have the full backing of Generals Monro and Haking in his decisions. While Haig has allowed truces 'on certain exceptional occasions',[39] he most certainly does not want what amounts to fraternisation becoming a regular event, and presumably the decision of his Generals on this occasion is that 1500 wounded Australian soldiers is not exceptional enough. It will be the later expressed view of the official British historian, Brigadier-General Sir James Edmonds, in a letter to Bean, that there were lots of unofficial truces in such circumstances as this, and the mistake the Australians made at Fromelles was to ask for permission from their Divisional Commander, instead of just going ahead on the quiet.)

Major Murdoch is stunned, devastated, scarcely crediting such callousness. Are they really going to leave hundreds of their men out there, boiling in the sun, their life-blood ebbing out of them, all because some British officers think it is not quite the done thing? His view, and the view of many, is that as this is an Australian operational matter, to do with Australian soldiers, what the Englishmen in GHQ think about it is neither here nor there. But, the decision is taken. Military protocol trumps all of national loyalty, human decency, common sense and *mercy*, mother. Even when Major Murdoch does later arrange a partial truce with the German officer opposite, and some more wounded soldiers are retrieved, it is called off after two hours, following orders from higher up, and his men know 'Major Murdoch is in trouble'.[40]

In the meantime, once McCay's decision becomes known, officers in the line have no choice but to stop stretcher-bearers from doing their work.

What makes the matter all the more appalling is that there is no compelling reason of war to leave men out there to die. For just look to the right, where the 61st Division stretcher-bearers are gathering in their own men, completely untroubled by the Germans. Their truce has been straightforward – or at least the rejection of it has been delayed, allowing them crucial time to retrieve the men they can – and, clearly, Major-General Colin Mackenzie has had no concerns that he will get into trouble with his superiors. He is just following common sense.

But McCay will not budge,[41] and nor will any of his superiors.

'One account,' Norm Nicolson records in his diary, 'says that [the] General . . . did not approve of the Armistice as they were only Australians who were lying out there – common fellows, and not numbers of the British aristocracy or upper class. At any rate, he had no sympathy with these poor wretches, victims of his own incapacity, and ordered that, as it would look like an admission of defeat [for the truce to continue], that the Armistice was to cease, our men to be called in and then shots fired over the Germans' heads to warn them to go back.'[42]

At least stretcher-bearers can continue to go out for a certain distance along the communication saps that had been dug into No-Man's Land, for it is here that many wounded have crawled, to drop over the edge.

One of the 8th Field Ambulance stretcher-bearers, Private David Mason, is shocked from the first with the 'dead and wounded lying all over the place', but he does his best, and keeps going until such times as 'I had to come in the ambulance [myself, for] our knuckles were skin and bone through hitting the sides of the sap coming out with wounded. This is a day I will never forget.'[43]

In the meantime, as roll calls are being taken among the survivors of the battalions – gathered on the road by their Brigade HQs – it is only now that the true catastrophic consequences of the battle are becoming apparent, though it is far from uniform. Oddly, the men of the British 61st Division have escaped relatively lightly, precisely for the fact that they had been decimated early, had lost heart for the battle and withdrawn – with just 1547 casualties all up, and 31 prisoners taken. (By far the worst affected unit is the 2/1st Bucks, which has lost 322 men.) For the Australians, alas, the fact that two of their three brigades actually had succeeded in capturing the German line had meant that they had fed ever more men into the battle, many of whom they had subsequently lost.

And *how* they had lost them, even among such 'Reserve Battalions' as the 15th Brigade's 58th . . .

For they are, for the most part, in the image of Major Hutchinson – now suspended on the German wire, riddled with bullets – valiantly dead. Of the two companies that had gone over the top with the courageous Major, some 400 strong, just 163 men are left, with all the rest casualties.

The 59th Battalion, which had attacked first, as the furthest Australian assault battalion on the right, has been all but wiped out. No fewer than 800 had gone forward, occasioning 695 casualties, of whom 20 are officers.

Yet nowhere is it worse than with the 59th's brother battalion, the 60th. This time the previous day, they had mustered 887 fine Australian soldiers, drawn from Melbourne and towns in country Victoria such as Glenorchy, Kamarooka and Rainbow. This morning, there are just 106 soldiers and one shattered officer left – Lieutenant Tom Kerr from Gippsland, who has survived only after many narrow escapes – to answer the roll call. So devastated are their ranks that, even though a lowly Lieutenant, Kerr will be acting Battalion Commander for the next two days.

The 32nd Battalion is the worst hit of the 8th Brigade, with 701 Diggers and 17 officers unable to answer roll call, while the 31st Battalion has lost the services of 528 Diggers and 16 officers.

As to the 14th Brigade, they are marginally less devastated, but it is close. The 53rd Battalion soon lists 601 soldiers and 24 officers as casualties, while Lieutenant-Colonel Walter Cass's 54th Battalion counts 521 soldiers and 19 officers gone or maimed.

Among the survivors of the 55th Battalion – which has 339 casualties – on this morning is the dazed and exhausted Bert Bishop, collapsed on the ground among his comrades well back from the front-line, as a field kitchen arrives with hot stew and tea and proceeds to dole them out to these men, grown ten years older overnight, staring into the distance with those thousand-yard stares.

A Sergeant is reading out the names in their 'muster parade', and every now and then a desultory hand is raised to indicate the named soldier's presence, but sometimes the Sergeant reads a dozen names without any response whatsoever. Other times, a soldier calls out in response to an unanswered name, 'He's dead, Sergeant. I saw his body in the German trench just before we came back,' and the Sergeant makes a note. No one wants to meet anyone else's look, though occasionally there is a collective sharp intake of breath when it is confirmed that a particularly beloved figure from the battalion is missing, presumed dead. All up, they have 330 casualties.

Across all Australian battalions, there are no fewer than 'twelve sets of brothers . . . and two sets of fathers and sons'[44] who have been killed.

But now a soldier tells Bert that their battalion's machine-gunners can be found in yonder barn, across that field. Bert heads off towards it when he sees a man in the distance and stops. The loping way he walks. The way he kind of nods his head from side to side as he does so. The way his arms move in that oh so distinctive fashion. It is not that Bert has ever consciously noticed these things before, but by God he notices them now, and he knows his man. That is Robbo. And he is *alive*!

The two come together in the middle of the field, and Robbo is every bit as relieved to see him.

'Thank God,' he says, putting his hand on young Bert's shoulder, 'you're okay. Have you heard anything . . . yet?'

Oh . . . *God*. Is this it?

'I've heard nothing, Robbo,' Bert quavers. 'But I feared something was going to happen to Ray.' Bert can sense what is coming. In all the time he has known this hardened 30-year-old veteran, he has never seen Robbo like this, his voice choking, his eyes teary.

'It happened, Bert. Can you take it?'

'I've got to. Tell me, Robbo.'

'I guess when you were last over . . . you could see how difficult our set-up was . . .'

Robbo then tells him the story. The desperation of the situation. The Germans closing in from all sides. The request for volunteers and how Ray had heroically put his hand up to be one of them. How the other bloke who had volunteered had been shot, as had Ray . . . but he had kept throwing his grenades regardless. And now, the last part does not come easily to Robbo, but he has to tell it as it happened.

He'd got Ray back into the trench, and he was still alive, but it was really grim. Ray had blood pouring from several wounds, and his breathing had a strange rattle to it, but he was still alive . . .

So what could he do with the Germans closing fast? He had to make a run for it himself – they had successfully got the precious Lewis gun away, and the others were making their stand back in the Old German Line – so he had done so. But there is no doubt about it. 'He was dying fast,' Robbo finishes. 'I believe he was dead as I ran from dozens of Germans closing in.'[45]

For now, there is not a lot more to say. The two take their leave of each other, and Bert walks back to his billet, thinking of Ray, of Auntie Alice, of Margaret, the girl back on her family property, 'Tyrone', whose photo Ray carried in his wallet, the one he was sweet on.

Ray . . . dead? Can Ray really be *dead*, out there in No-Man's Land?

It is almost too much to take in all at once, though other mates of Ray's soon give Bert the same story, even reckoning 'he deserved a V.C. for it'.[46] And now he's likely dead.

Such a ghastly thing, on such a beautiful day. Near his billet at the barn, there is long green grass liberally sprinkled with buttercups, and Bert sinks down into it, hoping that after his wide-awake night, sleep might take him now to give him some relief, but it is no use. All he can think of is Ray. And then he hears the soft pad of footsteps coming through the long grass. It is one of his other mates from the platoon, Chris.

'So there you are,' he says. 'There's nothing doing. I want you to drink this, then have a sleep. I'll come for you if necessary.'

Chris gives him a mess tin of hot tea so heavily laced with rum it might be more proper to say it is rum lightly laced with tea, but in any case Chris stays with him until he is sure that Bert has drunk every drop – the first time in his whole life he has had this kind of alcohol. 'Now, you lie down and sleep,' Chris says,[47] and pats him on the shoulder reassuringly before heading off.

Again, Bert lies back, this time really starting to loosen his terrified grip on consciousness as first his belly warms to the rum and then some kind of loosening from it seeps into his soul. But that loosening does not first bring sleep; it brings tears, welling up from deep inside, which quickly turn into great, racking sobs, the first time he has cried in years. They grip him, they shake him, they course through him. He cries till he can cry no more and then still cries some more until . . . at last . . . comes sleep.

—

Among the Germans, there is that curious combination of joy and mourning that shows up among soldiers through the ages after recording a great victory . . . where they have nevertheless lost many cherished comrades. Though their casualties are relatively small compared with the enemy's – they have around 2000 – the same cannot be said of the men who had the misfortune to face the 5th Division.

'Our losses are very high especially at the 3rd Battalion,' Julius von Braun would record of his men of the 21st RIR. 'They come to 7 officers and officer deputies . . . and 288 sergeants and troops dead; 8 officers and 377 men wounded; 1 officer and 94 men are missing, most of them are probably buried under the collapsed *Brustwehren*, parapets. Much higher are the losses of the enemy . . .'[48]

AFTERNOON, 20 JULY 1916, FROMELLES, AT LAST

At last, after a harrowing journey of 60 miles and several hours, Charles Bean arrives before the Fromelles battlefield, in the early afternoon, to scenes of devastation, the shattered remains of a once strong community just after the cyclone has hit, with human debris scattered to all parts.

'We've had an awfully rough passage,' the first man he comes across tells him.[49] One appalled look at the battlefield of No-Man's Land shows Bean just how bad it is, as German machine guns continue to chatter and 'the wounded can be seen crawling into shell craters by the river'.[50]

As quickly as Bean can, he brushes off the British press officers, who want to inform correspondents that the attack 'had succeeded in its object'.[51] For Bean's own summation is unwavering. 'That is not true – it is the opposite.'[52]

And he doesn't want to speak to press officers; he wants to speak to *real* officers, and the soldiers themselves. The first senior officer he gets to is 'poor old Tivey, [who] looked quite over done – with eyes like boiled gooseberries'.[53] A small red gash on Tivey's bottom lip also tells something of the anguish he is feeling as, likely, he's bitten his lip rather than cry out loud.

Never in his time, Tivey tells Bean, has he seen anything like the fire his men were subjected to the night before. And nor has anyone else. 'Men who were at Anzac,' he relates ruefully, 'said that the shellfire in Gallipoli was child's play to this.'[54]

By now, the reality of what has happened has even sunk in for General McCay, and the bravado of his previous assertion that morning, that 'they'll get used to it',[55] has faded somewhat. Bean finds McCay 'terribly depressed and overwrought'.[56] After a desultory conversation, where Bean delicately probes just what has occurred, the Australian correspondent asks to speak with Pompey.

McCay advises that after Elliott's sleepless night, the Commanding Officer of the 15th Brigade has returned to his tent to snatch a couple of hours' sleep, but that he, McCay, is happy to wake him up.

Elliott arrives shortly afterwards, looking for all the world like a fellow 'who had just lost his wife'.[57] Every bit as depressed and over-wrought as McCay, Elliott 'looked down and could hardly speak'.[58] Still, the General does what he can, trying to explain to Bean just what kind of fire his men had been facing. Elliott believes that, beyond all the shell fire, 'there were five machine-guns in that salient firing at them'.[59]

Bean continues to take notes, as ever gathering whatever informa-tion he can. He is astonished, appalled, that Haking can have sacrificed '7,000 troops in a night for so small a result'.[60] Ideally, he will file some kind of story for the Australian and British newspapers within a couple of hours. The question is, just how much of this will he be able to get past the censors?

Some things, he knows, he won't be able to get into the paper, but he can at least get them down in his diary: 'The 61st Division, they said, were rather second rate territorials. Why <u>do</u> they put second rate terriers in with our men on a job like this?'[61] While appalled at the death and destruction, Bean is stunned by the courage of the rescuers. 'The sight of the wounded lying tortured and helpless in No-Man's-Land, within a stone's throw of safety but apparently without hope of it, made so strong an appeal that more than one Australian, taking his life in his hands, went out to tend them.'[62]

In all that confusion, the potential for both extraordinary humanity and terrible tragedy is manifest – and, on one occasion, both are dis-played. That mid-afternoon, from out of No-Man's Land, two German soldiers suddenly appear. Men reach for their rifles, but . . .

But wait! They're carrying something. A stretcher. And there is a badly wounded Australian soldier on it! Arriving at the Australian lines, the two German soldiers gently lay the wounded soldier down, salute the Diggers to whom they have been handing him over and then turn on their heels and begin to walk back across No-Man's Land.

Suddenly, two shots ring out. Both Germans drop, killed by other Diggers further along the line who have no idea of what has just occurred, but have seen German uniforms and acted accordingly.

—

Now in the late afternoon, it is Chris who comes to wake Bert Bishop. No urgency; there is no more battle to be had. But tea is on.

Bert rises from the green grass, slowly, carefully, still entirely racked by both grief and exhaustion.

'You're quite a few years older than you were this time yesterday,' Chris says.

After a 'tuppa tea', it is time for Bert to do something that he has been dreading. He must find his other cousin, Billy, and tell him of Ray's death. Knowing his platoon to be only a few hundred yards away, he heads off. Inside the tent he's directed to, he immediately recognises one of Billy's mates, who in turn recognises him.

'You're the bloke,' says this fellow slowly and carefully, 'who called on us that night at Moascar after the desert march, aren't you? You and he were cousins?'

With an apprehensive nod of the head, chilled to his core – for the bloke has used the past tense '*were* cousins' – Bert indicates he is one and the same.

'Come outside.'

The bloke explains what happened. They'd been in the first wave of the 54th Battalion to go out. He'd been right beside Billy when a shell had exploded nearby and a piece of shrapnel had hit him in the chest. 'I couldn't stay with him, of course, but from the glimpse I had I would say he was badly hurt. Making enquiries this morning I learned that he was brought in later, and was evacuated. I know no more.'[63]

But at least he is still alive, and that is something, a rock to clutch on to in the flood of grief that now threatens to carry Bert away.

Alas, it matters little, as only a short time later Bert learns that Billy died of his wounds in hospital, and that he, Bert, is the last of the three Bishop cousins still alive.

And now a message comes, that he must report to Battalion HQ.

Arriving, Bert is told peremptorily to go into a small building over the road, where he finds the Battalion Quarter-Master working his way through a whole pile of packs – those of the men who didn't make it and will never be able to open these packs again.

'There's a pack here. Name of Bishop. He was a relative of yours?'

'Yes . . . my cousin.'

'Would there be any likelihood of any personal effects being in the pack which you would like to take?'

'I think there would be.'

'Open the pack and go through it. From here all packs go back to base stores for reissue.'[64]

Almost feeling like he is snooping in Ray's diary, as close as the two had been to each other, Bert unfastens the clips on Ray's pack and finds the usual soldier's kit of overcoat, socks, blanket and spare clothing. And there, at the bottom, are two packages filled with letters, a notebook or two and many photos . . . one of which flutters to the floor.

It is lovely Margaret – the girl Bert had been sweet on who, nevertheless, had chosen Ray. Bert's eyes fill with tears as he gazes at her, overwhelmed by so many wonderful memories and the thought of what the news will do to her, the grief it will cause her and indeed all of their friends, and all of the Bishop family.

Oh, he can see Margaret now, galloping along on the grand family property 'Tyrone', on her horse, Tirry, her lustrous hair rising and falling with every glorious bound. And now, suddenly, crashing into that image comes another one, of what must happen now.

It is Margaret, seated on that same log where Bert had seen her kissing Ray just before they had left to join the army. And now she near collapses in grief, her head on her arms and she is sobbing as if she will never stop, her whole body racked with an emotional pain that has completely gripped her. Tirry is nuzzling her lovely hair and whinnying softly, trying to comfort her, but it is to no avail. Still she keeps crying, Bert's heart is breaking for her, and for Ray, and . . .

And a voice crashes into his sad reverie. 'Hey, Dig,' the Quarter-Master asks plaintively, 'how much longer are you going to take? It's my mess-time.'

The old soldier looks over Bert's shoulder and sees the photo of Margaret, so lovely, so young, so innocent, so oblivious at this point to all the terrible things there are in this world. 'What a lovely girl,' he says softly, obviously impressed. 'May I have a closer look?'

Picking the photo up, he examines her image closely. 'Was she a friend of your cousin?'

'Yes.'

'Have you a picture of your cousin?'

Bert takes his photo of Ray out of the pocket of his tunic and gives it to the Quarter-Master, who places it side by side with that of Margaret on the table. 'Two kids – two splendid Aussie kids,' says he, sadly. 'Were they engaged? How old were they?'

'They were each nineteen. They were sweethearts.'

The Quarter-Master hands the photos back and tells Bert to take all the time he needs.

'But it's your mess-time,' Bert says.

'My mess-time? It doesn't matter at all. Those two poor kids . . .'[65]

——

Those many poor kids.

Beyond the stretcher-bearers trying to impose some order on the dead and dying, the other key group are the Army Chaplains, many of them delivering the last rites, offering prayers and solace, and – most importantly for future reference – gathering information, as they accompany burying parties. Following instructions from the Adjutant-General, before the dead are buried, the Chaplains consult the identification discs that have been removed from the bodies and 'make a careful note of the names of those whom they bury in communal graves. Each grave will be marked by a piece of wood or anything suitable and on this will be written the Chaplain's initials and a number'.[66]

Those details are then passed on to the Graves Registration Unit, as the first steps in a long process where deaths and grave sites are confirmed, and the families informed.

Meantime, at 4.30 pm, there is hell to pay when General McCay calls on Colonel Pope at 14th Brigade HQ, only to find him fast asleep and – McCay would stoutly maintain – drunk. It is an accusation that Colonel Pope would equally vigorously deny, pointing out that as he had not slept for the previous 34 hours before putting his head down at 3 pm, confident at last that no German counter-attack was under way, he was indeed very fast asleep, that was all. For the moment, McCay instantly relieves him of his command, and begins the process that will see him sent home to Australia in ignominy.

—

Well back from the German lines on this afternoon, the German War Correspondent Wilhelm Scheuermann is collating his notes, and composing the words that will shortly be appearing in the German press. Like Bean, he has spent the day talking to officers and soldiers, and has a fair feel for what occurred. The consensus is that the Australians had been particularly impressive.

'They mostly consisted of war volunteers,' he would report, 'among them were many rich farmers, strong, youthful men, who without doubt have attacked with great boldness and proven themselves as skilled and tough in close combat. The heavy losses that they suffered during the storm and the complete lack of success of their immense losses have a very shattering effect on them. They had expected certain victory and based their hopes especially on the superiority of their artillery, of which they had been told of a lot. The officers made a good impression and showed themselves superior to the average of the English officers in education and nobility. The bravery of the troops and their endurance stand without any doubt. They showed themselves also in the horror of the hand-grenade battle surely not as fearfully as the majority of the newly recruited English soldiers.'[67]

A correspondent of note, Scheuermann is simply mystified at the insanity of the whole attack, and is keenly aware that he is not alone. 'The endeavour of the English against Fromelles has caused people to shake their heads everywhere . . .' he writes in his battle report for his newspaper, the *Norddeutsche Allgemeine Zeitung*, 'maybe even the French and the English themselves, because one could not imagine what the English wanted to do with it . . . The whole thing would appear somewhat mysterious, if we had not captured the English order of attack. From this it is clear that the English were of the opinion we'd pull our troops out of this front section to use them at the Somme. They wanted to prevent this, to hinder our forces and if possible to pull back reserves from the Somme. This plan did not work out for them at all, because the attacked Bavarian Division had fended off the superior force with this outstanding success, fully under their own power, without requesting a single gun from another position and even without needing the naturally made-ready reserves from the neighbour sections for even just one moment. Not one man and not one gun more have been used as scheduled from the start for the defence of this section.'[68]

As to the Australians, another German correspondent, George Querl, reports back to his readers, 'Sturdy lads, grown up with gold in all pockets, somewhat educated, sons of rich sheep-farmers, and heirs to the land . . . what once had brought their fathers to the wild colony lay in their expressions and eyes . . .'[69]

EVENING, 20 JULY 1916, FROMELLES, LIES, DAMNED LIES, AND OFFICIAL COMMUNIQUÉS

On this same devastating day, Charles Bean is nearly done. Having worked through the afternoon and into the early evening to write an article that will convey something of the devastation he has seen – while still passing the British censors – Bean races to Amiens, arriving at 8.15 pm, to send the story back to Australia. It is a close-run thing with those censors, but he does, in fact, manage to get the story through, which will, indeed, appear four days later in *The Sydney Morning Herald*, beneath a headline that Bean himself would never have chosen:

AUSTRALIANS ATTACK TRENCHES
TEMPORARY SUCCESS . . .
TAKE 200 PRISONERS

Yesterday evening, after a bombardment, an Australian force attacked the German trenches south of Armentières . . .

The Germans were ready for the attack and had managed to save a number of machine guns from the bombardment . . .

Our troops, in this attack, had to face shell fire which was heavier and more continuous than was even known in Gallipoli . . .

The manner in which they carried the operation through seems to have been worthy of all the traditions of Anzac. At least 200 prisoners were captured and several machine guns. Many Germans were killed. The losses amongst our troops engaged were severe.[70]

It is a job well done, Bean most particularly having successfully defined what had happened as an 'attack', not a mere 'raid', and most importantly recording the truth: the losses were 'severe'. For what else can you call nearly 2000 Australian soldiers killed in just fourteen hours?

True, the censor had knocked out one word, as '1st Army objected that there never was an *intense* bombardment'[71] – but it really is something, especially when put against other accounts and official responses.

As to the official communiqué from GHQ, however, it is the one picked up by most papers in Britain and indeed the English-speaking world:

Yesterday evening (Wednesday), to the south of Armentières, we carried out some important raids on a front of two miles. The Australians took part in the raids. About 140 Germans were made prisoners.[72]

In response, Bean is ropable. The chronicling in newspapers of blatant lies, worse still blatant lies put out by official channels, outrages his sensibilities. An 'important series of trench raids . . .' Really? It was an *attack*, a full-blown attack, and everyone knows it. 'What is the good of deliberate lying like that?' he writes in his diary. 'The Germans know it was an attack.'

Oh, but it doesn't stop there when it comes to outrageous official responses to the catastrophe. Most egregious is Haking's note to General McCay, which seeks to portray the whole attack – which he has conceived, prosecuted and championed all but to the bitter end – as a success:

I should be glad if you would convey to all ranks of the Division under your command my deep appreciation of the gallant and successful manner in which they carried the attack on the enemy's lines yesterday afternoon.

Officers and men displayed a fine spirit throughout the attack and drove back the enemy with true British vigour . . .

Although the division was unable to hold the position gained for a long time, the attack must have made a great impression on the enemy and fulfilled its main purpose which was to assist our Comrades who are fighting in the South and prevent the enemy from moving reserves away from our front in that direction. I wish you all a still more complete victory in your next attack and I hope that I shall be somewhere near it when it takes place.[73]

(Though Bean keeps his own counsel for now, the generally moderate and considered correspondent would be crisp in his condemnation of Haking in the *Official History* of the war, noting that 'it is difficult to conceive that the operation, as planned, was ever likely to succeed'.)[74]

———

Sir Douglas Haig – who has, after all, signed off the whole catastrophe, pushing it forward when even Haking had momentarily lost faith – also hails the 'success' of the action at Fromelles, for what else can he do? He sends his own cable to the commanding officers:

PLEASE CONVEY TO THE TROOPS ENGAGED LAST NIGHT MY APPRECIATION OF THEIR GALLANT EFFORTS AND OF THE CAREFUL AND THOROUGH PREPARATIONS MADE FOR IT. I WISH THEM TO REALISE THAT THEIR ENTERPRISE HAS NOT BEEN BY ANY MEANS IN VAIN AND THAT THE GALLANTRY WITH WHICH THEY CARRIED OUT THE ATTACK IS FULLY RECOGNISED.[75]

Once more, in the wake of the catastrophe, Haig is not particularly perturbed at the reports and is in little doubt where the problem lies, as he confides to his diary: 'The troops seem to have somewhat become disorganised. The reality of the fighting and shelling seems to have been greater than many had expected! So the experience must have been of value to all . . .'[76]

As to the leadership provided by his dear friend, Sir Richard Haking, Sir Douglas is not remotely concerned. This war can only be won by those prepared to attack at all costs, and, once again, Sir

Richard has shown that he can do that. Far from remove him from command as a butcher of men, Sir Douglas will shortly recommend him for a promotion, to take over an entire army, going from a Lieutenant-General to General.[77]

In any case, there is little time to focus on what went wrong at the moment, as so many other things are demanding Sir Douglas's attention. Not least of these is the forthcoming attack on Pozières. General Gough's view is that a division-sized attack of the Australians should go in, in the early hours of 22 July, at 1.30 am.

'I told him to go into all details carefully,' Sir Douglas writes in his diary that night, 'as 1st Australian Division had not been engaged [in France] before, and possibly overlooked the difficulties of this kind of fighting.'[78]

—

Right now, on the night of 20 July 1916 at Fromelles, those difficulties include having hundreds of men lying, dying, out in No-Man's Land, capable of being rescued and saved within minutes, if not for the brutal refusal to allow a truce. And yet, as soon as darkness falls, the attitude of the Australians in the front-line is clear.

For while Bean would put it prosaically, 'The horror of knowing that a mate – his living body the prey of flies and ants – is being slowly done to death within two minutes of the succour, to which, without military disadvantage, he could be brought, is less present to distant staffs than to officers and men in the line,'[79] the attitude of those men in the line could be put more succinctly:

Fuck McCay.

He may have refused to make a truce with the Germans, but that doesn't mean the survivors of the 8th, 14th and 15th Brigades are going to leave their wounded to their fate. For on this very night, dozens of men sally forth, crawling out to the spots where they have seen movement during the day, and helping whoever they find back to their trenches. In the words of Charles Bean, what follows is 'that magnificent tribute of devotion which the Australian soldier never failed to pay to his mates. For three days and nights, taking the chance of wounds and death, single men and parties continued to go out in answer to the appeal from No-Man's-Land.'[80]

As soon as dusk falls, four men in particular quickly move out into the lines in front of the 8th Brigade. They are Captain Frank Krinks and the three survivors of that early morning. They keep on keeping on, to bow to their vow, doing all possible to leave no one behind. And there's one now! Groaning, bleeding from his abdomen, they find Corporal Sydney Wells, still cruelly suspended on the barbed wire.

Gently they cut him down and get him on the stretcher, with a Novocastrian, John Wishart,[81] and Tommy Watts – a 19-year-old Sydneysider – taking a handle each of the rear end, and they quickly move back towards Australian lines.

A single shot rings out, and both Wishart and Watts fall. The bullet has been fired by a nervy Australian sentry who thought they might be Germans. It has gone through the neck of Johnny Wishart and into the head of Tommy Watts. Tommy is dead before he hits the ground; Johnny dies an agonising death a short time later.

Nearby, the younger brother of Captain Aubrey Liddelow, Roy, is also out looking for his sibling, when he is shot and badly wounded.

Such tragedies notwithstanding, the rescues go on. The general system, once the wounded are located, is not unlike the newly popular practice of surf life-saving back home. That is, you get the wounded bloke to climb onto your back, have him hold on for dear life, and then you just keep pushing yourself back to safety the best you can.

'It was no light work getting in with a heavy weight on your back,' one of the rescuers would explain, 'especially if he had a broken leg or arm and no stretcher bearer was handy. You had to lie down and get him on your back then rise and duck for your life with the chance of getting a bullet in you before you were safe.'[82]

And exactly that happens, many a time. 'Bearers sometimes endeavoured to apprise the enemy of the nature of their work by holding the stretchers over their heads,' Bean would record, 'but so many were wounded that they were eventually forbidden to go out by day . . .'[83]

It is not an exercise the British soldiers of the 61st Division are at all involved in. For one thing, they had far fewer men out in No-Man's Land to begin with. For another, their officers had organised a truce to get the men in. And for yet another, yes, many of them are having a champagne dinner . . .

Company Commander James Wyatt, of the 2/4th Battalion Gloucestershire Regiment, 183rd Brigade, 61st Division, records the occasion in his diary, an event marked with 'great joy', notwithstanding the fact that his battalion had had two officers killed and five wounded: 'We marched into [Estaires, two miles south of Sailly] by Coys independently and found our billets about 6.30 pm. Then we went to the "Hotel de Ville" and had a champagne dinner. It was not such an event for me of course as for the other fellows who had just escaped with their lives out of this rotten show . . . So you may imagine how those fellows enjoyed their dinner. The place was packed with people from all the Regts on the same track.'[84]

And let there be no doubt that the 61st Division's Commanding Officer, General Colin Mackenzie, is pleased with them. 'The Division has not only fought gallantly,' he will shortly address them all, 'but all ranks of every arm and service have carried out in the most exemplary and devoted manner, working every day and night an amount of work which has highly tested their endurance and discipline and merits my unqualified praise.'[85]

Pass the champers.

———

Back at Fromelles, just a few miles to the south-east, the rescuing goes on.

'This may be the last entry in this book,' Private Arthur Brunton writes in the diary he keeps for his wife, home in East Melbourne, 'for tonight after dark I go out between the lines to bring in the wounded. They have laid in No Man's Land all day. Fritz will probably fire upon us, though we will be unarmed. We drew lots who should go so that it was fair to everyone . . . And now I must bid my little wife farewell, perhaps for the last time, though I hope not. I will do my best.'[86]

Such brave ventures into No-Man's Land go on through the night, with no fewer than 300 badly wounded Diggers rescued, and they continue even beyond dawn.

Do the Germans shoot at them?

Not always. It is very much the luck of the draw whether Fritz draws a bead on you and fires, or whether, in the name of *Menschlichkeit*, humanity, they will allow badly wounded men another chance at life through the heroism of their mates. A blessedly heavy fog on this morning helps, as, though there is no official truce, it feels like the gods have voted for humanity, and a merciful German soldier can always claim he didn't see any stretcher-bearers.

21 JULY 1916 AND ONWARDS, FROMELLES, AN UNFORGETTABLE MOMENT

On this morning after the battle is over, Sergeant Simon Fraser, a 38-year-old farmer from Victoria, is with his mates from the 57th Battalion, carefully moving about in No-Man's Land, following one particularly agonised cry for stretcher-bearers, 'an appeal no man could stand against'. Searching for that voice, they are right up near the German entanglements of barbed wire when, praise the Lord, they find 'a fine haul of wounded'[87] and, with great difficulty, are able to bring them in.

Still, however, farmer Fraser is aware that none of these men is the source of that haunting cry he had heard, and so, once more risking life and limb, he heads out again.

This time, he finds him, 'a splendid specimen of humanity trying to wiggle into a trench with a big wound in his thigh'.[88] But he is a big bastard all right. All of 14 stone, and simply impossible to carry. Very quietly, desperately aware that, in this mist, sound carries as clearly as it does on water, Fraser gets the giant safely into an old trench and tells him to lie in silence, for he will be back for him shortly with stretcher-bearers. Then he hurries off.

Just an instant later, however, he hears it. It is like a whisper wafting in the mist, the struggling words of a man not far off breathing his last, but now singing out with the final bit of spirit he has in him:

Don't forget me, cobber...[89]

Fraser turns, and walks towards the voice.

There! Just 30 yards away is a badly wounded Digger. Quickly now, knowing that the mist will lift at any time, Fraser tells him he will be back, takes his bearings the best he can, and races back to his own trenches to get a stretcher and four volunteers, before they all head out once more.

There!

And there!

The stretcher-bears carry the huge man, while Fraser gets his 'cobber' onto his shoulders and struggles back to the Australian lines, in much the same way he used to be able to carry two bags of wheat on the farm back home.

Both men are saved.

Other sagas are more problematic, most particularly when the mist lifts and even the humane Germans can no longer maintain they see *nussink*. For, like the *Flying Dutchman*, there is one particular cove who keeps appearing and then disappearing. He is a blinded and dazed Australian officer who, every few hours, manages to rise from among the dead, stagger around looking for the Australian line, before sinking groundward once more. The Australians have tried everything to guide him, most particularly shouting '*This* way, this way, mate!'. And several brave souls have tried to race out and get him, only to be shot down themselves. Extraordinarily, the Germans have allowed it to go on, but on this afternoon, one sniper tires of the whole thing. Or perhaps he is showing mercy for a death that is inevitable. For the officer has no sooner risen to stagger about than a single shot rings out and the blinded Australian goes down, never to rise again.

Not far away, one Digger hiding in a shell hole likely hears the shot and stiffens. But the bullet is not for him. To his amazement, he is still alive. And so is his mate. For the last couple of days, the two have been lying doggo during the day and slowly crawling forward at night, living off the rations they take from their dead comrades. It is slow going, for his mate is badly wounded and has to be dragged, but this particularly resilient Digger won't leave him.

And so it goes, over the next few days, with great bravery shown by Diggers trying to save their mates.

On the second night, Corporal Hugh Knyvett goes out with some mates to a particular bridge that crossed the Laies, where the German machine guns had been able to focus much of their fire, causing nothing less than a small mountain of dead to be piled there. 'Not all were dead [though],' he would recount, 'for in some of the bodies that formed that pyramid life was breathing. Some were conscious but too weak to struggle from out that weight of flesh. Machine guns were still playing on this spot, and after we had lost half of our rescuing party, we were forbidden to go here again, as live men were too scarce.'[90]

Night after night, the rescues continue. '[We] carried till the mind refused its task and limbs sagged,' Private Jimmy Downing would recall, 'and always there were hundreds for whom each minute decreased the chances of life. Release came to very many of the stricken . . . [We] left the hopeless cases undisturbed for the sake of those whom the surgeons could save.'[91]

Many of the rescuers are stunned at the selflessness of the wounded they find. They discover legless men who have near bled out, who have gone for days and nights without food or drink, who have arms hanging by a thread of flesh, blinded men missing half their face, and men who hold their bowels in their hands, men whose faces are so badly shot away that when you try to give them a drink, 'it was literally impossible to decide where to put the water bottle' – and yet these men, as a rule, *still* direct them to blokes worse off than them.

Look in the drain, or among those bushes over there, they say. During the day, I heard a groan over there.[92]

—

For those in the Australian front-lines, their upset at the catastrophe and outrage at McCay's refusal to countenance a truce are compounded whenever the wind changes. When it is blowing from behind them, things are manageable, but when it comes from across No-Man's Land, 'the awful stench from the dead was unbearable. Men could not keep their food down and had to depend on the limited rum issue. Parties were sent out night after night with lime to cover the dead.'[93]

PART THREE

END GAME

This new force of ours is just realising – each man in
the infantry individually, for the first time in most
cases – that there is only one way out of this war for
an infantryman, and that is on his back; either sick,
wounded, or dead . . . There is no way out. They are
looking down the long road straight to the end.[1]
Charles Bean at Pozières

We French fight for our country, our ideals and our flag.
Australians appear to fight because they like to fight.[2]
A French observer of the Australians at Pozières

Chapter Fifteen

THE BATTLE OF POZIÈRES

On the 23rd July, my lads,
In the year 1916;
We charged for Pozières town, my lads,
Through hell on earth we'd been,
We took the trench, we took the wood,
At last we took the town,
The Germans could not throw us back,
Although they mowed us down,
The Germans could not throw us back,
Although they mowed us down.[1]

*Stanza 5 of song composed by Lance-Corporal Ben
Champion, A Company, 1st Battalion, AIF*

LATE MORNING, 21 JULY 1916, ALBERT, FIE, THE BATTLE IS NIGH

The car sweeping into the gracious, spacious grounds of this château on the edge of the town of Albert has been travelling hard all morning. No sooner has it come to a halt than out steps the lanky figure of Captain Charles Bean.

Still shattered by his experience at Fromelles the day before – he didn't sleep well the previous night, haunted by the thought of how many of his fellow Australians must still be out in No-Man's Land, dying – he is nevertheless determined *not* to miss out on the Australian attack going in at Pozières. He had left Fromelles at dawn.

Under the circumstances, it is understandable that his most urgent line of inquiry upon arrival is just when will the Pozières attack go in?

The answer to that question, as it happens, is being resolved in that château at the very time of Bean's arrival – a meeting is taking place within the quarters of the AIF's 1st Division's General, Sir Harold Walker.

For General Walker, the last three days have been tumultuous and anxiety-filled – enough to make his thinning red hair get thinner still, his light-ginger moustache bristle with rage and his blue eyes glaze over with fatigue. After being ordered by General Hubert Gough on 18 July to 'go into the line and attack Pozières tomorrow night!',[2] the two senior officers – General Walker and his Chief of Staff, Colonel Thomas Blamey – have been fighting a furious rearguard action since.

They had left that first meeting with Gough reeling, with Walker writing in his diary that night:

Scrappy & unsatisfactory orders from [Gough] – Hope I shall not be rushed into an ill-prepared operation, but fear I shall![3]

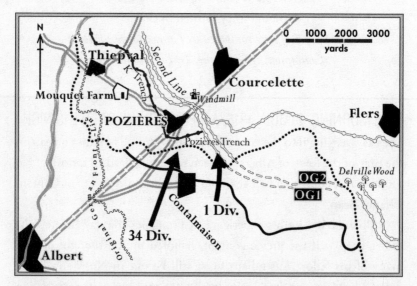

The British 34th and 1st Divisions on 14 July 1916

Those orders had rested on a telling background.

For General Haig, the resistance of Thiepval on the front-line and Pozières on the second line had been a problem for too long. In the first fortnight of the Battle of the Somme, attacks towards both villages had failed. Though some inroads had been made, denting the German line below Thiepval and allowing Allied forces to get closer to Pozières, Thiepval itself had remained strong as ever – a real problem. With the Somme forming one barrier on the right, the Thiepval barrier on the left means the Allies' 'gate' of possible penetration is a dangerously narrow one.

Clearly, the only way to get Thiepval is to come at it from a different angle, to push towards Pozières, secure its high ridge – marked by the Windmill site, which the second German trench system runs right in front of – and then advance north-west along that ridge, through a spot called Mouquet Farm, to take Thiepval from the rear.

And so, on the morning of 14 July, four more British divisions of the Fourth Army, under General Rawlinson, had gone in on a full-blown attack and captured 5000 yards of the German second line south-east of Pozières. Further advances brought them to within a few hundred yards of the village.

That evening, from 6 pm, the British artillery had lined up every heavy gun in the area and so pulverised Pozières that, before long, as the 34th Division's history would record, 'The whole place went up in brick dust, and when it was over no trace of a building could be seen anywhere. It was a wonderful sight, huge clouds of rose-coloured, brown, bluish black and white smoke rolling along together with flashes of bursts, the whole against a pale green-blue sky and bright evening sunlight.'[4]

And yet, *still* the Germans hadn't moved. No sooner had the big guns expended their ferocity than a furious, if dusty, Fritz emerged in force from his deep bunker – one of many in the basements of Pozières houses – and opened up on the advancing British soldiers.

Of course Fritz was still there in his hole, in obedience to General von Falkenhayn's policy of no retreat. Any ground lost had to be immediately recovered by counter-attack. Two days earlier, von Falkenhayn had shuffled his leadership and installed General Fritz von Below as Commander of the 1st Army, and that worthy had no sooner gained the position than issued Secret Army Order 575: 'I forbid the voluntary relinquishment of positions. Every commander is responsible for making each man in the Army aware about his determination to fight it out. The enemy must be made to pick his way forward over corpses.'[5]

Twice in the course of the attacks, the soldiers of the British Fourth Army had actually reached the first German defensive line, Pozières Trench, that lay at the base of the slopes leading up to the village, but on both occasions the German counter-attack had been so intense that the attackers had been thrown out once more.

Three days later, much the same thing happened when they had come across a particularly troublesome defensive point – a one-time sturdy stone home with stairs and a cellar, the whole thing reinforced with concrete and well-stocked with men, munitions and four machine guns. Most crucially, its second storey allows a great observation point over all those who would attack Pozières, and the men had consequently nicknamed it 'Gibraltar' for its rock-like imperturbability. (More prosaically, as is their wont, the Germans call it either the '*Blockhaus*' or '*Panzerturm*',[6] as in 'armoured turret'.)

All up, Rawlinson's Fourth Army has done well, but it has still not got hold of Pozières, so Haig sent for his most notable 'thruster' at hand, General Gough, the Commander of the Reserve Army – which has been attacking north of the Albert–Bapaume Road since 1 July – and simply instructed Gough to get the village 'with as little delay as possible'.[7]

Gough had been so eager to do exactly that that he had not first gone via Birdwood – who has yet to arrive – but instead called for General Walker, the commander of the (mostly) highly regarded Division of Birdwood's I Anzac Corps, to come to him directly. Gough and his senior staff were insistent that Walker send in his 1st Division immediately, on the same angle of attack as the failed 34th Division venture – advancing along a line broadly parallel with the old Albert–Bapaume Road.

Hence, the angst of the last few days.

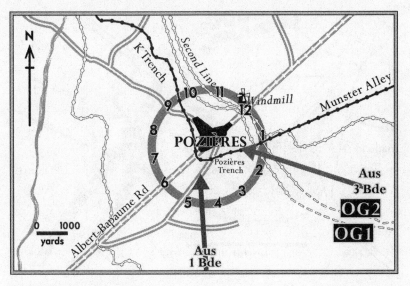

Poizières clock-face orientation

Firstly, Walker and Blamey had sought as much delay as possible, to allow both themselves and their troops time to survey the ground. Secondly, they had worked towards weaning General Gough and his senior officers off the 'disgraceful'[8] plan they had proposed for the AIF's 1st Division, and to instead embrace a plan of the 1st Division's own making.

For – call them innovative if you must – having actually *studied* the ground, Walker and Blamey had decided on, and refined, a different plan.

Instead of going straight up the Bapaume Road, right at the most formidable defences, as if attacking on a clock face from 6 pm straight at 12, where the coveted Windmill lies, Walker and Blamey want a flanking attack. They intend to capture that same road, the village being at the centre of the clock, by sending the 1st Brigade to attack it from the direction of four o'clock while the 3rd Brigade, on the right of the 1st Brigade, will attack from two o'clock – and the 2nd Brigade, kept in reserve, will be ready to move where most needed.

The 1st and 3rd Brigades would attack in three waves of two lines each. The waves would be a half-hour apart, each wave with a specific objective. A little like the plan at Fromelles, it would be for the first line

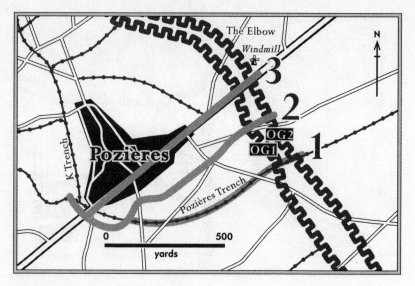

Three objectives of the AIF at Pozières

to take Pozières Trench, which crosses the Albert–Bapaume Road at nearly right angles and loops south-east below the village. Succeeding waves would take the peach and plum orchards, and then secure half the village itself, right up to the road.

Of course, just before each line went in, the artillery would shift its aim from one objective to the one just ahead.

A complication for the 3rd Brigade is that, as well as taking on the Germans in Pozières Trench, there would also be a heavy concentration of German soldiers in their second trench system immediately to the east. Known as Old German Lines 1 and 2 (OG1 and OG2), these two trenches intersect the 3rd Brigade's jumping-off trench. They run up to the Windmill at the top of the ridge before veering back west, forming a semicircle to the north of the village – rather as if those trenches are on the rim of the said clock, going from 2 to 12, and down to 10. On the western side of the village, effectively running on the clock rim from 6 to 9 – then leaving the clock face there and heading in the direction of Mouquet Farm – there is another heavily defended trench, K Trench, which the 3rd Brigade will have to deal with when they get to it.

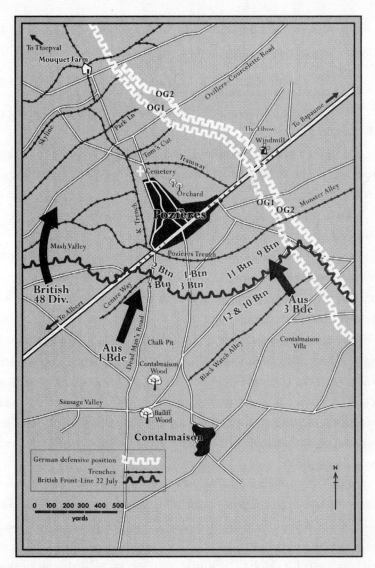

Pozières, 23 July 1916

And yet, while it had been one thing to come up with a better plan, it had been quite another to persuade Gough and his staff of its rightness. In the end, Walker had tackled an officer of Gough's staff – à la General Pompey Elliott taking Major Howard on a tour of the Fromelles battlements a week earlier – and *shown* him the lack of wisdom of Gough's plan against the brilliance of his own.

It proved to be a masterstroke. With German shells falling all around, Gough's man, Major Edward Beddington, could contain himself no longer.

'Is it necessary to go further?' he inquired plaintively.

'Not if you are convinced,' Walker replied.[9] 'What are you going to tell Gough?'

Again, such a direct question is not the British way, but, once it is presented in the Australian manner, there is little Beddington can do but answer directly.

'I shall recommend your plan . . .'[10] Beddington concedes. He is rewarded by Walker allowing him a hasty exit.

(For all that, Walker would later be frank when it came time to characterise Gough's command in this period: 'I always look back on those days as the very worst exhibition of Army commandship that occurred in the whole campaign . . .')[11]

This morning, upon his arrival, Bean's key question remains: *when*. There had been endless negotiations between Gough and Walker on that very subject, with Gough pushing for 'as quickly as possible'. Walker is not surprised, as he regards Gough as 'temperamentally'[12] inclined to rush attacks, but is himself insistent that they wait, particularly when he discovers there is a serious problem with the artillery plans.

By the time Walker and Blamey emerge from the meeting with Gough, however, to a waiting Bean, all is agreed: the attack will go in at 12.30 the following night of 23/24 July, in the first moonless pitch of the midnight hour. The time and date suits because it gives yet more precious hours for the 1st Division to prepare, and will also mean they will be attacking in tandem with the British 48th Division on their left, which will hopefully secure that ground to the west of the village, and the 19th Division on their right, which will advance 1000 yards east of Pozières.

The fact that the 48th had failed in an attack to take 'some trenches west of Pozières' just the night before, in part because their artillery had not been up to it, has been a subject of great discussion at the conference. When it is over, Bean finds his friend Brudenell White '[rightly] anxious' about it.[13]

And so is Walker.

'Walker said to me,' Bean records in his diary, 'that the 1st Australian Division would be knocked out by this attack though most people think they will succeed.'[14]

Typical of Bean, eager to see things for himself, he decides the next morning to walk with all the rest of the traffic pushing to the north-east to get a look at that night's proposed battle site from a high spot just back from it. He is so close that stray shells fall in the near distance, and even behind him.

Is *that* Pozières?

So pulverised is the whole thing that you can just see the rough contours of village's old layout – not by the shattered buildings, for they are indeed so shattered there is simply nothing of them left but brick-red powder – but by, as another soldier puts it, 'the shredded stumps and trunks of trees which once made the gardens or orchards or hedges behind the houses'.[15]

As for the Albert–Bapaume Road – built right through the middle of Pozières by the Romans back when Caligula was no more than a tyrant of a toddler in short pants – you can discern its course because that is where many of the shredded stumps are aligned. Poplar and plane trees, planted a century earlier by order of Napoleon, used to stand silent sentinel on both sides of the thoroughfare as odd travellers made their way through.

Never were there travellers like these Germans, though. Merciless in attack all through Belgium and the north of France, they are also, clearly, implacable in defence. Visible at the base of the slope that lies before the village is Pozières Trench, behind which lies a mostly standing copse of trees, with all their leaves blown off by the bombardments.

And there, high on the slopes on the upside of the village, Bean can see the second trench system, where stands a mound. This, he knows from his discussion with General Brudenell White, is the ruins of the

Windmill – the key objective of future Australian attacks, though tonight they're just going after the village. Ultimately, if they can get to the Windmill, they will control the highest point on the entire Somme battlefield.

But will the Australians be capable of achieving that?

The one thing the men themselves suspect is that it is going to be tough – that much is evident from the thick carpet of corpses that lie all around their positions, soldiers who have tried to do what they are about to embark upon, but who will never return. Their bodies lie everywhere, as do their body parts.

Most of the Australians – the 1st Brigade on the left and the 3rd Brigade on the right – have been substantially in position since the wee hours of the night of 19/20 July, at which point it had been thought they would be attacking in the early hours of the 21st. The two subsequent delays have given them more time, yes, but the waiting has also been exhausting, the more so because the men's breathing is labouring through the gas masks they have all been made to wear.

Their Hell on Earth consists of more than just the stench, the fear of death and the difficulty breathing, however. There is also the matter of German shells falling among them, regularly killing and maiming dozens at a time. The only consolation is that, however badly they are copping it, the Germans appear to be copping it worse. The Australian artillery, which has been systematically bombarding German positions for the last three days – since two o'clock on the morning of the 19th – is now firing as never before on the trench system the Australians must soon attack.

'They are firing like mad & have got the range to a nicety,' Private Archie Barwick of the 1st Division's 1st Brigade's 1st Battalion would record in his diary, with no little satisfaction.[16] 'The way they shell the wood in front of us is something terrific. All day long there are shells bursting in it from 3 in. to 12 [in.]. I can tell you the latter send the earth & stuff easily 300 ft high and go off with an ear-splitting roar. I have seen them uproot big trees, such is their power . . . I reckon for every shell the Germans send over we send 20.'[17]

—

Even as Walker and his senior officers are coming to grips in their HQ with the finer points of their plan of attack, a key German officer is arriving to report in at General Fritz von Below's First Army HQ, a massive white château in Bourlon Wood, just west of Cambrai, 15 miles north-east of Pozières.

Major-General Richard Ludwig Wellmann – that rarest of things, a quietly spoken Prussian officer – has already distinguished himself in recent weeks, being decorated with the *Roter Adlerorden*, Red Eagle II Class with Oak Leaves and Swords, for his valour in leadership of his 18th Reserve Division, which had performed so very well during the first 16 days in the Somme battle. (Such a decoration means little to a man who has already lost two of his three sons in this wretched war, but he is glad, at least, for the honour it has done his division.)

For now, von Below has given General Wellmann the task of helping to defend Pozières, and he is quick to get to grips, heading to forward positions to survey the ground and consult with his four Regimental Commanders.

—

Meanwhile, on this morning, in the settlement of Léalvillers, just north of Albert, Goldy Raws is feeling curiously . . . let down.

It has been such a long journey to get here, by train and foot, right to this spot just beyond direct shell attack from what apparently used to be the village of Pozières, and two nights ago he and the 23rd Battalion had joyously believed a report that they were right on the point of attacking the German positions – stripped down physically, fired up mentally and ready to go – only to find out the whole thing was a furphy. Instead of them, it is the 1st Division who will have the honour, and he and his men of the 2nd will have to wait their turn . . .

'I feel,' he writes to his sister Helen, 'as one who, having stripped himself of his clothes, has poised his body ready to leap into the swift icy current – and is held back. You have had all the tension and effort to get ready, and if by any chance we are not "thrown in" we won't have any of the glory.'[18]

And, yes, he and his mates continue to joke about what kind of wound they might be lucky enough to get when they do go in, whether it might be the most highly prized of all, a 'Blighty' – one bad enough to get you back to England but ideally with no long-term ill-effects – what the nurses might be like and so forth, but still there is that underlying anxiety. What if something goes wrong and they miss out altogether? They want to see action. Of course they know it's dangerous. That point had been made on their approach to Pozières, when the roads had suddenly been crowded with Red Cross cars and they had passed endless dumps of shells – when he had seen some massive 15-inch ones, he had shivered – but that hasn't put him or his mates off.

Rather, as Raws had written to his other sister, Gwen, just a couple of days earlier:

There is excitement that at last we have the Huns on the move. I do not think the stories of heavy casualties deter our men. Things like that you know must be, besides which most of the old hands have stood trench warfare quite long enough, and there is a feeling to get at the bastards at any cost.[19]

Whatever else happens, the one bit of good news is that at least his brother Alec is close by, going through the last bit of training with an Entrenching Battalion – a unit specifically devoted to digging state-of-the-art trenches. Apparently, Alec will be here within days. Goldy can't wait.

———

Alec Raws can't wait to see his brother either.

He is near the front-lines at last, having travelled to Steenwerck just across the border in Belgium, 'through towns and villages made famous by the war, in some of which the destruction wrought by the Hun artillery was plainly visible even from a distance'.[20]

The main thing, as he writes to his mother, is that he is 'well within range of the German guns at last!'.[21]

He is close enough that the ground shakes, he notes with some satisfaction, but there is something else he observes on breaks from supervising the digging of these practice trenches and taking up the shovel himself:

> Sometimes one sits on a grassy bank and has lunch, or perhaps a smoke, and a rest, while British and German shells go screaming overhead. It struck me yesterday evening how jolly awkward it would be if two met above my head.

Quite.

Still, the main thing is that he is getting closer to Goldy with the 2nd Division. All else being equal, Alec knows he will be posted to Goldy's 23rd Battalion within days, and he is feeling ever more comfortable being with the AIF here in France.

The English officers, for all that, are still hard to fathom, and Alec is not the only one who thinks so. On this morning, Alec is in the trenches with his rough mate Bill Gow, who is about to shave, when one of those English officers who believes it is correct form to occasionally be friendly to lesser beings happens to pass by. Bill has a filthy lather all over his face, the blade in his right hand, and he is earnestly peering at the little metal mirror stuck in the face of the sandbag parapet.

'Having a shave?' the Captain asks.

'Yes, sir,' says Bill, carefully containing himself.

'Still taking an interest in your personal appearance?' the Pommy muses. 'That's good.'

Bill rubs his face warily but manages what the Diggers call 'a shit-eating grin'. Against all odds, he has still not been rude.

'It is rather wet here,' the Captain continues, glancing down at his enormous waterproof rubber boots, up to his ankles in the massive puddle Bill is standing by.

'Wouldn't you be better getting up on the fire-step, out of the wet?' Bill asks encouragingly.

'Oh, I don't mind the wet,' the Captain replies heroically.

Bill, whose own boots have likely more holes than leather, nods and keeps ruminatively rubbing the now completely dry lather, through which his bristles are clearly sprouting like persistent weeds. The shit-eating grin has gone, replaced by something very close to a scowl.

Still the Captain won't move on! Just stays there, ankle-deep in the puddle.

'Oh, by the way, do tell me, my man, why you don't wet your brush?' asks the Captain. 'I've been standing here for five minutes watching you rub your face dry, and I'm awfully interested.'

It is more than flesh and blood can stand.

'Tell you why!' says Bill, shaking his drought-stricken brush in the Pommy Captain's face. 'Gawd strike me dead! Why, you've been standin' in me bloody shaving water for them five bloody minutes!'[22]

———

The thundering of hooves is the signal they have all been waiting for.

Attennnnnn-shun!

Galloping across country from his own HQ at Château Valvion by the village of Beauquesne, General Sir Douglas Haig is not only a Knight of the Realm, he *looks* like a knight of old as he arrives full tilt at Gough's HQ. For who else but the Commander-in-Chief of the BEF could enter in such grand manner? He is escorted by no fewer than two dozen horsemen of the 17th Lancers, hard men whose motto 'Death or Glory' is emblazoned on the skull and crossbones badge worn on their caps, while they have a red over white pennant on the end of each lance. (Impressive for some, though the Australians call all British cavalry 'donkey wallopers'.)

As the great man alights, the Honour Guard snaps to attention.

Of course, when Haig is making a visit there is a cluster of red tabs to meet him, along with any number of less exalted beings eager to receive him properly.

Haig returns their salute and quickly makes his way inside to Gough's private study. With the attack on Pozières now just hours away, there is much to discuss.

Haig has come, he makes clear to Gough, 'to make sure that the Australians have only been given a simple task'. After all, 'this is the first time that they will be taking part in a serious offensive on a big scale [against the German Forces]'.[23]

———

All day long, the British barrage of shells keeps hitting Pozières. The Germans suffering under it are in no doubt about what is doing the most damage.

It is the Allies' answer to 'Big Bertha', a massive gun they call 'Granny', sending down 15-inch shells every few minutes, just it has been for days, around the clock.

In his deep dugout with comrades of the 116th Regiment Reserve – part of the famously vigorous 66-year-old General Max von Boehn's IXth Corps – *Leutnant* Richard Sapper, artillery liaison officer, grits his teeth and prays for it to end. When the shells land close, the light in the dugout flickers and dies. Nails fall out of the wall, sending caps, coats and weapons to the floor. It is obvious that if the trench takes a direct hit, they will be unlikely to survive.

'After each impact,' he records, 'we were conscious of relief, that fate had granted us another four to six minutes before we might be forced to turn our back on life, having been buried alive, charred or suffocated and –'

And a new thunderclap, this one *very* close, followed by a clatter on the stairs.

'*A-a-alle sind tot!* E-e-veryone's dead!' they croak through burned lips. 'E-e-veryone's dead! E-e-veryone's dead!'[24]

They are the only two men who have escaped the dugout next to Sapper, and they report that 23 of their comrades are still down there, dead or trapped – who knows? A rescue team is dispatched immediately but is only able to drag out 'a soldier's boot with the remains of a charred leg'.[25]

—

As the sun begins to sink on this gorgeous summer's day, as the shells continue to land on both sides, the shrapnel flies and men die, there is a surge forward up the main communication trench for 1st Division Operations, known as Black Watch Alley, and into the Australian jumping-off trenches. Munitions, stretcher-bearers and Lewis gun teams with their heavy ammunition buckets and signallers with their clumsy field telephones and spools of wire move into position for what is to come.

To get there, all must pass through a spot called Sausage Gully – 'its constant traffic and busy life recalling to some of the troops their memories of the beach at Anzac'[26] – and by sundown it has become as busy as a kicked nest of ants. For beyond all the traffic, Sausage Gully is also where much of the Australian artillery is positioned, in a state of constant roaring – '18-pounders, 4 ½-inch howitzers, long-barrelled 60-pounders of five-inch bore'[27] – their crashing booms rolling over the Australians in the forward trenches, even as their shells roar so closely overhead that the men duck involuntarily.

By the erroneous count of Corporal Arthur Thomas of the 6th Battalion, for he exaggerates by a factor of two, 'about three thousand guns are being fired simultaneously and continuously, the gunners stripped to the waist . . .'[28]

On this evening, all the men of the 1st and 3rd Brigades who are due to go over the top are issued with two bombs and two empty sand-bags to take with them. The bombs are for the Germans, of course, and the sandbags to fill for themselves, to give them some protection against what the Germans are likely to do in reply. Some sign of that is what the German artillery is doing now, as it has clearly caught up from its rather lax shelling of the day before.

'They [are] pouring it in properly,' Archie Barwick records. 'Evidently they think we are massing men in a little gully just close to Contalmaison, but they are sadly out of it . . . I'll bet there is about 30 acres of ground that you couldn't ride a horse over for shell holes & some of them are 15 or 20 ft deep. It is a sight that has to be seen before you can form any idea of what it is like.'[29]

Oh, but the Diggers are getting an idea, and no mistake.

Just as the French had been at Verdun when exposed for the first time to that kind of shelling five months earlier, they are shocked. What chance has a man of living if above ground in the vicinity of one of those things? No chance. Witness what Archie and his mates had observed on their approach to these parts: 'All over the place . . . little white crosses, hastily erected to the brave fellows who broke this line and pushed them further on.'[30]

Your only hope is to be dug deeply into a trench that is not hit directly.

Consequently, much of the men's energy on this day is spent doing precisely that – digging deeply. Spiritually, emotionally, and with a shovel in their hands.

Dig, you bastards.

Throughout the afternoon, the soldiers of the 1st Division continue to dig, or huddle together once their trench is deep enough – and seem as calm as possible at a time when thousands of shells are exploding all around and deadly shrapnel is whizzing through the air. Terrified stretcher-bearers are flat out, ferrying the dead and grievously wounded bodies of their unlucky mates – some of the lucky ones have only lost a hand, clean – back from the front-lines. Christ Almighty, if this is what it is like *before* they go over the top, what is it going to be like *tonight*?

Those who can concentrate long enough write letters to loved ones.

To their left, they can hear the Fourth Army artillery roaring as never before; the sound of their own shells first roaring overhead then pounding German positions, hurling skyward bricks, huge clods of earth, tree branches and, occasionally, hopefully, Germans – though it is hard to tell. It is somehow comforting to the Australians to know that they are not alone in this, that at much the same time as they go over the top so too will the British soldiers.

As the sun goes down just behind Pozières, the light is perfect for the men to actually see many of the larger shells, fired from several miles behind, land on the German lines, at this distance 'falling like cricket balls'[31] and exploding as they hit the ground.

And now, as night falls, all of the guns in both the forward and rear positions start firing together, all aimed at the trenches the Australians will shortly be seeking to occupy. The exploding shells are so constant on the eastern skyline that the silhouette of what had been Pozières is constantly flickering 'fore a stuttering red glow, and the ground itself feels as if it is in the throes of a major earthquake. The German artillery is making heavy reply, convinced that a major attack is in the offing, raining shells down on both the Allied trenches and all the roads and trenches leading to the village, trying to destroy whatever reserves might be moving forward.

As ever, the flares rise and the shells fall and explode. The Germans are ensuring that No-Man's Land is as bright as day, and all who venture upon it will be torn asunder. Even those soldiers in reserve a few miles away can see what looks like the dawn of Hell.

'Flashes like summer lightning were quite continuous, making one flickering band of light,' one Digger would record in his diary. 'Every now and then a low lurid red flush, very angry, lit the horizon. All around the horizon shells were flashing and the pretty starlights making their graceful curves, a dozen or a score at a time in all quarters to east and north. Occasionally a red light or a rocket bursting into green stars, and the twinkle of shrapnel like the flash of a match which won't light or the glow of a match-end.'[32]

And the Germans are suffering all right, as they continue to be pounded by Allied artillery, just as they have been for most of the last three weeks. For all that, one ashen-faced soldier, with trembling hand, is still able to scratch out a note to his loved ones, with a particularly apposite return address in the top right-hand corner:

In Hell's trenches

Dear Luise and children,
My darlings, die Götter, the gods only know if I am writing
for the last time. We have now been two days in the front
trenches. It is not a trench, but a little ditch, shattered with
shells, with not the slightest cover and no protection. We've
made a hole, and there we sit day and night . . . We have
already lost about 50 men in two days, 6 killed, the others
wounded. We get nothing to eat or drink, and life is almost
unendurable . . . Here I have given up hope of life . . .
To my last moment I will think of you. There is really no
possibility that we shall see each other again. Should I fall –
then farewell . . .[33]

—

Bean, now back in his billet in Albert, is trying to work on this night
of 22 July. He is going through the copious notes he took at Fromelles,
attempting to understand just how the catastrophe occurred. However,
he is finding it exceedingly difficult to concentrate. Who can work on
the minutiae of troop movements at midnight by the Sugar-loaf when,
just half a mile away, the heavy guns are unleashing hell on the German
lines? Many of the shells are actually passing overhead, from artillery
positioned around the town.

Back at Gallipoli, an English correspondent had said of the
Australian's tightly tailored, just-the-facts-ma'am journalistic style,
'Bean! O, I think Bean actually counts the bullets.'[34]

Funny he should say that . . .

'Guns are banging off all round – about 40 or 50 to the minute,'
Bean records of this night, 'sometimes more all the time. Some are near
– one or two very big ones every five minutes or so whose great report

makes one jump and one can hear the shell climbing with the swish of a great rocket, or escaping steam.

'Every now and then waggons or motors, one or two waggons galloping through. Then the put-put of a despatch rider's motor cycle.'[35]

He keeps counting the artillery as the intensity increases, to the point that there is more than one launch a second. Seventy shells fired every minute!

Good God Almighty – if it is as frightening as this just having the shells go overhead, how appalling must it be on the receiving end?

Bean is not sure but, determined as ever to know more, he quickly packs up in readiness to move forward, to be closer to the front-line when the Australians go over the top.

—

'Around Pozières fire of the heaviest calibre was falling on our trenches,' *Unteroffizier* Heinrich Klußman, 77th RIR, would record of this time. 'We sat huddled in our dugout smoking pipes, cigars and cigarettes by the feeble light of a candle to calm our overstrained nerves because, with one hit, we could all be killed. The overhead cover received five direct hits. It held firm, despite the fact that the earth trembled and shook. Things did not go so well everywhere. The commander of 7th Company, Reserve *Leutnant* Reusche, was buried alive three times in an hour and a half, but on each occasion he was dug out in the nick of time by his men . . . The air was foul, decomposing corpses spread a disgusting stink . . .'[36]

LATE EVENING, POZIÈRES, 22 JULY 1916, TOMMY GUNS

By 10 pm, the barrage has begun to crescendo to its long, shattering climax, every gun firing, each one emitting clouds of choking smoke.

As one Digger would record of the prevailing feeling, 'There is only ever one question anyone wants to ask – "What time is it?" – and just about only one answer – "Dig, it's just a couple of minutes since you last asked me."'[37]

Strange how the day has raced by to this point, but from now on the minutes crawl past like dying caterpillars. Many of the men start to cough as the smoke gets thicker and . . . *norma . . . conversat . . . now . . . imposs.*

They check their ammunition belts for the umpteenth time, sharpen their bayonets, light another Woodbine from the butt of the last one, even while assessing the virtues of using the butts of their rifles as clubs. Or perhaps the sharpened shovels might be better?

Ten minutes past midnight. Time for the first move.

Their hearts in their mouths, their rifles in their hands, their stomachs holding something a lot stronger than mere butterflies that flutter by, they gather up their kits, their bags of bombs and their courage and make ready. For this attack, the soldiers of the 1st Division less 'hop the bags' than silently steal across them as quickly as they can – many have their boots wrapped in empty sandbags to silence their footfall. They keep crawling forward to previously laid 'jumping-off tapes' about 100 yards from the German lines, where they must lie in wait before the barrage on those lines is due to lift at 12.30 am sharp.

In No-Man's Land, they move not a muscle, whirl not a whisker, though the earth itself is shaking with the terrible emotion at what is being done to it. Or maybe it is them. Perhaps both.

Among these most forward soldiers is Lance-Corporal Harold 'Squatter' Preston of the 9th Battalion, who tries to press his body as close into the bosom of Mother Earth as possible. The advisability of this measure is emphasised when, 'neath the fading, flickering, ethereal light thrown by the endless flares, the men note that the German machine-gun bullets are now so low that 'we could see [them] cutting off the poppies almost against our heads'.[38]

Certain that he is about to stop a bullet, all Preston can do is jam his tin helmet, his 'battle-bowler', onto his head and bring the butt of his rifle to sit before his face, hoping for extra protection . . . but Christ knows if that is going to bloody work.

Nearby, his Sergeant is yelling something, but who knows what? Preston's ears are ringing with the cracking of bullets, shrapnel shells continue to burst all around, and some men who have been hit are groaning, screaming or death-rattling.

Next to Squatter Preston, a fellow soldier is 'crying like a baby', pausing only between sobs to repeat, 'We will never get out of this . . . we will *never* get out of this.'[39]

And Preston knows he might be right. Whereas they had gone out in darkness, that has all changed now. 'The flashes of the guns, the bursting of shells, and the Verey lights, made the night like day, and, as I lay flat to the ground as possible I was expecting to stop one any time.'[40]

Many of the Australian soldiers do, most often groaning softly as a piece of shrapnel cuts short their young lives.

The men are not long there when – seemingly impossible, but true – the barrage on the trenches ahead intensifies, causing the Germans to all but instantly reply with artillery and machine-gun fire.

And, *mein Gott*, then the Lord said let there be . . .

'Brilliant white flares rose from Pozières, close ahead, and to the right along the O.G. Lines, but the troops, crawling low, were mostly hidden by the fall of the ground and by thistle tufts which fringed the older shell-holes.'[41]

Just beyond Pozières Ridge, scattered between one and three miles back *von der Windmühle*, from the Windmill, the German artillery men of the 117th and 7th Infantry Divisions, together with those of the IV Corps, are working as never before. Following their strict routine, the officers in charge of the crews working the 120 field guns and 30 heavy guns are continually roaring above the cacophony of battle, '*Feeertig!* Ready!' and then '*Feuer!* Fire!'

An instant later, their guns erupt like angry volcanos, the shells disappearing as searing streaks of flame into the darkness, lobbing towards the Australian lines.

And again and again and again!

'*Feuer!*' '*Feuer!*' '*Feuer!*'

Lying out in *Niemandsland*, among his mates, a 19-year-old Lance-Corporal from the AIF's 1st Battalion, Ben Champion, is doing his best not to wet himself, but just cannot help it. 'I couldn't stop urinating . . .' he would recount in his diary. 'It seemed as if the earth opened up with a crash. The ground shook and trembled, and the concussion made our ears ring.'[42]

Despite his terror, Champion notes something else happening among himself and his mates, men for whom, previously, being seen to do anything remotely close to cuddling another might mark you as a 'poofta'. 'It is strange how men creep together for protection. Soon, instead of four paces interval between the men, we came down to lying alongside each other, and no motioning could make [us] move apart.'[43]

Lance-Corporal Archie Barwick is one of those charged with trying to keep the men of the 1st Battalion apart, but he soon gives up the uneven struggle as the whole situation intensifies.

Two minutes of hurricane fire.

The German assault intensifies – 'Feuer!' 'Feuer!' 'Feuer!' – now plastering the communication trenches leading to the front-lines with shrapnel shells, knowing they are sure to create murderous mayhem among the men moving forward.

Men of the third wave are torn asunder by the shelling, most particularly in the 3rd and 4th Battalions of the 1st Brigade. As Charles Bean would describe it, 'The road past Casualty Corner to Contalmaison was intermittently swept with shrapnel and high-explosive, and drenched with phosgene gas shell. At times the corner could only be passed by men running one at a time; those who were hit had to crawl away from the place as best they could, their mates having at that moment one paramount duty – to reach their starting-point for the attack.'[44]

Among those who make it is Archie Barwick, due to go over the top with the second wave of the 1st Battalion. 'A most uncanny feeling was in the air,' Barwick would record. 'The horizon was lit by the flames of the bursting shells and the still air was charged with the sweet-smelling Lachromatry gas and heavy with a sort of chloroform. Most of us were thinking of home and uttering silent prayers that we should not fail in this great attack, and so disgrace ourselves and the great name of Australia.'[45]

For some reason that he can't fathom, Archie personally has a surprising presentiment: 'As for myself, I had a confident feeling that I never had before and for the first time I felt absolutely sure of myself.'[46]

At last, however, it happens.

'Suddenly,' Lance-Corporal Ben Champion would recount, 'there was a pause for a second, and then we saw the barrage smoke move forward . . .'[47]

The Australian barrage is lifting off Pozières Trench, and shifting to the orchards behind.

She's *on*, mate!

—

In the German trenches, many a soldier is shattered – physically, emotionally, mentally – and not just because of the exploding shells and endless bullets. It is what goes with that, the privations . . . bordering on starvation. Things have been *so* grim in the last couple of days with the constant shell-fire that one soldier would recall how 'the water [in the shell hole] was green and full of muddy clay, but we had to use it to brew coffee, because the ration parties could not get through to us'.[48]

But still they have been confident.

At one point, the shout had gone up, '*Der Tommy ist am Angreifen!* Tommy is attacking!'[49] and all of his *Kameraden* had sparked up, ready to get to grips with them, only to be disappointed as none of the enemy had appeared.

'*Ach, wie schade! Wie verdammt schade!* What a shame, what a bloody shame!' the German soldier *Reservist* Rabe of the 11th Company RIR 15 would report. 'I had dug myself in so well and was equipped with piles of hand grenades and ammunition. We felt very certain of ourselves.'[50]

But now, a strange piercing sound comes from down the slopes . . .

—

Across the Australian lines, 1st Division officers look at their synchronised watches to confirm, take a deep breath, stand up, lift the whistle to their lips and give three quick, shrill blasts.

With a roar, the Australians are up and charging, determined to get to Pozières Trench before the Germans can recover from the mind-numbing effects of the bombardment, realise that the barrage has lifted and get to their posts. And so the Australians run – *hard* – straight into 'the pall of evil-smelling dense smoke hanging low to the ground, pierced everywhere with bright red flashes from the bursting shells, our own and the enemy's'.[51] The instant they are up, most feel an enormous sense of vulnerability for the first few steps, naked before and prey to the whims of the big guns and bullets. Their heads tingle uncomfortably, anticipating a bullet, but for some it is their family jewels that feel most exposed. After those few steps, however, they tingle no more – the urge to surge, to get into the attack, takes over.

Their legs pumping, their rifles thumping against their thighs, their bayonets forward, their lungs starting to burn – all of them know it is a matter of life or death.

'We made one mad rush at them,' Archie Barwick would record, 'and then Hell seemed let loose, for the Germans poured a torrent of high explosive shells, machine guns and shrapnel on us. It was something awful, for we were out in the open and unprotected and men fell fast as rain . . .'[52]

Some of those near Ben Champion, for example, to Archie's right, are 'an instant too late . . . and the machine guns opened and got Captain McKenzie and a row of chaps, and they stopped where they lay'.[53]

The surviving Australians charge on, giving it their all, a little like they did back at school in Bethungra and Gunning and Beechworth and Katherine and Ceduna and Geraldton and Mangrove Mountain and the Alice, when they did the 100-yard dash. Then, the white tape had awaited at the finish line, with sometimes their parents cheering them on, and victory would be a blue ribbon to pin to their puffed-up chest.

This time, it will be victory enough just to live, across what remains of that 100 yards of No-Man's Land.

For the most part, though, the Australian soldiers make it – *they make it!* – and jump right down into the German trenches.

'We swept into their front line like a torrent,' Archie records, 'shooting, bayoneting and clubbing like fury.'[54]

Most of the horrified, blinking Germans resist the best they can, while others give up the ghost quickly, begging for their lives: 'Mercy, *Kamerad!* MERCY, *Kamerad!*'

Sometimes the Australians show mercy, but more often . . . they show steel, ruthlessly applying Guiding Rule Number 8 of the *British Army Manual*: 'Four to six inches' penetration is sufficient to incapacitate and allow for a quick withdrawal, whereas if a bayonet is driven home too far it is often impossible to withdraw it. In such cases a round should be fired to break up the obstruction.'[55]

A few Germans show fight; more often, they show a clean pair of heels – in many places there is much less resistance and fewer Germans to kill than the Australians had been expecting.

Nevertheless, there are a few Squareheads who remain, and in this matter of life and death it is obvious that the more German deaths there are, the more Australian lives will be spared, and the battle that proceeds is as fast and furious as it is ferocious.

As ever, Private Preston is right to the fore of the fight, though perhaps more inclined to show mercy than the rest of his mates. One of those he spares proves to be *ein deutscher Armeearzt*, a German Army doctor, who is quickly sent back with the other prisoners.

The Australians of the 1st Brigade, meanwhile, continue to push forward when suddenly up ahead they see – *what is it?* – something white waving in the gloom. It turns out to be a grimy handkerchief being waved from the top of a dugout.

Hold your fire.

Slowly, tentatively, inch by inch, the figure holding the white hanky – clearly fearing he is about to be shot in cold blood – emerges from the dugout, puts his hands upon his head and walks towards them. And there are another 11 German soldiers behind him, also with their hands on their heads! (Apart from the right posture for surrender, the Australians like their prisoners that way – it is the best way to see if they have wristwatches. After a battle, it was not unknown for a Digger to be wearing half a dozen German watches up his forearm. He can sell or trade them later.)

Among the dozen prisoners of war are two doctors, one of whom had done some of his medical training in England. 'Well,' says he in thickly accented English, 'this is a blessing!'[56]

Those with him appear to have the same attitude – as glad as they are amazed to have made it out of this hell hole alive, and to be treated decently. They even shake hands with the Australians and offer them German cigarettes, marked *Heer & Flotte, Heidelberg*, special ration issue for those in the *Army & Navy*.

Together, some of these men who have been fighting each other tooth and nail, bayonets and bullets, have a durry.

Meantime, the Australians who have just taken Pozières Trench set about securing it, including – in what is fast becoming a Digger tradition – taking the German bodies and using them to build up their parapet.

'Our chances of survival,' one Digger would record, 'depended upon how quickly we could get underground; no time was wasted, for the enemy artillery was evidently aware of our position and was registering a concentrated fire on the area we were in.'[57]

For even over and above the shattering, chattering of the machine-gun fire from both sides, they can hear a much higher-pitched whistle than before – this time, the sound of a shell coming down in their area – and there is a pause as the pitch gets even higher still. Have their last moments on this earth come?

'The shells approaching or passing over sound for the world like railway trains coming nearer and nearer, till they reach you or pass you with a horrid shriek.'[58]

And then the night is filled with the angry hiss of shrapnel flying in every direction, all too often followed by the screams of the men it hits.

Even beyond the shelling, heavy German infantry resistance remains, with some Germans determined to hold on to their own section of trench against all comers. These, usually, prove to be the veterans, the ones the Germans refer to as *alte Hasen*, 'old hares', who know how to fight and are, in fact, prone to do anything *but* run. And, of course, each dugout must be checked for hidden Germans. (That checking traditionally involves throwing a bomb down the stairs or ladders and then listening for screams.)

Topside, the ferocious fighting goes on, and great acts of heroism from both sides are on display. Though the fighting on the left soon sees the Germans turn and run – 'All tiredness was forgotten,' Ben Champion would record, 'and we chased the Fritz's and got them, and then we turned round and dug like mad'[59] – likely nowhere is the clash so intense as over on the far right, from the Australian view, in the battle for OG1 and OG2, the German trenches that lead all the way to the Windmill.

It is a party from the 3rd Brigade's 9th Battalion that leads the push and begins to advance up the terrain between the OG1 and OG2, only

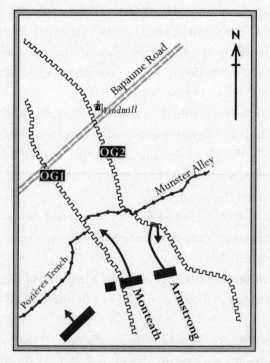

Attack on OG1 and OG2

to draw intense fire. It becomes so withering that they split into two, each side bombing their way up the trench on either side.

The one on the left, led by Lieutenant Charles Monteath, soon captures the junction of OG1 and Pozières Trench and is pushing on when they are confronted by a devastating obstacle. Up ahead, on ground higher, a platoon of German soldiers is firing at them from a concrete bunker and hurling numerous grenades.

Of course, the Australians fire and throw back, but there is a problem. While the German *Eierhandgranate*, an 'egg grenade', can be hurled as far as 50 yards, the Australians' own British Mills bomb is a much heavier device. Even the strongest man, the best cricketer, can only get it 40 yards. And the Germans have the further advantage of hurling downhill. The Australians are being slaughtered.

It is now that Private John Leak, a 22-year-old bullocky from Rockhampton – a man with the curious combination of having a baby face, singularly bushy eyebrows and wise eyes, as if he has been put together with spare parts, like the platypus – takes matters, and three grenades, into his own hands.

Yeah, there *is* no doubt the Germans can hurl long, but he is not sure if they can hurl straight – the way he once had as a champion schoolboy cricketer.

Scrambling out of his trench, he charges up the hill, his right arm poised as bullets kick up the dust at his feet like heavy rain.

He throws once.

Straight in over the stumps.

Screams ring out.

He throws a second and third time.

Two more explosions, more screams, and resultant carnage ahead as some of the survivors flee. In an instant, Private Leak has leapt up and over the German parapet, and he is suddenly right among three stunned German soldiers who have not been quick enough to get out. They look up to see – *mein Gott!* – a whirling dervish, seemingly with six arms and as many bayonets flashing by the light of the flares.

Within 30 seconds, all three Germans lie dead at Leak's feet. When

Lieutenant Monteath tentatively peers into the strongpoint shortly after, it is to find Leak calmly wiping the blood from his bayonet onto his felt hat, which he prefers to his helmet.

Trying to consolidate the position to the right, Squatter Preston and his mates soon find themselves in much the same situation – the German egg grenades continue to cause havoc, and their own bomb supply soon runs out. All they can do is throw up sandbag blocks on the trench they have already won and 'rely on rifle and bayonet until more grenades arrive. Men are spread out along the trench and the bombs are passed from man to man.'[60]

Ah, but Fritz is canny.

Though the Australians are reasonably secure where they are, when nearby Germans put helmets and caps on the muzzles of their rifles to parade them above the parapet, it is more than many of the Diggers can resist. Alas, once they rise up to take a shot, 'they themselves were shot by other Germans farther along the trench'.[61]

—

All those in the second wave can do after they've moved forward is wait as the seconds tick by, occasionally risking a quick look at the battlefield ahead, the wider scene illuminated by the endlessly wavering glow provided by the Germans' flares. Most terrifying is the fact that there appears to be no diminution of the bullets and shells coming from the German side – whatever is happening to them and the first wave, they are not being quelled.

But still they know, whatever the likelihood of their own destruction, they must go out into it. It is their duty.

Among them is Private Percy Smythe of the 3rd Battalion, one of four brothers from the Sydney suburb of Kogarah in the AIF. Closing his eyes and gritting his teeth, he can barely believe the concussive force of all the shells exploding around him. The time, he knows, must be near when they of the second wave are to go. At 1 am, the barrage will lift off the orchards and shift back to the road. It will be their mission to charge forward over the positions won by the first wave and take the orchards. Smythe feels ready for it, and the men are just waiting for the word from their Sergeant to go.

Suddenly, however, there is confusion. Instead of the expected signal at 1 am to charge – just as they hear the sound of the barrage moving forward – there comes the sound of a commotion in front, and then the shouts.

'Double back! Double back!'[62]

Instead of Smythe charging forward, other blokes who have gone further out into No-Man's Land ahead of him are running back down the slope. Percy is crushed.

'It seemed in that instant,' he would recount, 'that all our hopes were dashed to the ground, and that failure was to be our lot.'[63]

But wait!

Now there is another cry.

'Steady, boys, steady! Stick to it, lads!'[64]

It is Sergeant Jack Bubb, swearing in a manner to turn milk blue – as Jack, twice wounded at Gallipoli, is ever wont to do – which is useful. Many of the men who'd been wavering would rather face the Germans than an angry Bubb and, though there really has been confusion, the Sergeant soon sorts it out and the second wave is on its way once more. Smythe is relieved and watches them go, waiting only for the word that he must go forward with his machine-gun crew.

And now here is the first of the wounded men coming back. They include Jack Bubb, being half-carried by one of the men, though Jack keeps saying, 'I'm all right. I'm all right.'[65]

Next comes the cry over the staccato sound of machine guns in the near distance, and screams.

'Machine gunners forward!'

Percy springs up to go, restrained only by one of his mates who is momentarily wavering, telling him to wait.

'No,' says Percy firmly. 'We're not going to squib it.'[66]

Leaping like a long-tailed cat in a room full of rocking chairs, Percy is quickly out of the trench and heading off up the hill with all the rest, even though heavily burdened by his load of magazines.

—

Across much of Pozières Trench, the furious free-for-all continues. Germans and Australians become mixed, pushing back and forth each way along the trench, with neither sure if friend or foe is ahead of them, or if the figures behind are protecting their backs or are about to drive bayonets into them. As the second wave of Australians leapfrogs the first to try to take the next objective, many are met by German reinforcements, who have themselves been rushed forward. So many of the Germans attack Lieutenant Monteath, Private Leak and their comrades that the Australians are forced to retreat from their hard-won position 100 yards up the trenches of the Old German Lines. Fritz is coming on like a *madman* . . .

'We threw hand grenade after hand grenade ceaselessly,' *Unteroffizier* Paul Wabnik of the 3rd Company Infantry Regiment 157 would record. 'We fired round after round from our rifles, until the barrels glowed red hot.'[67]

As always, someone has to cover the Australian retreat to allow the others to get away. John Leak puts his hand up – and hurls some more grenades at the approaching Germans while he's at it.

'Leak was the last to withdraw at each stage,' the citation for John Leak's Victoria Cross will read, 'hurling bombs to cover his companions' retreat. By the time reinforcements arrived his courage and energy had done much to weaken the enemy's defence . . .'[68]

The Australians are soon attacking the post once more.

'Our courage began to falter in the face of overwhelming enemy strength,' *Unteroffizier* Paul Wabnik would recount, 'but Lt Neugebauer shouted loudly at us to hold on and threw one grenade after another . . . Our casualties were high; one comrade after another fell to the floor of the trench, shot through the head. The little group of fighters shrank steadily.'[69]

Still, the Germans fight on. Toe to toe the two sides go, bayonets clashing and sparking – parry, thrust, *in* – a scream, a gurgle, a death-rattle, and go again.

'First of all the blood ran to my head & I saw nothing,' Archie Barwick, now advanced to the second trench, would record of the overall experience of bayonet fighting. 'All seemed blank, then like a flash of lightning my senses returned, & I was cool, calm & collected . . . The next feeling was one of cold anger & I felt fit for anything . . . The incessant chatter of the machine guns was making a fine row & over all the heavy howitzers were falling fast, scattering death & destruction everywhere.'[70]

Men are falling all around, but Archie wields his bayonet with the best of them, with devastating results.

And sometimes it's not even something as sophisticated as a bayonet.

'Some of the men were gripped with trench frenzy and launched themselves at the enemy with spades,' *Unteroffizier* Wabnik's account runs, 'only to be beaten to death with rifle butts.'

The dead mount up, both their own and those of the Australians, who start to shout at them in the only German they know apart from 'Kaiser' and 'Berlin': '*HÄNDE HOCH!* HANDS UP!'

Some do give up.

Others don't.

'Obstinately we clung to our position and would not allow ourselves to be ejected,' *Unteroffizier* Wabnik would recount. Which is one thing. But with little ammunition for their rifles left, and only a handful of hand grenades – that is, around one a man – and their only machine gun already *kaputt*, it is obvious they cannot last long and must soon indeed put their *Hände hoch*. 'We prepared ourselves to be marched off to London. We destroyed the bolts of our weapons and waited. Morale was not exactly rosy . . .'

Suddenly, however, an excited whisper. One of Wabnik's sentries reports that a German soldier is crawling towards their position via a shallow ditch.

It shows there is a way out. Quickly, they start crawling away, right up until they are spotted and an Australian machine gun fires upon them. The Germans are up and running for their lives an instant later.

'Some of the men were killed or wounded. Physically completely drained, we . . . were down to eleven men.'[71]

Just 500 yards away, the panicked Germans are in such full retreat that Squatter Preston and his mates, together with some soldiers of the 11th Battalion, are able to chase them almost up to the old Windmill site, with those Germans who are overtaken being shot or bayoneted.

Out on the far left of the Australian line, the same thing happens, as the 1st Battalion's Archie Barwick would record:

'Men fell in all directions, but nothing could stop the boys now their blood was up. Into the trench they dashed & bayoneted & shot like fury. The Squareheads were thunderstruck by the violence of the assault & hopped out of their trench and ran for their life, with the boys after them hotfoot. They dropped everything they had; their one thought was to get away from the despised colonials.

'A and B Coy [of the 1st Battalion] were supposed to stay in this trench but no fear, on they went like a pack of hungry dogs, now they had tasted blood.'[72]

So cool are many of the Australians – despite the fact that 'the shell fire was now hellish & the noise deafening'[73] – that Archie Barwick

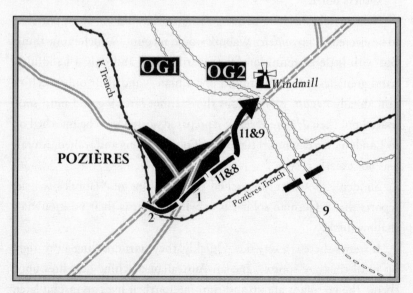

9th and 11th pursue Germans to Windmill

chronicles them going up the slope after the Germans, singing one of the Battalion's favourite tunes, 'I Want to Go Home'.[74]

Ah, sing it, boys!

I want to go home, I want to go home,
I don't want to go to the trenches no more
Where sausages and whizz-bangs are galore.
Take me over the sea, where the Allemand can't get at me,
Oh, my, I don't want to die,
I want to go home—[75]

The problem is that many of them *do* die, as Australian shells exact a terrible toll on the Australians themselves. They are not meant to be in this position at this time, and they must retreat.

It is Squatter Preston who realises – when he and his men reach the top of the ridge – that they have gone way beyond their objective. Gathering whatever men he can, he insists they head back.

Elsewhere, across the slopes of Pozières on the left flank, the progress of the 1st Brigade has been solid, bordering on spectacular.

All up, 60 Germans have been taken prisoner from Pozières Trench alone – many of them tough Silesian coalminers and foresters – while the Australians of the 1st Division are already well on their way to the 2000 casualties they will take in this initial onslaught, with a quarter of them killed.

At one point, when four Germans throw their hands in the air, a fifth only raises his hand to try to throw a grenade at the rampaging Australians – all five are cut down by the men born beneath the Southern Cross. In another case, a German soldier is seen to surrender, only to suddenly stick a bayonet in the stomach of the nearest Australian officer.

Through it all, the Australians are notable for their 'give it a go' mentality. For Charles Bean, the approach is best illustrated by a small incident that occurs as the 2nd Battalion successfully storms a trench on the far left. They have been so quick, and so surprised the German defenders, that one of the Australians manages to retrieve a water bottle that still contains – you bloody beauty – *hot* coffee.

'Don't drink it,' shouts one of his mates in warning, and another, 'It's poisoned!'

'Well, here's luck!' answers the finder,[76] gulping it down for all the world as if it's closing time at the Last Chance Saloon. He is fine – at least from the drink.

Just a couple of hours after the Allies have launched the attack, Pozières village is securely in the hands of the Australians – a significant achievement after three solid weeks of failure by other forces to achieve exactly that. Moreover, in the broad frontal attack that Pozières was the centrepiece of, everyone but the Australians had failed.

By the time Percy Smythe of the 3rd Battalion arrives at their final objective of the night – the trench along the southern side of the Albert–Bapaume Road – so many Germans have fled that it is secured without too much trouble, just after 1.30 am, when the barrage lifts off it.

Smythe is distressed, however, to hear that Captain Arthur Edwards, the Commanding Officer of A Company, has been killed – a furphy, as it turns out Edwards has only been badly wounded – and Smythe does

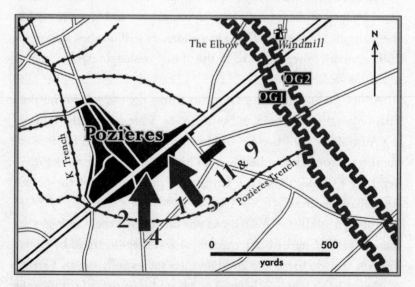

Third-line battalions of the 1st Brigade moving forward

as ordered by positioning himself in one of the dugouts scraped into the side of the trench.

'The Germans were sending over a lot of High-Explosive shrapnel and a few "whiz-bangs",' he would later recount of this consolidation phase in the wee hours, 'but, being very tired and sleepy, I dozed off, leaning doubled up against the wall of the dugout, and . . .'[77]

And never in his life has he had such a rude awakening.

Suddenly there is a whistle rising to a climax, an explosion, and this son of Jerilderie comes to, just in time to see something dark falling upon him, which he is momentarily sure is a dead body. But it's not. It's tons of earth, blown out by the German shell landing nearby and coming down right on him and his dugout.

'Got my head out and called for someone to come and dig me out, and a couple of chaps soon turned up with shovels. It was a great relief to get that awful weight of earth off my legs.'[78]

He is soon free and in another dugout with a couple of mates, Privates Dunn and Steer, 'when there was a sudden flash of fire just over our heads, accompanied by the roar of H.E. shrapnel'.

Dunn is shaken, Steer has blood pouring from a big hole in his leg, but Percy Smythe is all right.

'A man in the next dugout was killed by the same shell. A lot of those beastly H.E. shrapnel kept bursting close overhead, each time giving one a jar in the head like a blow from a fist.'[79]

And this is war for you. Smythe is so exhausted, so shattered by the experience, that he soon comes up with the only solution available. A better, more secure dugout is the one next door, with the chap killed by the piece of shrapnel to the head – he should have been wearing his helmet – so Smythe goes there. He has a look at the fellow's identity disc – it is Private Squires, a mate of a mate of his, which sort of makes him his mate, too – and it's sad all right. Look, at any other time, settling down to sleep next to a corpse would have shattered Smythe and he wouldn't have got a wink. However, it has been a long day and a longer night and, in the phenomenon noted since biblical times – severely shocked soldiers often go to sleep, or go mad – Percy is gone to the Land of Nod within a minute.

Archie Barwick, meanwhile, is taking matters into his own hands.

He and his mates have managed to get right to the edge of the wood, which they know is far enough, but as it seems all of their officers have been killed or wounded or are missing, they are near leaderless! What to do?

And yet, as I told you, it is not only in the realms of physics and mathematics that genius can strike.

Noting the single stripe on his arm that gives him the rank of Lance-Corporal, Archie realises that by taking off that one stripe, if he starts giving orders loudly enough, he might be mistaken for an officer, which is what is needed right now. A quick, surreptitious rip and it is done. The Lance-Corporal starts barking orders like a Colonel, Major or Captain, and in the semi-gloom no one knows the difference!

'I had nearly 300 men working like mad,' Archie would record proudly. 'I laid the line out myself and got them all along it and put other Sgts and Cpls in charge, while I walked along encouraging them, and the bullets and shells were flying thick, but somehow I had that feeling that this was my opportunity and I had no such thing as fear.'[80]

And it is working! In short order, the 300 Australian soldiers are digging like mad things. The trench gets progressively longer and deeper, while Archie, just one tiny rank above most of them, urges them on to ever-greater efforts and . . .

Oh Christ.

Right on daybreak, Archie, still busily impersonating an officer, looks up to see his 'worst enemy' appear, a man with whom he has had many clashes – Captain 'Blinker' McKenzie. He has been asking the men who is in charge here, and they are all pointing at Archie!

Oh *Christ*.

Just where Blinker has been for the last few hours is not clear, but Archie is clearly about to cop it. Blinker is heading this way, with intent.

But wait. Recognising that it is Archie in charge, instead of being angry, Blinker is *dumbfounded*.

The Captain puts out his hand and says, 'Henceforth I am your friend, Barwick, you have done me a good turn this night, and I have never deserved it.'[81]

And oh, the look on the other men's faces when they realise that they have been scrambling all night long on the orders of a mere Lance-Corporal!

'They were as puzzled as could be,' Archie would record, 'and they all gave me a hearty smile.'[82]

It is easy to forgive when they look at their handiwork. Because of Archie's subterfuge, the 1st Battalion now has a trench six feet deep into the black soil and can set to work building up the parapet and breastworks. They are ready for a German counter-attack, and their artillery barrage!

Not that it's over yet . . .

To their left, the men of the 2nd Australian Infantry Battalion can see in the growing light, just on the other side of the road, an extraordinary German defensive structure, two storeys high, all white, with several ominous slits from which to fire machine guns. On the western end is 'a low, square block tower'[83] and this 'concrete tower was exceedingly strong, and continued to stand practically undamaged after every trace of the house itself had been utterly blown away'.[84]

It is the German's *Blockhaus*, nicknamed 'Gibraltar' by the Australian troops, too good a target to ignore – even if it is 150 yards north of the road they have been ordered not to cross – for who controls it obviously controls this section of the front. Between them, Captain Ernest Herrod and Lieutenant Walter Waterhouse quickly work out a plan of attack, with the senior officer, Captain Herrod, taking the lead.

Rushing, for they must do this before true daylight, on Herrod's signal they start. To the right, Waterhouse takes a group of ten men on a circuitous route over the road and round, so that they can come at Gibraltar from behind, even as Captain Herrod sets his own men from the front.

And . . . *now!*

Up and over.

On the instant of the arranged time, Herrod's men charge forward, bursting through the door on their side at precisely the moment that Waterhouse's men are bursting through the back door.

One second, the 26 German soldiers are firing on the stealthy figures they can see over the road, and the next their front and back doors fly open and these giant figures from the other end of the world are upon them. No fewer than 25 of the Germans instantly surrender. Only one, a machine-gunner, is too distracted to notice the presence of the enemy, but he comes to understand quickly enough. A quick recce by the Australians discovers a large cellar below, 'from which a stairway leads down to a second and deeper chamber'.[85]

With 26 prisoners in tow, Captain Herrod quickly ushers the whole lot back to the Australian lines, together with the four captured German machine guns. It had been tempting to try to hold Gibraltar, but with the British and Australian barrage falling all around – and the Germans still just 50 yards away on the southern end of K Trench, their defensive digging on the western edge of the village – the risk of being overwhelmed by a successful German counter-attack was too great.

Before the battle, the Commander of the 117th Division, Major-General Ernst Kuntze, had been clear as only a senior German officer can be to his senior officers: 'Not an inch of trench must be abandoned to the enemy.' And if the enemy *does* occupy any ground, then all officers and soldiers on hand must 'drive him out at once by an immediate counterattack'.[86]

Kuntze had applied the same approach when he led his division to victory against the British at Loos in September 1915, and he insists on it being pursued now.

For the Commandant of Pozières, an *Hauptmann* with the unlikely name of Ponsonby Lyons, the capture of Pozières is not just critical, it is career threatening. For three weeks, the Germans have held the line against the best the British have thrown at them, and now the Australians have taken it? They must be removed at all costs. In the first glimmer of dawn, Hauptmann Lyons personally leads a counter-attack that attempts to drive a cleaver into the one area in which the Australians have not made progress, between the trenches occupied by

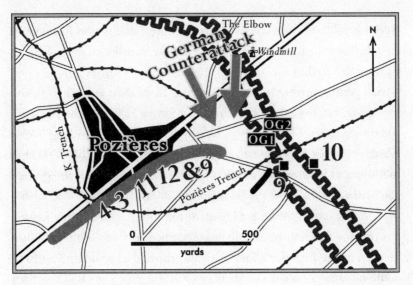

German counter-attack at Pozières

the Australians along the Albert–Bapaume Road, and the OG1 and OG2 trenches they have failed to occupy.

The German reinforcements summoned forward to join this attack have to cross the skyline atop Pozières Ridge where, in their hundreds, they are easily seen silhouetted against the sky by the Australians. Souvenir hunters 'ratting' Pozières village for mementos from dead German soldiers and their abandoned dugouts stop briefly, unable to resist shooting down easy targets. It is not every day that you flush the Hun into the open.

'The enemy came towards us . . . like swarms of ants rushing from shell hole to shell hole,' Squatter Preston would recount.[87] 'In our trench each man full of fight and confidence lined the parapet and emptied magazine after magazine . . . Men pulled one another down from the parapet to get a shot themselves . . . The machine-guns caused great losses and artillery which had been brought up tore great gaps in the oncoming lines, the attack just melted away.'[88]

Back to ratting . . .

Over on the far right, the fighting for the OG trenches goes on more fiercely than ever; the growing light gives ever better targets for both sides to shoot at. The most furious of these fights is led by a one-time

Adelaide solicitor and Gallipoli veteran of great distinction, Lieutenant Arthur Blackburn. Back on the day of the Dardanelles landing, Charles Bean would credit him – accompanied by a South Australian Corporal – with getting further inland against the Turks than any other surviving Anzac, before being obliged to retreat for the fact that others had not come with them. One theory as to why he has survived so long is that everything about him is so neatly tucked in, from his shirt tails to his chin to his ears to his arms by his side when he walks – no small thing when you live in a world where deadly shrapnel is always flying back and forth.

For Blackburn, pushing himself to the limits is just in his nature, but on this occasion he is fully accompanied to these limits by 70 of his men of the 10th Battalion. They hurl themselves again and again in bombing attacks on the Germans of OG1, for much of OG2 has been obliterated by the constant shelling. Bay after bay falls to their rushes, before the Germans rush back and retake bay after bay in turn, aided by their remaining machine-gunners in OG2, who are able to draw a bead on the invaders. Still, Blackburn and his men continue counter-attacking against the German counter-attacks as the fight crashes back and forth.

Blackburn leads the charge forward no fewer than seven times, losing half of his men in the process before they settle on a position close to the junction of Pozières Trench and OG1, and build a sandbag wall across to hold it – a final gain of 100 yards. For his 'most conspicuous bravery',[89] Lieutenant Blackburn is also awarded a Victoria Cross, no doubt tucked neatly into his vest somewhere.

It is the ground gained that is the true prize of the night, however, even if the men of the 3rd Brigade here are still 600 yards away from the Albert–Bapaume Road, and there is a gap of just under a quarter of a mile between them and the nearest Australian soldiers in the village.

———

The bottom right-hand quarter of the Pozières 'clock' is now in Australian hands. With the last protection of the limited light before daybreak, the men furiously dig their trenches, managing to get down to a depth of some four feet all along that road. And no fewer than 20 machine guns are now set up against whomever would try to come at them from the other side of the road.

All up, it has been an extraordinary advance, with the only disappointment being that, over on the right of the Australian axis of attack, another attempt to push up towards the Windmill via the OG Lines has failed. Once again, the Germans there have proven to be too deeply entrenched, with too many cleverly concealed and well-supplied machine-gun nests, to make any advance possible.

The fact that the Germans have held their positions in the OG Lines east of the road means they threaten the Australians' right flank, so they will sooner or later have to be dealt with, but for the moment it is indeed an impressive night's work. The key for the Australians now is going to be to hold on to the ground they have won, to allow them to push on from there, and in that exercise few are busier than Captain Ivor 'Margo' Margetts of the 12th Battalion – a much-loved sportsmaster from Hutchins School, Hobart. An athletic cove, he had been in Sydney representing the Tassie Aussie Rules team in an interstate carnival when war broke out, and he immediately joined up, distinguishing himself at Gallipoli, where he was among the first ashore.

As good with hard-bitten soldiers as he had been with children, he now has his men dig in at the northernmost position of the Albert–Bapaume Road. It is he who makes the running, steadying his men, organising their defences. The trench must be dug here, the Lewis guns over there, and we will stick the Company HQ in that shell hole over *there*. Hop to it, lads. Oh, and I need a casualty report sent back to Battalion HQ, so send a runner. And ask him to find out when our water and ammo replenishment will arrive.

Notwithstanding the German snipers who continue to take pot shots at them from the ruins on the other side of the road, there is a festive atmosphere among the men and lots of laughter. Many of the Australian soldiers smoke newly won German cigars and wear some of Fritz's wonderfully spiked helmets, the *Pickelhauben*.

Wait till the folks at home see this!

—

Some 300 yards to the south, in Pozières Trench, things are a lot less festive, though equally thankful. For his part, Archie Barwick can barely believe he is still alive.

'Well, thank God,' he finally finds time to begin his diary entry of the day. 'I have been spared to come through another fierce charge safely & with scarcely a scratch. I think Providence must watch over me, for my luck seems unnatural.'[90]

Right in the middle of Pozières, by the road with the 3rd Battalion, Percy Smythe feels much the same, with a twist: 'Every man wounded was regarded as being very lucky. I saw a madman rambling down the communication trench trying to catch hold of something he could see in the air, and I envied him.'[91]

When a German prisoner is brought back, a Sergeant wants to shoot him, but Percy and his mates won't hear of it. 'In our own affliction, we could well sympathise even with our enemies.'[92]

For the moment, things are calm – but how long will it last?

Chapter Sixteen

DIGGERS CAN'T BE CHOOSERS

The shelling at Pozières did not merely probe
character and nerve; it laid them stark naked as
no other experience of the A.I.F. ever did.[1]
Charles Bean

23–25 JULY 1916, POZIÈRES POUNDED

Far removed from that bloody exultation apparent in the Australian survivors in the front-line trenches, in the back areas there is mostly just blood – and lots of it. Stretcher-bearers work nineteen to the dozen bringing back wounded soldiers, and doctors and orderlies feverishly try to save their lives. One of those at work is the *deutsche Armeearzt*, the German Army doctor whom Squatter Preston had captured. Loyal to his *Eid des Hippokrates*, Hippocratic Oath, he is simply saving as many lives as he can, regardless of whether the grievously wounded are Australians or Germans.

Compounding the problems for all of them, though, are the probes of the German artillery, still seeking to gouge at sensitive points . . .

'Shells came in about 1 or 2 a second & everything was like day with the flares that were thrown up,' one stretcher-bearer, Frank Shoobridge, would record in his diary.[2] 'Wounded started coming in faster than we could get them away & the dugouts being full we had to put them out in the open where many of them got wounded again after we had dressed them . . . We were within 100 yards of the Aid post on our fifth trip . . . when a 5.9 [inch] shrapnel burst right above us.'[3]

For the stretcher-bearers, some of whom are pacifists choosing to serve their country in this manner – they won't carry a weapon or shoot anyone, but they are willing to be shot at – the job is somewhere between heartbreaking and backbreaking, and frequently both. And yet all are heartened when, to their amazement, at a collecting station, 'General Birdwood came round & talked to us – said the bearers had done good work.'[4]

Further back still, at Albert, the British soldiers soon become convinced that the Australians as a whole have done *great* work, most particularly when soldiers of the 1st Battalion march 100 German prisoners back beneath the Virgin Mary, whose arms, this time, are outstretched to greet them.

'The Tommies nearly went frantic with delight when they heard of the success of the Australians,' one soldier would recount proudly in his diary on 23 July 1916. 'They regard us as marvels, they had failed twice in their attacks on the wood & village, & we took it first time. We had a good reputation before but Australia's name stands higher today than ever it did before.'[5]

Yes, it has been an extraordinary day of history for Australian arms, but for General Haig it is just another day in his career. Other things are on his mind this morning as he writes to his wife:

My name is beginning to appear in the papers with favourable comments!
You must think I am turning into an Advertiser!
But that is not so . . .[6]

Whatever the truth, Haig has already made one key decision on this day, before breakfast, that will change the whole course of the battle. From now, all his Army and Corps Commanders are to cease making major, multi-division assaults and instead launch smaller, local attacks. Rather than looking for the big push, the big breakthrough, they must edge forward, trench by trench, gradually capturing important tactical features so that when the general attack *is* renewed, it will be better placed to succeed. Meantime, men and munitions – the key ingredients for success in that next big push – will be brought forward into the newly won areas.

For I Anzac Corps, it means their task is to focus first on two bits of important ground, Pozières Heights and then Mouquet Farm, as the ideal prelude for a general assault on Thiepval. The problem, in this case, is that the Anzacs are dependent on the British advances on both flanks going equally well, and alas . . . to their right, the British Fourth Army has stalled, and the 48th Division on their left, while making some headway, has not gained enough ground to make a difference.

Though the Australians have indeed done very well to take Pozières, the failure of the British to advance on both sides has left them exposed on both flanks.

—

In the end, for the Germans defending Pozières, the words of their commander, General Fritz von Below – 'The enemy must be made to pick his way forward over corpses'[7] – apply now more than ever.

Their first step is apparent in the early morning.

'A salvo of four big shells came over, and then the place was con-verted into an absolute Hell,' Percy Smythe records. 'It was awful. It seemed as if the whole face of the earth was being churned up. Clouds of earth and branches of trees were hurled skywards, while clods and lumps of chalk were falling all round. When a shell came near, the dense cloud of black smoke converted daylight into darkness, and the smell and the smuts were vile, but worst of all was the terrifying nerve-racking roar of the explosion, which was indescribable.'[8]

Later in the day, two major German drives are launched at Australian positions, with both repelled thanks chiefly to accurate rifle fire – a skill learned in the Australian bush and refined at Long Bay Rifle Range and again at Tel-el-Kebir – and, more particularly, the accurate British and Australian artillery, which targets the advancing Germans, leaving shattered corpses thickly scattered on the far slope of Pozières Ridge.

Where to from here, for the Australian forces?

Exactly.

The obvious move for Generals Walker and Blamey is to repeat what has worked so well to this point: unleash an overwhelming barrage on the German positions on the other side of the road through Pozières before sending their forces forward once more to capture the land where the village once stood. But that is the old tactic. Gough, following Haig's *diktat* of that morning – abandon big bombardments and large land grabs in favour of small attacks with smaller objectives – overrules Walker and Blamey. For, even beyond Haig, there is another factor that guides Gough. It's an issue of 'spend and save'. Haig has spent his saved up artillery ammunition to get this far; now Gough must save for a while until Haig says he can afford to spend big once again.

But what's this? New information suddenly changes everything. At noon, one of the aerial observers flies over where the Germans are meant to be.

But they aren't there!

'The whole of the village of Pozières north of the Road appeared deserted,' the report runs. 'All trenches in Pozières village are empty.'[9]

It is an assessment backed up by artillery observers with binoculars.

It looks as though the Germans have entirely abandoned Pozières! So, with that in mind, need they waste precious shells on quelling resistance that doesn't even appear to be there?

Gough says no and orders General Walker to simply send out local patrols. If all goes well, he says, the Australian 1st Division should be able to push through to Pozières cemetery on the far side of the village and join up with the British 48th Division, which is going to make another push.

Walker reluctantly agrees to General Gough's orders and passes them on to his own subordinates.

'To some of the front-line infantry, who throughout the day had been sniped at by parties of Germans still hidden in Pozières,' Bean would note delicately, 'it was rather exasperating to be informed that the place was empty.'[10]

Another sceptic is in Pozières at this time, under heavy German fire from across the road.

'How we used to love the air force when they sent messages of this sort!' Colonel Charles Hazel Elliott, commanding the 12th Battalion, would comment.[11]

Of course, it does not take long for the Allies to determine that, rather than gone or just a scattered few, hundreds of Germans are still in the area. Though they certainly have disappeared *above* ground, it soon turns out they are everywhere *below* ground – in the old cellars where the Pozières houses once stood, in the tunnels that have been dug to connect the cellars and in the myriad shell holes that abound all around.

Fierce skirmishing takes place throughout the rest of afternoon as the Australians try to clean out stronghold after stronghold by dropping grenades and phosphorous-like bombs – the latter designed to produce fire, billowing smoke and deep burns on whatever flesh it lands on – down the entranceways to the cellars, and catching or shooting all those who emerge. The Germans in turn are always able to use the tunnels to come up in different spots, as their dugouts always have two exits as a matter of military principle – precisely for situations like this. It allows them all too frequently to suddenly ambush the Australian attackers from *behind*, just as dedicated German riflemen are still able to exact a terrible toll.

All up, however, it is the Australians who have the better of it, with one Digger likening it to 'being out for a day's rabbiting'.[12]

For all that, the Germans are still able to bring down heavy artillery on the consolidated Australian positions as the day starts to finish.

Late in the afternoon, Lieutenant-Colonel Arthur Stevens, the Commanding Officer 2nd Battalion, and Lieutenant-Colonel Iven Mackay, Commanding Officer 4th Battalion, are trying to work out when best to move on reoccupying Gibraltar as they consult their maps, right by the appropriately named 'Dead Man's Road'. There are many of those about as they chat 'amid dozens of corpses and moaning wounded, mainly German'.[13]

Even as they are considering just how they might best advance their men – what precisely they must instruct their company commanders to do – they are interrupted by a runner eager to give them his message. His eyes darting left and right – spinning wildly, bouncing up and down – he gives them the envelope, hoping against hope that there will be no message in reply and he can be gone again in an instant. For who wants to stay longer than he has to in this, the most heavily shelled spot in all Pozières?

On the front of the envelope is marked *Urgent and secret*, and further inspection reveals it to be from General Gough. They open it quickly, knowing only too well that it will be of momentous import, likely affecting their whole plan of attack.

Oh.

Oh, dear:

```
A number of cases have lately occurred of men
failing to salute the army commander when he
is passing in his car, in spite of the fact that
the car carries his flag upon the bonnet. This
practice must cease.[14]
```

Such distractions notwithstanding, the Australians of the 2nd Battalion successfully retake Gibraltar, and bit by bit through the course of the evening of the 23rd begin to advance over the road in an effort to occupy the rest of Pozières – though, in parts, the German resistance remains strong, including the ongoing shelling of Australian positions.

On this evening, having a supper of bread and butter, bacon, cheese, sardines, sweet biscuits and chocolate, as the shells continue to fall, Percy Smythe is taking shelter the best he can in the trench by the road with his mates from the 3rd Battalion and is suddenly conscious that he and his men are not the only ones suffering.

'A little mouse came over to us to feed on the scraps,' he would record. 'It was quite tame, and seemed half silly, possibly suffering with shell-shock. A stray kitten was also wandering about the lines in a half-dazed manner.'[15]

On the far right of the Australian line, in the village early in the night, Captains Ivor Margetts and Alan Vowles – both highly regarded officers, adored by their men – cross the Albert–Bapaume Road with small patrols to determine where best to establish a new front-line. After discussion, it is agreed that while Margetts digs in with his men in this new position, which is about 150 yards on the far side of the road, Vowles will go back to bring up their two companies.

In the meantime, other patrols that have crossed the road achieve immediate success in terms of adding to their tally of killed, wounded and captured Germans, with one of the soldiers gleefully reporting, 'Altogether we killed 6 and captured 18 down the dugouts. The men had great sport chucking bombs down any hole they saw.'[16]

And that is not the only sport in such situations.

When one patrol is overdue to return, a search party is sent out, dodging flares and shell holes for some time . . . before, up ahead, a particularly incandescent flare reveals the lost patrol in a tight huddle in a shell hole, staring at the ground.

A soft voice rings out from one of them.

'Two heads are right!' he cries, before stooping further to pick up the pennies and his winnings from their impromptu game of two-up.[17]

There are signs everywhere of just how devastated the German defenders have been by the Australian attack, their previous existence here in ruins, just as the village is. Of course, there are dead German soldiers everywhere, but also a rich treasure trove. For the many Australian souvenir hunters, Ben Champion notes, there are 'trophies galore – helmets, badges, bombs, equipment, etc., enough to stock any large museum. This place, judging by the equipment, must have been very heavily garrisoned, and the men must have been blown to bits.'[18]

And what is this? It is a letter, blowin' in the wind, obviously written by a German soldier before the attack.[19] An Australian soldier tucks it into his pocket, to hand in later – such letters often prove to be vital sources of information.

(This one, as it turns out, once it is translated, proves to be far more personal in nature:

In Hell's trenches[20]

Dear Juise and children,
My darlings, the gods only know if I am writing for the last time . . . There is really no possibility that we shall see each other again. Should I fall – then farewell . . .)[21]

And yet, on this night, the German artillery is replying in kind, causing enormous damage of its own – with Fritz knowing their men, mostly underground, will be protected.

Just after 9 pm, Captain Margetts is in his forward position, taking shelter in a shell hole filled with wounded Australians and giving orders to one of his Sergeants, when a shell explodes above, sending out a shower of shrapnel in a vicious radius of ripped flesh. Amid all the screams, smoke and confusion, it is hard to work out who is freshly hit, but when one of Margetts' men, a stretcher-bearer attached to his company, Private George McKenzie, crawls over to him, after hearing the Captain weakly call his name – '*McKenzie! McKenzie . . .*'[22] – it is clear the news is bad.

'I have got one at last,' Margetts groans.[23]

Tenderly, McKenzie takes the scissors to open the Captain's shirt and quickly finds a wound the size of a penny over Margie's heart. The soldier dresses the wound the best he can and brings his water bottle up to the Captain's lips, but his officer is fading fast and soon falls silent, breathing shallowly.

Some 20 minutes later, Captain Margetts stirs. 'Is that you, McKenzie?' he whispers through barely open lips.

'Yes, sir . . .'

'If you get through this stink, lad, which I hope to the *God* above you do, let my people know how I got hit and died thinking of them.'[24]

With the last ounce of strength, of vitality, of life that Margetts has in him, he reaches out, clutches McKenzie's hand and . . . dies.

'I cried like a kid . . .' McKenzie would sorrowfully record. 'I think he went because he was too good for the beastliness of war . . .'

When the time comes to bury Margetts, McKenzie does it himself, removing what little personal effects the Captain has on him – to send home to his people.

'The only part of his property that I buried him with,' McKenzie would advise them, 'was a ring on his little finger which I could not get off without cutting his finger off, so I left it on him'.[25]

—

Over on the left of the Australian positions, the trench dug in the early hours of the morning by the men of the 1st Battalion under instruction from Archie Barwick is holding! When at 10 this evening they spy Germans massing, the Australians are thrilled.

'We all stood up in our excitement and shouted to them to come on, the thicker they were the better we liked them,' Archie would record, 'and promising them all sorts of nice things when they reached our trenches. But little hope had they against such cool and splendid rifle-men as the Australians. They never had a dog's chance.'[26]

—

Captain Alan Vowles, a rough, tough and tall West Australian like they just don't make them anymore, brings forward his and Margett's companies as the two had agreed and, with the shelling easing off, sends them fossicking for pockets of German resistance.

Just at that point of the darkest hours where it is drifting from being exceedingly late one night to very early the next morning, they find one promising set of stairs leading down to an open doorway, so they throw a bomb . . . for no reaction.

'Throw another one down,' Vowles says, sensing something.

Again, after the flash and explosion and billowing smoke, there is still no sound. Two of his men start to descend, only to hear voices from below.

Wait!

'*Parlez-vous français?*' Vowles calls down, relying on the fact that it is more likely for learned German officers to speak French than English, and even most of the common soldiers have picked up some of the language from two years in the estaminets. And, sure enough . . .

'*Oui!*' comes the Teutonically accented, guttural reply.[27]

Hold your fire!

In short order, no fewer than 17 furiously coughing and frightened German soldiers emerge from the darkness, hands in the air. One of them who speaks English informs the Australians that there is a Captain below.

That Captain, who has been in hiding here since he led the first early-morning counter-attack, an impeccably dressed man with an air of great authority, soon emerges and introduces himself.

'*Ich bin* Hauptmann Ponsonby Lyons,' he says, with his words translated into English by one of Vowles's men. A quick conversation ensues, which establishes two things of interest: Hauptmann Lyons has an English grandfather and . . .

'I am the Commandant of Pozières,' he says.

'Tell him that he *was* the commandant,' Vowles responds, 'but that I shall be happy to relieve him!'[28]

—

At 7 am the next morning, 24 July, Lieutenant-General Sixt von Armin, the Commanding Officer of Germany's IV Corps, which has responsibility for the Pozières sector, receives confirmation that all of the village has been lost.[29] It is, of course, bad news, but the fact that the Allies' attacks on both sides have been beaten back at least means that the narrow Australian penetration can be attacked with heavy artillery from both flanks.

Von Armin is quick to give his orders accordingly, and within the hour, on this otherwise beautiful day, all of holy hell breaks loose on the Australian positions, not with the expected six-inch shells, but – and Archie Barwick is now an expert in knowing the difference – '9.2 and 12 inchers'.

It is the beginning of the worst artillery bombardment that Australian soldiers will *ever* endure.

After the Germans first get the range, they specifically target the Australian trenches with enormous howitzer shells. To Barwick's ears, 'these enormous great shells sound just like an express train rushing through the air, & when they explode it is more like a ton of dynamite exploding. You can see them real plain sailing through the air on their frightful mission & everyone holds their breath & [braces] themselves for the frightful concussion that arises from explosion of these monsters . . .'[30]

Somehow, the collective resilience of the Australians is enough that they can still mount a formidable resistance. That much is obvious when, at mid-morning, another German attack appears on the ridge crest, only to meet the same fate as before – shot to pieces by Australians eager to give Fritz a bit (and more) of what they have been bloody well taking on their own for too long.

—

General Fritz von Below, the jowly commander of Germany's First Army, who has primary responsibility for defending the Somme Valley against the British thrusts, has called a crisis meeting, convened at First Army HQ in Bourlon Wood.

As ever, his Chief of Staff, Colonel Friedrich Karl 'Fritz' von Lossberg, is seated at his right shoulder. (Together, these two are known as '*die zwei Fritz*' – the two Fritzes – and are often criticised by the officer corps for too frequently risking their own lives by going to a different part of the front each day.) Also gathered around the large oaken table are the Commanding Generals of all four corps and nine divisions under von Below's command.

In his opening remarks, von Below could not be clearer. '*Meine Herren*,' he tells them, 'Pozières has fallen and must be taken back.'

Rather *sachlich*, matter-of-factly, General Max von Boehn – the Commanding Officer of IX Corps, which has responsibility for Pozières – comes to what appears to be a snap decision. 'General Wellmann,' he says, 'is entrusted with the re-conquest of Pozières . . .'[31]

All eyes turn to General Wellmann, the highly accomplished 57-year-old Commander of the 18th Reserve Division who is, quietly, stunned. They have the Commanders of the 7th and 117th Infantry Divisions present, both of whom are familiar with the local conditions – and yet *they* are not chosen?

'The whole thing,' Wellmann would note afterwards, 'was *eine überfallartige Überrumpelung*, a raid-like surprise attack, for me and the officers of my staff.'[32]

They have just arrived at the front themselves, after a quiet year in Artois, and *this* is to be their first task?

For now, all General Wellmann can do is stand, click his heels together, thank General von Boehn for the honour and assure him that his men will fulfil their duty. The two then retire with their two Chiefs of Staff to a small bedroom to discuss details.

'Following my suggestion,' General Wellmann would recount, 'the attack was set for tomorrow afternoon, because the attacks in the early morning hours here had always failed so far; now the English might not expect it in the afternoon.'[33]

There is much to do.

For General Wellmann is under no illusions. Retaking Pozières from *den Australiern* is going to be a singularly difficult task, even for one with such a magnificently upturned moustache as his, a phenomenon that is the envy of his peers.

—

Strangely, in Pozières village, there is just one pause in the carnage. In the early afternoon, both sides stop – even artillery crews must have lunch, and on this occasion they happen to coincide. At this point, despite the death, destruction and devastation all around, and the powdered remains of a once-bucolic village 'neath the Australians' feet, the birds are singing, the butterflies flutter by, and the most perfect of all perfect summer days is in full swing.

And then, mid-afternoon, the shelling resumes in force, more intense than ever before.

'The air sounded with one continuous whistle & roar from the big shells that were streaming through it, yes, in thousands,' Archie Barwick would later write. 'I stood with my watch in hand & counted in 5 minutes no less than 75 shells lob on an area no bigger than 4 acres, & not one of them was under a 9.2 & some were up to 15 in. All day long the ground rocked & swayed backwards & forwards from the concussion of this frightful bombardment . . .'[34]

Inevitably, with so many shells falling on the Australian front-line trenches over a full day, just what is trench and what is shell hole becomes problematic. Alas, under these circumstances, Diggers can't be choosers, and they only seek what shelter they can, where they can, praying for the bombardment to cease. The shells keep falling regardless, and by the time the sun starts to set, 'Pozières Wood & village was an onion bed . . .'[35]

And *still* it goes on.

'Everyone holds their breath and grips themselves for the frightful concussion that arises from the explosion of these monsters,' Barwick scrawls in his diary. 'They throw earth & stone, & men too, or rather what is left of them, to a height of easily 300 feet. Words fail to make anyone understand the terrible power possessed by these engines of destruction.'[36]

Meanwhile, another Digger, understandably nervous under the fierce barrage, ducks into the next bay to bludge a durry, only to find upon his return that all his mates in the bay he'd just left are dead. 'So smoking is good for your health,' he would tell anyone who would listen for the rest of his long life.[37]

Under such a bombardment, there is *no* safe place. The shells fall and those who take direct hits die instantly, while many of those in the vicinity are horribly wounded. Even those a good distance away risk having the walls of their trenches fall in on them. Time and again, after the explosion there are screams and cries for help, and survivors scramble to dig out buried comrades, until they hear a different scream . . . that of the next shell . . . and quickly take what cover they can find . . . until it explodes in turn.

By one account, 'the Huns simply poured high-explosive shells into our position. Trenches disappeared like paper in a storm. Where there had been trenches nobody could tell. The place was a series of huge shell holes, some 30-feet wide and 20-feet deep. Shells were so thick that they obscured the sun, smoke was so intense that one could not see, the row and noise was so terrific that men went mad, men simply stood and shook, their nervous system one entire wreck. Shell after shell planted itself in our lines, man after man was blown to pieces and yet not a man faltered.'[38]

The experience of Lance-Corporal Champion is similar. 'Continuous gunfire all the time,' he records in his diary. 'Of course, Fritz has his own late trenches marked off to a "T" on his maps, and can shoot back on them with accuracy. We were being continually bombarded, the trenches caving in, and we were digging each other out all day long. Soon our beautiful trench was nothing but a wide ditch, each side caving in making it shallower and wider.'[39]

And so it goes across the line, with the Australians really given no choice but to just suffer and survive the best they can. Early that night, the first attempt to take the OG Lines has one surprise success.

The 5th Battalion's Captain Cyril Lillie may only be 21 years old; may only be five foot nothing; may only be eight stone with his boots and backpack on and known as the 'Pink Kid' or 'The Kid' to the rest of the battalion because of his soft complexion, but he is a canny leader of men. He is able to get a mix from two companies of the 5th into the OG2 Lines, where they fight with the Squareheads like cats in a sack. And yet so quickly do the Germans themselves react, sending in a flood of well-provisioned bombing parties, that The Kid has no choice but to pull his men back to avoid being wiped out.

At least on the left of the Australian front, Pozières cemetery is captured by the 1st Brigade. A few of them even report that in the distance they'd glimpsed Mouquet Farm – inevitably referred to as 'Moo-cow Farm'[40] – which they must take.

Here, too, Private Thomas Cooke, a New Zealander serving with the Australians, had earned a Victoria Cross. Cooke had stuck to his post during a German attack and was found dead by his Lewis gun, thus setting 'a splendid example of determination and devotion to duty'.[41]

And then the bombardment ordered by General Richard Wellmann intensifies.

'One battery of 5.9-inch howitzers in particular,' Bean would note, 'began systematically to enfilade the trench-line [next to] the main road, sector by sector . . .'[42]

The situation is *appalling*.

'I can't imagine anything more concentrated than the German barrage at that stunt,' Private Frank Brent of the 8th Battalion would recount. 'The bay on our left, two or three chaps were killed, then the bay on our right went down. I said to the chap next to me, "We're next." I'd hardly said it before we were buried. I was quite unconscious, but they dug me out and [I woke up when] a pick hit me on the shoulder. I was sent down to the first aid post. I was given a tot of something, I wish it had been rum.'[43]

For those who have already been buried, the whine of the salvoes of yet more descending shells can be completely shattering, and some of the troops begin to lose their grip on sanity. 'Any amount of men were driven stark staring mad & more than one of them rushed out of the trench, over towards the Germans. Any amount of them could be seen crying & sobbing like children, their nerves completely gone. How on earth we stood it God alone knows. We were nearly all in a state of silliness & half dazed but still the Australians refused to give ground.'[44]

Major Verner Rowlands – once a Manly real-estate agent, now

responsible for the lives of a company of infantry – would report suddenly having 'eight men with shell-shock, praying to be paraded before the doctor'.[45]

After every explosion, survivors look to see who and what has been hit. One shell kills 15 Australian soldiers in one go, while another – a great 15-incher, says the Gallipoli veteran Archie Barwick – kills 40.

For Colonel Charles Elliott, '25th July was a fateful day for the Twelfth. I do not remember any other [bombardment] so severe . . . The great majority of the 375 casualties the battalion suffered were on this day.'[46]

For many of the Australian soldiers, this shelling doesn't seem quite fair. 'We beat Fritz,' Percy Smythe would note, 'beat him easy, he would not stand up and fight like a man, but fled before us, and then turned and tore us to pieces with his artillery.'[47]

—

Fritz certainly did.

At I Anzac HQ in Albert on this morning, Generals Birdwood and White go through the numbers of casualties and are not long in reaching their decision. Just as the French at Verdun had embraced the principle of *roulement*, constantly rotating divisions, so too are they now bound to pursue the policy of the day, bringing their divisions forward one by one into action, until they are 'bled white, and then taken away for a blood transfusion in some other more healthy area'.[48] It is clear that 1st Division is at that point now, and as the 1st Division War Diary records, '*At 1100 it was decided to withdraw the 1st Aust Infantry Division and replace it by the 2nd*'.[49]

—

It has been a long haul, but General Wellmann finally has his troops of the 18th Reserve Division, IX Corps, launched and attacking the Australian positions. It has not been easy. A few hours earlier, the

Commander of Infantry Regiment 157 had refused to attack because they were not yet prepared. He had only changed his mind when Wellmann told him, 'If IR 157 does not execute the ordered attack I'll see *den Kommandeur* court-martialled!'[50]

Now that the major attack is on, Wellmann's feelings change between '*himmelaufjauchzend*, exulting with utter joy' and '*zu Tode betrübt*, being in complete despair' as he follows the battle raging for hours continuously from the early morning.[51]

At 4 pm, he writes in his diary, '*Die Schlacht tobt ununterbrochen seit heute früh at Pozières*, the battle rages continuously since this morning at Pozières . . . I don't have time for writing more now.'[52]

At 5.30 pm, his major counter-attack is to go in, and his heavy artillery has already been smashing the Australian positions since 1.30. In the anxiety of it all, he is grateful to have help from on high:

Allmächtiger Gott im Himmel. Almighty God in Heaven, stand by us.[53]

Shortly thereafter, it is with some confidence that the German soldiers move forward. They have witnessed with their own eyes the terrible destruction wrought on the Australian positions over the last three days, most particularly since 1.30 that afternoon, and it defies belief that any force could still be alive.

Still, they must move quickly over the open ground, and so charge forward with fixed bayonets when – *meine Güte!*

Suddenly, from just up ahead, like demented kangaroos, surviving Australians come bouncing – in the dozens rather than the hundreds – beside themselves with savage joy that the shelling has at last stopped. And here are some of their tormentors before them, waiting to be shot for their trouble!

'The excited infantry,' the 2nd Battalion's Harry Hartnett would chronicle, 'could see Germans crawling over as quickly as they might from one shell crater to another, grey backs hopping from hole to hole. They blazed away hard . . .'[54]

Nothing if not brave, the Germans keep coming hard.

'When the Prussian Guards charged they got the shock of their lives,' Archie Barwick records, 'for they got cut to ribbons & the few remaining Australians actually hopped out after them with the bayonet. We took a few of them prisoners.'[55]

The infantry attack beaten back, the Germans' artillery explodes with fury, to the point that 'it seemed to onlookers scarcely possible that humanity could have endured such an ordeal. The place could be picked out for miles by pillars of red and black dust towering like a Broken Hill dust-storm . . .'[56]

Again the Germans attack. Again they are beaten back.

Mercifully, that evening of 25 July, the ordeal of the 1st Division is almost over. The first of the goggle-eyed soldiers of the 2nd Division arrive to take over their positions – a process that will take two nights in all. Alas, for the mightily relieved relieved, it is not simply a matter of filing back down the communication trenches – the Germans seem somehow aware of what is going on and shells follow them the whole way. Men who have survived against all odds for two whole days in this living hell are cut down.

'Last night about 11 o'clock we filed out & I think everyone breathed a silent prayer when they got clear of it,' Barwick records. 'I know I did for I never expected to come out alive.'[57]

The soldiers can barely believe it.

Open ground! Air that is not filled with shrapnel! Only a *distant* roar, and not the shrieks of shells exploding all around. Perhaps most extraordinary of all, there is hot stew and tea waiting for them. And then, after a march of just another three miles or so – taking them even further away from the front, so no one is complaining even though it is the middle of the night – they arrive at their bivouac area on the edge of Albert.

'We just simply threw ourselves down & slept as we were,' Barwick records in his diary, '& to many of us it was the first time we had closed our eyes for 6 nights, so you can imagine how we looked.'[58]

—

For his part, General Wellmann notes in his diary, '*Infantrie* Regiment 157 has *völlig versagt*, completely failed, in the attack . . . The attack of Regiment 86 has failed in enemy artillery barrage . . .'[59]

But, whatever else, it seems to have stopped the British attacking them, and that is really something. Not that General von Falkenhayn sees it that way. In a furious exchange with General von Below, he demands to know 'why Pozières has been lost . . . and why the counter-attack has collapsed, costing 2000 men but achieving nothing'.[60]

26 JULY 1916, NEAR ALBERT, NOT SO GRAND FROM THE GRANDSTAND

Good Lord Almighty.

Standing on the hill known as 'the Grandstand',[61] close to Albert and overlooking Pozières, General Walker is shocked.

In his entire 32 years in the military, he has never seen anything like it. He *would* be gazing upon the positions of his 1st Division troops if he could, but so extraordinarily heavy is the German bombardment that it is impossible to see a thing.

Now, when told before the Battle of Thermopylae that Persian arrows would be so numerous they'd block out the sun, Dienekes, a Spartan leader, reportedly replied that it was good news – he and his men 'could fight in the shade'.[62] But General Walker, his thin red hair now getting thinner by the *minute*, does not summon equal equanimity as he observes the shells raining down upon them as never before.

In the front-line trenches, the remaining soldiers of the 1st Division, together with the freshly arrived men of the 2nd, grit their teeth, pray to their Lord and, all too often . . . die anyway.

Now that the Germans can be confident that none of their own are still within the bounds of the Pozières village, there is nothing to prevent them firing heavy shells from all directions, and they continue to do so, at one point at a rough rate of eight shells a minute, by the count of the 2nd Battalion's Harry Hartnett. Just like at the Battle of Thermopylae, the sun really does disappear, and the landscape is blotted out, 'except for fleeting glimpses seen through a lift of fog'.[63]

From the German side, it looks much the same. 'The sky,' German soldier Friedrich Klahn, in Wellmann's 86th Regiment, records, 'was flecked with the bursts of shrapnel. The gigantic and phantasmagoric shapes of the high explosive could be made out through the yellowish grey dust, which extended over the boiling earth and reduced the sun to a dull yellow disc.'[64]

The shelling is so varied that it is hard to keep track, though Harry Hartnett has done his best: '[There were] gas shells musty with Chloroform, sweet scented tear shells, that made your eyes run with water, high bursting shrapnel with black smoke and a vicious high explosive rattle behind its heavy pellets, ugly green bursts, the colour of a fat silkworm, [and] huge black clouds, from the high explosive of his five-point-nines. Day and night the men worked through it, fighting this horrid machinery far over the horizon as if they were fighting Germans hand-to-hand, building up whatever is battered down, buried some of them not once, but again and again and again. What a barrage against such troops!'

Never has Harry been prouder of his mates. 'They went through it as you would go through a summer shower – too proud to bend their heads many of them, because their mates were looking.'

And even the officers are the same. 'I have to walk about as if I liked it,' one of Hartnett's Lieutenants tells him. 'What else can you do when your own men teach you to?'[65]

No one has seen anything like it! 'Later we experienced many hurricane bombardments,' Colonel Charles Elliott would be quoted as saying in a history of the 12th Battalion.[66] 'Lasting half an hour or more, of far greater intensity, but I do not remember any other so severe for such a long time . . . When I went up to arrange for our relief by the 19th Battalion, I could hardly find a trace of the trenches that had been so well dug the previous day.'[67]

Despite all that, some Australian soldiers manage to carry on, in their own fashion. At one point, when an officer makes his way to a part of K Trench that has been newly won, he sees four men of the 24th Battalion playing cards, even as the shells explode all around them. Of course they're anxious, but playing cards helps take their minds off it.

Above, on the parapet, is the corpse of their Sergeant, who, while playing with them just a short time before, had been killed. His dead hand of cards has been taken over by one of their mates. The officer notes it as an example of Australian sangfroid.

Alas, 'When the officer passed that way again, those four men were dead.'[68]

—

The thing that staggers the Germans most, however, is that, despite the extraordinary battering the enemy is taking, there is still fight in them.

'The British,' one sorrowful German report would have it, mistaking the men born 'neath the Southern Cross for their main country of origin, 'are an obstinate people who do not give up.'[69]

At noon on 26 July, high on the slopes of Pozières, a German artillery observer, scanning the Australian positions below with his binoculars, suddenly jerks his glasses back.

Was ist das denn?

They are trenches – newly dug trenches – snaking towards the Germans up the slope.

Still this extraordinary enemy intends to keep pushing upwards towards the ridge. It is a further inducement to shell such a desire out of them, and the artillery fire is increased further.

Of the many problems the Germans face, however, the complete Allied superiority in the sky over the Somme is a significant one, denying their own aviators the chance to guide that artillery fire. Those few German airmen who cross the lines rarely return to tell the tale. And yet, even for the British airmen, there is great risk. On his first mission of this war, on this very afternoon, Lieutenant Cecil Lewis is flying his frail two-seater BE2 over the OG Lines and has just taken his 22nd

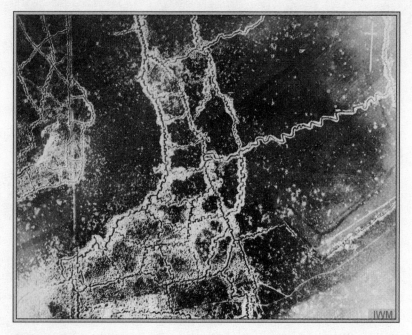

Typical aerial view of British and German First Word War trenches (this one between Loos and Hulluch, July 1917), IWM Q 45786

photograph when suddenly the Sergeant with him stiffens, cocks his gun and points: 'Fokker!'

Coming straight at them! Firing!

The Sergeant swivels his gun and presses the trigger.

Nothing. Stone-cold, motherless *nothing*.

'Jammed! Jammed!' he shouts while pulling frantically at the gun. *Still nothing.*

Lewis jerks hard on the joystick and tries to take his kite under the German. In an instant, there is a sharp crack, and the windscreen a foot in front of his face shows a hole. Mercifully, neither he nor the Sergeant is hit, though how the bullet missed, Lewis will never know.

'I stood the machine on its head,' Lewis will recount, 'and dived for home.'[70]

With the photos.

5 PM, 26 JULY 1916, POZIÈRES, FURIOUS FRITZ FIRES BACK

It is like an earthquake that simply won't stop. So heavy is the German bombardment that Walker and his senior staff are convinced the Germans must be about to launch a counter-attack to retake Pozières, so they order a barrage upon the German positions by the combined artillery batteries of I Anzac Corps and II Corps, and the British X Corps and II Corps.

Two villages down the road towards Bapaume, General Max von Boehn, the Commander of IX Corps, has replaced von Armin in charge of the Pozières front. While coordinating the planned counter-attack on Pozières village, he consults with the artillery officer whose job it is to play conductor to the orchestra of guns they have available.

The two of them become convinced that the hellish fire upon their own positions must presage another Allied attack, and so they increase German artillery fire even *more* – with the advantage being for the Germans, who can concentrate on a small target area. As the sun starts to set, a combined total of 350 German guns continue to pound to powder Pozières, while all the Australian soldiers can do is pray for it to end. Nothing in the war to date, not even Verdun, has reached this level of intensity. Even half a mile back from Pozières, the concussive force of the blasts constantly blows out carbide lamps.

In face of the whole conflagration, General Walker is furious, more glad than ever that the last of his 1st Division men will be pulled out tonight, but extrication proves to be no easy matter.

'My God, how they shelled us,' a Digger from the 6th Battalion records. 'The 24th Battalion took our place and in relieving us they made such a noise, that the Bosch heard us changing over and they shelled us like blazes, and it's a wonder any of us got out. We had no communication trench so had to cross in the open, so a battalion of men was at stake, and the silly blighters moved us out in single file and it was awful, dozens were killed, blown to bits, never shall I forget the 26th July 1916 . . .'[71]

The 1st Battalion's Ben Champion feels the same way, noting in his diary that, 'The 26th was our worst day . . . Of course, Fritz shelled us unmercifully, and charging over ground, and walking on the corpses of our A.I.F. men gave us the creeps . . .'[72]

Relieved at last by a battalion of the 2nd Brigade, Champion looks at his mates ruefully: 'What a mess of a Battalion . . . a scarecrow mob.'[73]

While delighted to get back to their own packs where they had left them – in a shed, guarded by the Q-store staff just outside Albert – that joy does not last long. Half the packs lie there unopened, sort of *staring* at them. The sight is so sad that many of the men, now that the threat of imminent death has passed, allow themselves to indulge in grief for their dead mates. And some of them engage in a delicate task, going through the personal effects to remove anything that might upset the family at home: semi-pornographic postcards, letters from women to whom they are not married or engaged, condoms and so forth. They get busy, as there are so *many* packs.

After just three days in the line, for example, the 1st Battalion has lost over half their men: 'Seven officers and 110 other ranks killed, four officers and 370 men wounded and 50 men missing.'[74]

A small parenthesis here.

Occasionally, *very* occasionally, however, something occurs that is very close to a miracle, where the list of those dead, wounded and Missing in Action can be reduced by one or two at a time.

Just such a thing occurs on this evening back up at Fromelles. To the stunned amazement of those manning the trenches, two ragged *real* scarecrow figures in khakis flop over the parapet – Diggers thought lost who had been out in No-Man's Land for nearly a week! One man had been shot in the arm; the other shot all over. But the first Digger had refused to leave his mate, and – after scavenging whatever rations and water they needed from the dead every day after the sun went down – dragged him a little further back every night, until they got to safety.

The next night, another man is rescued just in time. 'It's so good, matey, to see a real live man again,' he tells his rescuer. 'I've been talking to dead men for days. There was two men came up to speak to me who carried their heads under their arms!'[75]

The next night again, the Australians manning the trenches are even more stunned when another sole Digger makes it back, a man wounded in both legs and one arm, frankly more dead than alive, but now safe.

'He had not been able to reach the water himself,' the amazed army doctor who attended him would later recount, 'but had been able to keep his thirst down by sucking a strip of tunic which he had soaked in the shell hole water; by sucking very nearly continuously he had been able to get just sufficient water to keep him alive.'[76]

Back in Australia, of course, the news of such miracles is seized on by the families of all those Fromelles soldiers who are Missing in Action, proof that anything is possible. One holding on to such hope is Jessie Bowden, the wife of the 59th Battalion's Second-Lieutenant Jack Bowden, who *refuses* to believe the love of her life can be dead. *Not* Jack.

Close parenthesis.

—

The horrendous casualty rate at Pozières notwithstanding, there is no choice but to continue the changeover, as the 1st Division raggedly retreats, even as the men of the 2nd Division's 5th and 6th Brigades struggle forward. And what a struggle it is.

For men like Lieutenant Goldy Raws and his 23rd Battalion of the 6th Brigade – moving into Pozières positions at 10 pm on the night of 26 July – it is no easy matter to take over the 'trenches' left for them by the 1st Division, now advanced to the fields on the slopes above the site of the village. Walls have collapsed, massive craters are everywhere, and by the light of the flickering flares and exploding shells the 23rd Battalion men can see a ground littered with bloody bandages, ammunition boxes, broken rifles, dead soldiers and body parts – but no discernible trenches. In fact, in a task that would make Sisyphus weep, the survivors of the fearful shelling must completely re-dig every trench every day or two. What it means for the 23rd Battalion is that, while it is all very well for the 6th Brigade HQ to have given them maps, those drawings bear little resemblance to the shattered terrain in front of them.

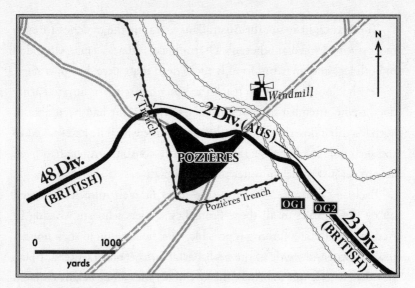

Position of the Australian 2nd Division, 27 July 1916

All Goldy and his men can do is get themselves into approximately the right spot and dig in the best they can before the sun comes up. With so much blood, the position of these men of the 23rd Battalion is like cattle taking up residence in an abattoir, peering into the darkness and wondering just when the workers will return.

Sure enough, with the first glow of dawn, so too do the shells roar down wherever the Germans have spied fresh trenches, just as their gunners start firing at all movement – and more Australian soldiers are killed.

With the 1st Division now fully out of the trenches of Pozières and heading back to the reserve area, it is now for the 2nd Division to complete their takeover and continue the advance. Their challenge will be to push on to the highest point of the ridge behind the village, the spot where the Windmill once stood. Obviously, if they can get it – and hold it – the Allies would be able to rain accurate shells down on German positions as far as seven miles away to Bapaume, with observers actually able to *direct* the fire right onto the Kaiser's mob.

Out on the far right flank, the 17th Battalion of the 5th Brigade is getting settled into the front-line. No sooner have they taken up position

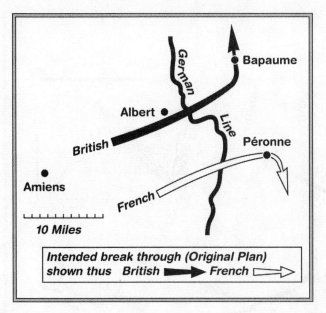

After a map by Charles Bean, *Official History of Australia in the War of 1914–1918*, Vol. III, p. 236

than they become aware that the Brits on their right are engaged in a grenade duel with the Germans.

The Australians can't stand it. Their hands twitch, their shoulders *ache* with the urge to throw. Reluctantly, their commanders give permission for the 17th's bombing platoons to head over there and get into it. And so they do, as what will be described as 'the greatest grenade battle of the war' unfolds.[77]

Bombing party after bombing party sallies forth, advancing against the resilient German defenders, who in turn rally to the sally and force the Australians back – with the two sides occasionally coming together in bitter hand-to-hand, bayonet-to-belly fighting. By 8.30 pm, the Australians have advanced 200 yards towards Munster Alley, the trench intersecting the OG Lines. By midnight, they've been beaten back again.

In the wee hours, however, Bean would record, 'On fresh bombs arriving another attempt was made on Munster Alley and about 60 yards of trench was regained by us. Hostile artillery enfilade fire was brought on the newly captured portion, but a barricade was built and the trench held.'[78]

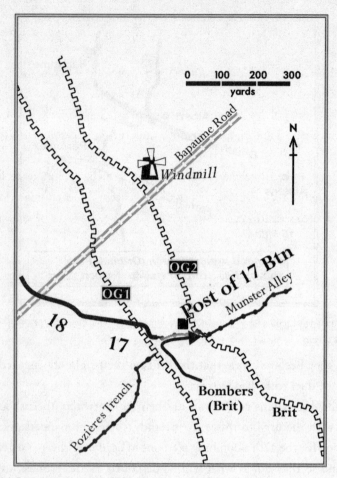

The 17th Battalion attacks the OG Lines

It is a battle that lasts over 12 hours, with all of 15,000 bombs thrown from the Australian side. The attack borders the positions held by the 68th British Brigade, whose Brigadier reports that it was only 'with great difficulty the ANZACs were persuaded to let me relieve them'.[79]

DAWN, 27 JULY 1916, WARLOY, SPECTRES FROM THE FOG

Marching in the morning mists. Soldiers coming this way, phantoms in the fog. Second-Lieutenant Albert Jacka and his men of the 14th Battalion – camped just out of Warloy, by the old village of Herrissart, waiting their turn to go forward – peer through the swirl to determine who it is.

Christ. It's the 1st Division AIF, now wholly relieved by the 2nd Division, who had finished their move up the night before. But, geez . . . just look at 'em! Yes, the 4th know that the 1st Divvie has been in the thick of a tough fight, but until now they'd had no idea just how tough.

'They looked like men who had been in hell,' Jacka's mate Edgar Rule would recount. 'Almost without exception each man looked drawn and haggard, and so dazed that they appeared to be walking in a dream, and their eyes looked glassy and starey. Quite a few were silly, and these were the only noisy ones in the crowd.'

And this was after they'd had a night's sleep and clean-up. What must they have been like before? Beyond their appearance, most shattering is the gaps in the ranks – about 50 per cent, well over 5000 of them! 'Some companies seemed to have been nearly wiped out . . . In all my experience I've never seen men so shaken up as these.'[80]

Is *this* to be our fate too? Is this what *we* will look like, once *we* have gone forward to relieve the 2nd Divvie? And which of *us* will be the ones now represented by the gaps in those ranks?

No chiacking now, no banter. Just a quiet breakfast follows as the shadow of the Valley of Death passes over them.

A short time later, at last back at their Tara Hill bivouac – the one area of green grass slope between the battlefront and Albert – the once mighty 2nd Battalion of the 1st Division throw down their packs. Just a few days earlier, when they had gathered at Warloy to hear the sermon of 'Fighting Mac', just before heading to Pozières, they had been 985 soldiers strong. Now, they can muster just 125 men still standing on their own two feet.

Of course, there is devastation and desperation among many of the survivors, for the things they have seen and done, for the comrades they have lost . . . but, as a body, there is also something else. As ever after a battle, the greater the devastation the survivors have survived, the more joyous they are to have done so. Many soldiers of the 2nd and

4th Battalions gather in the night around the mobile kitchen stoves and exult: 'See them get into that fat Hun. My God! A trench full of them . . . By God the boys let 'em have it. Billy Smith, he dropped his machine-gun, an' I chucked away me bombs – I wanted to get at 'em with my fists. God, what a time!'[81]

Other soldiers are haunted for reasons beyond the obvious. Better men than they – braver men, too – have been killed, slaughtered before their eyes. Of course, it's not their fault, but still they feel strangely guilty.

There is no doubt, however, that word of their exploits has spread. At one point, Lieutenant Charles Carrington is with a battalion of the Royal Warwickshires marching past these men of the 1st Division, when a tall, gaunt bloke in a slouch hat runs up.

'What lot are you?' he asks, friendly, but in an accent that seems to rely on vowels that are as squashed as Carrington's own vowels are rounded. 'You're the best looking crowd I've seen down here.'

Carrington is thrilled. 'That was a proud moment,' he would record. 'My regiment had been praised by an Australian.'[82]

In London, the Australian High Commissioner, Andrew Fisher, receives a very gratifying cable from an English officer of his acquaintance:

I'VE BEEN WATCHING . . . A FAMOUS AUSTRALIAN FORCE COME OUT OF ACTION. THEY HAVE FOUGHT SUCH A FIGHT THAT THE FAMOUS DIVISION OF BRITISH REGULAR TROOPS ON THEIR FLANK SENT THEM A MESSAGE TO SAY THEY WERE PROUD TO FIGHT BY THE SIDE OF THEM.[83]

Meanwhile, in a newly created military cemetery at Tara Hill, outside Albert, an army chaplain is holding a short service beside a long line of freshly dug graves, each one with the body of a 1st Division Digger who has perished overnight, covered in a blanket.

'I am the resurrection and the life . . .' the chaplain intones in the sunshine on this bucolic day. Nearby, a Lieutenant who is overseeing the burial of the men from his own company is taking the opportunity to write letters to families at home, to tell what he knows of how they died, as well as providing an affirmation of what fine soldiers they were, and how much they will be missed.

The chaplain goes on . . .

'Oh death, where is thy sting?

'Dust to dust, ashes to ashes . . .'[84]

As to their replacements of the 2nd Division, the question that must be addressed now is *when* and *how* are they going to take the Windmill? On this early afternoon, 27 July, at his dingy HQ in Toutencourt, General Gough is discussing just that with the Commanding Officer of the 2nd Division, General James Legge, a handsome man whose face appears to have weathered the war years lightly, at least in comparison to many of his rapidly ageing colleagues.

And Gough makes it clear to Legge from the first – just as he had a week before with the 1st Division's General Walker – that he expects *speed*, for the Australians to go in all but immediately, launching a series of moderate jabs to keep the Germans reeling.

'Once we allow him to get his breath back,' Gough has told Birdwood, 'we shall have to make another of these gigantic assaults by which time all the German defences will have been repaired and strengthened. I think our way keeps down casualties and brings the best results.'[85]

He warms to the same theme now. A week ago, General Walker had been strong and confident enough to resist, insisting on more time – and he had been strongly backed by Generals Birdwood and White.

On this occasion, Legge, a one-time brilliant barrister, educated at Sydney Grammar and the University of Sydney, and afterwards a Boer War veteran, would have been capable of mounting a strong argument against Gough's need for speed, just as he had once been a vocal critic of the landing at Gallipoli and, later, the attack at Lone Pine. But on this occasion, he mounts no such argument.

Waxing confident, Legge agrees to send his men in force, at all possible speed. For, despite the action being rushed, 'the atmosphere was one of extreme optimism', Bean would record of the mood at Legge's HQ.[86]

It is not, however, an optimism shared by Generals Birdwood and White later that afternoon at I Anzac Corps HQ, as they go over Legge's final plan, which is at least a vast improvement on that first proposed by Gough and his staff, simply a series of . . . . hammer blows by four battalions attacking successively *up* the Old German Lines. After consultation with Brudenell White, Legge had agreed it would be better to send the men over open ground with the troops of the 7th Brigade charging at OG1 and OG2 – with the first two waves to take the first line and the second two waves to take the second line, which includes the high point of the Windmill. They will be attacking, effectively, from the centre of the clock face to the 12, straight at the target – while the 5th Brigade will do the same on the right. Just one battalion of the 6th Brigade, meanwhile – Goldy Raws' 23rd – will attack on the left. Their job will be to gain 'elbow room' for the Allies by advancing on Mouquet Farm and pushing back those Germans situated in a trench on the Ovillers–Courcelette Road, which runs parallel to the Albert–Bapaume Road, who threaten to enfilade the attack of the 7th Brigade unless they are disposed of.

What most concerns Birdwood and White is the timing of the plan. At exclusively Legge's behest, the men are to attack at 12.15 am on 29 July, less than 36 hours hence, and no more than 48 hours after most of his men had arrived. That short duration means the men of the 2nd Division haven't had time to dig themselves trenches close to the jumping-off points, meaning the troops will have to assemble in the open, making them highly vulnerable to the German artillery, who will most certainly be *expecting* the attack.

And even then the trench they will launch from is badly placed. The 2nd Division will have to use the existing Tramway Trench, which lies at an angle to OG1, with men having to charge over an open quarter-mile to get to it.

And there are still more problems. As the ongoing shell fire has created terrible smoke and dust, it means that the artillery won't be able to properly register their guns. Legge has allowed for only one day of bombardment, which seems insufficient both to destroy the enemy's defensive barbed wire and ensure that it has been done thoroughly.

Yet the task set for the artillery is highly delicate. At 12.12 am, three minutes of hurricane fire would descend on OG1, before moving back to OG2 for ten minutes, before moving back again to the communication trenches where German reinforcements would be rushing forward.

And nor does it seem to Birdwood and White that Legge has a proper grasp of the need for heavy artillery, which – under normal circumstances – would have been given the job of levelling the OG trenches before the soldiers were sent forth. There seems to be a view afoot that it would be better to capture those trenches intact – which is all very well, so long as that can be accomplished. The other clear problem with the artillery is that because the Australian penetration is now a narrow finger, a salient, it means they can get their artillery no closer than 3000 yards – for fear of being destroyed by German artillery.

Legge and his senior staff seem so confident, however, that the I Anzac Corps men are swayed.

'General White, though full of misgiving,' Bean would chronicle, 'for once allowed the confidence of others to bear down his own judgment, and the date fixed by Legge was approved.'[87]

Quietly, Brudenell White is even more concerned than he lets on. 'I was sure things were not ready,' White tells Bean later, 'but everyone was so eager I gave my consent – through weakness I suppose . . .'[88]

What on *earth* is going on? In his HQ at Château Valvion this night, General Haig, who is hankering to secure Pozières Ridge, receives a report from his Artillery Commander, General Noel Birch, to the effect that the Australians of the 2nd Division had decided at the last moment that they would go at the Germans after midnight *without artillery support* and that, by the by, 'they did not believe machine gun fire could do them much harm'.[89]

Fortunately Birch had immediately gone to see General Gough, who arranged for the original artillery program to be carried out.

'The Australians,' General Haig notes in his diary, 'are splendid fellows but very ignorant.'[90]

All he can do now is hope that the Australian attack works . . .

Chapter Seventeen

A TILT AT THE WINDMILL

The much-glorified charge of the Light Brigade . . .
pale[s] by the side of the fearlessness and bravery of the
Australian and New Zealand farmer boys, and of the
London clerks, who charged into certain death at Pozières.[1]
Herr Karl von Weigand, Berlin correspondent for New York World

27 JULY 1916, OFF TO WAR FROM WARLOY

Christ Almighty.

This is it then. It is an extraordinary thing for these men of the 7th Brigade to march towards an all-but-certain fate – that within hours, many, if not most of them, will be dead or wounded – but they continue to do so, even with light banter.

And a long march it is, starting from their billets at Warloy at 6 pm and marching at a regulation two and a half miles per hour for 50 minutes – *left-right-left . . . leeeeft . . . leeeeft* – punctuated by a ten-minute break every hour. They are volunteers all, and this is their destiny, each step bringing them closer to the throbbing, flaring, booming horizon where, they know, they'll be attacking the Germans at last.

By the time they reach Tara Hill at around 8 pm, within coo-ee of Pozières, after ten miles of marching they are far from fresh. Yet no sooner have they arrived than they must march another two miles to the front trenches and go straight into the attack, charging at the

Germans over an open distance of more than a quarter of a mile!

That's the plan?

That's the plan.

Few are more stunned by how things are turning out than Captain Walter Granleese Boys of the 25th Battalion, a very *Australian* Australian bloke from Maryborough, Queensland, with enormous, capable hands. He is in sole charge of a company of 250 men, and it has been an *in extremis* miracle that they have found the right jumping-off point to begin with, after consulting a good map, a compass and uttering several prayers. But now they have to charge *400* yards? He can barely credit it.

The Allies' hurricane fire falls on the German trenches opposite, and the first of the four waves of Australians prepares to make its charge. It will be for the first two waves to get into OG1 and the third and fourth waves to get into OG2.

—

In their trenches east of the Albert–Bapaume Road, ready to go over the top, the Germans soon become aware of the forthcoming attack. Just before midnight, their sentries spot the beginnings of the enemy move: soldiers of the 5th Brigade massing on the other side of the road.

Speaking into their field telephones – calling for *Leuchtpatronen* . . . flares . . . *Maschinengewehre* . . . machine guns – they get almost instant results. Within minutes, those Australians huddling in their trenches in the darkness are illuminated as never before by German flares, and machine guns start chattering, even as shells start to explode all around them.

—

Watching closely from the German lines, *Leutnant* Richard Sapper, Artillery Liaison Officer of the 116th Field Artillery Regiment, is glad. 'Shells were landing everywhere with deafening crashes,' he would recount. 'And there – *Ja*, here we go! – searchlights came on, machine gun and rifle fire crackled along the trenches.'

Leutnant Sapper fires his red signal cartridges to help guide the artillery behind.

'Angrily our field guns opened up to our rear and our mortars and howitzers joined in, hammering and banging away. Now at last the whole orchestra was present. I listened with glee to the whistling, roaring and gurgling of our shells, which crashed down among the British. Great work you gunners. *Feuer! Feuer!* Give them everything you've got!'[2]

Around him, machine-gunners rush to their posts, while riflemen look down their barrels to their sights, waiting for the first sign of the enemy.

And here they come!

—

On the right of the Australian advance, the 5th Brigade are under such heavy fire that they can't really get moving. They do their best, trying to sneak forward, shell hole to shell hole, but under such heavy German fire it's hopeless, and the company commanders call it off.

In the Australian centre, the 7th Brigade storms forward into an even greater storm, a hail of machine-gun fire. 'They fell around me like flies,' Captain Walter Boys would recount of his comrades of the 25th Battalion, 'but on we went as if in a dream, while the smell of powder & din of guns, bombs etc, nearly turned my head. I reached the German barb-wire with *some* of my men, but could not get through . . .'[3]

One of those men is his great friend Lieutenant Vic Warry, who makes Captain Boys feel much the stronger for having him beside him. 'He fought splendidly and was right on top of the Germans when he went down. I nearly went mad when I saw him killed. Poor Vic, he died at the head of his men like a soldier . . .'[4]

That loss, however, is soon overtaken by the sharp difficulties ahead. For the barbed wire is substantially intact all along 7th Brigade's front!

The bombardment that had been meant to destroy it has not done so, with inevitable results. When the later waves of the 28th Battalion arrive, it is to see the first wave prone before the wire, surely ready to leap up once the blokes with the wire-cutters do their work . . .

And then they realise.

Those blokes are dead.

To their left, the soldiers of the 25th Battalion frantically try to find a way through, attempting to use the butts of their rifles to beat a path, trying to pull out the fencing stakes and using wire-cutters – even as the German machine-gunners, just 50 yards away, fire up to 600 bullets a minute and cut them down in droves.

In desperation, many men run up and down the line of barbed wire, thinking that at some point there must be an opening, but there is none. *There is none!* Only blasts of lead, tearing them apart.

Just to the left again of the 25th, the 26th Battalion is coming to equal grief. The German fire from the unbroken defences is furious; the wire is intact and there is no way through!

Yes, a few men, against all odds, have crashed into the German trenches, but it's clear that, overall, the 7th Brigade attack is a failure. The survivors have no choice but to go to ground. In desperation, one of the surviving company commanders, Captain Christian Johnson, takes his pocket torch and starts flashing messages down the hill using Morse Code to seek orders.

Hold . . . on . . . or . . . retreat? Hold . . . on . . . or . . . retreat? Hold . . . on . . . or . . . retreat?

There is no answer.

The only alternative is to give signaller Charles Rutsch a verbal message before sending him down the hill. 'If you signal "O.K.", [we'll] come back,' Captain Johnson yells at him over the roar of battle. 'If you send "H.O.", [we'll] hold on.'[5]

Given what has happened to his own devastated battalion – and the impossibility of communicating with anyone of superior rank – Captain Boys decides to take matters into his own hands and crawls along, relieving section after section and sending them back down

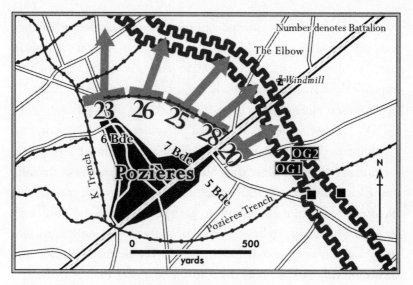

The Australian attack on Pozières Heights, 28 July 1916

the slopes to safety. A traditionalist, if Boys had been a sea-captain he would have viewed it a point of honour to be the last one to leave his sinking ship.

'I had to see all my men from the German lines before I could leave,' he would recount. But it proves not to be as easy as he'd hoped. And as yet more shells start to crash all around, getting to all his men proves to be as impossible as getting back himself.

Meanwhile, Goldy Raws and his company of the 23rd Battalion are in the thick of their own push on 'Moo-cow Farm', which will protect the left flank of the 7th Brigade and give them the elbow room they need. The 23rd's orders are to capture a manned German trench on the Courcelette Road – which runs roughly parallel to the Bapaume Road – about a quarter of a mile away, and dig in there.

As ever, through the smoke and screams, the bullets and scything shrapnel, fear stalks men like a wolf in the night trying to pick off stray sheep. And, as ever, they mostly push forward regardless, sticking tightly together and drawing strength from each other. This is not only what they have been trained to do; it is what they *must* do. Goldy's view is just as his brother Alec had put it in a letter to their father: 'I curse the systems of governments, the hideous fraud of a civilisation, which permits this dreadful welter of blood and suffering to have enveloped the world in modern times. And yet I go to join it, believing that the only hope for the salvation of the world is a speedy victory for the Allies.'[6]

More and more of them drop, but still the survivors push on.

'On and on we went, it seemed for miles,' Staff Sergeant Fred Hocking, in the same first wave as Goldy Raws, would recount.

Coming from the other direction, the German soldiers of the 10th and 12th Companies 86th RIR are just passing through the trenches of Mouquet Farm, pausing only to gaze in wonder at the 'wild artillery fire'[7] suddenly landing in front of them. It can only mean one thing: Tommy is about to launch an attack. The Germans rush forward accordingly, hoping to beat them to the foremost trench in the area – one they call '*Gierich Weg*', and the British, 'Park Lane'. Shrapnel reaps a terrible harvest among them as they proceed, but they still push forward because they must. They arrive just in time to see, emerging from the smoke and thunder, ethereal figures of fury running at them. The shout goes up: '*Tommy kommt*, Tommy comes!'[8]

—

In the vanguard of the 23rd Battalion, Hocking reaches their objective, the trench at Courcelette Road, but he can't be sure of it in the dark. All he knows is that the shadowy figures up ahead must be Germans!

'Stick the bayonet into them,' he roars, 'take no prisoners.'[9]

The Australians stick the bayonet into them; they take no prisoners. Many of the Germans flee back to the Old German Lines, leaving just a dozen of their *Kameraden* to fight on. Soon enough, these Germans, too, are running away. Hocking, seized with blood-lust, knows only one thing: 'My greatest desire in life is to kill one.'[10]

And he might have, but only an instant later a German machine-gunner in the Old German Lines sights him . . . '*Biff*, I was lying on the ground . . . I looked at my leg. Little spurts of blood were coming out.'[11]

All Hocking can do is start crawling back.

Where is the Courcelette Road? In the darkness, the confusion, the shell fire, it is extremely difficult for the Australians to discern its location. Before they know it, they have not only crossed the road but have gone 200 yards beyond it, arriving at the heavily defended Park Lane.

And things gets worse. Suddenly, the Australians are not only under attack from the Germans but, as Bean would detail, 'Many had run into their own barrage as well as the enemy's; and those on the Australian left had . . . been mistaken by the British troops for Germans, and fired on from the rear.'[12]

They are caught in a deadly debacle, brought on by their preparations having been too rushed. So too with the others, like Goldy and his men, who have got into Park Lane to fight a pitched battle with the German defenders, only to realise the area is untakeable. So they start to head back to where the Courcelette Road has been found – right where the final two waves of the 23rd Battalion are digging in.

It is the measure of Goldy Raws that, from leading like a raging wolf at the head of his pack, he is now at the back, shepherding his men more like a kindly sheepdog, with just one or two soldiers behind him. Corporal William Bagley, a Sydney hairdresser, is just 20 yards from Lieutenant Goldy Raws when suddenly there is the blinding flash of a shell exploding, and Lieutenant Raws is not there anymore! Bagley rushes on and, just seconds later, there is another sudden flash, and all goes dark and . . . heavy. (Bagley will remain all but buried for two hours, with only his head exposed. When he is finally dug out by his fellow Diggers, he is stone-cold deaf, can only speak in the barest whisper, is tremulous and has a terrible headache. But he is *alive*.)

———

Still going, Staff Sergeant Fred Hocking, leaving gouts of blood in the mud behind him, finally makes it back to the original Australian lines. His comrades, meantime, have now at least recognised Courcelette Road and are digging trenches beside it. It will prove to be the only gain of the entire attack. Elsewhere, the Germans have comprehensively beaten back the attacks of the 5th and 7th Brigades.

At 3 ack-emma, the Commanding Officer of the 26th Battalion, Colonel George Ferguson, further down the Pozières slopes, flashes with his torch the message for his men to come back, something they are able to do without trouble.

Others are not so fortunate – among them Captain Walter Boys, who continues to crawl among his men, seeing who is still alive, who can be helped and who can be told to get away while they still can and . . .

Suddenly daybreak is upon him. Boys realises he is trapped just 30 yards from OG1. He cannot move for fear of being shot, and his situation becomes more perilous as a mist settles all around, allowing the Germans to come out of their trenches to tend the Australian wounded. At this point, true, he could have surrendered, but Boys is made of sterner stuff. He stirs not a muscle, moves not a whisker. Truly, he barely breathes – so cold is it that a big, cloudy breath would give him away instantly.

———

At his HQ in Château Valvion, General Haig is ropable when he hears the full report of what has happened last night in the 2nd Division attack on Pozières. There are 2000 casualties for just about no gain, apart from the minor one by the 6th Brigade on the left.

As he marks in his diary, the causes of the disaster are obvious, starting with the fact that the jumping-off points for the 2nd Division had not been parallel with OG1. He even lists the most crucial flaws in his diary:

1. Attacking troops not formed up square opposite their objective . . .
2. The advance was made in the dark for a distance of 700 yards . . .[13]
3. One of the brigades had spent the day 2 miles in the rear . . .
4. The artillery bombardment was [poor][14]

Truthfully, General Legge himself is appalled by what has happened, realising that he really had been rushed and preparations had been insufficient. One British officer, Brigadier-General Howell of II Corps, comes across Legge that morning and would report finding him 'furious with the [Reserve] army; at least 1000 men lost for nothing'.[15]

Many years later, General Legge will go public with his anger, stating, 'Any apparent haste [I showed] should be properly ascribed to the daily pressure of the Reserve Army Commander [General Gough].'[16]

———

Captain Boys lies doggo through the whole day, completely unmoving as the sun beats down. Sweat trickles off him and the stench of his dead comrades makes him want to vomit. Just one move and he will surely be riddled with bullets. It is agony, and so distressed is Boys that, as he would recount, '[I was] almost off my head'.[17]

Even as he lies there, however, he is able to take note of the effect of the bombardment on the German wire – or lack thereof. Some shells, true, land accurately and blow the wire, but the majority are ineffectual.

EARLY AFTERNOON, 29 JULY 1916, 1ST ANZAC CORPS HQ, CONTAY, A GENERAL UNEASE TAKES HOLD

No, Sir Douglas Haig does not often get close to the front-lines. He is an overseer of the overall action, who makes strategic decisions by gazing at maps, rather than tactical ones by looking at the landscape itself.

He does occasionally drop in on different HQs of different corps and divisions, like the Anzac HQ at Contay, where on this day – in an office boasting a large wall map – he grants an audience to his nominal hosts, the Generals Birdwood and Brudenell White.

It is not a meeting of the minds, and when it comes to Birdwood, to whom he has never been close, Haig need not temper his temper, nor his remarks, in any way.

(Haig's feelings are strong. Just before this meeting, he had visited General Gough at his Reserve Army HQ – an officer, like General Haking, whom he continues to support through thick and thin, come what may – specifically to impress upon him that he and his most senior officers 'must supervise more closely the plans of the Anzac Corps. Some of their Divisional Generals are so ignorant and (like many Colonials) so conceited, that they cannot be trusted [to work out unaided the plans of attack].'[18]

In the here and now, Haig is convinced that Birdwood simply doesn't understand the conditions, and nor do the Australians. 'You can't come here after your victories in Gallipoli,' he says, his voice dripping with condescension, 'and imagine you can tackle this enemy as if you were fighting [Turkish irregulars] Bashi-Bazouks . . . !'[19]

Not a man given to emotional explosions, Haig nevertheless means it with a great deal of passion and quickly follows up. 'This is serious, scientific war,' he says, 'and you are up against the most scientific and the most military nation in Europe.'[20]

Why, look at all the mistakes you're making. Referring to the large map, Haig takes Birdwood and White through it. Yes, it is one thing to have taken Pozières, but Birdwood and his Australians must understand it 'had been captured thanks to a very thorough artillery preparation. Last year, the French had spent often a *fortnight* in taking such villages . . .'[21]

And don't talk to him about Legge. He had visited Legge some days prior and is convinced he is a 'bad stick' who showed a 'confidence [based] upon no production of knowledge and experience'.[22] On this occasion, Legge had blundered in to try to take the coveted Windmill site atop Pozières Ridge without first ensuring that their artillery had quelled most of the German resistance? Instead of that, their 'artillery bombardment was only for "one minute" before the attack, which was made soon after midnight . . .'[23]

And the men had been expected to charge home against the enemy's trench that was as much as 500 yards away – from Tramway Trench to OG1.

'Our experience,' Sir Douglas says firmly, 'is that about 150 yards is the limit for a successful charge.'[24]

(Oh, that Pompey Elliott could be here. His 15th Brigade had been wiped out at Fromelles just ten days ago after Haig's HQ had agreed to Haking's plan whereby his men would be asked to charge nearly three times that distance, *despite* Pompey pointing out the insanity of it. And if he could but know that now, such a short time later, Haig will issue a careful instruction to his commanders that no enemy positions are to be attacked 'without careful and methodical preparation',[25] he would surely explode.)

Haig goes on, making quite a few errors of fact, and though Brudenell White tries to correct him a couple of times, Haig's Chief of Staff, Brigadier-General Sir Launcelot Kiggell, intervenes with a raised hand to insist the great man continue casting his pearls uninterrupted.

When White *still* tries, it is Haig who is insistent: 'Listen to what I say, young man, I am giving you the benefit of my experience.'[26]

Haig is also critical of the fact that one of the brigades, after spending the day two miles in rear, 'had only marched up to Pozières after dark so, although the officers had reconnoitred their objective, the bulk of the troops were quite ignorant of the task before them'.[27]

(That sound? It is Pompey Elliott gnashing his teeth, even as he turns blue. So *now* General Haig places primacy on familiarity, whereas at Fromelles there had been no hesitation in sending troops who had barely laid eyes on the battlefield straight at entrenched positions, manned by Germans who had been there for 18 months.)

Now, while in the face of Haig's anger, General Birdwood looks as though he wishes the floor could swallow him whole, Brudenell White really is made of sterner stuff. And while Birdwood is incapable of answering the worst of Haig's barbs – 'Birdwood said nothing, probably being a little out of his depth,' is how Bean would describe it in his diary[28] – as he had not been the one actually putting the nuts and bolts of the attack together, Brudenell White most certainly can.

When Haig's fury is finally spent, he returns to English-gentleman mode and says simply, if distractedly, 'You have nice quarters here,' and is just reaching for the door when it is White who insists, 'I can't let you go, sir.'

'Why, what do you want of me?' asks Haig, stunned at the presumption.

While Haig's own Chief of Staff again looks on, aghast, trying to flash a warning to stop, the Australian begs to differ on a few points. 'Come to this map, sir,' says White. 'I cannot let you go when I know you are under a misapprehension on these points of which I know the truth to be different.'

Effecting the manner of an earnest teacher to a very smart student, he proceeds to talk Haig through it, by using his pointer. 'You said that the heavy artillery etc., etc., . . . The fact is they were . . . You said this . . . and this, and that . . . But the fact is . . . and so on and so on.'[29]

Quickly and quietly, the Australian tells the most powerful British military man in France just why he has got it wrong, while still managing to stay away from what they all know to be the core problem: Haig's protégé, General Gough, had pushed Legge into launching the attack before the 2nd Division was ready. Brudenell White does, however, defend Legge, assuring the Commander-in-Chief that, 'whatever his mannerisms . . . he did not undertake the task in any light hearted spirit'.[30]

And Haig hears him out, perhaps because in his view Brudenell White is an exception to the rule when it comes to Colonials and, as he will summate later, is clearly 'a sound capable soldier',[31] quite unlike Birdwood, who, while he has his uses, 'is not much use for directing *operations*. His tastes lie in making speeches to the Australian rank and file . . .'[32]

It is typical Brudenell White: quietly spoken but persuasive. 'He almost invariably swung his superiors to his view,' Charles Bean would note of his friend, '[while] with his inferiors, on a matter of principle, he was inflexible.'[33]

White's logic *is* rather compelling and, when he is done, Haig visibly softens to lay a fatherly hand on his shoulder. 'I dare say you are right, young man,' he says to the Australian, only a little over a decade his junior.[34]

Brudenell White softens in turn and assures General Haig, 'We have learnt our lesson and will be more thorough in future.'[35]

Despite it all, however, Haig, while underwhelmed at the effort of the 2nd Division, remains impressed by what the 1st Division accomplished. And however much he has enjoyed browbeating Birdwood in that afternoon's meeting, there is no point in being anything other than honest when writing in his diary later that evening: 'Still, the capture of Pozières by the Australians would live in history!'[36]

———

Finally, night has fallen. After no less than 20 hours and ten minutes of pretending with every ounce of his soul that he was dead, through an entire day and half a night, the whole time surrounded by corpses and bleeding men – 'It seemed years that 20 hours'[37] – Walter Boys is ready to make his move. With a thirst that borders on madness, he starts the long haul back.

Slowly, carefully, the back of his head tingling as he expects a bullet any moment, Captain Boys crawls down the slope. It takes hours but, finally, nearing midnight, he makes it back to his own lines.

'Somehow God watched over me, and I got through all right.'[38]

———

Whatever else, Haig's words have been heeded, as has the urging of General Brudenell White's long-held and oft-repeated view that it is 'useless to renew a defeated attack without changing the method'.[39]

And so, although Legge's 2nd Division is committed to launching another attack in an effort to take the Windmill at last, this time it will only be done after far more careful preparation. Deep consultation with

General White and the senior staff of I Anzac Corps quickly produces a new plan.

No more attacks when it is 'black as the pit from pole to pole' and confusion inevitably reigns, with catastrophe riding shotgun. Rather, the men will go in just before dusk, when *they* can see what they are doing from up close, and the Germans will struggle to see them from a distance. And then, if the Germans want to counter-attack, it will be *them* trying to move in the pitch dark while it is the Allies who will be firing from a position of strength.

But they must be precise. This time, they will go over the top at 9.15 pm exactly, when there is just 45 minutes of twilight left. Then they will be able to keep their bearings by keeping the Windmill mound at the top of the ridge in sight. There is, however, one complication with the new plan. For it all to work, the Allies will need a broad mass of men to get into the jumping-off positions in the daytime without the Germans seeing them, and this inevitably means further trenches will have to be dug, both to get the men there and to conceal them before they go over the top – a total of maybe 1400 yards of trench digging in all. This time, the jumping-off trenches will be parallel to the OG Lines, and no more than 250 yards away, so the attack on them can be 'square', as General Haig insists.

Given that the Germans will automatically bring down heavy fire on any digging they see, the construction of these trenches will have to be at night. Now, even though the jumping-off trenches are to be nothing like ordinary trenches – these new ones are just three feet wide and three feet deep – it will still take an extraordinary amount of labour. As each soldier is said to be capable of digging just two yards of trench in a night – which is to say 54 cubic feet, or a bit more than the space of three coffins – the Allies will need to dig over several nights. Initially, the hope had been that just one night would do the trick, but by now reality has set in and it is decided that the next attack will go in on the evening of 3 August, six days hence.

This time, the artillery will all be under the command of British heavy gun specialist, I Anzac Corps Artillery Commander, Major-General

William Napier. A no-nonsense, *big*-gun man who eats, breathes, thinks, loves and *lives* artillery, Napier has promised Legge that he will bring as far forward as he dares every heavy howitzer he has, and by using nine batteries of heavies, with four guns in each battery, he and his men will be able to bring down upon the enemy more than 5000 heavy shells over the ten hours preceding the attack going in. No one, now, talks of capturing the OG Lines intact.

EVENING, 29 JULY 1916, POZIÈRES, OH BROTHER WHERE ART THOU?

Alec Raws is thrilled. He has arrived at long last! After one *year* of waiting, of training, of corresponding, he is about to be reunited with his beloved younger brother. Beyond getting to grips with the task at hand – he has no sooner arrived than he is assigned to build those new trenches on this night of 29/30 July – what Alec wants most is to look for Goldy, of whom neither hide nor hair has been seen since the previous night.

Alec had even naively hoped that it might be possible to slip away from the task at hand to actively search for his hopefully just wounded brother in No-Man's Land, but, as it happens, it is clear from the first that he will be lucky to *stay alive* himself, let alone find Goldy. As a Lieutenant, Alec's role is to shepherd 50 men forward – each with his rifle over one shoulder and his shovel over the other – making sure that none straggle.

It is hard enough already for this dirty khaki snake to slither its way through the communication trenches that lead towards Pozières village, as the German artillery is shelling those thoroughfares. The men must regularly stop to clear away the dead or tend to the wounded. When they leave the remains of the village behind and get closer to where the nominal front-lines are meant to be, it is sheer bloody carnage. This close, it is like being out in a wild storm, with the thunder and lightning right on top of you, regularly wiping out whole sections of your comrades. At one point when the line stops, Alec pushes his way to the front of the blockage to find a shell has landed amidships, killing and wounding many men, cutting their snake in two.

'I would gladly have shot myself,' Alec would later recount, 'for I had not the slightest idea where our lines or the enemy's were, and the shells were coming at us from, it seemed, three directions.'[40]

Nevertheless, gathering himself much as he gathers his men to him, Alec works out what to do next, even as the shells continue to explode all around.

'I took a long drink of neat whisky and went up and down the bank trying to find a man who could tell us where we were. Eventually I found one. He led me along a broken track and we found a trench. He said he was sure it led to our lines.'[41]

Which is one thing – getting his men up and moving to get there is another. But through a process of bluff and bluster, orders and threats, Alec is indeed able to lead them out into No-Man's Land to the right spot, where they find the rest of the company. Which is the good news.

The bad news, as he would recount, is, 'Our leader was shot before we arrived, and the strain had sent two officers mad.'

It is for Alec and another officer to take charge and make sure their section of the trench is dug, despite the shells and ever-deadly machine guns. At least the men need no encouragement under such circumstances, as it is obvious that every shovelful deeper you go, the safer you are. With the burden of leadership on him, Alec is even more desperate that the men keep at it, as despite 'being shot at all the time . . . I knew that if we did not finish the job before daylight, a new assault planned for the next night would fail.'[42]

As the bullets fly, the shrapnel hisses and strikes, and the flares burst overhead, Alec has to give direct orders: even when your mate is killed beside you, there is no time to grieve – you have to *dig*. Your mate's body must be simply thrown aside – as ever, as part of the parapet between you and the Germans – and the same goes for those who are wounded, who must look after themselves and, if necessary, die through lack of care. Even those who go mad and turn into screaming, blubbering messes are on their own. Nothing can be done for them, because *nothing* is more important than this.

Dig, you bastards. DIG!

And now, a clash. In the first glow of dawn, a wild-eyed engineer, 'hopelessly rattled', takes it upon himself to tell Alec and his men that it is time to withdraw. But hang on, their part of the trench is not finished!

Alec draws his Webley revolver. 'Any man who stops digging will be shot.'[43]

They dig on until, 'amid a tornado of bursting shells', Alec allows his men to stop and withdraw. The trench is still not done, but they have no choice. Again he takes the rear to ensure no man is left behind, and again it is horrifying – some are cut down, and they all are cut off and lost.

Twice, shells explode close enough that Alec and the men nearest him are buried under mud, body parts and decaying corpses from past battles. 'I would, after struggling free from the earth, pick up a body by me to try to lift him out with me, and find him a decayed corpse. I pulled a head off . . . covered with blood. The horror was indescribable. In the dim misty light of dawn I collected about 50 men and sent them off, mad with terror, on the right track for home.'

Alec, meantime, stays back with two brave men to help the only unburied wounded man they can find, in an effort to save him.

'He was delirious. I tied one of his legs to his pack with one of my puttees.'[44]

Finally, they get away. Just another night at Pozières.

———

A few hours later, a meeting is held at I Anzac Corps HQ, 12 Rue de Noyelles – a pokey house on a pokey *rue* on the west side of Albert, well removed from their previous HQ at Château Lamont on the east side of town, where German shelling had become too intense. Around the table are the Generals Birdwood, Brudenell White and Legge, all flanked by their most senior officers, with the Commanders of I Anzac Corps making a surely tempting offer to the Commander of 2nd Division . . .

Would Legge like his men to be relieved?

What, *leave*, before the task assigned them is completed? This is not the way Legge and his senior officers see it. No, their broad view, as characterised by Charles Bean, is clear. 'Give it another go,' they say. 'There is no use leaving off after a set-back.'[45]

Even with 3500 casualties so far, the 2nd Division is not used up yet, with still 8000 soldiers left. They can still pack a punch to the Boche snout they so desperately deserve. They will proceed, albeit on a later schedule than before. As neither the communication trenches nor the jumping-off trenches are remotely close to being completed, the attack will now go in on the night of 1/2 August.

———

Where is Goldy?

After the insane horror of the night before, Alec Raws is now getting to grips with finding his beloved brother. Back in the Pozières Trench area, among the wounded, exhausted and sleeping survivors of the night, Alec wanders, introducing himself, asking questions, trying to find Goldy, trying to find, firstly, his brother's platoon. He must be here *somewhere*.

No one in the wider battalions seems to have definitively seen Goldy since two nights earlier, though Alec is impressed by how many soldiers and officers know his brother and speak of him reverentially. He keeps moving in the unfamiliar network of trenches, picking his way through sleeping men, dead men, bleeding men and the detritus of battle – from bloodied bandages and shell casings to ammunition boxes and severed limbs.

Aching for the familiar line of his brother's chin, the way he carries himself, the distinctive slope of his shoulder, Alec keeps moving, fighting a rising sense of panic that Goldy might be . . . gone. No, it couldn't be. He'd surely find him, just around the next bay of the trench. But after a couple of hours moving through the whole battalion – it takes much less time than it would have at the same hour yesterday – and finally finding those few survivors of Goldy's platoon, there is no denying it. Goldy is one of those missing. Oh, my Lord and Saviour, Jesus Christ, let it not be true. The effect on his parents and wider family, Alec knows, would be sheer devastation.

In hope of a miracle, that night he ventures into No-Man's Land once more. Despite assurances from the stretcher-bearers that Goldy isn't out there, Alec knows he has no choice. It is what his parents would want him to do, what Goldy would do for him, what he must do. Scrambling from shell hole to shell hole, calling out, scanning for the slightest sign of movement, trying to jump at the endless shadows that flit back and forth as the flares rise and fall, he is finally satisfied. There is no sign of Goldy in the area in which he was last seen.

—

The recent losses at Pozières are, of course, simply added to the latest casualty lists, and are no better or worse than usual. Yet there is no doubt that the overall length of all these casualty lists put together is now becoming a great concern.

'The Powers that be,' Chief of the Imperial General Staff, General William Robertson, in London, delicately writes to his friend and ally Sir Douglas Haig at this time, 'are beginning to get a little uneasy in regard to the situation[46] . . . In general, what is bothering them is the probability that we may soon have to face a bill of 200,000 to 300,000 casualties with no very great gains additional to the present. It is thought that the primary object – the relief on Verdun – has to some extent been achieved.'[47]

It is true, Haig allows in reply, that they have lost a lot of men in the last month. But still, as one who has always been ready to pay 'the price',[48] he is not unduly troubled by that. 'Our losses in July's fighting,' he notes to Robertson, 'totalled about 120,000 more than they would have been had we not attacked. They cannot be regarded as sufficient to justify any anxiety as to our ability to continue the offensive.'[49]

For the point remains. Though that is indeed quite a few casualties, and no small number of 'death-knocks' around the British Empire to 'convey the deep regret and sympathy of their Majesties, the King and Queen, as well as the Commonwealth Government in the loss that [you] and the army have sustained by the death of [your] son . . .'[50] the point is, the Germans are suffering nearly as much and are without an Empire to replenish their men. (Even as Haig writes, the conscription debate in Australia is warming up and the Commander-in-Chief of the British Forces in France is confident that a flood of previously reluctant Australians will soon be on their way.)

No, they must keep going with their methodical attacks on the Germans, simply wearing them down in this war of attrition.

'In another 6 weeks,' Haig assures Robertson, 'the Enemy should be hard put to it to find men!'[51]

Not all of those in positions of British leadership, however, see things the same way. A particularly trenchant critic is the one-time First Sea Lord and then Major with the 6th Battalion Royal Scots Fusiliers on the Western Front, Winston Churchill, who now finds himself back in London as a mere Member of Parliament on the Opposition benches. Never a man to fancy that he does not know a whole lot more than the Generals, Churchill is insistent that his views be shared in a memo circulated to Cabinet.

'Leaving personnel and coming to ground gained,' he notes, 'we have not conquered in a month's fighting as much ground as we were expected to gain in the first two hours. We have not advanced three miles in the direct line at any point . . . In personnel the results have been disastrous; in terrain they have been absolutely barren . . . From every point of view, therefore, the British offensive *per se* has been a great failure.'[52]

Haig does not see it like that at all, and, when the memo is passed on to him in France, is outraged by Churchill's presumption as much as his conclusions.

LATE AFTERNOON, 31 JULY 1916, POZIÈRES, A MAN PUSHED TO THE BRINK PUSHES FORWARD

That tall, skinny but rather stooped figure pushing forward through the falling twilight of the rise of eventide, towards the spot where he has been told the front-lines lie? From the first, he is remarkable for the fact that he is clearly not carrying a rifle, there being no telltale silhouette of a muzzle poking from the top of his right shoulder. And though the ginger-haired man with the piercing blue eyes is wearing khakis, he bears not a cane, or a pistol in a holster, or any other kind of accoutrement officers so frequently bear. He doesn't even bear a grudge . . . but we'll get to that.

He has neither the air of fierce determination about him of one who is about to do or die, nor the look of refined remoteness so often apparent in those whose job it is to tell others to do the same. No, he is just a man, poking forward, trying to find his way along a communication trench that will lead him directly to the most forward Australians here. He is resolute, without rage for the enemy nor rancour for the bastards who are making him do this. He is here with peaceful purpose, out of duty for his craft.

He is Charles Edwin Woodrow Bean, and of course he is alone. For not only is he the only Australian correspondent within coo-ee, but – a fact that deeply annoys him – the British correspondents focus only on British exploits, such as there are, even though, as he would shortly note in his diary, 'none of them come within shellfire . . . Every one of them is free to come where I do if they want – and goodness knows I'm careful and nervous enough; but they don't and the consequence is I suppose that they don't actually know what we have been doing.'[53]

(True, he will later note this as something of an exaggeration, due to the fact that he is overworked, but it reflects his feelings at the time.)

And so it is up to him to chronicle the Australian experience, their extraordinary courage, the grandeur of their achievement.

Besides, how can he *possibly* cover what is happening at Pozières without seeing it himself? Can he really look Australian soldiers in the eye, and even have them salute him as 'Captain', for that remains his nominal rank, if he has not experienced at least something of what it is to be in the trenches with them?

He cannot.

Following the exceedingly rough directions he has received, the 36-year-old pushes forward towards the centre of the Australian positions, through the devastation . . . *obliteration* . . . of what was once a village.

More appalled with every step, Bean heads to that part of the Allied front-line occupied by the Australian 5th and 6th Brigades.

And now there are *voices* up ahead. Whose? Ours? Theirs? Under the circumstances, it could be anyone, but Bean is relieved to find they are Australian soldiers after all, five of them, who give him rough directions – go along here to this shell hole, turn right at a group of six dead men and you'll find, etc. – to where the front-line now lies.

Following those directions closely and being obliged to stoop even further and run at one point to escape the worst of a burst of machine-gun fire, Bean finally arrives at a point where there are more live soldiers than dead ones, and then into what looks very much like a recognisable trench, though one still shattered by shells. It is held by the British – for he has lost his way and overshot the 2nd Division positions – but they are able to turn him round and show him the way.

But there prove to be so many craters, and they are so tightly clustered, just like the Australian soldiers of the 21st Battalion he finds, that it is all but impossible to work out just what was trench and what is shell hole. And, of course, as Bean continues to push along, in so many spots he can see dead Australians, sometimes as many as a dozen, mostly of the 28th Battalion, who had died in the first wave of the 6th Brigade attack in the early hours of 29 July. Their bodies and body parts even show up in a pattern to indicate where the shell that killed them must have landed, throwing them outwards. In other spots, there is not a mark on them, and it even looks as though they are sleeping, sitting up like Jacky, clearly having been killed by the concussive force. Even as the roar of shell fire continues to roll over him, nearly flattening his spirit with its force, Bean continues to nudge forward, through mostly deserted trenches that, he knows, hundreds of Australian lives have been lost and lamed to capture.

His aim is to get to the 19th Battalion over on the far right – the one in the foremost position closest to the Windmill. Again following directions from the few men he encounters, Bean finds himself on his hands and knees, crawling along behind what was once a hedge over the final 100 yards to reach the 19th. 'It was an eerie feeling clambering over craters, behind the hedge, with no sign of any trench anywhere or of any living thing,' Bean would recall.[54]

Every now and then, he catches sight of the shattered remains of the Windmill, high on the hill, which helps him get his bearings.

Some 30 minutes later, the forward survivors of the 19th Battalion are stunned to see a strange man with a notepad emerge from the gloom – surely the only unarmed officer for miles in any direction!

And Bean is in turn stunned to see them, a group of survivors almost as shattered as the landscape around: 'They had been in for seven days and were nearly at the end of their powers . . . They have had no fight – they have simply had to hang on in the line cut (i.e., traversed) by the German barrage . . . They are quite cut off from the right and the left except for journeys overground. There they live and are slowly pounded to death – they think there are only 250 of the battalion left . . .'[55]

As is ever his wont, Bean takes copious notes and asks as many questions as possible of these exhausted, shattered men.

When the time comes to go, the men of the 19th offer him a guide, a fellow by the name of Welsh, who – if he can't promise to get Bean back safely – can at least get him back safer than he would be on his own. Bean feels he has no choice, as otherwise he has no confidence he will be able to find his way, and the two set off.

'Everywhere were blackened men – torn and whole – dead for days,' he would recount of the return journey. 'About eight or ten big black shrapnel shells were thrown over as we went, but they were far behind us. At last the guide recognised the remains of a hedge to the left of us. We had gone too far, and we saw the dry white pad leading along a broken trench . . . we ducked under the railway. I knew the way now, so the runner left me – I hope he got home safe – good chap.'[56]

Soon enough, Bean is able to further get his bearings by coming out on what used to be the Albert–Bapaume Road, which he only recognises through its 'curious straightness'.[57] The road surface itself has completely disappeared under the constant shelling.

After following the path for some 20 minutes, as the crashing of the shells starts to recede just a little, Bean is soon greeted by the welcoming, friendly face of a man he knows and admires, Chaplain Major Walter Dexter, and two other men of the cloth, right by the road in Becourt Wood.

It is typical, brilliant, brave Dexter, who is a decorated veteran of the Boer War from before he started doing the work of the Lord. Scrounging the stuff he needs from God-knows-where, this chaplain of the Anglican Church, known as 'the Pinching Parson' for his ability in this very field,[58] has managed to put together a large billy of boiling water and is serving piping-hot tea and coffee to the endless stream of wounded who are making their way back from the front-lines. It is precisely the kind of restorative that Bean needs, and he pauses in his journey, deciding to spend the night with these good men in their dugout, on Dexter's convivial invitation.

Not that there is much time to chat, however. Bean must attend to his note-taking of the extraordinary things he has seen, while the chaplains busy themselves burying the dead. This is an urgent task, not just because so many bodies are decomposing but because senior officers have deemed it bad practice to leave them out in the open.

'It does not encourage new troops to see a sight like that,' Bean records. '[So] they simply turn them into the nearest shell hole and cover them up. No time to get identity disk – it is rotted away. So these poor chaps go down as "missing" unless someone has their disk already.'[59]

Most of the corpses buried, Dexter comes back to sort through the personal effects he has gathered, in order to put them in separate packages and, when those effects identify the dead soldier, send them back to the family. The chaplain is so doing when there is yet another explosion, close this time, and screams are heard. A German shell has just killed six soldiers and grievously wounded a couple of dozen more in a nearby wood. There will be yet more burying to do on this night.

God help *him*!

'I find this sort of shelling very trying when it's on,' Bean records in his diary, 'a scream and a sharp crash and a branch of a tree sailing up to the top of the wood and subsiding.' All up, he is convinced. 'I don't want to go through Pozières again. I have seen it now once – it was a quiet day.'[60]

2 AUGUST 1916, RESERVE ARMY HQ, TOUTENCOURT, A MATTER OF BLACK AND WHITE

At his HQ at Toutencourt on this morning of 2 August, General Gough is advised that General Brudenell White is on the phone. Gough, an officer with a certain *what-is-it?* in his voice at the best of times, is not pleased to hear it, suspecting only too well that it will be yet one more problem causing another dashed delay. Sure enough, in his educated but broad Australian accent, Brudenell White tells him exactly that – they will need to postpone the attack until two evenings hence, 4 August, as the Australians simply won't be ready beforehand.

'But General Legge has told me the opposite,' Gough replies, bristling.[61]

'Well,' the Australian says evenly, 'you can order them to attack if you like, but . . .'[62]

As Gough's mood turns blacker, the imperturbable Brudenell White proceeds to point out that not only are the jumping-off trenches not finished, but the enemy barbed wire has still not been cut, despite the British artillery having been targeting the fences heavily since the last attack. By leaving the attack until the night of 4 August, White insists, both tasks will be completed.

. . .

General Gough . . . ?

. . .

It goes against the grain, but Gough reluctantly agrees to Brudenell White's logic, and so informs General Legge that he will allow a two-day delay.

One of them, a Colonel Bridges, is not very pleased. 'This gives us a bit more time for preparation,' he harrumphs, 'and more time to the *Boche* too!'[63]

———

If only General Wellmann could find some fresh units, he most certainly would bring them forward during the extra time allowed. But there are none. Only a handful of replacements for casualties have arrived, and Wellmann complains to his diary that they are 'much too young'.[64] After nearly five weeks of the Battle of the Somme, the German Army is hollow-eyed with exhaustion, and there are simply no fresh reserves in bulk. Thus, all Wellmann's 18th Division can do is hold their positions in the OG Lines, among their dead comrades, blinking in the butchered darkness and wondering just when it is that the Australians will be back to attack. In fact, so expectant are the German soldiers that twice they report attacks that have not actually taken place. As Charles Bean would document, exhausted officers had seen Australians working on the jumping-off trench, assumed this must be the attack they'd all been waiting for and so called in a barrage. Once the Australians had duly retreated, those same officers triumphantly reported their attacks had been beaten off. But Wellmann is not fooled. In his *bones*, he knows there must be a big attack to come . . .

3 AUGUST 1916, CHÂTEAU VALVION, *DEUX HOMMES À CHEVAL*

The two men riding their fine steeds on this day are close. Though at 55 years old General Sir Douglas Haig is just under a decade older than General Hubert Gough, his relationship to the younger man is almost a paternal one, and Gough – who has served under Haig since the beginning of the Great War – is fiercely loyal to him in turn. Their talk, thus, is easy and frank, though Gough must break the news to Haig that the attack of the Australians at Pozières has been delayed one more time.

'From what he said,' Haig would later write in his diary, 'I concluded that the cause was due to the ignorance of the 2nd Australian Division, and that the GOC Legge was not much good.'[65]

The attack will now commence the next night, on 4 August, at 9.15 pm. All is set then. All that is left then is a vigorous ride to get their blood racing.

A-gallop, a-gallop, a-gallop awaaaaay.

—

The word goes around among the men of the 4th Division's 4th Brigade. It's time to leave Warloy and exchange their billets for bullets oncoming. They must prepare to go in and relieve the 2nd Division, which has now been in the line for well over a week.

Going into the battle proper then? The experienced soldiers know what to do – their laundry.

If they are likely to be suffering wounds, then their best hope of not getting those wounds infected – which perhaps could kill them – is to have a clean body inside clean clothes, and so they set to with a will. You pass the soap, and I'll provide the elbow grease.

—

The nicknames of most Diggers are obvious: 'Long'un' for the well-endowed fellow; 'Windy' for the bloke who once got very windy under shell fire; 'Gypsy' is one of their cobbers who lived in every state in Australia; 'Snow' for the blond bloke and 'Bluey' the redhead. Not so, however, 26-year-old engineer Captain Eric Webb, who is known as 'Azi' among the scientists of his usual milieu, from 'azimuth' – the number of degrees between due north and a certain reference point

– which is known to be his favourite word. No matter that most Diggers wouldn't know an azimuth if it bit them on the bum, the name had stuck and Azi, a veteran of Sir Douglas Mawson's famed 1911 expedition to Antarctica, is a popular officer within the 7th Field Company of engineers, highly regarded for both his leadership and his ability to sort out complexities. Both qualities are on call in the early hours of this morning as, with compass in hand, Azi manages to sort out the location in No-Man's Land for the final burst of digging for the jumping-off trench. By the first flush of dawn, it is done. All is now in readiness for the attack.

Tonight.

One officer making ready is Lieutenant Percy Cherry of the 7th Brigade's 7th Machine Gun Company, as his diary entries over these two days attest:

> 3 August. Attack delayed on account of the forward trenches not being finished. Men anxious to be given the word for action.
> 4 August. Attack tonight at all costs. Everything prepared. Feel confident of success.[66]

———

It has been far and away the most devastating five days of Alec Raws' life, filled with death, destruction, desperation and grieving. Nothing on Heaven and Earth could ever have prepared him for this living Hell.

In his delicate hand, he writes a letter to a friend in the Legislative Council of the Victorian Parliament, trying to capture just how extraordinary his situation is:

> One feels on a battlefield such as this that one can never survive, or that if the body lives the brain must go forever. For the horrors one sees and the never-ending shock of the shells is more than can be borne. Hell must

be a home to it. The Gallipoli veterans here say that the peninsula was a happy picnic to this push. You've read of Verdun – they say this knocks it hollow. My battalion has been in it for eight days, and one-third of it is left – all shattered at that. And they're sticking it still, incomparable heroes all. We are lousy, stinking, ragged, unshaven, sleepless. Even when we're back a bit we can't sleep for our own guns. I have one puttee, a dead man's helmet, another dead man's gas protector, a dead man's bayonet. My tunic is rotten with other men's blood and partly splattered with a comrade's brains. It is horrible, but why should you people at home not know? Several of my friends are raving mad. I met three officers out in No-Man's-Land the other night, all rambling and mad. Poor Devils! . . .

The sad part is that one can see no end of this. If we live tonight we have to go through tomorrow night and next week and next month. Poor wounded devils you meet on the stretchers are laughing with glee. One can not blame them. They are getting out of this.[67]

For now, Alec's main focus – beyond survival – remains unchanged. He wants either to find Goldy or to find out what happened to him. Where to from here? Well, at least Alec is known among his comrades for the fact that 'his reporter's training made him very reliable in the way of news, which he used to pick up and sift at headquarters'.[68] He is able to put the same skills to use now, trying to work out who saw what and when, and how this fits with other available information.

There are varying reports. The most promising one is a soldier who swears that on the night that Goldy disappeared, he had been in a hospital four miles the other side of Albert and had spoken to a medical officer who 'appeared to know Mr. Raws personally, and said that Mr. Raws had passed through his hands with wounds in his head, and been sent on',[69] but, alas, the soldier does not know the medical officer's name.

Another says that, coming back from Courcelette Road, one moment Lieutenant Raws was there and the next he wasn't. Still another claims, 'He was seen to fall, but to get up again, and say he was all right,'[70] though what happened afterwards is not clear.

The bottom line is that Goldy is still missing and – most galling of all to Alec – it had all happened as part of an insanely planned operation that had seen Australians rushed into action against a superior, entrenched force, over open ground. All this with insufficient artillery to protect them and ordered to do so by superior officers in remote HQs wantonly wanting to advance their forces, as they did their careers! The way Alec sees it, they ordered his brother's company forward *knowing* it would be carnage, only *hoping* it would be worse on the other side!

So strong is the sentiment in the centre of his soul that he will soon write to his oldest brother, Leonard: '[Goldy] must be accepted as missing finally. His death has proved a far greater shock to me than I thought possible.'

There is no way around it. He really would have to accept that he will never see his brother again, this side of Heaven.

'Before going in to this next affair, at the same dreadful spot,' he writes, 'I want to tell you, so that it may be on record, that I honestly believe Goldy and many other officers were murdered on the night you know of, through the incompetence, callousness, and personal vanity of those high in authority. I realise the seriousness of what I say, but I am so bitter, and the facts are so palpable, that it must be said . . .'[71]

The feeling in his breast is clear, as he will put it in another letter: 'I boil to see the war through in order, interalia, to do what I can to expose some things the Australian public never dream of.'[72]

Meanwhile, he has also been agitating for a Court of Enquiry to be held so that there is official force behind these queries, so that men can be pulled out of the line and ordered to answer questions. But, given that no fewer than 70 per cent of Goldy's original company has been killed or wounded by this time – let alone the even more devastated platoon he was with at the time – it is clearly going to be a difficult exercise. It is like trying to hold a murder trial for a bloke on a boat, when just about all the other passengers have been murdered too. And, yes, he does mean *murder*. Or did he mention that?

Alec finishes his letter and begins to make ready. The third big attack on German positions at Pozières is going in tonight, and he and his battalion are to be in the thick of it.

And so will Russell Bosisto of the 27th Battalion. This son of South Australia, with five sisters and devoted parents, is worried. Now, just hours before the battle, this only son writes to his beloved father, pouring out his angst about how things are so much worse here than at Gallipoli. The 27th is right on the front-line, about to go over the top. There is, of course, to be no retreat, and the only way out of here is to go forward, Dad. He also asks his father not to read the letter to the rest of the family and to prepare them for what might happen.

The piercingly blue-eyed 'Boss' has been in trouble more than usual of late, and has had such a wearing time of it in recent months that his mates have chipped him about the fact that his once jet-black hair is turning grey. He is not surprised – it may be about to get a lot greyer still. As a matter of fact, he has just come off what would have been a fortnight's stint of 'Field Punishment No. 2' – heavy labour – for having been found with grog in his kit. But they'd let him off the last two days, so he could join this battle.

No, really, they shouldn't have.

—

Things are strangely calm. Five days earlier, when the Australians had attacked, everything had been frenetic at this point before the whistle blew, as the 1st Division had been forced to rush materiel and men forward. Not this time.

This time, every man, every grenade and every ration box is where it should be. The trenches are dug. The artillery is as ready as it ever will be.

Now, with just over three hours to go before the attack begins, that artillery launches its final major barrage of intense fire on the German positions to be attacked – in exactly the same manner they have for the previous evenings. Yes, they have hopefully *trained* the Germans to understand that they can go into their dugouts and simply come out when it is over.

And so it is that, exactly as planned, at precisely 9 pip-emma, three hours after the heavy barrage had begun, it stops – only to resume, just as suddenly at 9.15, on OG1. The men of the 7th Brigade on the left and 5th Brigade on the right coil themselves like tightly wound springs.

They are positioned exactly as they had been on the night of 28/29 July, with the 7th Brigade in the prow of the attack, the 5th Brigade on its right flank and the 6th Brigade on its left, part going for the ridge and part looking to make 'elbow room' by working its way north along the Courcelette Road. They know that at 9.18 pm the artillery is going to lift off OG1 and pound OG2 for ten minutes, before moving again to 50 yards behind OG2 at 9.28, to prevent reinforcements rushing forward.

Anxiously, they wait for 9.18 pm.

There!

Even over the cacophony of machine-gun fire and exploding shells, the shrill blast of many whistles pierces the already shattered night.

With a roar, the Australians are up and moving forward, and things are immediately different. This time, the artillery fire on the Germans really has been so devastating that the Squareheads have had no choice but to retreat to their dugouts. And secondly, because the jumping-off trenches of the Australians are so much closer, at a maximum of 300 yards – where lies the outward kink in OG2 known as 'The Elbow' – that they are able to jump onto the still-blinking Germans in their dugouts before the Boche know what has hit them. Most of the Huns have not even had time to get to their machine guns, let alone set them up in their emplacements.

The fighting is as brief as it is brutal. The Australians kill and maim those who resist, and capture those who put their *HÄNDE HOCH!* By the time the barrage lifts off OG2 to go further to the German rear, some of those same Australian soldiers in the first wave of the 7th and 5th are able to join the second wave as they charge to OG2.

But where is it?

In the familiar plaint of Pozières, just what is trench and what is shell hole is not immediately apparent – though, in the case of the 5th Brigade, they are at least able to get a clue by spotting the line of stakes that had previously held up the rolls of defensive barbed wire. This is it! Here! Dig here!

Furiously the Australians set to – just as they have reclaimed OG2 from the Germans, they now must reclaim it from Mother Earth.

In the momentary confusion as to where the trench lies, however, the Australians present perfect targets. With one chatter of a machine gun, a whole group of them, just to the right of The Elbow, falls. One of those men is Captain Walter Boys of the 25th Battalion, who had survived the first attack against all odds, only to now be riddled through the abdomen and killed.

Out on the left flank of the Australian attack, the 23rd Battalion are engaged in much the same exercise as they had been on the night Goldy Raws had died, and his brother Alec is doing much of his fighting within 200 yards of where it had happened. They get to their objective, and then the trouble begins and the instinct of the Diggers is to do what they have always done notably well. They dig. Alec, like all the others, hurls clumps of dirt from his shovel so fast there are two clods in the air at any one time. No one needs orders; the bullets and shrapnel flying from both sides have their own way of encouraging them to go fast.

'The Gallipoli men,' Alec would recount, 'say that our fighting in this offensive far exceeds for strain and horror the Peninsula campaign. They say they would rather have a month at Gallipoli, with all its hardships, than one day of our Great Push.'

Twice, a shell lands within 20 yards of Alec and his mates, with inevitable results, as an instant later they become part of a conflagration of mud, blood and bodies. When it settles, seconds later, many find themselves completely covered by the crushing weight of earth. For a split second, everything is as black as . . . death. Either they are now in their graves for all eternity, and these are just the first seconds, or . . .

With a massive surge, Alec manages to get his bearings and pushes towards where there appears to be some movement, which must be *up*. As he bursts back through to the open air once more to take big, gasping breaths, it is almost as though, *in extremis*, Mother Earth has given birth to him once more.

Some of his mates do the same, while others don't. A frantic scrabbling at the dirt to try to find them ensues. Some they find and save . . . some they don't. Alec lies back, 'much dazed and very frightened'.[73] The shells keep landing.

As to being merely being knocked down by the concussive force of the explosion, that happens at least a dozen times and is too inconsequential to remark upon. Through it all, whatever he is feeling, Alec manages to maintain an extraordinary calm, with one of his fellow officers noting how, 'Given a job he was sure to carry it through, even under such difficult conditions as on that first night he entered the firing line . . . Raws was always cool, philosophical and quietly cheerful.'[74]

Just next to Alec, a soldier who is little more than a boy, a fellow they call 'Omeo' because he is from that tiny village in Victoria's high country, has just taken the pin out of his Mills bomb and is ready to throw – he is said to be the longest thrower in the 23rd, and this is where they need him most – when a German bullet drills him and he falls, the bomb rolling from his outstretched hand.

With his dying breath, the lad manages to say, 'Mick, the pin is out.'

Said Mick leaps, grabs and throws, just a couple of seconds before it explodes, saving them all.

This time, the attack works, all along the Australian line – a Battalion of the 6th Brigade and all of the 7th and 5th Brigades are at last into the OG Lines all along a 1200-yard front.

Among the men of the 7th Brigade's 27th Battalion, Russell Bosisto is right in the fiery thick of it. Whatever they have said about his constant AWLs, his predilection for impersonating an officer by putting the pips of a Lieutenant on his uniform to impress the French girls, and all of his shenanigans, no one has ever doubted his ability as a soldier when a donnybrook is on – he is right in the forefront of the 27th's attack. Suddenly a shell lands nearby, sending up heavy chunks of earth.

Everything is as black as . . . death. Either Russell is now in his grave for all eternity, and these are just the first seconds, or . . .

He struggles . . . and struggles . . . and struggles . . . and subsides.

This time, there will be no bursting forth from Mother Earth. She has claimed him, as his comrades surge on.

'They were in too great number to be stopped,' a rueful German officer will say later, before adding, admiringly, '. . . fine strong lads.'[75]

The next target for those lads, of course, is to get to the crest of Pozières Ridge, just 50 yards beyond OG2.

For in this particular battle, both sides know it: who wins the Windmill wins . . .

Chapter Eighteen
DÉJÀ VU, ALL OVER AGAIN

When the history comes to be written this battle of
Pozières ridge will certainly rank with the battle of
Pozières village and with the landing at Gallipoli
and the battle of August, 1915, as the four hardest
battles ever fought by the Australian troops – indeed,
among the hardest ever fought by any army.[1]
Charles Bean, The West Australian, 10 August 1916

2 AUGUST 1916, OUR FATHER, WHO ART IN HEAVEN

Attennnnnn-shun! Now, with just a short time to go before they will
be hurled into the line, no less a personage than General Birdwood
has arrived to inspect the 4th Division. Yes, Birdie is a man of many
failings, but the Australians retain a rough affection for him.

Whatever else, at least he turns up occasionally like this, just as
he did when these same men of the 2nd Division had been the first
to arrive in France, all those years ago . . . back in . . . April. And
Birdwood in turn likes the Australians, even fancies he has a rapport
with them that the other British Generals don't. It is about showing
familiarity, you see, demonstrating that you care for them as *men*, not
just as soldiers, almost – and this is the revolutionary part – dealing
with them as if they are not your peasants to do with as you will. And
for such an occasion as this, when a fresh division is about to go in,

he goes forward, wandering among the men, chatting here and there, asking them, 'Have you written home?' and so forth.

As he moves along the line, the English General asks one fellow, as if he has known him all his life, 'How is your father?'

The private in question, Mick, tells him straight up: 'My father is dead.'

Birdwood doesn't seem unduly perturbed by this sad piece of news and makes his way down the line. Returning back up the line, he comes across Mick again. 'Well, my good man,' the Commanding Officer of I Anzac Corps says, 'how is your father?'[2]

'He's still dead, sir,' says Mick.

The Birdwood inspection complete, the 4th Division, including 'Jacka's mob' of the 14th Battalion, move off. Within three hours, they are within coo-ee of the battle's roar.

'With the darkness,' Eddie Rule would record, 'came "wind up" – our knowledge that we were going into hell . . . made us very uneasy.'[3]

The roar of artillery fire rolls over them, as does the distant chatter of machine guns going nineteen to the dozen, even while the sky to the east pulses with angry flashes of light. And they are heading right into it.

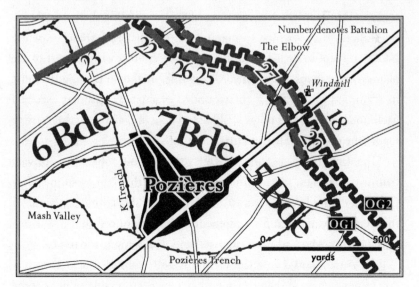

Pozières attack, 4 August 1916

Christ.

Well after dark, they get to Brickfields, outside Albert, just back from the front, where they are to bivouac for the night.

They try to sleep, though that constant *boom-BOOM-boom-BOOM* makes it hard. They're still two miles from the line and the ground is shaking *here*.

What must it be like in the middle of it?

Christ Almighty.

All the men of the 5th, 6th and 7th Brigades are, of course, more frantic than a Marseilles pox doctor. It's been one thing to take what's left of the German trenches; it's another now to dig them out again while holding them against both the Hun's artillery barrage and the inevitable counter-attack. They occasionally discover German dugouts still mercifully intact. (Some of these, as Archie Barwick would attest, are stunning: 'Their dugouts here are easily 20 feet below the surface and fitted, in some cases, with beds and tables and pianos and even electric light . . . They thought they were there for good apparently.')[4]

The most urgent priority is to try to impose order on chaos, as Sergeants look for Lieutenants, who are in turn looking for their Captains. A pecking order established, the highest-ranking officer starts shouting orders over the cacophony of exploding shells and whining bullets. They set men to digging out the shattered trenches, while NCOs are sent to the left and right to make contact with the rest of the platoon or, perhaps, the enemy. Meanwhile, their own Lewis guns must be set up, sandbags filled, the wounded evacuated, prisoners escorted back under guard and notes scribbled to give to dashing messengers to report the position. Hurry! Hurry! Hurry!

'The first thing I noticed after reaching our objective,' Private Clifford Sharman, an advancing gunner of the 7th Machine Gun Company would recall, 'was a man furiously shovelling earth out of the trench. I wondered for a moment and then noticed that it was one of the enemy who had been captured and was being made use of.'[5]

The Australians know the Germans will counter-attack; they just don't know when. If there is time, they may even be able to bury some of their dead and gather in stray limbs for some kind of decent burial in a shell hole – a commodity they don't lack, as new shell holes are being created all the time, producing more dead bodies and more stray limbs.

The Germans, knowing the battle is in the balance, plaster these positions from midnight with such intensive shelling that it exacts a dreadful toll among those Australians not yet properly dug in, which are many. But enough Australians still hold on to these hard-won positions that there is some confidence they will see off any counter-attack. Extraordinarily, so good is the Australian position that, though they are not yet quite to the ruins of the Windmill, they can see where the German artillery is coming from – flashes in the night reveal the location to be 1500 yards to their north-east, over by the town of Courcelette.

The key to holding this position is going to be well-situated machine guns with plenty of ammunition on hand, and it is for this reason that the 'particularly dashing'[6] Lieutenant Percy Cherry of the 7th Machine Gun Company – the man with the most fetching tilt to his slouch hat in the battalion and known to his Commanding Officer as one who is 'always smiling'[7] – arrives ahead of his men and immediately goes to the most advanced position, The Elbow, to work out precisely where to put his four water-cooled Vickers guns, together with the 20,000 rounds he has set aside for them.

His men follow close up. By the time Private Sharman arrives, Cherry is on top of the situation, has the positions sorted and quickly gets the men set up. They are just in time, but only just.

Within minutes, just as dawn is breaking, they see something! A large body of men is coming their way from the German lines. Surely German? Yes, probably, but in all the confusion there is no telling.

Fortunately, Cherry has organised a password: 'Dinkum! *Dinkum!* DINKUM!'[8]

Nothing.

Not only is there no reply password – '*Saeeda!*', which the Diggers had learned in Egypt is Arabic for 'good' – but there is no reply at all. Instead, they see the man who is in the lead move his hand above his head and raise it up and down, at which point the approaching group starts firing on them!

'Yes, they are Germans,' Lieutenant Cherry says calmly. 'Open fire.'[9]

In an instant, the Vickers guns are chattering, the approaching mob is scattered – killed, wounded or diving for shell holes – and the 7th Machine Gun Company is in a fight for the ages.

'The two machine guns simply slew them in dozens and broke up their attack . . .' Percy Cherry would record.[10] Ah, but the Germans are not finished yet. Even though they are no longer attacking en masse, many of them keep advancing, firing as they go.

Private Sharman is one of the first to be hit; a German bullet pierces his helmet to plough a neat furrow across his scalp. No matter, a mate takes his place on the Vickers while Sharman gathers himself, his hand grenades – and those of his fallen mates – and starts hoiking, *hard*.

'[I] found by making a little run along the trench and throwing hard,' he would recount, 'I could make them explode amongst the enemy . . .'

In that tepid dawn, meanwhile, Cherry can see him: a stately German officer brandishing a revolver and urging his men *vorwärts, vorwärts*, forward, forward, ever forward!

Even at this distance, Cherry tries his luck – the shot narrowly misses and alerts the German to his own presence.

The German officer fires back, and the two start to trade shots over a progressively shorter distance, as still the *Unteroffizier* herds and harries his men from shell hole to shell hole. Whatever the battle between the German and Australian soldiers, Cherry and the German officer keep track of each other, firing shot after shot until it is obvious either one or t'other must fall.

Finally, when they are just about within a stone's throw of each other, both men pop up and fire simultaneous shots. Cherry reels backward, hit in the head, and is only saved because the bullet has struck his steel helmet and *doesn't* penetrate. The German, though, has been hit near the heart and has his life ebbing out of him with every beat.

Under fire, Cherry crawls over and they manage to speak. The

German, who proves to speak passable English, has no rancour. This is war, *mein freund*. Would Cherry take some letters from his pocket that he has prepared against just this possibility?

Cherry agrees and folds the envelopes into his jacket.

'And so it ends,' says the German, just a few moments before he breathes his last.[11]

With their officer's death, many of those attacking throw their hands in the air and surrender. Cherry would record with great satisfaction in his diary, 'With my battery [of machine-guns] alone, we got 32 prisoners and 1 officer.'[12]

They prove to be from Schleswig-Holstein. One Australian who speaks a little German talks to them and later tells Clifford Sharman that, in his view, they 'are not very keen Germans'.[13]

The situation for much of the rest of the defending Australians, however, remains more than merely perilous. The *very* keen German soldiers of the 162nd Regiment – long-suffering members of General Wellmann's 18th Division – continue to flood forward.

Coming the other way, from the Pozières side, is Captain Cecil Maitland Foss, leading two companies from the 28th Battalion. An hour earlier, he had been told to get himself and his men urgently up to OG2, to tackle the German counter-attack there. It is no easy matter; to even get there, they had to 'move through a terrible barrage'.[14]

But once in place, Foss is as fearless as ever in leading his men forward, furiously firing on the German assault, even managing 'to establish a small machine gun post near the windmill'.[15]

Just like Colonel William Malone finally managing to lead his men to the heights of Chunuk Bair on the morning of 8 August 1915, the dawn brings the splendid vision of the Promised Land before him. In Malone's case, it had been the waterway of the Dardanelles. For Captain Foss and his men, it is first the village of Courcelette poking up through the mist and, yes, there beyond it is . . . Bapaume, just seven miles away!

After 36 days of what has been mostly a long string of disasters in the Battle of the Somme, this key goal, the high ground of Pozières, has been triumphantly captured by the Australians, led by one of their finest officers, Captain Maitland Foss.

No fewer than 14,000 men from both sides have died to possess this point. From here, their observers will be able to direct the lobbing of artillery shells onto all the juicy targets now in view for miles, or at any Hun who so much as scratches himself on the gentle slopes in front of these victorious soldiers.

The challenge now, though, is going to be whether or not the Australians can hold it. An indication of the dim view the Germans take on this development comes from the hurricane fire of shells that starts to land all around.

Dig, men, *dig!*

MORNING, 5 AUGUST 1916, BEHOLD THE PROMISED LAND

Scheiße! Is there a worse way to start the day?

At dawn, the exhausted Commander of the 18th Division, General Richard Wellmann, is given the news by an orderly: 'A new strong enemy attack during the night has broken into our position. The counterattack of our reserves is underway.'[16]

Wellmann is shocked, and fearful of the consequences. 'The enemy is in full possession of the dominant *Windmühlen-Höhe*, Windmill Heights,' he writes in his diary, 'and *das ist das Schlimmste*, this is the worst!'[17]

Quickly throwing on his uniform as his orderlies scurry hither and thither, General Wellmann has an urgent meeting with the most senior commanders of his two brigades.

'We agreed in the assessment of the situation so far that during the day a new counterattack would be completely pointless, and that the 18th Reserve Division was überhaupt nicht mehr imstande, not capable at all anymore to execute it alone, without any fresh forces.'[18]

Their best hope is that the local reserves currently attacking can clear the Australians off the ridge and give the Germans time to launch the major counter-attack later.

—

In full daylight, the view from the Windmill is every bit as spectacular as they had hoped.

The most staggering thing of all for two Lieutenants in Cherry's 7th Machine Gun Company is that from their high positions they can now gaze for the first time down the *other* side of the Pozières slopes.

'Far down the slope,' *The Times* would report, 'there were Germans moving. And in the distant landscape the German gun-teams limbered up and hurried away.'[19]

And now, look closer. See there!

They can spy 'a slow procession of white-hooded wagons . . . winding down from the distant village of Grévillers towards Courcelette, presumably bringing troops for some counter-attack'.[20]

And over there!

'A German battery could . . . be seen near Courcelette and a line of guns father back near Pys . . .'[21]

Quickly, the two Lieutenants from 7th Machine Gun Company call for a Forward Observation Officer of the 6th Field Artillery Brigade so he can direct the guns onto the aforementioned prizes. That officer

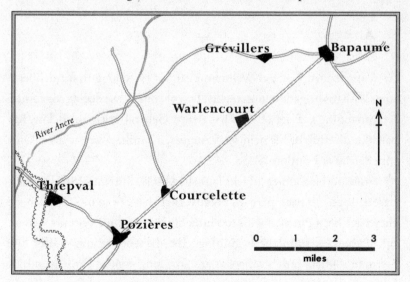

Courcelette, Grévillers and surrounds

soon arrives with binoculars, a map and an *attitude*. Now, now, they are going to let the dog see the rabbit!

Behind the officer comes a couple of artillery signallers trailing a spool of telegraph wire and, before long, Bob's your uncle! The artillery officer uses his glasses to work out the coordinates of the best targets, and an instant later Cherry's machine-gunners cheer as Australian shells start to land among those targets. And now the artillery officer takes his glasses and watches closely how the shells land, before barking into his field telephone, 'Left one hundred' . . . 'up one hundred' . . . 'that's bang on, now pour it into 'em!'

Their artillery is no longer shooting blind!

Best of all, their shells are 'playing havoc among some of the German batteries then in action'.[22]

Even General Wellmann feels the difference, noting that the British artillery are now shooting 'with astonishing precision . . .'[23]

And soon there will be another key bonus. The fact that the Australians control the Windmill site means the Germans *don't*, meaning the Huns can no longer see Australian positions. The Australian artillery can now move further up the Pozières slopes without the danger of being targeted.

———

At Warlencourt, General Wellmann cannot tarry long in his deliberations with his brigade commanders. For, of course, the deeply concerned Commanding Officer of the First Army, General Fritz von Below, has called a meeting of his own on 5 August, 12 miles away at his HQ in his château at Bourlon Wood.

None of the counter-attacks launched by Wellmann's 18th Division has made any impact, perhaps because there have been too few men, or they have been pursued with too little heart, or the men simply weren't up to the task from the beginning. The days of the universally fine German soldiers early in the war are now long gone, a consequence of having to dig deeper and deeper into their reserves, and Crown Prince

Rupprecht had even recently sent back some untrained reservists as, in his view, they were more a danger to themselves and the other soldiers than the enemy. General Wellmann might have done the same, but the situation is too desperate. For more than ten days now, the Germans have thrown everything at *die Australier* and *nothing* has stopped them – not artillery, not counter-attacks, not machine guns, not grenades. A breakthrough for the whole Western Front is threatened.

Yes, there is one half-hopeful report for General von Below, that 'the enemy had been at *der Windmühlen-Höhe* and beyond it, but has been expelled again by our *Artilleriefeuer*',[24] but few around the table actually believe it.

What is certain is that their own artillery is running out of ammunition, and supplies have become so dangerously low that General von Below has had no alternative but to order the conserving of shells. And at one point, one report from overnight has it that the German forces were so depleted that, 'In continuation of the enemy's attack, Courcelette would have been lost. Fortunately, the enemy does not attack.'[25]

Shortly thereafter, Wellmann confirms the truth about the failure of his latest counter-attack. '*Die Engländer*,' he writes bitterly, again mistaking the country of the soldiers concerned, 'have taken root at the windmill.'[26]

With heavy brow, General von Below orders General Max von Boehn to send his best remaining men of the IX Corps to counter-attack. All they can manage is to cobble together whatever units they can, under the command of General Wellmann.

But make no mistake – General von Below could not be more clear in his official communiqué to his Generals, including Wellmann: 'At any price, *Die Pozières Plateau* must be recovered, for if it were to remain in the hands of *die Briten*, it would give them an important advantage. Attacks will be made by successive waves 80 yards apart. Troops which first reach *die Plateau* must hold on until reinforced, whatever their losses. Any officer or man who fails to resist to the death on the ground won will be immediately courtmartialled.'[27]

Wunderbar.

In Wellmann's view, it is one thing to send out such grandiose communiqués and quite another to actually have to deal with the situation, which includes endless meetings like this with von Boehn and von Below, who are, in his view, 'more hindering than supportive' of his own divisional staff, 'stealing a lot of precious time'.[28]

Wellmann starts to marshal his forces to launch the major counter-attack using soldiers from five battalions, drawn from three different regiments – coalesced around the 63rd Regiment of the 12th Division. These men are Silesians and not highly regarded as fighting troops, but they will have to do. Together, they will go in either side of the Bapaume Road, supported by some pioneer troops who can re-dig the trenches once the ground is recaptured. And this time, together with soldiers and artillery, General Wellmann has obtained permission to attach every available *Flammenwerfer* and machine-gun unit from other divisions.[29]

'The time for the storm,' the faithful diarist Wellmann notes, 'is set by General Command at 4:30 in the morning.'[30]

There is much to do, including for Wellmann to move from his divisional headquarters in a cramped little château at Haplincourt to his Forward Command Post closer to Pozières, a house at Warlencourt where a telephone station has already been set up for him along with a *Scherenfernrohr* telescope – that curious contraption that resembles binoculars on legs. Gazing through it in the afternoon light, Wellmann can see the ruined remains of *der Windmühle*. Clearly, fighting is still going on all around it as shells explode and troops on his side of the hill continue to move forward.

The most pertinent factor, personally, however, is that from their viewpoint atop the heights, the Australian artillery observers can see *his* HQ. As Wellmann would chronicle, Warlencourt was 'soundly shelled while I was there, [but] shelter was not available'.[31]

———

At 3 pm, one of the 2nd Division's Artillery's Forward Observation Officers atop Pozières Ridge makes a significant observation:

Reported that there is every indication of a counter-attack at night.[32]

True. Down the slopes, and despite the barrage now upon them, there are clear signs of German forces moving forward in force. Some time overnight or tomorrow morning, they will surely come.

—

As Charles Bean, inevitably drawn back to the action despite his vow never to return, moves among the 2nd Division soldiers on this late afternoon – at a time when the German shelling is singularly intense – even he is stunned at just how eyeball-rollingly exhausted and bloodied they are, the very reflection of the village territory they now possess.

'Pozières has been a terrible sight all day,' he notes in his diary, 'steaming with pink and chestnut and . . . smoke. One knew that the brigades, which went in last night, were there today in that insatiable factory of ghastly wounds. The men are simply turned in there as into some ghastly great mincing machine. They have to stay there while shell after huge shell descends with a shriek close beside them – each one an acute mental torture – each shrieking tearing crash bringing a promise to each man – instantaneous – I will tear you into ghastly wounds – I will rend your flesh and pulp an arm or a leg – fling you, half a gaping quivering man like these that you see smashed round you, one by one, to lie there rotting and blackening like all the things you saw by the awful roadside, or in that sickening dusty crater. Ten or twenty times a minute. Every man in the trench has that instant fear thrust upon his shoulders – I don't care how brave he is – with a crash that is physical pain and strain to withstand.'[33]

More than a few Diggers become homesick for Gallipoli.

Under attack like that, and Gough wants them to keep going?

It can't be done.

In the end, there is only so much that flesh and blood – and, more to the point, bloodied flesh – can bear. It is General Birdwood who now steps in, insisting to Gough on this afternoon of 5 August that his 2nd Division must be pulled out immediately and their last remaining fresh division – the 4th Division, who have already been moved forward – sent in. It will be for them to take over the positions and secure them against all comers.

Gough agrees.

—

The word is out: it is time to *get* out. The 28th Battalion has done its job; they have taken the Windmill. Tonight the men of the 4th Division will finally be relieving them.

That afternoon, Captain Maitland Foss has every reason to be enormously satisfied.

Once again, he and his men have proved themselves in battle, have accomplished great things and have been able to withstand withering counter-attacks. Not that they are quite out of it yet. Even as they are making their way down the open slope to Tramway Trench, shells continue to fall all around them while the German artillery – sensing from prisoners that a changeover might be under way – probes like the blind man on sensitive spots and . . .

And then Foss goes down. Hard.

Two pieces of shrapnel have nearly severed his right leg. He has also suffered 'severe abdominal wounds . . .'[34]

His men are able to staunch the worst of the bleeding on his leg with a tourniquet, but his survival is going to be touch and go.

Captain Foss is just one of many 2nd Division casualties in the course of their 11 days in the line. By this time, the 2nd Division's original contingent of 11,000 infantry has been whittled down to just 3200 men still standing with rifle in hand. The cost notwithstanding, it has been an extraordinary achievement, as even Sir Douglas Haig acknowledges in his diary that evening:

> *The Australians gained all their objectives north of Pozières and beat off 3 counterattacks. A fine piece of work.*[35]

Throughout the night of 5/6 August, the German shelling continues to hit Australian positions from all directions, including their rear – the ever troublesome Thiepval remains in German hands, allowing them to fire artillery from a very close range. And yet, the fact that the German shell supply is so diminished means the artillery fire is more in the order of scattered rain than a thunderous downpour. It is shelling to keep the Australians back rather than a prelude to the planned major counter-attack, which – after one half-hearted effort coming from the direction of Courcelette is stopped by Australian machine-gun fire from OG2 – will have to wait until the following morning at dawn.

1.40 PM, 6 AUGUST 1916, ALBERT, TRUTH AND DARE

Jacka's mob, the 14th Battalion, will be among the last whole battalion of the 4th Division to move forward to take over the positions of the half-strength 26th and 28th Battalions of the 2nd Division. At last, they get the word. They are to pack up their digs just outside Albert, fall in and get going!

At 2.30 pm, they start marching towards the sound of the booming guns, booms that become ever louder and more terrifying with every mile the men march, moving first through the town of Albert, up and over the small hill on the other side, and then down – towards the action before, inevitably, they are told to wait.

Finally, by late afternoon, the word again comes to move forward.

But which way? Which of the many lead-in trenches leads to the one, that leads to the one, that leads to the one that they are ordered to take over?

When finding their way in Melbourne, they'd frequently had an actual map to work with; they *never* had to ask directions while disembowelled men are screaming for their lives just yards away, as shells explode and shrapnel whistles and machine-gun bullets buzz all around.

But, ask they must, and who better than their 'old Brig' – an exceedingly young man for his position, Colonel Charles Moreland Montague Dare, a 27-year-old Melbourne architect by training – who happens to be passing by on horseback. If the Commanding Officer of their own brigade doesn't know, who would?

'What, lost in daylight?!' Colonel Dare harrumphs. 'Don't know what you'll do in the dark.'[36]

Quite. They are finally saved when one of the 14th Battalion's own Majors comes back to guide them into the beginnings of Sausage Valley, 'a long, narrow valley, two or three hundred yards across',[37] completely dominated by heavily sheltered artillery batteries, lined up very nearly 'wheel to wheel' all along it, with yet more labyrinthine paths through it. By the time Jacka's mob reaches the head of the valley where the smallest kind of field guns, the 18-pounders, are, the newly arrived soldiers of 4th Division are 'a trifle deaf'.[38]

But the gun crews? They must be totally deaf, for, sweating and straining as they load and fire shell after shell, they barely blink at every explosion. Here at the top of the valley, the 14th Battalion men again must wait in the heat of day, getting what shade they can while watching the endless stream of wounded men, covered in blood, groaning, screaming, being carried back by the brave stretcher-bearers. It is not much of an advertisement for where they are going. But it is the awful truth of what they are likely facing themselves.

And yet not all of the sufferers are physically wounded, and not all need to be carried. 'One shell-shocked case . . . came along,' Edgar Rule would recall, 'the picture of terror, and trembling from head to foot. His legs trembled so much that they just about carried him, and that was all.'[39]

Oh, Jesus Christ Almighty.

Just what are they headed for in yonder trenches? There is only one way to find out.

As the heat of the sun starts to die down, they push forward and, after a long struggle, approach the front-line. Here, apparently, was a village, now just rubble, dust, splinters and the shattered remains of other things that once went with family homes – a child's doll, a sewing machine, a tambourine, a piece of broken wood . . . with violin strings attached. Ah, such sweet music it must have once played, only to finish like this.

And, of course, there are also dead soldiers – many of them. They lie face-down, face-up, 'arsapeek' – Digger slang for upside down – across each other, half-buried, half-severed, over by the track and even under-foot, hence that terrible spongy feeling as you tread warily forward. Those still with faces mostly bear the contorted grimaces of agony they had worn when they shuffled off this mortal coil. Few appear to be *Ruhe in Frieden*, Resting in Peace, whatever their families at home in Australia and Germany might take solace in when they hear the tragic news.

By the time the 14th Battalion's C Company, with Sergeant Edgar Rule in the lead and Lieutenant Dean in the rear, get close to their allotted position in relief of the 2nd Division's 28th Battalion, even Rule himself, an experienced campaigner, is spooked . . . and something more. 'I was more than terrified,' Sergeant Rule would recall. 'I had never before been so horrified in my life. The shelling, and the dead lying in all sorts of attitudes, were enough to send new men mad.'[40]

The men push on some 400 yards and come to 28th Battalion HQ, situated in an old Hun dugout, and pause for a moment, awaiting orders.

Pushing along the trench, coming the other way, is a just-relieved 28th Battalion officer, hurrying to get the hell out. (So relieved he may well be pissing his pants, by the look of him.)

'What,' Sergeant Rule asks, solicitous of the need for his own soldiers to have the same, 'have the men of your unit done with the blanket and waterproof that each one carried in?'

'You will be damned lucky,' the officer tosses back over his shoulder in reply, his voice getting more distant by the word, 'if you'll ever use a blanket again.'[41]

This, frankly, seems like a fair point under the circumstances, and all the more so because, as Rule feels, even if you did live through it, you probably still wouldn't be able to get any sleep. On the strength of this, he throws his blanket off his back and leaves it there, marching off. Now that specific orders have emerged, telling C Company which trench they are to take over – a support line with its left end on Pozières cemetery – they quickly crowd into it, such as it is.

'I've never seen men so closely packed in a trench,' Rule would recount. 'It was not a bit of wonder that men were being killed like rabbits. Every shell that got into the trench simply cleaned it out, and it was easy to see how one shell could smash up a dozen men.'[42]

The most important thing now is to secure the trenches that have been so hard won by their comrades of the 2nd Division. That means digging out once again all those trenches that have collapsed and throwing out all detritus that is cluttering up the floors, which most certainly includes dead bodies but also shattered rifles, empty boxes of ammunition and half-emptied *Machonochie* meat and veg tins. Of course, all over the Pozières slopes, others of their battalion and the wider 4th Division are doing the same – digging in, trying to maximise their chances of getting through the night.

Some 400 yards forward of Sergeant Rule's men of C Company in Tramway Trench, Jacka, with the 5th Platoon of B Company of the 14th Battalion, is settling into a German dugout right on the front-line on the ridge crest. He is a surprisingly small man for one with such a reputation, with nothing to him but muscle, gristle and bone. Of his many attributes, he is known from his VC onwards as being 'greased lightning'[43] with the bayonet.

Just over to their right, beyond The Elbow, another 4th Brigade Battalion, the 48th, is dug in and has already been there for a day. Their Commanding Officer, Lieutenant-Colonel Ray Leane – a 38-year-old Gallipoli veteran from Adelaide known as 'Bull' by his men for a

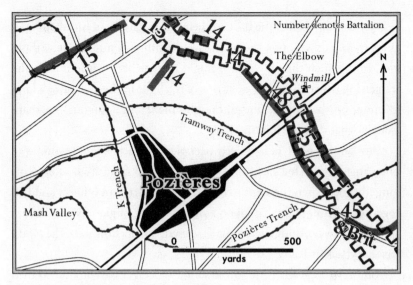

The 14th and 48th Battalions meet at The Elbow

certain undeniable resemblance to that powerful animal – now feels it more strongly than ever. He is sure a German counter-attack is just hours away. And Leane is not the only one expecting the Hun to soon be upon them.

Still not satisfied that he has all his men in the best defensive position, Sergeant Rule leaves half of them in the first position they have settled and orders the other half to follow him. But now here is the Commanding Officer of the 28th Battalion, the last officer of his unit to depart.

'What should I do?' Rule asks him simply.

'Get up to the front line and help your mates; you'll be attacked tonight.'[44]

Wishing Rule good luck and good night, the Lieutenant-Colonel promptly disappears.

Still, Sergeant Rule decides to do exactly that and leads his men through the darkness, picking their way up the slope, stumbling over the dead and dying. At one point, Sergeant Rule himself falls heavily; he picks himself up only to find one of his hands wet and clammy with another man's blood. And now a mighty explosion from behind.

Some of the men at the back of their group have been hit; shells continue to roar down upon them. The whole thing is a nightmare without end, from which the only escape might be that sleep without end, and it's getting worse. But now, at last, here is a light in the darkness, a faint glimmer on the hillside ahead, the glimmer from a dugout – perhaps exactly what they are looking for?

But careful now. Is it indeed occupied by their own? In this war, one can never be too careful. Taking his pistol from its holster, Rule gingerly goes down the steps to find . . . two Australian officers huddled together in front of a table, upon which a couple of gloomy candles are sputtering away. Both men look shattered, spent, finished. They gaze vacantly back at Rule.

'Sir,' says Sergeant Rule to the senior officer. 'I have about 40 men up on top. We have no orders, neither have we an officer. What shall I do with them?'

The officers stare. The candles sputter. Outside, the dull, muffled thud of landing shells and the distant chatter of machine-gun fire are a constant. Will they *never* answer?

Finally, the senior officer responds: 'How are your men standing it, Sergeant?'

'They are feeling the strain of it a little, sir.'

There is a long pause.

'All right, Sergeant,' the officer finally speaks, not with military authority but in the tired voice of a father who realises he is too old and weak to do anything more for his son. 'Take your men along the trench and attach them to the Company lying in support.'[45]

It is his way of saying, *You and your men are on your own here. We have done what we can, given our all, and have nothing left.*

Sergeant Rule moves on, and he and his men eventually find themselves back where they had started from, at the end of the support trench, which butts up against Pozières cemetery, among their comrades once more – or at least their surviving comrades.

Even though well back from the front-line, these support trenches are being shelled through the night as never before. All the men can do is huddle at the bottom of the trench, shoulder to shoulder, knee to knee, and pray that every succeeding, screeching shell doesn't land on them. Time and again, that happens to nearby bays, and they all must scramble along to help dig out the poor bastards who have been buried alive. But, for the moment at least, Sergeant Rule's bay stays intact.

Beyond the artillery, all are aware that their severest test may well be yet to come. What was it the Commanding Officer of the 28th Battalion had said as he left?

'You'll be attacked tonight.'[46]

———

Lieutenant-Colonel Raymond Leane is a man with a sure instinct, and much admired by his men. (And those men, by the by, are almost a family affair, as their numbers include Bull's brother, three of his nephews and a couple of other sprigs on the Leane family tree. The 48th even refer to themselves as the 'Joan of Arc' battalion, as it is 'Made-of-All-Leanes', as in, 'Maid of Orleans', and it won't be long before Charles Bean would describe 'The Bull' as 'the head of the most famous family of soldiers in Australian history . . .')[47]

But his own hunch about there being a German attack not far away is hardening into certainty. Since dawn that morning, just after his troops had arrived, Bull has been watching German activity, seen their troops moving forward, noted the observation balloons and, of course, suffered the heavy bombardment without end, and he has come to a conclusion.

It all looks to him to be 'indicative of the proximity of a counter-attack, probably during the next night'.[48]

Against that possibility, Bull now sends forward one of his best men, Sergeant David Austral Twining of Ballarat, first to reconnoitre the Windmill site and then to establish a strongpoint just to its right, next to the Albert–Bapaume Road, in a spot that proves to have 'no trenches . . . constructed, the place just being one mass of craters'.[49]

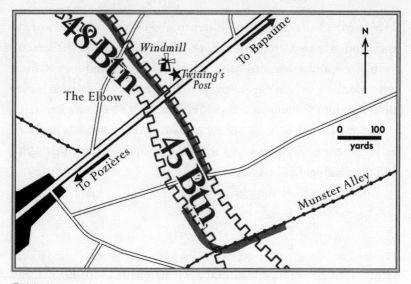

Twining's post

For the usually eternally cheery Twining, known to his many mates as 'Don Ack Toc' – his initials in 'signalese' – it is Hell on Earth to get the position set up with enough ammunition to make it viable. There are no communication trenches, so this means ration parties have to trek 400 yards up the slope under heavy artillery, making their way through the 'wounded carried back the same way',[50] but, by the wee hours, it is done. If the Germans *do* attack, there will be at least one very well placed Lewis gun waiting for them.

———

In preparation for the attack, from 9 pm the German artillery zeroes in on the Australian positions.

'Their guns were innumerable, and were exactly ranged,' the official history of Jacka's 14th Battalion would record. 'The drum fire was incessant, and continued all night with unabated fury . . . There were shells from the big 12-inch howitzers down to the little nerve-racking "whizbangs", there were high explosive shells with sulphur fumes . . . The very earth, lacerated and torn, rocked and dissolved under the weight and force of the metal blown into it. Both the earth and the heavens seemed rent by this concentrated effort of man's fury.'[51]

In the midst of what has become 'a heaving volcano',[52] many men of the 14th die, others are wounded and more than a few are knocked out by concussion as trenches are blown in.

'Most of the men,' the official history records, 'fortunately found cover in some untenanted and commodious German dugouts which had survived previous bombardments.'[53]

One of them is Albert Jacka, who, in a measure of his extraordinary sangfroid, actually manages to fall asleep.

While he slumbers, the barrage intensifies. For just as the darkest hour is before the dawn, so too in wartime is it often the noisiest as, presaging an attack scheduled for first light, the enemy unleashes everything they have.

Hurricane fire!

—

Some 500 yards to the east, over the lip of the flat, wide crest of Pozières Ridge, no fewer than 3000 German soldiers of the 18th and 12th Divisions, under the command of General Richard Wellmann, huddle tightly.

Die Stunde hat geschlagen. Now is the hour.

Among the men is *Leutnant* Zinnemann, a German officer in the 63rd Regiment. With tight commands, he briefs his troops. In a few minutes, they will leave their trenches to advance as close to the lip of the hill as they dare, hopefully without being seen. They must get into position so that as soon as the barrage ceases, they can charge up and over the hill and across the flat top to where they will find the enemy dug in but hopefully shattered. They will attack in two prongs, one on either side of the Albert–Bapaume Road, with the intent being to retake the entire 1200 yards of OG1 lines lost to the Australians, and once more establish the German line along the crest of the ridge.

Der Leutnant finishes briefing his officers with, 'OK, break a leg.'[54]

7 August German counter-attack

A little over 500 yards forward of Zinnemann, in his OG1 dugout near The Elbow, Albert Jacka stirs. His sixth sense alerts him that something may be up, and now he heads up the stairs of the dugout to look out onto No-Man's Land.

But in the semi-darkness, there is nothing apparent – apart from three shells a minute, landing within 50 yards of him. Absolutely nothing. Still uneasy, however, Jacka heads back down the stairs, remarking only to his men that things are 'just the same'.[55]

Or are they? It seems unlikely that a barrage of this intensity does not presage trouble. He stays alert, on principle.

—

'Let's go!' *Leutnant* Zinnemann shouts to his men in a hoarse whisper. 'Jump to it, go, go!'[56]

On the instant, they are up and out, charging up the gentle slope, even though bent double in the hope they will present smaller targets should they be seen.

Suddenly flares burst above, bathing them in light. *Scheiße!*

'Take cover! Stay still.'

Bullets crack past at short range, and Zinnemann is immediately concerned. 'The front is . . . on the alert,' he would record of his thoughts. 'That's bad. This isn't going to work! Assaults must have surprise . . .'[57]

Mercifully, however, return fire is not renewed. It is possible, just possible, they have not been seen. Now they must await the moment, precisely 4.30 am.

—

In his own dugout, 400 yards back from Jacka, Sergeant Edgar Rule has a sudden presentiment similar to Jacka's. Is there something of a diminution in the number of shells landing on this support line? Is the shelling moving further back, perhaps putting down a 'curtain' behind them to cut off whatever supporting troops might try to rush forward as the Germans themselves attack? Still, when Sergeant Rule mentions his fears to the officer nearby, Lieutenant Stanley Thompson, the Lieutenant laughs lightly and tells him to sit down again.

But Rule is not so easily persuaded. 'I'm getting my rifle and bombs ready, anyhow.'[58]

—

Leutnant Zinnemann checks his watch: 4.30 am. Confirming that the moment is nigh, the artillery barrage on the Australian positions suddenly moves back.

'*Vorwärts, los! Los!* Forward, go! Go!' he shouts to his men,[59] and the call is taken up along the line.

'Piercingly shrill "*Hurras*" shouts and roars fill the air.'[60]

In three waves, the 63rd Regiment charges forward as part of this mass flood of German soldiers on both sides of the Albert–Bapaume Road, with the arrowhead of the attack centred on what turns out to be Jacka's own 5th Platoon of the 14th Battalion, itself positioned in OG1, near The Elbow, on the left flank of the 48th Battalion.[61]

Sergeant Twining, meanwhile, is some 400 yards to Jacka's right, by the Windmill out in front of OG2, 150 yards in front of his own battalion, the 48th, and they don't have long to wait.

For there they are!

It is Sergeant Twining and his men by the Windmill who spy the swarming Germans first and immediately open fire. Alerted by the shots, waiting for just this moment, Lieutenant-Colonel 'Bull' Leane sends off his homing pigeons with messages and has SOS flares fired, calling for a protective box barrage in front of them.

It is substantially too late, and there are just too many Germans. Though Sergeant Twining and his men shoot many, nothing can stop most of the swarming Germans coming up and over the hill. All Sergeant Twining can do – even as the dozen men he started with are reduced to just six still standing – is keep firing, keep cutting a swathe into the Germans, including swivelling the machine gun around to fire on those who have gone past. Another man might have surrendered to the obvious – he is going to die unless he surrenders – but Twining keeps firing. (There is just something about Twining, a strange air of innocence, almost as if he is too young and pure to be killed in such a monstrous war. It somehow imparts confidence to those around him.) Shortly thereafter, a German machine gun operating from a shell hole just 300 yards away opens up and Twining loses another man . . . only for a shell to land right on that shell hole, knocking the gun crew out.

Twining fights on. He *always* fights on! Just over to his left, the Germans break through, and fierce combat breaks out . . .

Leutnant Zinnemann is with his men, surging forward as grenades thrown by the Australians start exploding all around. Men scream and fall; others keep racing on.

'Figures flit before us, right and left of us, huge bursts of fire – bullets fly everywhere – a machine gun rattles away. Germans can be seen going down. Cursing, moaning, the last of the grenades are thrown in the direction of the machine gun.'[62]

Just to Zinnemann's right, a soldier pulls the pin from a grenade and hauls his arm back in preparation to throw, when a shot rings out. He goes down hard, shrieking – *Er ist laut, so wird er in Ordnung sein*, he's loud, so he will be okay – and the *Leutnant's* batman is at the soldier's side in an instant. He grabs the grenade and hurls it, and everyone around throws themselves to the ground just before it explodes.

But now Zinnemann and his men are caught in the open as a chattering machine gun shatters their ranks. The survivors must stay down!

—

Miraculously, Sergeant Twining at the Windmill has *still* not been hit, though so many of his men have been that there are now just two of them left – him and the gunner Private Charles Tognini, a shopkeeper from Bunbury in civilian life, who is very proud, by the by, of having come sixth in the Bunbury Rifle Shooting Competition the year before. And he feels unlucky not to have finished even higher. But even Tognini is wounded, having taken a bad hit to his leg. Still, he is strong enough to keep his Lewis gun going, keep the Germans at enough of a distance that they can't throw bombs at them. That means they can only be stopped by bullets, and Tognini – with Twining handing the ammo up to him, loading the fresh magazines and spotting new targets – just keeps firing on suspicion at all spots where they think the Hun even *might* be tucked away. He is *not* going to come sixth this time!

—

Zinnemann and his men are still held up. The Germans are charging ahead in other parts, but here the fire is devastating.

'There are very few of us here forward,' the German would recount. 'The majority are dead and wounded; we can hear the [screams and groans]. We can't help hearing them and it grates on us . . .'[63]

Zinnemann is exhausted, dug in the best he can, when something strange happens. For the barest fraction of a second, he hears a howl, followed by 'an indescribably heavy leaden thud on my skull'.

It feels like his skull is caved in, like he is falling down a great hole, like he is about to die, and all he can do is thank the fact that 'the good Lord has made it swift . . . *"Leutnant! Leutnant!* Are you still alive?"'

Like a slap to the face, Zinnemann realises he *is* still alive and his batman is shouting at him.

'"August! August!" I shout . . . I am completely buried. Only my head is free. August can see I am alive.'

Like a madman, the worthy batman August tears away at the earth with his bare hands and calls for help. 'Hey, Antek, get over here, the *Leutnant* is buried!'

Finally he is free and yet, try as he might, Zinnemann cannot stop himself from 'weeping uncontrollably'.

'Leutnant,' August tells him kindly, 'you've got to crawl to the doctor. I'll help you.'

Zinnemann starts to crawl away.[64]

The other German soldiers keep going, most particularly on the right of the Albert–Bapaume Road, where they quickly overwhelm the thinly held OG2 trench and are soon into the OG1 positions. Right by the Windmill, the first of the three waves of Germans – totalling some 2000 soldiers – attack on a 1200-yard front, helped by a mist clinging to the hollows there that hides their advance. In a seeming instant, soldiers from the 157th and 63rd Regiments, aided by sections of machine-gunners, *Flammenwerfers* and pioneers, have broken through in the centre, on a 300-yard front at The Elbow!

—

Suddenly two German soldiers arrive at the entrance of Second-Lieutenant Albert Jacka's dugout and roll a grenade down into it. Most of the men are still asleep, but not Jacka, who, alerted by the sudden *clunk-clunk-clunk* of the grenade on the stairs, is able to dive to rough cover the instant before it explodes. In all the smoke, confusion and screams, it is Jacka who is first to react, whipping his Colt .45 from his holster and charging up the stairs.

There! Near the top, above him, through the smoke, he can dimly perceive what must be a Squarehead, and fires off a shot at much the same time as the German fires down at him.

The German falls, with a head now not so square after all. Jacka is okay. Heading back down the stairs, the Australian grabs his rifle, his bayonet, and whatever coughing and spluttering survivors he can, grimly telling them to 'fix bayonets'[65] and follow him.

—

At the Windmill, the stunned Twining and Tognini can now see, off to their left rear, the flood of German soldiers breaking through the OG Lines, having engulfed Australian positions at The Elbow. If they keep going and sweep across, the two soldiers of the 48th Battalion will be cut off. They quickly move the Lewis gun to the other side of their shell hole so they can fire on the enemy from behind. Clearly they are in a fight for their lives, and their only chance of survival is to shoot straight.

Tognini brings the gun roaring to life, even as Twining keeps up the supply of fresh magazines, popping his head up now and again to look for more Germans to kill. The two fight on.

As do the Australians positioned on either side of the German break-through, as those parts of the line still intact rally and start enfilading fire, 'taking full advantage of the magnificent target presented to them, and cut up the right flank of the attacking force severely'.[66]

—

Jacka and his men emerge from their dugout to find that, while many German soldiers are already moving down the slope from OG1 towards Pozières, all around them, as the official history of the 14th would record, 'Germans were mixed up with our men like players in rival football teams during a match.'[67]

Jacka's men quickly engage in activities that would have sent them from such a football field in disgrace, requiring dozens of zambucks to tend to the fallen Germans, before focusing on the next development!

There. Over to the left.

As they look across the flat-topped ridge, they can see that the Australian positions over at The Elbow have been overwhelmed by German soldiers, and no fewer than 40-odd from the 48th have been rounded up and taken prisoner. And, under heavy German guard, they are coming this way . . .

Get down!

Ducking into a nearby trench, Jacka and his mob lie doggo until Fritz is just 30 yards away . . . before jumping up all at once, and charging!

Jacka is in the lead, charging straight at the Germans, firing as he goes. He is quickly right on top of the Huns, a blur of movement – thrusting, parrying, stabbing and cutting them down. Supported by his seven comrades, they are soon together with . . . the Australian prisoners they have freed in the process! And suddenly, with a roar, they are joined by other Australian soldiers leaping up from dugouts, shell holes and trenches as the melee intensifies.

'A sensational and desperate, furious fight occurred,' the official history of the 14th would record, 'the odds against the Australians' counter-attack being at least twenty to one.'

There is no quarter asked for or given. When the 48th Battalion's Sergeant Cyril Beck sprints to Jacka's aid, he is suddenly killed by a random bullet, while another Sergeant has a leg blown off by a grenade.

The battle goes on.

This is close-quarters fighting, with the bayonet doing much of the work.

As Jacka keeps forging his way ahead, he suddenly sees the tops of four German soldiers in a shell hole, *aiming their rifles at him.* There is no time to react. As the first bullet hits, Jacka goes down, but he still manages to leap up again. Twice more he is hit, and twice more he leaps up, like a prize-fighter who has been struck hard but is eager to get up off the mat and strike blows of his own.

By the time Jacka is right upon them, the four shocked Germans

– how can this *schweinehund* still be *alive?* – throw down their rifles and put up their hands.

Jacka, still mightily aggrieved at the indignity of having the grenade thrown into his dugout and losing so many of his mates, not to mention being shot himself, shoots three of them through the head and bayonets the fourth. 'I had to do it,' he explains later. 'They would have killed me the moment I turned my back.'[68]

And now another shot from just behind. Jacka whirls around to see an enormous Hun, who must be all of 18 stone, bearing the stunned expression of one who has realised he has just missed out on shooting the Devil himself. The Hun is coming right at him, bayonet poised . . .

—

Back down at Tramway Trench with those of the 14th Battalion in reserve, Sergeant Rule is slipping a clip of cartridges into his rifle when a dishevelled and panicky Australian soldier comes running along, yelling out, 'Jacka is killed and the Huns have got the ridge!'[69]

—

Jacka fires right at the Hun's enormous belly and doesn't miss, the brute nearly falling right down on him. Around and about, the fight goes on and, despite his wounds, Jacka is soon into it once more.

From 500 yards away, the mesmerised Sergeant Rule now gazes at this most extraordinary spectacle on the ridge ahead, in this first gloomy glimmer of dawn: men running along the crest. Swiftly bringing his binoculars to bear, Rule can see it is his own boys flying at the Germans and firing point-blank. Some appear to have fallen to their knees to pray for their very lives. Some are fighting on and being bayoneted for their trouble.

'Huns and Aussies were scattered in ones and twos all along the side of the ridge,' he would later recount. 'It was such a mix-up it was hard to tell who were Huns and who were Aussies. Each Aussie seemed to be having a war all on his own, and the issue was not long in doubt.'[70]

The Australians win the encounter. In short order, some 80 German prisoners are being led back through the communication trenches, and Rule would record of them, 'They were certainly the most joyful looking lot of Huns I'd ever seen . . . They looked as if they were all off to a wedding . . .'[71]

Yes, they are prisoners, but at least they are *alive* and no longer fighting barking mad Australians, led by one iron lunatic who just won't lie down and die, no matter how often they shoot him. Later, when the stretcher-bearers are making their way back, bearing the wounded, Rule calls out, 'Who've you got there?'

'I don't know who *I've* got,' the fellow replies, 'but the bravest man in the Aussie Army is on that stretcher just ahead. It's Bert Jacka, and I wouldn't give a Gyppo piastre for him, he is knocked about dreadfully.'[72]

And so he is. As Jacka is carried down, the stretcher-bearers pause for a moment so his brother Bill, an officer in the same battalion, can get a look at him. Bill is shocked. For there is his brother Albert all right, but he looks 'like a lump of lard, absolutely bloodless . . .'[73]

'By Jove,' he thinks, 'you've had it, Albert. I won't see you again.'

Albert is carried away.

It is later estimated that the seven-times wounded Jacka – including one bad bullet graze to the head and another where a bullet passed through his body – has, with his half-dozen men, killed around 20 Germans in what Charles Bean will call 'the most dramatic and effective act of individual audacity in the history of the A.I.F.'.[74]

But thanks in large part to that audacity, his fellow Australian soldiers are able to rally and hold the crest after all!

'The position,' the official history of the 14th records, 'was now as follows: The first German waves, arriving under cover of darkness, had entered the Australian lines, and though a portion of it had been smashed by Jacka's violent attack, other portions were still scattered about our front. The succeeding waves, received by a hot fire, had been mostly destroyed or driven back, whilst their reserves, cut up by our artillery barrage, was unable to follow up the success of the first waves.'[75]

But it has come at a great cost. In fact, no group has been hit harder than Jacka's platoon, which has just four men left standing without need of medical attention, from an original complement of 52.

—

Even General Wellmann has become aware of Jacka's extraordinary exploits.

'The attack seems to have penetrated at some points,' he notes ruefully in his diary this morning, '[but was] thrown back by an English counterattack . . . Many Englishmen had been captured, but the counterattack not only tore the [OG trenches] from us again, but also most of our prisoners . . . We've already had the 1st, then the 2nd, and now the 4th Australian Division is against us.'[76]

—

At his own dugout HQ, Lieutenant-Colonel 'Bull' Leane is just going through the first of the casualty reports with his brother, Major Benjamin Leane, a dozen years his junior, by his side.

'War is hell!!!' the younger brother would soon note in his diary. 'We have had 48 hours of the most frightful time I ever wish to experience. Of the 900 odd men we took into the trenches at Pozières, we have tonight out less than 200. The remainder are all either killed or wounded. Gallipoli was a paradise to it. Pozières is a veritable charnel house. God! The sights one sees. How any of us are alive seems a miracle . . . I have seen men trembling in every limb, weeping like babies, cowering at every explosion . . .'[77]

On this occasion, Lieutenant-Colonel Leane is interrupted in his grim contemplation of just how bad the situation is by a wounded man. 'Begging your pardon, Sir, but Sergeant Twining has a message for you. He says, "I am the only one left. Do you still want me to hold the position?"'[78]

Bull Leane is stunned, scarcely able to credit that, somehow,

Sergeant Twining, in the most forward position of all, has survived.

He sends orders back: Thank you, Sergeant Twining, that will be enough.

Twining is able to walk back, still without a scratch, while Tognini, alas, is brought back by stretcher-bearers with serious wounds to his leg and arm, and has to be quickly put, yes, on the road to Rouen hospital.

—

In a sea of despair for the Allies in the Somme Valley, Pozières now stands as an island of *triumph*, the highest point now secured after five weeks of trying. Not that you'd know the grandeur of that triumph – the Germans won't even try to take it from the Australians from this point on – unless you were right there, or in the highest reaches of the British officer class.

'We have fought,' Charles Bean would note in his diary, 'the greatest battle in our history – one of the greatest in theirs – but not a suspicion of it would you get from the English papers.'[79]

The Australian correspondent is ropable. 'I can't help thinking,' he notes at a later point, 'it is another and far more important instance of jealousy.'[80]

Bean's transformation from transplanted Briton to proud Australian – indeed, the country's prime booster for the very notion of Australians being a separate breed from the British – is near complete. And there is ever more of it about, among the troops themselves.

For there now is the King!

Yes, it is King George V himself, the King of the United Kingdom and British Dominions and Emperor of India, just a few miles back from the front-line at Pozières, passing before the British and Australian troops, most of them just emerged from the devastating fight. His Majesty is in the company of one of his sons, the Prince of Wales, together with General Birdwood, and as his motorcade proceeds along the street of this village, the mostly bedraggled but still awestruck troops manage to raise a cheer and, of course, they all salute him.

As he salutes back from his open car, he looks, to the eyes of many of the Australians, surprisingly old for his 51 years, and also 'rather worried',[81] likely for many of the appalling things he has seen on this quick tour – all the death and destruction so confronting when seen in the flesh and not from the remote distance of newspapers.

Suddenly, however, amid the tired cheers and gasps of admiration just to be in the King's presence, a voice rings out. 'Good day, George! Hallo, George! How are you, George!'[82]

The King, 'utterly taken by surprise' at such familiarity as he has never heard in his entire public life, turns to see who it is.

Oh.

It is a garrulous Australian, 'a bronzed brown face and dark humorous eyes . . . a bold funny fellow' who has celebrated his surprising survival at Pozières by having a few drinks at a nearby estaminet – and likely more than a few. In response, the Tommies are 'awe-struck at such cheek and looked as though they expected someone to be shot',[83] while the other Australians mostly laugh at his sheer audacity.

The King – to the amazement of the Tommies – joins in the laughter, which relieves the tension somewhat, and His Majesty is soon gone in the mist. But not the merry Australian. For some time afterwards, he holds his own court of commoners on the corner, bursting forth on republicanism versus royalty . . .[84]

He is, needless to say, in favour of republicanism, floating the refreshing view – some would say a particularly Australian one – that it is not because a man is born to a royal family that he is necessarily any better than anyone else.

—

Finally, however, it is time for the last of the 4th Division to be withdrawn.

The word comes to them in the form of the relief troops actually turning up.

Now, normally, the arrival of the cavalry in this manner would see those relieved hightailing it as fast as their little legs can carry them, but this is a tad different for Edgar Rule and his mates of Jacka's mob. For the relief has arrived in the late afternoon when the shells are falling their thickest, and, given there is more cover in these deep trenches than in the shallow trenches, Jacka's mob will actually feel safer here overnight. They plan to leave early the next morning when the shell fire is less intense.

And so it proves. Their exit the next morning is nothing if not hairy, but most of them make it.

As they regain the back area, they happen to pass an English artillery officer who is earnestly peering through his glasses into the German lines.

'Can you see any Huns?' one of Eddie Rule's mates asks.

'No,' the English officer replies thoughtfully. 'I think you bastards have killed them all.'[85]

EPILOGUE

We Shall Keep the Faith

Oh! You who sleep in Flanders fields,

Sleep sweet – to rise anew . . .

We cherish too, the poppy red,

That grows on fields where valour led . . .

Fear not that ye have died for naught,

We've learned the lesson that you taught,

In Flanders fields.[1]

After reading the poem 'In Flanders Fields', an American woman, Miss Moina Michael from Good Hope in Georgia – credited with conceiving the idea of using poppies as a symbol of remembrance – wrote this famous reply in November 1918

Whoever planned the Battle of Fromelles was stupid, it was the greatest piece of stupidity since the Charge of the Light Brigade. We were in full view, the Germans chopped us to pieces . . . Haking was a rat bag, it was the worst piece of strategy. It was murder, we had no chance.[2]

Fred Kelly, 53rd Battalion, 101 years old, in 1998

Without doubt Pozières was the heaviest, bloodiest, rottenest stunt that ever the Australians were caught up in.[3]

Private Frank Brent, 8th Battalion, 1964 interview

Despite the Battle for Pozières Ridge being over, the rest of the battle to take Thiepval, of course, continued, with the same three Australian divisions all being rotated through over the next three weeks in their attempt to claim the key stepping stone to that prize, Mouquet Farm. In the end, although the Australians continued to inch forward, the task proved to be beyond their exhausted and depleted means, and the Canadian relief of the Australians began on 3 September 1916. (Those valiant Canadians would spend another three weeks taking Mouquet Farm, and Thiepval would fall on 26 September.)

In their six weeks in the line, the three Australian divisions had launched no fewer than 19 attacks and fended off nine major German counter-attacks, for a catastrophic final 'butcher's bill' of 23,000 Australian casualties, including 6800 killed – nearly as many in their graves from this six weeks at Pozières–Mouquet Farm as in the whole eight months at Gallipoli. Together with the catastrophe at Fromelles, in six and a half weeks the Australians in France had suffered 28,500 casualties for nearly 9000 soldiers killed. All up, well over half of the men in every infantry battalion that had arrived in France earlier in the year had by now been killed or wounded.

Among those killed was, tragically, Alec Raws. On 23 August, just as the 2nd Division was re-entering the line, Alec was bringing up the rear of the 23rd Battalion's B Company when a shell exploded nearby. He was found 'dead with three privates beside him. No wound marked his body, and it is probable that concussion from a shell caused instant death.'[4]

Before his death, Alec had been one of three officers presiding at a Court of Enquiry held at Berteaucourt on 12 August, which determined:

That in the case of Lieutenant R.G. Raws the evidence available is not sufficient to prove definitely his fate.
Recommendation – That Lieutenant R.G. Raws be posted as missing.[5]

With no grave, Goldy Raws is commemorated on the Villers-Bretonneux Memorial, France, in the list of 10,774 names of Australian soldiers who died in France and Belgium (a quarter of all the Australians who died there) but have no known grave. The news of his death reached his parents in Australia on 29 August 1916, their wedding anniversary, just before they received the news of the death of Alec. Alec, too, has no recognised grave, as his battlefield burial site disappeared later in the war, and his name is nestled just above Goldy's on the wall at Villers-Bretonneux. Together, forever.

———

The Battle of Fromelles did not, as General Haking claimed, do the 5th Division a 'great deal of good'. In fact, they were so shattered by the experience, and their ranks so thin, it was four months before they were judged capable of returning to fight once more in the Somme with the other Australian divisions.

'The men all looked very serious,' Bean would note of the returning blooded and now bloodied veterans, 'sturdy and solid, but not the least buoyancy about them.'[6]

Things had changed in the 5th's approach, however. When ordered to hop the bags in a particularly difficult attack near Flers on 23 October 1916, it seemed the days of instant obedience to organised insanity had finished. 'Brigadier-General [Pompey] Elliott,' Peter Pedersen noted in his book *The Anzacs: Gallipoli to the Western Front*, 'protested that the very idea of attacking was sheer lunacy; General McCay declared that he was not going ahead unless specifically ordered to by Birdwood.'[7]

Charles Bean would note in the *Official History of Australia in the War of 1914–1918* how, after Pozières, particularly, there was 'a certain bitterness towards the higher command. Some of the more thoughtful soldiers wondered . . . whether any sufficient object was being gained by this excessive strain and loss. The prevailing tactics – repeated shallow advances on narrow fronts – were dreaded and detested . . . it is not surprising if the effect on some intelligent men was a bitter conviction that they were being uselessly sacrificed.'[8]

In the end, the Battle of the Somme, which was ended by the exhaustion of both sides in the winter of 1916–17, was most staggering both for its catastrophic slaughter – with the forces of the British Empire, the French and the Germans losing over 1.1 million soldiers, killed and wounded between them – and for how little those deaths translated into advances or retreats. With 432,000 killed or wounded in the BEF to advance after four months no more than seven miles from its starting point, Pedersen would calculate that the advance cost 'about one man per inch . . .'[9]

At Verdun, of course, the calculus of catastrophe was as appalling. The French lost half a million killed and wounded; the Germans about 400,000. There, too, the severe winter of 1916 ended the battle.

But there were many bitter battles to come.

For the rest of the war, the Australian soldiers of all five divisions – the 3rd Division, under General John Monash, arrived in November 1916 after completing its training in Britain – fought hard in France, etching their names for perpetuity in such famous battles as Bullecourt, Messines, Menin Road, Polygon Wood, Broodseinde, Villers-Bretonneux, Hamel, Amiens, Mont St Quentin and the storming of the Hindenburg Line, and were perhaps the most highly regarded soldiers there.

Despite their renown, however, it was not until November 1917 that the five Australian divisions were able to combine into the one formation, the 'Australian Corps', which came under Australian leadership when John Monash took the helm in May 1918. For the rest of that final year of the war, they fought stunningly well, never suffering a defeat.

'[Let] me tell you what all French people think of you . . .' French President Georges Clemenceau told a gathering of exhausted Australian soldiers after the victory at the Battle of Hamel in July 1918, and German resistance began to crumble further. 'We knew you would fight a real fight, but we did not know that from the very beginning you would astonish the whole continent with your valour. I have come here for the simple purpose of seeing the Australians and telling them this. I shall go back tomorrow and say to my countrymen: "I have seen the Australians; I have looked into their eyes. I know that they, men who have fought great battles in the cause of freedom, will fight on alongside us, till the freedom for which we are all fighting is guaranteed for us and our children.'"[10]

When the Armistice came, at 11 am on 11 November 1918, London time, two minutes of silence whispered around the world, punctuated at silence's end by the haunting strains of 'The Last Post'. After four long and terrible years of war . . . peace came at last. The people danced, the people sang, the people cried with relief. There was very little work done on the day by the key protagonists of the war, with one notable exception.

For out on the old Fromelles battlefield that very afternoon, a nattily attired 37-year-old man is to be seen poking around among the skulls and bones, rusty bayonets and broken rifles. Who else could it be other than Charles Edwin Woodrow Bean – still deeply troubled by the battle he had so narrowly missed chronicling.

'We found the old no-man's land simply full of our dead . . .' he would recount. 'The skulls and bones and torn uniforms were lying around everywhere. I found a bit of Australian kit lying fifty yards from the corner of the salient, and the bones of an Australian officer and several men within 100 yards of it. Farther round, immediately on their flank, were a few British – you could tell by their leather equipment.'[11]

At this same time, Corporal Adolf Hitler, who had of course fought in this same battle, was in a hospital at Pasewalk in Pomerania, recovering from gas poisoning and weeping with fury that Germany had surrendered in what he'd describe as 'the greatest villainy of the century . . . There followed terrible days and even worse nights – I knew that all was lost . . . In these nights hatred grew in me for those responsible for this deed. In the days that followed, my own fate became known to me . . .'[12]

That fate, of course, was becoming the most famous dictator the world had ever seen, which, in turn, would bring him back to Fromelles . . .

For once risen to the position of Chancellor of Germany, *der Führer* sent the country's forces into France once more. And straight after France formally capitulated to Germany, on 22 June 1940, the German dictator's next port of call had been long planned. He went straight to Fromelles, to the site of the battle that moved him most, in the company of two of his comrades from the 16th Bavarian RIR. The next day, they, too, tramped the old battlefield, looked for their old trenches, worked out exactly where the Sugar-loaf had stood, and where the Australians and British had come from.

And yet, despite the fascination from the likes of Charles Bean and Adolf Hitler for what had happened at Fromelles, despite the fact that so many had been killed and wounded that terrible night, still, awareness of and reverence for the battle struggled to make much headway.

If not for the assiduous work of Charles Bean, much of the detail would *never* have come to the public attention. The depth of Bean's research, it must be noted, is staggering, as the copious research folders at the Australian War Memorial, filled with his notes and correspondence with survivors, bear testament. Oddly, the grieving Reverend John Garrard Raws never quite appreciated the significance of his sons' letters, how in their spidery pages lay so much of the horror that not only his sons but also their whole military generation had experienced on the Western Front.

When he was approached by Bean's nascent Australian War Memorial in 1927 for access to the letters, Reverend Raws loaned the only copies he had, begging the archivists to be careful with them as 'they are all I have left'.[13] And yet, he also noted, 'I doubt if they contain any information of note.'[14]

So graphic, however, were his son Alec's accounts – along with those of many others on the Western Front – that Bean was pressured to leave them out, a pressure he fiercely resisted. When Alec wrote, 'My tunic is rotten with other men's blood and partly splattered with a comrade's brains,'[15] that was *exactly* what it was like. And yet some veteran staff officers, as Ross Coulthart in his book *Charles Bean: If People Really Knew*, points out, thought such words 'overpitched and hysterical and showing the Australian as a weaker man than he really was'.[16]

But Bean would not budge to Australian pressure. The doubters had not been in those front-line trenches under fire, like he had. Pozières, he noted in the *Official History of Australia*, 'was not much visited by officers of the higher staffs'.[17] But *he* had visited. Those words would remain, and many words like them.

Pressure of a different kind came from Great Britain, most particularly after J. E. Edmonds, the British Official Historian, read the *Official History of Australia* in draft form and urged Bean to soften his account of Sir Richard Haking. But Bean would not, would not, he would not be moved . . . and eventually even Edmonds would quietly acknowledge to Bean, 'I don't think that [Haking], was much use after his wound . . . in 1914.'[18]

Bean's final account would form two chapters in the *Official History* entitled 'The Battle of Fromelles', and would appear in the third volume, published in 1929. Bean's reverence for the Battle of Pozières was also marked, and in 1946 he would note, 'The Windmill site . . . with the old mound still there – marks a ridge more densely sown with Australian sacrifice than any other place on earth.'[19]

As Director of the Australian War Memorial, Bean was instrumental in that sacred institution purchasing the ruins of that Windmill in 1932. And yet, while that event highlighted just how highly the officially titled Battle of Pozières was positioned in the public mind, the same could not be said for what had happened at Fromelles.

For not even the work of Charles Bean would see it recognised as a major 'battle' – a distinction that made all the difference in battle honours, monuments and reverence. As the then Premier of New South Wales, Barry O'Farrell, pointed out to me in 2014, the Anzac War Memorial at Hyde Park is just one of many memorials that does not acknowledge Fromelles as a battle. In 1921, the Battles Nomenclature Committee – a British body without a single Australian representative – decreed that Fromelles was a mere 'subsidiary attack', and so it has remained ever since.

All the Committee would allow was for all units in the Australian 5th Division to have the battle honour 'Somme 1916', on the ground that the action at Fromelles assisted the main offensive on the Somme. (There is some evidence that Fromelles was successful in that regard, as it was not until 16 September that another German division from Lille left to go to the Somme, followed on 27 September by 6 Bavarian Reserve Division – some small recompense for the slaughter.)

However, in typical Australian fashion, some battalions included 'Fromelles' on their banners anyway – and bugger the Brits – but this was only ever an unofficial claim to the honour, not official recognition.[20]

Neither of the autobiographies of General Sir William Birdwood and Sir Alexander Godley could find space for the very word 'Fromelles'.

Nevertheless, the survivors of the battle – the '19th of July men', they called themselves – did everything to keep the memory alive, and after the war would often gather on the anniversary of hopping the bags, to reminisce and, yes . . . to wonder at their extraordinary luck, too often with a sense of guilt, that they had somehow been spared.

Their last stand, effectively, took place in 1966, which was the 50th anniversary. On that occasion, it was Lieutenant David Doyle who made a speech at the Shrine of Remembrance in Melbourne. 'We have gathered,' he began, 'to quietly remember . . . the most dreadful experience of our lives . . .'[21]

His theme was sad wonderment that, all these years on, there seemed so little public recognition of what had happened that night. Up in Sydney on the same day, Fromelles survivors congregated at the Anzac Memorial at Hyde Park. 'Yesterday, they stood bare-headed, their faces showing the years between,' the *Herald* reported, 'as they remembered the bloody World War I Battle of Fromelles, 50 years ago to the day.'[22] At this point, the *Herald* noted, there were just 300 Fromelles survivors left alive across Australia.

The last Australian survivor of Fromelles was a Queenslander, August Band, who had been born in December 1895 and died on 31 October 2001, aged 106, three years after being awarded the Legion of Honour by a still appreciative French Government. With the 15th Field Company, he had been one of the men digging the sap across No-Man's Land in front of the 15th Brigade, which had to be abandoned. (The last known Australian veteran of Pozières is thought to have been Roy Longmore, who died on 21 June 2001 aged an extraordinary 107 years old.)

It was around the time of Band's death that interest in Fromelles was growing, due in large part to the publication of a series of books, including *Don't Forget Me, Cobber*, by Robin S. Corfield; *Fromelles 1916*, by Paul Cobb; *An Impression Which Will Never Fade: The True Story of an Original Anzac*, by Neville Kidd; *Fromelles*, by Peter Pedersen; *Fromelles and The Somme: Australians on the Western Front – 1916*, by Peter Burness; *The Lost Legions of Fromelles*, by Peter Barton; and *Fromelles*, by Patrick Lindsay.

—

The fate of those who survived the battles of Fromelles and Pozières was, of course, varied, both in terms of what happened to them in the rest of the war and afterwards.

General Sir Douglas Haig KT, GCB, OM, GCVO, KCIE, ADC, retained command of the BEF on the Western Front for the rest of the war, was promoted to Field Marshal and retired from the British Army in January 1920. Historians would be divided on the merits of his military career – though, for what it's worth, it is these words of the distinguished veteran become military historian B. H. Liddell-Hart that resonate most with this writer: '[Haig] was a man of supreme egoism and utter lack of scruple — who, to his overweening ambition, sacrificed hundreds of thousands of men . . . A man who gained his ends by trickery of a kind that was not merely immoral but criminal.'[23]

Most fascinating for me was that as late as 1925, Haig was *still* insisting that the verities of his military youth were still cogent in the modern age. 'I believe,' he said in a speech to the Royal College of Veterinary Surgeons, 'that the value of the horse and the opportunity for the horse in the future are likely to be as great as ever. Aeroplanes and tanks are only accessories to the men and the horse, and I feel sure that as time goes on you will find just as much use for the horse – the well-bred horse – as you have ever done in the past.'[24]

After Haig died at the age of 66 on 29 January 1928, his funeral was held at Westminster Abbey. Two of his pall-bearers were Field Marshal Ferdinand Foch and the French Inspector-General of the Army Henri-Philippe Pétain – the last of whom would go on to lead the Fascist-orientated collaborationist Vichy Government during the Second World War and would only narrowly escape the death penalty for treason.

Another pall-bearer was General Sir Hubert Gough GCB, GCMG, KCVO. The rest of his war had been a difficult one, most particularly being blamed for his Fifth Army completely collapsing in March 1918 as the Germans hurtled at them during Germany's last offensive, the *Kaiserschlacht*, the Kaiser's battle. Despite General Haig's attempts to protect him from the likes of Prime Minister Lloyd George and War Minister Lord Derby, Gough was sent home and replaced by General Rawlinson on 28 March 1918. Much of Gough's subsequent energies went into trying to rehabilitate his reputation, succeeding to the point of his being knighted in 1937. He died, at home, in 1963, one of the longest lived of the British Commanders of the Great War.

Another attendee at that funeral, General Sir Charles Monro GCB,GCSI, GCMG, outlived Haig by a year, after having filled many post-war roles, including Commander-in-Chief of the Indian Army, and Governor of Gibraltar.

———

General Sir Richard Haking GBE, KCB, KCMG was never called to account for his failure of command in the Great War. Just three weeks after Fromelles, General Haig even recommended that he be given command of the First Army. In response, there was vociferous protest from Haking's fellow officers, and even at Cabinet level, against even the possibility of him being so promoted, and the move was finally blocked, though not before Haking had served temporarily in the position for two months.[25] Haking consequently continued as Commander of XI Corps for the duration of the war. The final, alas unsuccessful, attempt to get rid of Haking occurred when a deputation from the Liberal Party went to a War Cabinet meeting on 11 April 1918 to make 'very serious protests against the retention of officers whom they considered incompetent, particularly . . . General Haking'.[26]

Despite such strong feeling against him, Haking continued with the British Army after the Armistice, was showered with honours such as KCMG in 1918 and GBE in 1921, and rose to the rank of full General in 1925. For all that, he would never be allowed to forget his role in the devastating debacle of Fromelles, with many of his own officers speaking out on it. One of them wrote to the British Official War Historian, noting that the whole episode, 'was as good an illustration as there was of the reckless extravagance in expenditure of life which ruled the minds of some of the subordinate commanders, like Gen. Haking, at this stage of the war. G.H.Q. [was guilty of] not seeing that a Corps Commander, left to himself, would always be tempted to win glory for his Corps by a spectacular success, and would be prodigal in using the divisions that passed through his hands for this purpose. The 61st Division . . . lost 50% of its attacking troops upon an objective which . . . could not possibly have been held against a counter-attack . . . Every man knew after the battle that the attack had been ordered against a position that was still, except in one part of the line, fully protected by wire, and manned by immovable machine-guns, and they lost faith in their more remote commanders as a result. Haking was always "Butcher Haking" after this battle.'[27]

In 1945, weeks after a second, but much less expensive – at least, for the British – victorious war against the Germans, Haking died from colon cancer in his bed, comfortably, and seemingly untroubled to the end by the *tens* of thousands of needless deaths he had caused.

—

By late August 1916, it was obvious that General Erich von Falkenhayn's Verdun venture had failed. Rather than knocking France, 'England's best sword', out of its hands, Verdun was one of the bloodiest stalemates in history, having caused 400,000 German casualties by this time, with France having suffered just a few more. And yet, France was still holding on valiantly to the fortress city, while the British forces were slowly, inexorably, making progress on the Somme, most particularly in the area around Pozières.

It was likely the former that wore von Falkenhayn down most, with a colleague noting of the 54-year-old at this time, 'The youthful general of 1914 has become an old man as a result of the failure at Verdun.'[28]

General von Falkenhayn was made to pay the price for the whole failure on 29 August, replaced in his position by General Paul von Hindenburg, despite the latter being nearly 70. That day, Prince Rupprecht, Falkenhayn's long-time opponent in the German Army, wrote in his diary, '*Endlich!* At long last!'[29]

Hindenburg shook hands with his predecessor at the moment of changeover, with von Falkenhayn whispering to him, '*Gott* help you and the Fatherland.'[30]

It would later be reported, 'Hindenburg made it a condition of his accepting the post that no further actions against Verdun should be attempted.'[31]

General von Falkenhayn, meanwhile, took command of the Ninth Army, which captured the Romanian capital of Bucharest in an admittedly brilliant three-month campaign, before leading Turkish forces in Palestine, where he met our mob once again in the shape of the Australian Light Horse in their famous and victorious charge at Beersheba, on 31 October 1917. (*RAH!*)

By the time of the Armistice, von Falkenhayn was commanding the Tenth Army in Belarus. He retired shortly afterwards, and devoted himself to writing his memoirs, a task he had completed before dying on 8 April 1922, in Potsdam.

—

Lieutenant-General William Birdwood GCB, GCSI, GCMG, GCVO, CIE, DSO, despite sometimes mixed reviews of his role in leading the

Anzacs, remained an Australian favourite and even coveted – and was considered for – the position of Governor-General of the country. (This despite the fact that, as Ross Coulthart notes in his biography of Bean, there would be claims that some of the Australian survivors of Pozières felt such ill-will towards the English General they even hooted at him at one point as he passed and called out 'Butcher'.)[32]

In 1938, Sir William was created Baron Birdwood of Anzac and Totnes, living the rest of his years quietly until dying on 17 May 1951. In Melbourne, The Shrine is on Birdwood Avenue.

—

Sir Cyril Brudenell White KCB, KCMG, KCVO, DSO was once described by Bean as 'the greatest man it has been my fortune to intimately know'[33] – and that intimacy saw White help Bean greatly as the latter wrote the *Official History*. Brudenell White remained a respected figure in Australia for the rest of his life, being knighted just after the war was over and going on to chair a variety of prestigious public and private institutions, before returning to the fray in 1939 at the outbreak of the Second World War, to again become Chief of the General Staff in March 1940. That role, alas, was tragically cut short in a Canberra plane crash in August 1940, which also saw the death of three Federal Cabinet Ministers.

—

Like General Haking, Major-General Sir James McCay KCMG, KBE, CB, VD suffered no check in his career for the debacle of Fromelles on his watch – and nor was he called to account for the outrage of having allowed the wounded Australian soldiers to die in No-Man's Land, rather than accept the German offer of a truce. He remained with the 5th Division until January 1917, when he became ill once again. Unsurprisingly, when word spread later that year that McCay might be taking over Monash's 3rd Division, there was something close to a revolt from his fellow Australian General, Sir William Birdwood. 'I told him,' Birdwood would later reveal, 'I didn't want the 3rd Division ruined like he had ruined the 5th!'[34]

McCay left the Australian Army the following year, was appointed as a KCMG in 1918 and KBE in 1919. Though he went on to forge a career in the business world, just like Haking, what happened at Fromelles would still haunt him. In his book, *Fromelles*, Peter Pedersen records, 'After the war, Australian veterans scrawled "Butcher McCay" in red paint outside a servicemen's club he was visiting, and one of the AIF's great heroes, Captain Albert Jacka VC, MC, publicly refused to shake his hand.'[35]

McCay died on 1 October 1930 of a kidney ailment, and is buried in Box Hill cemetery.[36] It would have been illuminating to know more of his side of the story, but, alas, he burned his papers before his death.

—

Colonel Harold Pope CB, BD fought long and hard to clear his name of the idea that he had been drunk on duty the day after the Fromelles attack, and succeeded to the point that by March 1917 Pope was back, in charge of the 52nd Battalion, where he acquitted himself well until being seriously wounded at the Battle of Messines in June, whereupon he was invalided home. He died on 13 May 1938 of heart disease.

—

General Pompey Elliott CB, CMG, DSO, DCM, VD continued on as a successful officer, loved by his men, for the rest of the war, being mentioned in dispatches seven times for his valour. No less than Charles Bean would credit his leadership at the battle of Polygon Wood with having 'snatched complete success from an almost desperate situation'.[37]

Still, he was never given a division to command. 'The reason for this,' Pompey's Intelligence Officer at Fromelles, Lieutenant David Doyle, would state more than 20 years later in a letter to the Editor of

Reveille, 'was General Elliott's inability to get on with British Officers. He couldn't understand them, and they couldn't understand him . . .'[38]

Throughout the war, Elliott never stopped grieving for those lost at Fromelles, and none more than Geoff McCrae. 'If I myself should fall in France,' he said, 'I should like to be buried near poor Geoff.'[39]

After the war, Elliott entered politics, becoming a Victorian Senator for the Nationalist Party for all of the 1920s. Much of his energy also went to helping returned soldiers in any way he could, as well as trying to ensure those who gave 'the order [to attack at Fromelles] may be made to realize their responsibility'.[40]

This rage was never more apparent than in an article he wrote for *The Duckboard*, the Official Organ of the Melbourne Branch of the Returned Sailors and Soldiers Imperial League of Australia. 'Haking must take the chief blame for this debacle,' he declared. 'The plan was his, and but for his insistence would have been abandoned almost at its birth. He can, however, shelter behind the weakness displayed by Monro, by Butler, and even by Haig himself at this critical juncture.'[41]

As Elliott was ever wont to do, he went on . . . 'The whole operation was so incredibly blundered from beginning to end that it is almost incomprehensible how the British Staff, who were responsible for it, could have consisted of trained professional soldiers of considerable reputation and experience, and why, in view of the outcome of this extraordinary adventure, any of them were retained in active command.'[42]

Elliott reeled off the many blunders made by Haking and McCay, with the acidic accuracy of one who dwelled on them most days of his life: 'Failure of the first duty of a commander – personal reconnaissance – resulting in selection of unsuitable ground . . . No-Man's-Land in front of centre of attack was too wide . . . Insufficient artillery preparation . . . Hurried and insufficient preparations resulting in mistakes by inexperienced junior staff officers . . .'[43]

And, of course, the consequences of the whole botched operation on his men haunted him to distraction, and perhaps more. He had recommended a Victoria Cross for Major Arthur Hutchinson, who had led that gallant charge to try to take out the Sugar-loaf, but, of course, it had been denied. For to award it would have required the authorities to acknowledge the 'shameful betrayal of gallant men', who had been 'hopelessly and helplessly massacred'.[44]

Likely suffering from post-traumatic stress, in March 1931 the 52-year-old Elliott first tried to gas himself, and when that failed was admitted to a private hospital in Malvern. In the lost watch of the early hours next morning, he succeeded in causing such a grievous wound to his arm he was found dead at dawn.

His State Funeral was attended by thousands of returned servicemen, who followed the gun-carriage bearing his coffin from his home at East Camberwell to his grave at Burwood Cemetery – standing to attention as his coffin was lowered into the grave and a 13-gun salute was fired. There was such an outpouring of emotion that the former Prime Minister Stanley Bruce would say of it, 'I have never seen a greater tribute.'[45]

—

Evacuated to England after the Fromelles battle, suffering from severe rheumatism, Lieutenant-Colonel Walter Cass CMG was able to meet up with the beautiful Canadian Army nursing sister Helena Holmes, whom he had been courting for five years, and they were married within three months.

On their wedding day, he wrote her a passionate letter, featuring his most fervent hope: 'I pray, dear, that the Great Architect of the Universe in weaving the pattern of the world for All time will afford us our share.'[46]

The Great Architect did not.

After Cass had recuperated from his rheumatism, he returned with Helena to live in Australia, where he became Director of Military Training in 1917, a position he retained for the rest of the war and for three years into peacetime, before filling a variety of official roles including Base Commandant in three states. In 1929, he had risen to the rank of Brigadier-General and become Base Commandant of the Third Military District in Melbourne when – with Helena and their five-year-old daughter, Angela, by his bedside – he died after an operation for appendicitis went wrong, still a relatively young man on 6 November 1931, aged just 55.

As one of his men would write of him, 'The leaders of the A.I.F. were mostly generous men, and marked for their sense of duty; but there were perhaps few in whom the recognition of duty was quite so strong, or sympathy with the rank and file so keen, as in Walter Cass.'[47]

Vale, Walter Cass. You were a good 'un. If I had been at Fromelles, I would have liked to have been led by you.

—

Lieutenant-Colonel Frederick Toll DSO, VD was awarded the Distinguished Service Order for his gallantry at Fromelles and then earned a bar to that DSO for his services in temporarily leading the 8th Brigade for a fortnight in November 1917. Highly regarded, he became a foundation member of the Returned Sailors' and Soldiers' Imperial League of Australia, was appointed a Member of the British Empire in 1939, and died on 6 November 1955 in Brisbane, aged 83.

—

Brave Lieutenant-Colonel David McConaghy CMG, DSO, who had led the 55th Battalion so well during the Battle of Fromelles, was killed at Hangard Wood, near Villers-Bretonneux, on 9 April 1918.

—

Captain Charles Arblaster was indeed taken prisoner by the Germans as they surged forward after dawn on 20 July, and was given quick treatment for his grievous wounds at a German military hospital, but lived only another four days. He died of septicaemia, aged just 21.

When Carlton played Fitzroy in the Aussie Grand Final of 1916, all of the Carlton players wore black armbands in memory of George Challis.

'The news that he had been killed in action,' *The Australasian* noted, 'arrived just when there was the first touch of spring in the air, and if there had been no war, instead of being in France, Challis would have been playing in the Premiership match on the M.C.G. Fifty thousand people would have cheered Challis for his speed and skill . . .'[48]

Private Arthur Brunton, who had written a farewell note to his wife before venturing into No-Man's Land to rescue fellow Diggers the night after the Fromelles battle . . . survived the night. And the war. He returned to his wife in 1919 and died in 1966.

In late 1916, Eddie Rule was completely stunned.

Albert Jacka . . . dead?

He can't believe it. Not *Jacka*. And yet, there is the news, black on white, the headline in the London paper:

Death of Jacka.
Australia's First V.C. Winner Dies of Wounds.[49]

And yet, when Eddie shares his misery with his mate George, to his astonishment, George starts laughing.

'I can see,' George says merrily, 'that you don't know the sequel to Bert's death.'

'What do you mean?'

George tells him the story. Back in England, to where Bert Jacka had been evacuated after his terrible injuries at Pozières, Jacka had found himself under siege from well-meaning people, including ladies of all descriptions, old and young, which would have been fine if he had been a ladies' man, but . . .

'Bert, as you know, was never a ladies' man, and he had very soon had as much attention as he could put up with. One day some of us were sitting around his bed when a request to see him came from a reporter of one of the London daily newspapers. Bert turned to one of the chaps. "Go to the door and tell the beggar I'm dead . . ." But Bert's far from dead, don't worry. We'll have him back with us yet.'[50]

And he was right. Jacka's mob soon boasted Jacka himself once more, now promoted to Lieutenant. And yet, as Rule would also detail, even so great a soldier as Jacka had been stalked by demons unleashed by the dreadful battle he had been through. 'During those months [away] the iron will was so badly shaken that the noise of a box-lid hurriedly closed would set up a physical shaking that would continue for hours at a stretch, during which time he was incapable of signing his name to an order or memo.'[51]

Jacka recovered enough to fight on, and did so, right up until, at Villers-Bretonneux in May 1918, he was gassed and had to be evacuated.

A measure of his fame was that, when landed in Melbourne later that year aboard *Euripides*, Albert Jacka VC, MC and Bar was greeted by an enormous crowd that included the Governor-General, Sir Ronald Craufurd Munro Ferguson – who stayed with them as Jacka joined a cavalcade of 85 cars that bore him to Melbourne Town Hall, where a reception awaited him, heavily peopled by who else but Jacka's mob, the 14th Battalion, who had mostly preceded him.

Of all his many feats, it was perhaps his action at Pozières that would be the most remembered. And yet, despite the fact that those most familiar with his actions believe he deserved a second Victoria Cross for Pozières – and even a third for another extraordinary feat of arms at Bullecourt – to go with the one awarded to him at Gallipoli, he received a slightly less glorious Military Cross, something that surprised and disappointed him.

In 1931, the authoritative *Reveille* magazine would report that Jacka considered his Pozières feat 'the greatest of all his personal exploits and rates it six times as high as his V.C. performance'.[52]

After running an electrical goods business with two members of the 14th Battalion, marrying his sweetheart and adopting a daughter, in the late 1920s Jacka entered politics and soon became the Mayor of St Kilda – which was useful, as his business did not survive the Great Depression.

Tragically, the ravages of war – particularly the gassing – never quite left him, and he died at Caulfield Military Hospital on 17 January 1932 of chronic kidney disease, aged just 39. His last words were to his weeping father, hovering by his son's deathbed: 'I'm still fighting, Dad.'[53]

He, too, was given a State Funeral, and his coffin lay at Anzac House as no fewer than 6000 people filed past to pay their respects. A thousand of Jacka's mob turned up to lead his funeral procession, and his coffin was carried into St Kilda Cemetery, borne by eight winners of the Victoria Cross. No man in Australian history has ever had such a send-off.

—

One Pozières veteran who would be awarded a Victoria Cross for his heroism later in the war was Lieutenant Percy Cherry VC MC for his derring-do on 26 March 1917, in leading his surviving men to capture the village of Lagnicourt . . . before he was killed by shell fire the next day.

—

Just six days after being wounded, and having his leg amputated, Captain Cecil Maitland Foss MC died, at No. 3 Casualty Clearing Station at Puchevillers on 11 August 1916. He was, said his friend Major Arnold Brown, a 'soldier, gentleman and leader – a man who would have risen high in the service had he survived'.[54] The death of the 25-year-old, it would be noted, 'cast a pall over the entire battalion'.[55]

—

The German soldier who took the proffered Bible from Private Edgar Parham as he lay dying at Fromelles was himself dying 20 years later. And he remembered. There was something that had been troubling him for many years.

'Search my old war kit for an English Bible,' he managed to rasp out to his brother in his final hours. 'Give it back . . .' And then, *'Lebewohl . . . Kamerad . . . Gott mit uns . . .* Goodbye . . . Comrade . . . God with us.'

Searching the kit, the brother found the Bible, marked with the words *E.W. Parham; mother* and *Australia.*

It proved to be enough, and in April 1937 the Bible was returned, providing some solace for Parham's 83-year-old widowed mother – as had the fact that a French farmer, ploughing his field a decade before, had found dear Edgar's skeleton, complete with identity disc, and he had been properly buried.

In return, Mrs Parham sent the brother, Karl Steinmetz, at *Hindenburgstraße 86a in Berlin-Wilmersdorf,* another Bible 'inscribed with *an aged mother's thanks* and her prayer that *'innocent men might never again be sent out to kill and be killed'.*[56]

—

The three surviving children of the widower who died at Fromelles, Captain Harry Paulin, now orphaned – Noel, Harold Jnr and Violet – were separated and sent to foster homes – never to see each other again.[57]

Sadly, Captain Paulin's message to his daughter did not arrive until she was in her 70s. It was passed on to her by a relative who had gone through the files of her father at the Australian War Memorial and come across the account. She burst into tears . . .

—

Sergeant David 'Don Ack Toc' Twining survived the war, and returned home to take up the post of Adjutant to the 27th Battalion in Adelaide. But, just like Pompey Elliott, the events of the war haunted him and simply would not let go. In 1931, he too took his life, being found dead in an office in the drill hall at Keswick Barracks. Brigadier-General Ray Leane, Twining's 48th Battalion Commander at Pozières, was one of the pall-bearers at his funeral. Another was his best mate from the same battalion, Harry Downes, who, with the two brothers Bill and Bert Watson, had formed an inseparable group of four. One of the officers of the battalion would later recall, 'In France . . . they worked together and played together. I can see them now in their hut – sparring with the gloves, to keep warm while merry quip and jest kept the onlookers in a continued state of laughter.'[58]

A grief-stricken Harry Downes wrote an obituary for David Twining in *Reveille*, which included the telling passage: 'To some people the war finished in 1918, but to those of us who understand, the Grim Reaper is still taking his toll, just as surely as he did at Messines or Passchendaele, and, to me, "Don Ack Toc" has gone to join his comrades of Gallipoli and Flanders, "killed in action" just as surely as if he had "stopped it" in the strenuous days of 1914–1918.'[59]

Downes knew precisely of that which he wrote, and, later that same year, tragically took his own life.

—

Though Norman Gibbins's body was buried in an unmarked battle-field grave on the day that he died, only a couple of days later he was exhumed and re-interred in Anzac Cemetery at Sailly graveyard, 'neath a large wooden cross, on which would be marked the words, courtesy of the one sister who remained tightly loyal to him, 'My beloved brother. Son of the late William Gibbins CE Australia.'[60]

Charles Bean would do Gibbins his due. 'You will not find him,' the correspondent and historian would note, 'where he ought to be – in the hall of V.C.'s; yet, like many who best earned that distinction,

I do not think he would have sought it, resting content with a reward infinitely more precious – the adoring trust, and gratitude of his mates, and the consciousness that, in an hour of need, he had served Australia well.'[61]

Vale, Gib. A hundred years on, mate, we remember you.

—

Ray Bishop's mother lived in hope, for the rest of her days, that her boy, Ray – first reported by 'Base Records' at Victoria Barracks, Melbourne, as Missing in Action – had been captured by the Germans and would one day make his way home to her. Of course, it was not to be, and more realistic members of the family realised the truth, most particularly when the army changed his status to Killed in Action – after a witness had come forward with a claim to have seen his dead body.

Bert Bishop MM mourned his cousins Ray and Billy Bishop – and Ray's elder brother, Harold, who had also been killed at Gueudecourt on the Somme on 5 November 1916 – for the rest of his own extraordinarily long life.

On 14 May 1919, Bert was awarded a Military Medal – for 'conspicuous gallantry and devotion to duty during operations at PERONNE . . . showing great courage and keenness under terrific enemy artillery and M.G. fire; going forward with his Lewis Gun . . .'[62]

Returned to Australia, Bert first took up a career as a journalist with his father's newspaper, *The Milton Times*, before going on a peripatetic career as a printer, then farmer up Wyong way, and then having a series of corner-stores on Sydney's North Shore. Along the way, he married one Edna Turnbull and raised a happy family. Many times, however, Bert, too, would wake in the night screaming, and Edna would have to calm him, 'Bert, Bert, Bert, the war is *over*, the war is *over*, and I am here.'[63]

For the rest of his life, he would frequently work on a manuscript of his war memoirs, which drew heavily on the letters he had sent home during the war. It was a process that went on for all of seven decades before, in 1991, he released *The Hell, the Humour and the Heartbreak – A Private's View of World War I*, a wonderful volume of personal reminiscences that I have drawn on heavily for this account. Just a few months after it was published, he died in his sleep, in his bed – some 75 years after his cousin Ray had died so violently in the early-morning hours of 20 July 1916. To his dying day, Bert lived in hope that Ray's remains might be discovered, so he could be given a proper burial.

———

Other Australian parents simply refused to accept that their loved ones were gone, killed in a brutal battle for practically no gain. Among them were the parents of Russell Bosisto, Ernest and Annie. Together with Russell's five sisters, they lived in hope that through some miracle he might still be alive – perhaps 'somewhere unable to write or suffering from loss of memory . . .'[64] Annie wrote hopefully to the Red Cross, seven months after he disappeared at Pozières. In a PS to her letter, she even noted, 'If you have good news will you kindly call and I will pay this end.'[65] But there is nothing, nothing, nothing, no news. All they have is their treasured photo of him in uniform in pride of place above the fireplace – looking so smart – as the family settles in to decades of mourning, wondering what happened to him.

———

The mother of Major Tom Elliott was another case in point, where no amount of writing anguished and oft-furious letters could make the remains of her boy appear. So profound was her grief at his loss that she would eventually be committed to an infamous mental institution, Callan Park Mental Hospital, 'diagnosed with delusional mania'.[66]

The author Ross McMullin would detail how, convinced Tom was still alive, she varied in her belief that he was now an important General in England, on secret missions to Austria, or perhaps even married to an Italian princess. The tragic truth, of course, was that his remains lay on the battlefield where he fell. But with no body ever recovered, Thomas Patrick Elliott is commemorated at VC Corner Australian Cemetery and Memorial at Fromelles.

His heartbroken mother died within a year of the war ending, victim of the Spanish flu. And yet the grieving for Tom would go on, including by the woman in Ausralia whom he was so sweet on, Alice Thurlow, the one to whom he was always writing letters. She never married, though she lived for another 60 years beyond his death. Yes, there had been another Australian soldier, Billy Waters, who had competed for her affections, but, after contracting gonorrhoea in France, he, too, had been killed in action, in 1917. As McMullin also details, Alice still had Tom's letters with her when she passed away.

—

Others, like the widow of the one-time bank manager from South Yarra, Jack Bowden – who had perished shortly after being one of only likely two members of the 59th Battalion to reach the German wire – would come to accept the obvious, even though there had been some early reports that he had been taken prisoner. After further investigation, however, his status was confirmed as Killed in Action on 2 January 1918.[67]

As a final act of acceptance, on 19 July 1918, Jessie Bowden placed an *in memoriam* in *The Argus*:

In loving memory of my dearly beloved husband, John Charles Bowden (Jack). 2nd Lieut Australian Imperial Forces, who was killed in action on or about 19th July 1916 somewhere in France. (Inserted by his sorrowing wife Jessie Bowden.)[68]

Only Bowden's sister, Mary Stocks, kept up hope that either Jack or his body would be found, and it was through this correspondence that, in 1918, a note was generated from the Berlin branch of the British Red Cross with this paragraph: Regarding this enquiry, please note that a search of the cards at the Nachweis Ero reveals that two cards exist.[69]

For whatever reason, however – surely because that report did not make its way to either Jessie Bowden or Mary Stocks – it was not pursued.

———

In January 1998, a French farmer was ploughing his field just up near where the Windmill of Pozières used to be, when his plough brought something to the surface. Bones?

Yes, covered in tattered cloth. He carefully dug around with his hands, and the remarkably complete remains of an Australian soldier emerged, replete with his pipe, tattered gasmask, penknife and razor, loaded rifle, with hooked quillion. (Later, it will emerge that, despite his being a private, the insignia of a Lieutenant was found inside his pants pocket. Very strange . . .) And here is his identity disc. The farmer scrapes away the mud with his index finger and holds it up to the bright sunshine. It is different to the usual scungy dog tags he has seen. Not regulation. *Qu'est-ce que c'est?* This one is of finer metal, clearly done with a lot of love. And what is the name on it?

R G Bosisto 27th bn

Eighty-two years after he had disappeared on that terrible night, Russell Bosisto, 'Boss', has at last been found. The farmer calls *les Gendarmes*. The Australian Embassy is soon contacted, who in turn informs the Commonwealth War Graves Commission. A long legal and forensic process has begun . . .

Finally, however, on 5 July 1998, in the presence of two of his weeping nieces, an honour guard from Russell's old outfit, the 10/27th Battalion, Royal South Australia Regiment, carries his coffin, draped in the Australian flag, in a slow march behind the United Mineworkers' Federation of Australia Pipe Band, to an open pit at Courcelette

Cemetery. As they approach the grave, the bagpipes stop, and they all slow-march to the beat of a sole bass drum.

After the brief service, the coffin is, with great respect and ceremony, lowered into the pit, so Boss can rest for all eternity, right by nine of his mates of the 27th Battalion, who had been killed in the same action, and within direct line of sight of the old Windmill – as the Australian Ambassador John Spender presides, accompanied by many dignitaries, including the Australian Minister for Defence, Ian McLachlan.

And those four old men, now stepping forward – after the Chaplain sprinkles holy water from an upturned helmet of the Great War – to throw handfuls of dirt onto the coffin below, who are they?

Well, friends, they are four surviving First World War Diggers, flown to France for the occasion by the Howard Government. One of them, Howard Pope, was from Bosisto's battalion, the 27th, and is now 101 years old. As Bosisto is laid beneath the sod in a recognised grave, at last, the four Diggers, led by Pope, salute. Others, including his nieces, step forward to take one of the many blood-red poppies available in a large white basket to drop down onto his grave.

The Honour Guard of the 10/27th Regiment fires 18 shots into the air, and the bugler sounds 'The Last Post', followed by 'Reveille'.

It is for the Minister for Veterans Affairs the Honourable Bruce Scott to conclude proceedings. 'As we lay him to rest beside 9 mates,' he intones, 'killed on the same day, in the same action, words written by warrior poet, Siegfried Sassoon, in 1916 – the year of Russell's death – sum up all I would wish him to hear:

'I quote:

"Yet, though my dreams that throng the darkened stair

"Can bring me no report of how you fare,

"Safe quit of wars, I speed you on your way

"up lonely, glimmering fields to find new day."

'Godspeed, Russell Bosisto.

'May You Rest In Peace.'[70]

It is over. Boss's headstone reads:

**Private Russell George Bosisto, 27th Battalion AIF
Only son of Ernest and Annie Bosisto. An Anzac
Finally at Rest.**

—

Of course, despite the recovery of Russell Bosisto, the vast majority of the missing remained unaccounted for – and therein lay a mystery that remained into the next century.

So entered Lambis Englezos, a charismatic and indefatigable Greek-born art teacher from Melbourne, an amateur First World War enthusiast to beat them all. When Robin S. Corfield's book *Don't Forget Me, Cobber* came out in 2000, Lambis was particularly struck by the profile of Lieutenant Jack Bowden, including the paragraph, 'When the war was over it was revealed that the Berlin branch of the Red Cross did have a card for John Charles Bowden and the confusion . . . resulted from the Germans believing him to be among those they buried in one of five large British Collective Graves outside the *Fasanen-Wäldchen*, Little Pheasant Wood . . .'[71]

According to Corfield's book, 'Pheasant Wood' was a forested patch of land just outside the village, not far from the light railway line that ran back from it. What intrigued Lambis was that, as one who had read just about all there was to read about Fromelles, he had never before even *heard* of any Little Pheasant Wood.

How could that be?

'It was extraordinary,' he later told me. 'Of all the 1336 "missing", Jack Bowden's file was the only one that mentioned Pheasant Wood. But there was no reference to such a place anywhere else, and, crucially, no one seemed to have a clue *where* it was . . .'

And so he began to think.

Familiar with many of the diaries of the Diggers already, Lambis recalled the words of the 29th Battalion's Private Bill Barry when he had come to after being captured: 'to my horror I was in the place where all the dead men were. I was sitting on the edge of a hole about forty feet long, twenty feet wide and fifteen feet deep and into this hole the dead were being thrown without any fuss or respect.'[72]

Surely that was the mass grave he was looking for? After all, it only made sense – even if a check of the records held by the Commonwealth War Graves Commission in the UK revealed no such mass burial sites had been discovered. But what then had the Germans done with the hundreds of dead Australians they must surely have recovered? The most obvious thing would have been to pile them onto carriages and transport them back from the lines along the light-rail track. But what then?

One thing Lambis knew was that the German way was to quickly bury the dead – both the enemy's and their own – to prevent the stench and the spread of disease.

In April 2002, with the missing of Fromelles buzzing constantly at the back of his mind, Lambis visited the old battle site. While there, he began to ask questions about Pheasant Wood, but still came to a dead-end every time. No one had heard of the *Fasanen-Wäldchen*, nor the French or English translations of that name.

Still he would not stop. He felt something in his bones. And the numbers, only very rough at that stage, seemed to back him up, as Lambis estimated over 200 of the missing were still unaccounted for.

Returning to Australia, he began to communicate his suspicions to friends and historians, and made inquiries at the Office of Australian War Graves, as well as the Australian Army History Unit. But his over-tures about the possibility of the existence of mass graves containing the bodies of unrecovered Australian soldiers were largely ignored in Canberra, with one official writing to him, 'we cannot do things on your gut feelings, we need a carefully prepared, logical dossier'.[73]

Lambis Englezos began to prepare exactly that, helped by a develop-ing core group of believers – 'Team Lambis', as author Patrick Lindsay would come to call them, in his riveting book on the whole subject, *Fromelles*. The team included John Fielding, deputy principal of a Sydney high school who was also a Lieutenant-Colonel in the Army Reserve, and Ward Selby, grandson of a Fromelles veteran and a mining executive whose work saw him spend much time in Europe.

One key source was the Red Cross's 'Wounded and Missing' files, containing information gathered by the Germans about the dead they had collected. Their protocol had been to lay the bodies out by nationality on a spot by the Grashof, take whatever identity discs and personal belongings they could gather from each corpse, put them in a bag, and send them to the Red Cross to be passed on to their families. And all of the information therein contained had been carefully detailed, and was still available if you knew where to look.

Taking Robin S. Corfield's book *Don't Forget Me, Cobber* as his fount of information, Lambis personally cross-referenced the Honour Roll of the dead in the book and went through no fewer than 1336 files of all those reported 'missing' after the battle was over. His final estimate was that 175 soldiers had been buried in Pheasant Wood's mass grave.

But where could it be?

And then came the inspiration. If such pits were freshly dug, perhaps aerial reconnaissance shots before and after the battle on the German side of the line might show a difference? Bingo. And hence the location of the necessary relevant aerial photographs could be ordered from the Imperial War Museum (IWM) in Britain.

It took some doing, but in 2004 the before and after photos arrived from the IWM. Taking his magnifying glass in his suburban Melbourne study, Lambis began perusing them. Looking at the photo of the area on the German side of the Fromelles line taken on 17 June 1916, he could see nothing unusual. Moving on to the next photo, taken on 29 July . . . *There!*

Sure enough, right by a spot where the *rail track* ran, by the *woods* that lay just down the slope of Fromelles, it was obvious that some pits had been dug since the last photo. Surely the pits being used by the Germans as mass graves? Surely that was where the bodies would be found? Surely he was, right now, looking at the very spot where the Pheasant Wood mass burial site lay?

After the media began to pick up the story, the wheels were set in motion, and it was decided by Defence Minister Robert Hill and Lieutenant-General Leahy that a presentation by Team Lambis would best settle the issue.

Alas, however, despite that presentation going ahead, they were met with something perilously close to a stone wall. To the bureaucrats, it seemed simply impossible to believe that there could be a mass grave of those proportions, undiscovered by the post-war recovery teams whose specific job it was to look for exactly that – let alone that it could remain undiscovered since. The panel officially decided that, while further investigation might be warranted, 'field studies are not recommended unless more compelling evidence is located to support the contention that the site was being used as a mass grave by the Germans in 1916'.[74]

This 'compelling evidence' was not long in showing up. At the behest of Lambis, Dr Lothar Saupe at the *Kriegsarchiv*, Bavarian Main State Archive's War Archive in Munich, finally found the critical document. It was an order written on 21 July 1916, the day the Battle of Fromelles was sputtering into nothing, by Oberst Julius Ritter von Braun, Commanding Officer of the 21st BRIR:

```
The English bodies will be buried in mass
graves immediately to the south of Pheasant
Wood. The removal of effects and identity discs
(in the same way as for the German bodies), on
which the number and company appearing on the
identity disc are recorded ... For the burial
of the dead, the company is to excavate mass
graves for approximately 400 bodies.[75]
```

This was the last piece of the puzzle.

In May 2007, with media pressure building on the Australian Government for the mystery to be solved, it commissioned the Glasgow University Archaeology Research Department (GUARD) to do a non-intrusive survey of the site. The survey – led by Dr Tony Pollard, Director of the Centre for Battlefield Archaeology, University of Glasgow, boasting sophisticated technology and including Peter Barton, who would go on to write the definitive work on the battle most particularly from the German side, *The Lost Legions of Fromelles* – confirmed an even scattering in the surface soil of war debris, along with two significant items of Australian origin, which was promising. The site was deemed 'of interest' by the team.

After gathering more supporting evidence from the Munich Archives, the government then commissioned GUARD to do a pre-liminary excavation of the site in May 2008. Again, Lambis Englezos was there for the occasion. He was fairly sure that he was right, and even *convinced* that the Australian remains would be discovered, but still . . . he was nervous. The very careful dig began, the archaeologists delicately removing centimetre after centimetre of topsoil on an area right in the middle of the site that Lambis had designated. After the first day, there was nothing. And so too throughout the second day – though there was 'waft', the technical word to indicate the rising smell of the dead.

And then, late on the second day, just as dusk is setting in, it happens.

A careful, if excited, shout goes up. One of the team has found something – it will prove to be a human arm, missing a hand. Lambis, when he finds out, is 'very relieved . . . and hopeful. Hopeful that the discovery will lead to them each being given the dignity of a grave of their own.' The dig is shut down for the day, and delayed the follow-ing morning as the Gendarmes arrive to confirm that the remains are archaeological in nature and not criminal. (In the Gendarmes' view, anyway.)

The dig continued.

Most staggering was how well-preserved many of the remains were within the heavily compressed clay, with identifiable hair and, fre-quently, evidence on their skeletal forms of just what battlefield wounds had killed them – from shattered skulls, indicating a bullet to the brain, to bayonet marks on ribs around the heart.

The dig went on, the beginning of a long process, and when finally completed, of the eight pits excavated, skeletons were found in five of them, together with many Australian and some British artefacts. While the bodies had been laid in some order in the first three pits, in the last two the soldiers appeared to have been just thrown in, higgledy-piggledy, from the edge of the pit. At the conclusion of this first excavation, the remains were effectively buried again, to await a political determination as to what to do. Should they be fully exhumed, identified and placed in individual graves? Or should, perhaps, a memorial be constructed to note that here lie Australian soldiers?

At the small memorial service to mark the end of the three-week excavation, a frail French lady appears – a very old, distinguished woman, accompanied by her grandson. It is Madame Marie-Paule Demassiet, who owns the ground the soldiers have been found on. 'This ground, *n'est plus le mien*, is no longer mine,' she says to the gathering. 'It belongs *aux soldats*, to the soldiers.'

It took a year, but after an agreement was reached between the Governments of Australia, Great Britain and France, full recovery commenced in May 2009. Excavation of the total area of the pits, 30 metres wide by 150 metres long, took five months. When it was done, no fewer than 250 soldiers – 'The Lost Diggers of Fromelles'[76] – were recovered to be examined, analysed and catalogued by a team of forensic archaeologists and anthropologists. Finally the remains of each soldier were prepared for DNA-based identification, due to take place *after* the Diggers – and several British soldiers – were laid to rest.

When the time came for reburial, it was decided that the men could not simply be re-interred in the same ground where they had been found, as the ground at Pheasant Wood itself was too damp. Instead, a parcel of civic land just 400 metres from the Pheasant Wood grave site was requisitioned, just down from the Fromelles village church.

The first of the reburials in the snow-covered graveyard took place on 30 January 2010 – each soldier in an oak casket, laid to rest with enormous ceremony, as a bugler sounded 'The Last Post'. And so it began. In one three-week period in early 2010, no fewer than 249 soldiers were buried. Many of the villagers from Fromelles, Aubers and places nearby would also attend, just to pay their respects to those who had died defending their forebears. The last of the soldiers was interred on the 94th anniversary of the battle, 19 July of that year.

Always, particular care was taken to place side by side men who had already been lying side by side for the last nine decades in those mass pits – now together for eternity. After the burials were complete, the long process got under way to identify each skeleton and inform the families. One obvious problem with getting DNA samples from family is that most of the remains recovered were from men who had died childless, so in most cases it was grand-nieces and grand-nephews who did the honours.

Among those identified were Ray Pflaum and Ray Bishop. If only Bert Bishop had lived to see the day.

With each name revealed, Lambis Englezos felt a stab of sadness. Having perused their files for so long, gazed at their photographs, read the correspondence from their anguished families, he *knew* these sons of Bunyip, of Northcote, of Brunswick, of South Melbourne. And now they were found – 144 bodies identified as this book goes to press. But still no Jack Bowden – something that makes Lambis feel more than slightly wistful.

'Every time I get the list of new names identified,' he told me in August 2015, 'I look for his name first. He was the one that led us to the grave site, and it would be only right if we have his remains beneath an identifiable headstone, to pay our respects.'

—

Eight decades after the Pozières battle was over, it was dirt from the Windmill site that was scattered on the coffin of Australia's Unknown Soldier when he was interred at the Australian War Memorial on 11 November 1993.

'We do not know this Australian's name and we never will,' Prime Minister Paul Keating famously intoned. 'We do not know his rank or his battalion. We do not know where he was born, nor precisely how and when he died. We do not know where in Australia he had made his home or when he left it for the battlefields of Europe. We do not know his age or his circumstances – whether he was from the city or the bush; what occupation he left to become a soldier; what religion, if he had a religion; if he was married or single. We do not know who loved him or whom he loved. If he had children we do not know who they are. His family is lost to us as he was lost to them. We will never know who this Australian was. Yet he has always been among those whom we have honoured. We know that he was one of the 45,000 Australians who died on the Western Front. One of the 416,000 Australians who volunteered for service in the First World War. One of the 324,000 Australians who served overseas in that war and one of the 60,000 Australians who died on foreign soil. One of the 100,000 Australians who have died in wars this century.

'He is <u>all</u> of them. And he is one of us . . .'[77]

Vale to him, and to his lost generation.

I weep.

With rage, too.

NOTES AND REFERENCES

BACKGROUND AND ACKNOWLEDGEMENTS

1. Bean, *Official History of Australia in the War of 1914–1918*, Vol. V, p. 110.
2. *Time* magazine, Vol. 186, No. 5, 2015, p. 11.

PROLOGUE

1. Lewis, p. 69.
2. Stevenson, Frances, p. 40.
3. Brown, 'The Old Windmill: Pozières' Tragic Landmark', *Reveille*, October 1932, p. 3.
4. Though, admittedly, a Prussian army had marched past the Pozières windmill before, in November 1870 during the Franco-Prussian War.
5. *Deutscher Reichsanzeiger*, 6 August 1914.
6. Charteris, pp. 125–6.
7. Recouly and Jones, p. 112.
8. Charlton, James (ed.), p. 35.
9. Haking, p. 103.
10. Douglas Haig, Final Dispatch, *Fourth Supplement to the London Gazette*, 10 April 1919, p. 4699, www.thegazette.co.uk/London/issue/31283/supplement/1.
11. De la Gorce, p. 102.
12. De Gaulle, p. 5.
13. Braithwaite, p. 121.
14. Strictly speaking, the term 'shrapnel' only applied in the First World War to the pellets that came out of a shrapnel shell. The chunks of metal from high-explosive (H.E.) shells that caused so many casualties were called 'shell shards' or 'fragments'. Because the soldiers themselves used 'shrapnel' to describe pellets and shell shards, I have employed the term to mean either.

15. Grant, p. 59.
16. Wichers, 'The Forgotten Victims of the North: French Civilians under German Occupation during World War I', *Armstrong Undergraduate Journal of History*, www.armstrong.edu/Initiatives/history_journal.
17. Taylor, p. 20.
18. Falkenhayn, p. 37.
19. Ibid., p. 38.
20. Ibid. (tenses changed).
21. Barton, p. 28.
22. Ibid.
23. *The Times*, 1 January 1915, p. 3.
24. Dash, 'Word War I: 100 Years Later', *Smithsonian*, 23 December 2011, www.smithsonianmag.com.
25. Van Emden, pp. 71–2.
26. *The Gazette*, 'World War One: The Christmas Truce of December 1914', www.thegazette.co.uk.
27. Jürgs, p. 232 (translated).
28. Lindsay, p. 26.
29. Stevenson, 4 April 1915, p. 40.
30. Haig, Douglas, *War Diaries & Letters*, p. 110.
31. Weber, *Hitler's First War* (English ed.), p. 81.
32. Weber, *Hitler's First War* (English ed.), p. 81; Weber, *Hitler's Erster Krieg* (German ed.), p. 110.
33. Weber, *Hitler's First War* (English ed.), p. 81.
34. Lee, p. 76.
35. Bean, *Official History of Australia in the War of 1914–1918*, Vol. III, p. 251.
36. Bristow, p. 65.
37. *The Nottingham Free Press*, 18 June 1915, p. 5.
38. *The Times*, 13 May 1915, p. 8.
39. Haking, p. 103.
40. Bristow, p. 128 (reported speech changed to direct speech).
41. Pedersen, *Fromelles*, p. 24.
42. Haig, Douglas, *War Diaries & Letters*, pp. 122–3.
43. *The Times*, 14 May 1915, p. 9.
44. McMullin, *Pompey Elliott*, p. 508.
45. Graves, p. 131 ('But they're all fucking dead' changed from reported speech to direct speech).
46. Macdonald, p. 493.
47. Ibid. (reported speech changed to direct speech).

48. Senior, p. 58.
49. Ibid., p. 59.
50. Bean, Diary, 31 January 1915, *Diaries & Notebooks*, AWM38 3DRL 606/37/1, pp. 39–40, www.awm.gov.au/collection/RCDIG1066738.
51. Carlyon, p. 50.
52. McMullin, *Pompey Elliott*, p. 205.
53. Farrar-Hockley, *Goughie*, p. 174.
54. Haig, Douglas, *War Diaries & Letters*, p. 216.
55. Ibid., p. 217.
56. Carlyon, p. 48 (reported speech changed to direct speech).

PART ONE: THE BATTLE KNELL IS NIGH

CHAPTER ONE: THE DRUMS OF WAR

1. Richard Job Gardiner, Letter, 9 January 1916, AWM 1DRL/0305, p. 10.
2. *The Argus*, 22 January 1916, p. 17.
3. Hartnett, p. 6.
4. Rule, Edgar, p. 12.
5. According to Robert Holden (*And the Band Played On: How Music Lifted the Anzac Spirit in the Battlefields of the First World War*), the arrival of one of the last Australian units to be evacuated from Gallipoli in December 1915 – the 13th Battalion – was welcomed in Lemnos by the pipe band of a Scottish regiment stationed on the island.
6. John Turnbull, Diary, 19 December 1916, AWM PR91/015, p. 24.
7. John Cosson, Diary, 21 December 1915, AWM 1DRL/0216, p. 10.
8. Goldy Raws to brother William Lennon, Letter, 7 January 1916, Lemnos, Raws, John and Robert letters, AWM 2DRL/0481, p. 50 of pdf (p. 27 of original document), www.awm.gov.au/collection/RCDIG0001092.
9. Bishop, *The Hell, the Humour and the Heartbreak*, p. 12.
10. In his memoir *The Hell, the Humour and the Heartbreak*, Bishop only mentions the names 'Hodgy and Robbo'. After consulting the AIF's Nominal Roll for the 9th reinforcements of the 5th Infantry Brigade, 19th Infantry Battalion (available at http://static.awm.gov.au/images/collection/bundled/RCDIG1067564.pdf) – the group with which Ray and Bert Bishop embarked from Sydney – I have figured these two men were probably Private Herbert Hodges, a 24-year-old dairyman

originally from Gloucester, England, and Private Thomas Roberts, a 32-year-old labourer of Penshurst, New South Wales.

11. *The Sydney Morning Herald*, 22 December 1915, p. 11.
12. Bishop, *The Hell, the Humour and the Heartbreak*, p. 5.
13. Hartnett, p. 3.
14. Lance Horniman, Letter, 27 February 1916, AWM 1DRL/0357, p. 3.
15. Bishop, *Dear All*, p. 3.
16. Hartnett, p. 3.
17. Falkenhayn, p. 249.
18. Ibid., p. 259.
19. Ibid., pp. 249–50.
20. Haig, Douglas, *War Diaries & Letters*, p. 177.
21. Churchill, *The World Crisis*, Vol. 3, p. 17.
22. Haig, Dorothy, p. 133.
23. Haig, Douglas, *War Diaries & Letters*, p. 171 (reported speech changed to direct speech).
24. Norman Nicolson, Letter, 16 March 1916, AWM 3DRL/2715, Vol. 3, p. 102.
25. Langford Colley-Priest, Diary, 29 March 1916, Mitchell Library, MLMSS 2439, Item 1, p. 40, http://acms.sl.nsw.gov.au.
26. Goldy Raws to family, Letter, 7 January 1916, Lemnos, Raws, John and Robert letters, AWM 2DRL/0481, p. 51 of pdf (p. 28 of original document), www.awm.gov.au/collection/RCDIG0001092.
27. Ellis, p. 35.
28. Apcar de Vine, Diary, 31 December 1915, AWM 1DRL/0240, p. 96.
29. Goldy Raws to family, Letter, 16 January 1916, Tel-el-Kebir, Raws, John and Robert letters, AWM 2DRL/0481, p. 53 of pdf (p. 3 of original document), www.awm.gov.au/collection/RCDIG0001092.
30. Goldy Raws, *Hail and Farewell*, 25 January 1916, Tel-el-Kebir, p. 66.
31. Ibid. For the sake of clarity to the reader, I have slightly altered his wording here, to fill out the biblical passage he referred to, in truncated fashion, to his father.
32. Bishop, *Dear All*, p. 5.
33. Ibid., p. 7.
34. Ibid.
35. Bishop, *The Hell, the Humour and the Heartbreak*, p. 15.
36. Bishop, *Dear All*, p. 7.
37. Ibid.
38. Falkenhayn, p. 243.
39. Sun Tzu, p. 220.

40. Falkenhayn, p. 240.
41. *The Army Quarterly*, Vol. III, p. 146.
42. Bean, Diary, 5 February 1916, *Diaries & Notebooks*, AWM38 3DRL 606/37/1, p. 58, www.awm.gov.au/collection/RCDIG1066752.
43. Bean, *Official History of Australia in the War of 1914–1918*, Vol. III, pp. 56–7.
44. Ibid., p. 56.
45. Bean, Diary, dated February to March 1916, *Diaries & Notebooks*, AWM38 3DRL 606/40/1, pp. 16–17, www.awm.gov.au/collection/RCDIG1066752.
46. Masefield, p. 222.
47. When they learned of it, the New Zealand Government did not appear to have been keen on the idea.
48. *Daily Herald* (Adelaide), 31 July 1914, p. 5, http://trove.nla.gov.au.
49. Bean, Diary, 31 January 1916, *Diaries & Notebooks*, AWM38 DRL606/36/1, p. 59, www.awm.gov.au/collection/RCDIG1066752.
50. Ibid.
51. McCarthy, p. 211.
52. Bean, *Official History of Australia in the War of 1914–1918*, Vol. III, p. 35.
53. McCarthy, p. 211.
54. Harold Elliott to George Henderson, Letter, 12 April 1916, AWM PR01279, p. 5.
55. Haig, Douglas, *War Diaries & Letters*, p. 179.
56. Samuel Topp, Letter, 25 February 1916, AWM 1DRL/0583, p. 24.
57. William Armstrong, Diary, 29 January–8 March 1916, AWM 1DRL/0059, p. 1.
58. Edgar Rule relied on his memory to write *Jacka's Mob*, and consequently some of the facts are distorted. Though in the book Twomey is recorded as being a Sergeant at this time, in fact he had not yet been promoted and was still a private.
59. Rule, pp. 14–15.
60. Albert Williams, 'A Soldier Looks Back', undated, AWM MSS 1337, p. 61.
61. Bean, *Official History of Australia in the War of 1914–1918*, Vol. III, pp. 48–9.
62. Athol Dunlop, Diary, 9 February 1916, AWM PR00676, pp. 45–6.
63. Paul Johanesen, Letter to parents, 3 March 1916, AWM PR87/018, p. 1.
64. Rule, p. 2.
65. Ibid.

66. Ibid.
67. Clarence Collier, Letter to parents, 12 April 1916, AWM 1DRL/206, p. 1.
68. Apcar de Vine, Diary, 13 February 1916, AWM 1DRL/0240, p. 102.
69. Hartnett, p. 17.
70. Ibid.
71. Downing, *To the Last Ridge*, p. 27.
72. Ellis, p. 37.
73. Horner, p. 113.
74. *The New York Times*, 28 April 1916, p. 3.
75. Meyer, p. 311.
76. Barbusse, p. 115.
77. Hatch, p. 36.
78. History World, World War One, Verdun, http://history-world.org/battle_of_verdun.htm.
79. Ibid.

CHAPTER TWO: REINSTOUSHMENTS TO THE FORE

1. Ellis, p. 34.
2. This detail drawn from Robert Goldthorpe Raws to family, Letter, 30 May 1915, AWM 2DRL/0481, www.awm.gov.au/collection/RCDIG0001092, p. 11: 'I can tell you now that we are in the Red Sea, and tomorrow we arrive in Suez. It is Sunday afternoon – the difficulty is to write letters. I had to break off just now for "Retreat" sounded, and on that call being played by the bugler all stand to attention facing, as a rule, the setting sun.'
3. Hatch, p. 36.
4. Tucker and Roberts, p. 913.
5. Marshall, p. 246.
6. Bean, *Official History of Australia in the War of 1914–1918*, Vol. III, p. 62.
7. Ibid.
8. William Robertson to Archibald Murray, Telegram, 1 March 1916, Item 8/1/20, Robertson Papers, Liddell Hart Centre for Military Archives, King's College, London.
9. Bean, *Official History of Australia in the War of 1914–1918*, Vol. III, p. 45.
10. Birdwood, *Khaki and Gown*, p. 300.
11. Archibald Winter, Diary, 25 April 1915, AWM PR89/163, p. 166.

12. Derham, p. 8.
13. Harold Elliott to George Henderson, Letter, 12 April 1916, AWM PR01279, p. 2.
14. Ibid., pp. 2–3.
15. McMullin, *Pompey Elliott*, p. 185 (reported speech changed to direct speech).
16. Harold Elliott to George Henderson, Letter, 12 April 1916, AWM PR01279, p. 2.
17. Ibid.
18. McMullin, *Pompey Elliott*, p. 182.
19. Ibid., p. 196.
20. Bean, Diary, 11 September 1916, *Diaries & Notebooks*, AWM38 3DRL 606, p. 22 (p. 21 of pdf), www.awm.gov.au/collection/RCDIG1066752.
21. Ibid., p. 24.
22. Ibid., p. 26.
23. Bean, *Official History of Australia in the War of 1914–1918*, Vol. III, p. 58.
24. Ibid., pp. 58–9.
25. Craig, p. 5.
26. John Raws to brother, Letter, 27 June 1916, AWM 2DRL/0481, p. 121, www.awm.gov.au/collection/RCDIG0001092.
27. Bean, *Official History of Australia in the War of 1914–1918*, Vol. III, p. 60.
28. Ibid.
29. McCarthy, p. 219.
30. Sloan, p. 257. In the original account, the words 'fuck' and 'c–nt' are completely dashed out, in respect of the sensibilities of 1938. I have restored them on the grounds they are the only two words that fit, and our contemporary sensibilities are less exacting.
31. Putkowski and Sykes, p. 68.
32. Crozier, p. 84.
33. Ibid.
34. Ibid.
35. Bishop, *The Hell, the Humour and the Heartbreak*, p. 22.
36. Drane, January 1915, *Complete Anzac Gallipoli War Diary*, http://bushroots.com.
37. Hartnett, p. 13.
38. Bishop, *The Hell, the Humour and the Heartbreak*, p. 23.
39. Ibid.
40. Ibid., p. 24.

41. Goldy Raws to mother, Letter, 8 March 1916, AWM 2DRL/0481, p. 59, www.awm.gov.au/collection/RCDIG0001092.
42. Downing, *Digger Dialects*, p. 41. The translation is 'reinforcements'.
43. Bishop, *The Hell, the Humour and the Heartbreak*, p. 31.
44. Ibid.
45. Bishop, *Dear All*, p. 21.
46. Goldy Raws to family, Letter, 30 May 1915, AWM 2DRL/0481, p. 14, www.awm.gov.au/collection/RCDIG0001092.
47. Bean, *Official History of Australia in the War of 1914–1918*, Vol. III, p. 13.
48. Newton, p. 78.
49. Renton, William to parents, Letter, 13 March 1916, AWM PR89/176, p. 1.
50. Geoffrey Serle, 'McCay, Sir James Whiteside (1864–1930)', http://adb.anu.edu.au.
51. *The Bulletin*, 8 October 1930, p. 14.
52. Norman Nicolson, Letter, 16 March 1916, AWM 3DRL/2715, Vol. 3, p. 111 (reported speech changed to direct speech). In fact, there is no such thing as an artillery division. What Nicolson means is 'form the new artillery brigades needed for the two new divisions (4th and 5th)'.
53. Ibid.
54. Ibid., p. 115.
55. Goldy Raws to family, Letter, 21 March 1916, AWM 2DRL/0481, p. 62, www.awm.gov.au/collection/RCDIG0001092.
56. Archie Barwick, Diary, 24 March 1916, MLMSS 1493, Box 1, Item 2, pp. 317–18, MLMSS 1493, http://acms.sl.nsw.gov.au.
57. Ibid., p. 318.
58. Ibid., p. 330.
59. Haig, Douglas, Diary, 27 March 1916, 'The Haig Papers from the National Library of Scotland'.
60. James Murray Aitken, Diary, 27 March 1916, AWM 1DRL/0013, p. 25.
61. Bean, *Official History of Australia in the War of 1914–1918*, Vol. III, p. 78, extract from diary of Brigadier H. C. Ferguson, 22nd A.F.A. Brigade.
62. Haig, Douglas, *War Diaries & Letters*, p. 183.
63. Though, technically, France's province of operations extends three miles north of the River Somme.
64. McMullin, *Farewell Dear People*, p. 34.
65. Norman Nicolson, Letter, 20 June 1916, AWM 3DRL/2715, Vol. 3, p. 248.
66. Williams, Harold, p. 21.

67. Harold Elliott to George Henderson, Letter, 12 April 1916, AWM PR01279, p. 3.
68. Pedersen, *Fromelles*, p. 31.
69. W. J. A. Allsop, Diary, 28 March 1916, MLMSS 1606, Item 1, pp. 135–6, http://acms.sl.nsw.gov.au.
70. Williams, Harold, p. 25.
71. Harold Elliott to George Henderson, Letter, 12 April 1916, AWM PR01279, p. 3.
72. Herbert Trangmar, Diary, undated, 1916, AWM 2DRL/0710, p. 100.
73. Harold Elliott to George Henderson, Letter, 12 April 1916, AWM PR01279, p. 3.
74. Ibid., p. 4.
75. McMullin, *Farewell Dear People*, p. 76.
76. Williams, Harold, p. 26.
77. Ellis, p. 42.
78. Bishop, *The Hell, the Humour and the Heartbreak*, p. 31.
79. Cook, p. 7.
80. Bishop, *The Hell, the Humour and the Heartbreak*, p. 32.
81. Ibid.
82. Pedersen, *The Anzacs*, p. 128.
83. Bishop, *The Hell, the Humour and the Heartbreak*, p. 33. Despite the rumours at the time, no men died on the desert march.
84. Herbert Trangmar, Diary, undated, 1916, AWM 2DRL/0710, p. 99.
85. Theodor Pflaum, Diary, 30 March 1916, AWM PR04009, p. 19. Pflaum used the abbreviation '14th Batt[ery]' in his diary. However, I think he meant 'Brigade'.
86. Langford Colley-Priest, Diary, 28 March 1916, MLMSS 2439, Item 1, p. 39, http://acms.sl.nsw.gov.au.
87. General Staff, Headquarters, 5th Australian Division War Diary, February–March 1916, p. 28, www.awm.gov.au/collection/RCDIG1000342.
88. Harold Elliott to George Henderson, Letter, 12 April 1916, AWM PR01279, p. 5 (reported speech changed to direct speech).
89. Ibid., p. 6.
90. Ibid.
91. Alfred Sheppeard, Diary, 27 May 1916, in Bean, *Diaries & Notebooks*, AWM38 3DRL 606/256/1, p. 178.
92. Bean, *Official History of Australia in the War of 1914–1918*, Vol. III, p. 291.
93. Harold Elliott to George Henderson, Letter, 12 April 1916, AWM PR01279, p. 4.

CHAPTER THREE: *MOI* AUSSIE

1. Newton, p. 79.
2. Harry Preston, Notebook, undated, AWM 2DRL/0811, p. 55.
3. Bean, *Official History of Australia in the War of 1914–1918*, Vol. III, p. 135.
4. Bishop, *The Hell, the Humour and the Heartbreak*, p. 35.
5. Ibid.
6. Bean, *Official History of Australia in the War of 1914–1918*, Vol. III, p. 408.
7. Major Base Records to Secretary, Letter, 11 August 1920, Norman Gibbins War Service Record, p. 120, http://recordsearch.naa.gov.au.
8. Bishop, *Dear All*, p. 22.
9. Norman Pearce, Diary, 28 March 1916, p. 27, http://acms.sl.nsw.gov.au.
10. Norman Nicolson, Letter, 4 May 1916, AWM 3DRL/2715, Vol. 3, p. 198.
11. Ibid., p. 201.
12. Bean, *Anzac to Amiens*, p. 217.
13. Bishop, *The Hell, the Humour and the Heartbreak*, p. 42.
14. Ellis, p. 51.
15. Rule, p. 17.
16. Bishop, *The Hell, the Humour and the Heartbreak*, p. 12.
17. Albert Williams, 'A Soldier Looks Back', undated, AWM MSS 1337, p. 72. In fact, the usual sign was 8 *chevaux* or 40 *hommes*.
18. Rule, p. 17.
19. Harry Preston, Diary, 2 April 1916, AWM 2DRL/0811, p. 55.
20. Bean, *Official History of Australia in the War of 1914–1918*, Vol. III, p. 205.
21. Housman, p. 39.
22. Goldy Raws to father, Letter, 21 March 1916, AWM 2DRL/0481, p. 67 (of pdf), www.awm.gov.au/collection/RCDIG0001092.
23. Ibid.
24. Ibid.
25. Charteris, pp. 143–4.
26. *The Chronicle* (Adelaide), 'A Brilliant Son of the Empire', 4 February 1928, p. 19, http://trove.nla.gov.au.
27. Birdwood, *Khaki and Gown*, p. 301.
28. Edmonds, Sir James, *Military Operations France and Belgium 1916*, Appendix No. 4, p. 34.

29. Mead, p. 351.
30. Eyre, p. 82.
31. Bean, *Official History of Australia in the War of 1914–1918*, Vol. III, p. 99.
32. Ibid.
33. Ibid., p. 97.
34. Hartnett, p. 52.
35. Henry Seymour Baker, Tasmanian Archive and Heritage Office, TAHO NS2661/1/30.
36. Hartnett, p. 28.
37. Ibid., pp. 26–7. This is a generic impression, rather than of this specific evening.
38. Ibid., p. 38.
39. Ibid., p. 27. This is a generic impression, rather than of this specific evening.
40. Aubrey R. Wiltshire, Diary, 15 April 1916, MLMSS 3058/Box 1/Item 5, http://acms.sl.nsw.gov.au.
41. Hartnett, p. 30 (tenses changed).
42. Alec Raws to mother, Letter, 15 July 1916, AWM 2DRL/0481, p. 128, www.awm.gov.au/collection/RCDIG0001092.
43. Ibid.
44. Bean, *Official History of Australia in the War of 1914–1918*, Vol. III, p. 127.
45. I have drawn heavily from Bean for this account.
46. Bean, *Official History of Australia in the War of 1914–1918*, Vol. III, p. 104.
47. Archie Barwick, Diary, MLMSS 1493, Box 1, Item 3, 18 May 1916, pp. 22–3, http://acms.sl.nsw.gov.au.
48. *The Sydney Morning Herald*, 19 July 1919, p. 7.
49. Gleichen, p. 273, https://openlibrary.org.
50. John Monash to wife, Letter, 20 June 1916, AWM 3DRL/2316, Vol. 1, p. 195, http://www.awm.gov.au/collection/RCDIG0000569.
51. Bean, *Official History of Australia in the War of 1914–1918*, Vol. III, pp. 451–2 (tenses changed).
52. Archie Barwick, Diary, MLMSS 1493, Box 1, Item 3, 18 May 1916, p. 23, http://acms.sl.nsw.gov.au.
53. Goldy Raws to father, Letter, 18 April 1916, p. 3, AWM 2DRL/0481, p. 69 (of pdf), www.awm.gov.au/collection/RCDIG0001092.
54. Ibid.
55. *Lille Post & L'Armee*, 14 June 1916, p. 93.

56. Bean, *Official History of Australia in the War of 1914–1918*, Vol. III, p. 107.

57. Hartnett, p. 34.

58. Bean, *Official History of Australia in the War of 1914–1918*, Vol. III, p. 87.

59. Ibid., p. 43.

60. Aubrey Wiltshire, Diary, 30 April 1916, MLMSS 3058/Box 1/Item 5, p. 56, http://acms.sl.nsw.gov.au.

61. Hartnett, p. 27.

62. Alec Raws to a friend, Letter, 20 July 1916, AWM 2DRL/0481, p. 135 (of pdf), www.awm.gov.au/collection/RCDIG0001092.

63. Bean, *Official History of Australia in the War of 1914–1918*, Vol. III, p. 133 (tenses changed).

64. Ibid. (tenses changed).

65. Ibid., p. 126.

66. Cooper, p. 30.

67. Bean, *Official History of Australia in the War of 1914–1918*, Vol. III, p. 189.

68. Ibid., p. 306.

69. Goldy Raws to father, Letter, 18 April 1916, AWM 2DRL/0481, p. 70 (of pdf), www.awm.gov.au/collection/RCDIG0001092.

70. Great Britain War Office, p. 30.

71. Hartnett, p. 51.

72. Albert Williams, 'A Soldier Looks Back', undated, AWM MSS 1337, p. 90.

73. Ibid., p. 93.

74. Levine, p. 183.

75. Albert Williams, 'A Soldier Looks Back', undated, AWM MSS 1337, p. 58.

76. Aubrey Wiltshire, Diary, 9 May 1916, MLMSS 3058/Box 1/Item 5, p. 63, http://acms.sl.nsw.gov.au.

77. Ibid., 14 June 1916, p. 93.

78. Ibid., 2 May 1916, p. 58.

79. Makepeace, 'Sex and the Somme', *Daily Mail Australia*, 29 October 2011, www.dailymail.co.uk.

80. Aubrey R. Wiltshire, Diary, 21 May 1916, MLMSS 3058/Box 1/Item 5, p. 71, http://acms.sl.nsw.gov.au.

81. Ibid., 1 July 1916, p. 110.

82. Maxwell, p. 28.

83. Butler, p. 152.

84. Makepeace, 'Sex and the Somme', *Daily Mail Australia*, 29 October 2011, www.dailymail.co.uk.

85. Weber, p. 167 (German ed.); Weber, p. 124 (English ed.).
86. Ibid., p. 167 (German ed.).
87. Ibid., p. 124 (English ed.).
88. Ibid., p. 124 (English ed.); ibid., p. 167 (German ed.).
89. Ibid., p. 168 (German ed.).
90. Ibid., p. 124 (English ed.).
91. Ibid.
92. Ibid., p. 123 (English ed.).
93. Ibid., p. 124 (English ed.).
94. Ibid., p. 184 (German ed.); Ibid., p. 136 (English ed.).

CHAPTER FOUR: *AUX ARMES AUSTRALIENS, FORMEZ VOS BATAILLONS!*

1. Trevor-Roper, pp. 232–3.
2. Rule, p. xi.
3. Bean, Diary, 8 April 1916, *Diaries & Notebooks*, AWM38 DRL 606/42/1, p. 20, www.awm.gov.au/collection/RCDIG1066752.
4. Haig, Douglas, *War Diaries & Letters*, p. 184.
5. Ibid.
6. Ibid., pp. 184–5.
7. Ibid., p. 185.
8. Ibid.
9. Aubrey Wiltshire, Diary, 14 April 1916, MLMSS 3058/Box 1/Item 5, p. 43, http://acms.sl.nsw.gov.au.
10. Ibid., 15 April 1916, p. 44.
11. Norman Pearce, Diary, 21 April 1916, MLMSS 8587, p. 34, http://acms.sl.nsw.gov.au.
12. Ibid., 29 April 1916, p. 36.
13. Bean, *Official History of Australia in the War of 1914–1918*, Vol. III, p. 195.
14. Ibid., p. 107.
15. Aubrey Wiltshire, Diary, 27 April 1916, MLMSS 3058/Box 1/Item 5, p. 54, http://acms.sl.nsw.gov.au.
16. Albert Williams, 'A Soldier Looks Back', undated, AWM MSS 1337, p. 81.
17. Bean, *Official History of Australia in the War of 1914–1918*, Vol. III, p. 74.
18. Hartnett, p. 47.
19. Bean, *Official History of Australia in the War of 1914–1918*, Vol. III, p. 78.

20. Hartnett, p. 50.
21. Aubrey Wiltshire, Diary, 26 June 1916, MLMSS 3058/Box 1/Item 5, p. 104, http://acms.sl.nsw.gov.au.
22. Still, Harry, Memoir, AWM PR00753, p. 36.
23. Alec Raws to mother, Letter, 18 July 1916, AWM 2DRL/0481, p. 132, www.awm.gov.au/collection/RCDIG0001092.
24. Bean, *Official History of Australia in the War of 1914–1918*, Vol. III, p. 124.
25. Ibid.
26. Kahan, p. 21.
27. Stevenson, Robert, p. 140.
28. McCarthy, p. 218.
29. Sladen, p. 193.
30. Ibid., p. 194.
31. *Auckland Star*, 24 June 1916, p. 13.
32. Murdoch, pp. 68–72.
33. Max Prisk, 'Sydney's First Anzac Day', *The Sydney Morning Herald*, 25 April 2008, www.smh.com.au.
34. Craig Tibbitts, '"Good Fearless Soldiers": Two Brothers at Pozières, 1916', 4 February 2014, AWM Blog, www.awm.gov.au/blog.
35. Alec Raws to father, Letter, 12 July 1915, AWM 2DRL/0481, p. 90, https://www.awm.gov.au/collection/RCDIG0001092.
36. Ibid., p. 91.
37. Goldy Raws to father, Letter, 26 April 1916, AWM 2DRL/0481, p. 71, www.awm.gov.au/collection/RCDIG0001092.
38. Ibid., p. 72.
39. Winter, Denis, pp. 56–7.
40. Gardner, p. 34.
41. Bean, Diary, 17 June 1916, *Diaries & Notebooks*, AWM38 3DRL 606/47/1, pp. 15–16, www.awm.gov.au/collection/RCDIG1066752.
42. Haig, Douglas, *War Diaries & Letters*, p. 184.
43. Robin Prior and Trevor Wilson, 'Rawlinson, Henry Seymour, Baron Rawlinson (1864–1925)', January 2011, Oxford Dictionary of National Biography, www.oxforddnb.com.
44. Robin Prior and Trevor Wilson, *Command on the Western Front*, p. 149.
45. Ibid., p. 152.
46. Bean, *Official History of Australia in the War of 1914–1918*, Vol. III, p. 190.
47. Ibid.
48. Domelier, p. 119.

49. Bean, *Official History of Australia in the War of 1914–1918*, Vol. III, p. 297.

50. Ibid., p. 334.

51. Rupert Campbell, Letter, 18 May 1916, AWM 3DRL/5087(B), p. 2.

52. Ibid., p. 4.

53. Ellis, p. 46.

54. Hartnett, p. 45. Though Hartnett did not apply this phrase to this specific incident, it was a generic term, also applied to Stokes mortar batteries.

55. Ellis, p. 80.

56. H. J. Maynard, 'Cookers in the Line', *Reveille*, 1 February 1936, p. 20.

57. Dudley Jackson, Diary, 28 May 1916, AWM 3DRL/3846, p. 49.

58. Ibid., p. 43.

59. As Bean notes, 'In the German records the hour appears as 9.40, the enemy time (mid-European plus one hour of "daylight-saving") being then two hours in advance of the British. The British and French advanced their clocks an hour on June 14.' *Official History of Australia in the War of 1914–1918*, Vol. III, p. 198.

60. Bean, *Official History of Australia in the War of 1914–1918*, Vol. III, p. 198.

61. Thomas Burnett, Letter, 8 May 1916, AWM 1DRL/0164, p. 2.

62. Gammage, p. 153.

63. Bean, *Official History of Australia in the War of 1914–1918*, Vol. III, p. 204.

64. Ibid.

65. Dudley Jackson, Diary, 5 May 1916, AWM 3DRL/3846, p. 43.

66. While Private Jackson refers to 'Barney Meacham' as an 'officer' in his diary, the AIF Nominal Roll lists a 'Private Bernard Meechan' of the 20th Battalion with no evidence of a subsequent promotion.

67. Dudley Jackson, Diary, 5 May 1916, AWM 3DRL/3846, p. 43.

68. Ibid.

69. Lucy, p. 223.

70. Dudley Jackson, Diary, 5 May 1916, AWM 3DRL/3846, p. 43.

71. Ibid., p. 44.

72. Bean, *Official History of Australia in the War of 1914–1918*, Vol. III, p. 204.

73. Gammage, p. 153.

74. Bean, *Official History of Australia in the War of 1914–1918*, Vol. III, p. 205.

75. Ibid.

76. Duffy, p. 53.

77. Bean, *Official History of Australia in the War of 1914–1918*, Vol. III, p. 203.
78. Hartnett, p. 34.
79. Bean, *Official History of Australia in the War of 1914–1918*, Vol. III, p. 201.
80. Ibid., p. 207.
81. Ibid.
82. Haig, Douglas, *War Diaries & Letters*, p. 186.
83. Alec Raws to mother, Letter, 16 May 1916, AWM 2DRL/0481, p. 104, www.awm.gov.au/collection/RCDIG0001092.
84. Alec Raws to sister, Letter, 21 May 1916, AWM 2DRL/0481, p. 106, www.awm.gov.au/collection/RCDIG0001092.

CHAPTER FIVE: WITH GOD ON OUR SIDE

1. Bean, *Official History of Australia in the War of 1914–1918*, Vol. III, p. 137.
2. McBride, p. 105.
3. Haig, Douglas, *War Diaries & Letters*, p. 187.
4. Moss, p. 176.
5. Rothenburg, p. 22.
6. Goldy Raws to mother, Letter, 30 May 1916, AWM 2DRL/0481, p. 76, www.awm.gov.au/collection/RCDIG0001092.
7. Goldy Raws to father, Letter, 22 May 1916, AWM 2DRL/0481, p. 75, www.awm.gov.au/collection/RCDIG0001092.
8. Ibid. (reported speech changed to direct speech).
9. Bean, Diary, 24 May 1916, p. 31, *Diaries & Notebooks*, AWM38 3DRL 606/44/1, www.awm.gov.au/collection/RCDIG1066752.
10. Scott, *Official History of Australia in the War of 1914–1918*, Vol. XI, p. 308.
11. Bean, Diary, 1 June 1916, p. 39, *Diaries & Notebooks*, AWM38 3DRL 606/44/1, www.awm.gov.au/collection/RCDIG1066752.
12. Haig, Douglas, *War Diaries & Letters*, p. 188 (reported speech changed to direct speech).
13. Ibid.
14. Ibid.
15. Bean, *Official History of Australia in the War of 1914–1918*, Vol. III, p. 297.
16. Knyvett, p. 160.

17. Ellis, p. 53.
18. Hartnett, p. 34.
19. Haig, Douglas, Diary, 1 June 1916.
20. Charteris, pp. 145–6.
21. Ibid.
22. Bean, *Official History of Australia in the War of 1914–1918*, Vol. III, p. 157 (reported speech changed to direct speech).
23. Sheffield, p. 145.
24. Haig did execute Australians, but they had to be serving in other than Australian units. John Sweeney from Tasmania, serving with the New Zealand Division, deserted and was convicted, sentenced and executed by firing squad in October 1916.
25. Ellis, p. 123.
26. Haig, Douglas, Diary, 3 March 1918, *War Diaries & Letters*, p. 386.
27. Fitzhardinge, p. 119.
28. Bean, Diary, 1 June 1916, *Diaries & Notebooks*, AWM38 3DRL 606/45/1, p. 39, www.awm.gov.au/collection/RCDIG1066752.
29. Ibid.
30. Aubrey Wiltshire, Diary, 1 June 1916, MLMSS 3058/Box 1/Item 5, p. 77, http://acms.sl.nsw.gov.au.
31. Murdoch to Bean, Letter, 1 June 1916, AWM 3DRL/33761 Bean, Diary, *Diaries & Notebooks*, AWM38 3DRL 606/45/1, p. 39, www.awm.gov.au/collection/RCDIG1066752 (reported speech changed to direct speech).
32. Ibid., p. 44.
33. Ibid., pp. 41–2 (reported speech changed to direct speech).
34. Aubrey Wiltshire, Diary, 1 June 1916, MLMSS 3058/Box 1/Item 5, p. 77, http://acms.sl.nsw.gov.au.
35. *The Argus*, 'Mr Hughes at Front', 9 June 1916, p. 7, http://trove.nla.gov.au.
36. Ibid. (reported speech changed to direct speech).
37. Lionel Oscar McCrae, Diary, 2 June 1916, AWM PR04752, p. 84.
38. Birdwood, Diary, 3 June 1916, AWM 3DRL/33761, p. 92 (of pdf), www.awm.gov.au/collection/RCDIG0000001.
39. Haking to Monro, Discussion with Second Army re Fromelles attack, 21 June 1916, First Army HQ, July 1916, WO95/164, p. 1.
40. Alec Raws to brother, Letter, 27 June 1916, AWM 2DRL/0481, p. 121, www.awm.gov.au/collection/RCDIG0001092 (reported speech changed to direct speech).
41. Ibid.

42. Ibid., p. 122 (reported speech changed to direct speech).
43. Ibid.
44. Alec Raws to mother, Letter, 3 June 1916, AWM 2DRL/0481, p. 111, www.awm.gov.au/collection/RCDIG0001092.
45. Alec Raws to brother, Letter, 6 June 1916, AWM 2DRL/0481, p. 112, www.awm.gov.au/collection/RCDIG0001092.
46. Alec Raws to mother, Letter, 3 June 1916, AWM 2DRL/0481, p. 111, www.awm.gov.au/collection/RCDIG0001092.
47. Bean, *Official History of Australia in the War of 1914–1918*, Vol. III, p. 315.
48. Crozier, p. 94.
49. Bean, *Official History of Australia in the War of 1914–1918*, Vol. III, pp. 257–8.
50. *The West Australian*, 4 September 1916, p. 6.
51. Kahan, p. 21.
52. Bean, *Official History of Australia in the War of 1914–1918*, Vol. III, p. 244.
53. 7th Infantry Brigade War Diary, 5 July 1916, AWM4 23/7/10, p. 2.
54. Bean, *Official History of Australia in the War of 1914–1918*, Vol. III, p. 251.
55. 'In ever loving memory of Captain Cecil Maitland Foss, M.C., 28th Battalion and Lieut. Henry Clinton Foss, 28th Battalion (late 10th Light Horse)', copy made by AWM, 1927, AWM 1DRL/0298, p. 4.
56. Browning, p. 114.
57. There are conflicting accounts of the number of Germans killed. I have gone with the figure in Browning, p. 116, and Kahan, p. 23.
58. Bean, *Official History of Australia in the War of 1914–1918*, Vol. III, p. 248 (reported speech changed to direct speech).
59. *The West Australian*, 4 September 1916, p. 6.
60. Edmonds, Sir James, *Military Operations in France and Belgium 1914*, p. 232.
61. Norman Nicolson, Letter, 11 June 1916, Vol. 3, AWM 3DRL/2715, pp. 231–2.
62. Rule, p. 21. Rule's description was for another raiding party but is still apt for this one.
63. Bean, *Official History of Australia in the War of 1914–1918*, Vol. III, p. 252.
64. Ibid., p. 253.
65. Austin, p. 154.
66. Bean, *Official History of Australia in the War of 1914–1918*, Vol. III, p. 254.

67. Ibid.
68. Austin, p. 155.
69. Ibid.
70. Bean, *Official History of Australia in the War of 1914–1918*, Vol. III, p. 258.
71. Summary of Proceedings Corps Commander Conference, 14 June 1916, First Army HQ, WO 95/164, pp. 3–4.
72. Ibid., p. 3 (reported speech changed to direct speech).
73. Bean, *Official History of Australia in the War of 1914–1918*, Vol. III, p. 258.
74. Ibid., p. 259.
75. Haig, Dorothy, p. 149.
76. Bristow, p. 24.
77. Haig, Douglas, *War Diaries & Letters*, p. 190.
78. Ibid., pp. 190–1.
79. Ibid., p. 191.
80. Samuels, p. 151.
81. Bean, Diary, 16 June 1916, *Diaries & Notebooks*, AWM38 3DRL 606/47/1, p. 5, www.awm.gov.au/collection/RCDIG1066752.
82. Walter Cass to Helena Holmes, Letter, 16 June 1916, SLV, MS15488, Series 1, Box 1, Folder 1A, p. 2.
83. Ibid., pp. 1–4.

CHAPTER SIX: 'ON THE ROAD TO ROUEN'

1. Cervantes, p. 231.
2. Churchill, *The World Crisis*, Vol. 6, p. 739.
3. Robert Harpley, Diary, 16 June 1916, AWM 3DRL/3663, pp. 3–4.
4. Bishop, *The Hell, the Humour and the Heartbreak*, p. 50.
5. McMullin, *Farewell Dear People*, p. 153.
6. Pompey Elliott to George McCrae (Geoffrey McCrae's father), Letter, 23 July 1916, AWM 1DRL/0427, www.awm.gov.au/collection/RCDIG0001274.
7. Pompey Elliott, Service Biography of Thomas Patrick Elliott, AWM 3DRL 2872, p. 1, www.awm.gov.au/collection/RCDIG0001321.
8. Herbert Henry Harris, Diary, 20 June 1916, MLMSS 2772/1, p. 26, http://acms.sl.nsw.gov.au.
9. Ibid., 26 June 1916, p. 31.
10. Ibid., 20 June 1916, p. 26.

11. Norman Nicolson, Letter, 20 June 1916, Vol. 3, AWM 3DRL/2715, p. 248.
12. William Birdwood, Diary, 20 June 1916, AWM 3DRL/3376 1/-, p. 101 (of pdf), www.awm.gov.au/collection/RCDIG0000001.
13. Frank Fox, p. 55, www.gutenberg.org.
14. *The Times*, 16 June 1916, p. 9.
15. *The Washington Post*, 27 June 1916, p. 2.
16. Bean, Diary, night from Thursday 22 June to Friday 23 June 1916, *Diaries & Notebooks*, AWM38 3DRL 606/47/1, p. 54, www.awm.gov.au/collection/RCDIG1066752.
17. Housman, *A Shropshire Lad*, p. 39.
18. Jünger, *Kriegstagebuch*, 24 June 1916, p. 127 (translated).
19. Ibid.
20. Hart and Steele, *The Somme*, ebook edition.
21. Jünger, *Kriegstagebuch*, 24 June 1916, p. 127 (translated).
22. Bean, *Official History of Australia in the War of 1914–1918*, Vol. III, p. 307.
23. Ibid.
24. This account is drawn heavily from Bean.
25. Bean, *Official History of Australia in the War of 1914–1918*, Vol. III, p. 308.
26. Sheldon, p. 127.
27. Ibid., p. 134.
28. Jünger, *Kriegstagebuch*, 24 June 1916, p. 128 (translated).
29. Bean, *Official History of Australia in the War of 1914–1918*, Vol. III, p. 286.
30. Diary quoted in T. Chalmers, *History of the 15th Battalion, The Highland Light Infantry* (John McCallum, Glasgow, 1934), p. 68, in Hart, p. 93.
31. Robert Harpley, Diary, 25 June 1916, AWM 3DRL/3663, p. 7.
32. Ibid.
33. Bishop, *The Hell, the Humour and the Heartbreak*, p. 53.
34. Ibid.
35. Robert Harpley, Diary, 25 June 1916, AWM 3DRL/3663, p. 6. A false report, as it turns out. The *City of Mexico* was in fact sunk off Beachy Head, England, by U-40 on 22 November 1916.
36. *The Riverine Grazier*, 10 July 1917, p. 4.
37. Ibid.
38. Ibid.
39. Ibid., 27 July 1917, p. 2.

40. Weber, p. 180 (German ed.); Weber, p. 133 (English ed.). This is a quote from the English edition and the German edition of Weber's book. The English translation has – in parts – been adjusted to be closer to the original German text.

41. Weber, p. 100 (English ed.).

42. Ibid., p. 137.

43. Jünger, *Kriegstagebuch*, 3 July 1916, p. 148 (translated).

44. Haking, *Company Training*, p. 21.

45. Geoffrey Christie-Miller, Memoir, Volume Two, IWM 80/32/1, Document 4776, p. 171.

46. John Williams, p. 148.

47. Paul Reed, 'The Boar's Head', Old Front Line Battlefields of WW1, http://battlefields1418.50megs.com.

48. Carlyon, p. 51.

49. Barton, p. 175.

50. Bean, *Official History of Australia in the War of 1914–1918*, Vol. III, p. 346.

51. Barton, p. 176.

52. Lytton, p. 42.

53. Blunden, p. 60.

54. Lytton, p. 42.

55. Alfred Sheppeard, Diary, 27 May 1916, AWM 2DRL/0956, p. 123.

56. Herbert Harris, Diary, 30 June 1916, MLMSS 2772/1, p. 33, http://acms.sl.nsw.gov.au.

57. Ibid.

58. Scott, p. 218.

59. Walter Cass to Helena Holmes, Letter, 12 July 1916, SLV, MS15488, Series 1, Box 1, Folder 1A, p. 2.

60. Bean, *Official History of Australia in the War of 1914–1918*, Vol. III, p. 326.

61. Neiberg, p. 199, footnote 29.

62. Haig, Douglas, *War Diaries & Letters*, p. 195.

63. Ibid., Wednesday 28 June 1916, p. 193.

64. Bean, *Official History of Australia in the War of 1914–1918*, Vol. III, p. 326.

65. Bean, *Letters from France*, pp. 71–2.

66. Bean, Diary, 30 June 1916, *Diaries & Notebooks*, AWM38 3DRL 606/48/1, p. 36 (p. 25 of pdf), www.awm.gov.au/collection/RCDIG1066752.

67. Bean, Diary, 28 June 1916, *Diaries & Notebooks*, AWM38 3DRL 606/47/1, pp. 69–70, www.awm.gov.au/collection/RCDIG1066752.

68. Ibid., 30 June 1916, AWM38 3DRL 606/48/1, p. 57.

PART TWO: HELL'S BELLS IN FROMELLES

1. Clapham (ed.), p. 95.

CHAPTER SEVEN: THE BATTLE OF THE SOMME

1. Weber, p. 14 (English ed.).
2. Haig, Douglas, *War Diaries & Letters*, p. 195.
3. Bean, Charles, Diary, 1 July 1916, *Diaries & Notebooks*, AWM38 3RDL606/48/1, pp. 48–9, www.awm.gov.au/collection/RCDIG1066752.
4. Corporal Arthur Thomas, Diary, 20 July 1916, AWM 3DRL/2206, p. 1, www.awm.gov.au/collection/RCDIG0001097.
5. Masefield, *The Battle of the Somme*, pp. 12–13, https://archive.org.
6. Ibid., pp. 13–14.
7. Ibid.
8. Ibid.
9. Talbot Kelly, p. 124.
10. Masefield, *The Battle of the Somme*, pp. 13–14, https://archive.org.
11. Buchan, p. 82.
12. Middlebrook, p. 56.
13. Ibid.
14. Ibid., p. 158.
15. Sheldon, p. 142.
16. Masefield, *The Battle of the Somme*, pp. 6–7, https://archive.org.
17. Maddocks, p. 146.
18. Crozier, p. 103.
19. Ibid., p. 104.
20. Middlebrook, Pen & Sword Military, Barnsley, 2006, p. 175.
21. Crozier, p. 106.
22. Kenyon, 'British Cavalry on the Western Front 1916–1918', doctoral thesis, Cranfield University, p. 46.
23. Crozier, p. 107.
24. Jünger, *Kriegstagebuch*, 1 July 1916, p. 147 (translated).
25. Ibid., 3 July 1916, p. 148 (translated).
26. Jünger, *In Stahlgewittern*, p. 59 (these English words are in the German edition).
27. Bardon, p. 451.
28. Crozier, p. 111.
29. Ibid.

30. Sheldon, p. 176.
31. Schoeck, p. 139.
32. Sheldon, p. 176.
33. Middlebrook, p. 235.
34. Lindsay, p. 59.
35. Mackenzie, p. 152.
36. Haig, Douglas, *War Diaries & Letters*, p. 197.
37. The prior week-long bombardment killed or wounded possibly as many as 10,000 Germans – more than they lost on 1 July (Passingham, p. 110).
38. Haig, Douglas, *War Diaries & Letters*, p. 198.
39. Ibid. (reported speech changed to direct speech).
40. Bert Bishop, *Dear All*, pp. 31–2.
41. Robert Harpley, Diary, 1 July 1916, AWM 3DRL/3663, p. 10.
42. Theodor Pflaum, Diary, 24 June 1916, AWM PR04009, p. 25.
43. Bishop, *The Hell, the Humour and the Heartbreak*, p. 55.
44. Ibid.
45. *The Times*, 3 July 1916, p. 8.
46. *Daily Express*, 3 July 1916, p. 1.
47. *Daily Chronicle*, 3 July 1916, p. 3.
48. *The Times*, 'New Tactics', 3 July 1916, p. 8.
49. Wade, 3–4 July 1916, p. 33.
50. Buchan, p. 42.
51. Afflerbach, p. 420 (translated).
52. Middlebrook, Penguin, p. 59.
53. McCarthy, p. 219.
54. Lance, Horniman, Letter to his parents, 2 July 1916, AWM 1DRL/0357, p. 2.
55. William Barry, Memoir, AWM PR00814, p. 32.
56. Ibid.
57. Alec Raws to sister, Letter, 4 July 1916, AWM 2DRL/0481, p. 124, www.awm.gov.au/collection/RCDIG0001092.
58. Ibid., p. 125.
59. G.H.Q. (Kiggell) to First, Second, Third Army Commanders, Order, 5 July 1916, WO 158/186.
60. Bean, *Official History of Australia in the War of 1914–1918*, Vol. III, p. 330.
61. Though the 29th Battalion's Bill Barry records this in his memoirs as occurring on the morning of the 7th, the 29th Battalion War Diary has it as happening on the morning of the 8th, which accords with Bean's *Official History*.

62. William Barry, Memoir, AWM PR00814, p. 33.
63. Ibid. (reported speech changed to direct speech).
64. Ibid. (reported speech changed to direct speech).
65. Ibid.
66. Ibid.
67. Ibid., p. 34 (reported speech changed to direct speech).
68. Ibid.
69. Bean, *Official History of Australia in the War of 1914–1918*, Vol. III, p. 328.
70. Ibid., p. 327.
71. Pedersen, *The Anzacs*, p. 138.
72. Bean, *Official History of Australia in the War of 1914–1918*, Vol. III, p. 328.
73. Ibid., p. 330.
74. In Eddie Rule's original account, this private is referred to only as 'Schaffner'. I suspect, however, he is referring to Private Leslie Norman Schaper, who appears on the AIF Nominal Roll for the 4th Division, 4th Brigade, 14th Battalion.
75. Rule, p. 23.
76. Gibbs, p. 180.
77. 'Haking Scheme of Attack to Hold Auber's Ridge', 9 July 1916, General Staff Headquarters, XI Corps, AWM4 1/22/4, Part 2, p. 1 (p. 19 of pdf), www.awm.gov.au/collection/RCDIG1004715.
78. Wray, p. 178.
79. 'Haking Scheme of Attack to Hold Auber's Ridge', 9 July 1916, General Staff Headquarters, XI Corps, AWM4 1/22/4, Part 2, p. 2 (p. 20 of pdf), www.awm.gov.au/collection/RCDIG1004715.
80. Aubrey Wiltshire, Diary, 14 June 1916, MLMSS 3058/Box 1/Item 5, p. 93, http://acms.sl.nsw.gov.au.
81. Bean, *Official History of Australia in the War of 1914–1918*, Vol. III, p. 373.
82. Edwin Tivey, Diary, 9 July 1916, AWM 3DRL/3058.
83. Goldy Raws to father, Letter, 9 July 1916, AWM 2DRL/0481, pp. 17–18 (pp. 82–3 of pdf), www.awm.gov.au/collection/RCDIG0001092.

CHAPTER EIGHT: DRIFTING TO A DECISION

1.   Ross McMullin, 'The Butcher of Fromelles', Wartime, Issue 27, 2004, p. 16.
2.   Arthur, *When the Bloody War is Over*, p. 97.
3.   Bean, *Official History of Australia in the War of 1914–1918*, Vol. III, p. 447.
4.   Hartnett, p. 52.
5.   Falkenhayn, *Die Oberste Heeresleitung*, p. 184 (German ed.).
6.   Falkenhayn, *The German General Staff*, p. 259 (English ed.).
7.   Reichsarchiv, *Der Weltkrieg 1914–1918 (The World War 1914–1918)*, Vol. 10, p. 202
8.   J. M. Bourne, 'Charteris, John (1877–1946)', Oxford Dictionary of National Biography, October 2008, www.oxforddnb.com.
9.   Charteris, p. 153.
10. Haking to Monro, Discussion with Second Army re Fromelles Attack, 21 June 1916, First Army HQ, WO 95/164, p. 1.
11. Notes on Subsidiary Operations, 11 July 1916, Military Headquarters Correspondence & Papers, First Army, WO 158/186, p. 1.
12. Pompey Elliott, 'The Battle of Fleurbaix or Fromelles', *The Duckboard*, Vol. 5, No. 9, 1 September 1930, p. 1.
13. Haig, Douglas, *War Diaries & Letters*, p. 122 (square brackets, denoting best guesses from the original handwriting, removed).
14. Bean, *Official History of Australia in the War of 1914–1918*, Vol. III, p. 332.
15. While Charles Bean's *Official History* has this as the equivalent of six divisions, in fact the minimum number of guns in any division's artillery was 72.
16. Bean, *Official History of Australia in the War of 1914–1918*, Vol. III, p. 332.
17. Ibid., p. 333.
18. While Bishop's book *The Hell, the Humour and the Heartbreak* states the 55th fell in at 9 pm, the 55th Battalion War Diary states 8.30 pm.
19. Bishop, *The Hell, the Humour and the Heartbreak*, p. 58.
20. Ibid., p. 57.
21. Ibid., p. 58 (reported speech changed to direct speech).
22. Ibid.
23. Empey, p. 157.
24. Bean, *Official History of Australia in the War of 1914–1918*, Vol. III, p. 189.
25. Graves, p. 164.

26. Alec Raws to sister, Letter, 27 June 1916, AWM 2DRL/0481, p. 123, www.awm.gov.au/collection/RCDIG0001092.
27. Bishop, *The Hell, the Humour and the Heartbreak*, p. 59.
28. Hutchinson, p. 23.
29. Bishop, *The Hell, the Humour and the Heartbreak*, p. 59.
30. Ellis, p. 79. I have replaced the word used in the account, 'blanky', with the word surely used on this occasion: 'bloody'.
31. Ibid.
32. Sloan, p. 64.
33. Miles, p. 122.
34. Pompey Elliott, 'The Battle of Fleurbaix or Fromelles', *The Duckboard*, Vol. 5, No. 9, 1 September 1930, pp. 3–4.
35. W. G. Shipway, 'My Memories of the First World War', IWM Document 749, Box 90/37/1, p. 11.
36. Geoffery Christie-Miller, Memoir, Volume Two, IWM 80/32/1, Document 4776, pp. 171–2.
37. Congreve, p. 71.
38. Hutchinson, p. 22.
39. Bristow, p. 39.
40. Hutchinson, p. 22.
41. Hanson, p. 53.
42. Ibid.
43. Edwin Tivey, Diary, 12 July 1916, AWM 3DRL/3058.
44. William Smith, 'Sapper's Diary: The Battle of Fromelles', *Reveille*, 1 July 1936, Vol. 9, No. 11, p. 14.
45. Bean, *Official History of Australia in the War of 1914–1918*, Vol. III, p. 451.
46. Farrar-Hockley, p. 200.
47. 'Haking Scheme of Attack to Hold Auber's Ridge', 9 July 1916, General Staff Headquarters, XIth Corps, AWM4 1/22/4, Part 2, p. 1 (p. 19 of pdf), www.awm.gov.au/collection/RCDIG1004715.
48. Senior, p. 116.
49. Ibid.
50. Bean, *Official History of Australia in the War of 1914–1918*, Vol. III, p. 335.
51. Reid, p. 208.
52. Renamed the Fifth Army on 30 October 1916.
53. This order is made official on 17 July 1916.
54. Neillands, p. 389.
55. Pompey Elliott, 'The Battle of Fleurbaix or Fromelles', *The Duckboard*, Vol. 5, No. 9, 1 September 1930, p. 9.

56. Pedersen, *The Anzacs*, p. 142.
57. Barrie, p. 19.
58. Haig, Douglas, Diary, 29 March 1916, *War Diaries & Letters*, p. 183.
59. Pedersen, *The Anzacs*, p. 142.

CHAPTER NINE: THE HORROR OF POMPEY

1. Tsouras (ed.), p. 474.
2. Pompey Elliott, 'The Battle of Fleurbaix or Fromelles', *The Duckboard*, Vol. 5, No. 9, 1 September 1930, p. 15.
3. Bean, *Official History of Australia in the War of 1914–1918*, Vol. III, p. 59.
4. Pompey Elliott, 'The Battle of Fleurbaix or Fromelles', *The Duckboard*, Vol. 5, No. 9, 1 September 1930, p. 2.
5. Ellis, p. 90.
6. Pedersen, *The Anzacs*, p. 162.
7. I have drawn heavily on Bean for this account.
8. Bean, *Official History of Australia in the War of 1914–1918*, Vol. III, p. 341.
9. Pompey Elliott, 'The Battle of Fleurbaix or Fromelles', *The Duckboard*, Vol. 5, No. 9, 1 September 1930, p. 4.
10. Ibid., p. 15.
11. Lindsay, p. 74.
12. Pompey Elliott, 'The Battle of Fleurbaix or Fromelles', *The Duckboard*, Vol. 5, No. 9, 1 September 1930, p. 10.
13. Ibid., p. 15.
14. McMullin, *Farewell Dear People*, p. 88.
15. Waldo Zander, Memoir, AWM 2DRL/0171, p. 1.
16. Ibid.
17. Pompey Elliott to Charles Bean, Letter, 17 August 1926, *Diaries & Notebooks*, AWM38 3DRL 606/243B/1, p. 116.
18. Pompey Elliott, 'The Battle of Fleurbaix or Fromelles', *The Duckboard*, Vol. 5, No. 9, 1 September 1930, p. 7.
19. Pompey Elliott to Charles Bean, Letter, 17 August 1926, AWM38 3DRL 606/243B/1, p. 116.
20. Ibid.
21. Pompey Elliott, 'The Battle of Fleurbaix or Fromelles', *The Duckboard*, Vol. 5, No. 9, 1 September 1930, pp. 6–7.
22. Pompey Elliott, 'Private Memorandum on Supersession', 25 May 1918, Elliott Papers, AWM 2DRL/0513, Series 5 Wallet 4, p. 6 (reported speech changed to direct speech).

23. Ibid. (reported speech changed to direct speech).
24. Ibid. (reported speech changed to direct speech).
25. McMullin, *Pompey Elliott*, pp. 205–6.
26. Bishop's account of this is that they were in there for a week the first time. In fact, they had spent just three full days in the front-line.
27. Bishop, *The Hell, the Humour and the Heartbreak*, p. 60.
28. Ibid., p. 61.
29. Bean, *Official History of Australia in the War of 1914–1918*, Vol. III, pp. 342–3.
30. Geoffrey Christie-Miller, Papers of Sir Geoffrey Christie-Miller, Memoir, Volume Two, IWM 80/32/1, Document 4776, pp. 176–7.
31. Barnes, p. 20.
32. *Berliner Tageblatt*, 1 August 1916, p. 1 (translated).
33. Ibid. (translated).
34. Braun, p. 49 (translated).
35. 'Findings Relating to the Enemy', 11.7.16–16.7.16, Report B. No. 6106, in Barton, Chapter Ten: Stand To, Make Ready.
36. Reichskriegsministerium, *Der Weltkrieg 1914–1918*, Vol. X, p. 413 (translated).
37. Ibid., p. 414 (translated).
38. Norman Nicolson, Diary, Vol. 3, 16 July 1916, AWM 3DRL/2715, p. 269.
39. Ibid., 15 July 1916, p. 265.
40. Hardie, p. 44.
41. 'Instructions for Infantry Brigadiers', 15 July 1916, 14th Brigade War Diary, July 1916, Appendix 32/1/15, AWM4 23/14/4, p. 38 (p. 40 of pdf), www.awm.gov.au/collection/RCDIG1016768.
42. Ibid. (p. 39 of pdf) (slightly modified to more resemble normal speech).
43. John Schroder to John Black, Letter, undated, in Bean, *Diaries & Notebooks*, 1928–1937, AWM38 3DRL 606/276/1, p. 148, www.awm. gov.au/collection/RCDIG1066752.
44. Harold Elliott to Belle Campbell, Letter, 26 August 1916, Elliott Papers, AWM 2DRL/0513, Series 3, Wallet 13, p. 4. In the letter held by the AWM, the word 'terribly' is crossed out.
45. Ibid.
46. Brudenell White to John Black (editor of *Reveille*), Letter, undated 1937, *Diaries & Notebooks*, 1928–1937, AWM38 3DRL 606/276/1, pp. 120–2, www.awm.gov.au/collection/RCDIG1066752.
47. Bean, *Official History of Australia in the War of 1914–1918*, Vol. III, p. 346.
48. Brudenell White to Charles Bean, Letter, 1 June 1926, *Diaries & Notebooks*, 1916–1934, AWM38 3DRL 606/243A/1, p. 69, www.awm. gov.au/collection/RCDIG1066752.

49. Major Howard, 'Report of Meeting Representatives First and Second Armies, 14 July 1916', Military Headquarters Correspondence & Papers, First Army, WO 158/186, p. 2.

50. McMullin, *Farewell Dear People*, p. 80.

51. Ibid. p. 84.

52. Bean, *Official History of Australia in the War of 1914–1918*, Vol. III, p. 345.

53. Pompey Elliott to Kate Elliott, Letter, 18 July 1916, Elliott Papers, AWM 2DRL/0513, Series 7, Box 6, Wallet 4, p. 51.

54. Andrew Rule, 'Lost and Found in Fromelles', *The Sydney Morning Herald*, 20 July 2010, www.smh.com.au.

55. Butler, 'Memorandum of Visit to First Army', 16 July 1916, Military Headquarters Correspondence & Papers, First Army, WO 158/186, p. 1.

56. Ibid., p. 2.

57. Bean, *Official History of Australia in the War of 1914–1918*, Vol. III, p. 347 (reported speech changed to direct speech).

58. Butler, 'Memorandum of Visit to First Army', 16 July 1916, Military Headquarters Correspondence & Papers, First Army, WO 158/186, p. 2.

59. Butler, 'Memorandum of Visit to First Army', 16 July 1916, Military Headquarters Correspondence & Papers, First Army, WO 158/186, p. 2 (reported speech changed to direct speech).

60. Butler, 'Memorandum of Visit to First Army', 16 July 1916, Military Headquarters Correspondence & Papers, First Army, WO 158/186, p. 2.

61. Senior, pp. 118–19.

62. Butler, 'Memorandum of Visit to First Army', 16 July 1916, Military Headquarters Correspondence & Papers, First Army, WO 158/186, p. 3.

63. Bean, *Official History of Australia in the War of 1914–1918*, Vol. III, p. 348 (reported speech changed to direct speech).

64. Haig, Douglas, *War Diaries & Letters*, p. 206.

65. Kidd, p. 243.

66. Pompey Elliott to Belle Campbell (sister-in-law), Letter, 17 December 1916, Elliott Papers, AWM 2DRL/0513, Series 3, Wallet 13, p. 16.

67. Author not stated, '53rd Battalion: Fromelles', in Bean, *Diaries & Notebooks*, AWM 3DRL 606/243A/1, p. 19, www.awm.gov.au/collection/RCDIG1066752.

68. Sydney Duckmanton, Diary, 17 July 1916, AWM PR03057.001.
69. James Stewart, Diary, 16 July 1916, AWM 3DRL/1459, p. 90.
70. Bean, *Official History of Australia in the War of 1914–1918*, Vol. III, p. 349.
71. 'Haking to First Army', Letter, 17 July 1916, General Staff Headquarters XI Corps, AWM4 1/22/4, Part 3, p. 1 (p. 8 of pdf), www.awm.gov.au/collection/RCDIG1004716.
72. Lindsay, p. 80.
73. 'Haking to First Army', Letter, 17 July 1916, General Staff Headquarters XI Corps, AWM4 1/22/4, Part 3, pp. 1–2 (pp. 8–9 of pdf), www.awm.gov.au/collection/RCDIG1004716.
74. Bean, Diary, 17 July 1916, *Diaries & Notebooks*, AWM38 3DRL 606/49/1, p. 61 (p. 55 of pdf), www.awm.gov.au/collection/RCDIG1066752.
75. Ibid.
76. Sir Charles Monro to Sir Douglas Haig, Message, 17 July 1916, Military Headquarters Correspondence & Papers, First Army, WO 158/186.
77. Sir Douglas Haig to Sir Charles Monro, ibid.
78. Bean, *Official History of Australia in the War of 1914–1918*, Vol. III, p. 350.
79. Ibid.
80. Author not stated, '53rd Battalion: Fromelles', in Bean, *Diaries & Notebooks*, AWM 3DRL 606/243A/1, p. 19, www.awm.gov.au/collection/RCDIG1066752.
81. Remarks from XI Corps Commander, 18 July 1916, AIF War Diaries, 1914–1918, Appendix F, General Staff, HQ Australian 5th Division, AWM4 1/50/5, Part 6, p. 4, www.awm.gov.au/collection/RCDIG1012124.
82. Final speech to 61st British Division, and Australian 5th Division from XI Corps Commander, 18 July 1916, AIF War Diaries, 1914–1918, Appendix F, General Staff, HQ Australian 5th Division, AWM4 1/50/5, Part 6, p. 6, www.awm.gov.au/collection/RCDIG1012124.
83. Bean, *Official History of Australia in the War of 1914–1918*, Vol. III, p. 468.
84. Ibid.
85. Ibid. (tense changed).
86. Suzanne Welborn, 'Pope, Harold (1873–1938)', Australian Dictionary of Biography, http://adb.anu.edu.au.

CHAPTER TEN: THE BATTLE OF FROMELLES

1. Ronald McInnis, Diary, 19 July 1916, AWM PR00917, p. 22, www. awm.gov.au/collection/RCDIG0000887.
2. Hitler, p. 165 (translated).
3. Pompey Elliott, 'The Battle of Fleurbaix or Fromelles', *The Duckboard*, Vol. 5, No. 9, 1 September 1930, p. 16.
4. Denny, p. 144.
5. Hutchinson, p. 24.
6. David Doyle to John Black, Letter, 6 July 1837, in Bean, *Diaries & Notebooks*, AWM38 3DRL 606/276/1, p. 142, www.awm.gov.au/ collection/RCDIG1066752.
7. Pompey Elliott to Kate Elliott, Letter, 19 July 1916, AWM 2DRL/0513, Series 7, Box 6, Wallet 4, p. 52.
8. Harold Williams to his mother, Letter, 17 July 1916, in Bean, Diaries, Notebooks and Folders, AWM38 3DRL 606/243A/1, p. 55, www. awm.gov.au/collection/RCDIG1066752.
9. Geoff McCrae to his parents, Letter, 11 April 1916, AWM 1DRL/0427, Series 2: Letters from Geoffrey Gordon McCrae to his family, 1914– 1916, p. 75, www.awm.gov.au/collection/RCDIG0001269.
10. Pompey Elliott to Belle Campbell (sister-in-law), Letter, 17 December 1916, Elliott Papers, 2DRL/0513, Series 3, Wallet 13, p. 16.
11. Tom Elliott to his sister, Letter, 19 July 1916, 3DRL/2872, p. 1, www. awm.gov.au/collection/3DRL/2872.
12. Bean, *Official History of Australia in the War of 1914–1918*, Vol. III, p. 394.
13. Walter Cass to Helena Holmes, Letter, 12 July 1916, SLV, MS15488, Series 1, Box 1, Folder 1A, p. 1.
14. James Green to 55th Battalion, Letter, undated, AWM PR02053, p. 1.
15. Gordon Maxfield to his father, Letter, 13 October 1916, AWM 1DRL/0489, p. 2.
16. Mackay, p. 167 (reported speech changed to direct speech).
17. Arthur, *Forgotten Voices of the Great War*, p. 184.
18. Douglas Horton, 'With the First Battalion at Pozières', Essay, AWM 1DRL/0359, p. 7. Horton originally wrote this essay under the pseudonym 'Cadmus'.
19. Dick Roberts, 'Memoirs of an Anzac', Memoir, AWM PR00395, p. 39.
20. Ibid.
21. Douglas Horton, 'With the First Battalion at Pozières', Essay, AWM 1DRL/0359, p. 7.

22. Ibid. (reported speech changed to direct speech).
23. Eyre, pp. 213–14.
24. Bean, *Official History of Australia in the War of 1914–1918*, Vol. III, p. 354.
25. Friedrich Wiedemann, 'The Battle at Fromelles on 19 and 20 July 1916', in Solleder, p. 214 (translated).
26. Leslie Martin to Jack (brother), Letter, 31 July 1916, AWM 1DRL/0483, p. 1.
27. Richard Haking, 'Note to Be Read Out to Troops', 16 July 1916, General Staff Headquarters, XI Corps, AWM4 1/22/4, Part 3, July 1916, p. 3 of pdf, www.awm.gov.au/collection/RCDIG1004716 (tenses changed).
28. Bean, *Official History of Australia in the War of 1914–1918*, Vol. III, p. 357.
29. Norman Nicolson, Diary, 19 July 1916, AWM 3DRL/2715, Vol. 3, p. 284.
30. Ibid., p. 285.
31. Herbert Fiveash, 41st Battery, 13th Field Artillery Brigade, typed manuscript, AWM MSS1217, p. 106.
32. Harold Williams, *The Gallant Company*, p. 55.
33. Ibid.
34. Fritz Wiedemann, '*Das Gefecht bei Fromelles*', in Solleder, *4 Jahre Westfront*, p. 214 (translated).
35. *Berliner Tageblatt*, 1 August 1916, p. 1 (translated).
36. Downing, *To the Last Ridge*, p. 22
37. Bishop, *The Hell, the Humour and the Heartbreak*, p. 61.
38. Ibid.
39. Ibid.
40. Ibid.
41. Bavarian War Archive, *Bayerisches Kriegsarchiv, Die Bayern im Großen Kriege*, p. 290 (translated).
42. Braun, p. 49.
43. Barton, p. 213.
44. William Smith, 'Sapper's Diary: The Battle of Fromelles', *Reveille*, 1 July 1936, Vol. 9, No. 11, p. 4.
45. Downing, *To the Last Ridge*, p. 23.
46. Smith, William, 'Sapper's Diary: The Battle of Fromelles,' *Reveille*, 1 July 1936, Vol. 9, No. 11, p. 4
47. Bean, *Official History of Australia in the War of 1914–1918*, Vol. III, p. 358.
48. Hartnett, p. 53 (reported speech changed to direct speech).
49. *Port Lincoln Times*, 'Visit of Salvation Army Chief', 19 August 1932, p. 7, http://trove.nla.gov.au.

50. John Bond, p. 115. This is from a similar meeting McKenzie held back in April, and I have presumed these well-known hymns would have served on this occasion too.

51. Douglas Bond, p. 165.

52. In his report afterward, the 55th Battalion's Lieutenant-Colonel McConaghy would note, 'I even saw men throwing Mills Grenades without withdrawing the safety pin. This was not peculiar to any one Battalion.' (Pedersen, *Fromelles*, p. 107)

53. Benjamin Champion, Diary, 19 July 1916, AWM 2DRL/0512, p. 87, www.awm.gov.au/collection/RCDIG0000977.

54. Tennyson ('The Charge of the Light Brigade'), p. 147.

55. Hartnett, p. 54.

56. Ibid.

57. Walter Downing, *Digger Dialects*, p. 23.

58. Benjamin Champion, Diary, 19 July 1916, AWM 2DRL/0512, p. 88, www.awm.gov.au/collection/RCDIG0000977.

59. Ibid.

60. Cobb, p. 169.

61. *Berliner Tageblatt*, 1 August 1916, p. 1 (translated).

62. *Norddeutsche Allgemeine Zeitung*, 3 August 1916, p. 1 (translated).

63. Barton, p. 187.

64. Pedersen, *Fromelles*, p. 66.

65. Bean, *Official History of Australia in the War of 1914–1918*, Vol. III, p. 362.

66. Knyvett, p. 175.

67. Ibid. (reported speech changed to direct speech).

68. Ibid. (reported speech changed to direct speech).

69. William Smith, 'Sapper's Diary: The Battle of Fromelles', *Reveille*, 1 July 1936, Vol. 9, No. 11, p. 4.

70. Lieutenant-Colonel F. W. Toll, 'Report on Operation "Assault on and Attempt to Consolidate Enemy's Trenches N10 c 13 to N10 c 14 on the 19th & 20th July 1916"', 21 July 1916, 31st Battalion War Diary, Appendix D, AWM4 23/48/12, p. 2.

71. Lieutenant-Colonel F. W. Toll, 'Report to G.O.C. 8th Infantry Brigade (General Tivey)', 21 July 1916, 31st Battalion War Diary, Appendix C, AWM4 23/48/12, p. 2.

72. Lieutenant-Colonel F. W. Toll, 'Report on Operation "Assault on and Attempt to Consolidate Enemy's Trenches N10 c 13 to N10 c 14 on the 19th & 20th July 1916"', 21 July 1916, 31st Battalion War Diary, Appendix D, AWM4 23/48/12, p. 1.

73. Lindsay, p. 93.

74. 'Narrative of Events, 17 July to 20th July 1916', 14th Brigade War Diary, Appendix B, AWM4 23/14/4, p. 3.
75. Kelshaw and Thornton, p. 54.
76. Barton, p. 188.
77. Ibid. (reported speech changed to direct speech).
78. 31st Battalion War Diary, Appendix D, 21 July 1916, AWM 23/48/12, p. 23.
79. Cyril Brudenell White to John Black (editor of *Reveille*), Letter, undated 1937, in Bean, *Diaries & Notebooks*, 1928–1937, AWM38 3DRL 606/276/1, pp. 120–2, www.awm.gov.au/collection/RCDIG1066752.
80. Geoffrey Christie-Miller, Memoir, Volume Two, IWM 80/32/1, Document 4776, p. 182.
81. Friedrich Wiedemann, 'The Battle at Fromelles on 19 and 20 July 1916', in Solleder, p. 216 (translated).
82. Ibid. (translated; reported speech changed to direct speech).
83. Ibid., p. 215 (translated).
84. *Berliner Tageblatt*, 1 August 1916, p. 1 (translated).

CHAPTER ELEVEN: THE BATTLE PROPER

1. McMullin, *Farewell Dear People*, p. 152.
2. *The Ararat Advertiser*, 'Australian Attack on Fromelles: Described by a German', 5 August 1916, p. 2, http://trove.nla.gov.au. The translation has been edited to be closer to the original German text (*Berliner Tageblatt*, 1 August 1916, p. 1).
3. Bean, *Official History of Australia in the War of 1914–1918*, Vol. III, p. 358.
4. Geoffrey Christie-Miller, Memoir, Volume Two, IWM 80/32/1, Document 4776, p. 180.
5. British Headquarters Branches and Services, General Staff, 1 September 1915 to 31 July 1915, 61st Division War Diary, PRO WO 95/3033/1, p. 122.
6. 'Tommy Atkins' is a generic name for an English soldier, as per the 'Dictionary of the Trenches'in Empey, p. 253: 'The name England gives to an English soldier, even if his name is Willie Jones.'
7. 2/1 Battalion Oxfordshire and Buckingham Light Infantry War Diary, 19 July 1916, National Archives, London, PRO WO 95/3066/2, p. 3.

8. Geoffrey Christie-Miller, Memoir, Volume Two, IWM 80/32/1, Document 4776, p. 179.

9. 2/1 Battalion Oxfordshire and Buckingham Light Infantry War Diary, 19 July 1916, National Archives, London, PRO WO 95/3066/2, p. 3.

10. Ibid., 'Plan of Attack', Appendix C, p. 6.

11. Major-General Mackenzie, Commander 61st Division, Report on Operations 15th to 19th of July 1916, Appendix X, in 61st Division British Headquarters Branches and Services, General Staff, September 1915 to May 1917, WO 95/3033/1, p. 2 (p. 122 of pdf), TNA.

12. *Norddeutsche Allgemeine Zeitung*, 3 August 1916, p. 1 (translated).

13. *Berliner Tageblatt*, 1 August 1916, p. 1 (translated).

14. Ibid. (translated).

15. Ibid. (translated).

16. *Norddeutsche Allgemeine Zeitung*, 3 August 1916, p. 1 (translated).

17. Pedersen, *Fromelles*, p. 57.

18. James Wyatt, Diary, 20 July 1916, IWM 83/12/1, Document 4160, p.10.

19. James Wyatt, in Pedersen, *Fromelles*, p. 57.

20. F. A. C. Hamilton, in ibid.

21. Geoffrey Christie-Miller, Memoir, Volume Two, IWM 80/32/1, Document 4776, p. 183.

22. 'Artillery Action by 61st Div and Attached Artillery, 21 July 1916', 61st Division's Report on Fromelles, WO 95/3033, p. 2.

23. Lindsay, p. 93.

24. John Ridley to his parents, Letter, 24 July 1916, AWM 3DRL/6428, p. 1.

25. Barton, p. 197.

26. William Smith, 'Sapper's Diary: The Battle of Fromelles', *Reveille*, 1 July 1936, Vol. 9, No. 11, p. 4.

27. Seal, p. 2.

28. David Malouf, *Fly Away Peter*, p. 82.

29. Hamilton, *Gallipoli Diary*, Vol. I, p. 211.

30. William Smith, 'Sapper's Diary: The Battle of Fromelles', *Reveille*, 1 July 1936, Vol. 9, No. 11, p. 4.

31. Ibid.

32. The 59th and 60th War Diaries appear to be in error on this matter, claiming they crossed the parapet at 6.45 pm. I suspect this is a confusion between writing in hours from Zero Hour – 6 hours 45 minutes from the beginning of the barrage at 11 am – and the actual clock time of deployment, 5.45 pm.

33. Hubert Fitton to his wife, Letter, 26 July 1916, AWM PR01689, p. 1.
34. Bean, *Official History of Australia in the War of 1914–1918*, Vol. III, p. 373.
35. Barton, p. 213.
36. Ibid.
37. Ibid., p. 218.
38. Herbert Fiveash, 41st Battery, 13th Field Artillery Brigade, AWM MSS1217, p. 106.
39. Knyvett, p. 177.
40. John Turnbull, Diary, 21 July 1916, AWM PR91/015, p. 18.
41. *Berliner Tageblatt*, 1 August 1916, p. 1 (translated).
42. Barton, p. 216.
43. Downing, *To the Last Ridge*, pp. 23–5.
44. 'Major Thomas Patrick Elliott, 60th Battalion', Australian Red Cross Society Wounded and Missing Enquiry Bureau Files, 1914–1918 War, AWM 1DRL/0428, Box 101, Wallet 1, p. 3, http://static.awm.gov.au/images/collection/bundled/RCDIG1061840.pdf.
45. Ibid.
46. Barton, p. 219.
47. *Norddeutsche Allgemeine Zeitung*, 3 August 1916, p. 2 (translated).
48. Friedrich Wiedemann, '*Das Gefecht bei Fromelles*' ('The Battle at Fromelles'), in Solleder, p. 215 (translated). In the original, Wiedemann refers to the enemy as being English, but this is likely after the fashion of the time, which referred to the Australians and New Zealanders collectively as being English – just as the English and Australians identified them all as Germans, without distinguishing between Saxons, Bavarians, Württembergers and Prussians.
49. Preliminary Instructions, 15th Australian Infantry Brigade Order No. 17, 16 July 1916, Appendix 9, 15th Brigade War Diary, AWM4 23/15/5, p. 36.
50. Bean, *Official History of Australia in the War of 1914–1918*, Vol. III, p. 366.
51. Corfield, *Don't Forget Me, Cobber*, p. 149.
52. John Turnbull, Diary, 21 July 1916, AWM PR91/015, p. 18.
53. Bean, *Official History of Australia in the War of 1914–1918*, Vol. III, p. 366.
54. John Turnbull, Diary, 21 July 1916, AWM PR91/015, p. 18.
55. Sheldon, p. 142 (English words); Lais, p. 17 (original German words). This detail taken from an account of the attack on the opening day of the Somme, in a similar situation.
56. *Berliner Tageblatt*, 1 August 1916, p. 1 (translated).

57. Bean, *Official History of Australia in the War of 1914–1918*, Vol. III, p. 365.
58. Ibid., p. 368.
59. Kelshaw and Thornton, p. 55.
60. Ibid., p. 59.
61. 'Captain Harry Paulin, 53rd Battalion', Australian Red Cross Society Wounded and Missing Enquiry Bureau Files, AWM 1DRL/0428, Box 211, Wallet 3, p. 7, http://static.awm.gov.au/images/collection/pdf/RCDIG1056810--1-.pdf.
62. Cobb, p. 125.
63. Pedersen, *Fromelles*, p. 74.
64. 'Lieutenant Colonel Ignatius Bertram Norris, 53rd Battalion', Australian Red Cross Society Wounded and Missing Enquiry Bureau Files, AWM 1DRL/0428, p. 4, http://static.awm.gov.au/images/collection/pdf/RCDIG1061761--1-.pdf.
65. Bean, *Anzac to Amiens*, p. 229.
66. Pedersen, *Fromelles*, p. 84 (tense changed).
67. Walter Cass, 'Report on Condition of German Trenches', 22 July 1916, 14th Brigade War Diary, Appendix, 32/1/15, AWM4 23/14/4, p. 90 (p. 95 of pdf), www.awm.gov.au/collection/RCDIG1016768.
68. Ibid.
69. Walter Cass, '54th Battalion Report on Operations 29th & 30th July "In the Field"', 21 July 1916, 14th Brigade War Diary, AWM4 23/14/4, p. 1, www.awm.gov.au/collection/RCDIG1016768.
70. Kelshaw and Thornton, p. 60.
71. Ibid.
72. Ibid., p. 61.
73. Wiedemann, 'Das Gefecht bei Fromelles', in: Solleder (ed.), *4 Jahre Westfront*, p. 216 [Translated. Reported Speech.]
74. Percy Chapman, Diary, undated, AWM 1DRL/0198, p. 64.
75. Ibid.
76. Sydney Donnan, Memoir, 3 February 1934, AWM 2DRL/0712, p. 5.
77. Weber, *Hitler's Erster Krieg*, p. 201 (German ed.); Weber, *Hitler's First War*, p. 148 (English ed.).
78. Bishop, *The Hell, the Humour and the Heartbreak*, p. 62.
79. Pedersen, *Fromelles*, p. 85.
80. Bishop, *The Hell, the Humour and the Heartbreak*, p. 62.
81. Ibid.
82. Ibid., p. 63.
83. Pederson, *Fromelles*, p. 86.

84. Bean, *Official History of Australia in the War of 1914–1918*, Vol. III, p. 383.

85. Frederick Toll, 'Report on Operation 19th & 20th July 1916', Appendix D, p. 3, 31st Battalion War Diary, AWM4 23/48/12, p. 196 (p. 24 of pdf), www.awm.gov.au/collection/RCDIG1005459.

86. Ibid., p. 377.

87. Australian 5th Division, General Staff Memorandum No. 8, Carrier Pigeons, 13 July 1916, Australian 5th Division War Diary, AWM4 1/50, p. 23.

88. 15th Australian Infantry Brigade Report on Action 19th/20th July 1916, 23 July 1916, 15th Brigade War Diary, AWM4 23/15/5, p. 74.

89. Bean, *Official History of Australia in the War of 1914–1918*, Vol. III, p. 361.

90. Friedrich Wiedemann, 'Das Gefecht bei Fromelles', in Solleder, p. 231 (translated).

91. Bean, *Official History of Australia in the War of 1914–1918*, Vol. III, p. 363.

CHAPTER TWELVE: A LAND FOR NO MAN

1. Bert Bishop to Harold Bishop, 26 July 1916, Letter, 'Private Bishop, Raymond Charles', Australian Red Cross Wounded and Missing Enquiry Bureau, AWM 1DRL/0428, Box 39, Wallet 10, p. 1, http://static.awm.gov.au/images/collection/pdf/RCDIG1038264--1-.pdf.

2. Corfield, *Hold Hard, Cobbers*, Vol. I, p. 34.

3. Elliott to 15th Brigade HQ, 7.18 pm, 19 July 1916, 15th Brigade War Diary, AWM4 23/15/5, p. 78.

4. McMullin, *Pompey Elliott*, p. 218.

5. Bishop, *The Hell, the Humour and the Heartbreak*, p. 63.

6. Ibid.

7. Sloan, p. 80.

8. Bishop, *The Hell, the Humour and the Heartbreak*, p. 64.

9. Ibid.

10. As revealed by Peter Barton in his book *The Lost Legions of Fromelles*, the Australians at Grashof were not seen again, apart from a few who came back and were greeted with scepticism when they claimed to have been halfway to Fromelles. The rest, for a time, convinced the Germans that the Australian advance was much deeper than it was. Unwisely

these men, whose names are unknown, dug in and fought through the night, until killed or captured. (Barton, p. 244)

11. Frederick Toll, 'Report on Operation 19th & 20th July 1916', 31st Battalion War Diary, AWM4 23/48/12, p. 6.

12. Ibid., p. 5.

13. Bean, *Official History of Australia in the War of 1914–1918*, Vol. III, p. 392.

14. Pompey Elliott, '15th Brigade Report on Action 19th/20th July 1916', 23 July 1916, 15th Brigade War Diary, AWM4 23/15/5, p. 2.

15. Colin Mackenzie, '61st Division Report on Operation 15th–19th July 1916', 61st Division War Diary, British Headquarters Branches and Services, General Staff, National Archives, WO 95/3033/1, p. 4.

16. Bean, *Official History of Australia in the War of 1914–1918*, Vol. III, p. 394.

17. Ibid., p. 393.

18. Ibid.

19. Ibid., pp. 394–5.

20. Pedersen, *Fromelles*, p. 90.

21. Bean, *Official History of Australia in the War of 1914–1918*, Vol. III, p. 395.

22. Pompey Elliott, 15th AIF Brigade, 'Report on Action 19th to 20th July 1916', Appendix No. 12, 15th Brigade War Diary, AWM4 23/15/5, p. 54.

23. Ibid.

24. Bean, *Official History of Australia in the War of 1914–1918*, Vol. III, p. 394.

25. *Berliner Tageblatt*, 1 August 1916, p. 2 (translated).

26. *Norddeutsche Allgemeine Zeitung*, 3 August 1916, p. 1 (translated).

27. *Berliner Tageblatt*, 1 August 1916, p. 2 (translated).

28. Ibid.

29. Williams, John, *Corporal Hitler and the Great War*, p. 142.

30. Ibid.

31. J. Bain to Violet Gibbins, Letter, 19 June 1918, AWM PR02053/3, p. 1.

32. Harry Still, Memoir, AWM PR00753, p. 38.

33. Percy Larbalestier to Violet Gibbins, Letter, 27 January 1917, AWM PR02053/3, p. 1.

34. Percy Chapman, Diary, undated, AWM 1DRL/0198, p. 64.

35. Walter Cass to Helena Holmes, Letter, 29 July 1916, SLV, MS15488, Series 1, Box 1, Folder 1A, p. 3.

36. *Norddeutsche Allgemeine Zeitung*, 3 August 1916, p. 1 (translated).

37. Bean, *Official History of Australia in the War of 1914–1918*, Vol. III, p. 402.
38. *Norddeutsche Allgemeine Zeitung*, 3 August 1916, p. 1 (translated).
39. Max Schneckenburger, *'Die Wacht am Rhein'* (poem), 1840; music to this poem composed by Karl Wilhelm, 1854.
40. Bean, *Official History of Australia in the War of 1914–1918*, Vol. III, p. 403.
41. Walter Cass to Helena Holmes, Letter, 29 July 1916, SLV, MS15488, Series 1, Box 1, Folder 1A, p. 1.
42. Bean, Charles, 'The Leadership of Norman Gibbins', *The Link*, 1 September 1926, p. 6.
43. Bean, *Official History of Australia in the War of 1914–1918*, Vol. III, p. 408.
44. Ibid., p. 409.
45. Percy Chapman to Violet Gibbins, Letter, 27 July 1916, AWM PR02053/3, p. 1.
46. Bert White to Violet Gibbins, Letter, 3 April 1918, in Bean, *Diaries & Notebooks*, AWM38 3DRL 606/243A/1, p. 1 (p. 60 of pdf), (reported speech changed to direct speech).
47. Percy Chapman, Diary, undated, AWM 1DRL/0198, p. 66 (p. 4 of Part II).
48. William Barry, Memoir, AWM PR00814, p. 38.
49. Ibid., pp. 38–9.
50. Ibid., p. 39.
51. Bean, *Official History of Australia in the War of 1914–1918*, Vol. III, p. 401.
52. Pompey Elliott to 15th Brigade HQ, Message, 15th Brigade War Diary, July 1916, AWM4 23/15/5, p. 79.
53. Theodor Pflaum, Diary, 19 July 1916, AWM PR04009, p. 27.
54. Ibid.
55. Ibid.
56. Ibid.
57. *The Herald* (Melbourne), 5 May 1937, p. 2.
58. Major-General Mackenzie, Commander 61st Division, 'Report on Operations 15th to 19th of July 1916', Appendix X, in 61st Division British Headquarters Branches and Services, General Staff, September 1915 to May 1917, WO 95/3033/1, p. 4 (p. 124 of pdf), TNA.
59. Bean, *Official History of Australia in the War of 1914–1918*, Vol. III, p. 397.
60. Ibid.

61. Bishop, *The Hell, the Humour and the Heartbreak*, p. 65.
62. Farrar-Hockley, p. 200 (reported speech changed to direct speech).

CHAPTER THIRTEEN: IN THE MIDNIGHT HOUR

1. Carlyon, p. 92 (Alfred Langan's letter to his father, 22 July 1916, privately held).
2. Bean, *Official History of Australia in the War of 1914–1918*, Vol. III, pp. 397–8.
3. McMullin, *Farewell Dear People*, p. 154.
4. Bean, *Official History of Australia in the War of 1914–1918*, Vol. III, p. 398.
5. Corfield, *Hold Hard, Cobbers*, Vol. I, p. 34.
6. Colin Mackenzie, '61st Division Report on Operations 15th to 20th July 1916', 61st Division War Diary, National Archives, PRO WO 95/3033/1, p. 4.
7. By 2 am, on the Australian front only, there are 4000 Germans making counter-attacks and another 2000 Germans holding their own line. This 6000 is probably double the number of Australians left alive and still holding on in the German trenches.
8. Bean, *Official History of Australia in the War of 1914–1918*, Vol. III, p. 417.
9. Pedersen, *Fromelles*, p. 92.
10. Waldo Zander, 'Narrative of experiences', AWM 2DRL/0171, p. 5.
11. Bean, *Official History of Australia in the War of 1914–1918*, Vol. III, p. 421.
12. Bishop, *The Hell, the Humour and the Heartbreak*, p. 65.
13. Ibid.
14. Ibid.
15. Sydney Donnan, Memoir, 3 February 1934, AWM 2DRL/0712, p. 6.
16. Bean, *Official History of Australia in the War of 1914–1918*, Vol. III, p. 418.
17. Ibid.
18. D. M. McConaghy, '55th Battalion Report on the Operations on the Night of 19th–20th of July 1916', Appendix A, 55th Battalion War Diary, AWM 23/72/5, p. 2.
19. Bean, *Official History of Australia in the War of 1914–1918*, Vol. III, p. 418.
20. Ibid.
21. Ibid., p. 422.

22. Captain Arthur White, 'Report on Operations 19–20 July 1916', 32nd Battalion War Diary, Appendix A, AWM4 23/49/12, p. 2 (p. 11 of pdf), www.awm.gov.au/collection/RCDIG1000619.

23. Theodor Pflaum, Diary, AWM PR04009, 19 July 1916, p. 27.

24. Captain Arthur White, 'Report on Operations 19–20 July 1916', 32nd Battalion War Diary, Appendix A, AWM4 23/49/12, p. 2 (p. 12 of pdf), www.awm.gov.au/collection/RCDIG1000619.

25. Theodor Pflaum, Diary, AWM PR04009, 19 July 1916, p. 27.

26. Waldo Zander, 'Narrative of experiences', AWM 2DRL/0171, p. 6.

27. Bean has accepted Colonel Toll's own timing here and placed this scene at 5.30 am. However, better evidence confirms that the events described took place around 4 am.

28. William Miles to Charles Bean, Letter, 30 July 1929, Bean, *Diaries & Notebooks*, AWM38 3DRL 606/243A/1, p. 90, www.awm.gov.au/collection/RCDIG1066752.

29. Ibid.

30. Bean, *Official History of Australia in the War of 1914–1918*, Vol. III, p. 429.

31. In his *Official History*, p. 408, Charles Bean has this sap getting through at midnight, but, I respectfully submit, he is mistaken. It is the account of Major Henry Bachtold, commanding 14th Field Company – confirmed by diary entries of other Diggers, and the account of Bert Bishop – that it was finished at 4 am.

32. Sydney Donnan, Memoir, 3 February 1934, AWM 2DRL/0712, p. 6.

33. David McConaghy, '55th Battalion Report on the Operations on the Night of 19th–20th of July 1916', Appendix A, 55th Battalion War Diary, AWM 23/72/5, p. 2.

34. This is a generic order, typical of this exact situation. My expert in the field, Dr Peter Williams, notes NCOs of all armies were trained to direct the fire of the men under them in this manner. In British Empire armies, the sequence of orders issued was first to tell the men where to look for the target, then tell them what the target was and finally tell them how many rounds to fire. If the target was a long way away, the NCO would also give the range.

35. Ibid.

36. Bean, *Official History of Australia in the War of 1914–1918*, Vol. III, p. 419.

37. Ibid., p. 420.

38. Ibid., p. 419.

39. Honours and Awards: Percy William Woods, AWM, http://static.awm.gov.au/images/collection/pdf/RCDIG1068131--44-.pdf.

40. Bean, *Official History of Australia in the War of 1914–1918*, Vol. III, p. 419.

41. Ibid., p. 427.

42. Downing, *To the Last Ridge*, p. 27.

43. Ibid.

44. Hutchinson, p. 28.

45. Bean, *Official History of Australia in the War of 1914–1918*, Vol. III, p. 427.

46. Richard Haking, 'Summary of Events in Connection with the Operations Carried out by the XI Corps on the 19th July, 1916, to the North of Fauquissart, and the Reports Thereon', First Army HQ, WO 95/165, p. 21.

47. Walter Cass, '54th Battalion Report on Operations 29th & 30th July "In the Field"', 21 July 1916, 14th Brigade War Diary, AWM4 23/14/4, p. 2.

48. Bean, *Official History of Australia in the War of 1914–1918*, Vol. III, p. 427.

49. Herbert Fiveash, 41st Battery, 13th Field Artillery Brigade, typed manuscript, AWM MSS1217, p. 1.

50. Francis Law, 'Recollections of the Battle of Fromelles, France, July 19th 1916', in Bean, *Diaries & Notebooks*, AWM38 3DRL 606/243A/1, p. 136, www.awm.gov.au/collection/RCDIG1066752 (reported speech changed to direct speech).

51. Percy Chapman to Violet Gibbins, Letter, 27 July 1916, AWM PR02053/3, p. 1.

52. Francis Law, 'Recollections of the Battle of Fromelles, France, July 19th 1916'.

53. Ibid.

54. Archibald Winter, Diary, 19–20 July 1916, AWM PR89/163.

55. Walter Cass, '54th Battalion Report on Operations 29th & 30th July "In the Field"', 21 July 1916, 14th Brigade War Diary, AWM4 23/14/4, p. 2.

56. Bishop, *The Hell, the Humour and the Heartbreak*, p. 66.

57. Bean, *Official History of Australia in the War of 1914–1918*, Vol. III, p. 433.

58. Walter Cass to Helena Holmes, Letter, 29 July 1916, SLV, MS15488, Series 1, Box 1, Folder 1A, p. 1.

59. Bean, *Official History of Australia in the War of 1914–1918*, Vol. III, p. 431.

60. Ibid., p. 433.

61. William Smith, 'Sapper's Diary: The Battle of Fromelles', *Reveille*, 1 July 1936, Vol. 9, No. 11, p. 14.
62. Walter Cass to Helena Holmes, Letter, 29 July 1916, SLV, MS15488, Series 1, Box 1, Folder 1A, p. 1.
63. William Smith, 'Sapper's Diary: The Battle of Fromelles', *Reveille*, 1 July 1936, Vol. 9, No. 11, p. 14.
64. Bert Bishop, in an extract from the *Ulladulla and Milton Times*, 30 September 1916 (written by Bert, from the trenches, 1 August 1916), in the file of Raymond C. Bishop, 55th Battalion, AWM 1DRL/123.
65. Charles Bean, 'The Leadership of Norman Gibbins', *The Link*, 1 September 1926, p. 6.
66. Bert White to Violet Gibbins, 3 April 1918, Letter, in Bean, *Diaries & Notebooks*, AWM38 3DRL 606/243A/1, p. 1 (reported speech changed to direct speech).
67. L. Davis to Violet Gibbins, Letter, 18 November 1916, AWM PR02053/3, p. 1.
68. Bert White to Violet Gibbins, 3 April 1918, Letter, in Bean, *Diaries & Notebooks*, AWM38 3DRL 606/243A/1, p. 1 (tense changed).
69. Percy Chapman to Violet Gibbins, Letter, 27 July 1916, AWM PR02053/3, p. 1.
70. Charles Monro to Douglas Haig, Advanced First Army HQ to Advanced GHQ, Daily Report, 20 July 1916, General Headquarters, WO 95/5.
71. *Norddeutsche Allgemeine Zeitung*, 3 August 1916, p. 2 (translated).
72. Ibid.

CHAPTER FOURTEEN: THE AFTERMATH

1. Downing, *To the Last Ridge*, p. 30.
2. Knyvett, p. 179.
3. Pedersen, *Fromelles*, p. 103.
4. Knyvett, p. 179.
5. Downing, *To the Last Ridge*, p. 10.
6. Herbert Fiveash, 41st Battery, 13th Field Artillery Brigade, typed manuscript, AWM MSS1217, p. 106.
7. Bean, *Official History of Australia in the War of 1914–1918*, Vol. III, p. 438.
8. Bean, Diary, 20 July 1916, *Diaries & Notebooks*, AWM38 3DRL 606/52/1, p. 10, www.awm.gov.au/collection/RCDIG1066752.
9. Bean, *Official History of Australia in the War of 1914–1918*, Vol. III, p. 443.

10. John Schroder to John Black, Letter, undated, in Bean, *Diaries & Notebooks*, AWM38 3DRL 606/276/1, p. 149, www.awm.gov.au/collection/RCDIG1066752.

11. Corfield, *Don't Forget Me, Cobber*, p. 223.

12. Freeman, Neil, to Editor of *Reveille*, Letter, 7 July 1937, in Bean, *Diaries & Notebooks*, AWM38 3DRL 606/276/1, www.awm.gov.au/collection/RCDIG1066752, p. 135 of pdf.

13. Corfield, *Don't Forget Me, Cobber*, p. 223.

14. McMullin, *Pompey Elliott*, p. 224.

15. John Schroder to John Black, Letter, undated, in Bean, *Diaries & Notebooks*, AWM38 3DRL 606/276/1, p. 5, www.awm.gov.au/collection/RCDIG1066752, p. 149 of pdf.

16. William Miles to Charles Bean, Letter, 30 July 1929, in Bean, *Diaries & Notebooks*, AWM38 3DRL 606/243A/1, p. 91, www.awm.gov.au/collection/RCDIG1066752.

17. Ibid., pp. 90–1.

18. Richard Haking, 'Report to Advanced 1st Army Headquarters', 24 July 1916, General Staff Headquarters, XI Corps, Part 3, AWM4 1/22/4, p. 1, www.awm.gov.au/collection/RCDIG1004716.

19. Ibid.

20. Bean, *Official History of Australia in the War of 1914–1918*, Vol. III, p. 438.

21. William Barry, Memoir, AWM PR00814, p. 39.

22. Ibid.

23. Bean, *Official History of Australia in the War of 1914–1918*, Vol. III, p. 437.

24. Weber, *Hitler's First War*, p. 148 (English ed.) (reported speech changed to direct speech).

25. William Barry, Memoir, AWM PR00814, p. 41.

26. Braun, p. 52.

27. Archie Barwick, Diary, 22 July 1916, MLMSS 1493, Box 1, Item 3, p. 233.

28. Duffy, p. 56.

29. Bean, *Official History of Australia in the War of 1914–1918*, Vol. III, p. 396.

30. Duffy, p. 56.

31. Richard Haking, 'Secret Order to Divisions', 16 July 1916, General Staff Headquarters, XI Corps, AWM4 1/22/4, Part 3, p. 3, www.awm.gov.au/collection/RCDIG1004716.

32. William Miles to Charles Bean, Letter, 30 July 1929, in Bean, *Diaries & Notebooks*, AWM38 3DRL 606/243A/1, p. 93, www.awm.gov.au/collection/RCDIG1066752.

33. Ibid., pp. 92–3.

34. Ibid., pp. 93–4 (reported speech changed to direct speech).

35. Ibid., p. 95 (reported speech changed to direct speech).

36. Ibid. (reported speech changed to direct speech).

37. Bean, *Official History of Australia in the War of 1914–1918*, Vol. III, p. 438.

38. Ibid., pp. 439–40.

39. Ibid., p. 440.

40. Norman Nicolson, Diary, 21 July 1916, Vol. 4, AWM 3DRL/2715, p. 36.

41. Charles Bean, oddly, was a great defender of General McCay's. In his *Official History*, he noted that 'the blame for the enterprise was thrown upon an unpopular but entirely innocent leader, General M'Cay. It is probably true that in the case of the Fromelles offensive M'Cay welcomed the early chance of commanding his division in action but, even had he been as thoroughly opposed to it as were White and Birdwood, the general appeal made by his superiors for assistance to the force struggling on the Somme might well have prevented any opposition on his part to the plans of his superiors.' Bean in fact went further, defending him also on the 2nd Battle of Krithia, and the desert march, saying that in none of these 'was he, in fact, any more responsible than the humblest private in his force, while in the case of the desert march he had actually protested against the order.' (Bean, *Official History of Australia in the War of 1914–1918*, Vol. III, p. 447) Pompey Elliott defends him as well in 'The Battle of Fleurbaix or Fromelles', *The Duckboard*, Vol. 5, No. 9, 1 September 1930, pp. 3–7.

42. Norman Nicolson, Diary, 21 July 1916, Vol. 4, AWM 3DRL/2715, pp. 35–6. Nicolson, it seems, has mistaken General McCay for an Englishman, a common enough assumption at the time when Commanding Officers of Australian divisions were more than likely to be English.

43. David Mason, Diary, 20 July 1916, AWM PR01435, p. 22.

44. The Hon. Warren Snowdon MHR, Minister for Defence Science and Personnel, Questions without Notice, 28 May 2008, *Hansard*, p. 3547.

45. Bishop, *The Hell, the Humour and the Heartbreak*, p. 66.

46. Bishop, *Dear All*, p. 28.

47. Bishop, *The Hell, the Humour and the Heartbreak*, p. 67.

48. Braun, p. 51.

49. Bean, Diary, 20 July 1916, *Diaries & Notebooks*, AWM38 3DRL 606/52/1, p. 11, www.awm.gov.au/collection/RCDIG1066752.

50. Ibid., p. 17.

51. Ibid., p. 26.

52. Ibid.
53. Ibid., p. 18.
54. Ibid.
55. William Miles to Charles Bean, Letter, 30 July 1929, in Bean, *Diaries & Notebooks*, AWM38 3DRL 606/243A/1, p. 91, www.awm.gov.au/collection/RCDIG1066752.
56. Bean, Diary, 20 July 1916, *Diaries & Notebooks*, AWM38 3DRL 606/52/1, p. 20, www.awm.gov.au/collection/RCDIG1066752.
57. Ibid.
58. Ibid.
59. Ibid., p. 17.
60. Bean, *Official History of Australia in the War of 1914–1918*, Vol. III, p. 444.
61. Bean, Diary, 20 July 1916, *Diaries & Notebooks*, AWM38 3DRL 606/52/1, pp. 25–6, www.awm.gov.au/collection/RCDIG1066752.
62. Bean, *Official History of Australia in the War of 1914–1918*, Vol. III, p. 438.
63. Bishop, *The Hell, the Humour and the Heartbreak*, p. 68.
64. Ibid.
65. Ibid., p. 71.
66. Lindsay, p. 146.
67. *Norddeutsche Allgemeine Zeitung*, 3 August 1916, p. 2 (translated).
68. Ibid.
69. *Berliner Tageblatt*, 1 August 1916, p. 1 (translated).
70. *The Sydney Morning Herald*, 24 July 1916, p. 9.
71. Bean, Diary, 20 July 1916, *Diaries & Notebooks*, AWM38 3DRL 606/52/1, pp. 22–3, www.awm.gov.au/collection/RCDIG1066752.
72. *The Mercury* (Hobart), 'The Western Front: Australians in Battle', 24 July 1916, p. 5, http://trove.nla.gov.au.
73. Lindsay, *Fromelles*, pp. 155–6
74. Bean, *Official History of Australia in the War of 1914–1918*, Vol. III, p. 444.
75. Caulfield, p. 187.
76. Haig, Douglas, *War Diaries & Letters*, p. 208.
77. This recommendation for a promotion by Haig was overruled.
78. Haig, Douglas, *War Diaries & Letters*, p. 208.
79. Bean, *Official History of Australia in the War of 1914–1918*, Vol. III, p. 440.
80. Ibid.
81. Sloan, p. 83.

82. Simon Fraser, Letter, 31 July 1916, AWM 1DRL/0300, p. 4.
83. Bean, *Official History of Australia in the War of 1914–1918*, Vol. III, p. 441.
84. James Wyatt, Diary, 20 July 1916, IWM 83/12/1, Document 4160, p. 10.
85. Geoffrey Christie-Miller, Memoir, Volume Two, IWM 80/32/1, Document 4776, p. 225.
86. Gammage, p. 160.
87. Simon Fraser, Letter, 31 July 1916, AWM 1DRL/0300, p. 4.
88. Ibid.
89. Ibid.
90. Knyvett, p. 180.
91. Downing, *To The Last Ridge*, p. 29.
92. Knyvett, p. 181 (reported speech changed to direct speech).
93. John Turnbull, Additional Notes in Diary, after November 1918, AWM PR91/015, p. 173.

PART THREE: END GAME

1. Bean, Diary, 24 September 1916, *Diaries & Notebooks*, AWM38 3DRL 606/60/1, pp. 7–8, www.awm.gov.au/collection/RCDIG1066752.
2. Matt Walsh, 'The Somme: A Brief Record of Australia's Involvement in the Battle of Pozières', Defence Reserves Association Inc. and the Military Police Association of Australia Inc., 2008, Army Museum of South Australia, www.amosa.org.au.

CHAPTER FIFTEEN: THE BATTLE OF POZIÈRES

1. Ben Champion, Diary, 26 July 1916, p. 96, AWM 2DRL/0512, www.awm.gov.au/collection/RCDIG0000977.
2. Bean, *Official History of Australia in the War of 1914–1918*, Vol. III, p. 468.
3. Harold Walker to Charles Bean, Letter, 13 August 1928, in Bean Papers, AWM38 3DRL 7953/34, Part 1, p. 2.
4. Shakespear, pp. 62–3.
5. Sheldon, p. 179.

6. Keech, Kindle Edition.
7. Bean, *Official History of Australia in the War of 1914–1918*, Vol. III, p. 468.
8. Harold Walker to Charles Bean, Letter, 13 August 1928, Bean Papers, AWM38 3DRL 7953/34, Part 1, p. 5.
9. Pedersen, *The Anzacs*, p. 166 (reported speech changed to direct speech).
10. Harold Walker to Charles Bean, Letter, 13 August 1928, Bean Papers, AWM38 3DRL 7953/34, Part 1, p. 6.
11. Ibid., p. 2.
12. James Edmonds to Charles Bean, Letter, 16 November 1927, Bean Papers, AWM38 3DRL 7953/34, Part 1, p. 2. Gough would hotly deny the charge, writing to the British Official Historian, 'I was not "temperamentally" addicted to attacks without careful reconnaissance and preparation, as the conduct of all my military operations fully bears out, including this one.' (ibid.)
13. Bean, Diary, 21 July 1916, *Diaries & Notebooks*, AWM38 3DRL 606/52/1, July 1916, p. 36 (p. 40 of pdf), www.awm.gov.au/collection/RCDIG1066752.
14. Ibid., p. 38 (p. 41 of pdf).
15. Hartnett, p. 64.
16. Archie Barwick, Diary, 21 July 1916, MLMSS 1493, Box 1, Item 3, p. 272, http://acms.sl.nsw.gov.au.
17. Ibid., pp. 272–3.
18. Goldy Raws to sister Helen, Letter, 22 July 1916, AWM 2DRL/0481, p. 84, www.awm.gov.au/collection/RCDIG0001092.
19. Goldy Raws to sister Gwen, Letter, 20 July 1916, AWM 2DRL/0481, p. 83, www.awm.gov.au/collection/RCDIG0001092. In the letter, the word where 'bastards' is has been blacked out. It is my assumption that 'bastards' is the word.
20. Alec Raws to mother, Letter, 18 July 1916, AWM 2DRL/0481, p. 130, www.awm.gov.au/collection/RCDIG0001092.
21. Ibid., p. 131.
22. Alec Raws to Hon. W. A. Watt, M.P., Letter, 25 July 1916, AWM 2DRL/0481, p. 2 (p. 139 of pdf), www.awm.gov.au/collection/RCDIG0001092 (reported speech changed to direct speech).
23. Haig, Douglas, *War Diaries & Letters*, p. 208.
24. Sheldon, p. 205.
25. Ibid.
26. Bean, *Official History of Australia in the War of 1914–1918*, Vol. III, p. 473.

27. Hartnett, p. 56.
28. Arthur Thomas, Diary, 21 July 1916, p. 4, www.awm.gov.au/collection/RCDIG0001096.
29. Archie Barwick, Diary, 22 July 1916, MLMSS 1493, Box 1, Item 3, p. 276, http://acms.sl.nsw.gov.au.
30. Archie Barwick, Diary, July 1916, MLMSS 1493, Box 1, Item 3, p. 266, http://acms.sl.nsw.gov.au.
31. Hartnett, p. 56.
32. Bean, *Official History of Australia in the War of 1914–1918*, Vol. III, p. 494.
33. Bean, *Official History of Australia in the War of 1914–1918*, Vol. III, p. 522.
34. McCarthy, p. 191.
35. Ibid., p. 235.
36. Sheldon, p. 203.
37. Hartnett, p. 57.
38. Harold Preston, 'John Leak's V.C.', *Reveille*, 1 August 1935, p. 30.
39. Ibid. (reported speech changed to direct speech).
40. Ibid.
41. Bean, *Official History of Australia in the War of 1914–1918*, Vol. III, p. 496.
42. Ben Champion, Diary, 23 July 1916, AWM 2DRL/0512, p. 90, www.awm.gov.au/collection/RCDIG0000977.
43. Ibid.
44. Bean, *Official History of Australia in the War of 1914–1918*, Vol. III, p. 495.
45. Barwick, *Condensed Diary*, MLMSS 7229, p. 58.
46. Ibid.
47. Ben Champion, Diary, 23 July 1916, AWM 2DRL/0512, pp. 90–1, www.awm.gov.au/collection/RCDIG0000977.
48. Sheldon, p. 201.
49. Ibid.
50. Ibid.
51. Hartnett, p. 57.
52. Barwick, *Condensed Diary*, MLMSS 7229, p. 58.
53. Ben Champion, Diary, 23 July 1916, AWM 2DRL/0512, p. 91, www.awm.gov.au/collection/RCDIG0000977.
54. Barwick, *Condensed Diary*, MLMSS 7229, p. 58.
55. Moss, p. 176.
56. Carlyon, p. 149.
57. Hartnett, p. 57.

58. Raws, *Hail and Farewell*, Letter from Alec to mother, 9 August 1916, p. 151.
59. Ben Champion, Diary, 23 July 1916, AWM 2DRL/0512, p. 91, www.awm.gov.au/collection/RCDIG0000977.
60. Harold Preston, 'John Leak's V.C.', *Reveille*, 1 August 1935, p. 31 (tenses changed).
61. Ibid.
62. Percy Smythe, Diary, 23 July 1916, in Betty Smythe (ed.), 'The World War I Diary of Percy Smythe', www.smythe.id.au/diary.
63. Ibid.
64. Ibid.
65. King, p. 158.
66. Ibid., p. 159.
67. Sheldon, p. 215 (English words); Guhr, p. 116 (original German words).
68. *Supplement to the London Gazette*, 9 September 1916, His Majesty's Stationery Office, p. 8871, www.thegazette.co.uk.
69. Ibid.
70. Archie Barwick, Diary, 23 July 1916, MLMSS 1493, Box 1, Item 6, pp. 134–6, http://acms.sl.nsw.gov.au.
71. Sheldon, pp. 215–16.
72. Archie Barwick, Diary, 23 July 1916, MLMSS 1493, Box 1, Item 3, p. 279, http://acms.sl.nsw.gov.au.
73. Ibid.
74. Ibid.
75. Empey, *Over the Top*, p. 29.
76. Bean, *Official History of Australia in the War of 1914–1918*, Vol. III, p. 519.
77. Percy Smythe, Diary, 23 July 1916, in Betty Smythe (ed.), 'The World War I Diary of Percy Smythe', www.smythe.id.au/diary.
78. Ibid.
79. Ibid.
80. Barwick, *Condensed Diary*, MLMSS 7229, p. 58.
81. Ibid.
82. Ibid.
83. Bean, *Official History of Australia in the War of 1914–1918*, Vol. III, p. 535.
84. Ibid., p. 536.
85. Ibid., p. 535 (tense changed).
86. Ibid., p. 546 (tense changed).
87. Harry Preston, Notebook, undated, AWM 2DRL/0811, p. 60.

88. Ibid., p. 59.
89. *The Sydney Morning Herald*, 'Captain Blackburn, V.C.', 29 September 1916, http://trove.nla.gov.au.
90. Archie Barwick, Diary, 23 July 1916, MLMSS 1493, Box 1, Item 3, p. 279, http://acms.sl.nsw.gov.au.
91. Percy Smythe to parents, Letter, published in *The Jerilderie Herald and Urana Advertiser*, 1st part, 30 March 1917, p. 3, http://trove.nla.gov.au.
92. Ibid.

CHAPTER SIXTEEN: DIGGERS CAN'T BE CHOOSERS

1. Bean, *Official History of Australia in the War of 1914–1918*, Vol. III, p. 660.
2. Carlyon, p. 149.
3. Frank Shoobridge, Diary, 23 July 1916, AWM PR00626.
4. Ibid.
5. Archie Barwick, Diary, 23 July 1916 cont., MLMSS 1493, Box 1, Item 4, pp. 6–7, http://acms.sl.nsw.gov.au.
6. Douglas Haig to Lady Haig, Letter, 23 July 1916, in Haig, Douglas, *War Diaries & Letters*, p. 209.
7. Sheldon, p. 179.
8. Percy Smythe to parents, Letter, published in *The Jerilderie Herald and Urana Advertiser*, 1st part, 30 March 1917, p. 3, http://trove.nla.gov.au.
9. Bean, *Official History of Australia in the War of 1914–1918*, Vol. III, p. 531 (tenses changed).
10. Ibid., p. 534.
11. Newton, p. 101.
12. Pedersen, *The Anzacs*, p. 170.
13. Bean, *Official History of Australia in the War of 1914–1918*, Vol. III, p. 537.
14. Ibid.
15. Percy Smythe, Diary, 23 July 1916, in Betty Smythe (ed.), 'The World War I Diary of Percy Smythe', www.smythe.id.au/diary.
16. Bean, *Official History of Australia in the War of 1914–1918*, Vol. III, p. 541.
17. Fair, pp. 33–4.
18. Ben Champion, Diary, 23 July 1916, AWM 2DRL/0512, p. 92, www.awm.gov.au/collection/RCDIG0000977.

19. I base this on the article in *The Anzac Bulletin*, 21 August 1916: 'On Saturday afternoon our heavy shells were tearing at regular intervals into the rear of the brickheaps and flinging up branches of trees and great clouds of black earth from the woods. A letter was found next day dated "In Hell's Trenches" . . .' Charles Bean has a different version in his *Official History*, suggesting that the German soldier was captured with the letter still in his pocket, in which case odds are he saw Luise and the children once again, after the war – but I have gone with the more contemporary, and in my view the more likely, account.

20. The unknown author of this letter was in Pozières Trench, on the east side of the village. For several days, he endured the bombardment, writing the letter it seems only hours before the Australian infantry attacked.

21. Bean, *Official History of Australia in the War of 1914–1918*, Vol. III, p. 522.

22. George McKenzie to Stephen Margetts, Letter, 22 September 1916, AWM 1DRL/0478, p. 2 (reported speech changed to direct speech).

23. Ibid.

24. Ibid.

25. 'Captain Ivor Stephen Margetts, 12th Battalion', AWM 1DRL/0428, Box 170, Wallet 12, p. 2, https://static.awm.gov.au/images/collection/pdf/RCDIG1053324--1-.pdf.

26. Barwick, *Condensed Diary*, MLMSS 7229, p. 58.

27. Bean, *Official History of Australia in the War of 1914–1918*, Vol. III, p. 542.

28. Ibid.

29. Bennett, p. 70.

30. Archie Barwick, Diary, 24 July 1916, MLMSS 1493, Box 1, Item 4, p. 10, http://acms.sl.nsw.gov.au.

31. Wellmann, p. 119 (translated).

32. Ibid., p. 118 (translated).

33. Ibid., p. 119 (translated).

34. Archie Barwick, Diary, 24 July 1916, MLMSS 1493, Box 1, Item 4, pp. 11–12, http://acms.sl.nsw.gov.au.

35. Ibid.

36. Ibid., pp. 10–11.

37. A Pozières veteran's story, told to Dr Peter Williams in the 1970s.

38. Carlyon, p. 157.

39. Ben Champion, Diary, 23 July 1916, AWM 2DRL/0512, p. 92, www.awm.gov.au/collection/RCDIG0000977.

40. Bennett, p. 188.
41. Auckland War Memorial Museum, Online Cenotaph, 'Thomas Cooke', www.aucklandmuseum.com/war-memorial/online-cenotaph.
42. Bean, *Official History of Australia in the War of 1914–1918*, Vol. III, p. 552.
43. Frank Brent, BBC4 Collections, The Great War Interviews, Part 1, www.youtube.com.
44. Archie Barwick, Diary, 24 July 1916, MLMSS 1493, Box 1, Item 4, pp. 12–13, http://acms.sl.nsw.gov.au.
45. Bean, *Official History of Australia in the War of 1914–1918*, Vol. III, p. 553.
46. Newton, p. 102.
47. Percy Smythe to parents, Letter, published in *The Jerilderie Herald and Urana Advertiser*, 1st part, 30 March 1917, p. 3, http://trove.nla.gov.au.
48. Carrington, p. 116.
49. 1st Division War Diary, 25 July 1916, AWM4 1/43/18, July 1916, p. 16.
50. Wellmann, p. 123 (translated).
51. Ibid. (translated).
52. Ibid. (translated).
53. Ibid. (translated).
54. Hartnett, p. 69.
55. Archie Barwick, Diary, 24 July 1916, MLMSS 1493, Box 1, Item 4, pp. 15–16, http://acms.sl.nsw.gov.au. In fact, there were no Prussian Guards present.
56. Hartnett, p. 69.
57. Archie Barwick, Diary, 26 July 1916, MLMSS 1493, Box 1, Item 4, p. 22, http://acms.sl.nsw.gov.au.
58. Archie Barwick, Diary, 26 July 1916, MLMSS 1493, Box 1, Item 4, p. 23, http://acms.sl.nsw.gov.au.
59. Wellmann, p. 124.
60. Duffy, p. 88 (reported speech changed to direct speech).
61. Middlebrook, p. 149.
62. Herodotus, *The Histories*, Book 7:226.
63. Hartnett, p. 68.
64. Klahn, p. 133 (translated).
65. Hartnett, p. 68.
66. Newton, p. 224.
67. Ibid.
68. Bean, *Official History of Australia in the War of 1914–1918*, Vol. III, p. 618.
69. Duffy, p. 189.

70. Lewis, Cecil, pp. 55–60.
71. Arthur Thomas, Diary, 27 July 1916, AWM 3DRL/2206, p. 10, www. awm.gov.au/collection/RCDIG0001096.
72. Ben Champion, Diary, AWM 2DRL/0512, 26 July 1916, pp. 92–3, www.awm.gov.au/collection/RCDIG0000977.
73. Ibid., p. 93.
74. Ibid., p. 94.
75. Knyvett, p. 184.
76. Kidd, p. 299.
77. Adkin, p. 175. Bean claims a little less, ranking it second to Lone Pine: 'There followed a bombing struggle which, with the exception of Lone Pine, was by far the heaviest in the experience of the A.I.F.' (Bean, *Official History of Australia in the War of 1914–1918*, Vol. III, p. 608)
78. 5th Brigade War Diary, AWM4 23/5/13, July 1916, p. 5.
79. Bean, *Official History of Australia in the War of 1914–1918*, Vol. III, p. 611.
80. Edgar Rule, p. 25.
81. Bean, *Official History of Australia in the War of 1914–1918*, Vol. III, p. 592.
82. Edmonds, Charles (Carrington's pseudonym), p. 37.
83. Hartnett, p. 63.
84. Henry Seymour Baker, TAHO NS2661/1/30.
85. Charlton, Peter, p. 172.
86. Bean, *Official History of Australia in the War of 1914–1918*, Vol. III, p. 619.
87. Ibid.
88. Bean, Diary, 4 August 1916, *Diaries & Notebooks*, AWM38 3DRL 606/54/1, p. 118, www.awm.gov.au/collection/RCDIG1066752.
89. Haig, Douglas, *War Diaries & Letters*, p. 210.
90. Ibid.

CHAPTER SEVENTEEN: A TILT AT THE WINDMILL

1. *The Sydney Morning Herald*, 18 August 1916, p. 7.
2. Sheldon, p. 206.
3. Carlyon, p. 180.
4. Walter Boys, Letter, 2 August 1916, AWM 1DRL/0142, p. 1.
5. Bean, *Official History of Australia in the War of 1914–1918*, Vol. III, p. 636.

6. Alec Raws to father, 'The Great Decision', Letter, 12 July 1915, AWM 2DRL/0481, p. 1 (p. 90 of pdf), www.awm.gov.au/collection/RCDIG0001092.

7. Bean, *Official History of Australia in the War of 1914–1918*, Vol. III, p. 640.

8. Ibid.

9. Fred Hocking to father, Letter, 16 August 1916, AWM PR88/161, p. 12.

10. Pedersen, *The Anzacs*, p. 180 (tense changed).

11. Fred Hocking to father, Letter, 16 August 1916, AWM PR88/161, pp. 12–13. Strangely, in the actual letter, Hocking writes 'bleed', not blood. I have amended for ease of reading.

12. Bean, *Official History of Australia in the War of 1914–1918*, Vol. III, pp. 640–1.

13. In fact, the generally accepted distance is 400 yards.

14. Haig, Douglas, *War Diaries & Letters*, pp. 210–11.

15. French and Reid, p. 103.

16. Ibid.

17. Pedersen, *The Anzacs*, p. 180.

18. Haig, Douglas, *War Diaries & Letters*, p. 211.

19. Bean, *Diaries & Notebooks*, AWM38 3DRL 606/244/1, p. 226 of pdf, www.awm.gov.au/collection/RCDIG1066752.

20. Brudenell White to Charles Bean, Letter, 1 May 1928, in Bean, *Diaries & Notebooks*, AWM38 3DRL 606/244/1, pp. 1–2 (pp. 186–7).

21. Haig, Douglas, *War Diaries & Letters*, p. 211.

22. Brudenell White to Charles Bean, Letter, 1 May 1928, in Bean, *Diaries & Notebooks*, AWM38 3DRL 606/244/1, p. 2 (pp. 186–7), www.awm.gov.au/collection/RCDIG1066752.

23. Haig, Douglas, *War Diaries & Letters*, pp. 210–1.

24. Ibid., p. 211 (reported speech changed to direct speech).

25. Edmonds, Sir James, *Military Operations in France and Belgium 1916* (Maps and Appendices), p. 34 (Appendix 13: O.A.D. 91, 2 August 1916).

26. Bean, *Diaries & Notebooks*, AWM38 3DRL 606/244/1, p. 226, www.awm.gov.au/collection/RCDIG1066752.

27. Haig, Douglas, *War Diaries & Letters*, pp. 210–1.

28. Bean, *Diaries & Notebooks*, AWM38 3DRL 606/244/1, p. 226, www.awm.gov.au/collection/RCDIG1066752.

29. Ibid.

30. Brudenell White to Charles Bean, Letter, 1 May 1928, in Bean, *Diaries & Notebooks*, AWM38 3DRL 606/244/1, p. 3, (p. 188 of pdf), www.awm.gov.au/collection/RCDIG1066752 (reported speech changed to direct speech).

31. Haig, Douglas, *War Diaries & Letters*, p. 225.

32. Ibid.

33. Bean, *Official History of Australia in the War of 1914–1918*, Vol. I, p. 74.

34. Ibid., Vol. III, p. 644.

35. Haig, Douglas, *War Diaries & Letters*, p. 211 (reported speech changed to direct speech).

36. Ibid. (tense changed).

37. Boys, Walter, Letter, 2 August 1916, AWM 1DRL/0142, p. 1.

38. Carlyon, p 180.

39. Bean, *Official History of Australia in the War of 1914–1918*, Vol. III, p. 807.

40. Alec Raws to sister, Letter, 8 August 1916, in Raws, *Hail and Farewell*, pp. 147–8.

41. Ibid.

42. Ibid.

43. Ibid. (reported speech changed to direct speech).

44. Ibid.

45. Bean, *Official History of Australia in the War of 1914–1918*, Vol. III, p. 644.

46. Churchill, *The World in Crisis*, Vol. 3, p. 34.

47. Haig, Douglas, *War Diaries & Letters*, p. 213.

48. Douglas Haig, Final Dispatch, *Fourth Supplement to the London Gazette*, 10 April 1919, p. 4699, www.thegazette.co.uk/London/issue/31283/supplement/1.

49. Haig, Douglas, *War Diaries & Letters*, pp. 213–4.

50. *The Border Morning Mail and Riverina Times*, 7 May 1915, p. 2.

51. Haig, Douglas, *War Diaries & Letters*, p. 214.

52. Winston Churchill, 'Criticism of the value of the Allied offensive on the Western Front', NA CAB 37/153/3, p. 4.

53. Bean, Diary, 12/13 August 1916, *Diaries & Notebooks*, AWM38 DRL606/54/1, p. 195, www.awm.gov.au/collection/RCDIG1066752.

54. Bean, *Official History of Australia in the War of 1914–1918*, Vol. III, p. 616.

55. Ibid.

56. Ibid., p. 617.

57. Ibid.

58. Interview with grandson, James Dexter, in Albany, 28 July 1915.

59. Bean, Diary, 1 August 1916, *Diaries & Notebooks*, AWM38 3DRL 606/54/1, p. 48, www.awm.gov.au/collection/RCDIG1066752.

60. Ibid., 31 July 1916, p. 47.

61. Bean, *Official History of Australia in the War of 1914–1918*, Vol. III, p. 664 (reported speech changed to direct speech).

62. Ibid.

63. Ibid., p. 665.

64. Wellmann, p. 137 (translated).

65. Haig, Douglas, *War Diaries & Letters*, p. 215.

66. Percy Cherry diary, courtesy of his great-nephew, Barry Bachelor, and the Bachelor family.

67. Alec Raws to Mr Norman Bayles M.L.C., Letter, 4 August 1916, AWM 2DRL/0481, p. 140 of pdf, www.awm.gov.au/collection/RCDIG0001092.

68. Alec Raws, Letter from a comrade, in Raws, *Hail and Farewell*, p. 159.

69. Raws, *Hail and Farewell*, p. 144.

70. Alec Raws to sister, Letter, 8 August 1916, in Raws, *Hail and Farewell*, p. 146.

71. Alec Raws to Leonard Raws (brother), Letter, 19 August 1916, AWM 2DRL/0481, p. 1 (p. 160 of pdf), www.awm.gov.au/collection/RCDIG0001092.

72. Ibid., 12 August 1916, p. 1 (p. 143 of pdf).

73. Alec Raws to mother, Letter, 9 August 1916, in Raws, *Hail and Farewell*, p. 150.

74. Alec Raws, Letter from a comrade, in Raws, *Hail and Farewell*, p. 158.

75. Bean, *Official History of Australia in the War of 1914–1918*, Vol. III, p. 685.

CHAPTER EIGHTEEN: DÉJÀ VU, ALL OVER AGAIN

1. Charles Bean, 'Fight for Pozières Ridge', *The West Australian*, 10 August 1916, p. 7, http://trove.nla.gov.au.

2. Maxwell, p. 67.

3. Rule, Edgar, p. 26.

4. Barwick, *Condensed Diary*, MLMSS 7229, p. 57.

5. Clifford Sharman, Memoir, AWM PR01239, pp. 41–2.

6. Bean, *Official History of Australia in the War of 1914–1918*, Vol. III, p. 693.

7. Letter from J. Beggs to Red Cross Society, 15 July 1917, Australian Red Cross Society Wounded and Missing Enquiry Bureau Files, AWM 1DRL/0428, p. 10.

8. Clifford Sharman, Memoir, AWM PR01239, p. 42.

9. Ibid.

10. Percy Cherry diary, courtesy of his great-nephew, Barry Bachelor, and the Bachelor family.

11. Bean, *Official History of Australia in the War of 1914–1918*, Vol. III, p. 649.

12. Percy Cherry diary, courtesy of his great-nephew, Barry Bachelor, and the Bachelor family.

13. Clifford Sharman, Memoir, AWM PR01239, p. 46.

14. Charlton, Peter, p. 203.

15. Ibid.

16. Wellmann, p. 141 (translated).

17. Ibid. (translated).

18. Ibid., p. 143 (translated).

19. *The Times*, 18 August 1916. *Pour l'anecdote*, this article is held by Barry Bachelor, of the Percy Cherry family, and across the top of it, in Cherry's handwriting, it reads, 'This is where I fought until wounded.'

20. Bean, *Official History of Australia in the War of 1914–1918*, Vol. III, p. 713.

21. Ibid.

22. Ibid.

23. Wellmann, p. 144.

24. Ibid., p. 143 (translated).

25. Ibid., p. 142 (translated).

26. Ibid., p. 145 (translated).

27. Bean, *Official History of Australia in the War of 1914–1918*, Vol. III, p. 699. In his footnote on p. 699, Charles Bean refers to Hill 60 (Pozières Heights). He says, 'This is almost certainly a mistake in the English translation for "Hill 160" or "161", the name by which the Germans knew the Pozières heights.' The discrepancy is most likely explained by the Germans using two sets of maps, depending on two different measurements for how many metres above sea level it is.

28. Wellmann, p. 146 (translated).

29. Edmonds, Sir James, *Military Operations in France and Belgium 1916*, p. 152.

30. Wellmann, p. 143 (translated).

31. Ibid., p. 144 (translated).

32. Headquarters 2nd Australian Division Artillery, War Dairy, 6 August 1916, AWM4 13/11/6, p. 7, www.awm.gov.au/collection/ RCDIG1014127.

33. Bean, Diary, 4 August 1916, *Diaries & Notebooks*, AWM38 3DRL 606/54/1, pp. 109–10, www.awm.gov.au/collection/RCDIG1066752.

34. 'Captain Cecil Maitland Foss, 28th Battalion', Australian Red Cross Society Wounded and Missing Enquiry Bureau Files, 1914–1918 War, AWM 1DRL/0428, pp. 2 and 9, http://static.awm.gov.au/images/ collection/pdf/RCDIG1062524--1-.pdf.

35. Haig, Douglas, *War Diaries & Letters*, p. 215.

36. Rule, Edgar, p. 26.

37. Ibid.

38. Ibid.

39. Ibid.

40. Ibid., p. 27.

41. Ibid.

42. Ibid.

43. Hogue, p. 258.

44. Rule, Edgar, p. 28.

45. Ibid., p. 28.

46. Ibid., p. 28.

47. Bean, *Official History of Australia in the War of 1914–1918*, Vol. I, p. 558.

48. Keech, p. 52.

49. 48th Battalion War Diary, 8 August 1916, AWM4 23/65, p. 3 of pdf, www.awm.gov.au/collection/RCDIG1006245.

50. Ibid.

51. Wanliss, p. 138.

52. Ibid., p. 135.

53. Ibid., p. 138.

54. Sheldon, p. 231.

55. Bean, *Official History of Australia in the War of 1914–1918*, Vol. III, p. 715.

56. Sheldon, p. 231.

57. Ibid.

58. Rule, Edgar, p. 29.

59. Sheldon, p. 231.

60. Ibid.

61. Wanliss, p. 138.

62. Sheldon, p. 231.

63. Ibid., p. 232.
64. Ibid., p. 234.
65. Lawriwsky, *Hard Jacka*, p. 195.
66. Wanliss, p. 139.
67. Ibid.
68. Rule, Edgar, p. 30.
69. Ibid., p. 29.
70. Ibid.
71. Ibid.
72. Ibid.
73. Grant, Ian, p. 85.
74. Bean, *Official History of Australia in the War of 1914–1918*, Vol. III, p. 720.
75. Wanliss, p. 141.
76. Wellmann, p. 147.
77. Benjamin Leane, Diary, 8 August 1916, AWM 1DRL/0412, www.awm.gov.au/collection/RCDIG0001007.
78. P. Burness, 'Pozières Hell', *Wartime Magazine*, Issue 22, 2003, p. 16.
79. Bean, Diary, 12/13 August 1916, *Diaries & Notebooks*, AWM38 3DRL 606/54/1, p. 197, www.awm.gov.au/collection/RCDIG1066752.
80. Ibid., 20 August 1916, AWM38 3DRL 606/55/1, pp. 83–4.
81. Stretcher-bearer Septimus Elmore, 6th Field Ambulance, Diary No. 5, , 10 August 1916, AWM MSS 1825, page 7 of typed copy, page 37.
82. Ibid.
83. Ibid., page 7 of typed copy, page 38.
84. Ibid.
85. Rule, Edgar, p. 35.

EPILOGUE

1. Saunders, p. 99.
2. Corfield, *Don't Forget Me, Cobber*, p. 420.
3. BBC4 Collections, The Great War Interviews, Part 1, www.youtube.com.
4. Alec Raws, Letter from a Comrade, in Raws, *Hail and Farewell*, p. 159.
5. Raws, *Hail and Farewell*, p. 144.
6. Bean, *Official History of Australia in the War of 1914–1918*, Vol. III, p. 890.
7. Pedersen, *The Anzacs*, p. 201.

8. Bean, *Official History of Australia in the War of 1914–1918*, Vol. III, pp. 871–2.

9. Pedersen, *The Anzacs*, p. 204.

10. Monash, *The Australian Victories in France*, http://gutenberg.net.au.

11. Bean, *Official History of Australia in the War of 1914–1918*, Vol. III, p. 395.

12. Hitler, *Mein Kampf*, p. 206 (English ed.).

13. *Inside History*, Issue 20, January–February 2014, p. 32.

14. Ibid.

15. Bean, *Official History of Australia in the War of 1914–1918*, Vol. III, p. 661.

16. Coulthart, p. 209.

17. Bean, *Official History of Australia in the War of 1914–1918*, Vol. III, p. 657.

18. Charlton, Peter, p. 115.

19. Coulthart, p. 219.

20. Fromelles is at least now recognised on the newer Australian Memorial in Hyde Park, London.

21. Ross McMullin, 'Fromelles: A Calamity for Australian Arms', *The Canberra Times*, 19 July 1986, p. 6, http://trove.nla.gov.au.

22. *The Sydney Morning Herald*, 20 July 1966, p. 4.

23. Mearsheimer, p. 60.

24. Bartlett and Hulton, p. 16.

25. In April 1918, Haig recommended Haking for command of all British forces in Italy – again knocked back.

26. Bristow, p. 177.

27. Landon to Brigadier-General Sir J. E. Edmonds, British Official War Historian, Letter, 2 April 1937, Official War Histories Correspondence & Papers, Loos, 1915–1928, CAB 45/135, pp. 2–4.

28. Foley, p. 257.

29. Sheldon, p. 263.

30. Hindenburg, p. 99.

31. Blucher, pp. 153–4.

32. Bean, Diary, 24 September 1916, *Diaries & Notebooks*, AWM38 3DRL 606/60/1, p. 2, www.awm.gov.au/collection/RCDIG1066752.

33. Bean, *Two Men I Knew*, p. xi.

34. Pedersen, *Fromelles*, p. 113.

35. Ibid.

36. Despite the heavy criticism of McCay over the years – including certainly by this writer – it is worth noting that Charles Bean emerged as a key defender. 'The blame for our losses was in Australia

and amongst the soldiers thrown exclusively, but quite unjustly, upon General McCay,' he noted, 'for which he was, in fact, no more responsible than the humblest private in his force.' (*The Duckboard*, 1 September 1930, p. 14)

37. Bean, *Official History of Australia in the War of 1914–1918*, Vol. IV, p. 832.

38. David Doyle to John Black, Letter, 6 July 1937, in Bean, *Diaries & Notebooks*, AWM38 3DRL 606/276/1, p. 144, www.awm.gov.au/collection/RCDIG1066752.

39. McMullin, *Pompey Elliott*, p. 253.

40. Harold Elliott to Emily (Milly) Edwards, Letter, 23 July 1916, Elliott Papers, AWM 2DRL/0513, 3/15, p. 3.

41. Pompey Elliott, 'The Battle of Fleurbaix or Fromelles', *The Duckboard*, Vol. 5, No. 9, 1 September 1930, p. 9.

42. Ibid., p. 12.

43. Ibid., p. 15.

44. McMullin, *Farewell Dear People*, p. 171.

45. Ross McMullin, 'Pompey Elliott: Our Most Revered Fighting General?', *The Sydney Morning Herald*, 22 April 2011, www.smh.com.au.

46. Walter Cass to Helena Holmes, Letter, 18 October 1916, SLV, MS15488, Series 1, Box 1, Folder 1A, p. 2.

47. L. D. Matthews, 'Cass, Walter Edmund Hutchinson (1876–1931)', Australian Dictionary of Biography, 1979, http://adb.anu.edu.au.

48. *The Queensland Times*, 8 September 1916, p. 3 (*The Australasian* quoted therein).

49. Rule, Edgar, p. 48.

50. Ibid.

51. Ibid., p. 49.

52. Newton Wanliss, 'A.I.F. Celebrities (9): Captain Jacka V.C., M.C. & Bar.' *Reveille*, 30 April 1931, pp. 7–8.

53. Stone, p. 32.

54. Charlton, Peter, p. 209.

55. Ibid.

56. *The Herald* (Melbourne), 5 May 1937, p. 8.

57. Marie Low, 'A Family Shattered', *Namoi Valley Independent*, 8 September 2015, www.nvi.com.au.

58. P. Burness, 'Pozières Hell', *Wartime Magazine*, Issue 22, 2003, p. 19.

59. Kate Morchel, 'Faces of War', *Wartime Magazine*, Issue 69, Summer 2015, p. 17.

60. Corfield, *Don't Forget Me, Cobber*, p. 142.

61. Bean, 'The Leadership of Norman Begins', *The Link*, 1 September 1926, p. 6.

62. Bert Bishop, Honours and Awards, AWM, http://static.awm.gov.au/images/collection/pdf/RCDIG1068559--39-.pdf.
63. Interview with their daughter, Pamela Goesch, 10 August 2015.
64. Annie Bosisto to the Red Cross, Letter, 6 March 1917, in 'Private Russell George Bosisto', Australian Red Cross Society Wounded and Missing Enquiry Bureau Files, AWM 1DRL/0428, p.10.
65. Ibid.
66. McMullin, *Farewell Dear People*, p. 164.
67. 'Bowden, John Charles', Discovering Anzacs, NAA Record Search, http://discoveringanzacs.naa.gov.au.
68. *The Argus*, 19 July 1918, p. 1, http://trove.nla.gov.au.
69. 'John Charles Bowden', First World War Red Cross Wounded and Missing Files, AWM 1DRL/0428, p. 35. www.awm.gov.au/people/rolls/R1482995.
70. Address by the Minister for Veterans' Affairs The Honourable Bruce Scott MP at the Funeral of Private Russell Bosisto, Courcelette Commonwealth Cemetery, France, 5 July 1998, Parliament of Australia, http://parlinfo.aph.gov.au.
71. Corfield, *Don't Forget Me, Cobber*, p. 436.
72. Bill Barry, Memoir, AWM PR00814, p. 41.
73. Corfield, *Don't Forget Me, Cobber*, p. 433.
74. Ibid., p. 441.
75. Ibid., pp. 433–5.
76. Leigh Dayton, 'Fromelles Soldiers Are Laid to Rest', *The Australian*, 24 February 2010, www.theaustralian.com.au.
77. 'Speech by the Prime Minister, the Hon. Paul J. Keating, MP, Funeral Service of the Unknown Australian Soldier, 11 November 1993', Parliament of Australia, http://parlinfo.aph.gov.au.

BIBLIOGRAPHY

Initials used:
AWM   Australian War Memorial, Canberra
IWM   Imperial War Museum, London
ML   Mitchell Library, Sydney
NAA   National Archives of Australia, Canberra
NLA   National Library of Australia, Canberra
SLNSW State Library of New South Wales, Sydney
SLV   State Library of Victoria, Melbourne
TNA   The National Archives, Kew, England
WO   War Office records held at The National Archives, Kew, England

BOOKS

Adkin, Mark, *The Western Front Companion*, Stackpole, Mechanicsburg, 2013

Afflerbach, Holger, *Falkenhayn. Politisches Denken und Handeln im Kaiserreich*, Oldenbourg, Munich, 1996

Arthur, Max, *Forgotten Voices of the Great War*, Ebury Press, London, 2002
——*When the Bloody War is Over: Soldiers' Songs from the First World War*, Piatkus, London, 2001

Austin, Ronald James, *As Rough as Bags: The History of the 6th Battalion, 1st AIF, 1914–1919*, R. J. & S. P. Austin, Melbourne, 1992

Baker-Carr, Christopher D'Arcy, *From Chauffeur to Brigadier*, Ernest Benn, London, 1930

Barbusse, Henri, *Under Fire,* Digireads, 2010

Bardon, Jonathon, *A History of Ireland in 250 Episodes: A Sweeping Single Narrative of Irish History from the End of the Ice Age to the Peace Settlement in Northern Ireland*, Gill and Macmillan, Dublin, 2009

Barnes, A. F., *The Story of the 2/5th Battalion Gloucestershire Regiment*, Crypt House Press, 1930, facsimile by Naval & Military Press, 2015

Barrie, Alexander, *War Underground*, Tom Donovan, London, 1961

Bartlett, Vernon and Hulton, Edward George Warris, *World Review*, Chatto & Windus, London, 1940

Barton, Peter, *The Lost Legions of Fromelles: The True Story of the Most Dramatic Battle in Australia's History*, Allen & Unwin, Sydney, 2014

Bavarian War Archive, *Bayerisches Kriegsarchiv, Die Bayern im Großen Kriege, 1914–1918*, self-published, Munich, 1923

Bean, Charles E. W., *Anzac to Amiens: A Shorter History of the Australian Fighting Service in the First World War*, AWM, Canberra, 1946

——*Letters from France*, Cassell, London, 1917

——*Official History of Australia in the War of 1914–1918*, Vol. I, The Story of Anzac: The First Phase, 11th Edition, Angus & Robertson, Sydney, 1941

——*Official History of Australia in the War of 1914–1918*, Vol. III – The Australian Imperial Force in France: 1916, 12th Edition, Angus and Robertson, Sydney, 1941

——*Official History of Australia in the War of 1914–1918*, Vol. IV – The Australian Imperial Force in France: 1917, 11th Edition, Angus and Robertson, Sydney, 1941

——*Official History of Australia in the War of 1914–1918*, Vol. V – The Australian Imperial Force in France: December 1917–May 1918, 8th Edition, Sydney, 1941

——*Two Men I Knew: William Bridges and Brudenell White*, Angus and Robertson, Sydney, 1957

Belford, Walter C., *'Legs-Eleven': Being the Story of the 11th Battalion (AIF) in the Great War of 1914–1918*, Imperial Printing, Perth, 1940

Bennett, Scott, *Pozières: The Anzac Story*, Scribe, Melbourne, 2013

Birdwood, William, *Khaki and Gown*, Ward, Lock, London, 1941

Bishop, Walter Herbert (Bert), *Dear All: Letters from World War I*, Pamela Goesch (ed.), Brynwood House, Sydney, 2010

——*The Hell, the Humour and the Heartbreak – A Private's View of World War I*, Kangaroo Press, Sydney, 1991

Blücher, Evelyn, *An English Wife in Berlin: A Private Memoir of Events, Politics, and Daily Life in Germany throughout the War and the Social Revolution of 1918*, Constable, London, 1921

Blunden, Edmund, *Undertones of War*, Penguin, London, 1936

Bond, Douglas, *Mr Pipes and the British Hymn Makers*, Christian Liberty Press, United Kingdom, 2007

Bond, John, *The Army that Went with the Boys*, Salvation Army, Melbourne, 1919

Braithwaite, William Stanley, *The Story of the Great War*, Forgotten Books, London, 2013

Braun, Julius Ritter von, *Das K. B. Reserve-Infanterie-Regiment Nr. 21: Nach den amtlichen Kriegstagebüchern bearbeitet* (*The Royal Bavarian Reserve Infantry Regiment No. 21: Edited based on the Official War Diaries*), Bavarian War Archive, Munich, 1923

Bristow, Adrian, *A Serious Disappointment: The Battle of Aubers Ridge 1915 and the Munitions Scandal*, Leo Cooper, London, 1995

Browning, Neville, *The Blue and White Diamond: The History of the 28th Battalion 1915–1919*, Advance Press, Perth, 2002

Buchan, John, *The Battle of the Somme: First Phase*, Thomas Nelson & Sons, New York, 1916

Burness, Peter, *Fromelles and the Somme: Australians on the Western Front – 1916*, Department of Veterans' Affairs, Canberra, 2006

Butler, A., *Official History of the Australian Army Medical Services 1914–1918*, Vol. III, Problems and Services, Halstead Press, Sydney, 1943

Carlyon, Les, *The Great War*, Macmillan, Sydney, 2006

Carrington, Charles, *Soldier from the Wars Returning*, Arrow Books, London, 1970

Caulfield, Michael, *The Unknown Anzacs: The Real Stories of Our National Legend*, Hachette, Sydney, 2013

Cervantes Saavedra, Miguel de, *The History of the Ingenious Gentleman Don Quixote of La Mancha*, Vol. 2, printed for Hurst, Robinson and Company, Edinburgh, London, 1822

Charlton, James (ed.), *The Military Quotation Book*, Thomas Dunn Books, New York, 2013

Charlton, Peter, *Pozières 1916*, Methuen Haynes, Sydney, 1986

Charteris, John, *At G.H.Q.*, Cassell, London, 1931

Churchill, Winston, *The World Crisis: Verdun, Jutland, the Somme, and U.S. intervention*, Charles Scribner's Sons, 1931

Clapham, Marcus (ed.), *The Wordsworth Book of First World War Poetry*, Wordsworth Editions, Ware, Hertfordshire, 1995

Cobb, Paul, *Fromelles 1916*, Tempus, Stroud (Gloucestershire), 2007

Congreve, Billy, *Armageddon Road: The Diaries of Billy Congreve*, William Kimber, London, 1982

Cook, Timothy J., *Snowy to the Somme: A Muddy and Bloody Campaign, 1916–1918*, Big Sky Publishing, Sydney, 2014

Cooper, Leo, *Sniping in France*, 1994

Corfield, Robin S., *Don't Forget Me, Cobber: The Battle of Fromelles*, Melbourne University Publishing, Melbourne, 2009

————*Hold Hard, Cobbers: The Story of the 57th and 60th and 57/60th Australian Infantry Battalions 1912–1990*, Vol. I: 1912–1930, 57/60th Battalion (AIF) Association, Melbourne, 1992

Coulthart, Ross, *Charles Bean*, HarperCollins, Sydney, 2014

——*Charles Bean, If People Really Knew*, Victoria Bolinda Audio, Melbourne, 2014

Craig, William, *My Adventures on the Australian Goldfields*, Cassell, London, 1903

Crozier, Frank P., *A Brass Hat in No Man's Land*, Jonathan Cape, London, 1930

Davis, Wade, *Into the Silence: The Great War, Mallory and the Conquest of Everest*, Vintage, 2012

Dawnay, G. P. and Headlam, Cuthbert (eds), Vol. III (October 1921 and January 1922), William Clowes & Sons, London

De Gaulle, Charles, *The Complete War Memoirs of Charles de Gaulle*, Simon & Schuster, New York, 1964

De la Gorce, Paul Marie, *The French Army: A Military-Political History*, Weidenfeld & Nicolson, London, 1963

Denny, Captain W. J., *The Diggers*, Hodder and Stoughton, London, 1919

Derham, Rosemary, *The Silence Ruse: Escape from Gallipoli – A Record and Memory of the Life of General Sir Brudenell White KCB KCMG KCVO DSO*, Oryx Publishing, Melbourne, 1998

Domelier, Henri, *Behind the Scenes at German Headquarters*, Hurst and Blackett, London, 1980

Downing, Walter Hubert, *Digger Dialects: A Collection of Slang Phrases Used by the Australian Soldiers on Active Service*, Lothian Book Publishing Company, Melbourne, 1919

——*To the Last Ridge*, H. H. Champion, Australasian Authors' Agency, Melbourne, 1920

Duffy, Christopher, *Through German Eyes: The British and the Somme 1916*, Phoenix, London, 2007

Dunn, James Churchill, *The War the Infantry Knew, 1914–1919: A Chronicle of Service in France and Belgium*, Abacus, London, 1988

Edmonds, Charles, *A Subaltern's War*, Anthony Mott, London, 1984

Edmonds, Sir James Edwards, *Military Operations in France and Belgium 1914*, Macmillan, London, 1926

——*Military Operations in France and Belgium 1916*, Imperial War Museum, London, 1932

——*Military Operations in France and Belgium 1916* (Maps and Appendices), Macmillan, London, 1938

Ellis, Alex D., *The Story of the Fifth Australian Division: Being an Authoritative Account of the Division's Doings in Egypt, France and Belgium*, Hodder and Stoughton, London, 1920

Empey, Arthur Guy, *From the Fire Step: The Experiences of an American Soldier in the British Army*, G. P. Putnam's Sons, London, 1917

——('An American Soldier Who Went'), *Over the Top*, G. P. Putnam's Sons, New York, 1918

Eyre, Giles E. M., *Somme Harvest*, Jarrolds, London, 1938, reprinted London Stamp Exchange, London, 1991

Fair, Roger, *A Treasury of Anzac Humour*, Jacaranda, Brisbane, 1964

Falkenhayn, Erich von, *Die Oberste Heeresleitung, 1914–1916, in ihren wichtigsten Entschließungen*, Mittler & Sohn, Berlin, 1920

——*The German General Staff and its Critical Decisions, 1914–1916*, Dodd, Mead and Company, New York, 1920

Farrar-Hockley, Anthony, *Goughie: The Life of General Sir Hubert Gough*, Granada, London, 1975

——*The Somme*, Pan, London, 1964

Finlayson, Damien, *Crumps and Camouflets: Australian Tunnelling Companies on the Western Front*, Big Sky, Sydney, 2010

Fitzhardinge, L. F., *The Little Digger: William Morris Hughes, A Political Biography, Volume Two*, Angus & Robertson, Sydney, 1979

Foch, Ferdinand, *The Memoirs of Marshal Foch*, T. Bentley Mott (transl.), Doubleday, Doran and Company, Garden City (NY), 1931

Foley, Robert T., *German Strategy and the Path to Verdun: Erich von Falkenhayn and the Development of Attrition, 1870–1916*, Cambridge University Press, Cambridge, 2005

French, David and Reid, Brian Holden, *British General Staff: Reform and Innovation, 1890–1939*, Frank Cass, London, 2005

Gammage, Bill, *The Broken Years*, Penguin, London, 1975

Gardner, Brian, *The Big Push: A Portrait of the Battle of the Somme*, Cassell, London, 1961

Gibbs, Philip, *Now It Can Be Told*, Harper and Brothers, New York, 1920

Gliddon, Gerald, *The Battle of the Somme: A Topographical History*, Sutton Publishing, Stroud, 1996

Grant, Ian, *Jacka, VC: Australia's Finest Fighting Soldier*, Macmillan, Melbourne, 1989

Grant, R. G., *World War I: The Definitive Visual Guide*, Dorling Kindersley, London, 2014

Graves, Robert, *Goodbye to All That*, Penguin, London, 1960

Grayson, Richard S., *Belfast Boys: How Unionists and Nationalists Fought and Died Together in the First World War*, Continuum UK, London, 2009

Great Britain War Office, *Field Service Pocket Book (1914)*, Harrison and
    Sons, London, 1914
Guhr, *Das 4. Schlesische Infanterie Regiment Nr. 157 im Frieden und im
    Kriege 1897–1919, The 4th Silesian IR157 in Peace and at War
    1897–1919*, (Anthology), Bernhard Sporn, Zeulenroda (Germany),
    1934
Haig, Dorothy M. V., *The Man I Knew: The Intimate Life-Story of Douglas
    Haig, Reprint 203 par J. Gielen, Ferme de l'Abbiette, Attin*, Moray
    Press, Edinburgh, 1935
Haig, Douglas, *War Diaries & Letters*, Sheffield, Gary and Bourne, John
    (eds), Weidenfeld & Nicolson, London, 2005
Haking, Richard Cyril Byrne, *Company Training*, Hugh Rees, London, 1913
Hamilton, Ian, *Gallipoli Diary*, Vol. I, Edward Arnold, London, 1920
Hardie, Frank, *The Political Influence of Queen Victoria, 1861–1901*, Frank
    Cass, London, 1963
Hart, Herbert, *The Devil's Own War: The Diary of Herbert Hart*, Exisle,
    Auckland, 2008
Hart, Peter and Steel, Nigel, *The Somme: The Darkest Hour on the Western
    Front*, Pegasus, New York, 2008
Hartnett, Henry ('Harry') George, *Over the Top*, Allen & Unwin, Sydney,
    2009
Hatch, Alden, *The De Gaulle Nobody Knows: An Intimate Biography of
    Charles de Gaulle*, Hawthorn Books, New York, 1960
Hindenburg, Paul von, *The Great War*
Hitler, Adolf, *Mein Kampf*, German edition (unabridged reprint),
    CreateSpace, USA, 2012
——*Mein Kampf*, English edition, Ralph Manheim (transl.), Houghton
    Mifflin, Boston, 1943
Hogue, Oliver, *Trooper Bluegum at the Dardanelles: Descriptive Narratives of
    the More Desperate Engagements on the Gallipoli Peninsula*, Andrew
    Melrose, London, 1916
Holden, Robert, *And the Band Played On: How Music Lifted the Anzac Spirit
    in the Battlefields of the First World War*, Hardie Grant Books,
    Melbourne, 2014
Holmes, Richard, *The Little Field Marshal: A Life of Sir John French*,
    Weidenfeld & Nicolson, London, 2004
Horner, David, *The Gunners: A History of Australian Artillery*, Allen &
    Unwin, Sydney, 1995
Housman, A. E., *A Shropshire Lad*, Branden Books, Wellesley,
    Massachusetts, 1896

Hutchinson, Garrie (ed.), *Eyewitness: Australians Write from the Front-Line*, Black Inc., Melbourne, 2005

Joachimsthaler, Achim, *Hitlers Weg begann in München, 1913–1923*, Herbig, Munich, 2000

Jünger, Ernst, *Im Antlitz des Weltkrieges: Fronterlebnisse deutscher Soldaten*, Neufeld & Henius, Berlin, 1930

——*In Stahlgewittern, Aus dem Tagebuch eines Stoßtruppführers*, Mittler & Sohn, Berlin, 1922

——*Kriegstagebuch: 1914–1918*, Klett-Cotta, Stuttgart, 2010

Jürgs, Michael, *Der Kleine Frieden im Großen Krieg: Westfront 1914; Als Deutsche, Franzosen und Briten gemeinsam Weihnachten feierten* (*The Little Peace in the Great War: Western Front 1914; When Germans, French and British Celebrated Christmas Together*), Pantheon, Munich, 2014

Kahan, Henry, *The 28th Battalion Australian Imperial Force: A Record of War Service*, Hesperian Press, Canberra, 2007

Keech, Graham, *Battleground Europe: Pozières*, Pen & Sword Military, South Yorkshire, 2011, Kindle Edition

Kidd, Neville and Harrison, Roy, *An Impression which will Never Fade: The True Story of an Original Anzac*, self-published, Sydney, 2000

King, Jonathan, *Western Front Diaries: The ANZAC's Own Story, Battle by Battle*, Simon & Schuster, Sydney, 2008

Klähn, Friedrich, *Geschichte des Reserve-Infanterie-Regiments Nr. 86 im Weltkriege*, Stalling, Oldenburg, 1925

Knyvett, Hugh R., *'Over There' with the Australians*, Charles Scribner's Sons, New York, 1918

Lais, Otto, *Bilder aus der Sommeschlacht des Weltkrieges: Erlebnisbericht von Otto Lais*, G. Braun, Karlsruhe, 1940

Lawriwsky, Michael, *Hard Jacka*, Mira Books, Sydney, 2007

Lee, Roger, *The Battle of Fromelles 1916*, Army History Unit, Canberra, 2010

Levine, Joshua, *Forgotten Voices on the Somme: The Most Devastating Battle of the Great War in the Words of Those who Survived*, Ebury, London, 2008

Lewis, Cecil, *Sagittarius Rising*, Corgi, London, 1969

Lewis, Jon, *The First World War*, Eyewitness Accounts, Robinson, London, 2003

Lindsay, Patrick, *Fromelles*, Hardie Grant Books, Melbourne, 2007

Lucy, John F., *There's a Devil in the Drum*, Naval and Military Press, 1992

Lytton, Neville, *The Press and the General Staff*, W. Collins Sons., London, 1920

Macdonald, Lyn, *1915: The Death of Innocence*, Headline, London, 1993

Mackay, Angus, *'Somewhere in Blood Soaked France': The Diary of Corporal Angus Mackay, Royal Scots, Machine Gun Corps 1914–1917*, Alasdair Sutherland (ed.), Gloucestershire Spellmount, Stroud, 2011

Mackenzie, Compton, *Gallipoli Memories*, Obscure Press, 2008

Maddocks, Graham, *Mountaban*, Leo Cooper, South Yorkshire, 1999

Malouf, David, *Fly Away Peter*

Marshall, Samuel Lyman Atwood, *World War I*, Houghton Mifflin, Boston, 1964

Masefield, John, *Letters from the Front 1915–1917*, Constable, London, 1984

Maxwell, Joe, *Hell's Bells and Mademoiselles*, Angus & Robertson, Sydney, 1932

McBride, Herbert, *A Rifleman Went to War: Twenty First Battalion Canadian Expeditionary Force*, Thomas G. Samworth, Plantersville, 1935

McCarthy, Dudley, *Gallipoli to the Somme: The Story of C.E.W. Bean*, John Ferguson, Sydney, 1983

McMullin, Ross, *Farewell Dear People: Biographies of Australia's Lost Generation*, Scribe, Melbourne, 2012

——*Pompey Elliott*, Scribe, Melbourne, 2009

Mead, Gary, *The Good Soldier: The Biography of Douglas Haig*, Atlantic Books, London, 2014

Mearsheimer, John J., *Liddell Hart and the Weight of History*

Meyer, G. J., *A World Undone: The Story of the Great War 1914–1918*, Bantam Dell, New York, 2006

Middlebrook, Martin, *The First Day on the Somme*, Pen & Sword Military, Barnsley, 2006

Miles, Captain Wilfrid, *History of the Great War: Military Operations in France and Belgium, 1916*, Vol. 8, Part 1, Macmillan and Co, London, 1938

Moses, John A. and Pugsley, Christopher (eds), *The German Empire and Britain's Pacific Dominions, 1871–1919: Essays on the Role of Australia and New Zealand in World Politics in the Age of Imperialism*, Regina Books, Claremont (CA), 2000

Moss, James Alfred, *Trench Warfare*, Geo. Banta, Menasha, Wisconsin, 1917

Murdoch, Brian, *Fighting Songs and Warring Words: Popular Lyrics of Two World Wars*, Routledge, London, 2002

Murdoch, Keith (ed.), *'The Day' – and After: War Speeches of the Rt Hon. W. M. Hughes*, Cassell, London, 1916

Neiberg, Michael, *The Second Battle of the Marne*, Indiana University Press, Bloomington, 2008

Neillands, Robin, *The Great War Generals*, Robinson, London, 1999

Newton, L. M., *The Story of the Twelfth*, John Burridge, Perth, 2000

O'Neill, Herbert Charles, *A History of the War*, T. C. & E. C. Jack, London, 1920

Passingham, Ian, *All the Kaiser's Men: The Life and Death of the German Soldier on the Western Front*, The History Press, Stroud, 2011

Pedersen, Peter, *The Anzacs: Gallipoli to the Western Front*, Penguin, Melbourne, 2007

——*Fromelles: French Flanders*, Leo Cooper, South Yorkshire, 2004

Prior, Robin and Wilson, Trevor, *Command on the Western Front*, Pen & Sword Military Classics, Barnsley, 1992

Putkowski, Julian and Sykes, Julian, *Shot at Dawn: Executions in World War One by Authority of the British Army Act*, Pen and Sword, United Kingdom, 1998

Rawlison of Trent, Henry Seymour, *The Life of General Lord Rawlinson of Trent: From his Journals and Letters*, Maurice, Frederick (ed.), Cassell, London, 1928

Raws, Alec and Goldy, *Hail and Farewell: Letters from Two Brothers Killed in France in 1916*, Margaret Young, Bill Gammage (eds), Kangaroo Press, Kenthurst (NSW), 1995

Recouly, Raymond and Jones, Mary Cadwalader, *Foch: The Winner of the War*, Charles Scribner's Sons, New York, 1920

Reichskriegsministerium, *Der Weltkrieg 1914–1918*, Vol. X, Mittler & Sohn, Berlin, 1936

Reid, Walter, *Douglas Haig, Architect of Victory*, Birlinn, Edinburgh, 2006

Ridley, John Gotch, *Born to be a Soldier: War Diary of Lieutenant John Gotch Ridley, MC, A Survivor of Fromelles*, Kelshaw, Jean and Thornton, Bruce (eds), Baptist Historical Society, NSW, 2010

Rothenburg, Gunther E., *The Art of War in the Age of Napoleon*, Batsford, London, 1977

Rule, Edgar ('Eddie'), *Jacka's Mob: A Narrative of the Great War*, Military Melbourne, Melbourne, 1999

Samuels, Martin, *Command or Control?: Command, Training and Tactics in the British and German Armies, 1888–1918*, Frank Cass, London, 1995

Saunders, Nicholas J., *The Poppy: A History of Conflict, Loss, Remembrance & Redemption*, Oneworld, London, 2014

Schoeck, Ellen, *I Was There: A Century of Alumni Stories about the University of Alberta*, University of Alberta Press, Edmonton, 2006

Scott, Ernest, *Official History of Australia in the War of 1914–1918*, Vol. XI, 'Australia During the War', Bean, Charles E. W. (ed.), 7th ed., University of Queensland Press, Brisbane, 1941

Seal, Graham, *Inventing Anzac: The Digger and National Mythology*, University of Queensland Press, Brisbane, 2004

Senior, Michael, *Haking: A Dutiful Soldier – Lieutenant General Sir Richard Haking, XI Corps Commander, 1915–18; A Study in Corps Command*, Pen & Sword Military, South Yorkshire, Kindle Edition, 2012

Shakespear, John, *The Thirty-Fourth Division 1915–1919: The Story of its Career from Ripon to the Rhine*, H. F. & G. Witherby, London, 1921

Sheffield, Gary, *The Chief: Douglas Haig and the British Army*, Aurum, London, 2012

Sheldon, Jack, *The German Army on the Somme 1914–1916*, Pen and Sword, Barnsley, 2005

Sladen, Douglas, *From Boundary Rider to Prime Minister: Hughes of Australia the Man of the Hour*, London, Hutchison, 1916

Sloan, Hannibal, *The Purple and the Gold: A History of the 30th Battalion*, 30th Battalion AIF Association, Sydney, 1938

Solleder, Fridolin (Hg.), *4 Jahre Westfront*, (*4 Years Western Front*) (anthology), Max Schick Verlag, Munich, 1932

Stevenson, Frances, *Lloyd George: A Diary*, Harper & Row, 1971

Stevenson, Robert C., *To Win the Battle: The 1st Australian Division in the Great War, 1914–18*, Cambridge University Press, Cambridge, 2013

Stone, Gerald, *1932*, Macmillan, Sydney

Strauss, Edward M. (transl.), *Poilu, the World War I Notebooks of Corporal Louis Barthas, Barrelmaker, 1914–1918*, Yale University Press, New Haven, 2014

Sun Tzu, *The Art of War*, El Paso Norte Press, El Paso, 2009

Talbot Kelly, R. B., *A Subaltern's Odyssey*, William Kimber, London, 1980

Taylor, A. J. P., *English History 1914–1945*, Oxford University Press, Oxford, 2001

Taylor, F. W. and Cusack, T. A., *Nulli Secundus: A History of the Second Battalion, AIF, 1914–1919*, New Century Press, Sydney, 1942

Tennyson, Alfred, *The Poetical Works of Alfred Tennyson, Poet Laureate*, Harper and Brothers, Publishers, New York, 1870

Terrain, John, *The Smoke and the Fire*, Pen & Sword Books Ltd, London, 1980

Trevor-Roper, H. R., *Hitler's Table Talk 1941–1944, His Private Conversations*, Phoenix, London, 2002

Tsouras, Peter (ed.), *The Greenhill Dictionary of Military Quotations*, Greenhill, London, 2000

Tucker, Spencer C. and Roberts, Priscilla Mary (eds), *The Encyclopaedia of World War I*, ABC CLIO, Santa Barbara (CA), 2005

Van Emden, Richard, *The Soldier's War: The Great War through Veterans'
    Eyes*, Bloomsbury, London, 2008
Wanliss, Newton, *History of the 14th Battalion: Being the Story of the
    Vicissitudes of an Australian Unit during the Great War*, The Arrow
    Printery, Melbourne, 1929
Weber, Thomas, *Hitlers erster Krieg: Der Gefreite Hitler im Weltkrieg –
    Mythos und Wahrheit*, German edition, Stephan Gebauer (transl.),
    Ullstein, Berlin, 2012
——*Hitler's First War: Adolf Hitler, the Men of the List Regiment, and the First
    World War*, English edition, Oxford University Press, Oxford, 2011
Wellmann, Richard Ludwig, *Mit der 18. Reserve-Division in Frankreich: 24.
    Februar 1915 bis 4. Oktober 1916*, Kameradschaftliche Vereinigung
    der Offiziere des ehemaligen Reserve-Infanterie-Regiments Nr. 31,
    Hamburg, 1925
Williams, Harold R., *The Gallant Company: An Australian Soldier's Story of
    1915–18*, Angus & Robertson, Sydney, 1933
Williams, John, *Corporal Hitler and the Great War 1914–1918*, Frank Cass,
    New York, 2005
Williams, John F., *Modernity, the Media and the Military: The Creation of
    National Mythologies on the Western Front 1914–1918*, Routledge,
    Abingdon/Oxon (UK), 2009
Winter, Denis, *Haig's Command*, Viking, London, 1991
Wray, Christopher, *Sir James Whiteside McCay: A Turbulent Life*, Oxford
    University Press, Oxford, 2002

DIARIES, LETTERS, PAPERS AND REPORTS

1st Division War Diary, 1916, AWM4 1/43/18, July 1916
2/1 Battalion Oxfordshire and Buckingham Light Infantry War Diary, July
    1916, TNA, WO 95/3066/2
5th Australian Division War Diary, Part I, July 1916, AWM4 1/50
5th Brigade War Diary, AWM4 23/5/13, July 1916
61st Division War Diary, 1 September 1915 to 31 July 1916, TNA, WO
    95/3033/1
Aitken, James Murray, Diary, AWM 1DRL/0013

Armstrong, William C., Diary, 29 January–8 March 1916, AWM
     1DRL/0059
Baker, Henry Seymour, no. 5367, 4th Field Ambulance, 4th Brigade, 4th
     Australian Division, Tasmanian Archive and Heritage Office,
     TAHO NS2661/1/30
Barry, William Charles ('Bill'), 'Playing the Game with the A.I.F. during the
     Great War', Memoir, AWM PR00814
Barwick, Archie, *Condensed Diary of Sergeant A. A. Barwick, 1st Battalion AIF,
     1914–1919*, MLMSS 7229, Family Edition, self-published, 1995
Bean, Charles, Papers, AWM38 3DRL 7953/34
Boys, Walter, Letters, 1916, AWM 1DRL/0142
Burnett, Thomas, Letters, 1916, AWM 1DRL/0164
Campbell, Rupert J., Letters, 1916, AWM 3DRL/5087(B)
Cass, Walter, Letters, 1916, SLV, MS15488, Series 1, Box 1, Folder 1A
Chapman, Percy, Diary, undated, AWM 1DRL/0198
Christie-Miller, Geoffrey, Papers of Sir Geoffrey Christie-Miller, Memoir,
     Volume Two, IWM 80/32/1, Document 4776
Churchill, Winston, 'Criticism of the value of the Allied offensive on the
     Western Front', CAB 37/153/3, TNA
Collier, Clarence, Letters, 1916, AWM 1DRL/206
Cosson, John, Diary, AWM 1DRL/0216
De Vine, Apcar, Diary, AWM 1DRL/0240
Donnan, Sydney, Memoir, 1934, AWM 2DRL/0712
Duckmanton, Sydney, Diary, 17 July 1916, AWM PR03057.001
Dunlop, Athol Cedric, Diary, 9 February 1916, AWM PR00676
Elliott, Harold E. ('Pompey'), Elliott Papers, AWM 2DRL/0513, Series 3,
     Wallet 13; Series 5, Wallet 4
——Letters, 1916, AWM PR01279
Elmore, Septimus, 6th Field Ambulance, Diary No. 5, August 1916, AWM
     MSS 1825
Fitton, Hubert, Letters, 1916, AWM PR01689
First Army Headquarters War Diary, June 1916, TNA, WO 95/164
——July 1916, TNA, WO 95/165
Fiveash, Herbert, 41st Battery, 13th Field Artillery Brigade, typed
     manuscript, AWM MSS1217
Foss, Captain Cecil Maitland, Private Record, AWM 1DRL/0298
Fraser, Simon, Letters, 1916, AWM 1DRL/0300
Gardiner, Richard Job, Letters, 1916, AWM 1DRL/0305
General Headquarters War Diaries, TNA, WO 95/5
Gibbins, Norman, Letters from fellow soldiers, AWM PR02053

Harpley, Robert, Diary, 1916, AWM 3DRL/3663
Hocking, Fred, Letters, 1916, AWM PR88/161
Horniman, Lance, Letters, 1916, AWM 1DRL/0357
Horton, Douglas, 'With the First Battalion at Pozières', Essay, AWM
     1DRL/0359
Jackson, Dudley, Diary, 1916, AWM 3DRL/3846
Johanesen, Paul, Letters, 1916, AWM PR87/018
Kenyon, David, 'British Cavalry on the Western Front 1916–1918', doctoral
     thesis, Cranfield University, Cranfield, United Kingdom, 2007
Martin, Leslie James, Letters, 1916, AWM 1DRL/0483
Mason, David, Diary, 1916, AWM PR01435
Maxfield, Gordon, Letters, 1916, AWM 1DRL/0489
McCrae, Lionel Oscar, Diary, 1916, AWM PR04752
Military Headquarters Correspondence & Papers, First Army, July 1916–5
     November 1916, TNA, WO 158/186
Nicolson, Norman, Diary and Letters, 1916, Vols 3 & 4, AWM 3DRL/2715
Official War Histories Correspondence & Papers, Loos, 1915–1928, CAB
     45/135
Pflaum, Theodor, Diary, 1916, AWM PR04009
Preston, Harry, Diary and Notebook, undated, AWM 2DRL/0811
Renton, William, Letters, 1916, AWM PR89/176
Ridley, John, Letters, 1916, AWM 3DRL/6428
Roberts, Richard ('Dick'), 'Memoirs of an Anzac', Memoir, AWM PR00395
Robertson, William, Robertson Papers, Liddell Hart Centre for Military
     Archives, King's College, London
Sharman, Clifford, Memoir, AWM PR01239
Sheppeard, Alfred Edward, Diary, 1916, AWM 2DRL/0956
Shipway, W. G., 'My Memories of the First World War', IWM 90/37/1,
     Document 749
Shoobridge, Frank, Diary, 1916, AWM PR00626
Stewart, James, Diary, 1916, AWM 3DRL/1459
Still, Harry, Memoir, 'Some Experiences of a Member of the Australian
     Imperial Forces 3rd July 1915 to 1st February 1920', AWM
     PR00753
Tivey, Edwin, Diary, 1916, AWM 3DRL/3058
Topp, Samuel, Letters, 1916, AWM 1DRL/0583
Trangmar, Herbert S., Diary, 1916, AWM 2DRL/0710
Turnbull, John, Diary, 1916, AWM PR91/015
Williams, Albert, 'A Soldier Looks Back', undated, AWM MSS 1337
Winter, Archibald Thomas, Diary, 1915, 1916, AWM PR89/163

Wyatt, James Digby, Diary, IWM 83/12/1, Document 4160

Zander, Waldo Hyman, 'Narrative of Experiences by Captain Waldo
        Hyman Zander, 30th Battalion, A.I.F. – with the 5th Australian
        Division at Fromelles, July 19th 1916', Memoir, AWM 2DRL/0171

JOURNALS AND MAGAZINES

The Army Quarterly, G. P. Dawnay and Cuthbert Headlam (eds), Vol. III,
        October 1921 and January 1922, William Clowes & Sons, London

Bean, Charles E. W., 'The Leadership of Norman Gibbins', *The Link*, 1
        September 1926

Brown, Arnold, 'The Old Windmill: Pozières' Tragic Landmark', *Reveille*,
        October 1932

Burness, P., 'Pozières Hell', *Wartime Magazine*, Issue 22, 2003

Ekins, Ashley, 'The Battle of Fromelles', *Wartime* 44 (2008), 18–23

Elliott, Harold Edward ('Pompey'), 'The Battle of Fleurbaix or Fromelles',
        The Duckboard, Vol. 5, No. 9, 1 September 1930

Journal of the Society for Army Historical Research, Summer 1984, Vol. 62,
        Number 250 (published by The Society for Army Historical Research)

Maynard, H. J., 'Cookers in the Line: The 55th Battalion's Apprenticeship at
        Fleurbaix', *Reveille*, 1 February 1936

McMullin, Ross, 'The Butcher of Fromelles', *Wartime*, Issue 27, 2004

Morchel, Kate, 'Faces of War', *Wartime Magazine*, Issue 69, Summer 2015

Preston, Harold, 'John Leak's V.C.', *Reveille*, 1 August 1935

Smith, William, 'Sapper's Diary: The Battle of Fromelles', *Reveille*, 1 July
        1936, Vol. 9, No. 11

Wanliss, Newton, 'A.I.F. Celebrities (9): Captain Jacka V.C., M.C. & Bar',
        Reveille, 30 April 1931

Wilson, Ross, 'Army on the Western Front, 1914–18', *War & Society*, Vol. 31,
        No. 1, March 2012

——'The Burial of the Dead: The British Army on the Western Front,
        1914–18', *War & Society*, Vol. 31, No. 1, March 2012

ONLINE SOURCES

XI Corps War Diary, Parts 2, 3, General Staff Headquarters, 1916, AWM4
    1/22/4, www.awm.gov.au/collection/RCDIG1000162
7th Brigade War Diary, 1916, AWM 23/7/10, www.awm.gov.au/collection/
    RCDIG1000566
14th Brigade War Diary, July 1916, AWM4 23/14/4, www.awm.gov.au/
    collection/RCDIG1000559
15th Brigade War Diary, July 1916, AWM4 23/15/5, www.awm.gov.au/
    collection/RCDIG1000558
31st Battalion War Diary, July 1916, AWM4 23/48/12, www.awm.gov.au/
    collection/RCDIG1000618
32nd Battalion War Diary, July 1916, AWM4 23/49/12, www.awm.gov.au/
    collection/RCDIG1000619
48th Battalion War Diary, August 1916, AWM4 23/65, www.awm.gov.au/
    collection/RCDIG1006245
55th Battalion War Diary, 1916, AWM 23/72/5, www.awm.gov.au/
    collection/RCDIG1000546
Address by the Minister for Veterans' Affairs The Honourable Bruce
    Scott MP at the Funeral of Private Russell Bosisto, Courcelette
    Commonwealth Cemetery, France, 5 July 1998, Parliament of
    Australia, http://parlinfo.aph.gov.au
AIF War Diaries, 1914–1918, Appendix F, General Staff, HQ 5th Australian
    Division, AWM4 1/50/5, Part 6, July 1916, www.awm.gov.au/
    collection/RCDIG 1012124
Allsop, W. J. A., Diary, 23 July 1915–1 July 1916, MLMSS 1606, Item 1,
    ML, SLNSW, http://acms.sl.nsw.gov.au
The Ararat Advertiser, 'Australian Attack on Fromelles: Described by a
    German', 5 August 1916, Trove, NLA, http://trove.nla.gov.au
The Argus, 'Fromelles 1916! A Glorious Failure', 10 April 1920, Trove, NLA,
    http://trove.nla.gov.au
——'Mr Hughes at Front', 9 June 1916, Trove, NLA, http://trove.nla.gov.au
Auckland War Memorial Museum, Online Cenotaph, 'Thomas Cooke',
    www.aucklandmuseum.com/war-memorial/online-cenotaph
Australian 2nd Division Artillery War Dairy, Headquarters, AWM4 13/11/6,
    August 1916, www.awm.gov.au/collection/RCDIG1014127

Barwick, Archie, Diary, MLMSS 1493, Box 1, Item 2–6 (12 September 1915–28 March 1916), ML, SLNSW, http://acms.sl.nsw.gov.au

——Diary, MLMSS 1493, Box 1, Item 3 (10 May 1916–23 July 1916), ML, SLNSW, http://acms.sl.nsw.gov.au

——Diary, MLMSS 1493, Box 1, Item 4 (23 July 1916–2 September 1916), ML, SLNSW, http://acms.sl.nsw.gov.au

——Diary, MLMSS 1493, Box 1, Item 6, ML, SLNSW, http://acms.sl.nsw.gov.au

Bean, Charles E. W., 'Fight for Pozières Ridge', *The West Australian*, 10 August 1916, http://trove.nla.gov.au

——*Official History of Australia in the War of 1914–1918*, Diaries, Notebooks and Folders, AWM38 3DRL 606, www.awm.gov.au/collection/RCDIG1066752

Birdwood, William, Diary, 'Personal Diary of Field Marshal Lord William Birdwood' (unpublished), 1 January 1916–1 January 1917, Series 1: Field Marshal Lord William Birdwood's Personal Diaries, 1915–1920, AWM 3DRL/3376 1, www.awm.gov.au/collection/RCDIG0000001

'Bishop, Private Raymond Charles', Australian Red Cross Society Wounded and Missing Enquiry Bureau Files, 1914–1918 War, AWM 1DRL/0428, Box 39, Wallet 10, http://static.awm.gov.au/images/collection/pdf/RCDIG1038264--1-.pdf

'Bosisto, Private Russell George', Australian Red Cross Society Wounded and Missing Enquiry Bureau Files, 1914–1918 War, AWM 1DRL/0428

Bourne, J. M., 'Charteris, John (1877–1946)', Oxford Dictionary of National Biography, Oxford University Press, October 2008, www.oxforddnb.com

'Bowden, John Charles', Australian Red Cross Society Wounded and Missing Enquiry Bureau Files, 1914–1918 War, AWM 1DRL/0428, www.awm.gov.au/people/rolls/R1482995

'Bowden, John Charles', Discovering Anzacs, NAA Record Search, http://discoveringanzacs.naa.gov.au

Brent, Frank, BBC4 Collections, The Great War Interviews, Part 1, www.youtube.com

Champion, Benjamin William, Diary (transcript), 1915–1918, AWM 2DRL/0512, www.awm.gov.au/collection/RCDIG0000977

The Chronicle (Adelaide), 'A Brilliant Son of the Empire', 4 February 1928, Trove, NLA, http://trove.nla.gov.au

Colley-Priest, Langford, Diary, MLMSS 2439, Item 1, ML, SLNSW, http://acms.sl.nsw.gov.au

Commonwealth Gazette, No. 176, 30 November 1916, The AIF Project, www.aif.adfa.edu.au

Daily Herald (Adelaide), 31 July 1914, Trove, National Library of Australia, http://trove.nla.gov.au

Dash, Mike, 'Word War I: 100 Years Later', *Smithsonian*, 23 December 2011, www.smithsonianmag.com

Dayton, Leigh, 'Fromelles Soldiers Are Laid to Rest', *The Australian*, 24 February 2010, www.theaustralian.com.au

Doyle, Arthur Conan, *A Visit to Three Fronts: June 1916*, Part 1: A Glimpse of the British Army, Project Gutenberg, 1 February 2006, www.gutenberg.org

Drane, T. E., *Complete Anzac Gallipoli War Diary*, Bushroots, 20 April 2009, http://bushroots.com

Elliott, Harold Edward ('Pompey'), Letters, 1916–1926, in Bean, Diaries, Notebooks and Folders, AWM38 3DRL 606/243B/1, www.awm.gov.au/collection/RCDIG1066752

'Elliott, Major Thomas Patrick, 60th Battalion', Australian Red Cross Society Wounded and Missing Enquiry Bureau Files, 1914–1918 War, AWM 1DRL/0428, Box 101, Wallet 1, http://static.awm.gov.au/images/collection/bundled/RCDIG1061840.pdf

Elliott, Tom, Private record of Thomas Patrick Elliott (Service Biography and Letter), AWM 3DRL 2872, www.awm.gov.au/collection/3DRL/2872

'Foss, Captain Cecil Maitland, 28th Battalion', Australian Red Cross Society Wounded and Missing Enquiry Bureau Files, 1914–1918 War, AWM 1DRL/0428, http://static.awm.gov.au/images/collection/pdf/RCDIG1062524--1-.pdf

Fox, Frank G.S.O., *G.H.Q. (Montreuil-Sur-Mer)*, Project Gutenberg, 5 September 2013, www.gutenberg.org

The Gazette, 'World War One: The Christmas Truce of December 1914', www.thegazette.co.uk

General Staff, Headquarters 5th Australian Division, War Diary, February–March 1916, AWM4 1/50/1, www.awm.gov.au

Gibbins, Norman, War Service Record, Barcode 4171528, NAA, http://recordsearch.naa.gov.au

Gleichen, Edward, *The Doings of the Fifteenth Infantry Brigade: August 1914 to March 1915*, W. Blackwood and Sons, Edinburgh, 1917, Open Library, https://openlibrary.org

Haig, Douglas, Diary, in Haig, Douglas, 'The Haig Papers from the
National Library of Scotland', Part 1, Haig's Autograph Great War
Diary (NLS 3155, No. 96, 97, 141–153), 1987, Sussex, Harvester
Microform, held at NLA, mfm 1820, http://catalogue.nla.gov.au/
Record/1064910
——Final Dispatch, *Fourth Supplement to the London Gazette*, 10 April
1919, www.thegazette.co.uk/London/issue/31283/supplement/1
Hanson, Neil, *The Unknown Soldier*, Doubleday, London, 2005
Harris, Herbert Henry, Diary, 1916, MLMSS 2772/1, SLNSW, http://acms.
sl.nsw.gov.au
History World, World War One, Verdun, http://history-world.org/battle_
of_verdun.htm
Keating, Paul, 'Speech by the Prime Minister, the Hon. Paul J. Keating, MP,
Funeral Service of the Unknown Australian Soldier, 11 November
1993', Parliament of Australia, http://parlinfo.aph.gov.au
Leane, Benjamin, Diary, 1916, AWM 1DRL/0412, www.awm.gov.au/
collection/RCDIG0001007
Low, Marie, 'A Family Shattered', *Namoi Valley Independent*, 8 September
2015, www.nvi.com.au
Makepeace, Clare, 'Sex and the Somme: The Officially Sanctioned Brothels
on the Front Line Laid Bare for the First Time', *Daily Mail
Australia*, 29 October 2011, www.dailymail.co.uk
'Margetts, Captain Ivor Stephen, 12th Battalion', Australian Red Cross
Society Wounded and Missing Enquiry Bureau Files, 1914–1918
War, AWM 1DRL/0428, Box 170, Wallet 12, p. 2, https://static.
awm.gov.au/images/collection/pdf/RCDIG1053324--1-.pdf
Masefield, John, *The Battle of the Somme*, Heinemann, London, 1919,
Internet Archive, https://archive.org
Matthews, L. D., 'Cass, Walter Edmund Hutchinson (1876–1931)',
Australian Dictionary of Biography, National Centre of Biography,
Australian National University, 1979, http://adb.anu.edu.au
McCrae, Geoff, Letters from Geoffrey Gordon McCrae to his family, 1914–
1916, Series 2, AWM 1DRL/0427, www.awm.gov.au/collection/
RCDIG0001269
McInnis, Ronald, Diary, 1916, AWM PR00917, www.awm.gov.au/
collection/RCDIG0000887
McMullin, Ross, 'Fromelles: A Calamity for Australian Arms', *The Canberra
Times*, 19 July 1986, Trove, NLA, http://trove.nla.gov.au
——'Pompey Elliott: Our Most Revered Fighting General?', *The Sydney
Morning Herald*, 22 April 2011, www.smh.com.au

The Mercury (Hobart), 'The Western Front: Australians in Battle', 24 July 1916, Trove, NLA, http://trove.nla.gov.au

Monash, John, *The Australian Victories in France in 1918*, Project Gutenberg, Australia, May 2013, http://gutenberg.net.au

——Letters, Vol. 1 (24 December 1914–4 March 1917), AWM 3DRL/2316, http://www.awm.gov.au/collection/RCDIG0000569

'Norris, Lieutenant Colonel Ignatius Bertram, 53rd Battalion', Australian Red Cross Society Wounded and Missing Enquiry Bureau Files, 1914–1918 War, AWM 1DRL/0428, http://static.awm.gov.au/images/collection/pdf/RCDIG1061761--1-.pdf.

'Paulin, Captain Harry, 53rd Battalion', Australian Red Cross Society Wounded and Missing Enquiry Bureau Files, 1914–1918 War, AWM 1DRL/0428, Box 211, Wallet 3, http://static.awm.gov.au/images/collection/pdf/RCDIG1056810--1-.pdf

Pearce, Norman, Diary, 1916, MLMSS 8587, SLNSW, http://acms.sl.nsw.gov.au

Port Lincoln Times, 'Visit of Salvation Army Chief', 19 August 1932, Trove, NLA, http://trove.nla.gov.au

Prior, Robin and Wilson, Trevor, 'Rawlinson, Henry Seymour, Baron Rawlinson (1864–1925)', January 2011, Oxford Dictionary of National Biography, Oxford University Press, www.oxforddnb.com

Prisk, Max, 'Sydney's First Anzac Day', *The Sydney Morning Herald*, 25 April 2008, www.smh.com.au

Raws, John Alexander ('Alec') and Robert Goldthorpe ('Goldy'), Letters, 1915, 1916, AWM 2DRL/0481, www.awm.gov.au/collection/RCDIG0001092

Reed, Paul, 'The Boar's Head', Old Front Line Battlefields of WW1, http://battlefields1418.50megs.com

Rule, Andrew, 'Lost and Found in Fromelles', *The Sydney Morning Herald*, 20 July 2010, www.smh.com.au

Serle, Geoffrey, 'McCay, Sir James Whiteside (1864–1930)', Australian Dictionary of Biography, National Centre of Biography, Australian National University, 1986, http://adb.anu.edu.au

Simkin, John, 'Frank Percy Crozier', September 1997, updated 2014, Spartacus Educational, http://spartacus-educational.com

Smythe, Betty (ed.), 'The World War I Diary of Percy Smythe', www.smythe.id.au/diary

The Sydney Morning Herald, 'Captain Blackburn, V.C.', 29 September 1916, http://trove.nla.gov.au

——'Mr Hughes Visits Western Front', 9 June 1916, Trove, NLA, http://trove.nla.gov.au

Thomas, Arthur, Diary, 1916–1918, AWM 3DRL/2206, www.awm.gov.au/
collection/RCDIG0001096

Tibbitts, Craig, '"Good Fearless Soldiers": Two Brothers at Pozières, 1916', 4
February 2014, AWM Blog, www.awm.gov.au/blog

Walsh, Matt, 'The Somme: A Brief Record of Australia's Involvement in
the Battle of Pozières', Defence Reserves Association Inc. and the
Military Police Association of Australia Inc., 2008, Army Museum
of South Australia, www.amosa.org.au

Welborn, Suzanne, 'Pope, Harold (1873–1938)', Australian Dictionary of
Biography, National Centre of Biography, Australian National
University, 1988, http://adb.anu.edu.au

Wichers, Shannon, 'The Forgotten Victims of the North: French Civilians
under German Occupation during World War I', *Armstrong
Undergraduate Journal of History*, Vol. 1, No. 2, Summer 2011,
www.armstrong.edu/Initiatives/history_journal

Wiltshire, Aubrey R., Diary, 1916, MLMSS 3058/Box 1/Item 5, ML,
SLNSW, http://acms.sl.nsw.gov.au

INDEX

166, 170, 191, 211, 247,
259, 309, 331, 348–9, 354,
356, 359–60, 362, 364–7,
369, 383, 398–400, 412,
420, 423, 430, 432, 435,
519, 523–4, 528, 533, 551,
555, 558, 566, 568, 571,
573, 582–3, 599, 622–3,
632–3, 640
'Imshi Artillery' 160
training 142–3, 192
Artillery Brigade 156, 458, 627
Ashurst, Corporal George 132
Asquith, Mrs 149
Asquith, Prime Minister 52,
140, 149, 201
Aubers 9
Aubers Ridge 11, 12, 14, 18,
20, 23–4, 26, 41–2, 111, 114,
183, 198, 208, 222, 260, 267,
269, 279–82, 292, 308–9,
311, 320, 325, 341, 378, 438
'Australia Will Be There' 228
Australian Corps 260, 658
Australian front-line,
Fromelles 299
Australian Imperial Force (AIF)
1st Brigade 51
2nd Brigade 51
3rd Brigade 51
4th Brigade 51
5th Brigade 43, 73, 87,
159, 575, 576, 582, 586,
587, 606, 616–18
6th Brigade 85, 87, 117,
174, 575, 582, 592, 606,
616
7th Brigade 80, 86, 582,
585, 587–9, 616–18
battalions 33
1st Battalion 85, 132, 155,

339, 340, 354, 507, 516,
528–9, 540, 545, 552, 559,
574
2nd Battalion 24, 31, 116,
127, 129, 142–3, 178, 351,
466, 541, 555, 556–7, 569,
579
12th Battalion 53, 79, 549,
555, 570
14th Battalion 54–6, 268,
621, 633–5, 636, 640, 643,
649, 673–4
15th Battalion 178
21st Battalion 606
22nd Battalion 143–4, 174
23rd Battalion 41, 77, 84,
119, 174, 271, 517, 519,
575–6, 589–91, 617
25th Battalion 586–8, 617
26th Battalion 188, 588,
592
27th Battalion 86, 118,
170, 185, 615, 618, 676,
680–2
28th Battalion 118,188,
588, 606, 625, 632–3, 635,
637, 639
30th Battalion 305, 424,
437, 441, 448
31st Battalion 310, 391–2,
406, 427, 447, 485
32nd Battalion 79, 93, 207,
310, 391–2, 406, 412, 427,
431, 433, 441, 447, 485
48th Battalion 636–7, 639,
643–4, 647–8, 676
52nd Battalion 53, 668
53rd Battalion 392, 406,
485
54th Battalion 392, 406,
412, 427, 485

121, 198, 200, 208, 316, 520,
658, 663
5th Infantry Brigade 4
British planes 64, 145, 257
Brown, Major Arnold 674
Brunton, Private Arthur 500,
672
Brustwehren 488
Bubb, Sergeant Jack 537
Buchan, John 230, 231
Buchheim 9
The Bulletin 81
'Butcher of Cape Helles' 254
Butler, Major-General 293–4,
318–21, 669

Cairo 40, 41, 46, 50, 53, 68, 75,
134, 138, 149, 157, 171, 352
Calais 52, 106, 139, 256, 257,
271
Camden, Sergeant Hugh 218–
19
Campbell, Rupert 158
Carrington, Lieutenant
Charles 580
Carter, Brigadier-General
Charles Herbert 308, 415,
439
Cass, Lieutenant-Colonel
Walter 72, 202, 228, 265,
337, 347, 363, 374, 394–5,
406, 412, 414, 424, 427, 445–
7, 450–3, 455, 457–9, 461–6,
670–1
casualties 1, 4, 15–16, 22, 26,
31, 35, 37, 42, 84, 156, 191,
222, 225, 248, 252, 253, 254,
258, 267, 280, 288, 294, 297–
8, 318, 350, 362, 364, 366,
379, 414, 438, 454, 458, 462,
474, 484–5, 487, 518, 538,

541, 566, 575, 581, 592, 602,
603, 604, 610, 632, 656, 666
Cavan Ulster Volunteers 251
cemetery 41, 135
Anzac 676
Box Hill 668
Burwood 670
Courcelette 681–2
military 580
Pozières 554, 565, 636,
638
St Kilda 674
'stiff's paddock' 135
VC Corner Australian
Cemetery 679
Challis, George 57, 310, 318,
672
Champion, Lance-Corporal
Ben 353, 355, 507, 528–31,
534, 557, 573
Chantilly 38
Chapman, Second-Lieutenant
Percy 396, 424, 428–30, 459,
467
Charleville 156, 312, 436
Charteris, Brigadier-General
John 3, 279, 292
Château de Beaurepaire 172
Château de la Motte aux
Bois 111, 175, 181, 201, 208
Château de Montigny 291
Château Lamont 601
Château Valvion 229, 291, 520,
583, 592, 610
Cherry, Lieutenant Percy 612,
623–5, 627–8
'Chinese attack' 269, 300, 343,
357, 359, 367, 371
chlorine gas 124
Chocques 268, 293, 294, 318,
320